Managerial
Applications of
System Dynamics
edited by Edward B. Roberts

Managerial Applications
of System Dynamics

MIT Press/Wright-Allen Series in System Dynamics

Jay W. Forrester, editor

Industrial Dynamics, Jay W. Forrester, 1961

Growth of a New Product: Effects of Capacity-Acquisition Policies, Ole C. Nord, 1963

Resource Acquisition in Corporate Growth, David W. Packer, 1964

Principles of Systems,* Jay W. Forrester, 1968

Urban Dynamics, Jay W. Forrester, 1969

Dynamics of Commodity Production Cycles,* Dennis L. Meadows, 1970

World Dynamics,* Jay W. Forrester, 1971

The Life Cycle of Economic Development,* Nathan B. Forrester, 1973

Toward Global Equilibrium: Collected Papers,* Dennis L. Meadows and Donella H. Meadows, eds., 1973

Study Notes in System Dynamics,* Michael R. Goodman, 1974

Readings in Urban Dynamics (vol. 1),* Nathaniel J. Mass, ed., 1974

Dynamics of Growth in a Finite World,* Dennis L. Meadows, William W. Behrens III, Donella H. Meadows, Roger F. Naill, Jørgen Randers, and Erich K. O. Zahn, 1974

Collected Papers of Jay W. Forrester,* Jay W. Forrester, 1975

Economic Cycles: An Analysis of Underlying Causes,* Nathaniel J. Mass, 1975

Readings in Urban Dynamics (vol. 2),* Walter W. Schroeder III, Robert E. Sweeney, and Louis Edward Alfeld, eds., 1975

Introduction to Urban Dynamics,* Louis Edward Alfeld and Alan K. Graham, 1976

Dynamo User's Manual (5th ed.), Alexander L. Pugh III, 1976

Managerial Applications of System Dynamics, Edward B. Roberts, ed., 1978

*Originally published by Wright-Allen Press and now distributed by The MIT Press.

Managerial Applications
of System Dynamics

Edward B. Roberts, editor

The MIT Press
Cambridge, Massachusetts,
and London, England

Second printing, 1984

First MIT Press paperback edition, 1981

Printed and bound in the United States of America.

Library of Congress Cataloging in Publication Data

Roberts, Edward Baer.
  Managerial applications of system dynamics.
  (MIT Press/Wright-Allen series in system dynamics)
  Bibliography: p.
  Includes index.
  1. Industrial management — Addresses, essays, lectures. I. Title.
HD31.R567   658.4   77-26952
ISBN 0-262-18088-X (hard)
        0-262-68035-1 (paper)

To Nancy

Other Books by Edward B. Roberts

The Dynamics of Research and Development. New York: Harper and Row, Publishers, Inc., 1964.

Systems Simulation for Regional Analysis: An Application to River Basin Planning (with H. R. Hamilton, et al.). Cambridge: The MIT Press, 1969.

The Persistent Poppy: A Computer-Aided Search for Heroin Policy (with G. Levin and G. Hirsch). Cambridge: Ballinger Publishing Company, 1975.

The Dynamics of Human Service Delivery (with G. Levin et al.). Cambridge: Ballinger Publishing Company, 1976.

Contents

Preface

This book provides an overview of past and continuing applications of system dynamics philosophy and methodology to managerial issues, especially in corporations. System dynamics is the application of feedback control systems principles and techniques to the modeling of social systems. At its inception at M.I.T. in 1957, the field was labelled ''industrial dynamics,'' but the academic work at M.I.T. and elsewhere soon expanded the focus to urban, economic, medical, ecological, and human systems, and the field is now more appropriately called ''system dynamics.'' Yet the foundations had been provided, in methodology and early demonstrations, for continuing private corporate development and application of the approach. By the early '60s academia ceased being the breeding ground for industrial usage of system dynamics, and action shifted to the larger corporations and consulting companies. Details of these managerial applications of system dynamics, however, have not been readily available to the interested public. This book for the first time documents the evidence of such work and provides a comprehensive overview of the managerial usage of system dynamics.

Managerial Applications is divided into six parts. The first part introduces the concepts, philosophy, and methodology of system dynamics. The remaining five parts deal with corporate functional areas of application, namely, manufacturing, marketing and distribution, research and development, and finance and control, with the final section treating societal problems. Each of the above six parts begins with an overview of the papers contained in that part and provides a summary of the circumstances leading up to the applications. These overviews reference related applications not included in this book, as well as some applications which are not documented at all in the public literature. Many of the papers provide complete descriptions of the modeling processes and results. In some cases, model documentations are within the papers, in others they are included as appendixes at the end of the book. In all, 36 chapters provide in-depth descriptions of over 25 applications to business and industrial situations and several applications to societal problems. Nine models are fully documented by listings in the chapters and the four appendixes.

The editor hopes that students of system dynamics, in university classes and in managerial roles, will find these many examples helpful in their personal growth and development and in creating additional successful applications.

Acknowledgments

As indicated in the first page footnote of each chapter, much of the book has previously been published in other journals. The editor is grateful for the cooperation of the numerous authors and their publishers in granting permission to reprint these works in this volume.

The effort to assemble this volume started many years ago, before much of the present contents of the book had in fact been written. The editor appreciates the encouragement of Jay W. Forrester throughout this entire period. He initiated the field of system dynamics, directed the earliest projects aimed at managerial applications, and has pioneered the broadening endeavors in social and economic systems. Jack Pugh, Henry Weil, and several other colleagues at Pugh-Roberts Associates, Inc. have not only been instrumental in generating many of the real-world applications of system dynamics, but they have also made helpful comments and suggestions about the book's structure and contents on numerous occasions during the period of its assembly. Jim Lyneis has also been very helpful with comments on targeting the book's contents for possible classroom use.

Naren Patni has borne up well as publisher under the abuses of author harassment, schedule slippages and the multiple annoyances of putting together a large volume. Lisa Kunstadter maintained her energetic and helpful efforts in all the dimensions of secretarial support needed in completing this work.

I am appreciative of all of the above for their aid and comfort, and especially grateful to my wife Nancy to whom I dedicate this volume. Nancy not only goaded me along in this project at not infrequent invervals, but became so involved as to emerge a collaborator, rather than merely an observer, in system dynamics.

Edward B. Roberts

Massachusetts Institute of Technology
Cambridge, Massachusetts
June 1977

Part One:
System Dynamics — Basic Concepts

Part 1 introduces the basic concepts and underlying methodology of system dynamics. Chapter 1 examines the various background developments in engineering and the management sciences that made system dynamics practicable for managerial purposes and presents the methods used in performing system dynamics work. Description of the methods begins with causal loop diagramming for visualizing and assessing complex system structures. This leads to a discussion of the positive and negative feedback loops pictured by the causal diagrams, and of the prototype behaviors generated by these loop structures. Formal system dynamics flow diagrams are presented with their emphasis on differentiating level and rate variables in a system representation. The chapter also introduces the techniques of formal equation-writing and discusses a simple example of hand-calculated simulation. References to more elaborate computer simulation methods end the chapter.

The non-technical reader should gain a broad appreciation of the elements of system dynamics applications by reading Chapter 1 alone. The more technically oriented reader will want to go beyond the materials presented in Chapter 1 for more detailed information (1,2,3,4).

Chapter 2 is a reprint of the first broadly distributed discussion and theoretical use of the system dynamics approach (then called ''industrial dynamics''). Jay Forrester's first modeling effort focused on the fluctuations of orders, shipments and inventories in multistage distribution systems. Although no specific organization is described by his model, the parameters chosen for the computer simulations are drawn from information on the appliance industry. (Appendix A of this volume contains an annotated listing of Forrester's production-distribution model.) First published in the *Harvard Business Review* in 1958 under the title ''Industrial Dynamics — A Major Breakthrough for Decision Makers,'' the article generated both wide acclaim (by managers especially) and wide controversy (particularly among some management scientists). The article was followed a few months later by a second paper in the *Harvard Business Review* in which advertising considerations were added to the basic production-distribution model (See Chapter 11 of this volume.)

The basic work embodied in Chapters 2 and 11 became the models for many industrial applications of system dynamics. One presentation in the literature that attributes its heritage to Forrester's initial model is Yurow's work on the textile industry, carried out as part of a broad effort by the U.S. Department of Commerce (5).

Chapters 3 and 4 illustrate the editor's concern that the successful implementation of changes be derived from model development and use. In most management science endeavors, even in industry, consideration of implementation requirements seems unfortunately to come as an afterthought. This book intends to give the implementation perspective precedence over discussion of specific applications. Early experiences at Minneapolis-Honeywell in building and implementing industrial dynamic models are described in Chapter 3 by Meyers and Roberts. Some of the editor's experiences, as well as those of Pugh-Roberts Associates, Inc., the primary consulting firm in the area of system dynamics, are presented in a process perspective in Chapter 4. The points outlined in that chapter can serve as a meaningful guideline for assessing in advance the likelihood of implementing results arising from a system dynamics project.

References

1. Forrester, Jay W. *Industrial Dynamics*. Cambridge, Mass.: The MIT Press, 1961.

2. Forrester, Jay W. *Principles of Systems*. Cambridge, Mass.: Wright-Allen Press, 1968.

3. Goodman, Michael R. *Study Notes in System Dynamics*. Cambridge, Mass.: Wright-Allen Press, 1974.

4. Pugh, Alexander L. III. *DYNAMO User's Manual*. Fifth edition. Cambridge, Mass.: The MIT Press, 1976.

5. Yurow, Jerome A. "Analysis and Computer Simulation of the Production and Distribution Systems of a Tufted Carpet Mill," *Journal of Industrial Engineering*, January 1967.

System Dynamics — An Introduction

Edward B. Roberts

Background and Overview

System dynamics is the application of feedback control systems principles and techniques to managerial, organizational, and socioeconomic problems. For managerial usage, system dynamics advocates seek to integrate the several functional areas of an organization into a conceptual and meaningful whole, and to provide an organized and quantitative basis for designing more effective organization policy.

Three advances, largely the result of military research and development, made feasible the system dynamics approach:

1. advances in feedback systems design and analysis;
2. progress in computer simulation techniques;
3. increasing experience in the modelling of decision-making processes.

First in importance were advances in the understanding and analysis of information-feedback systems. These originated in engineering experience with simple mechanical and electromechanical servomechanisms and were extended during and after World War II through work on complex electronic systems which included numerous subsystems and thousands of components. As the subtleties of information-feedback systems became more widely known, the existence of feedback mechanisms in managerial and economic organizations began to be explored. Norbert Wiener awakened world thought to the ever-presence in man and society of feedback control processes[1] and by the early 1950s Arnold Tustin[2] and Herbert Simon[3] had begun to illustrate the translations into economics and business.

Another basic development that underlies system dynamics practice is the use of simulation methods. For many years simulation has been an important part of engineering design. Wind tunnels, ship-towing tanks, scale models, pilot plants, and analog

The ''Background and Overview'' section of this chapter draws heavily from Edward B. Roberts, ''New Directions in Industrial Dynamics,'' *Industrial Management Review* (now published as the *Sloan Management Review*), Fall 1964. The ''Why Model?'' section is a slightly edited version of a portion of Levin, Roberts, Hirsch, *The Persistent Poppy: A Computer-Aided Search for Heroin Policy* (Cambridge: Ballinger Publishing, 1975), pp. 4–6.

computers have all been used to verify theories and plans before full-scale application. The success and increased use of these simulative approaches to pre-test products made reasonable their extension to problems of business design. With the advent of reliable, high-speed digital computers, the simulation of large industrial organizations became practical. The restrictions that had constrained the size and form of desired mathematical models were now eliminated. The costs of experimental changes in industrial organizations were quickly reduced by the mid-'50s to just a few dollars for a simulated decade of company life.

Finally, along with these other developments came a better understanding of human decision-making processes. The increased knowledge in this area had been necessitated by our military requirements for automatic and semi-automatic weapon control. The success of military research in this field brought insights into many tactical-level decisions and, more importantly, a confidence that human thought and action were *not* beyond scrutiny, understanding, representation, and even improvement. During the decade of the '50s the growth of behavioral science interests in studying and representing decision processes had approached a critical mass of enthusiasm and at least an initiation of useful output.

Professor Jay W. Forrester had pioneered in important ways in each of these engineering-related progress areas. His move in 1956 from head of the Computer Division (under which was developed the SAGE system) at the M.I.T. Lincoln Laboratory to a professorship in the M.I.T. School of Industrial Management, now the M.I.T. Alfred P. Sloan School of Management, signaled the beginning of the industrial dynamics program, now broadened in identification into the system dynamics area. Recruitment during the next year of three electrical engineering graduate students (Willard Fey, Alexander Pugh and the author) as full-time research assistants launched the development of a system dynamics research staff and the creation of a philosophy, supporting methodology and pilot applications.

The system dynamics philosophy rests on a belief that the behavior (or time history) of an organization is principally caused by the organization's structure. The structure includes not only the physical aspects of plant and production process but, more importantly, the policies and traditions, both tangible and intangible, that dominate decision-making in the organization. Such a structural framework contains sources of amplification, time lags, and information feedback similar to those found in complex engineering systems. Engineering and management systems containing these characteristics display complicated response patterns to relatively simple system or input changes. The analysis of large nonlinear systems of this sort is a major challenge to even the most experienced control systems engineer; effective and reliable redesign of such a system is still more difficult. The subtleties and complexities in the management area make these problems even more severe. Here the structural orientation of system dynamics provides a beginning for replacing confusion with order.

A second aspect of the system dynamics philosophy is the concept that organizations are viewed most effectively in terms of their common underlying flows instead of in terms of separate functions. The flows of people, money, materials, orders, and capital equipment, and the integrating flows of information can be identified in all organizations. The flow structure orientation causes the viewer (manager or analyst) to cross suborganization boundaries in a natural manner. It acts to dispel the component approach to organization that promotes interorganizational conflict and unrecognized suboptimization. A meaningful systems framework results from tracing cause-and-effect chains through the relevant flow paths.

The system dynamics methodology was developed to make practicable the evolving philosophy. The tools of flow diagramming, mathematical modeling, and computer simulation were used and modified to fit the new needs. Borrowing from signal-flow graphs of electrical engineering, cause-and-effect arrow diagramming was developed to portray visually the underlying managerial situation. More formal flow diagramming and equation-writing methods were created for the next steps of most system dynamics projects. Both the flow diagrams and equations represent organizational relationships as falling into two categories—levels and rates. The levels represent those aspects of the real world in which accumulations of resources exist: inventories (of goods or ideas), balances of funds, pools of employees. The second variable type, the rate, includes all activities within the system: flows of effort, the streams of information, the payments for expenses.

Once the organization problem (or opportunity) has been represented in levels and rates, most system dynamics projects employ computer simulation of the system models. This serves both for experimental determination of ideas for policy improvement and for experimental testing of the proposed policy changes. The M.I.T. group developed its original compiler and simulation program, called DYNAMO.[4] Alexander Pugh and Pugh-Roberts Associates Inc. have advanced, maintain and distribute the DYNAMO system for use on most modern digital computers, ranging from minicomputers to the largest systems. Its thoroughness in error-checking, speed of execution, and flexibility of output form make DYNAMO a major asset to the system dynamics effort. Systems of equations—linear and nonlinear, algebraic and differential—containing as many as several thousand variables can be handled efficiently by DYNAMO, even though the user has no knowledge of computer programming.

As the system dynamics philosophy developed, and as the techniques became available, the initial testing of system dynamics was begun at M.I.T. in cooperation with industrial sponsors. Gradually the results of that work began to diffuse to industry-at-large, producing the applications represented in this book.

The remainder of this chapter will examine the motivations for developing models of the system dynamics type and then present the detailed methodologies needed to achieve these models.

Why Model?

The system dynamics approach begins with an effort to understand the system of forces that has created a problem and continues to sustain it. Relevant data are gathered from a variety of sources, including literature, informed persons (managers, customers, competitors, experts) and specific quantitative studies. As soon as a rudimentary measure of understanding has been achieved, a formal model is developed. This model is initially in the format of a set of logical diagrams showing cause-and-effect relationships. As soon as feasible the visual model is translated into a mathematical version. The model is exposed to criticism, revised, exposed again and so on in an iterative process that continues as long as it proves to be useful. Just as the model is improved as a result of successive exposures to critics, a successively better understanding of the problem is achieved by the people who participate in the process. Their intuition about the probable consequences of proposed policies frequently proves to be less reliable than the model's meticulous mathematical approach.

This is not as surprising as it may first appear. Managerial systems contain as many as 100 or more variables that are known to be relevant and believed to be related to one another in various nonlinear fashions. The behavior of such a system is complex far beyond the capacity of intuition. Computer simulation is one of the most effective means available for supplementing and correcting human intuition.

A computer simulation model of the kind described here is a powerful conceptual device that can increase the role of reason at the expense of rhetoric in the determination of organizational policy. A model is not, as is sometimes supposed, a perfectly accurate representation of reality that can be trusted to make better decisions than people. It is a flexible tool that forces the people who use it to think harder and to confront one another, their common problems and themselves, directly and factually.

A computer model differs principally in complexity, precision and explicitness from the informal subjective explanation or ''mental model'' that people ordinarily construct to guide their actions toward a goal. It is an account of the total set of forces that are believed to have caused and to sustain some problematic state of affairs. Like the informal mental model, it is derived from a variety of data sources including facts, theories and educated guesses. Unlike the mental model, it is comprehensive, unambiguous, flexible and subject to rigorous logical manipulation and testing.

The flexibility of a model is its least understood virtue. If you and I disagree about some aspect of the causal structure of a problem, we can usually in a matter of minutes run the model twice and observe its behavior under each set of assumptions. I may on the basis of its behavior be forced to admit you were correct. Very often, however, we will both discover that our argument was trifling, since the phenomenon of interest to us may be unchanged by a change in assumptions.

A computer model constructed and used by a managerial policymaking group has the following advantages:

1. It requires managerial policymakers to improve and complete fully the rough mental sketch of the causes of the problem that they inevitably have in their heads.

2. In the process of formal model-building the builders discover and resolve various self-contradictions and ambiguities among their implicit assumptions about the problem.

3. Once the model is running, even in a rudimentary fashion, logical ''bootstrapping'' becomes possible. The consequences of promising but tentative formulations are tested in the model. Observation of model behavior gives rise to new hypotheses about structure.

4. Once an acceptable standard of validity has been achieved formal policy experiments reveal quickly the probable outcomes of many policy alternatives; novel policies may be discovered; "what if" situations can be explored.

5. An operating model is always complete, though in a sense never completed. Unlike many planning aids, which tend to be episodic and terminal (they provide assistance only at the moment the "report" is presented, not before or after), a model is organic and iterative. At any moment the model contains in readily-accessed form the present best understanding of the problem.

6. Sensitivity analysis of the model reveals the areas in which genuine debate (rather than caviling) is needed and guides empirical investigation to important questions. If the true values of many parameters are unknown (which is generally the case in corporate strategic planning), the ones that most affect model behavior need to be investigated first.

7. An operating model can be used to communicate with people who were not involved in building the model. By experimenting with changes in policies and model parameters and observing the effects of these changes on behavior, these people can be helped to better understand the dynamic forces at work in the real-world system.

Feedback Systems Analysis

A feedback system exists whenever an action-taker will later be influenced by the consequences of his actions. The consequences may be quick and directly apparent in results produced; as when one prospective buyer's bid at an auction influences a second bidder's price, which in turn feeds back to affect the first bidder's next decision. Or the consequences may be delayed though directly apparent in results produced; as when a farmer's decision as to how much to water his crops affects the later growth rate of the crops, which in turn influences the farmer's later watering decisions. Or the consequences may be both delayed and quite indirect in perceived results; as when a decision to increase the R&D budget leads to the hiring of more scientists, which may produce improved products and processes several years later, which may enhance the company's competitive position, in turn increasing sales and/or profits, which may then influence the decision on the R&D budget. In all these cases a "closing the loop" occurs; in all cases a delay, whether short or long, intervenes between initial action and fed-back results. Closed loops and time delays in consequences are characteristic of all feedback processes.

In real-world settings many people fail to recognize that they are part of many different complex social, economic and organizational feedback systems. The longer the time delays "around the loop" and the less direct the consequences, the more difficulties will be encountered in recognizing the feedback structures.

Hierarchy of Feedback Elements.   Throughout this chapter I shall refer to four hierarchically different levels of feedback system structure: variable, linkage (or link), feedback loop, and feedback system.

A *variable* is a quantity that is changeable as time evolves. The variable may be a decision, such as "sales rate" or "shipping rate," or it may be a quantity that is affected by such decisions, for example "order backlog" or "level of inventory," or it may be a changeable input to a decision, such as "desired employment" or "inventory deficiency." When the variable is not affected by other variables inside the system being analyzed, the variable is termed "exogenous," or outside of the system. A variable that is subject to effects of other variables inside the system is termed "endogenous."

A *linkage* (or *link*) is a cause-and-effect relationship between two variables. A link is shown by an arrow connecting the causal variable to the effect variable.

(ARROW)
(TAIL)   (HEAD)

The variable at the tail of the arrow causes a change in the variable at the head of the arrow.

Illustrated below are three linkages: desired employment affects hiring rate, inventory level influences goods shipped, and morale is a determinant of employee turnover.

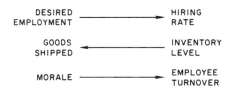

Figure 1   Cause-and-effect linkages.

A *feedback loop* consists of two or more linkages connected in such a way that, beginning with any variable, one can follow the arrows around and return to the starting variable. For example, all the alternatives described in the preceding section of this chapter form feedback loops, as indicated in Figure 2.

Implicit in every cause-and-effect illustration of a feedback loop are time delays: delays from each decision to each of its consequences and delays in feeding back information about each consequence to affect the next decision. If these time delays were accounted for explicitly in the feedback loop diagrams, we might show, for example, that the first buyer's bid at time t_1 affects the second buyer's bid at later time t_2, which stimulates the first buyer's bid at time t_3, in turn influencing the second buyer's bid at time t_4, and so on. For simplicity of appearance we omit these time delay notations from system dynamics feedback loop diagrams.

One common error among novices in system dynamics is to perceive feedback loops when multiple variables are connected together, but where the arrows cannot be followed around in a closed path. Such pieces of system structure may contain many

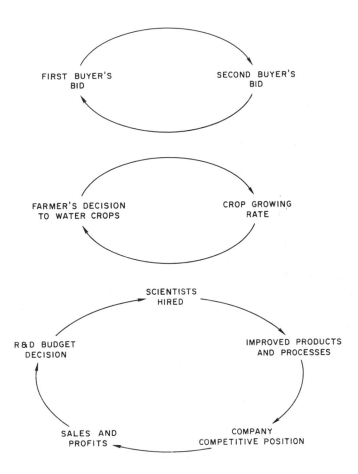

Figure 2   Sample feedback loops.

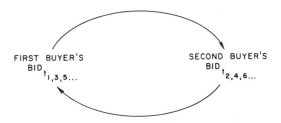

Figure 3   Feedback loop with time delays indicated.

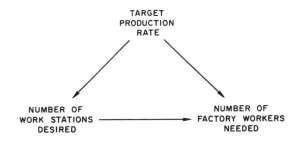

Figure 4   Multiple linkages, no feedback loop.

linkages but no loops. For example, in Figure 4 the target production rate is shown to influence the number of work stations desired in the factory, which in turn affects the number of factory workers who are needed. Target production rate also influences the number of factory workers needed. The three variables shown in the diagram are connected, but not in a closed feedback loop. The arrows cannot be followed around back to a starting point.

I define a *feedback system* as two or more connected feedback loops. The behavior of the variables in each feedback loop can propagate through the connections to affect variables in other loops within the feedback system. Figure 5 indicates some feedback systems which relate to the feedback loop examples shown earlier.

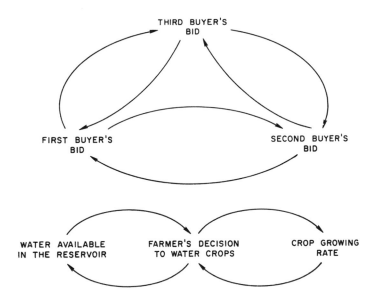

Figure 5   Sample feedback systems.

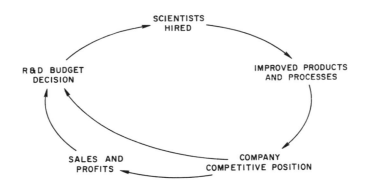

Figure 5 (cont'd.)

Complex organizational problems are embedded in such systems composed of many interconnected feedback loops. Formal analytical approaches become difficult to apply as feedback system complexity increases. This area of multi-loop feedback systems is the focus of system dynamics attention.

Causal Loop Diagrams.   In undertaking a system dynamics analysis of a managerial problem, the first step is to hypothesize the underlying structure of the system that is causing and maintaining the problem. This hypothesis is usually recorded and communicated to others in a "visual model," called a causal loop diagram. The causal loop diagram shows the existence of all major cause-and-effect links, indicates the "direction" of each linkage relationship, and denotes major feedback loops and their "polarity."

In developing a causal loop diagram each link is given a + or − "directional" sign, usually shown near the arrow head, and is referred to as a plus (or positive) or as a minus (negative) linkage.

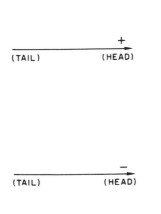

The + sign near the arrow head tells you that the variable at the tail and the variable at the head of the arrow change in the *same* direction. If the tail *increases*, the head *increases*. If the tail *decreases*, the head *decreases*.

The − sign near the arrow head tells you that the variable at the tail and the variable at the head of the arrow change in *opposite* directions. If the tail *increases*, the head *decreases*. If the tail *decreases*, the head *increases*.

As examples, for the links shown previously in Figure 1: an increase in desired employment should cause an increased hiring rate (plus linkage); a decreased inventory level tends to reduce goods shipped (plus linkage); and an increase in morale leads to a decline in employee turnover (minus linkage).

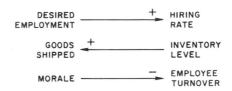

Figure 6   Linkages with directions indicated.

Just as linkages have two possible directions, feedback loops have two possible polarities, positive $(+)$ or negative $(-)$.

This symbol, found in the middle of a closed feedback loop, tells you that the loop acts to reinforce variable changes in the *same* direction as the change, contributing to sustained growth or decline of variables in the loop. The loop is called a *positive feedback* loop.

This symbol, found in the middle of a closed feedback loop, tells you that the loop acts to resist or to counter variable changes, thereby pushing toward a direction *opposite* to a change, contributing to fluctuation or to maintaining the equilibrium of the loop. The loop is called a *negative feedback loop*.

Two simple methods exist for determining the polarity of a feedback loop. The first approach traces behavior of a variable change around the closed loop. For example, in Figure 7(a) if the money in the bank were increased, the amount of interest added would increase, and the resulting amount of money in the bank would increase further. Going around the loop indicates reinforcement of the original change in the *same* direction as the change. Therefore, Figure 7(a) is a positive feedback loop, and so indicated by the symbol $+$.

Tracing Figure 7(b) suggests that if the amount of pollution rises, concern for pollution also rises, causing pollution controls to be increased, leading eventually to a decrease in the amount of pollution. Thus, in going around the loop an increase in a

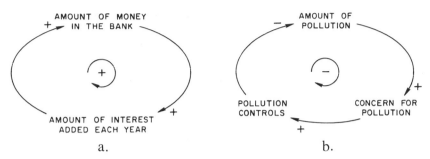

Figure 7   Causal loop diagrams.

variable leads to changes contributing to its decrease, a movement in the *opposite* direction. Therefore, Figure 7(b) is a negative feedback loop, and so indicated by the symbol —.

The second method for determining feedback loop polarity is even more simple. The negative linkages in the loop are counted. An odd number of negative links indicates a negative feedback loop. Zero or an even number of negative links indicates a positive feedback loop.

Applying the test to Figure 7, (a) has 0 negative links and is therefore a positive feedback loop; (b) has 1 (an odd number) negative link and is therefore a negative feedback loop. The mechanical counting approach tests consistently with the trace approach!

The beginner in system dynamics will want to practice developing causal loop diagrams of managerial and everyday situations. Similarly, experience is desirable in projecting the dynamic consequences of any given causal loop diagram. For these purposes Nancy Roberts has developed two kits, a Story Kit and a Diagram Kit, which she has successfully used in classes ranging from grade 5 in elementary school through executive programs at the M.I.T. Sloan School. An example from her Story Kit is shown below.[5]

STORY #5 - THE OIL CRISIS

One aspect of the oil crisis, as explained by an economist, was the starting of a "vicious circle." This vicious circle was begun by agreements made by the Arab oil producing countries in 1971 called the Teheran and Tripoli Agreements (named for the cities in which the meetings were held). Here these countries agreed to raise the price of oil. The rise in oil prices meant that these countries then made more money. They made so much more money that they could not possibly spend it all. Realizing this, these countries decided not to produce as much oil. They knew that eventually their oil supply would run out so they might as well make it last as long as possible.

Because there was less oil being produced in the world, and more oil was needed every day, a scarcity of oil developed. This scarcity of oil forced the oil prices to go up even higher, continuing the "vicious circle."

1. Draw a feedback diagram showing the "vicious circle" this economist points out.

A vicious circle is an example of a positive feedback loop. A positive feedback loop is one that continues going in the same direction, eventually exploding. A positive feedback loop is labeled with a ⊕ in its center.

2. Label each arrow with either a + or −.

One possible solution that Dr. Roberts suggests for this story situation is shown in Figure 8. The diagram suggests that as the price of oil goes up, profits increase, leading to a decline in the amount of oil countries need to produce. As oil production falls, the price of oil will rise further, indicating a positive feedback loop by the "tracing approach." An examination of the linkages indicates two (an even number) negative links, thereby also confirming positive feedback or self-reinforcing behavior.

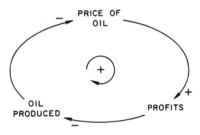

Figure 8   Example solution: the oil crisis causal loop diagram.

Causal loop diagrams have been used as a non-mathematical tool for organizational intervention.[6] Groups of key people have developed in common a set of causal loop diagrams that explain their organization's situation. The process of diagram development and the dynamic thinking that the diagrams encourage stimulate new policy insights and a collaborative approach to policy implementation. Causal loop diagramming has been used as a consulting technique in hospitals, medical schools, labor-management negotiation, and other areas needing group consensus in decision-making.

When used as part of a system dynamics modelling project, the causal loop diagrams become the primary and continuing basis for communicating the model's structure and contents to both participants and clients of the project. More formal flow diagrams and quantitative model development both usually follow the initial causal loop diagramming phase of activity.

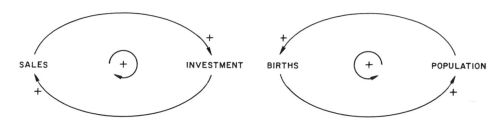

Figure 9 Positive feedback loops.

Positive Feedback Loop Behavior.   As defined earlier a positive feedback loop has very predictable behavior in response to a change induced in any of its variables. The loop can only act to reinforce or accelerate that initial change. As the simple examples in Figure 9 suggest, an increase in sales generates increased investment which leads to more sales that induce further investment, etc. Higher births increase population, leading to more births which add further to population, etc. Without constraints introduced by interaction with other feedback loops, each positive feedback loop can only produce exponential change.

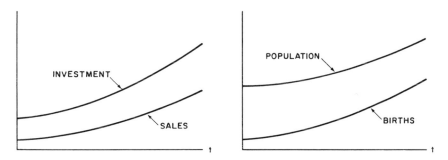

Figure 10 Positive feedback loop behaviors, accelerating upward.

If investment falls for any reason, the simple loop suggests that sales would then fall, causing investment to fall further, leading to more decline in sales, etc. This indicates that positive feedback loops can also produce exponential changes in a downward direction.

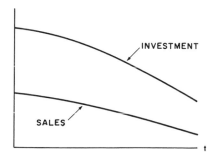

Figure 11 Positive feedback loop behavior, accelerating downward.

Positive feedback loops generate exponential change of all of their variables. Shifts in the relationships described by individual linkages in a positive loop can only affect the rate of exponential change, as shown in Figure 12. These exponential growth or decline patterns would continue forever, unless and until affected by impact from outside the loop, which of course always eventually occurs.

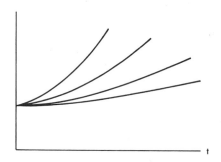

Figure 12   Alternate rates of positive loop explosion.

Negative Feedback Loop Behavior.   Negative feedback loops have greater variety in their behavioral possibilities than positive loops. In all cases a negative loop acts to counter the direction of initial change in any of its variables, but different forms of fluctuation or equilibrium-seeking behavior occur.

The simplest form of negative feedback loop behavior is gradual adjustment, without oscillation or fluctuation. For example, if target inventory in Figure 13 is increased, inventory order rate will initially rise, causing actual inventory to climb. But as actual inventory moves closer to target inventory, the actual inventory information feeds back to affect inventory order rate, and inventory order rate falls back toward its starting point. Equilibrium gets eventually reestablished in the loop.

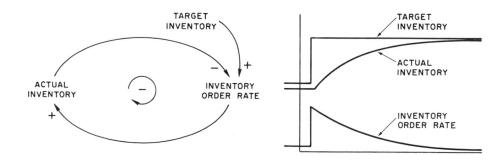

Figure 13   Simple negative feedback loop behavior: adjustment with no oscillation.

A second and very common type of negative feedback loop behavior is called "damped oscillation," i.e. the fluctuations about the equilibrium positions gradually fade away. To discuss this type of situation, let us examine the negative feedback loop shown in Figure 14. The higher the price of the commodity, the greater the rate at which farmers will plant the crop. This will lead to later increased harvest rate which will then add to market inventory. The higher inventory will tend to drive down market price leading to lower planting decisions by farmers. (This simplified diagram omits the feedback effect of price on consumers' buying rate, which would create a second interconnected feedback loop.)

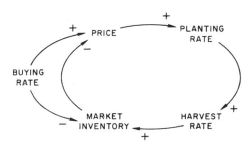

Figure 14   More complex negative feedback loop.

If weather severely decreased harvest rate during one growing season, the response over time of this supply loop would probably be the pattern of slowly stabilizing oscillations illustrated in Figure 15. This characteristic overshoot then undershoot, moving toward equilibrium, is sometimes referred to as "hunting" behavior, i.e. the loop is searching for its equilibrium position. The same behavior is found in many, if not most, negative feedback loops. It arises from the multiple delays and multiple variables that reflect accumulated information and decision processes in the negative loop. When multi-stage action-reaction situations are embedded in a negative feedback loop, that loop can exhibit fluctuating behavior.

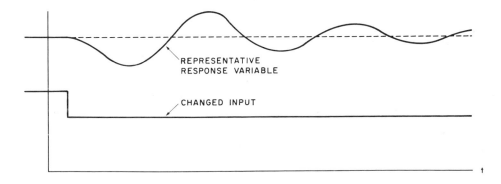

Figure 15   Damped oscillatory behavior of a negative feedback loop.

It is possible, by adjustment of decision rules and/or delays in such a loop, to cause the oscillatory behavior to become either stable or explosive, rather than decaying. Figure 16 illustrates these other situations, less frequently encountered in real life.[7]

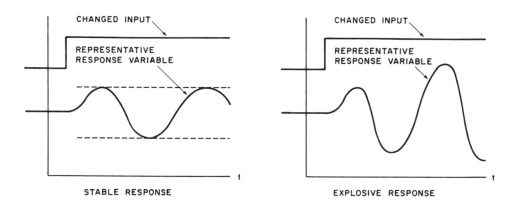

Figure 16   Stable and explosive oscillatory patterns of negative feedback loop behavior.

Mathematical Analysis of Feedback Systems.   For single feedback loops, positive or negative, mathematical techniques exist that permit explicit predictions of the consequences that will be produced over time by any change in feedback loop input or linkage structure. These same mathematical methods can be applied to rigorous analysis of multi-loop feedback systems.[8]

Unfortunately, these mathematics are not yet sufficiently powerful to deal rigorously with complex nonlinear multi-loop feedback systems of the type commonly encountered in real managerial issues. For example, none of the actual cases presented in this volume can be treated rigorously using analytical mathematics, without first undertaking major simplifications. This would require, in essence, "throwing out the baby with the bath water." For real feedback systems problems of managerial significance, the analysis method of present choice must be computer simulation modelling.

Simulation Modelling

A model is a purposeful representation of something, real or imaginary. A simulation model is a model that produces behavior over some period of time; it is dynamic instead of static.[9] The values of all variables in a simulation model are calculated at each point in simulated time. Time is then advanced one simulated increment, and new values of all variables are computed, using the previous values as a base. A simulation model thus "bootstraps" its way over any desired duration of simulated time.

The system dynamics type of simulation model is particularly easy to understand. Three kinds of variables are used, along with formal flow diagramming and equation-writing notations that focus upon the three variable types.

Kinds of variables.   From a system dynamics perspective all systems can be represented in terms of level and rate variables, with auxiliary variables used for added clarity and simplicity.

A *level* is an accumulation, or an integration, over time of flows or changes that come into and go out of the level. Inventories, cash balances, manpower pools, order backlogs are levels, respectively, of goods, money, people and order flows. Inventories accumulate units received minus units delivered. Cash balances integrate over time the flow of receipts minus expenditures. Manpower pools reflect hiring minus firing and/or quit rates, accumulated over some time period. Economists refer to level variables as stocks, mathematicians recognize them as integrations.

In addition to accumulating tangible flows, as indicated above, a level can be an integration of information over time. For example, perceived product quality image no doubt represents customer accumulation of intangible impressions stemming from information flows over an extended duration. Similarly, scientific knowledge is an information level variable. All averages are special cases of such information levels, e.g. average sales is an integration of company sales data over the averaging period.

The second variable type is a *rate*, a flow, decision, action or behavior that changes over time as a function of the influences acting upon it. Receipts, deliveries, expenditures, hiring, and quitting are examples of the tangible flows that occur during time intervals. Message rates and learning are comparable information rates. Economists refer to rate variables as flows.

One way to distinguish levels from rates is to consider the sudden stopping of all action in the system. Under this condition all rates would instantly become zero or nonexistent; levels would be exactly what they were before the action stopped. As an example, if a retail store is closed on Sunday, the Sunday rate of sales is zero. But the Sunday level of inventory is precisely what it was on Saturday night, at the time of closing.

All tangible variables are either levels or rates, i.e. they are either accumulations of previous flows or are presently flowing. But there is one more type of information variable, which we call an *auxiliary*. Auxiliary variables are combinations of information inputs into concepts. The concepts are used as inputs to rate decisions. Auxiliary concepts can refer both to any tangible variable as well as to any information variable. For example, the concept of a "desired inventory" is an auxiliary variable, representing perhaps some multiple of an average sales rate. Note that the "desired inventory" is not a level—it does not accumulate flows into it or out of it—nor is "desired inventory" a rate of flow itself. Consider also the auxiliary variable "inventory deficiency," the difference between desired inventory (an auxiliary) and actual inventory (a tangible level). Auxiliary concepts are used in models to clarify and simplify the representation of rate variables.

Figure 17 summarizes the types of variables used in system dynamics models and where they are found.

Tangible Variables	**Information (or Intangible) Variables**
Levels	Levels
Rates	Rates
	Auxiliaries

Figure 17   Kinds of variables.

Formal flow diagrams.   In visually representing a system dynamics model, causal loop diagrams as described earlier are usually used for general purposes of communication. However, for formal documentation of a model (and sometimes for use during the detailed structuring of the model prior to equation writing), formal flow diagrams can be developed. The formats shown below are the standard schematic conventions used throughout this volume and in all system dynamics work.

The three variable types listed earlier are each represented by a unique symbol. The level is shown as a box, with the name of the level variable indicated inside the box. One or more rates are usually shown adding to the level; one or more rates are usually shown subtracting from the level.

Figure 18   Level symbol.

Rates are illustrated in any one of three ways, depending upon personal preferences and/or space available in the diagram. In all cases the rate symbol suggests a valve, controlling a flow. The name of the rate variable is usually indicated in or near the symbol.

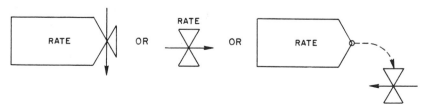

Figure 19   Alternate rate symbols.

The flows that are controlled by the rates are usually shown differently, depending on the type of quantity involved. System dynamics models have commonly used the six types of arrow designators indicated in Figure 20. Any other arrow symbol can be specified when convenient.

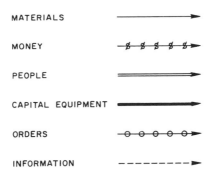

Figure 20   Alternate flow designators.

Flows originate somewhere and terminate somewhere. When the origin or termination is of relevance to a modelled situation, it is inevitably a level variable itself. But sometimes the origin of a flow is treated as essentially limitless, or at least outside of the model-builder's concern. In such cases the flow's origin is called a *source*. Similarly, when the destination of a flow is not of interest, it is called a *sink*. Both sources and sinks are shown as little clouds.

Figure 21   Source and sink symbols.

An auxiliary variable is shown by a circle with the variable named within. An auxiliary is always an information variable, with only information inputs and outputs.

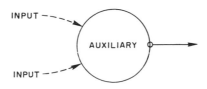

Figure 22   Auxiliary symbol.

A few other symbols will complete the designation of items included in formal system dynamics flow diagrams. In addition to the variable symbols shown above, all models include many *constant* terms, i.e. parameters of the model whose values are assumed to be unchanging throughout a particular computer simulation. Constants are pictured as in Figure 23, the name of the constant being underlined, with an information arrow going to the variable that is affected by the constant.

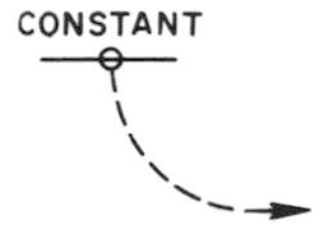

CONSTANT

Figure 23   Constant symbol.

Complex models are often diagrammed in multiple displays. This creates situations in which variables pictured on one diagram are used in another diagram. These variable cross-references are shown by including the name of the other diagram's variable in parentheses.

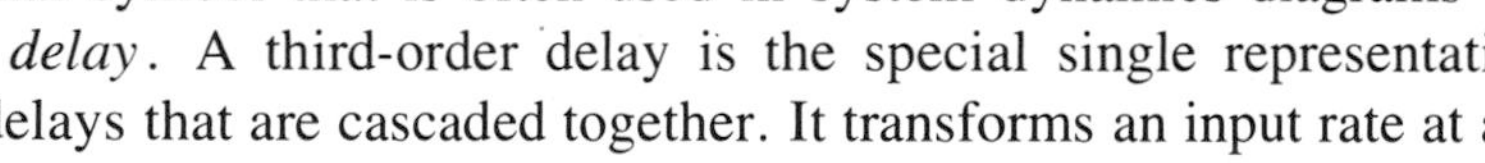

(INFLUENCING VARIABLE THAT IS ON OTHER DIAGRAM)   (VARIABLE BEING INFLUENCED ON OTHER DIAGRAM)

Figure 24   Symbols for diagrams cross-referencing.

The final symbol that is often used in system dynamics diagrams represents a *third-order delay*. A third-order delay is the special single representation of three first-order delays that are cascaded together. It transforms an input rate at a moment in time into an output rate distributed over an extended period of time. Figure 25 indicates the third-order delay symbol as based upon a level symbol with added features. The D3 in the upper-right box signifies a third-order delay, and the constant named in the bottom-right box is the time-constant of the delay. The rate flowing out of the middle-right box is given no further symbolic designation except its name.

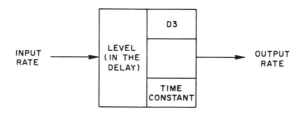

Figure 25   Third-order delay symbol.

As an example of an overall formal flow diagram let us illustrate in Figure 26 a diagram that would correspond to the earlier causal loop diagram of Figure 14. The diagram assumes that the rate of harvesting is a third-order delayed result of the planting rate, and that neither the source of the planting nor the destination of the buying is of interest to the model. It also introduces another variable, the rate of change of price, which had not been included in the less specific causal loop diagram.

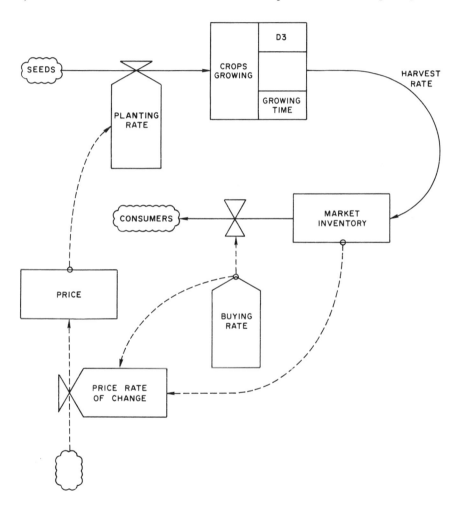

Figure 26   Possible formal flow diagram for Figure 14.

Equations.   Equations permit expressing model relationships in explicit quantitative terms that can then be simulated manually or by computer. The equation types correspond to the variable types described and illustrated in the prior sections. The model developer represents in equation form his or her best current understanding of the situation being modelled. Equations are not chiseled in stone; they are intended to be changed as the model builder's insights change.

In system dynamics modelling each variable in each equation must indicate the specific point in time or time period to which it refers. As shown in Figure 27, .K refers to the current point in time, .J refers to the previous point in time (one time interval ago), and .L represents the next point in time (one time interval into the future). The most recent time interval is denoted by .JK and the next time interval by .KL. Each time interval has the duration DT (Delta Time), whose value is specified at the outset of each simulation of a model.

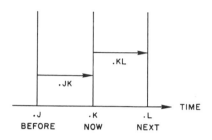

Figure 27   Time notation.

Level equations describe the system's state at each point in time. There are two types of level equations. One type represents measurable quantities such as the level of inventory, knowledge, or the number of employees. Equations for this type of levels take the following form:

L   LEVEL.K = LEVEL.J + (DT) (RATEIN.JK-RATEOUT.JK)

This equation form indicates that a level at the current point in time (.K) is equal to its value at the previous point in time (.J) plus the net change that took place over the past time interval (.JK). Net change is the resultant of flows into and out of the level (there may be several in each direction) multiplied by the appropriate time interval (DT) used in the simulation. Levels do not change instantaneously, but are subject to rates of change having this cumulative effect over time. For example, market inventory as shown in Figure 26 is the accumulation over time of harvest rate flowing in and buying rate flowing out.

L   MKINV.K = MKINV.J + (DT) (HARV.JK-BUY.JK)

MKINV—MarKet INVentory (bushels)
DT—Delta Time (time interval for calculations) (months)
HARV—HARVest rate (bushels per month)
BUY—BUYing rate (bushels per month)

The second type of level equation represents an average of another quantity that serves as a descriptor of the system's state. Such a quantity might be either a level or an auxiliary variable. One use of this type of level equation is to simulate the delay between the time a condition develops in a system and the time it is perceived by decision-makers and others. Another use is to average a rate of change, since rates of change cannot be observed at any one point in time and must be measured by the effect they have over time. Examples of such levels are consumer's perception of product quality and average rate of sales. This type of level equation has the following forms:

L   LEVEL.K = LEVEL.J + (DT) (1/TA) (QUANT.J-LEVEL.J)

or

L   LEVEL.K = LEVEL.J + (DT) (1/TA) (RATE.JK-LEVEL.J)

These forms indicate that the value of the level at the present point in time is equal to the level at the previous point in time adjusted by a change over the last time interval. That change is some fraction (1/TA) (TA represents the time for adjustment of the average or perception) of the difference between the value of the quantity or rate of change being averaged and the previous value of the level, multiplied by the time interval being used. This mathematical averaging process is referred to as exponential smoothing. It causes changes in the level to occur gradually at a rate determined by the value of the adjustment time (TA).

For example, an extension of Figure 26 might include an average rate of buying over some period of time, which would be written as:

L   AVBUY.K = AVBUY.J + (DT) (1/AVTB) (BUY.JK-AVBUY.J)

AVBUY—AVerage BUYing rate (bushels per month)
DT—Delta Time (time interval for calculations) (months)
AVTB—AVeraging Time for Buying rate (months)
BUY—BUYing rate (bushels per month)

In many system dynamics model equations, this averaging process is represented by the following equivalent shorthand:[10]

L   LEVEL.K = SMOOTH(QUANT.K,TA)

or

L   LEVEL.K = SMOOTH(RATE.JK,TA)

For example, using this notation the equation for average rate of buying would then be written as:

L   AVBUY.K = SMOOTH(BUY.JK,AVTB)

AVBUY—AVerage BUYing rate (bushels per month)
SMOOTH—special notation for exponential SMOOTHing or
        averaging equation
BUY—BUYing rate (bushels per month)
AVTB—AVeraging Time for Buying rate (months)

Rate equations are based on the state of the system at the current point in time (.K) and indicate rates of change that will occur over the next time interval (.KL). These equations take the following form:

R   RATE.KL = f(LEVEL.K,AUX.K)

As indicated, rates during the next time period are functions of level and/or auxiliary variable values at the current point in time.

For example, the rate of payment of accounts payable may be approximately a constant fraction of the bills outstanding.

$$R \quad PACPY.KL = \frac{ACPAY.K}{ATPAP}$$

PACPY—rate of Payment of ACcounts PaYable ($/month)
ACPAY—ACcounts PAYable (dollars)
ATPAP—Average Time for Paying Accounts Payable (months)

As another example, the rate of ordering goods for inventory may be a function of the gap between target inventory and actual inventory, as was shown in Figure 13.

$$R \quad INVOR.KL = \frac{TINV.K - INV.K}{TAI}$$

INVOR—INVentory Order Rate (units per week)
TINV—Target INVentory (units)
INV—actual INVentory (units)
TAI—Time for Adjusting Inventory (weeks)

Auxiliary equations represent informational concepts that are used as inputs to other auxiliary equations or to rate equations. They take the following forms:

$$A \quad AUX.K = f(LEVEL.K, AUX.K)$$

Auxiliaries are computed at the current point in time from level and other auxiliary values at the current point in time.

For example, extending the Figure 26 diagram, an auxiliary equation may be written for the size of inventory relative to current average demand.

$$A \quad RIS.K = \frac{MKINV.K}{AVBUY.K}$$

RIS—Relative Inventory Size (months)
MKINV—MarKet INVentory (bushels)
AVBUY—AVerage BUYing rate (bushels per month)

As another example, the total backlog of orders may equal the sum of backlogs of orders for three different product lines.

$$A \quad TBKLG.K = BKLGA.K + BKLGB.K + BKLGC.K$$

TBKLG—Total BacKLoG (orders)
BKLGA—BacKLoG, product line A (orders)
BKLGB—BacKLoG, product line B (orders)
BKLGC—BacKLoG, product line C (orders)

Most formats for auxiliary and rate equations in system dynamics models are straightforward algebraic expressions, as indicated in the several examples above. One equation form that is very useful and appears throughout system dynamics models does, however, require some explanation. It is the following special tabular, rather than algebraic, expression:

A   Y.K = TABLE(YTB,X.K,L,H,I)

or

R   Y.KL = TABLE(YTB,X.K,L,H,I)

This type of equation indicates a functional relationship between an independent (X) and dependent variable (Y). L, H, and I describe the low end L, high end H, and interval I between points in a set of values of the independent variable. YTB is an associated table (designated by T) of constant values of the dependent variable that correspond to each of the values of the X variable. Thus,

A   Y.K = TABLE(YTB,X.K,0,5,1)

T   YTB = 3,7,9,11,13,14

would represent the following functional relationship:

X	0	1	2	3	4	5
Y	3	7	9	11	13	14

This equation is represented graphically in Figure 28.

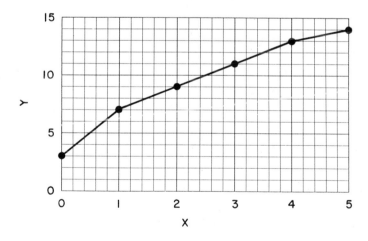

Figure 28 Sample table function.

If the planting rate of Figure 26 were to be represented as a tabular function of price, the graph might look like Figure 29.

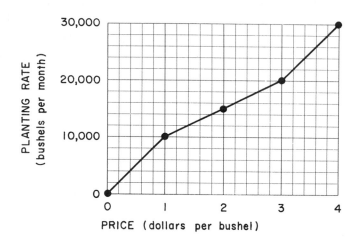

Figure 29   Planting rate as function of price.

The equations for this graph would be:

R   PLNT.KL = TABLE(PLTTB,PRICE.K,0,4,1)
T   PLTTB = 0,10000,15000,20000,30000

PLNT—PLaNTing rate (bushels per month)
TABLE—special TABLE function notation
PLTTB—PLanTing rate data TaBle (bushels per month)
PRICE—PRICE (dollars per bushel)

Many other special functional relationships may be useful in constructing system dynamics models. One more that is frequently used is the equation format for a third-order delay, corresponding to the symbol shown in Figure 25. This is simply written:

R   OUT.KL = DELAY3(IN.JK,TC)

OUT—OUTput rate (units per time period)
DELAY3—special notation for a third-order delay
IN—INput rate (units per time period)
TC—Time Constant of the delay (time periods)

This equation transforms an input rate at a moment in time into an output rate distributed over an extended period of time, as shown in Figure 30. More information about exponential delays can be found in Chapter 9 of Forrester, *Industrial Dynamics* (Cambridge: The MIT Press, 1961).

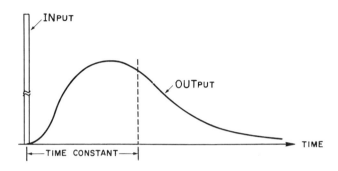

Figure 30   Behavior over time of third-order delay.

Simulation Calculations.   Once a model's equations have been written, simulation calculations of the model can be made over any desired time period into the future. At each point in time the status of the system (i.e., the value of its levels) is determined based on the known prior status and the changes (i.e. the values of the rates) that had taken place during the prior time interval. With this updated status, the new set of changes can be calculated that will take place during the next time interval (by calculating the values of the auxiliary and then the rate equations). The newly calculated changes permit the next updating of the system's status (i.e. its levels), and the simulation calculation can thus carry forward indefinitely.

Let us create a simple example to illustrate how a simulation is carried out. Assume that a purchaser tries to maintain his inventory equal to four weeks of average usage during the most recent six weeks. Furthermore, assume that he responds to any deficiencies in his inventory position slowly, over an eight week period, but that he receives shipments of his inventory orders on average two weeks after he places those orders. Finally, assume that his usage has been steady for several months at one hundred units per week, but goes up in the third week of the simulation to one hundred twenty units per week and remains at that rate.

The causal loop diagram for this example is shown in Figure 31. It indicates that one major negative feedback loop dominates the situation, with changes in usage providing complicating external effects through several linkages.

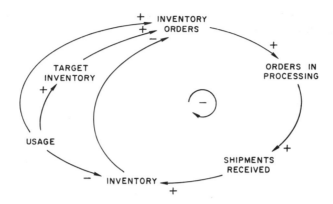

Figure 31   Inventory system causal loop diagram.

Going into somewhat more specific detail, we construct the formal flow diagram shown in Figure 32.

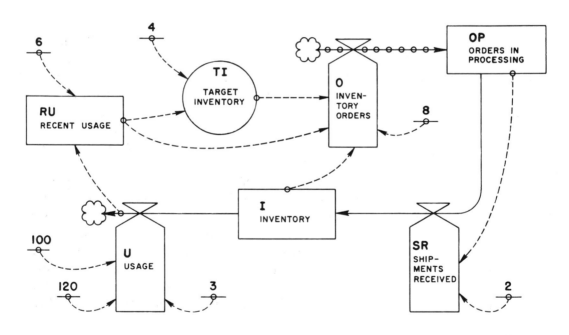

Figure 32   Inventory system flow diagram.

Let us now write the equations for this situation. The abbreviations used are those shown in the diagram of Figure 32. Inventory I is the accumulation over time of shipments received minus usage.

L $I.K = I.J + (DT)(SR.JK - U.JK)$ 1

We must specify the initial condition (at the start of the simulation, TIME = 0) for inventory, as well as for all other levels. Given that the purchaser has been trying to maintain an inventory of 4 weeks of usage, and usage has been steady at 100 units per week, we will indicate this in the iNitial condition equation.

N $I = (4)(100)$ 2

A second level equation is for the purchaser's orders for inventory refilling that are being processed OP. This equation cumulates over time the purchaser's inventory order rate minus the shipments received by the purchaser.

L $OP.K = OP.J + (DT)(O.JK-SR.JK)$ 3

The initial inventory orders in process reflect the previously steady order rate of 100 units per week and the speedy 2 weeks order-processing time.

N $OP = (2)(100)$ 4

The third level in the system is the recent usage RU, an average over the past 6 weeks of the usage rate. This will be written here as an exponential averaging equation.

L $RU.K = RU.J + (DT)(1/6)(U.JK-RU.J)$ 5

If we wanted to use the shorthand notation described earlier, we would write the equation using the SMOOTH function. The equation written below is completely equivalent to Equation 5.

L $RU.K = SMOOTH(U.JK,6)$

Given that conditions in the system have been steady, recent usage can be equated initially with current usage of 100 units per week.

N $RU = 100$ 6

The one auxiliary in the system, target inventory TI, is equal to 4 weeks of average usage.

A $TI.K = (4)(RU.K)$ 7

The purchaser's order rate O for inventory replenishment seeks to adjust actual inventory to target inventory over the next 8 weeks. In addition, of course, the purchaser must order his recent usage so as to maintain his proper orders-in-process position. These two components of the inventory order rate are indicated in Equation 8.

R $O.KL = (1/8)(TI.K-I.K) + RU.K$ 8

The shipments received SR by the purchaser, reflecting a 2 weeks order-filling delay, are therefore just half the inventory orders-in-process.

R $SR.KL = (1/2)(OP.K)$ 9

The final equation that needs to be written is for the usage rate U, which was indicated at 100 units per week prior to week 3 and 120 units per week from week 3 thereafter.

R   U.KL = 100, TIME < 3   10
            120, TIME ⩾ 3

A special notation is usually used in system dynamics models for this kind of change, called the STEP function. That representation of Equation 10 would be:

R   U.KL = 100 + STEP(20,3)

It indicates that U would step from 100 to 100 + 20 at TIME = 3.

      With these ten equations for the system now completely specified, we can go on to the simulation calculations. Beginning with TIME = 0, we can calculate the initial conditions of the three level equations,

TIME (weeks)	I (units)	OP (units)	RU (units/wk)	TI (units)	O (units/wk)	SR (units/wk)	U (units/wk)
0	400	200	100	400	100	100	100

as indicated by their respective initial condition equations. Values of Equations 7 through 10 are then calculated from the equations, filling in their respective boxes. Now that all values for TIME = 0 are calculated, we move time forward by one interval, chosen here to be 1 week, and calculate all values at TIME = 1 for the levels (Equations 1, 3 and 5), then the auxiliary (Equation 7), and then the rates (Equations 8, 9 and 10), filling in the boxes as we go. Going on to weeks 2 and 3 we repeat the same sequence of calculations, noting that as specified the value of U changes in week 3 to 120 units per week.

TIME	I	OP	RU	TI	O	SR	U
0	400	200	100	400	100	100	100
1	400	200	100	400	100	100	100
2	400	200	100	400	100	100	100
3	400	200	100	400	100	100	120

      With this change in usage rate other values now begin to change in the calculations for TIME = 4, still merely following the equations as stated above (and rounding off to whole numbers for ease). Let us review this set of calculations carefully.

TIME	I	OP	RU	TI	O	SR	U
4	380	200	103	412	107	100	120

Following each of the equations, term for term, at TIME = 4:

I = 400 + (1)(100-120) = 380
OP = 200 + (1)(100-100) = 200
RU = 100 + (1)(1/6)(120-100) = 103
TI = (4)(103) = 412
O = (1/8)(412-380) + 103 = 107
SR = (1/2)(200) = 100
U = 120

Now, going on in the same manner through week 30, we keep filling in the boxes.

TIME	I	OP	RU	TI	O	SR	U
0	400	200	100	400	100	100	100
1	400	200	100	400	100	100	100
2	400	200	100	400	100	100	100
3	400	200	100	400	100	100	120
4	380	200	103	412	107	100	120
5	360	207	106	424	114	104	120
6	344	217	108	432	119	109	120
7	333	227	110	440	123	114	120
8	327	236	112	448	127	118	120
9	325	245	113	452	129	123	120
10	328	251	114	456	130	126	120
11	334	255	115	460	131	128	120
12	342	258	116	464	131	129	120
13	351	260	117	468	132	130	120
14	361	262	118	472	132	131	120
15	372	263	118	472	131	132	120
16	384	262	118	472	129	131	120
17	395	260	118	472	128	130	120
18	405	258	118	472	126	129	120
19	414	255	118	472	125	128	120
20	422	252	118	472	124	126	120
21	428	250	118	472	124	125	120
22	433	249	118	472	123	125	120
23	438	247	118	472	122	124	120
24	442	245	118	472	122	123	120
25	445	244	118	472	121	122	120
26	447	243	118	472	121	122	120
27	449	242	118	472	121	121	120
28	450	242	118	472	121	121	120
29	451	242	118	472	121	121	120
30	452	242	118	472	121	121	120

Plotting the results of this hand-calculated simulation in Figure 33 produces clearly the indications of a simple negative feedback loop adjustment process, orders slightly overshooting the target of 120 units per week and gradually falling back toward the indicated equilibrium rate, with the other variables changing correspondingly. (Numerical round-off in this hand-calculation makes the adjustment slightly incomplete.) The simulation can be carried forward as much further into the future as desired, but the transient changes have stopped essentially by week 25.

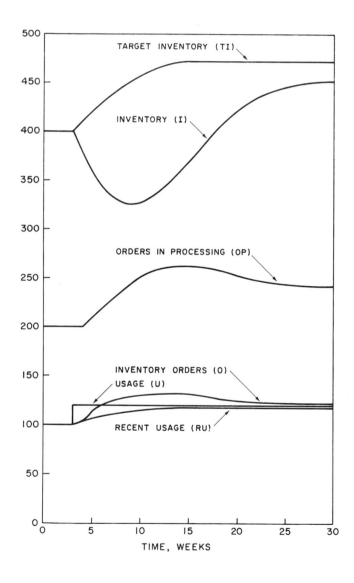

Figure 33   Graphical display of hand-calculated simulation. (SR omitted in order to avoid crowding of curves)

Computer Simulation. In carrying out a model simulation, the computer does precisely the same kinds of calculations as indicated in the preceding section above. It presents tabulated printouts of the results in the same manner, and generates similar graphical displays of the outcomes as were shown in Figure 33.

The DYNAMO (DYNAmic MOdels) compiler-simulator language used in system dynamics models is maintained by Alexander L. Pugh III and Pugh-Roberts Associates, Inc. It is now in use on a world-wide basis in many different configurations—for batch processing and time-sharing—for mini-computers and large "maxi-computers"—and has extensive special features for linear programming[11] or gaming, etc.

System dynamics models can be simulated readily using other compilers/languages such as CSMP or FORTRAN, but the model builder must be much more competent in computer techniques and the mathematics of his system to use these other languages, with no apparent advantage provided by these alternatives. DYNAMO does not require the user to have any prior knowledge of computer programming, and translates equations of the form shown in an earlier section into the needed computer code for simulating the model and producing its output printouts and plots.

Notes

1. See Wiener, Norbert, *Cybernetics* (New York: John Wiley & Sons, Inc., 1948).

2. The reference made is to Tustin, Arnold, *The Mechanism of Economic Systems* (Cambridge: Harvard University Press, 1953).

3. See Simon, Herbert A., "On the Application of Servomechanism Theory in the Study of Production Control," *Econometrica*, vol. 20, no. 2, April 1952, pp. 247–268. Reprinted as Chapter 5 of this volume.

4. For more information on DYNAMO see Pugh, Alexander L. III, *DYNAMO User's Manual*, fifth edition (Cambridge: The M.I.T. Press, 1976).

5. Nancy Roberts, "Teaching Dynamic Feedback Systems Thinking: An Elementary View"; "Dynamic Feedback Systems Diagram Kit"; "Dynamic Feedback Systems Story Kit" (unpublished manuscripts, 1975).

6. For an example of this type of application see Stearns et al., "System Intervention: New Help for Hospitals," *Health Care Management Review*, vol. 1, no. 4, Fall 1976, pp. 9–18.

7. More information on the specific technical conditions that lead to the various negative feedback loop behaviors is available in Jay W. Forrester, *Principles of Systems* (Cambridge: Wright-Allen Press, 1968), pp. 2–3 to 2–16.

8. The curious reader wanting to learn more about these methods of feedback systems analysis should read: R. C. Dorf, *Modern Control Systems* (Second Edition), (Reading, Mass.: Addison-Wesley Publishing Co., Inc., 1974).

9. Actually, a "simulation" is essentially identical to a "model," from a dictionary perspective. U.S. technical usage, however, includes the time-orientation. In the U.S.S.R., in contrast, "simulation" refers to all modelling.

10. In using DYNAMO this special SMOOTH function for a level equation should be used with an A notation instead of the L as shown here.

11. More complete technical information, including a wide variety of special functions that are helpful to the model builder, is available in Pugh, *DYNAMO User's Manual*, Fifth Edition (Cambridge: The MIT Press, 1976).

2

Industrial Dynamics:
A Major Breakthrough for Decision Makers

Jay W. Forrester

Management is on the verge of a major breakthrough in understanding how industrial company success depends on the interaction between the flows of information, materials, money, manpower, and capital equipment. The way these five flow systems interlock to amplify one another and to cause change and fluctuation will form a basis for anticipating the effects of decisions, policies, organizational forms, and investment choices.

My aim in this article is to look ahead at the specific kinds of progress which will be achieved and at the concepts which will make this progress possible. While I shall suggest certain ways of thinking about management that should be helpful to executives today in working on inventory control, production scheduling, advertising, sales, and other problems, my primary concern here is not with techniques and prescriptions. Rather, I am interested in the development of a professional approach to management.

Business leaders, like leaders in other areas, are influenced by an "image of the future." Their ideas about where they are going may be clear or vague, but in any event they have a subtle and far-reaching impact on administrative thinking and decisions. A look at some promising new concepts of management should, I believe, convince even the skeptical executive that his job is developing into much more than an art, that conceptual skill will play an increasingly vital role in company success, and that management is fast becoming second to none as an exciting, dynamic, and intellectually demanding profession.

TOWARD A THEORY

To develop the status of a profession, management must discover the underlying principles which unify its separate aspects. It must develop a basic theory of behavior.

This article is based on studies made possible through the support of the Sloan Research Fund of the Sloan School of Industrial Management at the Massachusetts Institute of Technology, the Ford Foundation, and the use of the IBM/704 computer at the Massachusetts Institute of Technology Computation Center. It first appeared in *Harvard Business Review* 36, no. 4 (July-August 1958), pp. 37–66. (© 1958 by the President and Fellows of Harvard College, all rights reserved.)

It must learn how to convert experiences and particular case examples into a contribution to this general theory. And, finally, it must be able to employ the basic principles of the theory as a useful practical guide for explaining and solving new problems as they arise. By accomplishing these aims, management will become a true profession during the next generation.

The task of management is to interrelate the flows of information, materials, manpower, money, and capital equipment so as to achieve a higher standard of living, stability of employment, profit to the owners, and rewards appropriate to the success of the managers. Looked at in this way, its goals are rooted as deeply in the public interest as the broad objectives of the legal, medical, and engineering professions.

In the past, with management considered more of an art than a profession, education and practice have been highly fragmentized. Manufacturing, finance, distribution, organization, advertising, and research have too often been viewed as separate skills and not as part of a unified system. Too often management education consists of gathering current industrial practice and presenting it to the student as a sequence of unrelated subjects. Similarly, in his work in industry the manager specializes within departments where his experience perpetuates the atmosphere of unrelated compartmentalization.

The next big step in management education will be the development of a basis for fitting together the many management functions into a meaningful whole. Around this central core specialized subjects and experience will take on more significance. Men can be developed more rapidly. They will be able to start from a point now accessible only through long training or fortuitous experience.

Such strides will far exceed in importance recent steps in using computing machines to execute clerical tasks or in applying operations research methods to isolated company problems. For we can expect to gain, during the next 25 years, a far better understanding of the dynamic, ever-changing forces which shape the destiny of a company. This understanding will lead to better usage of available information, to improved understanding of advertising effectiveness and the dynamic behavior of the consumer market, and to company policies that keep pace with technological change.

Beyond these achievements, there will be improvements in company organization resulting from a sounder basis for effective decentralization, from altering the relationships between line and staff tasks in the company, from the more effective utilization of scientific manpower, and from reducing the routine duties and enhancing the creativity of managers. And executives will gain in "clairvoyance." For example, they will be able to anticipate clearly (as I shall illustrate later in the article):

1. how small changes in retail sales can lead to large swings in factory production,
2. how reducing clerical delays may fail to improve management decisions significantly,
3. how a factory manager may find himself unable to fill orders although at all times able to produce more goods than are being sold to consumers, and
4. how an advertising policy can have a magnifying effect on production variations.

TOOLS OF PROGRESS

The new management concepts will rest in part on recent advances in the data-processing industry, in part on military research (which has given us an improved understanding of decision making and experience in analyzing and simulating the characteristics of complex systems), and largely on 20 years of research in information-feedback systems.

Electronic Data Processing.   The performance of electronic computers has increased annually by a factor of nearly 10 per year over the last decade; in almost every year we have seen a tenfold increase in speed, memory capacity, or reliability. This represents a technological change greater than that effected in going from chemical to atomic explosives. Society cannot absorb so big a change in a mere ten years. We therefore have a tremendous untapped backlog of potential devices and applications.

Viewing data processing in another way, we can trace the shifting frontiers of the field by dividing progress into five-year periods:

1. From 1945 to 1950 was the period of electronic research and the demonstration that machines having many thousand vacuum tubes would indeed operate.
2. From 1950 to 1955 was the pioneering period in applying computers to the solution of scientific and engineering problems.
3. During the present period, 1955 to 1960, electronic machines are being substituted for clerical effort in commercial organizations.
4. From 1960 to 1965 we can expect to see the application of digital computers to physical process control. Already there are digital machine tool controls and the SAGE air defense system; we can look forward to dramatic improvements in processes, to reduction of capital investment requirements in the oil and chemical industries, and to civilian air traffic control systems, all based upon new kinds of information utilization for control purposes.
5. From 1965 to 1970 we should see all these developments converging into pioneering improvements in the central management process. The routine, repetitive types of decisions will become more formalized, while management creativeness will be directed to *how* decisions and policies should be made rather than to the actual repetitive making of such decisions.

During the 1965–1970 period of widespread company testing of new management methods, electronic data processing will be an essential tool. Let me emphasize, however, that it is no more the focal point of the future management profession than a slide rule is the essence of engineering.

Decision Making.   Historically, military necessity has often led not only to new devices like aircraft and digital computers but also to new organizational forms and to a new understanding of social forces. These developments have then been adapted to civilian usage.

Such new exploration is now happening in the military *command* (or *management*) function. As the pace of warfare has quickened, there has of necessity been a shift of emphasis from the tactical decision (moment-by-moment direction of the battle) to strategic planning (preparing for possible eventualities, establishing policy, and determining in advance how tactical decisions *will* be made). The battle commander can no longer plot the course of his enemy on a chart and personally calculate the aiming point. In fact, with a ballistic missile he would have no time even to select his defensive weapon.

Likewise in business: as the pace of technological change quickens, corporate management, even at the lower levels, must focus more and more on the *strategic* problems of running the business and less and less on the everyday operating problems.

In the systems development for the military, it has been amply demonstrated that carefully selected formal rules can lead to tactical decisions that excel those made by human judgment under the pressure of time and with insufficient experience and practice. Furthermore, it has been found that men are just as adaptable to the more abstract strategic planning as they are to tactical decision making, once their outlook has been lifted to the broader and longer-range picture.

Simulation.   Also from military research we have available the methods of simulation for determining the behavior of complex systems. These techniques have reached the state of development where they can now be usefully applied to industrial organizations. Simulation is being used in the design of air defense systems and in engineering work. For example, in planning the development of a river basin, numbers in a digital computer represent water volumes, flow rates, electric demand, and rainfall. A few seconds of computer time can solve a whole day of systems operation. Dams can be located and designed for an optimum compromise between power generation, irrigation, navigation, and flood control.

In business, simulation means setting up in a digital computer the conditions which describe company operations. On the basis of the descriptions and assumptions about the company, the computer then generates the resulting charts of information concerning finance, manpower, product movement, and so on. Different management policies and market assumptions can be tested to determine their effect on company success.

To use simulation studies will not require undue mathematical ability. To be sure, details of setting up a model will need to be handled by experts because there are special skills required and pitfalls to be avoided. However, the job of directing the situations to be explored, judging the assumptions, and interpreting the results will be within the ability of the type of men we now see in management schools and executive development programs.

Feedback Control.   Systems of information feedback control are fundamental to all life and human endeavor, from the slow pace of biological evolution to the launching of the latest satellite. A feedback control system exists whenever the environment causes a decision which in turn affects the original environment. To illustrate:

1. A thermostat receives temperature information, decides to start the furnace, and changes the temperature.
2. A person senses that he may fall, corrects his balance, and thereby is able to stand erect.
3. In business, orders and inventory levels lead to manufacturing decisions which fill orders and correct inventories.
4. A profitable industry attracts competitors until, to use the economist's terms, the profit margin is reduced to equilibrium with other economic forces.
5. The competitive need for a new product leads to research and development expenditure that produces technological change.

All of these are information feedback-control loops. The regenerative process is continuous, and new results lead to new decisions which keep the system in continuous motion.

The study of feedback systems deals with the way information is used for the purpose of control. It helps us to understand how the amount of corrective action and the time delays in interconnected systems can lead to unstable fluctuation. Driving an automobile provides a good example; the information and control loop extends from steering wheel, to auto, to street, to eye, to hand, and back to steering wheel. Suppose the driver were blindfolded and drove only by instructions from his front-seat companion. The resulting information delay and distortion would cause erratic driving. If the blindfolded driver could get instructions only on where he had been from a companion who could see only through the rear window, his driving would be even more erratic.

Yet this is analogous to the situation in business. Top executives do not see the salesmen calling on customers, do not see the prospective buyers watching a TV commercial. They do not attend the board meetings of competitors. They do not have a clear view of the road ahead. The only thing they can tell with reasonable certainty (and even here there is sometimes doubt) is what happened to wages, sales, material costs, interest rates, and so on last year.

Smoother Operations.   The quality of management control depends upon what information executives use and for what they use it, as well as on their skills as administrators. As a system the company has certain characteristics which are completely independent of individual functions or departments, just as an electronic computer has certain characteristics as a system of parts. For instance, there is what the engineer might call "amplification," caused by inventory accumulation, filling of supply pipelines, and inept extrapolation of trends. There are delays in decisions, shipping, communications, and accounting. These all combine to cause production fluctuations, construction of excess plant capacity, creation of company-generated rather than customer-generated seasonal sales, and detrimental advertising policies.

Without an awareness of basic information-flow principles, it is only through costly errors that managers can develop an effective intuitive judgment. For example, in a company manufacturing consumer durables, it was discovered, after all data became available, that in a certain year retail sales had varied by 30 percent. In the same year the inventory and ordering practices in the distribution system and at the factory caused this small retail variation to be amplified to a four-to-one, or 400 percent, variation in factory production. The estimated avoidable costs of increasing and decreasing production and of carrying excess inventory were equal to the normal anticipated profit margin! (We shall see later how this could happen.)

Feedback theory explains how decisions, delays, and predictions can produce either good control or dramatically unstable operation. It relates sales promotion to production swings, purchasing and pricing policies to inventory fluctuations, and typical life cycles of products to the need for research.

PRODUCTION AND DISTRIBUTION

How do the concepts and approaches I have been discussing apply to specific business problems? Or, to be more precise, how do the delays, amplifications, and oscillations in the circuital flow of information in a company affect its operations?

Now, in order to illustrate, I must compromise one of the main ideas I have specified; namely, that the system (meaning not the paperwork forms and procedures, but the interrelationships between all the company operations) behaves according to the characteristics of the whole and not according to the characteristics of individual parts. For the sake of brevity, I shall have to limit myself to the production and distribution functions, forgetting research, engineering, sales, and, until a later point in the article, promotional effort. In a sense this is a subsystem, with its own complex of interrelationships that can be studied as such, but it is not *the* whole. Even within this production-distribution subsystem, I shall have space to include only the flows of information and materials. Omitted altogether are considerations of money, manpower, and capital equipment.

If I can make the principles of the new approach clear, however, it should not be difficult for the reader to extend his own picture to include the areas that I must omit.

Needed Information.   To begin the study of our example, we need to know three kinds of information about the system: its organizational structure, the delays in decisions and actions, and the policies governing purchases and inventories.

1. **Organizational structure.** Figure 1 shows a typical organizational structure for the production and distribution functions in a hard goods industry like household appliances. If we examine the basic internal behavior of the system when customer orders are independently specified, we will see that, even with very simple retail sales changes and with no other external disturbances affecting the company, typical manufacturing and distribution practices can generate the types of business disturbances which are often blamed on conditions outside the company. Random, meaningless sales fluctuations can be converted into annual, seasonal production cycles. Advertising and price discount policies of an industry can create two- and three-year sales cycles. Factory capacity, even though

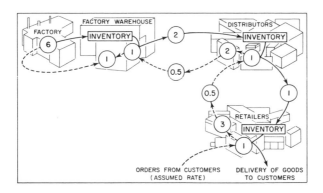

Figure 1 Organization of production-distribution system

always exceeding retail sales, can seem to fall short of meeting demand with the result that production capacity is overexpanded.

Examining Figure 1 more closely, we see that the bottom box represents the retail level. Next above are the distributors, and at the left the factory and factory warehouse. The dotted lines show the information flow, here consisting of orders for goods flowing upward. The solid lines show the shipment of goods flowing downward.

2. **Delays in decisions and actions.** To be able to determine some of the dynamic characteristics of this system we must also know the delays in the flow of information and goods. The time delays are shown on the diagram in weeks and are reasonable values for a consumer durable product line.

Delivery of goods to the consumer averages a week after the customer places an order. At the retail level, the *accounting* and *purchasing* delays average three weeks between the time of a sale and the time when that sale is reflected in an order sent out to obtain a replacement. *Mailing* delay for the order is half a week. The distributor takes a week to *process the order,* and *shipment* of goods to the retailer takes another week. Similar delays exist between the distributor and the *factory warehouse.* The *factory lead time* averages six weeks between a decision to change production rate and the time that factory output reaches the new level. Note that three levels of inventory exist—factory, distributor, and retailer.

3. **Policy on purchasing orders and inventories.** To complete the initial description of our example, we need to know the policies followed in placing orders and maintaining inventory at each distribution level. Let us consider three principal types of orders: (a) orders which directly reflect sales, (b) orders to adjust inventories with changes in business volume, and (c) orders to fill the supply lines with in-process orders and shipments. Let us suppose further that orders are treated in the following ways:

• After a sales analysis and purchasing delay (three, two, and one weeks for the three levels), orders to the next higher level of the system include the actual sales made by the ordering level.

• After a time for averaging out sales fluctuations (eight weeks), a gradual upward or downward adjustment is made in inventories as the rate of sales increases or decreases.

• The orders in process (orders in the mail, unfilled orders at the supplier, and goods in transit) are proportional to the level of business activity and to the length of time required to fill an order. Both an increased sales volume and an increased delivery lead time necessarily result in increased total orders in the supply pipeline.

The ordering rate will also depend on some presumption about future sales. Prediction methods that amount to extending forward (extrapolating) the present sales trend will in general produce a more unstable and fluctuating system. For our example, however, we will use the conservative practice of basing the ordering rate on the assumption that sales are most likely to continue at their present level.

Simulation Methods.   Before we can determine how our system will function over a period of time, all of the above rather general descriptions of the system must be expressed in explicit quantitative form. Illustrations of these relationships are shown in Figure 2.

The next step is to determine how the system as a whole behaves. To do so, we might use some pattern of consumer purchases as an input and observe the resulting inventory and production changes. A very good test would be to see what happens after a small sudden change in retail sales. The effect on the company system can be obtained by "simulation" methods—simulation being the technique of obtaining results from a model. For the industrial system, simulation consists of tracing through, step by step, the actual flow of orders, goods, and information, and observing the series of new decisions required. For example, our production-distribution system might be simulated by a group of men around a table, one to represent retailers, another the postal service, another transportation, another the factory, and so on. Five minutes might represent a week, and in each time interval the proper purchase orders and deliveries would be made according to the rules illustrated in Figure 2. Alternatively, the whole exercise can be done by one person in tabular form on paper. Better still, the entire sequence can be programed on a digital computer.

Digital computer simulation was used to obtain the results in Figure 3. A sudden 10 percent increase in retail sales was introduced in January. The resulting fluctuations are shown in order rates, factory output, factory warehouse inventory, and unfilled orders. (Retail orders are here given as an input which is independent of what happens in the production-distribution system itself. Retail orders are, of course, not actually independent since they are affected by availability of the product and by advertising, a point to be discussed later.)

To determine the behavior of a system by simulating the performance of its parts requires that one describe exactly, and in detail, the characteristics which are to be included. The validity of the outcome of the system studies depends on the judgment of what is pertinent to include in the system description. The following examples show some of the kinds of relationships that are needed in the study of the production-distribution functions of EXHIBIT I:

(1) The inventory level at retail at the end of any time period is the inventory at the beginning of the period, plus goods received, minus goods delivered during the period. The relationship can be expressed as:

$$I_{r,k} = I_{r,j} + \Delta t R_{d,jk} - \Delta t S_{r,jk}$$

which says that the inventory at retail, I_r, at time k is equal to the inventory one time period earlier at time j, plus the goods received in the time interval (the length of the time interval, Δt, multiplied by the rate at which goods are received from the distributor, R_d, over the time interval j to k) minus the goods delivered (Δt multiplied by the rate of sales to customers, S_r, in the interval j to k).

Δt must be a solution time interval that is short compared with any significant time delays which are to be represented in the system. (Δt is here 1/20 of a week, since third-order exponential delays as short as half a week — the mailing delays — are used in the system description.)

(2) Similarly, unfilled orders equal previous unfilled orders plus new orders minus shipments; that is:

$$U_{r,k} = U_{r,j} + \Delta t N_{r,jk} - \Delta t S_{r,jk}$$

where U_r represents unfilled orders at the retail level; N_r is the rate of receipt of new orders; and S_r is the rate of delivery of goods.

(3) Shipments by the retailers are dependent on various factors, here assumed to be the normal order-processing delay, d_{ur}, the level of unfilled orders, U_r, and the physical ability to fill orders based on a ratio of actual inventory level, I_r, to a desirable level of inventory, D_r. Expressed mathematically:

$$S_{r,kl} = \frac{U_{r,k}}{d_{ur}} \sqrt{\frac{I_{r,k}}{D_{r,k}}}$$

This is to represent the aggregate of many retailers each selling a multiplicity of catalogue items in the product line.

(4) We need to know the rate at which the retail level purchases from the distributor level. This reflects (a) the rate of customer purchases from retail plus (b) the rate necessary to adjust the retail inventories plus (c) the adjusting of orders in process in the pipeline between retailers and distributors. The mathematical statement is:

$$P_{r,kl} = P_{c,jk} + \frac{1}{d_{ir}} [(D_{r,k} + d_{pr}A_{r,k}) - (I_{r,k} + G_{r,k})]$$

This says that the purchasing rate by retailers, P_r, in the next time interval, kl, is equal to the purchasing rate by customers, P_c, in the previous time interval, jk, as it is thought to be after data-processing delays (provided by another equation), plus an allowance for inventory and pipeline adjustments which are made gradually over the length of time, d_{ir}.

The "desired ownership," consisting of the desired inventory, D_r, plus the orders which need to be in process to sustain the current business level (obtained by multiplying the total delay, d_{pr}, a variable time, in filling orders by the average rate of recent sales, $A_{r,k}$), is:

$$(D_{r,k} + d_{pr} A_{r,k})$$

The "actual ownership," represented by the present inventory, I_r, plus the actual orders in process, G_r, is:

$$I_{r,k} + G_{r,k}$$

Some 40 relationships of the above type serve to relate orders, shipments, purchases, mailing delays, shipping delays, factory lead time, and so forth. It is not the purpose of this article to do more than illustrate the nature of the relationships which are required. Much study of any particular industrial system would be necessary to determine the relationships that meaningfully portray its behavior. Line executives must set the stage for such a study, and specify assumptions to be used and results to be sought, but the detailed work is for the experts.

Figure 2   Formal quantitative statements of the relationships in Figure 1

Fluctuating Behavior.   Because of accounting, purchasing, and mailing delays, the increase in distributors' orders from retailers lags about a month in reaching the 10 percent level. It is important to note, however, that the rise does not stop at 10 percent. Instead it reaches a peak of 16 percent in March because of the new orders that have been added at the retail level (a) to increase inventories somewhat and (b) to raise the level of orders and goods in transit in the supply pipeline by 10 percent to correspond to the 10 percent increase in sales rate. These inventory and pipeline increments occur as "transient" or "nonrepeating" additions to the order rate and, when they have been satisfied, the retailers' orders to the distributors drop back to the enduring 10 percent increase.

The factory warehouse orders from distributors show an even greater swing. The upturn in orders at the factory warehouse lags the upturn at the distributor level. The incoming order level for distributors is above retail sales for four months, reaching a 16 percent increase in March, which is readily mistaken for a corresponding true and enduring increase in business volume of the same amount. The distributors' orders to the factory, therefore, include not only the 16 percent increase in orders they them-

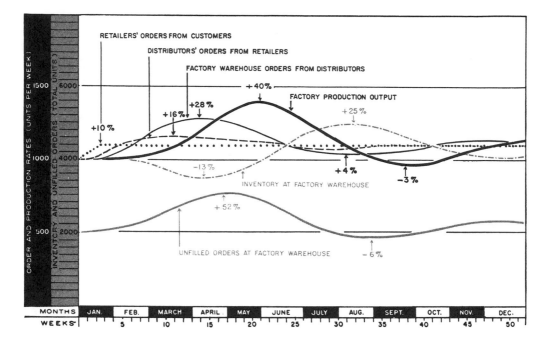

Figure 3   Response of production-distribution system to a sudden 10 percent increase in retail sales

selves receive but also a corresponding increase for distributor inventories and for orders and goods in transit between distributor and factory. As a result, orders at the factory warehouse reach in April a peak of 28 percent above the previous December.

Let us turn now to manufacturing orders. They are placed on the basis of the increasing factory warehouse orders and the falling warehouse inventory, which drops 13 percent. As a result, the factory output, delayed by a factory lead time of six weeks in this example and then a week of data-processing delays, reaches a peak in June which is 40 percent above December. While retail sales are still at 10 percent above December, the factory increase is four times as great.

Note that all of these effects are reversible, another very important point. As retailers satisfy their inventory requirements, they decrease their order rate. The distributors find they have built up an order rate, an inventory, and a supply-line rate in excess of needs. They take the excess out of current orders to the factory so that in August this order rate is 6 percent *below* retail sales and 4 percent above the previous December. In September and October factory output drops to 3 percent below December and 13 percent below current retail sales.

As a direct result of the typical organizational form shown in Figure 1 and of the customary inventory and ordering policies described, over a year is required before all ordering and manufacturing rates stabilize at their proper levels corresponding to the 10 percent retail sales increase. Ironically, this increase was minor compared to the fluctuations in company operations.

Retail Sales Variations.   The problem of unexpected variations in retail sales will now be examined. Imagine first that our system has operated in the past with constant sales, and then sales rise and fall gradually over a one-year interval.

Figure 4 shows the way in which an annual retail sales variation is accentuated as orders travel toward the factory. Retail sales have been stable at 1,000 per week in the past, and in January they start rising toward a 10 percent increase at the end of March. They fall to 10 percent below "normal" by the end of September and return to normal by the end of December.

The initial upswing in orders and factory output is much like that in Figure 3 except that the initial peaks are lower and later. However, at the time the system would naturally rebound from its overproduction state, it is given an additional downward shove by the declining retail sales, which are amplified for the same reasons as previously discussed. As a combined result, factory orders from distributors reach a low of 32 percent below normal in October, and factory output falls to 52 percent below normal in November.

If the following year were shown, we would see factory production continuing to fluctuate between peaks and valleys which are about 50 percent above and below normal, factory inventory fluctuating from 35 percent below to 42 percent above, distributor inventory from 28 percent below to 25 percent above, and retail inventory from 9.6 percent below to 9.3 percent above. During the same year the total inventory in the system varies from 21 percent below normal to 20 percent above, which is less

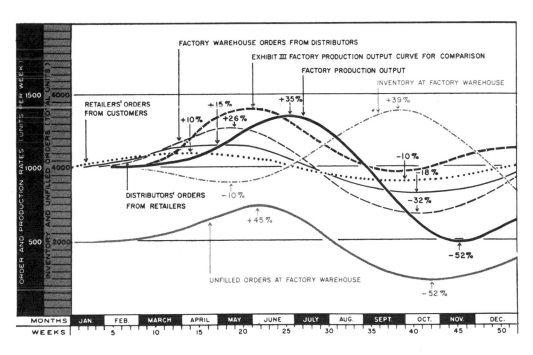

Figure 4   Response of production-distribution system to a 10 percent annual rise and fall in retail sales

than the sum of the separate distribution level peaks because the peaks are reached at different times.

Random Fluctuations.   Note that the curves of Figures 3 and 4 are smooth and free of the short-term random fluctuations which are seen in most charts of actual industrial orders. Uncertainty and random behavior can be inserted into systems studies of this type, as shown in Figure 5. Here the size of orders placed by distributors has been made subject to a week-by-week random uncertainty. Because of the tendency of factory scheduling to smooth out short-run order fluctuations, and because little amplification exists between distributor orders and the factory, the factory output is almost identical to that of Figure 3.

However, if the random-buying fluctuation is introduced in *consumer* purchases, more amplification develops. An oscillatory system like this will respond to the random disturbances by fluctuating at a speed determined by the characteristics of the system itself, rather than in a pattern that is easily traceable to the external disturbance (in this case, a tendency toward peak-to-peak production fluctuations some seven to ten months apart).

Even if there is no average change in retail sales level (as in Figure 3) and no regular periodic change (as in Figure 4), the system will, if it is naturally oscillatory, convert random events into upswings and downswings in orders and production:

Figure 6 shows four years of week-by-week consumer purchases containing random deviations from the average, but no meaningful changes in sales rate. Also shown is the resulting factory production output for the production-distribution system described earlier in the article.

The system, by virtue of its policies, organization, and delays, tends to amplify those retail sales changes to which the system is sensitive. Retail sales fluctuate from week to week over a range of 10 percent or 15 percent with one week falling 31

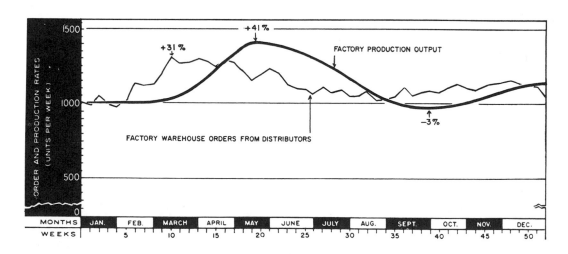

Figure 5   Random short-run uncertainty in distributor purchases

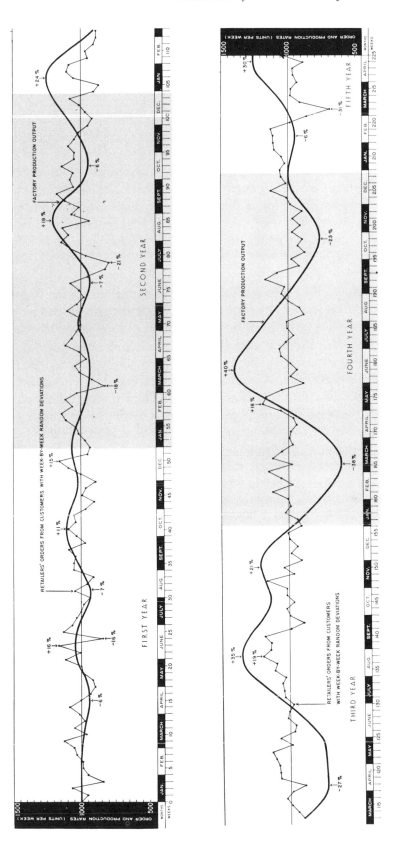

Figure 6　Effects of random deviations in retail sales on factory production

percent. Factory output rises and falls over periods of several months with amplitudes of 20 percent, 30 percent, and 40 percent away from the average.

Just as waves in a bathtub build up slowly when disturbed by a small movement of the hand, so it takes most of the first year to build up serious amplitudes in the factory production swings. These waves then feed on the sales fluctuations. By the time of the third or fourth year, examination of the factory production curve could easily lead the casual observer who lacked the retail sales information to conclude that a seasonal sales pattern was present.

I know of company situations in which such an erroneous conclusion about seasonal sales has led to the establishment of employment, inventory, and advertising policies which in succeeding years *caused* a seasonal manufacturing pattern and thereby confirmed the original error. The possibility of this happening in any company should be carefully considered in the design of management policies to give optimum stability to operations.

Production Limitation.   So far we have considered simple situations that lack many important realities. Additional characteristics of a company can be added as we become ready. In the preceding figures we assumed the factory was able to produce at whatever level was desired. In a more realistic situation, with limited factory capacity, some surprising new effects develop.

Figure 7 shows the effect of a maximum factory capacity 10 percent above the average sales level. As before, the system is completely stabilized at the start of the first year; then it is assumed that retail sales rise and fall 10 percent during each year.

Retail sales never exceed production capacity. Yet, because of the inventory and pipeline effects, distributor orders to the factory *do* exceed its capacity. Furthermore, as factory deliveries become slower, distributors begin to order further in advance of needs and still more orders are put into the system. As a result, the factory operates at full capacity for four and one-half months during the first year.

Then, inventory demands are filled at a time that coincides with falling retail sales. In the last half of the year, falling retail sales and inventory liquidation combine with the reduction of in-process orders which results from improving delivery. In September and October we see a combination of rapidly falling factory orders, a swiftly declining backlog of unfilled orders, and a suddenly rising factory inventory. The natural result is to curtail production from its maximum level to 52 percent *below* normal.

Unlike the first year, we now enter the second year in a state of imbalance with production curtailed, orders rising, and inventory falling. The result in the second year is an accentuation of the first-year performance. Factory orders from distributors rise to 49 percent above normal and show a broadened peak which is sustained by the distributors' tendency to order ahead when deliveries become slow. Factory production runs at full capacity for eight months to meet demand from the distributors. Unfilled orders at the factory rise to 337 percent above normal and represent a backlog which is six weeks of production higher than normal. In the meantime factory inventory has been depleted from the normal four weeks' production to less than a week.

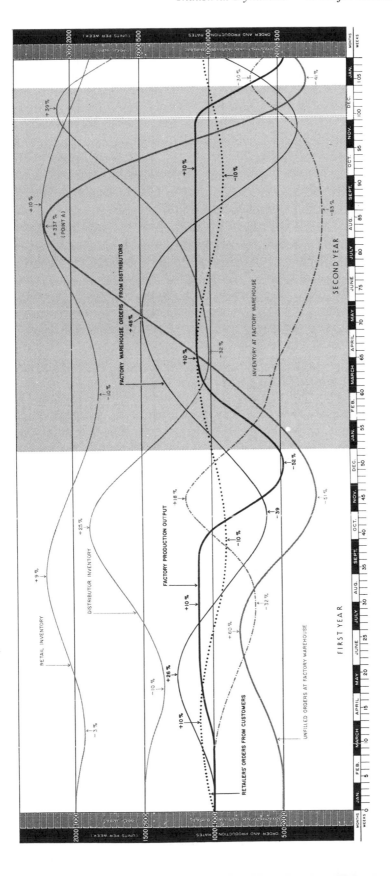

Figure 7 Effect of fluctuating retail sales on factory with manufacturing capacity limited to 10 percent above average sales level

In spite of low factory inventory and slow deliveries, note that retail inventories deviate only 10 percent and that actually there is little likelihood of losing retail sales.

Note that at point A in the 84th week shipments equal incoming orders; inventory is constant. This is therefore the point at which unfilled orders reach a peak and start down. Again, since the factory has produced in excess of sales for eight months and because the long-run average production must equal retail sales, manufacturing must be sharply curtailed in the remaining four months. It drops to a minimum of 54 percent below normal and produces at a level below average retail sales for a period of 14 weeks.

In succeeding years the system would act much as it did in the second year, though unfilled orders at the factory would go to somewhat higher peaks.

We see in Figure 7 an occurrence which may lead a company to overexpand production capacity. For 12 months in the second year, inventory was below the desired level; for 9 months from the first of November until July the order backlog was rising. Viewed from the circumstances at the factory, this condition might easily lead management to undertake expansion plans—even though retail sales never exceed production capacity.

IMPROVING CONTROL

To explain the behavior of an industrial organization is only the first step. After adequately representing the current operations of a particular company or industry, the next step is to determine ways to improve management control for company success.

Faster Order Handling.   To improve industrial stability and to make the company less vulnerable to external influences, executives may consider various alternatives. For instance, they might wish to explore the effect of reduced clerical and data-processing delays, which is often suggested as a quick and easy step toward better management control. However, companies often find the results disappointing, a point illustrated in Figure 8. Here, the clerical delays assumed in Figure 1 (the three, two, and one weeks of sales analysis and purchasing time) have been reduced to one-third their previous values. But the effect is only slight improvement: the production peaks are reduced from five times to four times the retail sales changes. Because clerical delays are such a small factor in the operation of the system as a whole, no amount of speedup can radically change over-all performance.

What about changes in ordering procedures? One possibility would be to place retail orders directly with the factory. The result is shown in Figure 9. When the inventory accumulation, fluctuation of in-process orders, and delays of one of the three stages are removed, production overshoot is 27 percent instead of the 40 percent in Figure 10.

The foregoing raises an interesting question about industries having more than three distribution levels. For example, in the textile industry, which shows marked instability, there are often four or five distribution levels from yarn manufacture to the

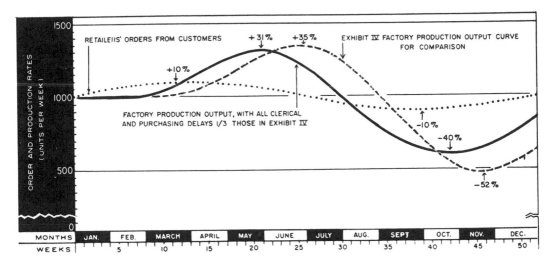

Figure 8   Effect of reducing clerical delays

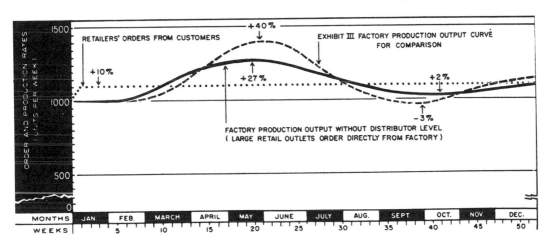

Figure 9   Distributor level eliminated

final consumer. May not a good deal of instability be caused by the existence of so many levels?

Better Sales Data.   Another way to improve factory production stability is to have reliable retail sales information on which to base factory production schedules. Figure 10 assumes that we have "reasonably" reliable retail sales data that are eight weeks late in becoming available to management. (This lag allows for time to collect the data and average out short-run random fluctuations.) By reliable data we mean here that the retail sales information is good enough so that we are willing to give it six times as much weight in scheduling production as we do to the actual orders received at the factory.

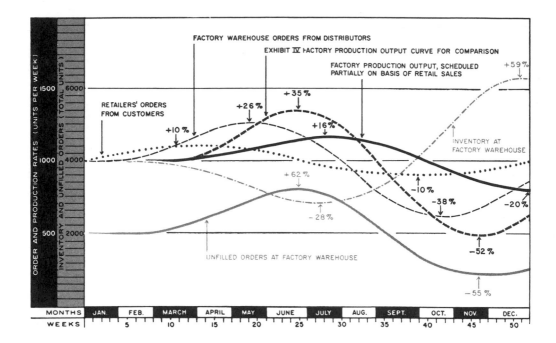

Figure 10   Effect on factory schedules of using reasonably reliable sales data

The first production peak is 16 percent above the start, instead of 35 percent as in Figure 4. Later peaks are two times the retail sales changes, instead of five times as in Figure 4. The supply pipeline and inventory changes at the retailer and distributor levels are being met more from factory inventory and less from peaks in production, which necessitates larger swings in factory inventory, in the unfilled order backlog, or in both.

The need for confidence in the retail sales information is apparent in October, when the factory output is being reduced only gradually in spite of incoming orders being down nearly 40 percent from normal, and in spite of a rapidly falling backlog of orders and a rapidly rising inventory. To achieve this degree of stabilization of production, one must be able to let factory inventory fluctuate from 35 percent below normal to 60 percent above.

Inventory Adjustment.   The behavior of a simple production-distribution system like that shown in the figures is probably more affected by the practices followed in adjusting inventories and in-process orders than by any other single characteristic. The amount of inventory change and its timing are both important. These points deserve special emphasis, and should be considered with especial care by decision-making executives.

To illustrate what can be accomplished, in Figure 11 we take the same production-distribution system as before but assume that management has changed the rapidity with which the inventory corrections are made (but not the total amount of

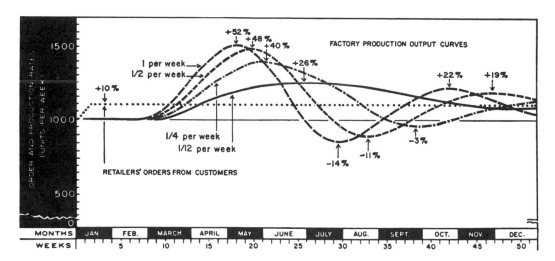

Figure 11   Changing the time to make inventory and in-process order corrections

Note: Fractions refer to amount of remaining imbalance corrected in following week

adjustments made). Management has specified that an inventory correction should be based on sales smoothed over the previous eight weeks (exponential smoothing with eight weeks time constant) so that in no case can the adjustment follow a sales change more rapidly than the delay introduced by the smoothing. The question is what time interval to specify for making inventory correction. When inventories are lower than desired for the current level of business activity, how much of the difference or imbalance should be added to the orders sent to the factory in the next week?

The factory output curves portray the data management needs for a decision. Each curve is based on a different correction rate—a different fraction per week of any inventory discrepancy which is to be corrected through adjustment of the ordering rate to the next higher supply level. (This is the d_{ir} term defined in the fourth point in Figure 2.) This correction rate varies from the top curve, in which orders for any imbalance in inventory and in-process orders are fully placed in the following week, to the lowest curve, in which only $^1/_{12}$ of any *remaining* imbalance is corrected in the following week. The lowest curve leads to about 60 percent of an initial imbalance being corrected in 12 weeks and 85 percent corrected in 24 weeks.

We see that the production fluctuations for the 1-week correction (the top curve) reach 52 percent above, 14 percent below, and 22 percent above the initial value as a result of a sudden 10 percent rise in retail sales. There is an interval of 24 weeks between successive peaks. At the other extreme, the 12-week correction time (the lowest curve) leads to peaks of only 25 percent above, 3 percent below, and 14 percent above the initial value as the production rate approaches the 10 percent higher level. The interval between peaks is longer—34 weeks. As for the curve for the 4-week correction, it is the same as that used in Figure 3 and is the basic system used in the other figures.

We see from Figure 11 that the more gradual inventory correction to business level changes leads to improved stability. Further, the reduction of manufacturing fluctuation is achieved without increasing the inventory extremes.

Figure 12 presents, for various correction times, peak percentage changes in inventory at each level in the system and the total change for the sum of all inventories in the system. The total inventory changes are less than the sum of the separate levels because the extremes do not occur at the same time.

Under many forecasting methods, the kind of gradual adjustment of inventories I have described is impossible. The unstabilizing effects are accentuated by superimposing changes in sales, in-process orders, and inventories.

EFFECT OF ADVERTISING

To show how we would begin introducing into our model additional realism which would be a part of actual company operations, we will now look at *one* of the many effects of advertising. Incorporating this aspect illustrates the step-by-step approach of adding new features to our analysis. An adequate representation of a complete company would, of course, be a very large task. In a single article one can only illustrate the possibilities.

Role in System.   First we need a schematic diagram of the advertising and marketing behavior which is to be considered. Figure 13 is oversimplified but will serve our present purposes. It includes the production-distribution organization set forth in Figure 1 and adds (1) an advertising function and (2) a special segment of the market, prospective purchasers. We assume that advertising expenditure decisions are based on (a) sales, particularly as reflected in the factory production schedule, and (b) excess inventories.

Now let us look more closely at the relationships shown in Figure 13:

1. A time interval of six weeks is allowed for analysis of sales conditions, waiting to be sure of business trends, and the reaching of a decision to change the advertising expenditure rate.
2. Acting on advertising decisions by agencies and media is assumed to require four weeks.
3. Full buyer awareness of the advertising is assumed to develop over a period of eight weeks after the appearance of a new level of advertising.

Adjustment time	Retail		Distributor		Factory		Total	
1 week	− 3.8%	to + 5.6%	− 10.9%	to + 12.9%	− 14.3%	to + 32.3%	− 7.1%	to + 13.6%
2 weeks	− 4.0	to + 5.4	− 11.3	to + 13.5	− 13.9	to + 30.2	− 7.3	to + 13.6
4 weeks	− 4.3	to + 5.5	− 11.5	to + 12.9	− 12.7	to + 24.6	− 7.4	to + 12.2
12 weeks	− 4.8	to + 5.3	− 11.3	to + 8.9	− 10.2	to + 13.2	− 7.4	to + 8.2

Figure 12   Effect of correction time on inventories

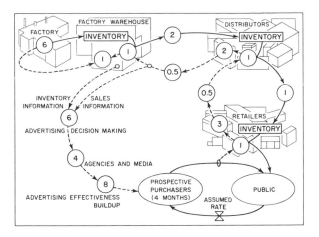

Figure 13   Advertising and consumer market

4. The rate at which consumers become prospective buyers is determined by such factors as the rate of wear-out of their existing household appliances and new housing construction.
5. The average time that prospective buyers contemplate purchase and during which they are subject to advertising influence is assumed to be four months in the presence of an "average" level of advertising.
6. Each 10 percent change in the advertising level is taken to shorten or lengthen by one week the four-month period during which the average prospective buyer considers his purchase.

Obviously, this underrates the impact of advertising; in reality it would normally affect not only the timing of purchases but also the size of the potential market. But even so, as we shall see, it plays a most important role in the working of the system.

Aggravated Production Cycle.   Now we can compare the effect of different advertising policies. What are the implications of gearing the advertising budget to the incoming sales dollar, for example, rather than to a preconceived plan?

Figure 14 shows the behavior of the system illustrated in Figure 13 when management's policy is to let advertising be proportional to expected sales, as represented by scheduled factory production. To see how the system responds to a market change, we here let the rate of appearance of *prospective* purchasers suddenly increase 10 percent. This builds up the pool of prospective purchasers, and gradually over 20 weeks the rate of consumer buying increases. Beginning with the twelfth week, factory production starts to rise; because of the factors earlier described, it exceeds the increase in retail sales.

The decision that leads to increased factory output also leads to a higher advertising commitment. This influences the pool of prospective buyers and further increases the retail sales between the eighteenth and thirty-sixth weeks. However, this retail sales rate, which rises in 43 weeks to 16 percent above the start, is 6 percent above the new

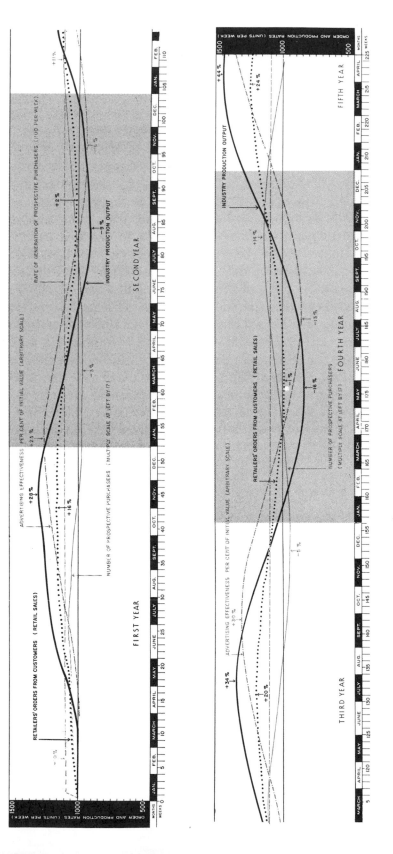

Figure 14   Effect of advertising when geared to sales

rate of generation of prospective buyers. After the twenty-third week, when retail sales surpass the 10 percent increase in new prospective purchasers, the pool of prospective purchasers starts to decrease. The decreasing pool of prospective purchasers becomes the controlling factor after 43 weeks, and retail sales start to fall despite a still rising advertising effectiveness.

We then see falling retail sales and a more rapidly falling production rate. The consequent fall in advertising commitments and effectiveness lets retail sales sink to a still lower level. Retail sales fall for nearly a full year, from October of the first year to September of the second year. In the meantime, retail sales have been below average demand since March of the second year because buyers are reverting to a slightly longer average wait before purchasing (since advertising has been cut back).

The pool of prospective buyers starts to rise in March of the second year; by September it overpowers the falling advertising effectiveness and retail sales start to rise again.

Because of the sequence of production swings that are greater than retail sales swings, advertising that is proportional to production plans, and a slight advertising influence on how soon the average prospective buyer makes his purchase, there is created a two-year production cycle which rises and falls some 30 percent above and below the new 10 percent increase in average demand. Furthermore, the amplitude of the production swings is gradually increasing and will do so until the swings are curbed by manufacturing limitations, lost sales due to delays in shipments, and other factors.

This pattern, with nearly two years elapsing between production peaks, reminds us of recent occurrences in household appliances and some other industries. It indicates that advertising is a *possible* cause of long cyclic disturbances. It would be premature to assume that advertising is *the* cause, however, until many other factors (e.g., consumer credit, sales forecasting methods, price discounting, and growth and saturation characteristics of the market) are also studied.

Longer-Run Effects.   To make our study still more realistic, let us introduce a few more factors and project the behavior of the system over a longer period.

Figure 15 portrays the results obtained from a more elaborate model of the company. It is based on the same kind of production-distribution-advertising system as that used in Figure 14, and on the added assumptions that (1) consumer purchases follow a random pattern which, while not affecting the long-run average of sales, does affect week-by-week sales, and (2) factory production capacity is limited to 40 percent above the value of the initial sales level.

As in Figure 14, a sudden, permanent 10 percent increase in the rate of appearance of prospective customers is followed by long, approximately two-year, fluctuations. Superimposed on this broad pattern are shorter disturbances which are caused by the system's response to random fluctuations in retail sales.

During the third year, production just reaches the maximum production capacity; not until the fourth and fifth years does the cyclic behavior of the industry reach an amplitude where the capacity limit is strongly evident. Periods of 8 months appear when the industry is producing at full capacity and much in excess of retail demand.

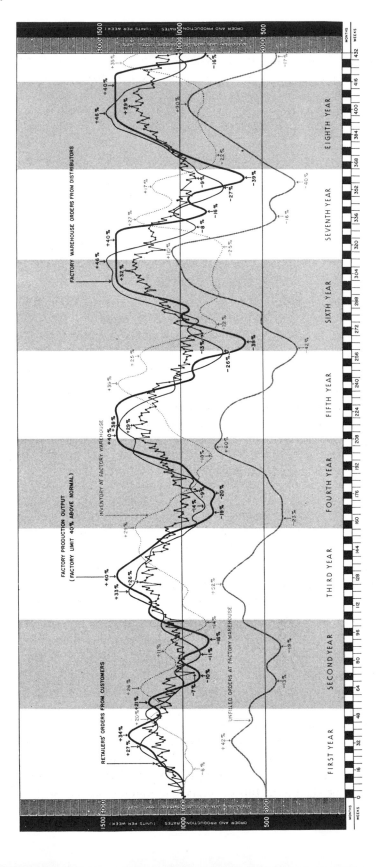

Figure 15 Composite model with advertising, a factory limit 40 percent above normal, and randomized retail sales

These periods are likely to lead to production-capacity expansion, with consequent heightening of the peaks and deepening of the recessions in the following periods.

The preceding discussion has shown how deferrability of purchase can join with other influences (advertising in the above) to produce fluctuating conditions in an industry. Economic conditions and price discounts can also interact with purchase deferrability. For example, the farm equipment industry sells to a market which can defer purchases for several years. Sales are then concentrated, depending not only on years of farm prosperity but also on the history of machine usage and the existing inventory in the hands of the customer.

How can this "roller-coaster" effect be reduced? What can flatten out the cycles? Management policies themselves are an important influence. As it is, the production and inventory policies in this example are helping to accentuate the detrimental effect from the advertising policy. Yet advertising policy might have been most effective in smoothing out the peaks and valleys in Figures 14 and 15 if the effort had been consciously planned to stabilize sales. Another management tool for stabilizing production and sales is pricing policy.

COMPLETE ANALYSIS

I have indicated only in a crude way what can be learned from the study of a company's system of operations. The examples used have included simplified flows of information and materials but not capital equipment, manpower, or money. In actual practice, management would want to have all the latter elements included in the model.

For instance, by adding money flow, including the factors determining the cost of carrying inventory, of changing production levels, and of losses from special inventory clearance sales, executives would be able to get direct profit comparisons between various methods of operation. The model could include the restrictions imposed by available labor supply, maximum hiring and training rate, overtime, and policies regarding work-force reduction.

To set up a dynamic model for simulating company or industry behavior, one must adequately describe the real system which it represents. Getting the data will often be difficult. However, the kinds of information needed involve the basic characteristics of the company. We need factory lead time, inventory policies, construction time for new plants, union contract provisions, and advertising policy. These are the same items that one considers and tries to interrelate in the everyday management of a business.

In a complete company model more intangible items must also be specified, such as the likelihood of results from research expenditures, consumer response to advertising, and market behavior. Many of these quantities will be unknown at first; a few can be measured; some can be closely estimated; others will be guessed at. Today these factors are combined intuitively, and sometimes quite effectively, but the systems-analysis approach should help reduce the margin of error.

When the exact value of an operating characteristic cannot be established, one can test the system with a range of possible values. Sometimes the system will be found insensitive to most differences in value of a factor; in one of the cases earlier described, for example, a speedup in data processing was found to have little effect on the behavior of the total operation. In such cases it does not make too much difference what assumption management directs the researchers to make about the activity so long as the quantity or relationship assigned is "in the right ball park." By contrast, if it is found that the system is highly sensitive, additional effort can be put into determining the correct value. At the very least, the risks of not knowing it become apparent.

SHAPE OF THE FUTURE

Industrial dynamics is in an early stage of development. At a few isolated places, in both companies and universities, research is under way as an outgrowth of military or operations research projects, but the full impact of the new approach will not be felt for one or two decades.

What kinds of advances are in prospect? When are they likely to be made? Obviously, any predictions that we make are subject to the usual "ifs" (business conditions, military pressures, and so on), but we can now foresee what is *probable.*

Two-Stage Progress.   Progress will come in two stages. It is likely that the next five years will be devoted to exploratory research, development of basic analytical techniques, handling of enough specific industrial situations to demonstrate success, and establishment of new academic programs for training future managers.

After this period there will come general recognition of the advantage enjoyed by the pioneering managements who have been the first to improve their understanding of the interrelationships between separate company functions and between the company and its markets, its industry, and the national economy. Competitive pressures will then lead other managements to seek the same advantage.

In other words, the company will come to be recognized not as a collection of separate functions but as a system in which the *flows* of information, materials, manpower, capital equipment, and money set up forces that determine the basic tendencies toward growth, fluctuation, and decline. I want to emphasize the idea of movement here because it is not just the simple three-dimensional relationships of functions that counts, but the constant ebb and flow of change in these functions—their relationships as *dynamic* activities. Such a concept is complicated and not easy to grasp. And, as with any major social change, a new approach to the management process will take time—time to develop ideas, time to test them, time to train a new generation of managers, and time for these men to reach positions of responsibility.

Many companies are already developing the background skills that will be needed. Computers that are now being acquired for other purposes can be used as systems simulators. Operations research departments can expand into the broader activity of studying management systems. Simulation techniques, feedback-control system theory, and analysis of decision processes are being developed in the engineering and research departments of many firms.

It is already clear that some companies will lead, rather than be overtaken by, these changes. For them, research on the management process is a part of the long-range planning of company improvement. But such companies are still the exception. In case after case we have the anomaly of thorough systems studies on products and almost none on the behavior and future prospects of the company itself. Research on devices is fashionable; research toward better management has yet to be fully appreciated. At the same time more companies fail from poor management than from poor engineering.

Areas for Study. What is the nature of the job to be done in the immediate future? I believe that business and educational leaders should concentrate on six high-priority areas for research:

1. Money flow. Models such as those used to illustrate this article must be extended to include money flow and costs in addition to information and materials flow. It will then be possible to see how the financial position of the company and its profitability depend on operating decisions.

2. Consumer market and advertising. The way now seems clear to establish an orderly behavioral structure to explain our experiences and our empirical knowledge of marketing, advertising, and consumer behavior. We should work toward a single unified market model to cover the entire life cycle of a product from the period of launching through sales and profit growth, profitability decline and sales volume saturation, and finally sales decline as the product is overtaken by new technological advances. The growth and decay curves of different products would, of course, be different; but large classes of products can probably be represented by the same model of marketing and technological relationships. In such a model account will be taken not only of the action of the company and its competitors but also of the flow of consumers from possible users to prospective buyers, owners, repeat buyers (based on life and usage characteristics of the product), and secondhand buyers (if any).

3. Capital investment. A long-range representation of company growth must include the motivations and decisions which lead to construction, use, and discard of capital equipment. It must include sources of investment funds whether equity, debt, or retained earnings. Potential productivity increases from modern capital equipment must be related to older equipment already in use. The tendencies during the early growth phase of a product to overexpand capital investment must be related to the product life cycle.

4. Research and development. While not so well understood as other aspects of company operations, research and development are crucial to company growth and to a succession of profitable products. A clear understanding of the relationship of research to profit and capital investment is necessary for proper representation of long-term forces on company growth. The very long lead times, longer than generally supposed, between research policy decisions and the resulting

influence on company profit must be properly related to current financial resources, production capacity, and market development.

5. Economic conditions. Although, as the exhibits show, major company crises are often of internal origin, others are initiated by outside conditions and are amplified internally. Ultimately, a truly satisfactory explanation and prediction of company evolution must incorporate the influences of national and international economics. We now know much about the separate parts of the economy, but we should not trust our intuitive estimate of what a development here or a change there implies for the behavior of the economic system as a whole.

6. Case studies. As the methods earlier described are developed, they must be tested in real situations. This will help us develop the means to cope with the complexities of actual management problems; it will also help us to guide research to the areas of greatest payoff.

The six preceding areas are being incorporated in the Industrial Dynamics Program at the Industrial Management School of the Massachusetts Institute of Technology. The research is being sponsored by foundation funds and also through cooperative research arrangements with interested industrial companies. To provide men competent to carry forward this work, both in research and in companies, industrial dynamics graduate courses and thesis research have already been inaugurated. Also, direct participation of men from cooperating companies will provide nuclei of talent in industry.

The industrial dynamics program at M.I.T. is aimed at four goals:

1. To develop in the manager a better intuitive feel for the time-varying behavior of industrial and economic systems. The study of particular situations, as in the figures in this article, improves one's judgment about the factors influencing company success. The results are beneficial even before one feels that he has reached an accurate quantitative formulation of company behavior that will have reliable predictive value.

2. To provide a background showing how the major aspects of a company are related to one another, so that the developing manager can derive the greatest benefit from his work experience. His operating experience should be more meaningful if he has a better understanding of how his immediate environment is related to the other company functions.

3. To help predict the future course of an existing organization. Very often present decisions determine future company welfare five years or more ahead. We have seen in the figures how underlying, unchanging characteristics of a company can cause erratic manifestations in operations. We can hope, eventually, for better ability to see where present company practices will lead.

4. To improve the future prospects of a company. Beyond prediction lies the ability to redesign an organization and its policies so that it stands a better chance of success. We have seen in the figures a preview of how one might explore and evaluate proposed changes in the company.

Effect on Manager.   What do these new developments mean to the manager? How will they affect his position in the company?

Just as automation requires new skills at the worker level, so will improved methods require new abilities at the management level. The executive of the future will be concerned not so much with actual operating decisions as with the *basis* for wise operating decisions. He will be concerned not so much with day-to-day crises as with the establishment of policies and plans that minimize emergencies.

He will be able to do these jobs with a considerable amount of sophistication and skill. He will have a basis for understanding the implications of market trends and the probable behavior of consumer demand. He will recognize the ebb and flow of forces which interact to generate fluctuating economic conditions. He will be able to relate the changing factors in research, investment, and marketing to the life cycle of a product. He will be able to relate different financing methods with their relative advantages and risks to the uncertainties of market and economic conditions. He will know how to devise organizational forms that are efficient and encourage the creativity of people.

We can expect changes in various management responsibilities. There will be a merging of many line-and-staff functions. Today, the kind of systems studies discussed in this article would be the province of staff specialists. Yet the results will determine the future success of the company; the conclusions will be only as valid as the assumptions on which the studies are based, the answers no more pertinent than the questions asked. Therefore, systems planning must, in time, be the tool of the responsible manager. It is by nature a thoughtful process of weighing the past and present, not to reach the immediate decision of the moment but to derive guiding principles for the future.

All of this will lead to a more decisive separation of policy making from operations, with the dividing line much lower in the organization than at present. New ways to predict the interaction between company functions will speed up the movement toward decentralized management. In the past, power has been concentrated at the top in order to improve over-all integration and control. With increased understanding of the company operation, we can expect that improved definition of objectives and more pertinent standards for the measurement of managerial success will permit managers at the lower levels to take on more operating responsibility. Senior executives will then be free to give more attention to product innovation, economic conditions, and the organizational changes that will enhance man's creativity.

3

Industrial Dynamics
and the Honeywell Experience

R.J. Meyers and A.R. Roberts

We would like, in this paper, to present our view of the place and function of industrial dynamics in applied research and in management. We will comment on its future prospects and present several suggestions on needed developments.

The position will be taken that the successful application of industrial dynamics in research and in management depends upon successful treatment of a somewhat broader and more basic problem—the "management science implementation problem." The "implementation problem" is here defined as the failure to make the newer, usually more productive, and often more sophisticated[1] analytic and problem solving procedures and processes a part of the accepted, ongoing management practices of some major organizational activity. We will propose a solution to that problem.

A major objective of the Management Research and the Marketing Research and Planning functions in the Honeywell Residential and Commercial Divisions is to become regular working members of the management teams taking part in the Divisions' continuing search for performance improvement. More succinctly the objective is to have the research approach (which we will soon define) become standard operating procedure where it seems to fit. We are making progress in that direction and it is on the basis of that experience that we would like to express our opinions, share some thoughts with you, and make some recommendations for future work.

When we were approximately a year along in our management research program it became clear to us that we lapsed too often into discussion of the tools rather than the function. We were spending more time than we should talking about, and working at, getting acceptance of the building of industrial dynamics and econometric models, and the use of quantitative and/or computer-based information and analysis systems. We have stopped that. We now work mostly at making the research process or function more productive and, we might say, more implementable.

The main themes or topics emerge: models, research, management, implementation, industrial dynamics. We would like to discuss them in that order so that we can place our main topics, industrial dynamics and the management science implementation question, in proper perspective; so that we can embed our main thoughts in a broader view of the whole management scene.

Model has become one of the buzz words of our culture. As a noun and as a verb it has been used to describe quite disparate activities, and as such has often created an aura of "scientificness". It might, then, be worthwhile to catalogue those activities and propose some order of "worth" or value. Models are, or have been, used to:

1. stimulate the creation of productive alternatives;
2. test alternatives in the simulation mode;
3. predict;
4. optimize;
5. express theory, structure, or assumed relationships;
6. train;
7. computerize arithmetic operations;
8. capture logic used or procedure followed;
9. summarize and combine estimates or beliefs;
10. monitor activities to achieve consistency.

We would propose that uses 1, 2, 3, and 4 are the most valuable, in that order. Why? Because we feel that the most important activity in which models can be used is the continual search for performance improvement in some activity in an organization.

An important part of that search for performance improvement is the research process to which we alluded earlier. We would define the research procedure as a six-step process involving:

1. the specification of current practice, usually in some kind of quantitative model;
2. the creation of alternatives to that present practice;
3. the selection and test of promising alternatives through model simulations;
4. field test of those alternatives which proved most productive in the model simulations;
5. implementation of the chosen alternatives; and,
6. measurement of the accomplishment of the implemented alternative(s).

If one were to argue that the main objective of applied research and the main objective of management in itself is to constantly move to higher levels of accomplishment; and, if we were to say, as we have, that the research process is an integral part of that search for performance improvement; and, if we define the research process as we have in the six steps above, it is possible to see why we have created the order of importance of activities that we have. That is, we have said that if one is to achieve performance improvement, by definition, one has to develop better ways of doing things. And in doing that one must, of necessity, create alternatives to present practices.

There has been a great deal of discussion in the management science literature of the difficulties involved in building models, of the difficulties involved in getting acceptance of the models and the alternatives chosen for implementation. We would submit, though, that the most critical activity is not the building of the model nor the gaining of acceptance of the alternatives. The most critical activity is that of alternatives that will stand the test — the simulation tests and more particularly the field tests.

We like to feel that it is possible to quantitatively rate the research activity in a manner something like this. We would expect that a good or productive research activity or process would be one which would result in the creation of four or five alternatives which have a great deal of potential for increasing objective achievement in the area concerned.[2] After the four or five seemingly productive alternatives have been created they would next be tested in the simulation model. The hope would be that with a good simulation model it would be possible to test these alternatives realistically and that out of the four or five alternatives created two or three would stand up under the simulation tests. The two or three, or even one or two, most attractive alternatives that have survived the simulation test would then be field tested under actual operating conditions. Again the measure of the goodness, as it were, of these alternatives, would be the number of created alternatives that survived the field test. The expectation would be that at least one or two alternatives would survive the field test and would appear to be quite productive in increasing our objective achievement. Then, of the one or two (or hopefully two or three) alternatives that survive the field test, the one that seems most implementable (or that seems to rate best in a combination of implementability and productivity) would be selected for implementation — for incorporation in present practice. Now the final measure of the research process would be the objective achievement increase that was actually experienced with this new alternative, as compared to past practice.

One now has a structure for describing, carrying out, organizing, and rating the research process. If our particular definition of the research process were accepted, if the six activities define a most desirable research process, one could see why we have selected activities 1, 2, 3, and 4, in that order, as being the most valuable. The reason for this is that we argue that of the six steps in the research process, the one that has received the least attention, but yet is the most important, would be the second one, the creation of alternatives to present practice.

There has been so much attention given in the literature to the creation of models and to the selling of solutions, as it were, that there really has not been enough attention given to the actual mechanics or environment most conducive to the creation of productive alternatives. We consider this to be the greatest gap in the present discussions of management science or operations research. We would then argue that the most important use that can be made of a model would be that of stimulating the creation of productive alternatives. A second most important use of the model then would be the testing of those created alternatives in the simulation mode. It would seem quite necessary to be able to conduct valid tests of the alternatives created. A third most important activity follows naturally from the second in the sense that prediction is a necessary part of the test; prediction not in the usual forecasting sense but in the sense of predicting the outcome of different practices. In summary then, the most important use that can be made of models, we feel, is to create alternatives, to test alternatives, and to predict the outcome of these alternatives.

It may seem strange that we have considered item 4, optimizing, as being the fourth most desirable use of models, since it would seem to follow that if one could optimize, one would accomplish the three previous steps. However, we would choose 1, 2, and 3 mainly on the basis of generality; that is, in practically all situations it is possible to create alternatives, test alternatives, and predict the outcome of the choices being made. In contrast, in most industrial situations which we have experienced we find it very, very difficult to develop algorithms which optimize the complex of objectives which exists in a given situation. We feel that in the most general case one could at least do some sort of hill climbing towards the complex of goals that exist in people's minds; that is, it is possible to develop alternatives which cause us to do a little better in increasing the achievement of one or more objectives without decreasing the achievement of other objectives, and therefore have some net effect in the usual welfare sense (though, parenthetically, we do not overlook the great difficulty of the welfare concept as it has been articulated over the years in economic theory). We find, on the other hand, that optimization is not as general a procedure as some sort of hill climbing or general performance improvement activity, and would have to rate optimization behind the other three uses of models.

In the first three steps of the research process models play a very important role. We, in our work at Honeywell, use a variety of models, all the way from simple logical "if-then" models (used to capture current practice) to econometric type models, analysis of variance models, regression models and industrial dynamics models. Each seems to have its place and function. In this paper we will discuss only the place and function of industrial dynamics models.

Industrial dynamics models, by definition, are most helpful and most useful when the relationships that one wishes to portray, and the environment in which one wishes to test alternatives, are feedback loop situations. Or where the feedback loop concept seems to be most helpful in creating ideas, in testing alternatives, and in making predictions. Since the feedback loop concept describes a great many situations, the industrial dynamics model and the descriptive framework provided by Forrester prove to be most useful.

Generally speaking, industrial dynamics models are somewhat more understandable to operating people, as a matter of fact, quite a bit more understandable to operating people than econometric models. While econometric models may be more specific in the quantification of relationships and in the articulation of simultaneous relationships, industrial dynamics models seem to express relationships much as operating management people do. A limitation, of course, is that in some situations it is not necessary, and in some cases not even particularly helpful, to look at the situation as a feedback loop situation. There are many situations in which we work where the events are more easily conceptualized looked at as straight line cause and effect, without any particular feedback in the servomechanism sense. In those cases, obviously, the industrial dynamics model and its framework makes no particular contribution and sometimes can be a detriment. Even in cases where it might be possible to structure a series of problems in industrial dynamics models, we find it quite useful to structure these problems in several different molds and model types simply to avoid giving the impression that we put every problem into the industrial dynamics "bag". That is, we are not "industrial dynamicists", we are model builders and model builders only insofar as model building can be useful in the research process.

There has, of course, been a fair amount of controversy over the relative usefulness of industrial dynamics. We would tend to feel that many of the points made in those debates are not terribly relevant. It has been common practice for innovators to claim a bit much for their innovations, and it has been quite common in the history of science for innovative people to be somewhat stubborn in arguing the virtues of their particular "baby". It is easy for them to overlook some of the defects; but we would not consider that something to become exercised about. We simply attribute this to the biased pride of parenthood, and would say that it is not the function of the creative innovator, struggling as he is against the inertia of the society around him, to build up a very balanced view. We would rather feel that users of the creation developed by the innovative person should provide the balance. It is quite unrealistic to ask innovators to be even-handed in their discussions of their particular development. We would simply take the view that industrial dynamics is not the solution to all problems, is not the best approach to be used in all applied research. But it is in many cases an extremely useful way to formulate the relationships that exist in some situations, to uncover the underlying phenomenon, and to make valid predictions of what might result from alternatives to, or changes made in, any particular system. Given the argument that industrial dynamics is a very useful way to model, we then should pay credit to Professor Forrester for developing a particular set of techniques and explanatory devices for bringing these techniques to management scientists, and let the matter rest there.

It is obvious, then, that we feel that any quarrel with Forrester's unevenness in argument or Forrester's argumentativeness in his presentations as not worth getting exercised about. Having said that, and having paid what we think is due credit to one of the pioneer developments of management science in the last ten years, we would then go on to say that there is work to be done in making the industrial dynamics concept, analytical approach, and output more accessible to management. It is in that area that we would make recommendations. One recommendation would be to provide more generality in the computing capability. We think it is becoming too restrictive to have to use the DYNAMO compiler, which at the moment runs on the IBM/7094. In our case, we have shifted over to developing the capability to run the industrial dynamics in FORTRAN. We developed this because we wanted to have the ability to run industrial dynamics models on Honeywell computers, for obvious competitive and image reasons. After we had developed the capability of building and running industrial dynamics models in the FORTRAN mode we discovered that Robert Lewellyn at North

Carolina State University had developed a system called FORDYN, which is a set of FORTRAN routines for doing most of what DYNAMO does. Now, we feel that we have pushed along a little further because we have not simply replicated the output formats produced by the DYNAMO compiler and the FORDYN routines, but have developed the ability to create quite different formats. We found, in our work with the operating people who are using the industrial dynamics models (and who are helping us to build the models) that the people tended to work a little better with numerical output rather than graphical output. This is what they had been used to working with. Secondly, we found that if one blocked out the output in terms of 13 week blocks, one could represent quarters of the year. And our people tend to think in terms of quarter-year periods. This is their continuous interaction with a fairly sophisticated production planning and control system, and a highly computerized order processing and inventory control system, all keyed around plans and goals set by quarters. We found it to be very useful to block out our output in thirteen week periods and then have the people trace the development of variables through the quarters and from quarter to quarter in attempting to understand the dynamics of the systems under study. The DYNAMO output and the FORDYN output list variables in a quite different way. They list all the variables for any one time period together, and then all the variables in the next time period together, and so on. We found that this format made it almost impossible for the operating people with whom we worked to trace the flow of a particular variable in the numerical output.

We have further found that we would like very much to run multiple simulations of a particular model with a variety of values for parameters to see the effect on one or two principal variables. We have then developed the technique of running a model a considerable number of times and storing the output on several tape drives. Then we go back and pull out one or two or some limited subset, of the variables for display in printed output. What we say is, ''I am not so much interested in looking at a display of the output of twelve variables under a whole variety of conditions. What I would rather do is to have a display under which I can compare the performance of one or two variables under a variety of conditions.'' By retaining a great deal of flexibility in our intermediate storage of results and our formatting of output we have found it possible to present output which can be analyzed in several ways by the operating people with whom we work. Greater insight is therefore achieved of the dynamics of the systems that we are studying and the effect of different alternatives created. In conclusion, then, we would say that industrial dynamics is one very valuable tool in our kit of modeling tools and we find it to be quite unproductive to quibble about whether this is the most important tool or whether some other type of tool is more important. Our view is a very simple one. Industrial dynamics models are very valuable models. They give a great deal of insight into the dynamics of systems that we look at, they help stimulate the creation of alternatives, and they are very useful in testing alternatives.

We like to use industrial dynamics, we work very hard at using it, and we feel that it is a great assist to us in our research effort. The improvements we suggest really follow the line of increasing versatility in output, and of clarifying the presentation of the model formulations so that they can be more easily understood by people not technically trained in model building. We are attempting to make the construction of models a little easier, are attempting to lay out the models and schematics and computer programs in such a way that when people return to a model after being away from it for three or four weeks it is possible for them to recall easily the relationships in the model. We are doing a great deal in this area, and we would hope that other people who are interested in industrial dynamics and who work in the same area would acquaint us with their work so that there might be some cross fertilization and feedback of ideas between us. If any of you are so working we would be very happy to know of your work and of course would be delighted to show you what we are doing so that we both can do a better job in applying industrial dynamics models.

We said earlier that the second of our main topics was the management science implementation question. We have used implementation in two senses in our discussion. In one case we defined implementation as making the research process an integral and standard part of management practice. Later on we talked about the implementation of chosen alternatives. We would like to conclude this paper with some thoughts on the first sense of implementation, which, of course, is the more critical one. How can one make the research process and some of the more formal techniques that have been described in the literature an integral part of management. We would suggest that there are two activities which should go on in parallel, or simultaneously, to promote or to solve the implementation problem. The two activities could be described as follows. The development of very simple models which in many cases do nothing more than simply formalize thought processes and analytical processes that have been a part of the manager's operating technique and style for many years. For example, we have seen some planning models which, on the face, seem to be nothing more than computerized printout of the profit and loss statements and balance sheets that have been the stock and trade of most planners. In other cases we have seen so called risk analysis models which are nothing more than the numbers that result from gathering the opinions of a variety of marketing and production people as to what the probability density functions are which describe estimates of annual sales volume and production costs for varieties of products. These so-called models have the virtue of being easily understood and are acceptable to management because they are following common practice and procedures. There is nothing new that has to be learned. The computer is just making it much easier to carry out the arithmetic and making it possible to consider a large variety of alternatives and to help the person in his display of information and his thoughts about that information. We feel that this activity is quite important because it moves the person into what is a familiar area in his model building. At least the subject matter is quite understandable to him and one avoids the creation of fears and all sorts of psychological hangups. We would suggest, however, that this device or this approach does have one serious weakness. Periodically a manager remarks that with all the talk about model building and computers and research and so on, we have not shown them any more than what they have been able to see over the years with their own handwork on pads of paper. Questions are raised as to what is new in the whole situation other than higher speed, fancy computer output, and so on. We have run into this kind of comment periodically and if we did not have, "in the back of our pocket", as it were, alternative approaches, I feel that we long since would have lost the opportunity to build credibility for the research process and the model building approach. We therefore feel that it is quite necessary to have parallel with this kind of simplistic type modeling, a more sophisticated model which is aimed at establishing causal relationships. There are many areas where the "hip-shooting" businessman has a difficult time either developing or substantiating beliefs about causal relationships. It is in those areas where formal model building and the more sophisticated models and research type approaches can make the greatest contribution by developing the causal relationships between independent and dependent variables. We then would feel that the best of all possible plans would be one in which there would be parallel, simultaneous efforts aimed at building simplistic models (which are easily understood and which represent no real psychological shocks to the manager) and developing causal relationship models which answer questions which people have been unable to answer before. The causal relationship models enable people to make predictions and influence events in a way in which they have never been able to before. We would argue that the combination of these two approaches builds the kind of personal credibility that an organization or activity needs to get acceptance of it as an integral part of management.

The preceding comments suggest a parallel or dual approach. As an alternate, a serial approach might be used in attempting to achieve successful implementation. This approach is tied to the first step in the previously described research process, because that is where it is possible to obtain the management involvement crucial to successful action on the other steps. A key tactic suggested here is that of using a two-step process in capturing current practice. In the first step the model builder captures what the manager believes is happening. Only in the second step or stage is an attempt made to capture what is really happening. Here, we feel that if the model builder tries to operate external to the system he will fail in his implementation efforts. He needs the participation and involvement of those in the system if he is to succeed. We would elaborate the concept as follows.

Many model builders' *first* step is capturing current practice, where the professional model builder himself conceives and constructs a model capturing what is actually happening. When this approach is followed, the "burden of proof" is placed upon the model builder, for he must demonstrate that his model, which most likely is in terms unfamiliar to management, is a proper representation of the operations.

The better approach is to *initially* capture in the model exactly what the manager *believes* is happening. Once in operation, the "burden of proof" then belongs to the manager to explain the differences between the model's predictions and actual practice. In some cases, at this point in the model's development the researcher may be surprised to see how well the manager's experienced "feel" of the business performs as a model. When this occurs, further work is refinement of the manager's own model. Since the manager has now shown that he "knew all along" how the basic forces interacted, he should be a willing contributor to such further work.

When the model based upon the manager's "feel" of the business does not effectively predict the real world, you have a different problem.

If you are fortunate, the manager will want to discover why his original model is not an effective predictor. This may stem from his personal intellectual curiosity, a desire to more fully understand his organization, or a belief that a more refined model will help him to solve a pressing problem. If such a manager feels that the model building effort does not jeopardize his objectives within the line organization, you can expect continuing interest and effort from him.

In contrast, the manager who does not want to continue to refine the model may feel this way for a number of reasons:

1. Having developed his own "conceptual model" of the operation from many years of experience, he may not be readily able to offer fresh new alternatives.
2. He may see *little or no value* in answering the "academic" question of why discrepancies exist between the model and his operation.
3. The manager's list of objectives and priorities may force him, in his opinion, to let the model building work sit, while more urgent operating problems are solved.

The researcher must expect these reactions and must have postured himself in advance to deal with them.

If reason 1 occurs, the researcher is presented with the obligation (and opportunity) to suggest alternative models or elements of the manager's model which help explain the deviations between the manager's model and reality. This means that the researcher should have been at work on his own model during the time he has been quantifying the the manager's model. It is most important to recognize that *only now* once the manager agrees there is a *problem* (i.e., a difference between his own conceptual model and reality), should the researcher offer a *solution* (a better model).

To prevent reason 2 from occurring the researcher must first ensure that the model will have credibility from the viewpoint of the manager.

a. It must explicitly consider variables the manager feels are relevant.
b. The results must not *grossly* contradict his feel for his operation.
c. The researcher must be adept at the *art* of portraying the model to management using the terminology and formats that management is comfortable with, as well as the *science* of creating an operating model on the computer.

The researcher may also need to establish that the "problem" (as defined above) is significant enough to justify the work required. He then must get the manager's agreement that the potential benefit (performance improvement) clearly is greater than the cost of model refinement.

Reason 3 is dealt with by having top management commitment to the researcher effort *prior* to the work beginning, so that conflicts in objectives and priorities will be resolved in favor of the research effort.

We said earlier that we would like to express some opinions on industrial dynamics and on the implementation question; that we would like to share some thoughts with you; that we would like to make some recommendations for future work; and that we would like to propose a solution to the implementation problem. We hope that we have done so in a constructive way.

Notes

1. More sophisticated in that they are cognizant of more of the factors at work in a real-life situation, are more explicit in their articulation of relationships among those factors, and are more correct in their ordering according to relative impact or influence.

2. In this paper we will not concern ourselves with the question of most desirable objective structure. We are taking as given the objectives arrived at in the area under study and have simply said that the use of models in the research process would be aimed at maximizing the achievement of the objectives already arrived at and agreed upon.

4

Strategies for Effective Implementation of Complex Corporate Models

Edward B. Roberts

Various compendia of modelling applications demonstrate clearly the penetration of complex models into all domains. (See References 1-7.) Yet how much impact are these myriad models producing? House and Tyndall (8), reviewing public policy modelling, lament that "the majority [of models]. . . . have seldom, if ever, been used by the level of policy maker we are concerned with." Brewer's (9) fascinating discourse on urban models goes even further: "The initial, underlying assumptions of the model-builders assured that policy-makers would have little use for their products." Except for routine operations-level models, how many complex models are really used by decision-makers to make decisions, or by policy makers to formulate strategy and policy? The prime asset of model-building is the breadth of its practice; the prime liability is the narrowness of its implementation.

Perhaps the fault lies in the origins of managerial model-making — the translation of methods and principles of the physical sciences into wartime operations research. The presumption of transferability of the scientific method accompanied the movement of physicists and mathematicians into the arena of managerial problem analysis. If hypothesis, data, and analysis lead to proof and new knowledge in science, shouldn't similar processes lead to change in organizations? The answer is obvious — NO! Organizational changes (or decisions or policies) do not instantly flow from evidence, deductive logic, and mathematical optimization.

The usual theorized sequencing of activities in a model-building project is:

> problem identification
> model development (including data gathering), and exercising
> recommendations
> implementation

This chapter is based on a paper presented at the International Symposium on Model- and Computer-Based Corporate Planning, University of Cologne, Germany, March 14–16, 1972. It has been published in *Interfaces*, vol. 7, no. 5 (November 1977). (©1977, The Institute of Management Sciences.)

But the implementation stage seldom occurs. Indeed, to produce implementation of change the needed perspective is that implementation requires a continuous process point-of-view that affects all stages of modelling.

Selection of the area for a modelling project, development of the model, and design of change recommendations all have implementation-affecting aspects, which I shall discuss here. My conclusions derive from eighteen years of developing and applying system dynamics models in a wide variety of real-world settings, with the past thirteen years' experience amplified by the further extensive efforts of my consulting colleagues.

Project Selection

Table 1.   **PROJECT SELECTION**

1. SOLVE A PROBLEM, OR REALIZE AN OPPORTUNITY
2. PROBLEM OR OPPORTUNITY MUST BE IMPORTANT TO "CLIENT"
3. OBJECTIVES MUST BE CREDIBLE

The first area to be discussed in regard to implementation of complex models is the selection of the project setting for the complex modelling. My first point in this regard is that you must be trying to solve a real problem. In response to the potential charge that this is obvious, I would argue that most corporate models do not meet the first criterion. That is, most models were not built to solve a problem; they were instead built merely to represent (or simulate) a corporation. If you build general-purpose corporate models, you should assume in advance that you will achieve little or no implementation of results. You must build models that are motivated by a real problem that exists. Alternatively, an apparent opportunity for the corporation is also suitable, but it must be perceived as realistic, not blue-sky.

Secondly, the problem or opportunity you select has to be seen as important by the "client" of your project, whom I define as the individual or small group whose approval is needed for change to be implemented. Whoever is the client of a project—whether company president or factory foreman—the problem has to be important to him. Many unsuccessful corporate models have indeed focussed on problems, but unfortunately on issues not very significant to the person paying the bill, or, more importantly, unimportant to the one whose approval was needed. In these cases implementation either did not occur or was only temporary. As one example, the very first application done by the M.I.T. industrial dynamics group in 1958 was to a production problem at the Sprague Electric Company (discussed in chapters 6 and 7). Yet the problem was not really important to the president of the company who was in fact the client of the project. The president was sponsoring the project, directly funding all of its activities, but the problem consisted of fluctuations in one product line that constituted only five percent of the total business of the company. The president was not going to get excited one way or the other about anything that happened to this particular problem. Consequently, it would be unrealistic to believe that he would devote very much time, energy or personal effort on behalf of the project or on the change recommendations that came out of the project. If you want to achieve changes in an organization as a result of your corporate modelling work, the problem or opportunity that you select must be important to the client. Otherwise, that client will neither pay much attention to the modelling effort, nor bother with its resulting recommendations.

The third item in Table 1 is that the objectives of your project must be credible. Credible, in this case, means believable to the client. The client must in advance or at least during the very early stages of the project believe that the types of changes you are seeking to achieve in this project situation are within the grasp of the organization—plausible given the resources and experiences of the organization—rather than "blue-sky" or a "mad scientist's dream" or "playing in the management science sand-box." The objectives should not require an advancement of technology beyond the organization's capability. They must not demand allocation of corporate funds of a greater magnitude than the corporation would reasonably be willing to expend. The techniques that are going to be needed to carry out the problem must be understandable to the management people involved. These conditions will help establish serious interest and involvement in the model-building by those whose later approval will be needed for implementation. This credibility criterion may often constrain the scope of at least early modelling efforts in an organization. Demonstration of usefulness may permit more ambitious efforts to be undertaken later, with serious purpose and expectation. If you fail on any one of these criteria, you are likely also to fail to achieve implemented changes in the organization as a result of the project undertaken. You can initiate the modelling project, you can carry it out, but nothing will happen as a result of the work you do.

Modelling Process

Table 2. **MODELLING PROCESS**

1. MAXIMUM IN-HOUSE INVOLVEMENT
2. EXPEDITE INITIAL MODEL DEVELOPMENT
3. MODEL DETAIL SUFFICIENT FOR PERSUASIVENESS
4. VALIDITY TESTING GEARED TO MANAGEMENT ASSURANCE
5. MEASURES OF EFFECTIVENESS DESIGNED INTO MODEL AND CONSISTENT WITH REAL-WORLD MEASURES

Once the project focus is established the work should be carried out with careful attention to other implementation facilitators. Here too several issues need consideration. The first point relates to who should be doing the modelling work. What should be the relative roles of insiders and outsiders? Clearly the client should be involved as much as possible, perhaps only indirectly, however, through his key aides or line assistants. Client delegation of this participative role to a low level staff member or to the management science group itself may be a harbinger of no-implementation. The boss needs to be involved to understand, to trust, and to be willing to act.

Beyond the client himself (or his trusted aides), additional in-house involvement is desirable whenever possible. This principle does not preclude the use of outside consultants to the extent they are necessary and available to supplement the inside skills. The greater the extent to which the job can be done effectively inside the organization, the better the likelihood that the job will result in implemented changes. The more that outsiders have to be relied upon, the more likely are problems of communication and continuity. Outside domination of the project is also likely to make more difficult the identification of an inside champion for the results. Of course, working with incompetent insiders, if only they are available, is not an acceptable alternative. A joint task force of several insiders collaborating with outside consultants is often an effective compromise.

Second — and I think this is an important point — you should expedite the initial model development to the point of early meaningful model operation. My view of corporate modelling is that you never develop from the outset *the* corporate model of a problem. You develop *an* initial corporate model of the problem; later you develop a second corporate model of the problem, and still later perhaps even a third version, and so on. In each case you may iterate, adding new variables, modifying your assumptions. But the point I am emphasizing here is that the first model for the particular problem should be expedited so that you have a developed and operating model running on the computer soon after the project begins. How quickly this is done depends on the circumstances. In our corporate consulting work we have found that in a project that might last nine months to a year before organizational changes can begin, first model results in three months are highly desirable. They provide reassurances to the client as to what is involved in all aspects of the modelling work, indicate the general direction that later finer answers might take, and of course provide important guidance on needed data collection as well as model enrichment and enlargement.

The third point I emphasize with respect to the process of modelling is that the model should have detail sufficient to be persuasively inclusive. I am not hedging on the issue of level of aggregation; I am specifying the issue of aggregation. How much detail do you need in a model? Enough to be persuasive to the client. If the client demands more detail, then you must provide more detail. If the client does not demand more detail, if he is willing to look at the problem in a more gross fashion, then his satisfaction is a sufficient condition. You first meet the client's need for detail. After that, you meet your need — your own personal need for adequate problem representation. But the client in most cases will probably demand greater detail than the model builder thinks is necessary. In this case, from an implementation point of view, the client is the boss. You must provide the level of detail that causes him to be persuaded that you have properly taken into account his issues, his questions, his level of concerns. Otherwise he will not believe the model you have built, he will not accept it, and he will not use it. In my experience, models need about twice as many equations to convince the boss as are needed to convince the model-builder. This tends to increase model size and requires careful coaching of the client by the model-builder to keep the client informed and relaxed about model content.

By the way, this is an important issue on which I disagree with Forrester's writings. He argues that one should model a problem at a level sufficient only to demonstrate the major feedback mechanisms that are at work. Forrester is right theoretically, if you want to consider what you the model-builder need to gain understanding of a problem. But Forrester is wrong practically, if you are concerned with what it takes to cause results to be implemented. To achieve implementation you usually must go far beyond merely a gross feedback representation of the problem.

The fourth "process" point is that the validity testing of a model must be geared to the level that will give the client assurance that the model is adequate, regardless of whether the client's criteria include eye-balling, historical comparison, R^2 calculations, or even spectral density functions! Many different validity testing schemes have been successfully used in system dynamics modelling projects. In some of our system dynamics cases we have done model-validation testing over five years historically, because in our judgment that was the relevant historical period about which management was concerned (see chapter 25, for example). In those instances management wanted the assurance that the model was consistent with its experiences for that period of time. In one case of modelling an economic development activity (10), we used a ten year period of historical validation, because that seemed like a reasonable data-base against which to gain assurance that what the model was doing was reasonable. In other cases, statistical testing has been used (see chapter 8, for example). In still other cases, no equivalent data-base has existed against which the model could be tested, and validity testing was limited to client and model-builder subjective analysis of individual equations, or to general analysis of overall simulation results. In each case the validity testing was based upon what it took to gain client assurance, and that indeed should be the criterion of emphasis.

Finally, with respect to the modelling process, when you begin trying to develop a complex corporate model you should decide upon the measures of effectiveness of results that you are seeking in the real world. These measures should explicitly be included as part of what you model. You model the measures against which you will test the implementation, and within the simulation model itself you provide an opportunity of asking how that measure of effectiveness will change as a result of historical policies vs. proposed policies or alternative strategies. For greatest likelihood of implementation, the modelled effectiveness measures should be consistent with real world measures that can be applied within the real organization; to have a theoretical measure alone is not going to be adequate for implementation.

Recommendations for Change

Table 3.   **RECOMMENDATIONS FOR CHANGE**

1. ACCOUNT FOR ABILITY TO ABSORB CHANGE
2. CONSIDER POSSIBLE IMPACT ON OTHER SYSTEMS
3. ACCOMPANY BY MANAGEMENT RE-EDUCATION AND/OR BY EX-
   PLICIT DECISION RULES

As the model is exercised for development of insights toward decision or policy change, further conditions must be met if the likelihood of implementation is to be increased. When potential recommendations are considered, the organization's ability to absorb the associated change must be assessed. Optimization of your model against your stated criteria may suggest that Policy X is the best policy to adopt. However, can the organization accept the consequences of attempted installation of Policy X? If your answer is no, then clearly you should not be recommending Policy X, even though the model may say that Policy X is good. You must then contemplate and come up with some Policy Y. Policy Y may be less good according to your initial criteria of effectiveness, but more likely to be absorbed into the organization. Remember again, our overall criterion of model effectiveness must be dependent upon *implemented* change, implemented improvement. A theoretically optimum result that is never implemented because the organization could not absorb it, generates no change or improvement. A less theoretically good change which is accepted, generates positive results. The model-builder and the organization both profit from implementation of moderate change proposals leading to some successful results; both lose from grandiose plans which fail to be moved ahead.

Pre-recommendations need also to be examined in terms of their possible impact on parts of the organization other than those included in the initial model system boundaries. Nothing is so embarrassing and so defeating of implementation than unanticipated consequences in unanticipated areas of an organization. You must ask of any corporate model you build: Have I been sufficiently oriented to interdependencies? As you recommend a solution in one area, are you liable to be getting the organization into problems in another area? This is very often done. No model is global for an organization. Every model is to some extent a subsystem-model. Every model has left out some considerations. You left them out because you thought they were not important to the problem. That is not to say that they are unimportant to the solution. A policy for improving suborganization A may well improve A but that policy could impact suborganization B. The policy's implementation may cross problem areas even though the initial problems were identifiably separate when they were analyzed. I can point to issues relating to attempted implementations that we have engaged in, where we did not take into account the cross-functional impact of recommended changes. Consequently sometimes opposition to a policy was unexpected and came from a part of the organization that did not participate in the initial work. In other instances the policies were in fact implemented and difficulties later arose from the implementation because of unexpected consequences in other parts of the organization. You must ask in some manner the cross-functional, cross-matrix, cross-organizational question: Will this recommendation impact other systems or other parts of the system?

Finally, most recommendations for change that are made as a result of working with a complex corporate model are strategy recommendation or broad policy recommendations. They tend not to be very detailed in character. In order to be carried out, however, such recommended changes either have to be accompanied by a reeducation program for management or explicit decision rules. Education programs should be started by asking how much new insight, new information, behavioral change, or shifted concepts or values does management need before they can follow through with this strategy or policy. Even when reeducation is not required, explicit procedures of operation no doubt will have to accompany gross strategies and policies. It will not be sufficient merely to say, you are running the company wrong; you should run the company this way instead. That approach would not be adequate for assuring that implementation will occur. In most corporate cases you will need to do both: you need to be explicit as to the decision rules and action plans for implementation and you have to carry out a thorough reeducation program for many members of management.

General Considerations

Table 4.   **GENERAL CONSIDERATIONS**

1. IMPLEMENTATION ORIENTATION FROM OUTSET
2. WORK CONTINUES UNTIL IMPLEMENTATION ACHIEVED
3. PROJECT PROCESS DESIGNED TO PRODUCE:
   IMPLEMENTABLE RESULTS
   DESIRE TO IMPLEMENT
   ENVIRONMENT THAT ENABLES IMPLEMENTATION

My final area of comment with respect to implementation are some general perspectives, all of which I believe are violated regularly in corporate modelling. First, from the outset of the work everybody associated with the project should have an implementation orientation. This means that right at the beginning you start by worrying about point of entry in the organization, membership in a project team, level of commitment to work, etc. All these issues are posed with respect to questions of how will this contribute to the likelihood of implementation whenever the project reaches the point of having recommendations. That perspective must start, however, at the beginning of the project, not at the end. Almost all management science projects, not limited merely to complex corporate models, have the wrong assumption about where implementation fits in. Nearly all books on problem solving, model-building, or information systems start with analysis, problem finding, and problem solution. They typically go through long lists of steps involved in their relevant technical process and the last item says implementation and education, or installation and education. This classic approach is completely wrong. From the beginning of any project the implementation issues that will arise should be considered. Such issues are relevant with respect to problem finding, group composition, and choice of problem analysis method. At every point of the problem approach, you should be asking, "Are we doing this with an implementation perspective?"

Secondly, the core of the project work group should stay essentially together until implementation is achieved. The people who had the commitment from the beginning for identification and analysis of the problem should not break up their working relationship when they submit a technical report containing recommendations. They should have as part of their responsibility the assisting of the organization in achievement of implementation, working together to consider problems that will arise and so forth.

Let me give you a very simple example of this, arising in the area of applied mathematical programming modelling. A classical management science case involved sophisticated production scheduling activity, first applied in a paint factory. The implementation was finally started, and the academics involved withdrew from the problem to go back to the university to write their book on their significant management science achievement. The implementation, however, stopped inside of six months of the initial completion of study and "acceptance" of recommendations. Why? One simple reason was that the decision rules were all calculated in terms of gallons of paint. The factory ran into a production problem when it tried to figure out what to do about half-gallons. This perhaps laughable situation was one of the major stumbling blocks that caused implementation to end. We encountered a similar problem at the Sprague Electric project, carried out at M.I.T. at about the same period of time as the work described above. Sprague management said, "We accept your concept of new operating policies, but we can't carry them out." Why? They said, "We need an inventory priority list." We asked, "How did you get along until now without such a list?" They answered: "Well, this is a very big change, and we need a list to help us out." Nothing happened until the M.I.T. team generated an inventory prioritizing computer program for them and implemented it. This effort had nothing technically to do with the M.I.T.-developed organization model for Sprague, but it was clearly essential so that management would go ahead with the implementation of our recommended decision rules. The work group that attacks an analytical problem must have the commitment and follow through to help all the way through until implementation is achieved. If they drop the ball, there is a good likelihood implementation will crash or fall between the cracks some place before final results are attained.

The last point for consideration in terms of overall perspective is that the project process should be designed so that it will produce results that are implementable—practicable and within the grasp of the organization. The organization must also desire to implement. The modelling team must see to it that relevant people in the organization have been educated, that they are persuaded that the change is worthwhile. The modelling team should have helped them to overcome their resistance barriers, motivated them to see the benefits—all that is part of effecting a desire to implement. Finally, you must also create an environment that enables the implementation to go forward. In many organizations, this will be a far broader task than all the corporate modelling activities that were undertaken. This may engage you in significant human organizational development work; it may require that you have a *behavioral* scientist as part of your team (not just another *management* scientist), an applied psychologist who will help you anticipate and overcome those classes of issues within the organization.

Attention to these ideas regarding modelling focus, work process, and recommendation development will increase significantly the likelihood that models will have impact. But these ideas can only work in the presence of a client, an individual or group who can approve the implementation of change. Yet many modelling activities today are carried out in clientless settings, where no one is decision-maker. The "world models" exemplify this situation. Here implementation can still be a relevant goal, but even more difficult to attain. The model-builder can set his initial and realistic goals to be those of stimulating public awareness, concern, or alarm. But he must seek from the then alerted public those few prospective clients for change who might be willing to work toward more serious implementation-focused modelling undertakings. Otherwise, our grand technology of model-building will permeate wider and wider horizons of promise, with but disappointingly little promise fulfilled.

References

1. Drake, A. W.; Kenney, R. L. and Morse, P. H. (editors). *Analysis of Public Systems*. Cambridge: M.I.T. Press, 1972.

2. Gass, Saul I. and Sisson, Roger L. (editors). *A Guide to Models in Governmental Planning and Operations*. Washington: Environmental Protection Agency, 1974.

3. Forrester, Jay W. *Collected Papers of Jay W. Forrester*. Cambridge: Wright-Allen Press, 1975.

4. Grochla, Erwin and Szyperski, Norbert (editors). *Modell-und Computer Gestutzte Unternehmungs-Planung*. Wiesbaden: Betriebs-wirtschaftlicher Verlag, 1973.

5. Guetzkow, Harold; Kotler, Philip and Schultz, Randall L. (editors). *Simulation in Social and Administrative Science*. Englewood Cliffs, New Jersey: Prentice-Hall, Inc., 1972.

6. Meadows, Dennis L. and Meadows, Donella H. (editors). *Toward Global Equilibrium: Collected Papers*. Cambridge: Wright-Allen Press, 1973.

7. Schreiber, Albert N. (editor). *Corporate Simulation Models*. Seattle: University of Washington, 1970.

8. House, Peter W. and Tyndall, Gene R. "Models and Policy Making," in Gass and Sisson, Reference 2 above.

9. Brewer, Garry D. *Politicians, Bureaucrats, and the Consultant*. New York: Basic Books, 1973, p. 288.

10. Hamilton, Henry R., et al. *System Simulation for Regional Analysis*. Cambridge: M.I.T. Press, 1969.

Part Two:
System Dynamics in Manufacturing

The system dynamics applications described in this book appropriately begin in the general area of manufacturing. The name, "industrial dynamics," predecessor of the more general current designator "system dynamics," suggests the fluctuations, instabilities and time changes that are so common to many industrial production activities. Observers of industrial behavior have long paid attention to the short-term cyclical patterns in production, inventory and employment in key manufacturing industries. Another classic problem of fluctuations in the manufacturing area is the longer-term cycles in capital investment, capacity utilization, prices and profitability. Almost all industries dominated by heavy capital investment requirements exhibit these long-term cycles.

Industrial dynamics began with the illustrative work on production-distribution systems problems, previously described in Chapter 2. Its first practical application was in the work done with the Sprague Electric Company on the problem of production-inventory-employment fluctuations. This work, described in Chapters 6 and 7, focuses on problems of steady-state dynamics (in contrast to the transient dynamics encountered in product life cycle or corporate growth phenomena), and examines the feedback systems that produce fluctuations around the steady-state or equilibrium conditions of the organizations. Chapter 1 of this book points out how even a single negative feedback loop can lead to oscillatory or fluctuating behavior. The interaction of multiple negative feedback loops, so often found in industrial situations, almost inevitably leads to fluctuating system behavior that results in higher manufacturing costs and greater employment instability, with negative impacts on all other areas of operation.

The articles included in this section are all limited to the dynamics of fluctuations around the steady-state. Although much work has been done in applying industrial dynamics to corporate growth problems [4,5,9], no article-length version of these works is currently available. Representative of this class of transient dynamics work are the M.I.T. studies aimed at uncovering the key factors that lead some young manufacturing firms to achieve steady successful growth, while others experience boom-or-bust periods producing chaos and often company failure. Figure 1 represents part of the total company system that produces these alternatives of success or failure.

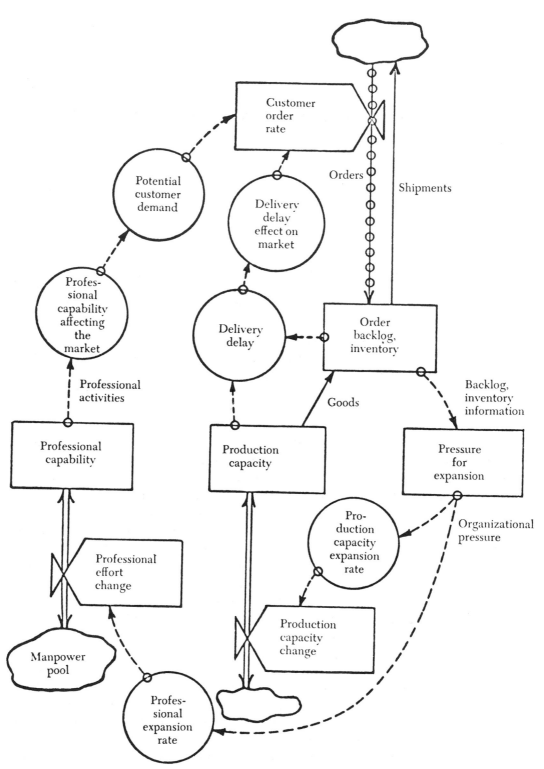

Figure 1   Corporate growth system
Reprinted with permission of publishers, from Edward B. Roberts, "New
Directions in Industrial Dynamics,"*Industrial Management Review,* vol. 6,
no. 1, Fall 1964, p. 8.

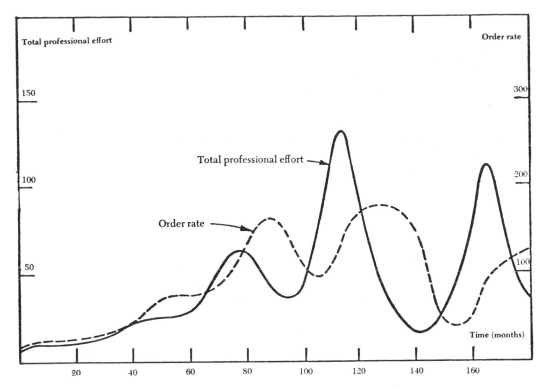

Figure 2 Basic corporate growth system behavior
Reprinted with permission of publishers, from Edward B. Roberts, "New Directions in Industrial Dynamics," *Industrial Management Review,* vol. 6, no. 1, Fall 1964, p. 9.

The diagram is derived from a monograph by David Packer [5], a former member of the M.I.T. Industrial Dynamics Research Group, and since then a long-time staff member at Digital Equipment Corporation. Digital Equipment's sponsorship of the M.I.T. industrial dynamics project on growth of young firms began when Digital's sales were only a few million dollars.

Packer's monograph traces the problems of corporate growth to two major company policies or response behaviors and their effects on the market place. The first is the manner in which the company increases the size of its professional staff, both technical and managerial. The second is the manner in which the company decides on expansion of production capacity, both in terms of increased plant and work force. The diagram indicates that in many young firms resources are acquired in response to pressures built up within the firm. The changed organizational capabilities then feedback upon the market place to affect customer order rate, which, in time, modifies the expansion pressures within the firm. This complex closed-loop system, containing at least four other smaller feedback loops, creates the frequently witnessed fluctuating growth illustrated in the fifteen-year organization history shown in Figure 2.

Detailed examination of the Packer model shows that a key determinant after the first five years of growth is a company's inability to absorb smoothly the increased professional manpower needed to develop new products, provide customer service, and manage production efficiently. The hypothetical company simulated in Figure 2 re-creates the problems of so many temporarily successful new organizations. The highly capable group that founded the company could develop, sell and produce their products so long as the total talent needed to manage the business was small. But with success came the requirement for larger numbers of top-notch people, difficult to find and even more difficult to train. The rapid expansion of professional staff presented a new demand on the limited experienced manpower for the training and effective absorption of the new recruits. These problems result in a reduction of the company's marketing efforts and effectiveness; consequently capacity rises more quickly than orders and resulting pressures necessitate cutbacks in the scope of operations. The cycle repeats, however, since the reduced organization can once again meet the demands of the market, and the growth phase begins again. This boom-or-bust cycle with a period of about three-and-one-half years is typical of the technically-based companies that have sprung up during the past twenty-five years. Solutions to this problem lie in a better understanding of growth dynamics, the impact of resource acquisition and allocation policies, and the necessity for monitoring the sources of market feedback information.

Chapter 5 by Herbert A. Simon of Carnegie-Mellon University, the first article of Part 2, presents an analytical representation of the feedback loops involved in produc-tion and inventory control. This work precedes by several years the system dynamics work at M.I.T. Simon's paper and Cooper's earlier related work indicate that Carnegie Tech in the early '50s had the potential for developing a feedback analysis approach to management problems. But by the late '50s, when Forrester organized the M.I.T. Industrial Dynamics Research Group, the Carnegie Tech approach had shifted away considerably from a feedback orientation. Simon's article is the only paper in this book that discusses mathematical analysis of feedback system problems. Such analysis is useful when possible, but unfortunately cannot be employed when the system structure is somewhat more complex. Even as simple a structure as a fifth-order feedback system approaches the limit of applicability of closed-form solution techniques. More compli-cated systems require the use of cut-and- try methods of numerical analysis or the simulation modeling featured in system dynamics work. The references at the end of Chapter 5 provide an excellent background in feedback systems analysis and its early applications in economics.

Chapters 6 and 7 present two views of the first industrial application carried out by the M.I.T. Industrial Dynamics Research Group, working with and supported by a grant-in-aid from the Sprague Electric Company. Jay Forrester conceived the model and directed all project work, with the assistance of several graduate student research assistants. Willard Fey, one of the first three research assistants in the M.I.T. group, had responsibility for the project during its implementation phase, and published Chap-ter 6 in the fall of 1962. Fey revised the article in January 1965, by adding an Author's Note, after Sprague essentially discontinued use of the policies recommended by the M.I.T. study. Fey is now Associate Professor at Georgia Institute of Technology.

Bruce Carlson's views on the work at Sprague Electric, as reprinted in Chapter 7, were published between the first and second versions of Fey's article. Carlson had been the principal liaison with the M.I.T. group during its working period at Sprague, advancing during the project from Statistical Assistant to the President, responsible for Sprague's industrial engineering activity among others, to Vice President–Corporate Planning and Systems.

Despite the eventual discontinuance of the recommended policies, the Sprague study was successful from several perspectives. First, as per the figures cited by Fey and Carlson, the policies did clearly generate cost savings and productivity increases that provided significant annual return on the project investment by Sprague. Second, the analysis, the model, and the resulting policies are directly translatable to numerous other manufacturing organizations. In fact, P. R. Mallory and Company, one of Sprague's major competitors in the capacitor field, was among the first to start a system dynamics effort that produced a model nearly identical to the Sprague model. Unfortunately, no public writeup documenting the Mallory effort and results is available. Another application of substantially the same model is described by Schlager in his case study of Company A in Chapter 8. Third, the Sprague project produced vital insights into the importance and unique problems of implementation, some of which Fey discusses at the conclusion of his article. Further discussion of this work from an implementation perspective appears in Chapter 9.

In Chapter 8 Kenneth Schlager describes three applications of system dynamics to manufacturing firms. During his year as a Sloan Fellow at M.I.T. Schlager undertook for his thesis an industrial dynamics analysis of the copper and aluminum industries [6]. Shortly after his return to Milwaukee, Schlager began teaching an evening course in industrial dynamics at Marquette University and did related consulting. The firm described as Company A in the article seems to be Badger Meter Manufacturing Company, which Schlager eventually joined on a full-time basis, and rose to the position of Vice President of the Systems Division before leaving the company. Although Schlager's article does not provide strong clues to the identity of Companies B and C, both were in the Milwaukee area, Company B producing heavy industrial equipment and Company C operating in the instruments and controls fields.

Chapter 9 is an extended editor's note arising from a comparison of the Fey and Carlson papers on Sprague Electric and the Schlager paper that treats primarily Badger Meter, providing an intended postscript to Chapters 6, 7 and 8.

Chapter 10 features a previously unpublished description of work carried out by several M.I.T. system dynamics research assistants in cooperation with a small precision machining company in the Boston suburbs. The firm, a job-shop producer of metal parts and fixtures, is here labelled the Precision Company. Its problem involves the interplay of several negative feedback loops, relating both manufacturing and marketing activities to customer decision processes. As with many other articles, it could therefore as easily be included in another section of the book, in this case Part 3 on marketing and distribution. The focus is on the alternating allocation of management time and effort between production and marketing. This classical dynamic problem arises in a variety of managerial situations, including research and development groups (see Chapters 19 and 20) [2,11], consulting firms [10] and manufacturing organizations. A thoroughly annotated presentation of the equations of the Precision Company model is provided in Appendix B of this book.

In addition to the articles included in Part II, Chapters 12, 13, 15, 23 and 25 also refer to system dynamics applications in manufacturing-related situations.

Manufacturing has probably been the area of most widespread application of system dynamics. Unfortunately, space limitations prevent inclusion of additional publications in this area. One set of studies deserving mention is the effort by the Technical Analysis Division of the U.S. Department of Commerce's National Bureau of Standards to apply system dynamics to problems of textiles, apparel and building construction. The in-house effort at Commerce, though hindered by lack of trained staff, resulted in a major application to textiles of a modified version of Forrester's production-distribution model (see Chapter 2) [12]. Several major system dynamics reports were also developed under contract research [1,7,8,9], one of them described in Chapter 13. Another application of the system dynamics approach to the textile industry is the work done by Zymelman using an analog computer representation of his model [13]. In the late '50s, Zymelman had worked at the M.I.T. Center for International Studies on a large-scale economic dynamics modeling project directed by Edward Holland. The project initially used analog computers, but converted to DYNAMO modeling when the analog approach ceased to be practicable [3]. Analog computers work quite satisfactorily when the model is limited to the size developed by Zymelman in his textile analysis. In fact, analog techniques are especially desirable for classroom demonstration and simple feedback systems analysis, and have been employed effectively in basic system dynamics courses at M.I.T.

Company secrecy and lack of orientation toward publication of in-house work have restricted the flow of information about numerous manufacturing applications of system dynamics. However, a review of past issues of the *System Dynamics Newsletter* clearly indicates that manufacturing applications have been undertaken by Boeing, Eastman Kodak, FMC Corporation, General Electric, General Radio, Honeywell, IBM, Lockheed Missiles and Space Company, Raytheon, and Texas Instruments among others in the United States, and by several non-U.S. companies, including Hitachi and Toyo Kogyo in Japan, Geigy Chemicals in Switzerland, and Compania de Acero del Pacifico in Chile. (The *M.I.T. System Dynamics Newsletter* is published annually by the M.I.T. System Dynamics Group, and may be purchased from the Group, M.I.T. E40-253, Cambridge, Massachusetts 02139.) Also, no publication yet documents the successful long-term system dynamics collaboration between the M.I.T. System Dynamics Group and the Cummins Engine Company.

References

1. *Advanced Systems Analysis of Textile Industry Problems.* Cambridge, Mass.: Pugh-Roberts Associates, Inc., March 1966.

2. Beaumariage, Donald C. *A Dynamic Model Study of a Military Product Development Organization.* Unpublished M.I.T. S.M. thesis, 1960.

3. Holland, Edward P. with Robert W. Gillespie. *Experiments on a Simulated Underdeveloped Economy: Development Plans and Balance-of-Payment Policies.* Cambridge, Mass.: The MIT Press, 1963.

4. Nord, Ole C. *Growth of a New Product: Effects of Capacity-Acquisition Policies.* Cambridge, Mass.: The MIT Press, 1963.

5. Packer, David W. *Resource Acquisition in Corporate Growth.* Cambridge, Mass.: The MIT Press, 1964.

6. Schlager, Kenneth J. *Systems Analysis of the Copper and Aluminum Industries: An Industrual Dynamics Study.* Unpublished M.I.T. S.M. thesis, 1961.

7. *Systems Analysis of an Apparel Company.* Cambridge, Mass.: Pugh-Roberts Associates, Inc., July 1967.

8. *Systems Analysis of the Apparel Industry.* Cambridge, Mass.: Pugh-Roberts Associates, Inc., September 1967.

9. *Systems Analysis of a Textile Firm.* Cambridge, Mass.: Pugh-Roberts Associates, Inc., July 1967.

10. Weil, Henry B. *Workload Fluctuations in a Management Consulting Firm.* Unpublished M.I.T. S.B. thesis, 1965.

11. Welles, Gilbert III. *An Analysis of the Dynamic Behavior of a Research and Development Organization.* Unpublished M.I.T. S.M. thesis, 1963.

12. Yurow, Jerome A. "Analysis and Computer Simulation of the Production and Distribution Systems of a Tufted Carpet Mill," *Journal of Industrial Engineering,* January 1967.

13. Zymelman, Manuel. "A Stabilization Policy for the Cotton Textile Cycle," *Management Science,* March 1965.

5

On the Application of Servomechanism Theory in the Study of Production Control

Herbert A. Simon

1. INTRODUCTION

THIS PAPER is of an exploratory character. Powerful, and extremely general, techniques have been developed in the past decade for the analysis of electrical and mechanical control systems and servomechanisms. There are obvious analogies between such systems and the human systems, usually called production control systems, that are used to plan and schedule production in business concerns. The depth or superficiality of these analogies can be tested by subjecting a fairly simple, but relatively concrete, example of a production control system to some of the techniques of analysis usually employed for servomechanisms. No attempt will be made, in this introductory essay, to do justice to the full range of analytic tools available to the servomechanism engineer for synthesizing control systems. Our intent is to give an elementary introduction to servomechanism theory and to determine its applicability to production control problems.

It might be pointed out that the notion of a servomechanism incorporating human links is by no means novel. In particular, many gun-sighting servos involve such a link. The idea of social, as distinguished from purely physiological, links is relatively new. However, Richard M. Goodwin [12] has arrived independently at the same idea as a means for studying market behavior and business cycles. The applicability of servomechanism models to the theory of the firm has been discussed by my colleague, W. W. Cooper [8] (see references at the end of paper). Two dynamic macrosystems that have been represented by analogue circuits (and in one case experimentally investigated) may also be re-

The author is indebted to W. W. Cooper, C. Klahr, and David Rosenblatt, and to staff members of the Cowles Commission for numerous helpful suggestions. The research for this paper was undertaken in the author's capacity as a consultant to the Cowles Commission for Research in Economics under its contract with the RAND Corporation. The paper appeared in *ECONOMETRICA* 20, number 2 (April 1952).

garded as servomechanisms [**9, 10**]. All such systems would be included in Wiener's [**11**] general program for cybernetics.

Some preliminary remarks are necessary, first to characterize servomechanism theory, and second, to describe the production control system we will study.

Servomechanism theory. Many of the systems with which electrical and mechanical engineering deal are described, at least approximately, by systems of linear differential or integro-differential equations with constant coefficients. Included are electrical networks with lumped constants, and among these (or their mechanical analogues) are many of the systems known as "controllers," "regulators," and "servomechanisms." We will not attempt here to distinguish these terms precisely, but instead set forth an example of such a system.

Consider a system consisting of a house, or other enclosed space, a gas furnace, and a thermostat that controls the rate of gas flow in the furnace.[2] The temperature setting of the thermostat (that is, the desired house temperature) will be referred to as the *input* of the system, desig-

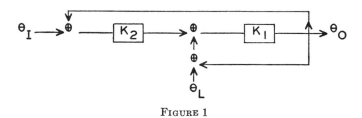

FIGURE 1

nated by θ_I ; the actual house temperature will be referred to as the *output*, θ_O ; their difference, $\theta_I - \theta_O$, as the *error*, ϵ; and the outside temperature as the load, θ_L .[3] All variables are functions of time.

The system is so constructed that the rate of gas flow in the furnace, and hence the rate at which heat is supplied to the house, is a function of the error (in the simplest case, proportional to the error). Further, this function relating the error to the output is selected so that the error will tend to be reduced, whatever the load imposed on the system.

[2] In order to preserve as close an analogy as possible with the production control system to be described later, we will assume a thermostat that is continuous in operation, instead of the more familiar on-off thermostat. The system described here is analysed in reference [4, pp. 298–303].

[3] In our example, the input is generally fixed, while the load is variable. This is the typical case of the controller; and the input is frequently referred to as the *standard*. The term "servomechanism" more commonly refers to a system in which the input is variable and the variable load absent. However, in many important engineering systems both variable input and variable load are present.

The system just described is shown in Figure 1. The equations that describe the system are

(1.1)
$$\frac{d\theta_0}{dt} = f(\epsilon) - k(\theta_O - \theta_L),$$

(1.2)
$$\epsilon = \theta_I - \theta_O.$$

The symbols $\oplus$ indicate differential devices (subtraction); the box K_2 corresponds to $f(\epsilon)$; and the box K_1 to the integration [from equation (1.1)] which gives θ_O as a function of $f(\epsilon)$ and $(\theta_O - \theta_L)$.

Two important features of this system should be noted. The first is the *control loop*, or feedback loop (the upper loop in Figure 1), by means of which (a) the output is compared with the input and (b) their difference is fed back into the system to alter the output in the direction of reducing the difference.

The second important feature is shown by the directional arrows. The input and load affect the behavior of the system (and, in particular, the output and error) but are themselves unaffected by it. Hence, variables not included in the loop may be regarded as independent and may be assumed to have any arbitrary time paths. This kind of relationship is sometimes referred to as *unilateral coupling*, or *cascading*. A reciprocal relation must be represented by a closed loop (such as the lower loop in Figure 1).

In a physical servomechanism, cascading is made possible by the fact that the closed portion of the system involves very little energy in comparison with the energy of the independent variables (as in a solar system with large central sun and small planets) or, more generally, draws its energy from an independent power source (as in an amplifier). It is this characteristic of the system that permits the output to follow the input without disturbing the path of the input. A servomechanism, then, is a system (1) unilaterally coupled to an input and a load, (2) with one or more feedback loops whereby the output is compared with the input, and (3) with a source of energy controlled by the error that tends to bring the output in line with the input. If the load is bilaterally coupled with the output, then the former must be included in the system and cannot be treated as an independent variable.

The most powerful technique for treating servomechanisms employs the Laplace transform. (See [2, Chapter 2; 3]). The Laplace transform of the input may be interpreted as its decomposition into its component frequencies (i.e., it is very closely related to the Fourier integral). The Laplace transform of the entire servosystem connecting input with output describes its behavior in filtering (altering amplitude and phase) the frequencies occurring in the input. The Laplace transform of the output, which is the product of the two previous transforms, is the representation of the output in terms of component frequencies. (In this statement we disregard the load, which enters as another input.)

The system is studied by determining the Laplace transform of the servo, multiplying this by various input transforms, and analyzing the resulting kinds of behavior of the output. We are interested in the stability of the output (which is related to its transient response) and in its steady-state behavior for various inputs. By defining a criterion function (a function of the output) we may compare the merits of alternative servos for controlling an output under specified conditions.

Production control. In this paper we shall consider the control of the rate of production of a single item. The item is supposed to be manufactured to standard specifications, placed in stock, and shipped out on order of customers. The item is manufactured continuously, and control consists in issuing instructions that vary continuously the quantity to be manufactured per day (or other unit of time).

The aim of the control system is to minimize the cost of manufacture over a period of time. This cost, or the variable part of it, is assumed to depend upon (1) the variations in the manufacturing rate (i.e., it costs more to make 1,000 items if the manufacturing rate fluctuates than if it is constant); and (2) the inventory of finished goods (i.e., increase in this inventory involves carrying costs, decrease in the inventory below a certain point involves delay in filling customers' orders). Hence, the criterion by which we will judge the system will be some function of the magnitudes of the fluctuations in manufacturing rate and the inventory of finished goods.

We will take as our input the optimum inventory (θ_I). Since this will be assumed constant throughout our problem, it may be taken as zero. The actual inventory of finished goods will be taken as the output (θ_o).[4] The error (ϵ) will then be the deficiency (positive or negative) of inventory $(\theta_I - \theta_o)$. Customers' orders per unit of time will be treated as the load (θ_L). We need two additional variables, the actual production rate per unit of time (μ), and the rate of planned production or, more accurately, planned new production per unit of time (η).

Assume that, on the basis of information about orders and the inventory excess or deficiency, instructions are issued daily (in our model, continuously) for the manufacturing rate of the product of a certain number of units. At some later date, the lag being determined by the time required for production, the units of product put into production at the initial time are actually produced and added to inventory. Meanwhile, customers' orders have been daily (continuously) withdrawn from inventory. Information regarding the inventory level is in turn fed

---

[4] The actual inventory may be either positive or negative. A negative inventory is simply a backlog of customers' orders. Wherever the term "inventory" is used in this paper it should be interpreted as "inventory of finished product or backlog of orders." Depending on the commodity to be produced, the optimum inventory may also be either positive or negative. The former is the case in a plant that ships from stock; the latter, in a plant that manufactures on order.

back to be compared daily (continuously) with the optimum inventory, and the calculated error employed, in turn, to redetermine the planned production rate.

This system obviously possesses the characteristics of a servomechanism. It is unilaterally coupled to the load and input (customers' orders and optimum inventory). It has a feedback loop: error → planned production → actual production → inventory → error. The error initiates a change in planned production in such a direction as to reduce the error.

In succeeding sections systems will be described for accomplishing the functions just listed. We will start with some highly simplified structures, and add complications as we proceed.

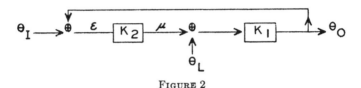

FIGURE 2

2. A SIMPLE SYSTEM FOR INVENTORY CONTROL

We will consider two systems. In the first we will be concerned only with the control of inventories; we will base production decisions only on information about inventories (and will ignore information about orders); and we will assume a zero time lag for production. In the second system all these restrictions will be removed.

Description of the system. The first system is shown in Figure 2, which is identical with Figure 1 except for the absence of the lower loop that appears in the former. In this system, it is assumed that μ is identically equal to η. That is, the rate of production at time t is equal to the rate at which new production is scheduled at time t. This implies that production plans are carried out without an appreciable time lag. The equations of the system are

$$(2.1) \qquad \theta_o(t) = K_1[\mu(t) - \theta_L(t)],$$

$$(2.2) \qquad \mu(t) = K_2[\epsilon(t)],$$

$$(2.3) \qquad \epsilon(t) = \theta_I(t) - \theta_o(t).$$

K_1 and K_2 are linear operators whose form will be specified. Equation (2.3) is a definition. Equation (2.2) represents a rule of decision—it specifies the rate of production that will be scheduled (and achieved) as a function of the excess and deficiency of inventory. The precise form of (2.1) is determined by the conditions of the problem since, by definition,

$$(2.4) \qquad \frac{d\theta_o}{dt} = \mu - \theta_L.$$

Hence, if we wish to design a servomechanism of the class described that meets some criterion of optimality, we have at our disposal only the operator K_2—the decision rule.

Our equations (2.1)–(2.4) can be restated in terms of the Laplace transforms of the quantities involved. The real variable t is replaced by the complex variable p. The Laplace transform of $y(t)$, written $\mathcal{L}[y(t)] = y^*(p)$, is defined by

$$(2.5) \qquad y^*(p) = \int_0^\infty y(t)e^{-pt}\,dt.$$

This integral exists for a wide class of functions, although in some cases it must be defined as a Lebesgue integral rather than a Riemann integral. The inverse transformation is

$$(2.6) \qquad y(t) = \frac{1}{2\pi}\int_{b-j\infty}^{b+j\infty} y^*(p)e^{pt}\,dp,$$

where the path of integration runs parallel to the imaginary axis along the line: real part of $p = b$.[5]

It can be shown that the Laplace transform of the derivative of a function that is initially zero is p times the transform of the function. Using this relationship, we can transform the terms of (2.4) and obtain (2.7), below. Comparing (2.7) with (2.1), we see that the operator K_1 in the t domain (integration) corresponds, in the p domain, to multiplication by $1/p$. In equations (2.8) and (2.9) we write the relations in the p domain that are obtained by transforming (2.2) and (2.3), respectively. We then have

$$(2.7) \qquad \theta_o(p) = (1/p)[\mu(p) - \theta_L(p)],$$

$$(2.8) \qquad \mu(p) = K_2(p)\cdot\epsilon(p),$$

$$(2.9) \qquad \epsilon(p) = \theta_I(p) - \theta_o(p),$$

where $\theta_o(p)$, etc., represent the Laplace transforms of $\theta_o(t)$, etc., respectively. [Since the argument of each function indicates whether it is defined in the p domain or the t domain, in these equations and those following we omit the asterisk (*) in writing a transform.] If we now assume $\theta_I \equiv 0$ and introduce the *system transform*,

$$(2.10) \qquad Y(p) = \frac{\theta_o(p)}{\theta_L(p)},$$

we derive from (2.7)–(2.9)

$$(2.11) \qquad Y(p) = \frac{-1/p}{1 + (K_2/p)} = \frac{-1}{p + K_2(p)}.$$

[5] No attempt will be made in this paper at mathematical rigor. Virtually all the mathematical tools employed here will be found in [2, Chapter 11] and [3]. The latter also contains (pp. 332–357) a very useful table of Laplace transform pairs.

Theorems about the Laplace transform. The behavior of the system under varying load can be discussed in terms of the properties of the system transform, $Y(p)$. As a basis for this discussion we will outline some results from Laplace transform theory without attempting proofs or complete rigor in their statement.

A system will be termed *stable* if the output remains bounded (in the t domain) for all bounded inputs (in the t domain). The equation obtained by setting the denominator of $Y(p)$ equal to zero we call the characteristic equation of $Y(p)$. In our particular system we have

$$(2.12) \qquad\qquad p + K_2(p) = 0.$$

Provided that the numerator of $Y(p)$ has no finite poles, the system will be stable if and only if all the roots of the characteristic equation have negative real parts.

Let $W(t)$ be the inverse transform of $Y(p)$, as defined in (2.6). We call $W(t)$ the *weighting function* of the system. Multiplication in the p domain corresponds to convolution in the t domain. Hence, we have, from (2.10),

$$(2.13) \qquad\qquad \theta_o(t) = \int_0^\infty W(\tau)\theta_L(t - \tau) \, d\tau.$$

Equation (2.13) relates the time path of the output to the weighting function of the system and the time path of the load. Generally, however, we do not employ this relationship. Instead, we multiply the Laplace transform of $\theta_L(t)$ by the system transform and then take the inverse transform of this product, obtaining $\theta(t)$ directly. Indeed, it is this procedure, together with the availability of tables of transform pairs, that makes the Laplace transform method particularly powerful.

Two additional theorems, which hold when the indicated limits exist, will prove useful:

$$(2.14) \qquad\qquad \operatorname*{Lim}_{t\to\infty} y(t) = \operatorname*{Lim}_{p\to 0} py(p),$$

$$(2.15) \qquad\qquad \operatorname*{Lim}_{t\to 0} y(t) = \operatorname*{Lim}_{p\to\infty} py(p).$$

In particular, (2.14) enables us to calculate immediately the steady state output for given load and system transform without transforming again to the t domain.

Steady-state and transient behavior. We return now to the task of discovering for our particular system a transform, $K_2(p)$, that will induce appropriate behavior of $\theta_o(t)$. By "appropriate" behavior we mean that we wish $\theta_o(t)$ to be as small as possible. We consider first the steady-state behavior, which we will study by means of (2.14).

$$(2.16) \qquad \operatorname*{Lim}_{t\to\infty} \theta_o(t) = \operatorname*{Lim}_{p\to 0} p\theta_o(p) = \operatorname*{Lim}_{p\to 0} \frac{p\theta_L(p)}{p + k_2(p)} .$$

A. Suppose that up to the time $t = 0$, orders have been zero, and that after that time they are received at the rate of 1 order per unit of time,

(2.17) $\theta_L(t) = 0$ for $t < 0$; $\theta_L(t) = 1$ for $t \geqslant 0$.

We have

(2.18) $\mathcal{L}[\theta_L(t)] = \theta_L(p) = 1/p$.

Hence,

(2.19) $\underset{t \to \infty}{\text{Lim}} \, \theta_0(t) = \underset{p \to 0}{\text{Lim}} - \dfrac{1}{p + K_2(p)}$.

Therefore, we wish the denominator of the right-hand side of (2.19) to become very large as p approaches zero. This can be accomplished, for example, by setting

(2.20) $K_2 = (1/p^k)\,(a + bp)$ with $k \geqslant 1, a > 0, b > 0$.

Rapid convergence is assured by making a large.

B. Suppose, now, that up to the time $t = 0$ orders have been zero, and that after that time they are received at the rate of t^n orders per unit of time,

(2.21) $\theta_L(t) = 0$ for $t < 0$; $\theta_L(t) = t^n$ for $t \geqslant 0$.

We have

(2.22) $\mathcal{L}[\theta_L(t)] = \theta_L(p) = \dfrac{n!}{p^{n+1}}$.

In this case we can assure a zero steady-state error with K_2 of the same form as (2.20) but with $k \geqslant (n + 1)$.

C. Suppose that $\theta_L(t)$ is sinusoidal:

(2.21) $\theta_L(t) = 0$ for $t < 0$,

(2.22) $\theta_L(t) = A/2[e^{i\omega t} + e^{-i\omega t}] = A \cos \omega t$, for $t \geqslant 0$.

Here we cannot use the method of the previous two cases since it can be shown that $\text{Lim}_{t \to \infty}\,\theta_0(t)$ does not exist. Instead, we use the result that if $\theta_L(t)$ is sinusoidal, $\theta_0(t)$ will be sinusoidal (aside from the transient term), with the same frequency but altered amplitude and phase. That is,

(2.23) $\underset{t \to \infty}{\text{Lim}} \, \theta_0(t) = B \cos (\omega t + \psi)$.

The amplitude, B, of the output is given by

(2.24) $B = A[Y(i\omega)Y(-i\omega)]^{\frac{1}{2}}$.

If, for example, $K_2 = (a/p) + b$, we have

(2.25) $Y(p) = \dfrac{-1}{p + K_2(p)} = \dfrac{-p}{p^2 + bp + a} = \dfrac{-p}{(p - p_1)(p - p_2)}$,

where p_1 and p_2 are the roots of the characteristic equation.

$$(2.26) \quad Y(i\omega)Y(-i\omega) = \frac{-i\omega}{(i\omega - p_1)(i\omega - p_2)} \cdot \frac{i\omega}{(-i\omega - p_1)(-i\omega - p_2)}$$

$$= \frac{\omega^2}{(\omega^2 + p_1^2)(\omega^2 + p_2^2)},$$

$$(2.27) \quad B = A\omega[(\omega^2 + p_1^2)(\omega^2 + p_2^2)]^{-\frac{1}{2}}.$$

For given p_1, p_2, as ω approaches zero, B approaches zero; as ω grows large, B approaches A/ω. When p_1 and p_2 are equal, B approaches its maximum for $\omega = p_1$. This maximum is $B = A/2p_1$. Hence we see that by selecting K_2 so that the characteristic function has large roots we guarantee rapid damping of θ_O for sinusoidal loads.[6]

We have now indicated the properties that our decision rule (the operator K_2) must possess to assure small or vanishing steady-state inventory excesses and deficiencies for various loads.

Next, let us interpret these results in the t domain. Suppose that $Y(p)$ is an algebraic expression,

$$(2.28) \quad Y(p) = \frac{b_m p^m + b_{m-1} p^{m-1} + \cdots + b_0}{a_n p^n + a_{n-1} p^{n-1} + \cdots + a_0}.$$

Then the equation in the t domain obtained by transforming (2.10) is

$$(2.29) \quad a_n \frac{d^n \theta_O}{dt^n} + a_{n-1} \frac{d^{n-1} \theta_O}{dt^{n-1}} + \cdots a_0 \theta_O$$
$$= b_m \frac{d^m \theta_L}{dt^m} + b_{m-1} \frac{d^{m-1} \theta_L}{dt^{m-1}} + \cdots + b_0 \theta_L.$$

If, for example, $Y(p)$ is defined by (2.25), we have

$$(2.30) \quad \frac{d^2 \theta_O}{dt^2} + b \frac{d\theta_O}{dt} + a\theta_O = \frac{-d\theta_L}{dt}.$$

From this equation we can verify the conclusions already reached above. For example, in A, we had $d\theta_L/dt = 0$ for $t \geqslant 0$. Here the general solution of (2.30) is

$$(2.31) \quad \theta_O = Me^{p_1 t} + Ne^{p_2 t},$$

where p_1 and p_2 are the roots of the characteristic equation,

$$(2.32) \quad p = \frac{-b \pm \sqrt{b^2 - 4a}}{2}.$$

---

[6] In analogy with the fact that a wide class of functions can be represented by Fourier sums of sinusoidal functions, the steady-state analysis of arbitrary loads can often be handled in servomechanism theory by decomposing the function representing the load into a weighted integral of sinusoidal leads with continuously varying frequencies. For this reason, the restriction of the load in the steady-state analysis of subsequent sections of the paper to a simple sinusoid does not involve any essential loss of generality with respect to the form of the function representing customers' orders. See, however, footnote 8.

Since $a > 0$, $b > 0$, p_1 and p_2 will be real and negative or complex with negative real part, and hence (2.31) will converge to zero as t increases.

If, on the contrary, we had $d\theta_L/dt = 1$ for $t \geqslant 0$, the general solution of (2.30) would be

$$(2.33) \qquad \theta_o = Me^{p_1 t} + Ne^{p_2 t} + (1/a).$$

Then the system transform (2.25) would yield a steady-state error of $1/a$ as $t \to \infty$. Again this result can be obtained directly by substitution of (2.25) and $\theta_L(p) = 1/p^2$ in (2.16). Moreover the transient part of θ_o will be rapidly damped if the negative real parts of p_1 and p_2 are large.

Returning to the case of a sinusoidal load,

$$(2.34) \qquad \theta_L(p) = \mathcal{L}[\cos \omega t] = \frac{\omega}{p^2 + \omega^2}$$

with the system function of (2.25), we have

$$(2.35) \qquad \begin{aligned} \theta_o(p) &= \frac{-p\omega}{(p - p_1)(p - p_2)(p^2 + \omega^2)} \\ &= \frac{A}{(p - p_1)} + \frac{B}{(p - p_2)} + \frac{Cp + D}{p^2 + \omega^2}. \end{aligned}$$

The transform of this is

$$(2.36) \qquad \theta_o(t) = Ae^{p_1 t} + Be^{p_2 t} + E \cos (\omega t + \psi).$$

The final term of (2.36) we have already encountered in (2.23)—it is the steady-state response to the sinusoidal load. The first two terms represent the transient response which, again, will be rapidly damped if p_1 and p_2 have large negative real parts.

Stability of the system. We stated in the section before last that a system will be stable if the roots of the characteristic equation of the system transform have negative real parts. In the section just preceding we noticed that the transient response of the system is independent of the load and is determined by the roots of the characteristic equation. If the roots have large negative real parts, the transient will be strongly damped. These results suggest that many properties of the system can be determined directly by examination of the roots of the characteristic equation. We next carry out this program for various choices of K_2.[7]

---

[7] We will not employ in this paper some of the procedures, such as Nyquist's rule, widely used in servomechanism analysis to determine whether a system has any roots with positive real parts. For Nyquist's rule, see [2, pp. 67–75] and [5, Chapter V]. It may be appropriate at this point to emphasize the exploratory intent of this paper. Emphasis has been placed on formulating the problem in the language of servomechanism theory, determining the criteria for evaluating the merit of a control system, and surveying the general basis in servomechanism theory for approaching such problems. For a more adequate account of the wide collection of analytic and graphical tools at the disposal of the servomechanism engineer for synthesizing a control element that has the desired characteristics, the reader must turn to the references at the end of the paper.

A. Let $K_2 = a/p$ with a real. Then $p_0 = \pm\sqrt{a}$, and the system is unstable since at least one of the roots has a nonnegative real part.

B. Let $K_2 = a/p + b$, with a and b real. Then $p_0 = (-b \pm\sqrt{b^2 - 4a})/2$, and the system is stable if $a > 0$, $b > 0$; otherwise, unstable. This result has already appeared from (2.31) and (2.32).

C. Let $K_2 = a/p + b + cp$, with a, b, c real. Then $p_0 = [-b \pm \sqrt{b^2 - 4a(c + 1)}]/2(c + 1)$, and the system is stable if a, b, and $(c + 1)$ all have the same sign; otherwise, unstable.

Interpretation of the decision operator. The operator K_2 represents a rule of decision. Since $\mu(p) = K_2(p)\cdot\epsilon(p)$, this rule determines on the basis of information as to the current deficit or excess of inventory $[\epsilon(p)]$, at what rate $[\mu(p)]$ manufacture should be carried on. Among the operators that have been examined and found to possess satisfactory properties is $K_2 = a/p + b$, with a and b large positive constants. With this operator, equation (2.2) becomes

$$(2.37) \qquad \frac{d\mu(t)}{dt} = a\epsilon(t) + b\frac{d\epsilon(t)}{dt},$$

which, interpreted, means: the rate of production should be increased or decreased by an amount proportional to the deficiency or excess of inventory plus an amount proportional to the rate at which the inventory is decreasing. The constants of proportionality, a and b, should be large if it is desired to keep the inventory within narrow bounds. The relation $b^2 > 4a$ should be preserved if oscillation is to be avoided.

All of this is obvious to common sense. What is perhaps not obvious is that derivative control [e.g., the final term in (2.37)] is essential to the stability of the system. To base changes in production rate only upon the size of inventory (setting $b = 0$) would introduce undamped fluctuations in the system. (Compare A and B of the previous section.)

3. SYSTEM WITH PRODUCTION LAG

With this preliminary analysis of a simple system we are ready to study a system that approximates more closely to the problems we would expect to encounter in actual situations. The most important features missing from the previous system are a production lag and the availability of information about new orders. In actual cases a period of time will elapse from the moment when instructions are issued to increase the rate of production to the moment when the increased flow of goods is actually produced.

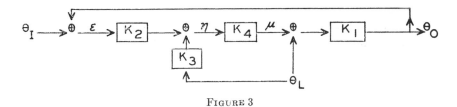

FIGURE 3

Description of the system. In Figure 3 is shown a system with a pro duction lag. The equations of this system are

(3.1) $$\theta_O = K_1(\mu - \theta_L),$$

(3.2) $$\mu = K_4\eta,$$

(3.3) $$\eta = K_2\epsilon + K_3\theta_L,$$

(3.4) $$\epsilon = \theta_I - \theta_O.$$

The new variable $\eta(t)$ represents the instructions at time t as to the production rate; $\mu(t)$ now represents the actual rate of production of finished goods at time t. $\mu(p)$ and $\eta(p)$ are connected (3.2) by the "production lag operator," K_4. As before, we will have, by definition, $K_1 = 1/p$. The operators K_2 and K_3 correspond to the decision rule, which now depends both on inventory level and rate of new orders. Both operators are at our disposal in seeking an optimal scheduling rule. It remains to find a plausible form for K_4.

The simplest assumption is that the production lag is a fixed time period, τ. That is,

(3.5) $$\mu(t) = \eta(t - \tau).$$

This means that if a given rate of production is decided upon at a certain time, this rate of production of finished items will be realized τ units of time later. The operator transform $K_4(p)$ corresponding to (3.5) is

(3.6) $$K_4(p) = e^{-\tau p}.$$

Substituting the known functions $K_1(p)$ and $K_4(p)$ in the system equations and solving for the system transform, we get

(3.7) $$Y(p) = \frac{\theta_O(p)}{\theta_L(p)} = \frac{(e^{-\tau p}K_3 - 1)}{p + e^{-\tau p}K_2}.$$

A comparison of (3.7) with (2.11) reveals that both numerator and denominator have been affected by the introduction of the production lag. Hence we shall have to re-examine the entire situation.

Feedforward of information about new orders. Consideration of the numerator of (3.7) shows that the control of inventory is not a trivial problem. If we set $K_3 = 1$, the numerator becomes $(e^{-\tau p} - 1)$, which approaches zero only as p approaches $2n\pi i/\tau$, where n is zero or an integer. Hence, this procedure would stabilize the inventory perfectly only for a sinusoidal load whose frequency is an exact multiple of the frequency corresponding to the production lag. At best we can say that the system will perform better with the operator $K_3 = 1$ than without any information about orders, but by no means perfectly.

Why not set $K_3 = e^{\tau p}$? Then we would have $(e^{-\tau p}K_3 - 1) \equiv 0$. Define the variable ϕ so that

(3.8) $$\phi(p) = e^{\tau p}\theta_L(p).$$

Taking the inverse transforms of both sides, we find

(3.9) $\phi(t) = \theta_L(t + \tau).$

Hence, setting $K_3 = e^{\tau p}$ corresponds to predicting the value of θ_L for τ units of time in advance of the actual receipt of orders. Again the result is intuitively obvious. If we could predict orders over the time interval τ, we could schedule production in anticipation of the actual receipt of these orders and avoid any inventory fluctuation whatsoever. We will not explore further the problem of forecasting $\theta_L(t + \tau)$, but will consider optimal decision rules when future orders are not known with certainty.[8]

Feedback of information about inventories. We consider next the denominator of (3.7). Because of the sinusoidal character of $e^{-\tau p}$, this will behave roughly like $(p + K_2)$. Hence, the system will behave in the same general manner as the system analyzed in the second section. Moreover, because of equation (2.14) we may expect the same general behavior in the steady state of this system as of the system of Section 2.

The roots of the characteristic equation

(3.10) $p^2 + (a + bp)e^{-\tau p} = 0$

are not easily evaluated. We will not investigate further here the roots of this transcendental equation. Instead, we will suggest a method of replacing the fixed lag, with operator $e^{-\tau p}$, by a distributed lag, with operator $a^2/(a^2 + p^2)$, which retains the algebraic character of the system transform and avoids the difficulties encountered in handling (3.10).

In place of $\mu(t) = \eta(t - \tau)$ we write

(3.11) $\mu(t) = \int_0^t P(\tau)\eta(t - \tau)\, d\tau,$

where

$$\int_0^\infty P(\tau)\, d\tau = 1.$$

$P(\tau)$ may be regarded, then, as the probability that the lag in producing a particular scheduled item will be of length τ. For large values

---

[8] In work that is continuing on this problem in an Air Forces project at Carnegie Institute of Technology, an attempt is being made to reformulate the problem in stochastic terms. In this approach the customer order function is regarded as an autocorrelated function rather than a sum of superimposed sinusoidal functions. When the problem is looked at in this way, the rather artificial distinction we have maintained between the prediction problem and the filtering problem tends to disappear. The stochastic approach, as applied to servomechanism theory, is largely the work of Norbert Wiener. See References [6], and [2, Chapters VI–VIII]. Our work has not yet progressed far enough to indicate the range of usefulness of the stochastic methods in relation to problems of the kind considered here.

of τ we would expect $P(\tau)$ to be zero, or at least very small. If (3.11) holds, we have, by (2.13),

(3.12) $\mu(p) = P(p)\eta(p).$

For example, suppose $P(\tau) = a^2\tau e^{-a\tau}$. Then $P(p) = a^2/(a^2 + p^2)$, and

(3.13) $\theta_O = \dfrac{\left(\dfrac{a^2}{a^2 + p^2}\, K_3 - 1\right)\theta_L}{p + \dfrac{a^2}{a^2 + p^2}\, K_2}.$

If we define $\bar{\tau} = \displaystyle\int_0^\infty \tau P(\tau)\, d\tau = 2/a$ as the *mean lag*, we see that the mean lag is still independent of η. The system transform defined by (3.13) can be analyzed by the methods previously employed to determine suitable forms for K_3 and K_2.

For example, if we take $K_3 = 1$, $K_2 = (b + cp^2)$,

(3.14) $Y(p) = \dfrac{-p^2}{p^3 + a^2cp^2 + a^2p + a^2b}.$

This has zero steady-state error for $\theta_L = 1/p^2$, i.e., for $\theta_L = t$ $(t \geqslant 0)$. The parameters b and c can now be given such values that the real parts of the roots of the characteristic equation will be negative, and the system consequently stable. The necessary and sufficient conditions for this are $c > b > 0$.

4. CONTROL OF INVENTORIES AND PRODUCTION-RATE FLUCTUATIONS

The general criterion for the optimality of a production control system of the sort we are analyzing is that cost of production, in some sense, be minimized.

Large inventories involve interest costs, possible costs through physical depreciation in storage, warehousing costs, etc. An inventory deficiency (excessive negative inventory), on the other hand, involves a "cost" in the sense of delay in filling orders, and consequent customer ill will. It appears reasonable to include in the cost of production, therefore, an element that represents the cost of excess or deficiency in inventories, say $\xi_1(\theta_O)$. In first approximation we may take ξ_1 proportional to $|\theta_O|$, or to θ_O^2.

It also appears reasonable to assume that the cost of producing a given quantity of output over a period of time is minimized if output is constant during that time. If we represent the output as a constant plus an oscillating function with zero mean—$\mu(t) = M + \mu(t)$—then we may assume that the rate at which cost is being incurred is a function of M and of the frequency and amplitude of $\mu(t)$.

Now, from equation (3.1), we know that

(4.1) $\theta_O(p) = (1/p)\mu(p) - (1/p)\theta_L(p),$

that is,

(4.2) $\dfrac{d\theta_O(t)}{dt} = \mu(t) - \theta_L(t).$

Hence, if we succeed in stabilizing θ_0 at $\theta_0 = 0$, μ will not be constant but will follow $\theta_L(t)$. Conversely, if we stabilize μ, θ_0 will not be constant, but will follow the integral of $\theta_L(t)$. We cannot devise a system that will simultaneously eliminate inventory and production fluctuations, but must, instead, establish a criterion that is some weighted average of these.

Analysis of a specific criterion. To be specific, we consider the steady state of the system under sinusoidal inputs and outputs. This assumption is consistent with the system (4.2). In fact, in the steady state, if θ_L is sinusoidal, θ_0 and μ will be sinusoidal with the same period. We assume that the cost associated with μ is proportional to the square of the amplitude of its oscillation, i.e., that it is of the form $\rho \mid B \mid^2$, where $\mid B \mid$ is the amplitude. Similarly, we assume that the cost of holding inventories is $\sigma \mid C \mid^2$, where $\mid C \mid$ is the amplitude of θ_0.

We let

(4.3) $$\theta_L(t) = a \cos \omega t,$$

(4.4) $$\mu(t) = b \cos \omega t + \beta \sin \omega t,$$

(4.5) $$\theta_0(t) = c \cos \omega t + \gamma \sin \omega t,$$

with a, b, β, c, γ real, whence

(4.6) $$\omega\gamma = b - a, \qquad -\omega c = \beta.$$

We wish now to minimize

(4.7) $$\rho(b^2 + \beta^2) + \sigma(c^2 + \gamma^2) = \xi$$

subject to (4.6). Substituting for c and γ from (4.6) into (4.7), taking derivatives of ξ with respect to b and β, and setting these equal to zero, we find

(4.8) $$b = \frac{a\sigma}{\rho\omega^2 + \sigma}, \qquad \beta = 0,$$

(4.9) $$c = 0, \qquad \gamma = \frac{a\rho\omega}{(\rho\omega^2 + \sigma)}.$$

For small ω: $b \to a$, $\gamma \to 0$. For large ω: $b \to 0$, $\gamma \to 0$, $\omega\gamma \to -a$.

Interpreting these results, we find that the optimal decision-rule will adjust the production rate and hold inventories down for long-period fluctuations in orders, but will stabilize production and permit inventories to fluctuate for rapid fluctuations in orders. In the latter case, the inventory excess or deficiency will remain small ($\gamma \to 0$) because the period of oscillation is short. The amplitude of manufacturing fluctuations (b) will vary inversely with ω. The magnitude of inventory fluctuations (γ) will have a maximum for $\omega^2 = \sigma/\rho$.

An alternative criterion. In the previous section we used the quadratic cost function (4.7). Interesting results are obtained by using the linear function,

(4.10) $$\zeta = \rho \mid \sqrt{b^2 + \beta^2} \mid + \sigma \mid \sqrt{c^2 + \gamma^2} \mid.$$

Minimizing ζ after substitution for c and γ from (4.6), we find as optimum values

(4.11) $$\beta = 0, \quad c = 0.$$

But for b we find

(4.12) $$b = 0 \text{ for } \omega > \sigma/\rho, \quad b = a \text{ for } \omega < \sigma/\rho.$$

Correspondingly, for γ,

(4.13) $$\gamma = -a \text{ for } \omega > \sigma/\rho, \quad \gamma = 0 \text{ for } \omega < \sigma/\rho.$$

Writing $Z(p) = \mu(p)/\theta_L(p)$, we see that for optimum results, $Z(p)$ should have the characteristics of an ideal low-pass filter: it should transmit without distortion all frequencies below $2\pi\sigma/\rho$ and should filter out all frequencies above $2\pi\sigma/\rho$. The meaning of this requirement in terms of a decision rule can be interpreted by the same methods as those used for the quadratic cost functions in succeeding sections.

Requirements for the system transform. Returning to the quadratic cost function of Section 4, we must now determine what kind of a system transform will satisfy (4.4)–(4.5) with b, β, c, γ given by (4.8)–(4.9). For brevity we write $\theta_0(p)/\theta_L(p) = Y(p)$, $\mu(p)/\theta_L(p) = Z(p)$. Then, from (4.1),

(4.14) $$Z(p) = 1 + pY(p).$$

The optimum transform $Z(p)$ is found readily as follows. Recalling (2.13) we can write the output $\mu(t)$ for a sinusoidal load $e^{i\omega t}$,

(4.15) $$\mu(t) = \int_0^\infty Z(\tau)e^{i\omega(t-\tau)} \, d\tau = e^{i\omega t} \int_0^\infty Z(\tau)e^{-i\omega\tau} \, d\tau.$$

But the factor under the integral sign of the right-hand side of (4.15) is, by definition, $Z(i\omega)$. That is, for a sinusoidal load with period $2\pi\omega$, we will have

(4.16) $$\mu(t) = Z(i\omega)\theta_L(t).$$

We see immediately that

(4.17) $$Z(i\omega) = \frac{b}{a} = \frac{\sigma}{\rho\omega^2 + \sigma}.$$

Hence,

(4.18) $$Z(p) = \frac{\sigma}{-\rho p^2 + \sigma},$$

and, from (4.9),

(4.19) $$Y(p) = \frac{\rho p}{-\rho p^2 + \sigma}.$$

The characteristic equations of $Z(p)$ and $Y(p)$, however, have real roots of opposite signs, $p = \pm(\sigma/\rho)^{\frac{1}{2}}$. Hence a system with these transforms would be unstable. The transient output would increase exponentially.

The reason for this somewhat unpleasant result is that we have designed the transform to minimize costs for steady-state operation. This will not, in general, minimize cost when the system is passing from one steady-state to another. Clearly, for $\theta_L(t) = T_A$, a constant, ($t \geqslant 0$), we want

(4.20) $\mu(t) = T +$ a transient term,

(4.21) $\theta_0(t) = 0 +$ a transient term.

The transient term in (4.20) should be such that $\mu(t)$ will not overshoot—that is, the system should be over-damped. This implies that the roots of the characteristic equation of $Z(p)$ should be negative and real.

To get the desired steady-state behavior of $\mu(t)$ for the indicated load we require that $\mathrm{Lim}_{p\to 0}\, pZ(p)(T/p) = \mathrm{Lim}_{p\to 0}\, Z(p)T = T$. From (4.21) we infer that $\theta_0(t)$ should be heavily damped, with $\mathrm{Lim}_{p\to 0}\, Y(p)T = 0$. From (4.14) we see that the latter condition is a sufficient condition that $\mathrm{Lim}_{p\to 0}\, Z(p)T = T$.

As can be seen from inspection, these limiting conditions are satisfied by the transforms of (4.18) and (4.19) although, because of instability, the conditions on the transients are not. To remedy this situation we replace the denominator of $Y(p)$ by $(\sqrt{\rho}p + \sqrt{\sigma})^2$. The resulting transform,

(4.22) $$Y(p) = \frac{-\rho p}{(\rho^{\frac{1}{2}}p + \sigma^{\frac{1}{2}})^2},$$

is critically damped and approaches the transform of (4.19) for large p. The characteristic equation has the two equal negative real roots: $p_0 = -(\sigma/\rho)^{\frac{1}{2}}$. The transient term in $\mu(t)$ will be of the form $Ate^{-p_0 t}$.

Construction of the decision rule. We return now to the problem of finding a K_3 and K_2 that will realize the $Y(p)$ of (4.22). We will first explore the simple case where $K_4 = 1$ (no production lag). In this case

(4.23) $$Y(p) = \frac{K_3 - 1}{p + K_2}.$$

If we now set $K_3 = 1 - \rho p$, $K_2 = \rho p^2 + [2(\rho\sigma)^{\frac{1}{2}} - 1]p + \sigma$ and substitute in (4.23), the result is (4.22). Moreover, we will have for $Z(p)$,

(4.24) $$Z(p) = \frac{2\sqrt{\rho\sigma}p + \sigma}{(\sqrt{\rho}p + \sqrt{\sigma})^2}.$$

Since, in the case of zero time lag, $\mu(t) = \eta(t)$, (4.24) gives the following rule for determining $\eta(t)$:

(4.25) $$\rho\frac{d^2\eta}{dt^2} + 2\sqrt{\rho\sigma}\frac{d\eta}{dt} + \sigma\eta(t) = 2\sqrt{\rho\sigma}\frac{d\theta_L}{dt} + \sigma\theta_L(t).$$

In the case where there is a fixed production lag, $K_4 = e^{-\tau p}$, we have

$$(4.26) \qquad Y(p) = \frac{e^{-\tau p}K_3 - 1}{p + e^{-\tau p}K_2}, \qquad Z(p) = \frac{e^{-\tau p}(K_2 + pK_3)}{p + e^{-\tau p}K_2}.$$

If we define $X(p) = \eta(p)/\theta_L(p)$, we obtain from (3.2) and (4.26)

$$(4.27) \qquad\qquad X(p) = \frac{K_2 + pK_3}{p + e^{-\tau p}K_2}.$$

Giving K_2 and K_3 the same values as in the previous case, we get

$$(4.28) \qquad X(p) = \frac{2\sqrt{\rho\sigma}\,p + \sigma}{p(1 - e^{-\tau p}) + e^{-\tau p}(\sqrt{\rho}p + \sqrt{\sigma})^2}.$$

The corresponding decision rule is

$$(4.29) \qquad \begin{aligned} \frac{d\eta(t)}{dt} &= (1 - 2\sqrt{\rho\sigma})\,\frac{d\eta(t - \tau)}{dt} - \rho\,\frac{d^2\eta(t - \tau)}{dt^2} \\ &\qquad - \sigma\eta(t - \tau) + 2\sqrt{\rho\sigma}\,\frac{d\theta_L(t)}{dt} + \sigma\theta_L(t). \end{aligned}$$

This rule we may take as a realizable approximation to the rule that would minimize costs. For the limiting cases as $p \to \infty$ and $p \to 0$, it has the same properties as the rule derived from (4.24).

5. FURTHER CONSIDERATION OF THE COST CRITERION

The cost criteria developed in Section 4 are undoubtedly greatly oversimplified. In this section we will consider possible methods of constructing a more realistic criterion. In particular, we wish to introduce a more complete analysis of that part of the cost function that depends on rate of manufacture.

We suppose that the cost of manufacture is the sum of three components:

1. Variable costs proportional to the rate of manufacture (e.g., cost of materials). Since these costs are determined by the number of orders to be filled, and hence are independent of the control system, we may continue to ignore them.

2. Fixed costs proportional to plant capacity, i.e., to the maximum rate of manufacturing activity. The previous section indicates how these costs can be handled in designing the control system.

3. Sticky costs proportional to the rate of manufacture when this is constant, but not capable of being reduced immediately as the rate of manufacture declines. In first approximation we may assume that as the rate of manufacture increases from a stable level, sticky costs will increase proportionately, but that if the rate of manufacture decreases, there is a fixed upper limit to the rate at which sticky costs will decrease.

Suppose (Figure 4) that $\mu(t)$ is subject to oscillation of period $2/\alpha$ and amplitude A. The slope of μ will be $\pm A\alpha$. Suppose, further, that sticky costs, $\xi(t)$ can only decrease with a slope of $-\beta$, but can increase as rapidly as μ.

The ordinate of $\mu(0)$ is A; the slope of $\mu(t)$ is $-A\alpha$ in the interval $0 \leqslant t < 1/\alpha$, $A\alpha$ in the interval $1/\alpha \leqslant t < 2/\alpha$. The ordinate of $\xi(0)$ is A; the slope of $\xi(t)$ is $-\beta$ in the interval $0 \leqslant t < t_a$; $A\alpha$ in the interval $t_a \leqslant t < 2/\alpha$. The integral of $\xi(t) - \mu(t)$ over the interval $0 \leqslant t < 2/\alpha$ is then the area of the triangle whose vertices are indicated

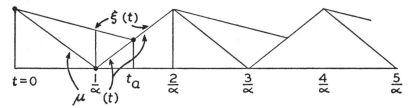

FIGURE 4

by dots. This area is $\frac{1}{2}$ the ordinate $\xi(1/\alpha)$ times t_a: $\xi(1/\alpha) = A - (\beta/\alpha)$. The value of t_a is given by

$$(5.1) \qquad A\alpha[t_a - (1/\alpha)] = A - \beta t_a$$

or

$$(5.2) \qquad t_a = \frac{2A}{A\alpha + \beta}.$$

Hence,

$$(5.3) \qquad \int_0^{2/\alpha} [\xi - \mu]\, dt = \frac{A\alpha - \beta}{2\alpha} \cdot \frac{2A}{A\alpha + \beta} = \frac{A}{\alpha}\frac{(A\alpha - \beta)}{(A\alpha + \beta)}.$$

If 1 is an integral multiple of $2/\alpha$, then

$$(5.4) \qquad \int_0^1 (\xi - \mu)\, dt = \frac{\alpha}{2}\int_0^{2/\alpha} (\xi - \mu) = \frac{A}{2}\frac{(A\alpha - \beta)}{(A\alpha + \beta)} = C.$$

But, for this same interval, $\int_0^1 \mu\, dt = A/2$; hence we have for the ratio of sticky costs to production

$$(5.5) \qquad C \cdot \frac{2}{A} = \frac{(A\alpha - \beta)}{(A\alpha + \beta)}.$$

It follows that sticky costs will be increased by an increase in the amplitude of the oscillations of $\mu(t)$—behaving, in this respect, like fixed costs—and will also be increased by an increase in the frequency of μ. In designing our optimal criterion we disregarded this latter consideration. Hence, the design of the decision rule can be improved by decreasing the response of $\mu(t)$ to $\theta_L(t)$ for high frequencies of the latter at the expense of increasing somewhat the response of $\theta_o(t)$. Again it is reassuring that our results coincide with common sense.

Assumption of a sinusoidal oscillation of μ and of ξ leads to the same kind of result. Finally, fixed costs and variable costs can be subsumed as a limiting case of sticky costs by considering a range of different cost categories, each with its characteristic β. The β for variable costs would be infinite; for fixed costs, zero. If we can define some kind of an average β, this can be used as a basis for our criterion of manufacturing costs.

6. CONCLUSION

The general conclusion to be drawn from our explorations, however tentative these have been, is that the basic approach and fundamental techniques of servomechanism theory can indeed be applied fruitfully to the analysis and design of decisional procedures for controlling the rate of manufacturing activity. To be sure, most of the conclusions we have reached could, at least in a qualitative sense, be reached intuitively. But even here, intuition has been aided by the frame of reference that servomechanism theory provides. Moreover, the more exact procedures permit statement of our results with a degree of precision that could not be attained without them. Even in this very early stage the theory permits actual numbers to be inserted for the construction of specific decision rules that would apply, with a considerable degree of realism, to actual situations.

Carnegie Institute of Technology

7. REFERENCES

The following list of references covers some of the more systematic and lucid introductions to servomechanism theory. They are listed in order from the relatively elementary treatments to the more advanced or specialized.

[1] LAUER, H., R. LESNICK, AND L. E. MATSON, *Servomechanism Fundamentals*, New York: McGraw-Hill, 1947. An introductory treatment employing differential equations rather than the Laplace transform. Analyzes in detail the behavior of a few very simple engineering servos, and gives a clear picture of the servo concept.

[2] JAMES, H. M., N. B. NICHOLS, AND R. S. PHILLIPS (eds.), *Theory of Servomechanisms*, New York: McGraw-Hill, 1947. Chapter I, "Servo Systems," gives a good introduction to basic concepts. Chapter 2, "Mathematical Background," gives an excellent introduction to the Laplace transform, its physical meaning, and its relation to the weighting function. General design principles and techniques are discussed in Chapter 4, and more advanced topics in other chapters.

[3] GARDNER, M. F., AND J. L. BARNES, *Transients in Linear Systems*, Vol. I, New York: John Wiley and Sons, 1942. A clear, systematic exposition of Laplace transform theory and methods.

[4] BROWN, G. S., AND D. P. CAMPBELL, *Principles of Servomechanisms*, New York: John Wiley and Sons, 1948. Parallel to [3], but with more emphasis on system design, and less on analysis.

[5] McCOLL, L. A., *Fundamental Theory of Servomechanisms*, New York: Van Nostrand, 1945. An elegant brief treatment stressing fundamental concepts and employing Laplace transform methods.

[6] WIENER, N., *The Extrapolation, Interpolation, and Smoothing of Stationary Time Series*, New York: John Wiley and Sons, 1949. An approach to the problem of forecasting a stochastic input or load. (See also [2], Chapters VI–VIII.)

[7] OLDENBOURG, R. C., AND H. SARTORIUS, *The Dynamics of Automatic Controls*, American Society of Mechanical Engineers, 1948. A systematic treatment of controllers, using Laplace transform methods. Includes extensive discussion of fixed lags, nonlinearities, and discontinuous regulation. (On the last point, see also [2], Chapter V; [5], Chapter X and Appendix; and [3], Chapter IX.)

Excellent bibliographies will be found in [3], [4], [5], and [7]. For discussions and examples of the use of servomechanisms in the study of economic systems see all the following:

[8] COOPER, W. W., "A Proposal for Extending the Theory of the Firm," *Quarterly Journal of Economics*, Vol. 65, February, 1951, pp. 87–109.

[9] MOREHOUSE, N. F., R. H. STROTZ, AND S. J. HORWITZ, "An Electro-Analog Method for Investigating Problems in Econometric Dynamics: Inventory Oscillations," ECONOMETRICA, Vol. 18, October, 1950, pp. 313–328.

[10] ENKE, STEPHEN, "Equilibrium Among Spatially Separated Markets: Solution by Electric Analogue," ECONOMETRICA, Vol. 19, January, 1951, pp. 40–47.

[11] WIENER, NORBERT, *Cybernetics*, New York: John Wiley and Sons, 1948.

[12] GOODWIN, RICHARD M., "Econometrics in Business-Cycle Analysis," Chapter 22 in Alvin H. Hansen, *Business Cycles and National Income*, New York: W. W. Norton and Co., 1951.

6

An Industrial Dynamics Case Study

Willard R. Fey

I. INTRODUCTION

Several years ago an Industrial Dynamics project was started at
M.I.T.'s School of Industrial Management to study and improve one product
line manufactured by the Sprague Electric Company. This study progressed
through the stages of system study, problem definition, model formulation,
model analysis, policy improvement, and new policy implementation. It is
now in a period of evaluation both of the changes produced in the system
by the new policies and of the lessons learned about carrying out a successful Industrial Dynamics study. This paper is a part of the latter evaluation, since it describes some of the problems that arose, the mistakes
that were made, and the lessons that were learned at each stage of the
analysis.

The objective of the Sprague Project was to understand the forces
that influenced dynamic behavior in one product line, and to find means of
changing the system to improve profits and employment stability. The
project began at a time prior to the development of much of the philosophy
and methodology of Industrial Dynamics.   This paper is intended to present a description of the problems that arose, the mistakes that were
made, and the lessons that were learned during the study.

The project proceeded through a series of steps which included:
study of the physical system, definition of the company's objectives, selection of the major problems, development of hypotheses relating to the

This article is based on a project directed by Professor Jay W. Forrester of M.I.T. and sponsored by
the Sprague Electric Company. It first appeared in the *Industrial Management Review* (currently published as the *Sloan Management Review*) 4, no. 1 (Fall 1962), pp. 79–99. (ⓒ 1962 by the Industrial
Management Review Association; all rights reserved.)

causes of the problems, model formulation, model analysis, development of better policies, introduction of the proposed policies into the operating system, and evaluation of the results.

The analysis was based upon an Industrial Dynamics model of the product line which contained representations of the firm's structure, its labor market, and its customers. Simulations on a large-scale digital computer* were run to produce the time response of the variables in the model for various input conditions and policy and parameter changes.

II. INITIAL STUDY

The Sprague Project began early in 1957 with the study of plant operations. The product line of high quality electronic components had been active for over ten years. It was in the mature phase of its life cycle, that is, the period after research and development and intensive market expansion when a company's operating structure becomes relatively fixed and the extent of the market is fairly well defined.

The product line contained several thousand active catalogue items used in large military and industrial systems in which reliability and accuracy were required. Inventories were carried for about 10 per cent of the catalogue items. Although some of the manufacturing operations required machines, the majority of the work was done by hand.

There were many customers, whose total weekly order volume fluctuated widely. The individual order size also varied substantially and requested delivery time ran from two weeks ago to a year in the future. The company had several competitors in this field.

Much detailed data on individual catalogue items and the total line accompanied the observations which led to the above description. Opinions and information were obtained from everyone associated with the line, and technical data on the production process and the characteristics of the product were studied. This added up to a considerable volume of unorganized information which presented many seemingly unrelated problems.

A substantial part of the first year was spent building a model of the company's production-inventory operations based on traditional order-by-order, item-by-item statistical simulation. The model was massive, difficult to understand, and oriented not at all toward the company's aggregate managerial decisions of employment, inventory and delivery delay control and their interaction with the market. It attempted to represent

---

*Computations were performed on the IBM 704 and 709 computers at the M.I.T. Computation Center.

every operation and transaction that occurred in the company in the hope that the important problems and their solutions would become clear when the model was analyzed. No progress was made, however, until it became evident that (a) the system study should develop a feeling for the company's objectives and the major dynamic problems and their causes, rather than be a general fact-finding expedition, (b) the system should be visualized as a whole, and (c) recognition should be given to the relationship between the aggregate decisions (like employment policy), system behavior as a whole, and individual item decisions which are made within the limits set by the aggregate policies.

III. DEFINITION OF PROBLEMS

The worth of a research project in large part is determined by the problems that are selected for study. The study of small or meaningless problems will produce corresponding results. A study of major problems, although it sometimes fails to produce quantitative solutions, can still provide extremely useful understanding. The search in this case was for the dynamic problems which were most important relative to the company's objectives. No attempt was made to restrict the problems to those produced by linear systems or to those that would yield optimum solutions. There was, therefore, no formal way of finding the major problems; they instead had to emerge from an understanding of the company's objectives and the overall nature of the system.

The company's objectives important to this study were profits and employment stability for its own sake. The major problems relative to these objectives were the long term cyclic nature of the product's industry and the tendency for wider fluctuations to occur in production than in sales.

a. Long-term Fluctuations in the Industry

A long-term cycle, about two years in duration, appeared in all system variables. This problem arose in large part because the customers tended to follow a policy of ordering ahead as the company's service delay became long and holding orders back when the delay was short. The company's employment decisions which directly affected the delay time were thus reflected in the customers' ordering rate. This problem forced a study of the interaction between the customers, the company, and the company's labor market. The labor market was the only factor market involved because this was a product line of predominantly hand-made items. Therefore, production output was directly controlled by the size of the work force.

b. Wider Variation of Production than of Sales

The second major problem was the greater variation of production and employment than of sales. This was created when management followed a policy of trying to maintain inventory at its desired level and of quickly correcting deviations from the ideal. Thus, when sales were rising and inventory was falling, inventory was reordered at a rate equal to the sales rate plus an additional amount needed to replace the units that had already been depleted. The depletion occurred in a rising sales situation even when inventory orders equalled sales because it took time to get the orders through the factory. During that manufacturing time, sales rose above the receipts of finished inventory units, and inventory fell. The added replacement orders placed an extra burden on the factory in busy periods, and the production rate exceeded the sales rate. In addition, the desired inventory level rose as sales did. Therefore, still more inventory orders were written to raise inventory to a level above the previous normal.

IV. STUDY OF THE SYSTEM

A review of data already collected and a second study of the system clarified the importance of the structure described below.

A customer, private or military, orders a group of high-quality systems from a system manufacturer (i.e., component customer). This manufacturer, who does not have an inventory of finished systems, has to design the system (if it has not been ordered before), make a parts list, check this against parts inventories, schedule production, obtain necessary parts, employees, and capital equipment, manufacture the system, and ship the product to the buyer. The manufacturer tries to make employees, parts, and capital equipment come together at the proper time, so that production time is not wasted. If employees, capital equipment, or parts are needed, they are ordered. Seeing that the proper resources are on hand, and the desire to establish an inventory for quick access on rush orders leads to the prime contractor placing orders for electronic components with the subject company or one of the competitors.

The selection of the component supplier is influenced by quality, speed and reliability of delivery, price, habit (convenience), and contractual conditions, as well as less rational forces. The timing of an order depends upon the expected delivery time and the time at which the customer needs the units.

The above is a description of one customer's operations with respect to one order. In fact, there are many customers, each continually receiving orders. Each operates differently in terms of quantities and timing, although each performs all of the functions described in roughly the same sequence in order to produce the necessary systems.

At the components manufacturer, the sales department receives the order and sends it to the engineering department. There, units are designed or specifications verified, and manufacturing orders are written. The orders proceed to manufacturing, where an inventory search is performed if the order is for an inventory item. Orders that can be filled from inventory are sent through a short final process, packaged and shipped. Orders that cannot be filled because of low inventory, or because they are not for stock items, go to production to be made-to-order. Each such order is scheduled, manufactured and shipped to the customer.

Several actions are necessary to support the manufacturing process. (1) Units to replenish inventory; these inventory orders go through the same manufacturing process that made-to-order customer orders use. (2) Factory priority decisions are made to decide the sequence in which customer and inventory orders are produced. (3) Decisions to hire or lay off production workers are made based on the average sales level and the factory backlog of work. A decision to hire increases the productive work force only after delays in obtaining the people and training them. A decision to reduce workers decreases the work force only after the required notice delay. (4) Decisions are made to reorder raw materials and to increase or replace capital equipment. These lead to the acquisition of the required items after appropriate delays.

The chain of events and decisions which results from a prime customer's order for a large electronic system can be displayed graphically by means of the flow diagram shown in Figure 1. This diagram represents the structure of the socio-economic system of interest, and it was used as the basic outline for the simulation model which ultimately formed the heart of this study.

V. MODEL DESCRIPTION

The purpose of the model which is described below was to represent the physical system in such a way that the previously defined problems could be meaningfully studied and understood and new policies and parameters could be tested before their use in actual operations. The following steps were taken, based on the problems and the system study:

1. The major sectors of the system to be included were selected.
2. The level of aggregation of the variables was determined.

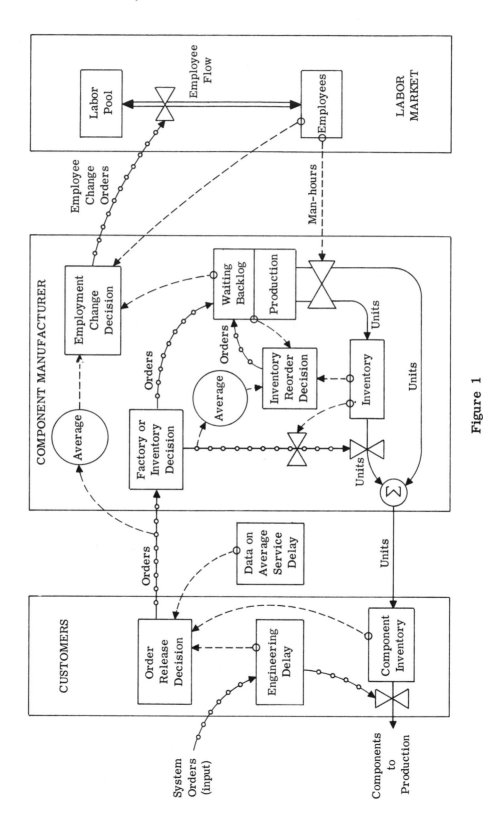

Figure 1

Detailed view showing the principal system components of customers, firm, and labor market. Delays in the flow channels are not indicated.

3. The physical flows (decisions) and levels (inventories, backlogs, etc.) necessary in each sector were chosen.
4. The information to be used in each decision was defined.
5. The mathematical form of the equation for each variable was stated.
6. The values of the physical constants used in the equations were determined.

All variables and constants had to have physical meaning so that anyone in the company could clearly understand the model and any new policy that could be tested in the model would work in the operating system.

The model incorporated those parts of the system that related to the defined problems. Included were the customers and their ordering and production-planning operations, the company with its inventory and production system, and the one factor of production (labor) which controlled the output. It was found that raw materials, capital equipment, costs, and prices did not have a significant influence on the decisions and actions in the system within the normal range of operations. Since the problems were of a highly aggregated nature involving all catalogue items and operations and since changes in the mix of the incoming orders and inventory were small relative to other variations, the model dealt with the total flows of units ordered, units produced and employees. Distinctions were not made between catalogue items, different customer orders or employees in different production departments. Some of these considerations are currently under study to produce further improvements, but they were not necessary for studying the problems treated here. Notice that the sectors to be included, the level of aggregation and the physical flows were based on the problems under study. Had other problems been chosen, a different model would have been necessary. For example, this model will not answer the question: What is the most efficient lot size for catalogue item XYZ?

Equations were written to describe the system's actions. These were in the form of first-order, nonlinear, difference equations designed for simulation of the model's time behavior on an IBM 704 computer. The time delays inherent in the flows of materials, men, information, and orders were not explicitly shown in Figure 1, but were included in the equation set.

a. Demand for Electronic Components

The customers were represented by three functions: component inventory, backlog of components to be ordered, and the component-ordering decision. Equation 1L, representing the component inventory, is an example of a representative equation. Only a few of the more important equations are included in this paper as examples. A complete list of the equations can be found in Chapter 17 of Industrial Dynamics by Professor Jay W. Forrester.

$$\text{IFAC.K} = \text{IFAC.J} + (\text{DT})(\text{UAIC.JK} - \text{URMC.JK}) \qquad (1\text{L})^{*}$$

IFAC   - Inventory, Finished, Actual, at Customer (units),
DT   - Delta Time (weeks),
UAIC   - Units Arriving at Inventory at Customer (units/week),
URMC   - Units Received in Manufacturing at Customer (units/week).

In Equation 1L, IFAC.K is the inventory level at the present time. It is equal to the inventory at the previous solution time (IFAC.J) plus the difference between what was added (DT)(UAIC.JK) and what was depleted (DT)(URMC.JK) during the interval. UAIC and URMC are the rates of flow into and out of the inventory, respectively.

The critical customer characteristic is the rate of release of orders to suppliers. The customer controls this rate by varying the length of time component orders are held in engineering before being released to the supplier. This engineering holding delay is set so that the total component acquisition delay (engineering holding delay plus supplier lead time plus buffer time in the customer's component inventory) will equal the production planning lead time. This assures that components arrive at the proper time for production. The customer order release rate, therefore, is equal to the backlog of orders to be released divided by the engineering holding delay. Assuming a constant backlog, an increasing supplier delay will result in a decreasing engineering holding delay, and an increasing order release rate. A decreasing supplier delay results in an increasing holding delay, and a decreasing order release rate.

b. The Company's Inventory-Production System

After delays in the customers' purchasing department, the mail, and the component suppliers' sales office, the orders encounter the first decision at the manufacturer: Should the order be made to order or sent from inventory? The policy is that if the order can be filled from inven-

---

* The four letters preceding the period represent the variable (IFAC means Inventory, Finished, Actual, at Customer), and the one or two letters following the period is a time subscript. A single time letter indicates that the variable takes on its value at the specified instant of time (K is taken as the present instant; J is the instant preceding K with a time DT separating J and K). A double letter indicates that the variable takes on and holds its value during the time interval specified (JK or KL). These two variable types are referred to as levels and rates, respectively. Variables with no time notation are parameters that do not change with time.

tory, it should be; if not, it must be made to order. Orders for inventory-type items must undergo an inventory search. Orders found in stock are filled. Orders for inventory items not in stock or for non-inventory items are made to order. The fraction of orders filled from inventory is a function of inventory as shown in Figure 2. As inventory increases, the portion taken from inventory increases. There are always some orders for special items, so the percentage filled can never be 100 per cent, even with infinite inventory.

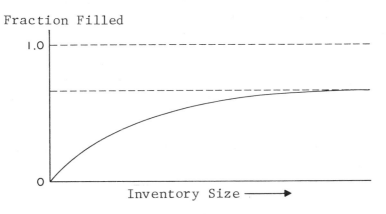

Figure 2
Fraction of Orders Filled from Inventory.

Orders to be made to order go to production to be scheduled and produced. The production process is represented in two parts. First, there is a waiting delay caused by the excess of orders above the manufacturing capacity. Second, there is a manufacturing delay necessary because of the technology of the process itself. The second delay is constant, but the first is a function of the backlog and the output rate.

Output rate is equivalent to the average productivity per employee times the number of employees. Since there are inventory replenishment orders in the factory as well as customer orders, the output for customers is not the total output. It is a fraction of the total determined by the relation between the number of customer orders and inventory orders in the backlog. No priority is assumed in the model for either type, although some customer units are expedited in the real system. The inventory output is the difference between total production and customer production.

The inventory reorder decision is based on the average outflow of units from inventory, the desired and actual values of inventory, and the desired and actual values of inventory orders in production. Imbalances between the desired and actual values are adjusted over a period of time, ASRS.

$$\text{UMSS.KL} = \text{AOIS.K} + (\frac{1}{\text{ASRS}})(\text{IFIS.K} - \text{IFAS.K} + \text{IDPS.K} - \text{IAPS.K}) \qquad \text{(2R)}$$

UMSS	-	Units to be Made for Stock at Supplier (units/week),
AOIS	-	Average Outflow from Inventory at Supplier (units/week),
ASRS	-	constAnt defining Speed of inventory Reorder at Supplier (weeks),
IFIS	-	Inventory, Finished, Ideal, at Supplier (units),
IFAS	-	Inventory, Finished, Actual, at Supplier (units),
IDPS	-	Inventory orders Desired in Production at Supplier (units),
IAPS	-	Inventory orders Actually in Production at Supplier (units).

A negative value of UMSS indicates cancellation of orders. This is reasonable as long as the cancellations do not exceed the backlog in the waiting delay. Further cancellation implies the dismantling of already started units and is unrealistic.

Desired inventory (IFIS) is a desired number of weeks of average sales. Desired orders in production (ISPD) is production lead time times average sales.

The employment decision (hiring and layoff rates) eventually leads to changes in the number of productive employees by shifting people between the labor pool and the employee pool. A hiring decision is followed by an acquisition delay and a training delay. A layoff decision is followed by a notice delay. The decision itself is based on the difference between desired (MDMS) and actual (MNES) employees adjusted over a time period, DLSS.

$$\text{MLHS.KL} = (\frac{1}{\text{DLSS}})(\text{MDMS.K} - \text{MNES.K}) \qquad \text{(3R)}$$

MLHS	-	Men to be Laid off or Hired at Supplier (men/week),
DLSS	-	Delay in the change of Labor force Size at Supplier (weeks),
MDMS	-	Men Desired in Manufacturing at the Supplier (men),
MNES	-	Men, Net, Employed at Supplier (men).

The desired employee term (MDMS) has two components, the employees needed to sustain the production output at the average sales rate, and those needed to adjust the backlog toward its acceptable level. As backlog rises, hiring increases; and as sales increase, hiring increases. As backlog and/or sales decline, layoff begins. It is assumed that the labor pool is able to supply all employment requirements.

The last part of the model includes the calculation and transmission to the customer of the suppliers' average lead time. This delay is a variable depending on the state of the supplier's inventory and the backlog in manufacturing.

In Figure 1 it can be seen that there are two paths that an incoming order can take through the supplier's system. It can be filled from inventory, or it can be made to order. In the former instance, no manufacturing is required, so the order is filled quickly. When the order goes through manufacturing, it is delayed by the normal processing time plus the time necessary to pass through the waiting lines before each process stage. Thus, there are two paths, one with a more or less fixed delay of short duration, and one of longer length which is variable and related to the size of the in-process backlog.

The delay information is the average delay associated with the total output. The total output is the sum of the outputs from the two paths. To find the average delay associated with this total, a weighted average of the delays in the two paths is used (as shown in Equation 4A).

$$DBVS.K = \frac{(USIS.JK)(DICS)}{USIS.JK + USMS.JK} + \frac{(USMS.JK)(DCOS.K)}{USIS.JK + USMS.JK} \quad (4A)$$

DBVS - Delay, average, for total of Both paths, Variable at Supplier (weeks),

USIS - Units Sent from Inventory at Supplier (units/week),

DICS - Delay in Inventory-filling Channel at Supplier (weeks),

USMS - Units sent to Shipping from Manufacturing at Supplier (units/week),

DCOS - Delay of Customer Orders in manufacturing path at Supplier (weeks).

DBVS is the average total delay that units leaving the supplier have experienced. The first term of Equation 4A is the fraction of the total output that came from inventory (USIS.JK/USIS.JK + USMS.JK) times the delay in filling from inventory (DICS). The second term represents the fraction of the total output that was made to order times the delay in the factory path (DCOS). The average service delay will change when the manufacturing time changes or when the proportion of units filled from inventory varies.

This information is necessary because the customers use this information in making their order release decision. When the delay time rises, the customers order ahead to insure that they have the units at the time they need them. Information about the supplier delay is relayed to the customers through a delay which represents the time it takes for customers to become aware of and act upon changes experienced in the supplier's delay.

The model's structure and simulated behavior were studied and it was decided that the equations adequately represented the real world decisions and operations. They could not be completely accurate, but they were useful for understanding the two problems of interest.

The equations included parameters that required numerical values before simulations could be made. These parameters included, for example, the average delay times in all the flow channels and operating departments, the average sales rate of the product, and the average production lead time.

The methods used to obtain these parameters varied considerably depending on the type of parameter and the sector involved. The company parameters, where possible, were based on samples of orders that had passed through the functions, as opposed to regression-type methods that dealt with the aggregate variables. Occasionally it was necessary to estimate parameters based on the testimony of the decision maker and/or other people associated with the situation. The customer parameters were based on estimates by company personnel familiar with the customers' ordering patterns and on studies of similar functions in the company. Reasonable ranges were then chosen and used to test the model's sensitivity. Only a few of the customer parameters turned out to be sensitive and thereby deserving of further study. The most important of these was the time the customer needed to become aware of and use the information about the delivery delay.

The last parameter was the computation interval (DT). This constant had to be made small enough so that the assumption that rates are constant during the solution interval did not introduce large errors. In the simulations, DT was set at one-tenth of a week. The use of a one week interval made almost no difference in the values of the variables.

VI. MODEL ANALYSIS

The objectives of the model analysis were (1) to develop an understanding of the relationship between the structure of the model and the behavior it produced, particularly with respect to the important problems, and (2) to verify the adequacy of the model as a representation of the real system relative to the problems under study so that the understanding derived was meaningful and potentially useful.

a. System Dynamics

The problems under study in this case were the long-term cyclic pattern in all system variables and the tendency in the company for employment and production to vary more widely than sales. The model clearly exhibited these problems for a wide variety of input ordering (system orders to the customers) patterns including instantaneous changes of various amounts, sinusoidal fluctuations, random disturbances and ramp type rises and declines.

Different values of parameters and different decision policies were tried with these inputs in order to determine the sensitive parts of the model. Such changes produced variations in the magnitude of the fluctuations and the size of the production overshoot, but the existence and causes of the problems remained.

The following description of the system's behavior can be traced in Figure 1.

Suppose that system orders to the customers (extreme left of Figure 1) begins to increase. The customers' backlog of orders in engineering rises and forces their orders for components to increase. As the component supplier's sales rise, the unfilled order backlog in manufacturing increases because the labor force that produced the output has not yet been changed. In this period, input orders exceed production output. As unfilled backlog grows, both the factory lead time and total service time increase.

The rising orders and backlog induce hiring. However, there are delays between the increase in sales and the desire to hire and between the desire to hire and the acquisition of fully productive employees. As a result, a sizable backlog accumulates before enough workers are hired and trained to raise the production rate to equal the order rate, and thereby stabilize backlog. Further hiring drives production above orders, and backlog declines toward an acceptable level.

Meanwhile, assume that the orders for systems to the customers have returned to their average value and remained there. The customers began to order ahead on the basis of the expected suppliers' lead time in order to keep their production lines in operation. Then, even though the system orders return to normal, the customers continue to increase their component orders because the service delay is increasing. They continue to order at a rate higher than normal until the delay falls to its usual value.

When the delay seen by the customers finally begins to decline (sometimes 10 weeks after the decline actually starts), the customers order less far ahead. They also reduce orders below normal, since their backlog of engineering orders has been depleted by excess ordering. This is the beginning of a period when the customers order less than normal because the lead time is short and there is not much to order. During this lower-than-normal order period, the component manufacturer reduces his work force below normal. When the customers build up their backlog and the service time rises, the component orders are again increased to restart the cycle. The cycles are self-perpetuating and need only a minor disturbance (i.e., the temporarily increased prime system orders) to start the process.

This cyclic shifting of orders from the customers' engineering department backlog to the component manufacturers' backlog and back again continues only as long as two conditions persist. These are (a) the customers' practice of ordering ahead as service delay increases and holding back orders as the delay declines, and (b) the component manufacturers' inability to prevent their service delay from varying enough to be recognized by the customers. If customers were to stop basing order releases on expected service delay or if suppliers could maintain a constant service delay, the long-term oscillatory tendencies of this system would disappear.

The second problem was that suppliers' production variations were wider than sales changes. This was due to the short-term adjustment in inventory ordering. When sales rise, inventory declines. When this fall in inventory is quickly corrected by sending inventory orders to the factory, the load on the factory includes the excess sales orders that can not be filled from inventory and these inventory orders. Since the inventory orders have to build the inventory back up to its original level as well as prevent a further decline due to the higher sales, total load on the factory is greater than just the added sales.

The target level of inventory also rises with sales, and an additional stress is placed on the factory by the orders intended to raise inventory above its old level. When hiring is not done quickly, factory backlog rises and the manufacturing delay increases. In response to longer factory delay, orders for inventory items are placed sooner, and the factory load is still heavier. Thus, policies associated with the company's inventory control cause greater changes in work force and production rate than originally occur in sales.

This problem was present as long as inventory adjustment was rapid and the desired inventory level was based on short-term average sales. If peak inventory could be timed so that it occurred before the peak in sales, this would make a decline in inventory desirable at the peak of sales stress. Production rate would then be less than the sales rate by the amount that inventory declined each week.

b. Validation of the Model

The model was accepted as adequate (not perfect) representation of the real system relative to the problems under study for two reasons. The functions included in the model and the way in which the functions were interconnected conformed to our and management's view of the system structure. Since the model represented the system in easily identifiable physical terms, the flows, decisions, inventories, etc., could be discussed and studied directly in factory and office by everyone. Secondly, the response of the model contained the short-term random factors, the long-term cyclic components, and the lag relationships between variables that were present in actual data. The amplitudes and periods of the fluctuations in individual variables and the time lags between variables were all close to the actual values for a range of reasonable inputs to the customer in the complete model and to the company in the partial, company-only, system. Simulations were also performed using the company sector along with the independent input being actual orders from the customers to the company. The pattern of lags and amplitudes was again similar to the actual behavior.

VII. IMPROVED POLICIES

The problem of improving the behavior of this system was not a simple one. While there were methods for finding optimum decision policies relative to a single objective and a single input pattern in a simple, linear feedback system, there were no such methods for complex (100 or more dynamic interrelated variables), nonlinear models in which there were several objectives whose forms differ from those commonly used in traditional optimization techniques. Furthermore, any new policies suggested would not only have to perform well for the expected types of inputs (in this case fluctuations around a steady average value), but also would have to provide a certain level of protection in the event the input should develop a sizable trend either up or down.

With formal optimization ruled out, there were two possible approaches to improvement. One was the simulation of the model for all combinations of values of the parameters. The second was the modification of the system structure based on an understanding of the causes of the problems and of the general principles of information-feedback system behavior. The exhaustive parameter variation method would certainly have provided some improvement. However, the system modification had a much greater potential. Thus, the search for improvement concentrated on structure variation, and led to the following decisions.

a. Inventory Ordering and Production Priority Policies

The reservoirs which were of principal concern relative to management's objectives (profits and employment stability) were found to be inventory, unfilled order backlog (because it influenced the service delay), and employment level. The decisions which were supposed to control them were found to be the inventory reorder decision, which controlled inventory, and the employment decision, which controlled backlog and employment. The question was then asked: Can each decision actually control the variable intended without interfering with other decisions? The answer in the inventory reorder case was that it could not, as inventory was the aggregate accumulated difference between production and shipments. Since sending orders into production does not directly control the employment level which produces the production rate, the orders only divert working time from customer orders.

The first change, then, was to shift the inventory adjustment process into the labor decision where all effective aggregate control resides. A new basis had to be selected for the generation of inventory orders. Since high productivity was desired, it seemed desirable to generate inventory orders only as they were needed to keep all production workers continuously busy. A priority list of inventory items needed was used as a guide to decide which type of unit to make for inventory.

b. Factory Priority

The long-term cyclic behavior of the industry to a large extent was due to the customers' reaction to variations in the delivery time. Variations in this delay were caused primarily by variations in the factory backlog relative to the work force. In times of high sales the backlog and delay rose. A sizable part of this backlog contained orders for inventory. Since there was no clear-cut and supervised priority for customer orders, these orders frequently waited while inventory orders were made. The establishment of such a customer-first priority was necessary to reduce both the delay itself and its variability. This would tend to suppress the system's oscillatory tendencies and provide a competitively desirable short delay.

c. Employment Policies

The problem of production overshooting sales would be improved by building inventory at slack times rather than in high sales periods. An equation was designed to specify the desired factory work force in such a way that, when combined with the new inventory-ordering policy, it would maintain a stable work force and force inventory accumulation at the proper time (i.e., when sales were falling). It was to be calculated each week and was based on long-term average sales (to provide a stable basic work force), inventory adjustment over a long period of time (so inventory absorbs as much of the sales fluctuation as possible), and backlog adjustment (to keep service delay short and stable and thereby reduce the long-term cycle). The equation had the following form:

$$\frac{\text{Employment}}{\text{Desired}} = \frac{\text{long-term average sales}}{\substack{\text{average productivity} \\ \text{per man per week}}} + \frac{\text{Desired inventory - Actual inventory}}{(\text{Average Productivity})(\text{Inventory adjustment time})}$$

(5A)

The backlog term had the same form as the inventory term except the numerator was actual minus desired backlog. It was not included in (5A) because the changes in priority and loading in the factory had kept the delay in control, so the term was inoperative. Notice that by averaging sales over a long period (one year) and by taking a long time to adjust inventory, desired employment will be insensitive to short-term changes in sales. If employment changes were small and inventory orders were generated to keep workers uniformly busy, most inventory would be made in slack sales times.

The parameters in this new decision had to be quite specific values. These values were determined by simulating the model using the new policies with different parameter values for a range of possible inputs to the customer sector. The selected parameters had to provide stable employment and service delay for any expected inputs having the form of variations around a nearly constant long-term average, while preventing major inventory changes if usage should suddenly change substantially. The parameter values could be no better than the assumptions that were made about the form of the system structure and the range of input functions. Major changes in any of these would force a change in the values or in the form of the policies.

An important part of the improvement process was the formulation of policies and procedures that had clear physical meaning. This was important (a) for one's own understanding of system behavior, (b) so that implementation would be possible given the existing system, and (c) so the people who had to use the policies could understand them and their limitations and could change them if necessary.

VIII. INTRODUCTION OF NEW POLICIES INTO THE SYSTEM

Changes were recommended in factory procedure (customer orders made first), inventory-ordering procedure (generated to maintain a constant, efficient factory work load from a priority list), and employment decision making (total authorized employment each week based on the calculation from an equation). The implementation of these new policies required making the changes work properly in the operating system, while resisting the temptation to make a greater number of less important modifications which would involve a great deal more work. There is a general tendency to believe that large behavior changes can only arise from major physical dislocation and drastic changes in policies and/or paper work flows. While there was no reason to believe this in this study, the appeal of the fallacy was irresistible. Therefore, much planning and work was aimed at changes which were unnecessary to achieve the major revisions in system behavior. Actually, no changes in personnel authority or location or production technique were necessary for these changes. All that was required was the regular generation of two or three easily obtainable pieces of information, fifteen minutes of secretarial time each week for the decision calculation, and the slightly changed attitudes of workers, foremen, and plant managers.

The procedure for the employment decision change included (a) establishment of several new information channels, (b) trial calculation for several months, and (c) gradual use of the new rule. The plant priority and inventory changes came about through encouragement over several months. There was no discontinuity in procedures or operations at any time. In fact, to some degree the customer-first production and the inventory ordering to maintain an efficient work load had always been in operation.

The implementation was introduced through the joint effort of the M.I.T. research group and several company people. The approach was to develop an understanding in the people concerned of the meaning of the changes and to motivate them to use the rules both to improve operations and to make more time available for other tasks. Therefore, the changes did not connote a loss in authority or individuality; rather they mechanized some time-consuming decision-making tasks, thereby freeing time for other considerations.

Attention was given to all minor practical details and problems so that incompatibility with the system's structure did not interfere with the use of the new policies. An attempt was made to consider the social, psychological, and physical realities in the over-all information-feedback system to promote the fastest, best understood, and most lasting modifications.

IX. EVALUATION OF SYSTEM BEHAVIOR

By the time the new hiring decision had been in use for six months and the modified factory priority and inventory-ordering policies somewhat longer, there were characteristics of the system's behavior which indicated that improvements in labor and production stability, productivity, and sales were taking place. Most of the gains were attributed to the recommended modifications because no other changes capable of producing such major alterations in behavior could be found in the system, and the areas and magnitudes of the changes predicted agreed with the results.

For comparative purposes, data for employment, production, inventory, sales, and productivity were available for past years. The recommended labor decision was first formally used in operations in the latter part of 1961. However, no sharp discontinuity in practice occurred. Although a quantitative statement of the recommended employment level was not made until late in the year, it had been evident for several months that the work force was too large. In addition, both customer-first production and inventory order generation (to keep workers busy) had always been in operation to some degree. The degree of their use was increased. However, even at present, none of the recommendations is used all the time. Therefore, the large change in dynamic behavior and the improvement in productivity and stability are remarkable given the small degree of change in operating procedures. Continued improvement can be anticipated.

Seven months after implementation of the new hiring decision, data for the past thirteen month period was analyzed, and the results showed that improvement was evident in several places. Average labor productivity had improved and was still rising. A comparable work force could sustain a production rate almost 12 per cent higher than was possible a year earlier. The sensitivity of employment and production to variations in sales had declined greatly because inventory was being forced to fall at peak sales (rather than rise as in the past), thereby relieving factory pressure at a time of crisis. Inventory could be built up during slack sales periods. Inventory level was lower in terms of both units and weeks of sales on hand. The average incoming orders were 16 per cent higher and more uniform than thirteen months before.

a. Higher Productivity

Average productivity as measured by a twenty-week exponential average of weekly productivity (productivity equals units produced divided by man-hours worked) had increased in the thirteen-month period by 11.8 per cent, and was still rising. An 11.8 per cent increase in productivity will allow a 10.5 per cent decrease in employment, if production is to be held constant.

b. Improved Employment Stability

Improvement in employment stability (smaller variation in work force for a given change in sales) was also evident.

The pattern of sales variation is best shown by a thirty-week exponential average. This average was at a peak at the beginning of the data period. A decline of 6.5 per cent occurred during the next six months. This was followed by a steady rise of 23 per cent, to 16 per cent above the previous peak, where it remained. Employment had a similar pattern of steady-decline-rise-steady, but the magnitudes of the changes were very different. During the 7 per cent decline in average sales, employment fell 38 per cent. During the 23 per cent sales rise, employment rose only 38 per cent back to its original value. Therefore, three times as large a sales variation failed to change the size of the employment adjustment.

Two factors caused this improvement. The first was the rise in productivity. The second was the use of inventory to ease factory pressure at peak sales by cutting back inventory production and allowing the stock to fall. At the first peak employment, inventory was rising at a rate (in units per week) of 10 per cent of the average sales rate. At peak employment after the changes, inventory was falling at a rate of over 11 per cent of the original average sales rate. This was a difference in factory stress of 21 per cent of sales. Had inventory been rising at its original rate at the second employment peak, that peak would have been 16 per cent greater than it was. Had productivity been equal to the original value, employment would have been an additional 12 per cent higher, which would have increased the second employment peak by 28 per cent. Somewhat more than 57 per cent of this improvement in stability was due to better inventory control.

A third potential influence in the employment variation was the rate at which order backlog was changing. This was not considered here because the backlog was falling at about the same rate at both employment peaks.

c. Higher, Smoother Sales

At the beginning of the thirteen-month period, the thirty-week exponential average of incoming orders was at a peak. It declined slowly for about six months to a low of 6.5 per cent below the peak. A steady rise in the average followed for three months to a point 15 per cent above the previous peak. In the last four months of the data period, the average rose slowly and uniformly to 16.7 per cent above the beginning peak. In the last fifteen weeks of data, the average was contained in the +14.7 to +16.7 per cent range. At no other time during the period had the average stayed within a 2 per cent range for more than nine weeks. Although the causes were not clear, the sales level was less erratic and substantially higher than before. This was at least partially due to a shorter, less erratic, delivery delay.

d. Lower Inventories

At the beginning of the period, total inventory stood at about its normal level. The inventory was 13.4 per cent lower a year later. In terms of weeks of average sales on hand, the figures were 7.4 weeks and 5.5 weeks, respectively. The trend even at the low level was still downward. Since there had as yet been no inventory build-up phase using the new policies, the outcome was somewhat uncertain. However, there was good reason to believe that the average level of inventory over a complete cycle could be reduced by 10 to 20 per cent without impairing the ability to fill orders.

REFERENCES

Forrester, Jay W., Industrial Dynamics, M.I.T. Press 1961.

> The background and equations for the model used in this study are presented in Chapters 17 and 18.

Fey, Willard R., An Industrial Dynamics Study of an Electronic Components Manufacturer - Transactions of the Fifth Annual Conference of the American Production and Inventory Control Society held in Boston, September 27 and 28, 1962.

> A more detailed description of the changes in the system's behavior that occurred after the new policies went into operation can be found here.

Author's Note to Chapter 6

Evaluation after Two Years. In the second year, the company did not adhere as closely to the hiring decision formula as it had in the first year of its use. More rapid adjustments in employment were made in response to downward sales changes than were indicated by the rule. This was the declining phase of the cycle in this product line and in the electronics industry generally. The customer-first priority system and the creation of inventory orders as needed continued to operate fairly well. Labor productivity rose another ten per cent during this second year. Employment, production and delivery delay became more volatile, but they did not return to their former excess over adjustment.

The gradual return to the old ways of making the employment decision continued in the third year. The trend probably will continue and, in the absence of strong pressures from the M.I.T. group, the use of the employment rule should disappear completely by the fourth or fifth year. The inventory ordering and production priority systems should persist. Productivity should continue to rise, but less rapidly.

Return to the Old Employment Policies. The new employment rule was used faithfully for the first year and a half for two reasons. The M.I.T. people were constantly in touch with the progress, giving encouragement, working out problems, and by their presence, putting pressure on company decision makers to use the rule. In addition no strong counterpressures were present from product line or overall company problems. Starting in the second year all of these conditions began to change.

It had been understood that M.I.T.'s participation would end after the policies had been implemented. Therefore, outside involvement (pressure) began

Willard R. Fey, the author of the Chapter 6 article, recorded the additional comments indicated here on January 28, 1965.

to decline in the second year. After three and a half years the company was receiving no M.I.T. assistance.

Also during the second year counterpressures began to build up. Sales in the line began to fall in response to the normal cyclic forces. Declining sales brought fears of obsolescence and increasing inventories. A fall in total industry sales occurred at about the same time so to the product line problems was added a company-wide cost consciousness which focused on inventory reduction. It was also likely that the making of the employment decision served as a creative outlet for the decision makers. Having a secretary spend 15 minutes a week calculating the decision never was very satisfying.

The reduction in positive pressures and the emergence of counterpressures led to deviation from the rule. This was rationalized by the observation that the use of the decision for over a year had not smoothed out the cycle (though it had been reduced). It would have been necessary to adhere rather strictly to the rule for about a cycle and a half (three years) in order to suppress a large part of the cycle. Even then normal disturbances, military budgeting procedures, and the behavior of competitors would still have provided a measurable two-year cycle. The patience to wait for three years and endure some difficult times and strong pressures (even with a constantly rising productivity) is a rare commodity in today's world. It must also be fortified with courage, self-confidence and great belief in system dynamics principles.

While it is true that the new employment decision did not become a permanent part, in its quantitative form, of the product line, it is still partially influential and positive results were realized. From the company's point of view "the record of operations since the new policies were introduced clearly shows improvements."* The study stimulated a great deal of company introspection which led to new thinking and activities in several areas. The changes in inventory ordering and factory priority are still in operation and should remain so.

The Sprague Project in its successful aspects also played a major role in developing the techniques and procedures of industrial dynamics. Its shortcomings pointed the way for much of our research effort. This is particularly true now in the area of human factors in the managerial feedback system. Here the implementation problems forced an awareness of the importance of the human being in the business system and indicated fruitful quantitative approaches to such studies.

---

*Carlson, Bruce R., "An Industrialist Views Industrial Dynamics," *Industrial Management Review*, Vol. 6, no. 1, Fall, 1964, p. 18 (included as Chapter 7 of this volume).

7

An Industrialist Views Industrial Dynamics

Bruce R. Carlson

Research and engineering have long been the animating spirit of the Sprague Electric Company, the nation's largest producer of capacitors and other electronic and electrical circuit components. On the average, profits over the years have been the largest when the percentage of new products has been the highest. This has led the company to rejoice in the pervasiveness of change, and it has made management enthusiastic about the search for better ways of doing things that applies to the field of management as well as product development.

The Sprague Company first came into contact with industrial dynamics as a result of a study initiated in 1957 under the guidance of Professor Jay W. Forrester of M.I.T., the object of which was to see if there were things we would do to improve the operation of our important product lines by applying quantitative analytical techniques. At that time, a team of M.I.T. staff members was formed to study one of the Sprague Company's products using whatever tools of applied research and management science they might consider applicable.

The product under study was a high-quality miniature tubular capacitor which had been developed by Sprague some ten years earlier and which had reached maturity in the terms of the manufacturing process and the extent of the available market. This line contained several thousand active catalog items used in large military and industrial systems and was sold to many customers whose total weekly order volume fluctuated widely.

The M.I.T. team spent the better part of the first year building a rather complex model of the company's production-inventory operations utilizing more or less conventional order-by-order, item-by-item statistical simulation of the Monte Carlo type. As the study progressed, Professor Forrester became increasingly concerned that the model was not oriented toward the managerial decisions surrounding the product or toward their interaction with the market in a way that would lead to fundamental improvements in the behavior of the system. He had already begun to recognize that the system had characteristics of information feedback which would make it appropriate for the type of simulation model he was then beginning to formalize under the term "industrial dynamics."

Accordingly, in 1958 Professor Forrester strongly recommended that the Sprague study give greater recognition to the relationships among aggregate delays and decisions and system behavior as a whole. Thus, almost without realizing it, Sprague Electric Company became the first industrial concern to explore the application of industrial dynamics simulations to an actual business situation.

This paper was presented to the management session of the 18th Annual Conference of the Instrument Society of America in Chicago, Illinois on September 10, 1963. It first appeared in the *Industrial Management Review* (currently published as the *Sloan Management Review*) 6, no. 1 (Fall 1964), pp. 15–20. (© 1964 by the Industrial Management Review Association; all rights reserved.)

The project is still continuing, but it has evolved from a search for techniques of applied problem-solving to longer-range research leading to the development of new insights into the causes of system behavior. In the course of this evolution, we have learned a great deal about the difficulties of this type of research; but we have also made significant gains in the understanding of our own operations and have been able to improve them in a number of respects..These problems and benefits should be apparent from the following brief review of the Sprague project and the industrial dynamics model that we have developed.

Development of the Project

For nearly two years the project team, including both M.I.T. and company personnel, devoted its time to studying the physical system, quantifying management objectives and the operation of the line in question, formulating hypotheses explaining the causes of the system behavior, and—most importantly—building and simulating models on a large-scale digital computer.°

Once the decision was reached to study the problem from an industrial dynamics point of view, various approaches evolved from increasing understanding of the nature of the system as it related to the company's major objectives: the achievement of profits, and, to a lesser extent, the maintenance of employment stability.

There appeared to be two major problems about which considerable insight could be gained from the model simulations: 1. The interaction between the company's response to a fluctuating order rate and the customer's response to changes in the time required to deliver an order. 2. The effect of inventory re-ordering practices that tended to cause inventory to rise when sales were rising and to fall when sales were falling rather than to act as a cushion to absorb short-run fluctuations in the order rate.

The structure of the model itself was based largely on logical deduction concerning the behavior of the company's customers, on descriptions by operating personnel of what was being done in the existing system and the reasons therefore, and, of course, on available historical data on such variables as orders, backlogs, inventories, shipments, and man-hours worked. One of the early lessons learned was that unnecessary detail quickly obscures important facts. In other words, the model should include explicitly *only* the dynamically important components of the system; but care must be taken to include *all* of these. Our present model incorporates the customer and his ordering decisions, the company with its inventory and production system, and the one factor of production—labor—which controls. the output. It was found that raw materials, capital equipment, costs, and prices do not significantly influence decisions and actions in the system within the normal range of operations. It was also hypothesized that changes in the mix of individual products within the line under study would have only small effects in comparison to other variables. Accordingly, the model deals only with the total flow of orders, production, and man-hours worked. No distinctions are made between different catalog items, between different customers, between orders for immediate delivery and those for future delivery, and between individual production departments or operations.

The resulting model has the virtue of being relatively simple and sufficiently general to be applicable with minor modification to any product the company makes which is in a relatively mature phase of its life cycle. As will be seen later, it has the drawback of being more abstract than operating personnel are accustomed to in a manufacturing business, where day-to-day decisions must be made in terms of specific products, individual customers, and separate operating departments. The Sprague model illustrates nothing about detailed production and inventory control procedures; its sole quantitative result is a decision rule which is being used for weekly calculations of the desired employment level in the product line studied. Its primary value, therefore, has been the insights derived from testing various hypotheses of why the system behaves as it does *in the aggregate*.

Complete descriptions of the Sprague model are available elsewhere to those interested.[1] The model consists of something

°Computations were performed on the I.B.M. 704 and 709 computers at the M.I.T. Computation Center.

[1]See [1] and [2].

less than 200 nonlinear, nonsimultaneous first-order differential equations involving some 150 parameters of the system. It is written in the DYNAMO computer language developed at M.I.T. expressly for the development of industrial dynamics models. The model has been used to make more than 100 simulation runs to test the response of the system to various inputs. The results of these simulations show the short-term random factors, the long-term cyclical components, and time lags between variables that are observed in the actual data. The amplitudes and periods of fluctuation are close to the actual values for a range of reasonable inputs to (1) the customer sector, in the complete feedback system model, and to (2) the company sector. In a few simulations of the company sector alone, data about actual orders from customers were used as an independent input.

Application of the Model

By early in 1961 the study had progressed to the point where certain inventory ordering, production priority, and employment policies were formulated in such a way that the desired balance between a stable work force and stable inventories was maintained. One important suggestion was to assure that the production scheduler always had a priority list of program stock items that could be produced whenever capacity exceeded that necessary for customer orders. The second proposal was a corollary to the first; it reaffirmed and strengthened the company's policy of always giving first priority to units for which there was a customer order in the house. Thus, on the one hand customer orders are always scheduled first; on the other, production employees are always assured of work. Finally, total authorized employment each week was to be based on a new decision rule based on long-term average sales (to provide a stable basic work force) and inventory adjustment over a long period of time (to make inventory absorb as much of the sales fluctuation as possible). One of the interesting results of the rule developed was that the changes in priorities and factory routing so improved the service delay that the system became insensitive to backlogs, which had previously been one of the major indicators on which operating personnel had relied in their employment and scheduling decisions.

Implementation of the new policies began early in 1961, and the weekly employment decision rule was being used on a routine basis by September of that year. Middle-line managers had been fully informed about the project from the start and were often asked to give advice on various points, but they did not really participate actively in the project until the implementation phase was reached. In the early phases of the implementation, much time and effort was spent by both company and M.I.T. personnel in educating line management by explaining in detail the new policies and what they were designed to achieve. In return, the managers pointed out a number of additional problems that the study team helped to solve, such as the determination of inventory reorder points, systems changes necessitated to generate more easily the information required to operate the new policies, and so forth. Over a period of time, considerable interest developed in the application of the new employment decision rule, and it was followed very closely.

It should be emphasized at this point that the new policies, and particularly the employment decision rule, did not replace the existing system completely but rather served as an additional input to decisions that were then and still are being made by operating management. There are occasions when the rule is disregarded; it is very difficult for line managers who are conditioned by years of experience to reacting intuitively to sudden changes in business conditions to accept with complete faith the relatively slow reaction times called for by the policies of the industrial dynamics model. The important thing, however, is that despite occasional deliberate deviations, the new policies continue to influence the decision-maker and he to influence the policies, which have undergone a number of minor modifications.

Accomplishments of the Project

On the basis of the company's experience to date, it is clear that a number of tangible accomplishments are directly attributable to the application of the model. These are as follows:

1. Comparisons of data before and after implementation of the new policies show that productivity, measured in units per man-hour, is up 12 per cent. This is partly

the result of the more stable employment called for by the new decision rule and partly the result of aggressive methods improvement programs.

2. The production cycle has been slightly shortened, as a result of the higher productivity and improved scheduling procedures.

3. The inventory level is being used to absorb factory pressure in periods of peak sales by cutting back inventory production and allowing the inventory level to fall. In one period of peak employment before the changes, inventory was rising at the rate of 10 per cent of the average sales rate. At peak employment after the changes, inventory was falling at the rate of over 11 per cent of the average sales rate, and this contributed to a variation in employment that was considerably less than would probably have occurred under the old policies.

4. Inventory is better balanced because of certain procedural changes suggested in the course of the study and due to the use of computer-established reorder points.

No attempt has been made to measure exactly the effect on profits of the new policies. This would be a very difficult and costly undertaking requiring extensive changes in company-wide accounting systems, which are not deemed worthwhile in view of the fact that the study has been confined to one product line among approximately 50 on which profit information must be compiled. Instead, all concerned have agreed that the record of operations since the new policies were introduced clearly shows improvements. Some of these improvements have resulted from the application of conventional systems and procedures and quantitative decision-making techniques; but it seems clear that these improvements derive in large measure from the insights provided by the model simulations.

In one major respect, however, the Sprague industrial dynamics project has not had the predicted effect. This is in the area of long-term fluctuations in demand and the interaction between Sprague's own actions and those of its customers in a closed-loop feedback system. It had been assumed from the start of the project that the long-term fluctuations arose in large part because each customer tends to order farther ahead as the company's service delay becomes long and to hold orders back when the delay becomes short. In other words, the company's employment decisions, which directly affect the delay time, are reflected in the customer's ordering rate. Thus it was hoped that the policy modifications in accordance with the model might damp out fluctuations in the incoming order rate. Unfortunately, this has not been achieved; after nearly two years, incoming orders for the product in question are fluctuating as widely as ever, and it has been necessary to modify the employment decision rule in recognition of this fact. The importance of the closed feedback concept in virtually all socio-economic systems is one of the cornerstones of the industrial dynamics approach. The Sprague project does not, to date, support that part of this concept which implies that a relatively few easily discernible factors interact to form feedback loops which dominate the behavior of a given system.

Evaluation of the Sprague Experience

The three most important problems in industrial dynamics in light of the Sprague experience are (1) the scope of industrial dynamics models, (2) the level of aggregation of model variables, and (3) the validation of industrial dynamics models.

With respect to model scope, it is not clear that in the Sprague project we have learned how to determine what the scope should be, or whether the amount of detail finally included in our model is the right amount. In this stage of the development of industrial dynamics, primary reliance must be placed on intuitive judgment in determining scope. For example, because the Sprague model omitted explicit representation of the company's competitors, there is some question whether the company's market is adequately represented.

Another problem arises from the necessity to include, in order to have a closed feedback loop, a model sector representing the company's customers, about whose operating policies little is actually known. We have postulated certain apparently logical responses by the customer to the delivery delay he sees on Sprague's part, but we do not know enough about what determines his ordering decisions to say that our customer sector is a correct representation of what really happens. The fact that operation of the new policies has not yet had any noticeable effect on the fluctuations in incoming orders reinforces this feeling, although it may be that insufficient time has elapsed for the feedback effect to be noticed.

With respect to the aggregation of variables, no systematic way has been developed for aggregating nonlinear elements of the system. For example, in the Sprague model we are aggregating orders from different kinds of customers in a number of different industries, and we are aggregating orders calling for immediate delivery and orders calling for extended future deliveries. We hope this is justified because the differences among these various categories are not dynamically important, but there is no way to be sure of this. With all the random fluctuations in the available information about real-world phenomena, it is virtually impossible to detect underlying causal mechanisms from existing data. We are therefore forced to rely on the opinions of operating people who are close enough to a given activity to have formed opinions about what is important in it—but who are also close enough to have biased views. It may be that the only way to determine that an appropriate level of aggregation has been selected is to build numerous models with different degrees of aggregation and examine how their responses to similar inputs differ.

With respect to the validation of industrial dynamics models, Professor Forrester has stated:

"The significance of a model depends upon how well it serves its purpose. The purpose of industrial dynamics models is to aid in designing better management systems. The final test of satisfying this purpose must await the evaluation of the better management. In the meantime, the significance of models should be judged by the importance of the objectives to which they are addressed and their ability to predict the results of system design changes."[2]

The present Sprague model has "served its purpose" in that it has led to the design of improved management policies relating to important operating objectives of the company. It has demonstrated an ability to predict the results of system design changes

in some areas, but not with respect to the important objective of damping out large fluctuations in the order rate. However, we are sufficiently satisfied with the results to date that we are planning to apply the model with appropriate modifications to at least one other product line and probably later on to still others.

New Applications of the Method

Industrial dynamics as a discipline is increasingly concerned with the more intangible aspects of industrial behavior. This may be because the problems of scope and aggregation are most obvious in production-distribution systems of the type represented by this first Sprague model. Moreover, in such systems, available data are apt to be very noisy, making it difficult to sort out the really significant causal relationships that must be represented in a model. Another difficulty in applying industrial dynamics to these more tangible problems is that the system changes suggested by industrial dynamics models may be in direct conflict with other, more conventional control techniques. It may, therefore, be very difficult to apply the new policies in one area of a company's operation without applying them throughout, and this broad application may well entail dropping some cherished control procedures and devising new ones to more adequately measure system response.

The industrial dynamics project at Sprague Electric is following a similar evolution, in that we are now considering the application of industrial dynamics to higher level problems in contrast to the relatively low-level production-distribution system represented by our present model. Higher level problems deal with such things as new product growth, divisional growth, or total corporate growth; in general, they are more important, have a longer range, and are more difficult to solve. Most significantly, they deal more with intangibles, and the benefits of a study are likely to come more from insights gained in making the study than from any mathematical decision rules that may emerge.

Applied to solving tangible problems, industrial dynamics is slower and more costly

[2]Forrester, [2], p. 115.

than conventional operations research techniques; to date industrial dynamics applied to tangible problems has probably yielded smaller payoffs, although it has certainly pointed out some important shortcomings of certain widely accepted analytical procedures. Industrial dynamics will make its major contribution by providing new insights into why things happen the way they do, especially when dealing with the more intangible problems that occur at higher management levels. For example, it clearly shows the importance of reaction times in decision-making and points out the tendency of managers at all levels to overcompensate for fluctuations in the system which result from the delays and amplifications in the system itself.

Industrial dynamics will profoundly influence the development of other management science techniques. This has happened already at Sprague Electric, where we are continuing to devote a portion of our management research effort to more conventional areas of management science. The conceptual relevance of industrial dynamics is more widely accepted today in the business schools than it is in industry, and the experience of Sprague Electric Company and others with this powerful new philosophy may help to bring it to the attention of more and more business managers.

References

1 Fey, Willard R., "An Industrial Dynamics Case Study," *Industrial Management Review* 3, Fall, 1962, pp. 79-99.

2 Forrester, Jay W., *Industrial Dynamics*, Cambridge, Mass., The M.I.T. Press, 1961.

8

How Managers Use Industrial Dynamics

Kenneth J. Schlager

Professor Jay W. Forrester's book, *Industrial Dynamics*,[1] touched off a new approach to development of improved systems of managerial decision-making. Since its publication, I've helped apply industrial dynamics in three companies in the Milwaukee area, and this experience has revealed many practical problems in its implementation. The first of these applications relates to the planning and control of production, inventories, and employment in a company manufacturing a high-volume assembly-line product. A second application concerns a company manufacturing custom-made low-volume specialty machinery products. The third application treats of product development decisions in a highly technical industry. My purpose here is to examine these three applications in hope that they will provide some insights for future use of industrial dynamics.

It is the methodology—i.e., the problem-solving sequence—that is actually practiced in any application of industrial dynamics. The problem-solving sequence enumerated below differs slightly from that described by Forrester as his steps in "enterprise design." These changes more strongly emphasize data collection and analysis, and they consider problems of implementing the model after it has been developed and tested:

1. Define the problem to be solved and the goals to be achieved.
2. Describe the system.
3. Develop an industrial dynamics simulation model of the system.
4. Collect the initial data needed for model operation.
5. Experiment with the model to determine improved information-decision systems for the company involved.
6. Implement the selected information-decision system in actual company operations.

The General Approach

Problem definition in the industrial dynamics sequence is a formidable task. In none of the three company applications was there any obvious problem adaptable to an industrial dynamics solution. This isn't to say that there weren't problems existing in each of the three companies. It's just that these problems, some quite perplexing and serious, didn't stand out sharply as being amenable to the industrial dynamics methodology.

Then, too, each of the companies realized the research nature of the project, and at first all were quite curious to determine the effectiveness of industrial dynamics independent of any particular problem facing the company. Inspiration for initiation of the program in each company was not any particular problem but rather a general expectation that industrial dynamics might improve over-all management of the company.

This paper was originally published in *Instrumentation Technology* (formerly *ISI Journal*) in March 1964. It is an adaptation of a presentation to the management session of the 18th Annual Conference of the Instrument Society of America in Chicago, Illinois on September 10, 1963.

After a few weeks of general familiarization with company operations, a specific problem was selected for study, becoming better-defined and being modified as the existing situation became evident. It seems quite clear from the experience in these companies that the development, application, and implementation of an industrial dynamics model are themselves a feedback process. Problem definition was modified during the system description and model development and, to a lesser extent, throughout the remaining phases of the study.

In two of the companies, development of the model was aided considerably by company employees who had previously studied industrial dynamics in my evening course at Marquette University. In one of these companies, the former students represented each of the primary functional areas in the organization—manufacturing, engineering, sales, and accounting. Their familiarity with both the company and industrial dynamics techniques expedited the task of model formulation. These employees also served an important role as enthusiasts for the project, reassuring hesitant colleagues when internal resistance to the project raised barriers to further progress.

Data collection and analysis provided some experiences that might modify previous thinking on the preferred methodology in industrial dynamics. While I still completely accept Forrester's viewpoint, which calls for system description and model development before extensive data collection, it seems from the results of the program in these three companies that a more extensive data collection and analysis phase is required to render the model useful in actual company operations.

Two kinds of data were collected. One class of data ("constant data") was needed to supply constants for operation of the model. Typical constant terms were work-in-process times and inventory-adjustment periods. Although this class of data suffices for model operation, it provides no check on the validity of the model as a representation of a real-life system.

To provide a measure of model validity, a second class of data was collected and analyzed to provide a historical sequence of the same variables synthetically developed by the model. The purpose here, of course, was to determine if the model behaved like the real system when it was excited by the same exogenous inputs. To achieve such validity, the critical constants in the model —those constants to which model operation is sensitive—must be determined accurately with meaningful data from company operations. During early phases of the projects in two of the companies, data collection and analysis were hurriedly performed; but difficulties were encountered in demonstrating validity, and the data-collection phase had to be redone. I believe these validity tests of the model, using historical data, are an absolute necessity. Few managements would care to make changes in company policy based on a model whose validity had never been checked.

Model experimentation on an IBM 7090 computer was first performed varying parameters and modifying decision rules one at a time in successive runs. Sensitivity of the model to various policies was examined in this manner. Later, a more systematic approach using statistical experimental design techniques was followed to study interactions of combined changes in the system. Since a primary purpose of the systems approach to management is to study complex interactions between elements within the system, experimental design of the model tests is quite critical. A parameter that is unimportant in one combination of system parameters may become quite critical with a different set of system constants. For this reason, it's important to design the experimental simulations to expose these complex interactions.

Bonini[3] has discussed the necessity for and the detailed development of a series of computer simulation runs experimentally designed using the factorial method. In all three company applications considered here, a random rather than factorial method of parameter value selection was used. This had the advantage of being independent of the number of variables in the model. Although statistical experimental design is useful in determining the combination of parameters to reveal interactions, the most important changes made to the model are usually structural in nature and will never be discovered by variations in parameters alone.

Stabilizing Production and Employment

Company A* is a manufacturer of instruments for liquid flow measurement. Although the market for products of the company is stable, significant fluctuations in production and employment mark most of the firm's history, especially since the end of World War II. These internal fluctuations have been considerably greater than seasonal or other longer cyclical fluctuations in company sales.

The situation existing at the onset of the project was similar in many respects to the customer-producer-employment case study outlined by Forrester in his book.[3] Moreover, top management of the company was well aware of the problems of unstable production and employment. A program for leveling production was already under way when the industrial dynamics project was started, and there is little question that stability in some form would have been achieved without the model. But the model did provide two things in this change of managerial policy:

1. An economic justification for the new policy.
2. A detailed decision rule that considered interactions between production, employment, overtime, and inventory in the system.

Although the firm's flow meters varied over a range of sizes and characteristics, production of most of the product line was on an assembly-line basis. Some standardization had been achieved in recent years. Despite product variations, it was meaningful to think of production in terms of aggregated units per week, a common practice in the company's short-term planning.

The possibility of a reasonable aggregation of products and the adoption of some segments of Forrester's customer-producer-employment model made it possible to develop an industrial dynamics model in a few months. This model differed from the original model in the following respects:

1. A more extensive cost structure was formulated in the financial sector of the model.
2. Manufacturing and production-inventory control sectors were subdivided into detailed subsectors for parts fabrication, two

classes of subassembly, and final assembly and test.
3. The personnel sector in the model included provisions for overtime as well as hiring and layoff.
4. Purchasing function was disaggregated into three classes of purchased items—castings, piece parts, and other materials.

All known costs related to production-inventory-employment were included to evaluate the cost benefits of greater stability. This cost formulation was necessary to demonstrate the value of improved stability to management and to select a combination of policies with a cost performance superior to the previously existing system. Such an economic measure of improvement was vital because some opinion-makers in the company had held employment stability to be an uneconomic luxury.

More detailed representation in the other sectors was necessary to define more explicitly the new decision policies. Experience soon proved that employment policies had to be detailed in terms of the type of employment—parts, subassembly or assembly—and the over-all number of personnel involved. Less detailed policies left too much to arbitrary judgment because operations in each of the shops differed significantly.

Data collection and analysis and model experimentation were based on the years 1961 and 1962. Use of actual data provided a realistic system input and also presented a more dramatic demonstration to management of the benefits of industrial dynamics. Confronting management with a more profitable set of policies tested over a recent period of company history can be extemely persuasive.

Final outcome of the initial stage of the project was a recommended set of aggregate production, inventory, and employment policies. These policies have since been adopted by the company, and actual behavior of the firm differs only slightly from the behavior represented in the model. Variations are the result of product changes and temporary labor shortages not considered in the model.

Productivity has improved and costs have

been reduced with the new system. Some cost reductions corresponded to those calculated in the model simulation runs. But total cost reduction has greatly exceeded calculated values because of unforeseen greater improvement in productivity over that of previous years. This extra increase in productivity appears to have originated from two sources:

1. The practice of hiring temporary summer employees, who greatly reduced over-all productivity in the past, has been discontinued.

2. Level production has made it possible to exercise tight control over labor and material cost variances that were not meaningful before because of fluctuating production.

Benefits of the new policies are evident in actual reduction of payroll, overtime, and inventory costs in the last few years. Using ultimate total costs indicated by computer simulation runs of the model as a reference base of 100, the following costs trend was recorded: 1961, 114; 1962, 110; and 1963, 104.

Total cost approached 100 by the end of 1963, realizing the full potential indicated by the model. Initiated in 1962, the program was fully implemented in 1963. The above costs reflect payroll, overtime, and inventory costs computed using a constant productivity factor. Secondary effects that resulted from increased productivity were roughly equivalent in amount to the cost savings indicated above.

Company A's model is now being expanded to include a more detailed marketing sector and a plant-equipment investment sector to increase its usefulness for long-range planning.

Project Management of Custom Products

Company B manufactures industrial machinery with a high value per unit sale. Most of the products are made to customer specifications, and all include some special features unique to each order. The production cycle is long compared to Company A, where the complete cycle can be measured in hours; it varies from a few weeks to as much as four months on large orders.

Early attempts to formulate a model using an approach like that followed in Company A met with little success. Because each order was partly unique, product aggregation wasn't meaningful. We then tried a somewhat different tack, using direct labor hours as a common unit of production. But this formulation was also meaningless because it didn't explicitly consider constraints imposed by individual order schedules. The manager was unable to really control production in the aggregate because production was controlled by the project schedules for each order. Finally, we saw that the company operation was really a collection of projects and that any realistic model must recognize this. So the company model was conceived as a flow of projects rather than as a flow of goods.

Sales input was expressed not in units per period of time but as an individual project order with specific man-hour and material requirements. Output of the system was a series of project completions resulting from application of engineering and manufacturing effort in a number of departments.

The model was set up in this way: After an order is received, its cost is estimated and it is scheduled for engineering and production. Initial estimating errors in cost and schedule are simulated by biasing the cost and schedule estimates above or below their true values. These estimating errors are randomly selected from a statistical distribution—based on historical company data—that is stored in the program.

Using these initial estimates, personnel are assigned to the project in various departments in the company. Assignments are sequenced beginning with the initial activity in engineering to the final tasks in assembly prior to delivery. Because this project is only one of many in process in the plant at one time, personnel are allocated to it in competition with other projects according to some priority rule.

Initial costs and schedule estimates err, of course, and work progress usually differs from what was expected because of varying productivity and interference with other projects. The project does not proceed exactly on schedule, but information on its current status is fed back to permit modification of original personnel assignments. Status information is delayed and subject to error just as in the real-life situation being portrayed.

The goal of experimentation with the

model was development of an improved information-decision system for the management of multi-project company operations. Answers to such questions as the following were needed:

1. What kind of information, of what accuracy and timing, best satisfies requirements of the system?

2. What priority decision rule best uses company personnel and equipment resources, minimizes work-in-process inventory, and complies with scheduled delivery dates?

3. How is the system affected by changes in sales mix?

Answers to these questions are being used to formulate a new information-decision system for application to a major product line within Company B. After success has been shown in this product line, the system will be extended to the rest of the firm. Now the project is in the implementation phase. Only time and experience will demonstrate the real value of the system; but if simulation test results are indicative, a major improvement is possible.

Product Development Decision-making

The applications in Company A and Company B were concerned with managing "inputs"—allocating internal resources—of each firm. Product line "output" was considered fixed. In the third application, this product mix provides the prime focus of attention.

The question posed by Company C was how a firm in the instruments and control-systems industry, where fast-changing products have decreasing life-cycle periods, should decide to initiate a new product or terminate an old one. Company C's research and development department had already begun to use critical-path methods for project scheduling, but the primary motivating objective of the industrial dynamics program centered upon selecting projects for product development and budgeting. A product strategy was desired.

In one respect this third model resembled the one developed for Company B. It was a project-centered model that contained a collection of projects in various states of completion. Unlike the former case, however, these projects were not special job orders for specific machines but rather products being developed for sale over a number of years. Outside input to the third model was not a specific order; it was the life-cycle sales potential of a product.

Much is owed, in this third application, to the original work of Roberts,[4] who has developed a general industrial dynamics model for research and development. Although the primary focus of Roberts' model is on activity in the military or space fields, many of his concepts and formulations are directly useful in a commercial product development model.

Primary inputs to the model are the potential sales of a series of existing and future products in various stages of their life cycles. Information relating to these product life cycles is, however, only imperfectly known within the company. Forecasting errors are simulated in model operation by delaying and distorting true potential sales information, and the imperfect information is used to project future value of a product to the company.

To arrive at a benefit-cost measure of product worth to the company, future benefit estimates are combined with estimates of the funds required to develop and market the product. Product selection and scheduling are based on the estimated benefit-cost ratios. Those products with ratios less than unity are rejected, but those with higher benefit-cost ratios are scheduled for development with a time urgency that is greater for larger ratios. One decision rule that was tested scheduled project durations varying from one year for high-value products to five years for low-value products. In the multiple-product version, this basic time might be modified by availability of technical personnel within the company.

After the basic schedule has been established, personnel are assigned and the development project is initiated. Project operation is simulated in a manner similar to that described for Company B. Errors in initial estimates and the actual rate of accomplishment introduce a discrepancy between desired rate of progress established by the schedule and actual rate of progress observed. In the inner feedback loop of the model, changes in personnel assignments are made to adjust actual progress to the current schedule. At the same time, value of the product is being constantly reevaluated in the outer loop of the system to determine whether the project should be continued or a different development schedule seems appropriate.

Experimental simulation runs conducted with the model have evaluated the comparative importance of such system variables as:

1. Effect of long-range sales forecast errors.
2. Length of the planning period, i.e., the time span in the future for which estimates are made.
3. Effect of initial errors in development cost estimates.
4. Effect of shorter and longer product life cycles.
5. Effect of changing technology.
6. Effect of various project selection decision rules.

Actual historical product sales data were used to confirm the validity of the model and to evaluate various changes to the current procedures used in selecting new products. Confidence in the value of the model has increased in Company C to the point where the model is now being considered for full-time operation in product selection and budgeting.

Implementing the System

With the model developed, data collected, experimental simulation runs performed, and a potentially profitable set of new information needs and decision rules determined, the industrial dynamics project may still falter in the operational implementation phase. Failure is assured if the systems engineer assumes that the potential demonstrated by computer simulation will carry the project through by its own weight.

Typically, phases of the program prior to implementation are accomplished by a few people who are intensely interested in the project. Data for the model are often collected by piecing together fragmentary records that are not available or suitable for daily operations. In many ways, these earlier phases resemble the development of engineering prototype equipment, so it is not surprising that procedures used to show benefits of the model are not entirely suitable for an operational system. Many an interesting prototype has proved impractical in production.

Lack of any operationally practical information system was the most significant bottleneck experienced in implementing the three industrial dynamics systems just discussed. Though it was usually possible to gather a typical set of data for demonstration purposes, obtaining data on an operational basis was more difficult. The answer is revision of the current system rather than superposition of a new system on the existing network. In the long run, no company should sponsor two competing and conflicting information systems.

Finally, there is a human barrier. Many companies making a satisfactory profit and growing at a reasonable rate do not become extremely excited about profit optimization.[5] Uncertainties of change often seem to outweigh promised benefits of a new system. None of the three companies involved in the industrial dynamics projects I have described was in dire financial condition, and two of them were having some of their best years. The sense of urgency needed by top managers to implement the industrial dynamics system did not arise from grim effort to save the companies but from a desire to improve continually their operations.

Human problems of program implementation, however, were alleviated in the three companies by two factors:

1. Continuing top-management support.
2. Technical and moral support by lower-echelon personnel who were familiar with industrial dynamics.

This second factor was especially important. I found it difficult as an outsider to develop a model, collect data, and carry out the remainder of the project without considerable support at middle and top levels of management. Ultimately the success of the project will be, and should be, judged by its contribution to company profitability. But success of an industrial dynamics project is more likely if company personnel are informed and personally committed to it.

Appendix

A block diagram of the Company A model is shown in the figure on the opposite page. The model is divided into seven sectors.

Marketing Sector

Meter sales orders for Company A and its competitors depend on the number of residential housing starts, the number of new metering systems installed in existing housing, and the number of meters replaced. Housing starts and new metering systems are treated as exogenous inputs to the model. An endogenous treatment of these variables would have involved the entire construction industry—an unnecessarily complex extension of the model. Meter replacement orders are internally developed, however, based on the inventory of meters in existing housing units.

The external inputs of housing starts and new community water metering systems are added to meters being replaced to develop the total sales of water meters in the industry. Total orders are then subdivided between Company A and the rest of the industry based on a market-share division dependent on delivery time, product quality, and price. These orders are time-delayed to reflect the time elapsed in bid negotiations and order processing. The final output of the sector is the sales order input to Company A. An option in the program allows for the insertion of historical data for Company A sales orders, thus bypassing most of the marketing sector. This option was used in some of the simulation test runs to enter the historical sales of 1961 and 1962 for comparison purposes.

The relationships just described make up the "A" portion of the marketing sector as depicted in the illustration. The "B" part of the sector receives meter shipments from Company A and its competitors. These meters are accumulated in a service inventory which determines the rate of replacement orders. This replacement rate is generated based on the number of meters in service and the meter life. Strictly speaking, meters in service should be categorized by years in service so that replacements can be made a function of meter life, but the existing data did not permit such a division. An extensive data-collection effort is now in progress at the company to provide the data necessary for a more complete development of the marketing sector.

Physical Distribution Sector

Incoming orders are subdivided in the physical distribution sector into two categories: orders to be filled directly from finished goods inventory and orders requiring special product features to comply with customer specifications.

This separation is significant at Company A because it is only in recent years that any orders of the first category were possible. Prior to the recent development of a new meter, all orders were of the second category requiring options in the final assembly of the meter. Currently, a substantial percentage of incoming orders are filled from a finished inventory of the new meter. This standardization and ability to produce to inventory has resulted in significant savings and production flexibility.

Order separation is based on the level of finished goods inventory. At higher levels of inventory, inventory-filled orders are increased. This formulation is quite realistic at Company A because even within the new product type there are a number of meter sizes and two options based on prevailing weather conditions in different areas of the country. A larger inventory will definitely increase the probability that a meter will be available in stock up to a certain inventory level, beyond which the probability is not further increased because some municipalities insist on special product features.

Customer orders are sent directly to the manufacturing sector. Inventory orders are shipped after a short delay from inventory.

Production-inventory Control Sector

Production orders for meters, subassemblies, and parts are originated in the production-inventory control sector. Orders for finished meters are based on a sales forecast using the exponential smoothing method and an adjustment of finished meter inventory. The difference between actual inventory and desired inventory is adjusted over a time interval. This inventory difference, added to the sales forecast, is the production level for the coming period. Provision is made for varying the length of the decision period between production level decisions.

Subassembly and parts orders are based on average finished meter production and the level of subassembly and parts inventories. Finished meter production is smoothed to fix average production. All production orders are then transmitted to the manufacturing sector.

Manufacturing Sector

Production orders accumulate in backlogs for parts, subassemblies, and finished meter production. The finished meter backlog differs from the other two in having two order sources—customer orders and inventory orders. The other backlogs receive only inventory orders.

In each of the manufacturing sub-sectors, production is paced by incoming orders unless manpower, material, or capital equipment availability restricts production to a lower level. Manpower limitations are partially alleviated by

Model of the Production-Inventory Employment System for Company A

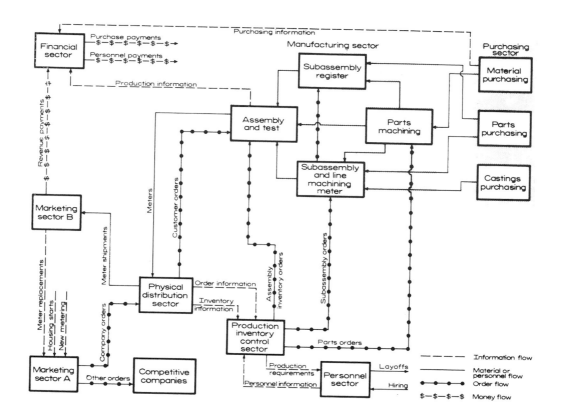

Marketing. Meter sales orders are generated based on housing starts, new metering programs for previously unmetered housing units and replacement of meters in service.

Physical distribution. Incoming orders are subdivided in this sector between those to be filled from inventory and those requiring special production. Meter inventories are also maintained in the sector.

Production-inventory control. Based on average sales orders, current production rate and accumulated inventories, inventory orders of assembled meters, subassemblies and parts are developed to control the volume of production.

Manufacturing. In the manufacturing sector, parts,

subassemblies and finished meters are produced based on customer and inventory orders received as limited by availability of men, material and equipment.

Purchasing. Castings, piece parts and other material (mostly rubber and bar and strip stock) are procured based on the average production rates in the various shops and the level of material inventories.

Personnel. The number of hourly and salaried personnel together with the scheduling of overtime is determined based on production requirements.

Financial. Cash flows resulting from incoming revenue and outgoing payments are tabulated in this sector. A detailed cost accounting of labor and material payments is also included.

an option to schedule overtime which is, however, also limited by the over-all employment policy formulated in the personnel sector. Plant-equipment capacity places a ceiling on the maximum production possible. Material shortages may limit production below that required if raw material inventories are below normal. Production is completed in each of the sub-sectors after a production time delay and is stored in an in-production inventory bank. Parts are withdrawn into subassembly production, and subassemblies are sent to final meter assembly.

Subassembly orders initiate production in two subassembly areas—bare meters and registers. This separation was necessary to reflect the differing production technologies in the two areas.

Personnel Sector

The number of company personnel and the over-all level of overtime are controlled in the personnel sector. Changes in the number of hourly personnel are based on the difference between the personnel desired and the personnel currently employed as modified by overtime and undertime allowances. Personnel desired relates to average production rate. This personnel gap is adjusted over a period of time. Overtime and undertime allowances prevent hiring and layoffs within specified limits. Hourly personnel are divided among the various shops according to production requirements. Salaried personnel are expressed as a percentage of long-term average sales.

Purchasing Sector

Materials and parts needed for production are procured and stored in the purchasing sector. Purchasing operations are subdivided into three subsectors, castings, parts, and other materials (rubber, supplies, and bar and strip stock). The purchasing rate for each of these categories is based on the production rate of the user shop together with an adjustment of the raw material inventory. Suitable delays are included to reflect procurement lead times.

Financial Sector

Company cash flow information is maintained in the financial sector. An inward flow of cash is generated by revenue received from the sale of meters. Cash level is reduced by a variety of payments for purchased materials, salaries, and wages. Hourly labor costs are particularly detailed because they interact critically with the aggregate production-employment decision rule. Regular payroll, overtime, hiring-layoff, and inventory costs are all calculated during the simulation run. Profit and cost variables computed in this sector permit an evaluation of the effectiveness of particular policies tested in model simulation.

References

1 Forrester, J. W., *Industrial Dynamics*, M.I.T. Press, Cambridge, 1961.

2 Bonini, C. P., *Simulation of Information and Decision Systems in the Firm*, unpublished Ph.D. thesis, Carnegie Institute of Technology, 1962.

3 Schall, W. C., "Industrial Dynamics," *Instrument Society of America Journal*, September, 1962.

4 Roberts, E. B., *The Dynamics of Research and Development*, unpublished Ph.D. thesis, M.I.T., 1962.

5 Cyert, R. M., and March, J. G., *A Behavioral Theory of the Firm*, Prentice-Hall, 1963.

Some Insights into Implementation

Edward B. Roberts

Many aspects of the Badger Meter problem situation and model (Company A of Chapter 8) are strongly similar to Sprague Electric (Chapters 6 and 7), as were the kind and magnitude of initial successful results produced by policy implementation. Major differences do show up, however, in Kenneth Schlager's clear orientation to implementation considerations, as well as in the apparent permanence of his implemented changes in contrast with the transient usage of the policies at Sprague. A comparison of Schlager's comments on the Badger Meter case with those of Fey and Carlson referring to the work at Sprague Electric, supplemented by other known facets of both activities, should help develop better insights into strategies for effective application of system dynamics. In hindsight, it seems that meaningful contrasts arose in the initiation, principal execution, and support and follow-up activities. These differences will be highlighted by re-stating affirmatively ten of the hypothesized principles for effective implementation of system dynamics (or of any other form of corporate modelling and simulation activities) that were outlined previously in Chapter 4, along with the contrasting evidences.

1. For effectiveness a project should be initiated as a serious problem-solving oriented effort. This was not the situation with the Sprague project. It was undertaken because Jay Forrester and Robert C. Sprague, founder and President of Sprague Electric Company, had deservedly high mutual respect for each other, and Sprague was interested in experimenting with the newer approaches of management science. Curiosity or fascination with system dynamics, while admirable, does not set the proper framework for an application endeavor. It generates an orientation toward research rather than results, and sets the wrong tone throughout the organization. In contrast the Badger work was undertaken as part of a program for levelling production fluctuations that was already underway in the company. If the atmosphere surrounding the project initiation is one of an "academic exercise," success will be difficult to achieve.

2. The problem undertaken should offer reasonable opportunity for significant improvement in the organization's performance. At Sprague the study was focused on one product line out of about fifty; at Badger all but about the five percent that were ''special'' products were included in the model. An effort that concentrates on one line only is certainly important to that line's management, but it can hardly be critical to top management of the company if it represents only five percent of sales, is a product in its mature stage, and is expected soon to be declining further. At Badger the top management were already on-board the problem being tackled and the profitability of the total corporation was at stake. To argue that a problem must offer significant improvement opportunities for the organization undertaking or sponsoring the work is not the same as arguing that it must be a top management problem. Certainly top management problems usually proffer greater payoff possibilities for not necessarily greater project outlay. But an appropriately important project initiated by and/or for a middle manager is also meaningful for a system dynamics approach. What is critical from an implementation perspective is that the problem selected must be important to the project's ''client.'' With the president of Sprague Electric as the client, stabilizing the oscillations of a product accounting for only five percent of the firm's sales lacks substantive justification as providing a ''reasonable opportunity for significant improvement.''

3. To the maximum degree possible the project work should be executed by knowledgeable in-house employees. At the least a mixed task force of insiders and outside consultants should collaborate closely on all aspects of the job. At Sprague the work was done completely by an M.I.T. research team, which only seldom met with Sprague employees during the problem and model formulation and development stages. No in-house education program on system dynamics was created and only few of Sprague's management received cursory briefings on system dynamics in general. In defense it should be noted that very little formal education in system dynamics was then available, even at M.I.T. But company education or involvement seemed relatively remote considerations at the outset of that project. Active company involvement is essential not only to ensure adequacy and accuracy of model formulation, but also to provide the people-basis for implementation of resulting recommended changes. At Badger, the project was initiated by several managers from different company functional areas who were jointly studying system dynamics in Schlager's evening course at Marquette University. They brought Schlager in as a consultant and the desired collaborative involvement naturally followed. The strategy of using mixed task forces of insiders who are just beginning to learn system dynamics with experienced outsiders is one that has often been used effectively to get the job done competently, while avoiding the possible delay of several years for in-house self-education. This mixed team approach appears to be especially suitable for companies that are in the early stages of experience with system dynamics endeavors.

4. Model development should be expedited, with a first operating model targeted for no more than several months after project initiation. For numerous reasons, having a model in operating condition quickly is good practice. First, it provides reassurances to the boss or client that real progress is being made. He can begin generating more confidence about the direction of the project once even crude model results become available for review and criticism. Second, the model becomes a tangible communications vehicle. No doubt many managers and staff related to the project's problem area will be unfamiliar with modelling and simulation. They will also be uncertain as to the real targets of the project, and may possibly feel threatened as to the forms of outcomes that are possible. The early model operation, while needing to be represented carefully as being both simplified and tentative, should help alleviate some of these difficulties. Further, because the model necessitates explicit statements, it will emphasize early in the process those areas of formulation that need greater clarification. Third, as early model results are generated they will naturally be checked with care against available knowledge, including any collected quantitative data. Such early validity tests help to point up areas of suspect formulation, areas needing more careful data gathering for improving the accuracy of formulation. Similarly, running sensitivity tests with the early model versions also generates new priorities, i.e., the sensitivity tests point up the relatively few parameters and functional forms whose values critically affect the model's simulated behavior. These areas demand more careful analysis, research, data generation, and model building. This emphasis on getting *an* operating model quickly can be followed in even the longest total duration projects. In the development of a model of the Susquehanna River Basin,[1] a project which eventually lasted through four formal contractual phases of work covering five years, the first model was operative within several months, and all model changes were made in incremental fashion from then on. At all points during the project, the model represented an up-to-date statement of progress on knowledge gained about the regional development situation being assessed. Schlager too reports that his modelling effort required only a few months' development time, whereas the Sprague work reportedly took two to four years, depending on the source referenced. This contrast is perhaps most unfair, however, in that the Sprague project was the first industrial application by the M.I.T. Industrial Dynamics Research Group, whereas the Badger project was substantially a copy of the Sprague model. Yet, regardless of cause, it would be difficult to sustain management interest and enthusiasm over a multi-year period without tangible interim results feedback.

4a. Successful model implementers may more often be followers than innovators, as suggested by the comments in 4 above. Never would the author knowingly discourage innovation, but it usually does take longer to solve a problem that no one else has previously tackled. An important motivation for this book was to make available to all a much larger library of application situations and models, thereby making the art of "following" a more practicable alternative. By reducing the uncertainty and the duration of project effort of many possible system dynamics uses, the innovators who solved the problems the first time have made important contributions. But it was much easier for P. R. Mallory and Company essentially to copy the published model of Sprague, and for Badger to more-or-less copy the same model, than for them to have reinvented their own models. Of course, in corporate modelling and simulation, especially for strategic areas, competitive tradeoffs do exist between innovating and following just the same as they exist in product research and development. But for most companies, "followership" will probably turn out to be an adequate and acceptable approach. The Sprague example being cited, for instance, could profitably be applied today by the vast majority of the world's manufacturing companies, with only minor adjustments needed in each case.

5. *The effective model will contain a level of detail sufficient to demonstrate the problem system, and sufficient to persuade participating management of the model's adequacy.* Only the appearance of tautology exists in the last clause of that sentence. For a model to lead to implemented results, management must be convinced the model is adequate, that it contains what management considers to be key uncertainty areas. The system dynamics philosophy has often led to the development of minimal models in terms of number of variables and level of aggregation. "Use only the content *necessary* to demonstrate the problem" has been the guiding maxim. This practice is clearly illustrated in the Sprague model. Fey reports in Chapter 6, "The model incorporated only those parts of the system that related to the defined problems." And Carlson continues in Chapter 7, "The resulting model has the virtue of being relatively simple . . . As will be seen later, it has the drawback of being more abstract than operating personnel are accustomed to in a manufacturing business . . ." And Carlson explicitly raises questions about adequacy of the model's treatment of competitors, customers, and different classes of orders. The Badger model in contrast added a much more detailed manufacturing representation, a more detailed personnel sector, three classes of purchasing decisions, and an extensive cost sector. All these additions were designed to heighten Badger management's confidence in the model, not necessarily to improve the analytical possibilities or more accurately to represent the underlying problems. For a model to be useful for application, management needs to be confident of its contents. Otherwise even the elegant model is useless.

6. *Model validity testing must be geared to management assurance criteria.* Forrester has made this same point often, i.e., that predefined so-called "objective" validity measures (such as 95 percent confidence levels of statistical tests, or levels of achieved Chi-square ratings) are really arbitrary and do not usually coincide with the measures of model suitability that would please the management concerned with the problem.[2] Yet too often would-be system dynamics practitioners have misread Forrester to be suggesting that if management acceptance could somehow be gained, an appropriate level of concern for model accuracy can be skipped. Fey represents that much detailed data were gathered in the process of problem and model conceptualization and formulation at Sprague. (See Chapter 6.) He also indicates that the model's structure and simulated behavior were studied by the M.I.T. team and company officials and that the equations were agreed upon as adequately representing the real world situation. But despite this orientation to model validity it appears that Schlager again went one or more steps further in gaining management confidence about the validity of the model and its results. In Chapter 8 he reports a "more extensive data collection and analysis phase," as well as the use of statistical experimental design techniques as means of bolstering management's confidence in the model validity.

7. *Measures of effectiveness of alternative policies should be designed into the model and should be consistent with real-world evaluation methods.* This means that if profitability and employment stability are to be the bases for comparing new policies to old, those measures should be incorporated as part of the model. In the Sprague situation, neither desired result was included as a measure in the model. No cost or profits sector was even included in the Sprague project model, and a simple cash flow sector was added only as an after-thought in Forrester's text writeup of the case.[3] Moreover, such model measures should correspond to available real-company measures, or at least to measures that might be made available. In this regard, Carlson is quoted: ''No attempt has been made to measure exactly the effect on profits of the new policies. This would be a very difficult and costly undertaking requiring extensive changes in company-wide accounting systems . . .'' In contrast in the Badger project specific costs-benefits simulations of alternative policies were used as the basis for the recommendations and for performance prediction and after-the-fact evaluation. ''Confronting management with a more profitable set of policies tested over a recent period of company history can be extremely persuasive,''reminds Schlager.

8. *Design of recommendations for change must explicitly consider their compatibility with all other parts of the unchanged management system.* A system model often does not contain enough of the total company system to be adequate by itself for evaluating the appropriateness of new policy proposals. For example, are proposed new authority structures compatible with other arrangements in the company? Is the reporting requirement commensurate with the data processing group's capacity? Are the personnel needs within achievement range of the company's human resources now or potentially available? Two aspects of the Sprague policies seem unsuitable from this view. First, that one line was to be operated in dramatically different ways, with different philosophy, reporting system and decision processes from the other fifty, seemed inherently incompatible. Fey attempts to minimize these disharmonies but fails to be persuasive in light of Carlson's testimony of difficulties. Schlager's advice seems appropriate: ''In the long run, no company should sponsor two competing and conflicting information systems, ''and this certainly extends to conflicting management systems. Second, the Sprague implementation led to an implicit downgrading of managerial authority, though no change was desired here. When fifteen minutes of a secretary's time, once a week, becomes the whole basis for a production manager's previously discretionary managerial behavior, a downgrading has occurred. Even Fey reports that this arrangement was never very satisfying. No wonder that on occasion, even when the system dynamics policies were in maximum use, the rule was disregarded.

9. *For implementation of desired policy changes, the recommendations must be accompanied by an extensive program of management reeducation, by explicitly designed decision rules that support the new policies, or more likely by both.* Forrester has argued extensively that system dynamics is policy-oriented, rather than decision-oriented. The distinction is appropriate and well-intentioned, but the practitioner of system dynamics needs to be prepared to go beyond mere policy advocacy if he wants successful implementation to follow his work. Change is difficult to help bring about in

organizations. The system dynamics analyst/consultant must be prepared to be an effective change agent for that role will usually be needed, whether or not requested. For management truly to accept new policies, their thinking must have gone through some transitional process, an unlikely occurrance without a deliberate program. The needed management rethinking of their outlooks regarding the relevant policy areas might follow a system dynamics analytic phase, or better still accompany it by intimate management involvement from the problem conceptualization on through the rest of the project duration. This reeducation regarding the alternate policies goes beyond the general understanding of system dynamics that was advocated in Principle 3 listed above. As a minimum, and not really sufficient to replace the managerial change of views, explicit decision rules for putting the new policies into effect need to be spelled out, of course, in conjunction with those who will have to use those decision rules. Both reeducation and explicit decision rules were lacking at Sprague; to some extent, both were present at Badger, although still greater attention might have been given to managerial reeducation.

10.   *For successful implementation, the model builder must be implementation-committed from the outset and must continue to assist its attainment until success is achieved.* Almost all management consultants and far too many in-house management staffs see their role as completed with the filing and perhaps verbal acceptance of recommended changes. But this state merely produces fancy reports on the shelves or buried in bottom drawers, and no change. Change needs to be championed in organizations; lack of these champions leads to a reinforced lack of change-resources (see Chapter 26) and nothing happens. In both the Sprague and Badger cases the consultants continued to work to gain implementation. But the M.I.T. team quit too soon, and their encouragement of and pressure on Sprague decision-makers vanished with their decline of participation. Schlager not only pushed hard for implementation, he designed his activities to have permanent effect by building his detailed decision rules into a newly developed management information system that he helped create. Moreover, he then followed his system work into Badger, initially as part-time Director of Management Systems, and later as a full-time employee, rising to Vice President of the Systems Division.

The last principle cited here, of the need for implementation-committed model-builders, is a problem that must be faced by the entire management science community. The professional management science organizations are run, their journals are edited, and the papers are authored generally by management science academicians, rather than practitioners. Yet the real guts of management science problems are encountered in the practice rather than in the theory. In TIMS-ORSA meetings I have often participated in the arguments between those seeking a stronger orientation toward real application and those seeking to maintain the dominance of theory. Until recently, the champions for theory have been clearly in the vanguard. It appears, however, that a shift is gradually occurring as leaders of the foremost management science graduate schools are increasingly willing to forsake (in part, at least) the comforts of the ivory tower for the decreased elegance of an orientation toward implementation of managerial change. University faculty members have not yet accepted (nor do they seek) a new self-image as agents of change who measure their achievements in terms of implemented results, rather than solely in numbers of published papers or even in terms of well-trained students. But at least a new direction is being set, if only slowly. With this academic legitimacy as a base it should then become possible also to evaluate corporate management science staffs and counsel in measures of their implementations, rather than of their elegant reports or advice. More, and more useful, implementations might then be produced.

Notes

1. Hamilton, et al., *Systems Simulation for Regional Analysis* (Cambridge, Mass.: The MIT Press, 1969).

2. Forrester, Jay W. *Industrial Dynamics* (Cambridge, Mass.: The MIT Press, 1961), pp. 115–129.

3. Ibid., pp. 240–242.

10

Systems Analysis of Workload Fluctuations: A Case Study of the Precision Company

Edward B. Roberts

Description of the Problem

The Precision Company is a job shop supplier of high quality machine parts. The company gets most of its orders through competitive bidding, its customers being primarily large electronic systems firms in the Boston area. Bid requests are examined by Precision's engineering department which decides whether the company wants to compete for particular jobs. Bids, quoting price and estimated delay for the delivery of completed work, are then prepared and sent to potential customers. There are occasional price and quality differences between Precision and its competition, but the president of Precision feels that the customer's decision to accept a bid is primarily influenced by the quoted delivery delay. Precision usually quotes the delay that is currently being experienced by orders in its work backlog.

Precision now has a pressing problem, a production crisis. This problem is not new, it occurs periodically. At the moment Precision has a large backlog of orders that will cause longer delays between receipt of new orders and completion of work. Strong pressure is being exerted to deliver on time even though the company has already cut back on its maintenance work and is using overtime to accelerate production. Precision wants to eliminate the present problem and prevent these recurring production crises. It sees no reason this cannot be done because the use of these products by its customers does not fluctuate so widely, though previous efforts have not produced significant stabilization.

The objective of this systems analysis is to increase profitability of Precision's operations by reducing costly fluctuations in employment, productivity, and the use of overtime. Presumably this may require achieving some stabilization of incoming orders.

This paper is based on a study performed at a precision metal-working shop in the suburban Boston area. The company's name and some details have been changed to assure anonymity. Several members of the M.I.T. Industrial Dynamics Research Group were involved in this study. Ole C. Nord was the principal M.I.T. staff member who authored the internal M.I.T. memoranda on which this synopsis is based. The author appreciates the assistance of Robert C. Payette in development of the revised version of the Precision Company model. The documented computer model for the Precision case appears in Appendix B of this book.

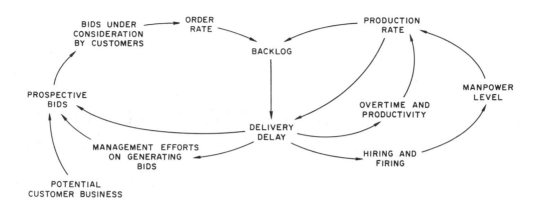

Figure 1   Basic system structure

A Systems Approach to the Precision Case

The fundamental reasons behind the workload problem at Precision are not obvious. Those reasons can be guessed at and new policies devised based on past experience that are believed adequate to resolve the difficulties. This route is very risky. It is not intuitively obvious which policies cause which changes in total system behavior. The route that will be taken in this paper is longer but more promising—that of a systems analysis based on the Industrial Dynamics approach.[1]

An industrial dynamics analysis of the situation focuses on structure and behavior. Structure is the set of policies and factors that determine overall behavior through time. The basic structure relevant to the present problem seems to be that shown in Figure 1.

The diagram indicates the flows of information, people and orders that have been determined to be relevant to the problem at hand. Judgment factors are used in deciding what elements of company practices interact. This judgment or intuition, however, is not used to draw conclusions about the total system behavior over time that is generated by these interactions. The flows or interactions between different variables will be described in greater detail below. Later the behavior that this structure generates will be described. This is accomplished by expressing the relationships of the structure in mathematical form and using a computer to simulate the effects for a period of time.[2] It will become more apparent why the fluctuations experienced by Precision are caused by the structure of information and decision flows. The structure will then be changed and the resulting improved behavior described and tested.

Description of the Existing System Structure.

In order to emphasize the closed loop structure, the system of Precision Company flows of information governed by successive decision policies will be described in terms of three major feedback loops. There are in fact six loops but to describe all of these overlapping loops would involve excessive repetition.

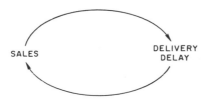

Figure 2 A simple feedback loop

An example of a closed loop of cause and effect is shown in Figure 2.

Each arrow points in the direction of the effect. Sales have a direct effect on delivery delay. The delay in delivery has a direct effect on sales. The difficulty about multi-loop structures is that causes and effects are not immediate and behavior is not obvious. An increase in sales today only has an effect on deliveries at some later date when orders are in production. Similarly delivery conditions only have effects on sales at some later date when customers realize the new delivery conditions and change their ordering pattern.

Sales loop. The first feedback loop in the Precision case that will be discussed is the so-called "sales loop". This loop is actually two loops that are described together for the sake of clarity. Figure 3 illustrates the sales loop.

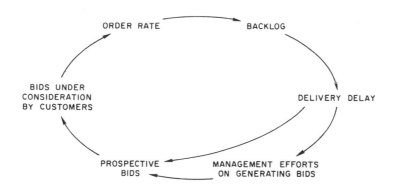

Figure 3 Sales loop

Because the variables successively determine one another, the description can be started at any point, with the incoming order rate for instance. The incoming order rate adds to the backlog. The delivery delay is the sum of the time required for a new order to move through the backlog of work awaiting production, for it to be produced, and for it to be shipped to the customer. At any time a first approximation of the delivery delay can be found by dividing production rate into the backlog of unfilled orders.

Delivery delay influences the fraction of total management effort that is devoted to bidding for new orders as follows:

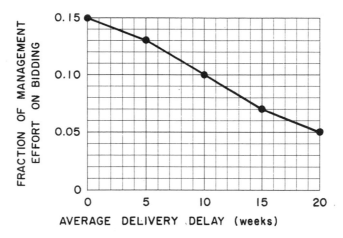

Figure 4   Fraction of management effort on bidding

Figure 4 indicates that with longer delivery delays more management attention is devoted to expediting existing orders in production and to placating customer complaints, and therefore less attention is devoted to prospective orders. Shorter delivery delays, on the other hand, indicate that the backlog is running low, and more work is needed to keep the workforce productively employed.

This bidding-marketing effort in turn influences the number of bid opportunities and submitted bids generated, as shown in Figure 5. And the number of bids influences what the order rate will be several weeks later.

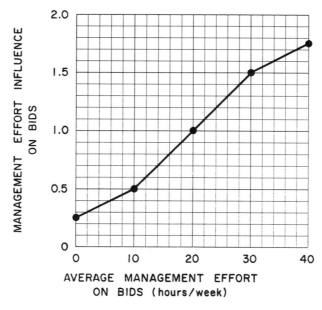

Figure 5   Influence of management effort on bids

The variables in the loop do not affect each other immediately. A change in prospective bids only influences order rate after several weeks. A change in order rate only produces gradual changes in backlog since backlog is an accumulation of orders coming in less orders completed. Backlog changes are reflected in changes in delivery delay. Delivery delay changes induce changes in management effort toward bidding after several weeks. Changes in management effort in turn result in changes in bids generated one or more months later.

Figure 3 also shows a direct effect of delivery delay on prospective business, because customers curtail the number of Precision Company bids accepted as a result of longer delivery delay. The direct effect of delivery delay on customer acceptance of bids is assumed to be of the form shown below in Figure 6.

Figure 6   Influence of delivery delay on bids accepted

Production and manpower loop.   The second major feedback loop is shown in Figure 7, and connects backlog, delivery delay, changes in manpower, employment level and production rate.

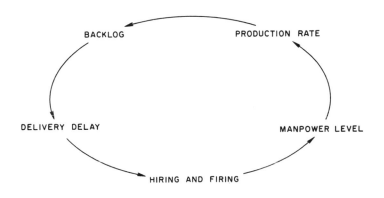

Figure 7   Production and manpower loop

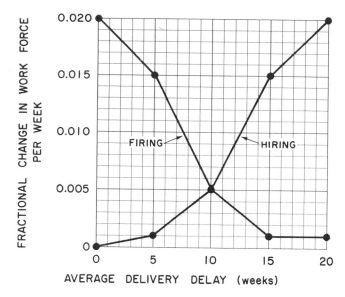

Figure 8 Manpower change policy

Changes in production rates gradually cause changes in backlog, the accumulation of orders received less orders produced. Backlog changes determine delivery delay changes. Precision's employment policy is pressure responsive, based largely on delivery delay and its implications for future workload.

Almost always some men are joining the company and some men leaving. When delivery delay is high the fraction of men leaving is low and the fraction of new men is high. The opposite holds when delivery delay is low. The influence of delivery delay on employment is not immediate. For employment level decisions, the company reacts to delivery delay averaged over several weeks. Company hiring decisions only have an effect about four to eight weeks later when a man can actually be recruited to join the company and becomes fully productive in the shop. The production start rate is directly proportional to the effective level of trained manpower.

A four week leadtime is normal for production orders in process. When production is completed, backlog is reduced. The change in backlog in turn affects delivery delay.

Productivity loop.   The final loop to be described relates production rate to backlog and to the use of overtime to affect productivity, and is shown as Figure 9. It too combines two feedback loops that act in the same manner.

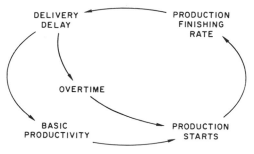

Figure 9 Overtime and productivity loop

Company policy is to use overtime to increase the production rate when delivery delay is high. Under workload pressures basic productivity also rises somewhat when delivery delay is high. In contrast, when delivery delay is low, no overtime is used and more maintenance and repair work is performed, reducing basic productivity per man below normal, as shown in Figure 10.

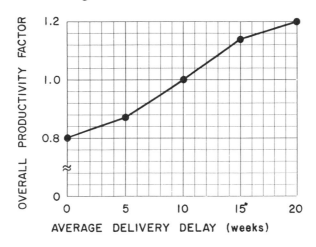

Figure 10   Productivity function, combining basic and overtime effects

The direct effect of productivity is on the production start rate. After about a four week delay to account for the usual in-process time, production finishing rate is affected. Changes in production finishing rate in turn influence calculated delivery delay, the ratio of backlog to average production finishing rate.

Careful examination of Figure 1 indicates that the production and employment loop and the productivity loop form two more feedback loops of closed cause and effect chains. These are the result of overlaps in interactions, add no new dimension to the analysis, and will not be discussed here.

Behavior of Present System

In this section the behavior produced by the system structure is examined. Because the interactions are complex, total system behavior cannot be determined directly. A computer has produced the results over a period of time by simulating changes in the system over a series of small intervals and updating the various states of the system each time.[3]

Figure 11 shows the response of the system to a 20% step increase in potential customer business. This smooth step increase is not a situation one would expect to happen in reality. However, it is used here as a basic analytical simulation run of the model. The response to a step change is highly informative, indicating the oscillating tendencies of the system. In making the run the system is initially set to equilibrium conditions and shows no change until week 5 when the potential customer business is increased 20%.

The results shown in Figure 11 are sustained periodic fluctuations of all variables. Delivery delay, normally 10 weeks in duration, peaks at the times of week 28, week 90, and week 156. The delay times at these peaks are approximately 12.5, 12.9, and

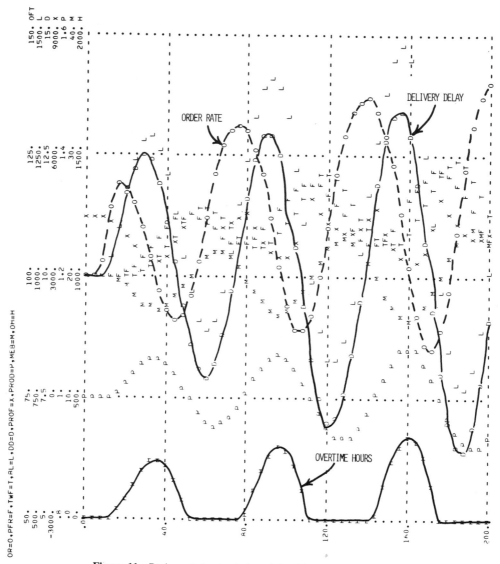

Figure 11   Basic analytic simulation of Precision Model: step function
response.

13.4 weeks, respectively. The deviation between successive peaks and the normal 10
week value of delivery delay increases by about 3% each time. These results are
sufficient to indicate that all fluctuations experienced by Precision will tend to grow
very slowly. The interval between successive peaks in Figure 11 is about 62 weeks. As
this response resulted from a step change in input, feedback theory predicts that this
same 62 weeks "natural" period of oscillation, or interval between peaks, will tend to
reappear under a wide variety of types of changes in potential customer business.[4] An
example will be shown below.

A closer examination of Figure 11 shows that the increase in potential business
produces an increase in order rate starting about six weeks later. This causes backlog
and delivery delay to rise. Overtime is used and productivity increases but not enough
to fully compensate for the order rate increase. In the period of week 10 to week 30

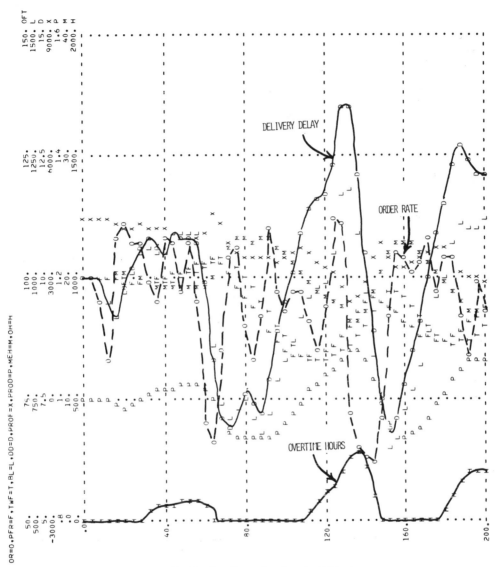

Figure 12 Random fluctuations in potential business.

backlog and delivery delay grow, causing a shift in organizational attention away from bidding efforts toward production and delivery problems. Less managerial time is spent on generating new orders and the prospective bids fall because of this and because of longer delivery delays.

By about week 20 the order rate begins to fall and by about week 32 the situation has begun to reverse. The reversal is accelerated by the hiring of new men that starts about week 15 and peaks at week 40. The period of reversal continues until week 60. Delivery delay and backlog are falling, more bids are generated by Precision and workers are not added as quickly. By week 60 the order rate picks up again and the whole upward cycle starts over again as more employees leave the company. This in turn produces the later recurring pattern of fluctuations.

Figure 12 shows system behavior under a more realistic condition, random or

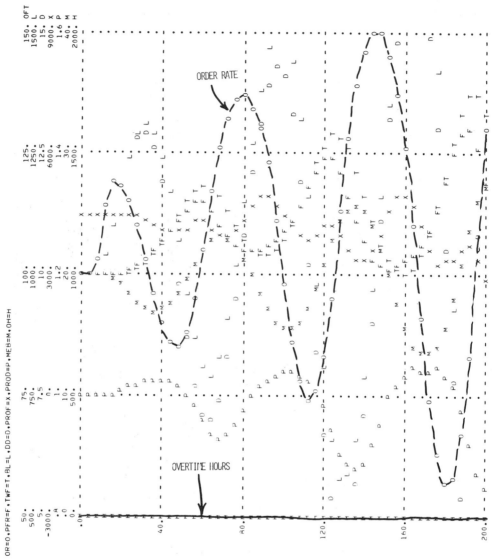

Figure 13   Policy of no overtime.

erratic variations in the potential customer business. For this simulation run the mean value of potential business was held constant but the actual value was varied from month to month by use of a normal random number generator with a standard deviation of 20%. As anticipated earlier, the same basic pattern of about 62 week periods between successive peaks reappears. Backlog peaks at week 132 and again at week 200 - a 68 week interval not unlike the expected 62 week interval. This demonstrates that there is a fundamental weakness in the present structure of the system. The network of information flows and decision policies of the Precision Company has produced sustained and even growing oscillations, instead of averaging out the monthly disturbances.

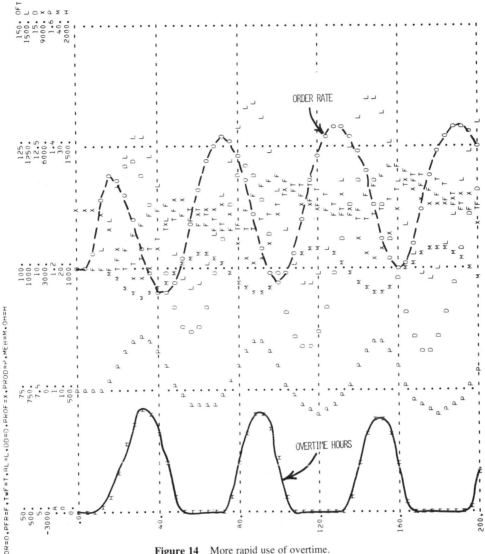

Figure 14   More rapid use of overtime.

Failure of Intuitive Approaches at Precision

Many attempts to change Precision's situation are suggested by consideration of the circumstances. Intuitively, it might seem that a policy of no overtime might eliminate some excesses of Precision's responses, and contribute to important profit improvement. But, as Figure 13 shows, a no overtime policy (when simulated by the computer) produces even worse overall results, and a deteriorating trend in profits.

In contrast, especially after Figure 13 is examined, it might seem reasonable to try a policy of more rapid use of overtime. Perhaps this approach would prevent the buildup of backlog, thereby keeping delivery delay within a moderate range of fluctuations. Yet, as Figure 14 shows, again no significant differences, and certainly no important profit improvements, are produced by this simulated policy change.

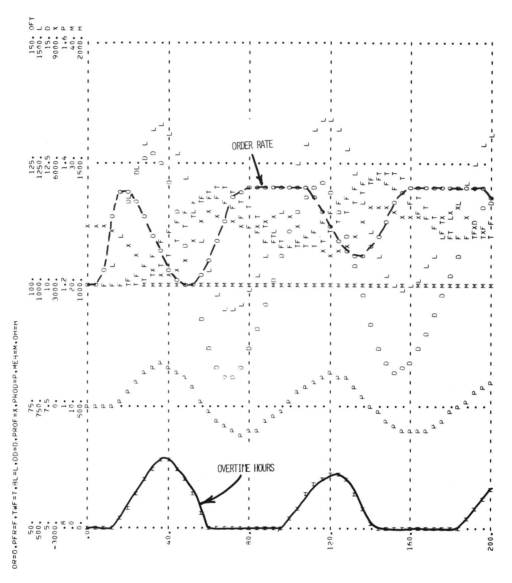

Figure 15   Policy of constant management effort toward generating business.

What about trying to stabilize Precision by eliminating its internal manpower allocation fluctuations? While it might be difficult to implement in the real Precision organization, the computer permits testing a policy of constant selling effort. The results indicated in Figure 15 show a more sluggish set of fluctuations, but not much overall improvement in profitability.

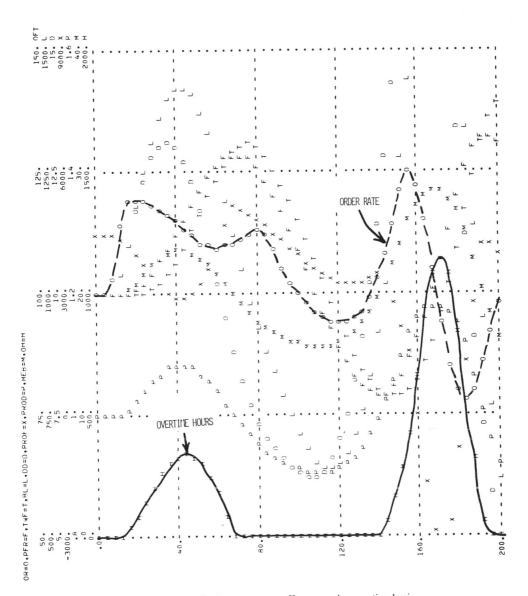

Figure 16 Countercyclical management effort toward generating business.

Perhaps the sales effort should be phased to try to counter the cycles previously observed. The effects of an attempt at such a countercyclical approach are simulated in Figure 16, leading unfortunately to even far worse instability and poor profits performance.

As a final intuition-based try, perhaps basing delivery quotations on forecasts of

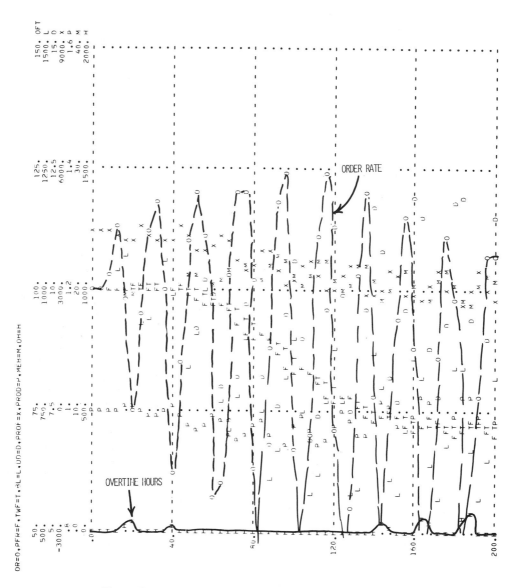

Figure 17 Bids based on projected, rather than current, delivery delay.

future delivery conditions (instead of on the present condition) will help produce stability. But Precision does not respond favorably to such an attempt, as illustrated in Figure 17.

This series of intuitively-based corrective-oriented policies include many of the common suggestions for treating problems similar to those encountered by the Precision Company. But none of them, as demonstrated by Figures 13 through 17, has succeeded in controlling the performance results produced by Precision's structure. Unaided managerial intuition appears inadequate to cope with even the relatively simple feedback loop structure of the Precision Company.

Designing Improved Policies at Precision

The problems encountered at Precision were manifested as undesirable oscillations in the behavior of the system, severely impacting profitability. They were caused by the structure of policies used by management. This situation can be changed.

The best solution to the problem is not to be found merely by adjusting the existing information flows and the decision variables until the problem disappears. This approach in general will not work because the problem lies in the structure, the nature of the information flows and their connections. In this case company policies must be reformulated: hiring can no longer depend on a pressure-based response to delivery delay but must be derived from rational consideration of the incoming order rate and other variables, and an explicit bidding policy needs to be developed. The new policy results described below were derived through analysis and trial of various stabilizing policies. Although only the final results are presented here, the process to obtain these is long and far from simple. It is a part of the total feedback systems analysis approach.

Manpower policy.   Instead of responding to delivery delay in making decisions about changes in manpower, Precision should consciously and logically respond to incoming order rate and to backlog. Figure 18 shows the flow of information leading to manpower changes under the improved policies.

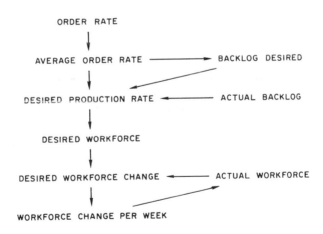

Figure 18 Improved manpower policy

The order rate may vary from week to week or from month to month, therefore the order rate information utilized is averaged over several weeks; in this case 12 weeks was found to be an appropriate order-smoothing time. From average orders, the desired backlog, equivalent to 10 weeks of orders, is determined. The desired production rate is made up of two components; the first and usually the largest is the average order rate. The second component takes account of the difference between actual backlog and desired backlog; 10% of the difference is added to the desired production rate, indicating that Precision will try to correct the imbalance in backlog position in about 10 weeks.

DESIRED PRODUCTION RATE = AVERAGE ORDER RATE
+ (10%)(DESIRED BACKLOG −
ACTUAL BACKLOG)

The normal production rate per week determines the level of manpower desired at normal productivity. The indicated change in work force desired per week is set as a fraction of the difference between the targeted and actual work force:

(10%)(DESIRED WORK FORCE − ACTUAL WORK FORCE)

The actual rates of men being hired and of men leaving each week are shown in Figure 19.

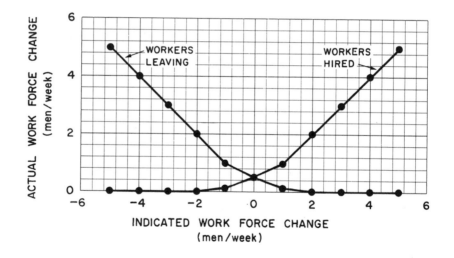

Figure 19   New manpower policy

Bidding effort policy.   The existing Precision Company policy of bidding efforts had been largely unplanned. By default the fraction of total available management time devoted to bidding was dependent on the pressures caused by delivery delays. The new manpower policy should help to stabilize delivery delay. In addition there should be an explicit policy on managerial effort devoted to bidding, in order to ensure stability of Precision's workload.

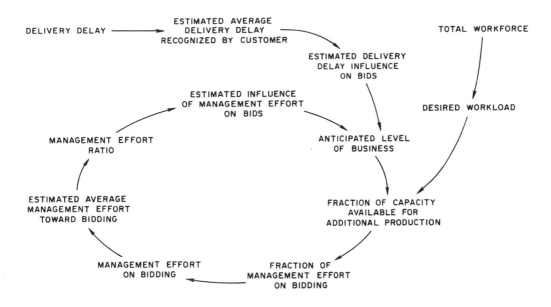

Figure 20 New bidding policy

Precision estimates that customers respond slowly to changes in actual delivery delay at the company; actual delivery delay is averaged over 20 weeks. Figure 21 shows Precision's estimate of the influence of delivery delay on customer acceptance of bids. On the "best" estimate curve, for example, Figure 21 illustrates that Precision estimates that when its delivery delay is 50 percent longer than normal, Precision will lose half of the bids it would otherwise receive.

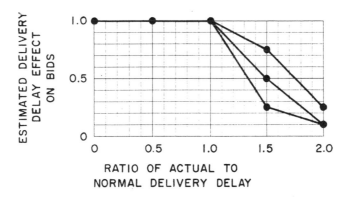

Figure 21 Company estimate of delivery delay effect on bids

The best estimate is so indicated; it will be used in the new policy analyses but the high and low estimates are also possible and will be tested, with results reported later in this chapter.

As shown by Figure 20 the anticipated level of business is determined by the average order rate and the estimated influences of delivery delay and of management efforts on the bids.

At any time the fraction of capacity available for additional production is equal to:

$$\frac{\text{DESIRED WORK LOAD} - \text{ANTICIPATED WORK LOAD}}{\text{DESIRED WORK LOAD}}$$

This fraction is used to determine what portion of available management time should be expended on bidding efforts, as indicated in Figure 22.

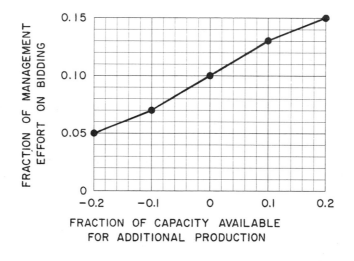

Figure 22   New policy on management
bidding efforts

The size of management effort toward bidding is given by total management effort available, regarded as a constant in the Precision situation, and by the fraction of that effort spent on bidding. The efforts of management on bidding will vary considerably within policy limits in order to try to stabilize the level of orders. The company estimates that the management effort toward bidding affects the market response about four weeks later. The ratio of this effort to normal bidding effort is the management bidding effort ratio.

The new structure of Precision policies and the connecting flows of information, orders, and personnel are summarized in Figure 23.

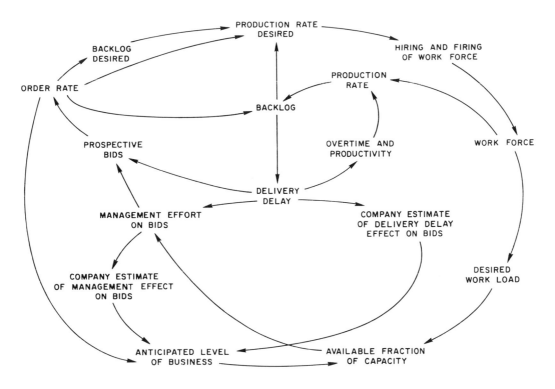

Figure 23   Structure of new Precision policies

Behavior of Precision Model with Improved Policies

The structure of the system now incorporates no new interactions between the company and its customers. The new employment and bidding policies are concerned with actions within the company. The behavior of this system under a 20% step increase in potential customer business, shown in Figure 24, is much more stable and shows fewer fluctuations than did behavior resulting from the original system (as was shown in Figure 11). Delivery delay has a peak value in Figure 24 of 12.2 weeks at week 24 and gradually returns to its normal value of 10 weeks without much oscillation.

Originally the delivery delay buildup put pressure on the company. In turn Precision reacted in an uncoordinated way that relieved the immediate problem but created recurring crises. Now, under the new policies, desired work load and labor force levels are determined by Precision management whose actions are directed to maintain lasting system stability around these established goals. Previously Precision was using delivery delay as a measure of performance but the company was continually kept off balance as delivery delay conditions changed in reaction to company changes of direction.

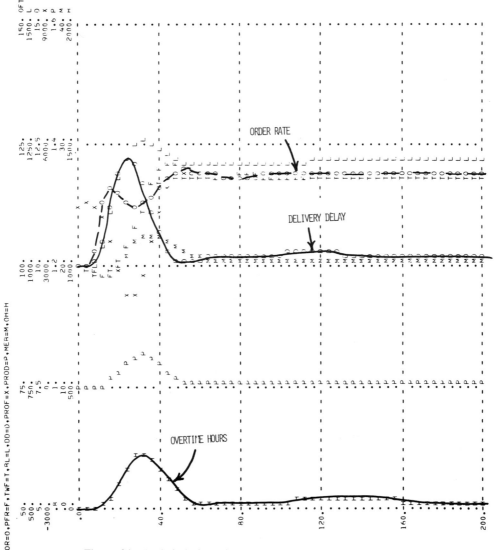

Figure 24   Analytical simulation of improved Precision Model: step function response.

Figure 25 shows system response to the same randomly fluctuating values of potential customer business as was previously illustrated in Figure 12. System behavior is now significantly damped, that is Precision's reactions are smaller than the random input. There has been a major improvement in Precision's performance compared to the original system.

Sensitivity of behavior to estimates of new policies.   At this point the stable mode of behavior resulting from the new employment and bidding policies is known to apply only under the assumed relationships. By testing variations in these assumed relationships, the sensitivity of basic system stability will be verified. Basic model behavior is in fact insensitive to a reasonable range of estimate errors. The following changes have little effect and produce substantially the same behavior as was shown in Figure 24:

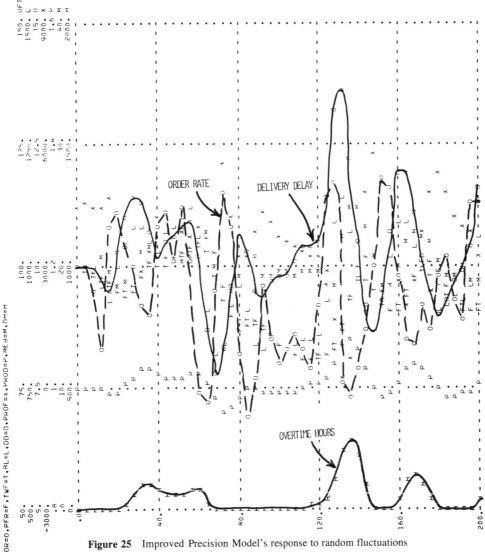

Figure 25   Improved Precision Model's response to random fluctuations in potential business.

changing management effort influence on bids from the best to a high or a low estimate;

changing delivery delay influence on bids from the best to a high or a low estimate, as shown in Figure 21;

doubling or halving the four week delay in averaging management effort on bid activities;

doubling or halving the 20 week delay in averaging delivery delay influence on customer bid acceptance policy;

lengthening the customer delay in consideration of bids from six to twelve weeks;

changing the formulation that had resulted in productivity variations from 80% to 120% of normal, to a constant 100% of normal productivity regardless of delivery delay.

Conclusions

The problem of workload fluctuations at the Precision Company has been examined and the structure of information and decision flows causing that problem has been described. The structure has been changed and tested under new policies and for a reasonable range of error estimates. Precision's problem appears to have been eliminated under all these circumstances.

This chapter has provided an example of a particular situation and the factors that were judged to be important to that situation. One general conclusion that may be drawn from this study, however, is that fluctuations are often not externally caused but are internally generated. Problems of the nature of Precision's can best be examined in terms of closed feedback loops of cause and effect, and of the delays between these causes and effects. Even when a systems analysis as detailed as this one cannot be carried out, management analysis should consider the underlying system structure as a probable source of performance problems.

Notes

1. See Jay W. Forrester, *Industrial Dynamics* (Cambridge, Mass.: The MIT Press, 1961).

2. Appendix B contains the detailed description of the computer model.

3. Appendix B contains a listing of the computer model equations written in the DYNAMO language and the definitions of terms used in the model. Detailed explanation of DYNAMO is contained in A. L. Pugh III, *DYNAMO User's Manual*, fifth edition (Cambridge, Mass.: The MIT Press, 1976). That appendix also documents specific model conditions that produced each of the computer outputs shown in this chapter.

4. This behavior of feedback systems is illustrated and explained in *Industrial Dynamics* (see note 1) pp. 175, 177–180.

Part Three:
The Dynamics of Marketing and Distribution

A feedback-oriented approach to analyzing management problems and designing management policies finds numerous applications in the marketing and distribution aspects of the firm. The market so often provides the visible closure and feedback to corporate actions. Changes in price, promotion, product newness and quality, delivery delay and other dimensions of customer service affect market response. Market feedback includes orders in particular, but also customer satisfaction and needs, corporate reputation, and pressures for change.

From its start system dynamics modeling has been applied to phenomena of the marketplace, including the distribution systems that bring the product to market. Forrester's first model (Chapter 2) focused on the dynamics of multi-stage distribution systems, with their built-in time delays, amplification, and distortion of information. At each model stage the customer's ordering behavior is affected by information fed back from his supplier as to the expected delivery time of the goods ordered. The retailer tends to order further in advance if he expects the distributor to take longer in filling orders. The problem of slow deliveries by a supplier leads to heavier orders being received by the supplier, thus further slowing down his service. When cascaded through three or four stages of distribution channels, this type of amplification produces wide swings at the factory sector in orders and production, a common problem symptom in many multi-staged industries.

This early concern over the effect of delivery delay feedback on customer ordering patterns shows up again in the Sprague model (Chapters 6 and 7) as the only market feedback. Also in the Precision case (Chapter 10) and in Nord's work on product growth [5], the feedback of delivery delay information to the market has a primary effect on sales, although in these models longer delivery times discourage orders. For a period of time the graduate research assistants at M.I.T. were jokingly renaming their group the Delivery Delay Feedback Research Group, in recognition of the apparent ever-presence of this phenomenon in early industrial dynamics models.

However, three of the five articles selected for this Part do not involve delivery delay market feedback, but rather feature other forms of market interaction. The first

185

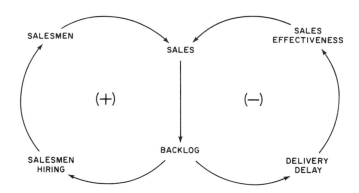

Figure 1   Market feedback loops from chapter 12

paper by Forrester (Chapter 11) discusses the dynamics of advertising. Without the aid of a simulation model, Forrester describes the kinds of market results that may be produced by varying advertising and/or price.

Forrester's article in Chapter 12 builds on one of his earlier papers that is not included in this book [2]. Chapter 12 ties together a two-loop market system with a capacity-ordering feedback loop. The two loops, one positive and one negative, produce a wide variety of possible patterns of corporate development, including sales growth, fluctuation and stagnation. These loops are shown in simplified form in Figure 1. The behavior produced by Forrester's model arises from the shifting dominance between these two loops and the chapter serves as an excellent tutorial in the behavior of simple feedback loops separately and in combination.

Chapter 13 analyzes the operations of a small raincoat manufacturer, identified in this case study as the Everdry Company. The article focuses on the interplay between production and market forces. In this aspect it resembles the Precision case of Chapter 10, although the two model structures are not similar. Chapter 13 synopsizes one of four system dynamics reports on textiles and apparel prepared by Pugh-Roberts Associates, Inc. under contract to the National Bureau of Standards (see Part 2 introduction for more detail). Treatment of retailer and distribution issues in Chapter 13 goes far beyond the limited aspects of inventory and order processing considered in Chapter 2. Other aspects of retailing are covered in Chapters 15 and 25.

The Everdry study was actually undertaken for the Department of Commerce, with Everdry merely being a cooperative firm. This led to certain conflicts between Everdry's and Commerce's interests and resulted in a delay of about one year before the changes suggested by the study were implemented. The results that were produced by the implementation are consistent with those indicated by the model. Equations for the model are presented in Appendix C at the end of this book.

In Chapter 14, Richard Wright, now a faculty member at Georgia Institute of Technology, describes work he undertook while an instructor at M.I.T. The series of modeling attempts to solve Scannell Trucking firm's operational problems were very revealing and, as related by Wright in his article, the findings were later successfully implemented.

Thomas Manetsch's article (Chapter 15) is based on his Ph.D. dissertation. His model of the production and distribution system of the U.S. plywood industry is of the same general type as Forrester's model of Chapter 2. A primary feature of Manetsch's work is the modeling of price determination. The dynamics of pricing has not been included in many system dynamics models, except for the works on commodity markets [4,9], and the treatment accorded in the works described in Chapters 13, 25, 29, 30, and 31. Yurow's article [10] illustrates another distribution system model similar to Chapter 15. Manetsch's model is represented in differential equation form and analog-type diagrams, similar to the Zymelman work [11] and different from the DYNAMO notation usually adopted in system dynamics works.

In addition to the works cited thusfar, numerous other published system dynamics efforts contain marketing orientations. For example, Chapters 16, 18, 19, 20, 21, and 22 relate various aspects of research and development to marketing. In particular, the editor's work on R&D project management focuses on the customer-company interrelationships in sponsored R&D work [6]. Chapters 24, 25, 28, 29 and 31 also treat the application of system dynamics to aspects of marketing.

Space limitations prevent including other marketing-related papers, including Helmut Weymar's interesting analysis of the company-market interactions in which advertising is the primary dynamic mechanism [8]. As a research assistant in the early M.I.T. system dynamics program, Weymar directed a cooperative project sponsored by Minute Maid Corporation prior to its merger with Coca-Cola. That project involved development of two major marketing models. The first related to the pricing, promotion and distribution of the Hi-C line of fruit drinks; the second was an overall study of Minute Maid's participation in the commodity market for oranges. The oranges market work was later followed up in related work [3].

Commodities have long been an area of special interest in the system dynamics program at M.I.T. [1,4,7,9]. For years the two-weeks M.I.T. summer course on system dynamics used commodity dynamics as the basis for teaching model formulation and computer simulation. Many varied commodities such as cattle, sugar and copper have been examined. The basic commodity models usually include the two negative feedback loops shown in Figure 2 reflecting supply and demand. As discussed in Chapter 1, each of these loops by itself can produce oscillatory behavior in market price and in supply/demand. In combination these two negative loops almost necessarily lead to fluctuating market conditions.

More sophisticated system dynamics commodity market models include representations of producer inventories and of conscious decisions to release goods from these inventories to the market. Pricing is based on inventory coverage, i.e. market inventories relative to the demand rate, rather than absolute inventory levels. Some commodity models have included price expectations, based on current price level and recent rate of change of prices, as influences upon producer and consumer decisions, bringing speculative factors to bear on the markets. Government control loops have been added,

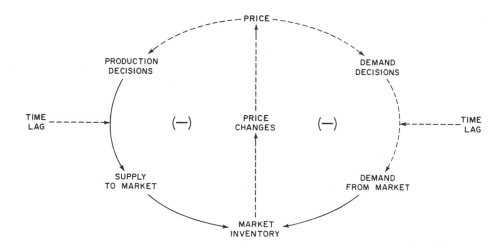

Figure 2   Basic commodity feedback loops

taking into account such policies as limits on production, buying and selling from government buffer inventories, and controls on price. These commodity markets have been good areas for system dynamics application, and private communications substantiate that many uses of these models have been made by professional commodity traders.

A review of several years' issues of the M.I.T. *System Dynamics Newsletter* shows many other applications of system dynamics in marketing. The Reuben H. Donnelly Corporation has studied salesmen allocation modeling through system dynamics. Goodyear Tire and Rubber has examined alternative distribution inventory systems via system dynamics models. Toyota Motor Distribution Company has used system dynamics models in examining alternative approaches to automobile distribution, while still another Japanese firm, Toa Nenryo, an affiliate of Exxon, developed a supply-demand model for petroleum products in Japan.

In retailing (in addition to Chapters 2, 13, 15, and 25) work has been undertaken for Morton Shoe Stores in regard to the management of a leased department merchandising operation. A series of system dynamics simulation models — interactive management games — have been developed for Montgomery Ward. Named as the Decision Dynamics Workshop, these games were implemented effectively and were used for training several hundred store and merchandising managers over a two year period. A series of confidential M.I.T. staff memos documents system dynamics work sponsored by Stop and Shop (a large chain of supermarkets) aimed at designing new approaches to individual store management incentives and controls.

References
1. Ballmer, Ray W. *Copper Market Fluctuations: An Industrial Dynamics Study* (unpublished M.I.T. S.M. thesis, 1960).

2. Forrester, Jay W. "Common Foundations Underlying Engineering and Management," *IEEE Spectrum*, vol. 1, no. 9 (September 1964). Also published in *Collected Papers of Jay W. Forrester*. Cambridge, Mass.: Wright-Allen Press, Inc., 1975.

3. Goldberg, Ray A. *Agribusiness Coordination: A Systems Approach to the Wheat, Soybean, and Florida Orange Economies*. Boston: Harvard Graduate School of Business Administration, 1968.

4. Meadows, Dennis L. *Dynamics of Commodity Production Cycles*. Cambridge, Mass.: Wright-Allen Press, Inc., 1970.

5. Nord, Ole C. *Growth of a New Product: Effects of Capacity-Acquisition Policies*. Cambridge, Mass.: The MIT Press, 1963.

6. Roberts, Edward B. *The Dynamics of Research and Development*. New York: Harper & Row, 1964.

7. Schlager, Kenneth J. *Systems Analysis of the Copper and Aluminum Industries: An Industrial Dynamics Study* (unpublished M.I.T. S.M. thesis, 1961).

8. Weymar, F. Helmut. "Industrial Dynamics: Interaction Between the Firm and its Market." In Alderson and Shapiro (eds.), *Marketing and the Computer*. Englewood Cliffs, N.J.: Prentice-Hall, 1963.

9. Weymar, F. Helmut. *The Dynamics of the World Cocoa Market*. Cambridge, Mass.: The MIT Press, 1968.

10. Yurow, Jerome A. "Analysis and Computer Simulation of the Production and Distribution Systems of a Tufted Carpet Mill," *Journal of Industrial Engineering*, January 1967.

11. Zymelman, Manuel. "A Stabilization Policy for the Cotton Textile Cycle," *Management Science*, March 1965.

Advertising: A Problem in Industrial Dynamics

Jay W. Forrester

How well is the impact of advertising on other company operations taken into account in advertising policies?

How adequate — in aim and contents as well as in amount — is advertising research?

How can a sudden change in advertising expenditures designed to get prospects to buy quicker create havoc in other distribution operations and in the factory?

What are the time effects of a periodic sales promotion on the costs of manufacture and of distribution?

How does the mission and social justification of advertising vary from stage to stage in a product's life cycle?

The thoughtful top executive looks at advertising differently from most advertising managers, copywriters, and researchers. He sees advertising as but *one* of many tools available to management for influencing the forces that determine company success. Having no personal involvement in advertising, he readily agrees that it is a powerful and important influence in our present-day economy, but he does not think of it as an end in itself. He would properly feel that its goal is not merely to generate impact or consumer awareness, that its primary purpose is not even merely to sell. Instead, advertising should operate as part of a team for creating long-range profitable company success — with a special emphasis on those words "long-range" and "profitable."

This viewpoint makes quite a difference. If we look at advertising the way so many specialists do, much of the current thinking and research about the subject might make sense. But if we look at advertising from a top-management viewpoint, a great deal of the work that has been going on does not add up at all.

I think it is time that we ask some different kinds of questions about advertising — questions that I would like to see more executives pressing upon their

This article was first prepared as a speech, "The Relationship of Advertising to Corporate Management," and published in *Proceedings of the Fourth Annual Conference of the Advertising Research Foundation,* October 2, 1958. It was revised to appear in *Harvard Business Review* 37, no. 2 (March-April 1959), pp. 100–110. (© 1959 by the President and Fellows of Harvard College, all rights reserved.)

advertising managers and research agencies, and that more scholars and educators should be looking into. In this article I shall suggest the kinds of inquiries which I have in mind, and outline briefly a new way of thinking that should help provide answers to them.

LEADING PROBLEMS

The worries which the top executive has—or might well have—about advertising do not concern matters such as readable copy, exciting graphics, program ratings, and choice of media. To him, such topics should be of only secondary importance. The real problems are far more basic. They include such matters as the time and scope relationships of advertising to other company functions, the aims and nature of advertising research, and the relationship of the agency to the company client.

Purposes and Functions.   For example, how adequately do advertising policies and measurements recognize some of the very long-delayed responses and aftereffects that exist? Advertising campaigns that look successful from the short-term view of a few weeks may have delayed reactions that are detrimental over a period of several years. Advertising schedules improperly related to market and production conditions can produce disastrous shifts in the *timing* of sales without increasing long-run total sales; or can produce peaks and valleys in the sales pattern which do nothing but increase factory and distribution costs. As for measurements made on this season's advertising effectiveness, they may be seriously misinterpreted because they include a long series of past market, product, and advertising conditions.

Again, consider the narrowness of scope of many advertising operations. How well are they integrated with product design and production? All too often product improvement exists only in the advertising office and not in the engineering and manufacturing departments. Too often advertising creates a product image which is not supported by the product itself; or it builds a picture of a company personality which is not reflected by company salesmen and service men. Advertising is often used as a fire department to cope with crises which might better have been handled as a coordinated program of fire prevention.

What is the purpose of advertising? Advertising is part of the flow of communications which ties our economic system together. But does advertising always communicate? It often tries to sell qualities that are not present in the product. At the other extreme, it often fails to mention features that set the product apart from and above its competitors. If there is any serious effort to communicate, it seems to get lost in an advertising-industry fascination with the psychological behavior of the consumer. The emphasis seems to be on how to force the consumer in a certain direction or on how to get the buyer to purchase in spite of himself.

Direction of Research.   At a different level there is the question of what advertisers are asking of their advertising research agencies and organizations. It seems to me that most of advertising research is superficial and deals with symptoms, not causes.

Let us begin by setting a standard. What is true research? It should be the seeking for fundamental principles. It should be the search for laws governing physical or social behavior. The successful results of such an effort have enduring value in explaining and predicting what happens.

Research is not the mere measurement of performance. In fact, performance measurement lies at the opposite end of the product sequence from research. Over-all performance measurement may tell us something of the *quality* of the prior research, but the measurement itself does *not* constitute the research. Take, for example, the relationship of physical research to a specific product. In producing jet engines we start by studying the characteristics of new metals and the chemistry of fuels, and by extending our knowledge of the laws of thermodynamics. That is research. The results have some permanence. Not only will they be useful in future jet engines, but also they will contribute to the entire fields of metallurgy and power generation. On the research foundation, we carry out development, product design, production, sale, installation, and use. Then and only then, do we finally verify the effectiveness of our efforts by measuring the performance of the equipment produced. And note that this measurement of performance is not the research but the ultimate *evaluation* of the quality of the original research, as well as of the succeeding design and production.

By contrast, advertising seems to start at the design step. The advertising is turned out, and then a performance measurement is attempted. The research step has been skipped, and the final measurement is misleadingly called research.

What would the research step include if it were not skipped? The company should, I believe, strive for lasting answers to such basic questions as:

What is the real relationship of a secondhand market to new-product sales?

What fraction of sales represents the actual rate of product usage and what fraction represents a one-time building up of the necessary product inventory in the customer's hands?

What are the typical phases in the development of a style fad as a guide to future design plans? [3]

Is advertising being used as a tool to help to stabilize factory production and employment, or is it causing cyclical fluctuation in orders and profits?

When are sales being primarily influenced by advertising, when by underlying demand and need, when by general economic conditions?

Are we measuring how many television sets are tuned to programs, or how many magazine advertisements are being noticed, when we should be determining how well the public is satisfied with our product?

Do current sales correlated against the latest advertising campaign tell us whether or not we are, for example, merely selling in March what we would otherwise have sold in June?

Are we attributing to advertising results which really arise from price changes?

Is advertising trying to overcome a product deficiency which might better be corrected in the laboratory?

In short, it seems to me that most advertising research measures the composite results of campaigns and does not establish enduring principles to guide future work. Much stands to be gained by changing the emphasis of research, by asking different questions and seeking different answers. We have—or are rapidly acquiring—the know-how. Will we get the right direction and support from top management?

In time, the answer is certain to be yes. Already some companies are beginning research programs into the true nature and purpose of advertising [2] . Also, some consulting organizations and academic institutions are beginning to delve into the basic market forces and their interactions rather than being content with gross over-all measurements of sales changes [1].

Effort and Organization.   Businessmen might well be uneasy about advertising research for still other reasons. For one thing, is the *amount* of it anywhere near adequate? I doubt that there is any other function in industry where management bases so much expenditure on such scanty knowledge. The advertising industry spends 2 percent or 3 percent of its gross dollar volume on what it calls "research," and even if this were really true research, the small amount would be surprising. However, I estimate that less than a tenth of this amount would be considered research *plus* development as these terms are defined in the engineering and product-research departments of companies. In other words, probably no more than one-fifth of 1 percent of total advertising expenditure is used to achieve an enduring understanding of how to spend the other 99.8 percent.

Apparently, therefore, the advertising industry as a whole is characterized by a different attitude toward research and progress than, say, the electronic, chemical, or aircraft industries in their product research. Why? I do not feel that the explanation has much to do with the ethics, ideals, or innate competence of advertising men; in these respects they seem to measure up as well as other people (best-selling books to the contrary). But I do suspect that superficial, defeatist attitudes toward research reflect the way the industry is organized and the way responsibilities are subdivided. For example:

1. Advertising *should* be an integral part of corporate operation. The amount, timing, character, and objectives of outlays *should* be geared to the status of product research, manufacturing, inventories, and price, and to the moral and ethical standards by which the corporation wishes to be known. Instead, in actual practice, advertising is separated by barriers even stronger than those that impede the integration of other corporate functions! Not only is advertising in a separate corporate department where there is little access to information about marketing and distribution operations, let alone operations in manufacturing or research, but most of the work is carried out in a separate company—the advertising agency.

2. To compound the difficulties which agencies would have under the best of circumstances (and those difficulties would be considerable in view of the present state of the art), it has become the practice for companies to judge the performance of an agency on immediate results. This short-range view is accentuated by our practices of rapid executive rotation and by our short-term executive evaluation methods such as the return-on-investment measure. I have even noticed that one television survey service plans to have viewers' sets permanently wired to a central electronic computer. The advertiser can then learn his audience rating every 90

seconds. In such an environment can management expect dedication to the long-run welfare of the corporation when this conflicts with the immediate present?

For example, over a period of 20 or 30 years, a number of our large corporations have developed a reputation for honesty and the delivery of the best value that the existing technology could provide. Such a reputation will persist for 10 years or more whether or not currently justified. It is to be expected that under extreme pressure for immediate results, marketing and pricing methods could take advantage of this carefully built reputation to the detriment of future customer confidence.

TIME RELATIONSHIPS

So much for the problems of advertising. To deal constructively with these problems I want to suggest an approach that I call "industrial dynamics," and which is described in my previous *Harvard Business Review* article ("Industrial Dynamics: A Major Breakthrough for Decision Makers," July–August 1958; see Paper 1 in this volume). In general terms, this means recognizing the company not as a collection of separate functions but as a system in which the *flows* of information, materials, manpower, capital equipment, and money set up forces that determine the basic tendencies toward growth, fluctuation, and decline.

Such an approach has a great deal to offer advertising because it takes *time relationships* into account. Proper recognition of the effects of time in advertising and market actions should go far in clarifying the existing controversies in the advertising field. For instance, answering the argument over the social value of advertising in our economic system depends on the relationship of advertising to the life cycle of the particular product. Advertising can be the mainspring of our capitalist system when it is used to communicate information about new products, but when used to sustain continued sales growth beyond the saturation level of an older product, it can actually increase costs, produce an economic loss, and eventually lead to the downfall of the very product whose success it was intended to enhance.

Effects of Sudden Increase. Of the many possible illustrations of time effects in advertising I shall take only a few. A good example to start with is the campaign designed to get customers to buy more quickly. Such campaigns are, of course, fairly common, and a typical situation can be simplified without doing too much injustice to reality.

To begin, what are some of the effects on an industry as a whole of consumers' decisions to defer purchases for a while? A hypothetical product market (or, more precisely, a subgroup of consumers) is shown in Figure 1. Here is a pool of "prospective customers" who are aware of their impending need to buy a product but who have not yet purchased it. To see what can happen, assume that the inflow of prospective customers is constant. This represents a demand which is created by natural circumstances and not by advertising. For example, it might represent the demand for refrigerators on the part of house builders where the builder knows as soon as he starts a house that he will need to purchase a refrigerator.

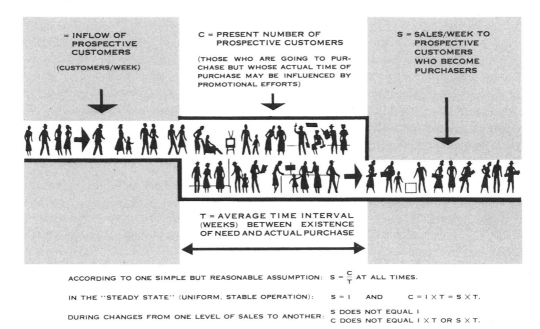

According to one simple but reasonable assumption: $S = \frac{C}{T}$ at all times.

In the "steady state" (uniform, stable operation): $S = I$ and $C = I \times T = S \times T$.

During changes from one level of sales to another: S does not equal I. C does not equal $I \times T$ or $S \times T$.

Figure 1   Constant inflow of customers

On the average, the prospective customer will exist as such for a certain period of time before actually buying. This period may be very different for different products—for refrigerators it may be 20 weeks, for raincoats 20 days. If advertising has *any* effect on these prospective customers, it must take the form of influencing the average length of time before they make a purchase. (Note that we are talking about only one possible effect of advertising. In this part of the market, advertising can affect the time of purchase but not total long-term sales. Long-term sales are controlled entirely by the inflow of prospective customers, here assumed constant but, in reality, affected by still other dynamic aspects of advertising.)

Looking at Figure 2, we see some effects of a sudden change in advertising expenditure rate. Taking the curves in order, from the top of the chart to the bottom:

1. The curve at the top shows the increase in advertising.
2. The second curve shows a buildup in what I call advertising "pressure." By this I simply mean the persuasiveness of the advertising to the prospective customer. It builds up more gradually than the actual increase in advertising because of the time that is required for the advertising campaign to achieve full effect.
3. The third curve shows the decrease in the average waiting time, a change which results from increased advertising pressure.
4. Reducing the average waiting time before purchase causes the total number of prospective customers in the pool to decrease. This is shown in the fourth curve.
5. In the last curve, at the bottom of Figure 2, we see the actual sales rate. It rises as the waiting time is reduced and the pool of prospective customers is partially depleted. Sales then fall again to the initial rate. It is impossible for sales to stay at a higher

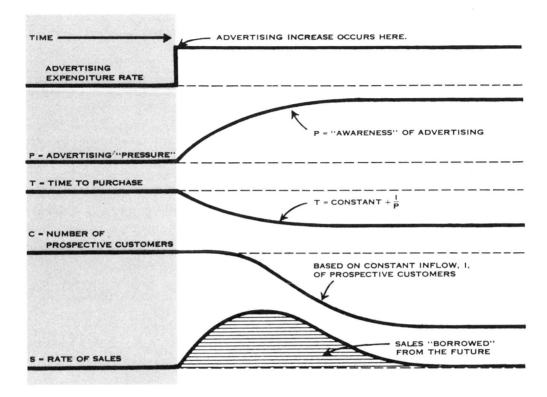

Figure 2   Effects of sudden advertising increase

level because in the circumstances, as set forth in Figure 1, the inflow of new prospective customers is constant.

Note that as soon as steady-state conditions have been reestablished, the outflow or sales rate must necessarily equal the inflow of prospective customers. The shaded area under the last curve of Figure 2 therefore represents sales "borrowed" from the future.

If the time from the beginning of the advertising campaign to the peak of the sales curve should be several weeks or several months long, it would be very easy and natural for management to mistake the rising sales level for a permanent improvement attributable to the advertising campaign itself.

Campaign Aftermath.   See now what happens when the advertising campaign is terminated. Figure 3 is like Figure 2 except that the advertising campaign increases, runs at a higher level for a period of time, and then returns to its original level. Advertising pressure rises gradually, reaches a saturation, and, after the end of the advertising campaign, falls off. Likewise, the average delay before the prospective customer buys is reduced, reaches a new lower value, and, after the end of the advertising campaign, rises gradually to its original length of time. The initial increase in sales causes the number of prospective customers in the pool to drop to a lower level. After the end of the advertising campaign, as the lowest curve shows, the system relaxes back to its initial longer waiting period during which time sales fall below their average value.

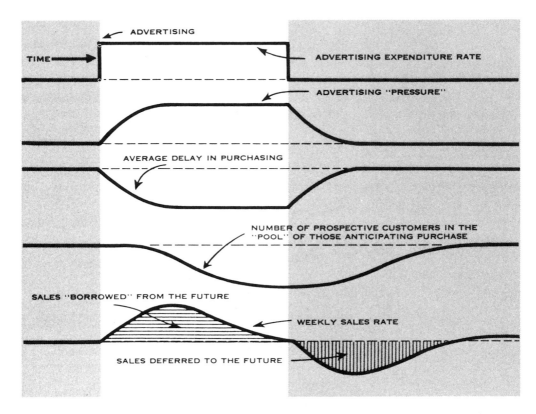

Figure 3   Effects of terminating campaign

The net result of the campaign: sales have simply been moved from the second shaded section of the curve to the first shaded section without affecting the total sales for the entire period. I believe that we would expect the behavior shown here to be an important part of the market pattern in consumer durable goods. It may even be very significant in clothing and expendables.

Fluctuations Exaggerated.   Earlier I referred to the troublesome tendency to think of advertising as a subject by itself, without relating its behavior to the behavior of other company operations and vice versa. Let us now, therefore, trace the effects of an advertising change more deeply into the company, adding retail and factory sales to our distribution picture. In Figure 4 we see another series of response curves (all hypothetical, yet reflecting a considerable amount of composite company experience):

1. In the first curve we assume that the inflow of prospective customers has suddenly increased because the need for or popularity of the product has increased.
2. As the market grows, we find in the second curve that the number of buyer prospects in the pool will gradually rise.
3. Actual sales will correspondingly begin to increase, as shown by the third curve.
4. When retail sales increase, it is customary, as we all know, for higher inventory levels to be carried at the different levels of distribution. Also, for a higher level of

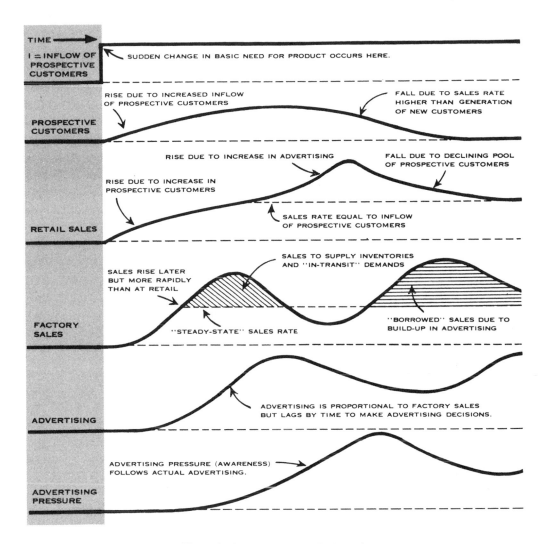

Figure 4 Permanent increase in demand

business there must be more orders and goods in transit in the supply pipelines of the system. Consequently, as we see in the fourth curve, the factory sales start rising. They are later than retail sales because of the time delays in the placing of orders. However, once they start to rise, they rise more rapidly and to a higher peak than the actual retail sales because of the inventory and pipeline influences.

5. In many companies the advertising level is, in fact, determined as a fraction of the sales and production forecast. In the fifth curve is shown the rise in advertising expenditure which might follow the factory sales in such a company. This advertising expenditure is delayed by the length of time necessary to make advertising decisions and to act on them.

6. The curve at the bottom shows the advertising pressure or awareness on the part of the prospective consumers.

Note that as advertising pressure begins to rise, it further boosts the rising retail sales curve (third curve). This new retail rise occurs at a time when the factory sales have already satisfied the initial inventory demands of the system and have fallen to their new steady-state level corresponding to the new rate of inflow of prospective customers. The peak in the middle of the retail sales curve then produces another peak at the factory (fourth curve).

This kind of graphical analysis is totally unsatisfactory except to convey an impression of *some* of the time relationships that management should analyze. In a system of this kind, with retail sales affecting factory sales, which in turn affect advertising, which in turn affect retail sales, it is necessary to treat the entire system as a closed-loop, information-feedback system to learn its behavior. The over-all behavior is not divulged by any analysis of one piece at a time.

The need is for the more comprehensive type of analysis outlined in my previous *Harvard Business Review* article (Paper 1 in this volume). Turning back to that article (particularly Figure 15), the interested reader can see in some detail how changes in the level of advertising expenditures proportional to planned sales might, in a typical distribution system, produce devastating peaks and valleys in the factory production and inventory curves. Can management afford not to know more about these effects?

Periodic Sales Promotion.   Let us turn now to some other time effects of advertising, as shown in Figure 5.

Numerous products are promoted both by advertising and by price discounts on a periodic basis. As a result, a sales pattern of the sort illustrated in Figure 5 can develop. Sales rise during the promotion but fall sharply thereafter as customers use their accumulated stocks of the product. Sales then begin to rise back toward normal as

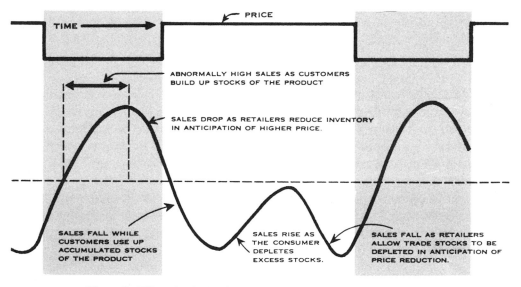

Figure 5 Effect of periodic price-reduction sales promotions on factory sales

customers deplete their excess stocks and reenter the market. Sales from the factory then take another sharp drop as *retailers* allow their stocks to be depleted in anticipation of restocking at lower prices during the forthcoming sales promotion.

Again we have a price and advertising pattern that probably has little effect on total long-run sales but can have serious repercussions on the cost of manufacture and distribution.

Product Life Cycle. Figure 6 shows the typical life cycle of a product from its introduction as an innovation through the phases of market growth, market maturity, and finally sales decline as it is replaced by some successor. The typical profitability peak rises to its maximum value ahead of the sales peak and then declines, sometimes to the point of unprofitability. This kind of growth pattern has, of course, a different duration for different products. For automobiles it may be 90 years long; for hula hoops it is probably 90 days.

It might be worthwhile to ponder the mission and extent of advertising during this life cycle. During product introduction, advertising tells customers of the existence of the new product. This is communication in its most useful form and is essential to the growth and development of our economy. In the market growth phase, competing product designs will show true product technological differentiation. Here advertising serves to stress the relative merits of differing products, thus helping to crystallize the most effective and acceptable design and to enhance product utility.

Advertising as a percentage of sales probably falls during the market growth period because total sales are rising so rapidly. In fact, we might expect a minimum fraction of sales going into advertising near the end of this phase because it is often characterized by demand exceeding production capacity with very little incentive to attempt to expand the market more rapidly.

As market maturity sets in, sales begin to hit the saturation level. Here the serious problems develop. Poor products fall by the wayside. Those that remain tend to be similar to one another, for the reasons given in Figure 6. Advertising may attempt to create product differentiation which does not, in fact, exist in the actual design. It sometimes becomes a shouting contest to attract customers by sheer volume.

It is in this phase that advertising becomes vulnerable to social criticism. I believe that we can trace much of the popular writing against advertising today to the fact that an unusually large number of our products are now in the market maturity phase. This simultaneous appearance of many products at the same stage of their life cycle has its origins in World War II. The big wartime and postwar upsurge in technological development which took place has now brought many new products to the market maturity phase together. This can be seen in such industrial lines as automobiles, synthetic textile fibers, household appliances, frozen foods, packaged food mixes, television sets, soaps, and detergents.

After the reshuffle which takes place during the market maturity phase, price, quality, and service will probably take precedence over sheer advertising volume in the selling of products. This last phase of the product life cycle may still be highly successful for many companies. We will see those firms in the profit struggle that have

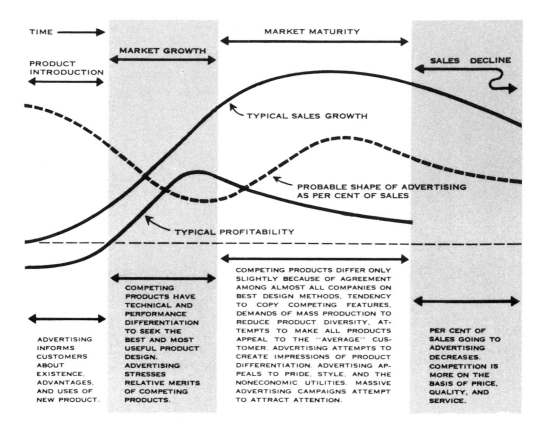

Figure 6   Typical life cycle of a product

made a sufficiently early start in laying the foundation for customer satisfaction and confidence. For other companies the market maturity phase simply marks the last desperate attempt to continue living as they did in the highly profitable market growth period. But at this point a company which persists in living in the past sooner or later awakes to find itself bankrupt.

Relation to Investment.   Advertising also affects capital investment, as shown in Figure 7. It was noted earlier that management often steps up the percentage and also the total volume of advertising in the maturity phase of the product life cycle. If this promotional effort has any effect, it will probably be to sustain market growth at the expense of a more rapid fall in later sales.

Now, one finds in many industrial situations that extrapolating the current market trend is a highly favored technique in planning future production plant capacity. Note in comparing the two curves in Figure 7 how advertising can contribute to overestimating production capacity and thus lead to excess and unused production facilities at a later time.

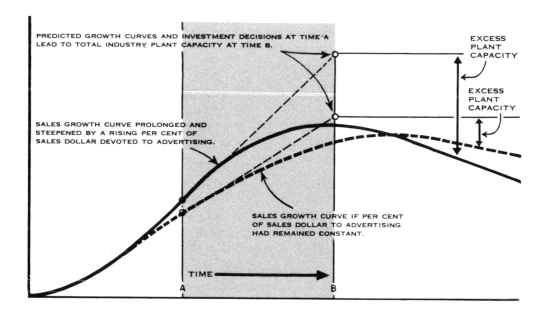

Figure 7 Possible interaction of promotional efforts and capital investment

CONCLUSION

I have described only some fragments of the dynamic marketing picture in which advertising plays a role. Numerous other critical time relationships also exist.

In trying to assess the combined implications of these many factors, intuition is totally unreliable (though it may provide dependable judgments on individual questions). We must turn instead to methods developed in the study of engineering and military-weapons systems. The most effective procedure follows five steps:

1. The available intuition, judgment, and experience about the firm's operations are drawn together.
2. These estimates and guesses are formulated mathematically into a single coherent system—or model. Such a formulation can be sufficiently comprehensive to include all the practical considerations that seem important.
3. The behavior of this sytem is then studied through digital computer simulation methods. The consequences of errors in the initial guesses can be determined and corrections made. At this point analysts are in a position to determine which factors and relationships are critical in company operations and which are unimportant. For example, the choice of advertising media might not have so much impact on the *company* as the timing of promotion campaigns.
4. After the critical factors have been identified, field measurements can be devised to secure needed data. This sequential approach conserves effort in the expensive field phase of the program.

5. The series of steps is repeated on a continuing basis to refine one's understanding and to introduce newly discovered factors.

Research into the fundamental nature of the industrial system and the consumer market is already getting under way in a number of places. Some industrial companies are beginning it, and so are a few consulting firms and a number of universities.

At the present time, perhaps only one-tenth of one percent of the nation's advertising budget goes toward what can properly be called "research and development" for improving advertising effectiveness. I venture to predict that, within a few years, 5 percent of total advertising expenditures will be devoted to true research and development, not including field measurement of advertising campaign results. Percentagewise, this is a tremendous increase—but is not every bit of it needed? The advertising industry seems to be built on a foundation of sand. Until management takes as much interest in understanding advertising in a conceptual way as it does in understanding physics and new products, the situation will not improve.

The challenge and new frontier in our capitalist society during the next three decades is not space flight but the science of management and economics. It is in management and economics, not on the moon or Mars, that the current international competition will be won. The American corporation is the heart of the American economic system. How well we fare will depend on how well American corporate management understands its job.

References

1. Alderson, Wroe. "Measuring the Sales Effectiveness of Advertising—A Progress Report," *Proceedings of the Fourth Annual Conference of the Advertising Research Foundation,* October 2, 1958.

2. "A Profit Yardstick for Advertising," *Business Week,* November 22, 1958, p. 49.

3. Robinson, Dwight E. "Fashion Theory and Product Design," *Harvard Business Review* 36, no. 6 (November–December 1958), p. 126.

12
Market Growth as Influenced by Capital Investment

Jay W. Forrester

INTRODUCTION TO SYSTEMS

To speak of systems implies a structure of interacting functions. Both the separate functions and the interrelationships as defined by the structure contribute to the system behavior. To describe a system, one must describe not only the separate functions but their method of interconnection. To identify the structure of a specific system, one should understand the fundamental nature of the structure common to all dynamic systems.

A dynamic system is one which changes with the progress of time. The parts interact to create a progression of system conditions. There is a basic structure common to all such systems, whether they be the systems encountered in engineering, in management, in economics, in nature, in psychology, or in any purposeful relationship of components.

The theory of system structure will here be described and exemplified in terms of four steps in a hierarchy:

> Closed boundary
> > Feedback loops
> > > Levels
> > > Rates
> > > > Goal
> > > > Observed condition
> > > > Discrepancy
> > > > Desired action

This paper was presented at the Ninth Annual Paul D. Converse Awards Symposium, University of Illinois, on April 13, 1967. Computer time for work reported herein was supported by Project MAC at M.I.T. under the Office of Naval Research contract no. Nonr-4102(01). The paper first appeared in the *Industrial Management Review* (currently published as the *Sloan Management Review*) 9, no. 2 (Winter 1968), pp. 83–105. (© 1968 by the Industrial Management Review Association; all rights reserved.)

If one has a theory of structure and confidence that the structure is universal in its applicability, such a theory greatly expedites the process of identifying and classifying the available information about an actual system. It is here asserted that such a theory of structure does exist, that it can be precisely stated, that it can be rigorously applied, and that it is of major practical value in organizing knowledge. The four hierarchies in the general theory of structure will now be discussed briefly and then illustrated by an example.*

CLOSED BOUNDARY

In defining a system, we start at the broadest perspective with the concept of the closed boundary. The boundary encloses the system of interest. It states that the modes of behavior under study are created by the interaction of the system components within the boundary. The boundary implies that no influences from outside of the boundary are necessary for generating the particular behavior being investigated. So saying, it follows that the behavior of interest must be identified before the boundary can be determined. From this it follows that one starts not with the construction of a model of a system but rather one starts by identifying a problem, a set of symptoms, and a behavior mode which is the subject of study. Without a purpose, there can be no answer to the question of what system components are important. Without a purpose, it is impossible to define the system boundary.

But given a purpose, one should then define the boundary which encloses the smallest permissible number of components. One asks not if a component is merely present in the system. Instead, one asks if the behavior of interest will disappear or be improperly represented if the component is omitted. If the component can be omitted without defeating the purpose of the system study, the component should be excluded and the boundary thereby made smaller. An essential basis for identifying and organizing a system structure is to have a sharply and properly defined purpose.

FEEDBACK LOOPS AS BUILDING BLOCKS

Inside the closed boundary one finds a structure of interacting feedback loops. The feedback loop is the structural setting within which all decisions are made. The feedback loop is a closed path. A decision is based on the observed state of the system. The decision produces action which alters the state of the system and the new state gives rise to new information as the input to further decisions. The feedback loop implies the circularity of cause and effect, where the system produces the decision which produces the action which produces change in the system. One has not properly identified the structure surrounding a decision point until the loops are closed between the consequences of the decision and the influence of those consequences on future decisions.

LEVEL AND RATE VARIABLES

Within the feedback loop we find the next lower hierarchy of structure. To represent the activity within a feedback loop requires two and only two distinctly

---

*For a more complete discussion of structure see [1].

different kinds of variables—the levels and the rates. The levels represent the system condition at any point in time. In engineering, the level variables are often referred to as the system state variables. In economics, the system levels are often spoken of as stocks. The levels are the accumulations within the system. Mathematically they are integrations.

The rate variables represent the system activity. The rate equations are the policy statements in the system which define how the existing conditions of the system produce a decision stream controlling action.

The clear separation of system concepts into the two classes of variables—levels and rates—has interesting and useful consequences. The level variables are the integrations of those rates of flow which cause the particular level to change. It follows that a level variable depends only on the associated rates and never depends on any other level variable. Furthermore, in any system, be it mechanical, physical, or social, rates of flow are not instantaneously observable. No rate of flow can depend on the simultaneous value of any other rate. Rates depend only on the values of the level variables. If levels depend only on rates and rates depend only on levels, it follows that any path through the structure of a system will encounter alternating level and rate variables.

POLICY STRUCTURE

An important substructure exists within the equation that defines a rate variable. A rate equation defining a rate variable is a statement of system policy.* Such a policy statement describes how and why decisions are made. A policy statement incorporates four components—the goal of the decision point, the observed conditions as a basis for decision, the discrepancy between goal and observed conditions, and the desired action based on the discrepancy.

A decision is made for a purpose. The purpose implies a goal that the decision process is trying to achieve. The policy statement that determines a rate variable does so in an attempt to bring the system toward the goal. The goal is sometimes adequately represented as a constant objective; more often the goal is itself a result of the past history of the system that has established traditions to guide present action. Whether or not the goal is actually achieved depends on how the system as a whole responds to the particular decision point. Usually, the competition for resource allocation results in the system falling short of most of the goals. The goal at the particular decision point is compared with the observed system condition as a guide to action.

One must distinguish observed conditions from the actual conditions of a system. A system model must incorporate both actual and apparent system levels (the levels describe the condition or state of the system). Where an important difference can exist between what the system is and what it is thought to be (and these differences are especially prevalent in the marketing sector of a company), one represents both, and explicitly shows how the apparent states arise out of the true states. A decision can be based only on the observed conditions, that is, the available information. Very often,

---

*For a more complete description of a policy statement see [2, chapter 10].

substantial deviations exist between the true conditions of a system and the observed conditions. The discrepancy can arise from delay in recognizing changes in the system, random error, bias in not wanting to believe what is visible, distortion, insensitivity, and misinterpretation of meaning.

The policy statement makes a comparison of the goal and apparent condition to detect a discrepancy. The discrepancy may be in the form of a difference, a ratio, or some other indicator of lack of agreement.

On the basis of the discrepancy, the policy describes the action to be taken.

A SYSTEM EXAMPLE IN MARKETING

The preceding concepts of system structure will now be illustrated in terms of a set of relationships often encountered in the growth of a new product.

Marketing couples the resources of a company to the desires of the customers. As such it represents the interface across which flow goods, services, money, and information. But these flows across the boundary are a consequence of interactions within the company, within the market, and between the two. Market dynamics can be understood only in the context created by other company functions because these other functions produce the variables with which marketing must deal.

As stressed above, one can identify a system only in terms of an objective. Here the objective is to identify and to explain one of the systems which can cause stagnation of sales growth even in the presence of an unlimited market. In particular, we deal here with that system which causes sales stagnation, or even sales decline, to arise out of an overly cautious capital investment policy. In this system inadequate capacity limits the growth in product sales.

Figure 1 illustrates the scope of the system being considered. The closed boundary surrounds the relationships shown. No other influences from the outside are necessary for creating the sales growth and stagnation patterns which will presently be developed.

Within the closed boundary the system consists of interacting feedback loops as illustrated in Figure 1. Three major loops are shown. Loop 1 is a positive feedback loop involving the marketing effort here described in terms of hiring of salesmen. It provides the driving power for sales growth. Only positive feedback loops can produce sustained growth. A positive loop is one in which activity changes the condition of the system in such a direction as to produce still greater activity. Assuming a favorable set of conditions around the loop, here is a situation in which salesmen book orders followed by product delivery which generates revenue which produces the sales budget which permits hiring still more salesmen. In short, salesmen produce revenue to pay for the further expansion of the sales effort.

However, Loop 2, on the upper right, involves delivery delay and sales effectiveness and can make the product sufficiently unattractive that the sales loop is no longer able to generate revenue greater than its current expenditures. The delivery delay in Loop 2 can convert the salesmen-hiring in Loop 1 from positive-feedback growth behavior to negative-feedback goal-seeking behavior. Negative loops are goal seeking and adjust activity toward some target value. Here Loop 2 is a negative feedback loop

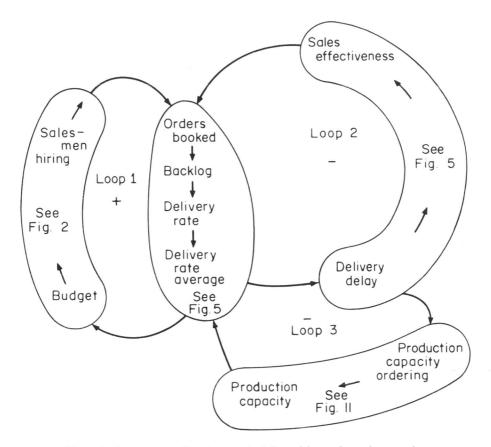

Figure 1 Loop structure for sales growth, delivery delay, and capacity expansion

and tends to adjust the incoming order rate to equal the production capacity. It is common to think of the order rate as determining the production capacity, but under many circumstances production capacity is instead determining the order rate. This phenomenon takes place within Loop 2. Orders booked increase the order backlog which increases the delivery delay which makes the product less attractive and reduces the order rate. Were the order rate to be sustained above the production capacity, the backlog and the delivery delay would continue to increase until the product could no longer be sold.

Production capacity is determined in Loop 3. Here a very simplified capital investment policy will be represented to keep the example within permissible size. The ordering of new production capacity is a function of delivery delay only. Rising order backlog, as indicated by delivery delay, is taken as an indication of inadequate capacity, and orders for more capacity are placed. These orders, after an acquisition delay, add to the production capacity. Loop 3 is a negative feedback loop which is attempting to change production capacity to adjust the order backlog to a value determined by a management goal for proper delivery delay. As the delivery delay rises, production capacity is raised to bring down the delivery delay.

These loops will be examined in turn to show their detailed structure and their behavior. The flow diagrams and system equations define a complete simulation model of the simplified company-market system so that the time sequences implied by the system description can be computed and plotted.*

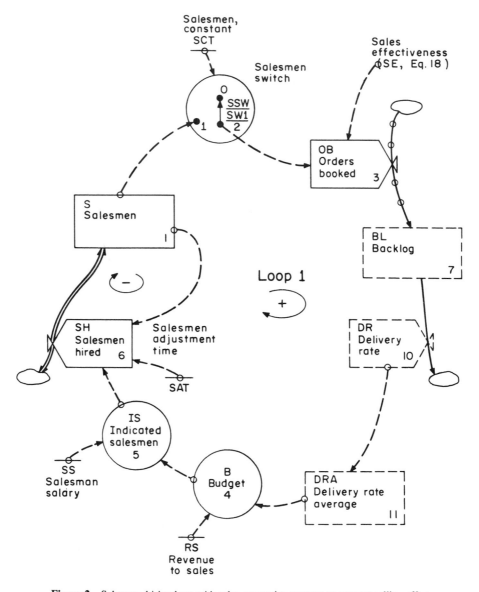

Figure 2   Salesmen-hiring loop with sales generating revenue to support selling effort

*The detailed equations and their descriptions are given in the Appendix.   Equation structure is described in [2]. Equation details conform to the DYNAMO compiler as described in [3].

SALESMEN-HIRING LOOP

The detailed structure of the positive feedback loop governing the hiring and level of salesmen is shown in Figure 2.

In the flow diagrams, the level equations are shown as rectangles, as for salesmen in this figure. The rate variables are shown by the valve symbol, as for salesmen hired. The circles are "auxiliary" variables which are algebraically substitutable into the following rate equations and are structurally part of the rate equation.

Considering that the auxiliary variables are part of the associated rate variables, we see in Figure 2 the alternating rate and level substructure within a feedback loop. The salesmen-hiring rate feeds the salesmen level. The salesmen level controls the orders booked rate. Orders booked as a rate flows into the backlog level. The backlog level is depleted by the delivery rate. The delivery rate is an input to the delivery rate average, which is a level. (All averages are generated by an accumulation process and, by both mathematical form and structural location, are necessarily system levels.) The delivery rate average, being a level, feeds into the salesmen-hired rate.

In Figure 2 the "Salesmen Switch" SSW at the top of the figure has been put in to agree with the specific equations in the Appendix. The switch allows activation or deactivation of the loop in simulation model runs. For the purpose of this discussion it should be considered in Position 1.

The positive feedback character of Loop 1 shown in Figure 2 gives this market system its growth tendencies. With a sufficiently attractive product and a sufficiently high fraction of revenue devoted to the sales budget, conditions are such that salesmen produce orders booked which increases backlog which increases delivery rate which increases the budget which increases the indicated salesmen that can be supported which causes a salesmen-hiring rate which increases the number of salesmen.

Such a positive feedback loop has an exponential growth character as shown in Figure 3. Here, Loop 1 alone causes ever-increasing growth without limit in the loop variables. The growth rate depends on the delays around the loop and on the conversion coefficients that determine loop amplification. Delays around the loop occur in the order backlog, in the delivery rate averaging, which here represents the billing and collection delay, and in the salesmen adjustment time SAT, which here represents the delays in budgeting and the delay in finding and training salesmen. The value of 20 months for SAT is probably shorter than correct for most systems. If any of these delays are increased, the growth rate will be slower.

The effect of changing the gain around the sales-hiring loop in Figure 2 can be shown by making a large change in the sales effectiveness. If sales effectiveness is reduced, it means that a given number of salesmen will book fewer orders and produce less revenue and thereby support a smaller sales budget. If the sales effectiveness were made small enough, a given number of salesmen would produce revenues too small to support themselves. Under these circumstances the indicated salesmen would be fewer than the existing number of salesmen, and salesmen-hiring would become salesmen reduction. Under such circumstances, the positive feedback loop would have been

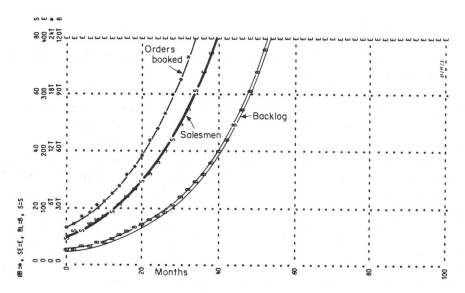

Figure 3   Unlimited exponential growth in Loop 1

converted to a negative feedback loop tending toward zero salesmen and zero activity. This change in sales effectiveness is shown in Figure 4. Here conditions are as in Figure 3 until week 36. At week 36 the sales effectiveness has been reduced from 400 units per man-month (400 units per month sold by each salesman) to 100 units per man-month. In other words, the imaginary condition has been created where the product is four times harder to sell. Orders booked drop immediately but rise again by a small amount because the number of salesmen is still increasing. After the time for the lower order rate to propagate through the order backlog and the delay in delivery rate averaging, the number of salesmen starts to decline, and, along with the declining salesmen, there is a corresponding decline in orders booked and in backlog. Figure 4 is included to give a feeling for the behavior of the loop in Figure 2. The sudden change in product attractiveness and the fourfold decrease in sales effectiveness would of course not be expected in an actual system.

MARKET LOOP

In Figure 5, the major loop, Loop 2 from Figure 1, connects delivery delay of the market, generates sales effectiveness, and influences the rate of orders booked. A minor loop relates order backlog and production capacity to generate the delivery rate.

The delivery delay of a product is given approximately by the ratio of backlog to delivery rate. In other words, the time to fill an order is indicated by how long the present delivery rate will require to work its way through the present order backlog. The delivery delay indicated DDI is the ratio of the present backlog to the present short-term average of the delivery rate DRA. But this present condition of delivery delay, as implied by present backlog and present delivery rate, ordinarily does not

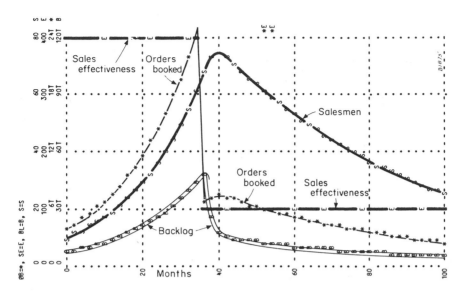

Figure 4   Initial growth in Loop 1 followed by decline when sales effectiveness is reduced

immediately reach the attention of decision makers within the system. The delivery delay recognized by the company DDRC is a delayed version of delivery delay indicated DDI. The delivery delay recognized by the company is an input to the production capacity ordering decision and also forms the basis of delivery quotations to the market. The market takes time to respond to changing delivery delay quotations, so a further delay intervenes before the delivery delay is recognized by the market, at DDRM. On the basis of DDRM the attractiveness of the product to the customers is determined. Figure 6 shows the general kind of relationship which must necessarily exist between delivery delay and sales effectiveness. The figure shows the sales effectiveness from delay as a multiplier SEDM, which is a fraction given in terms of its maximum value. The maximum value of unity occurs at zero delivery delay. For very small increases in delivery delay the sales are unaffected. As delivery delay becomes long enough to be of concern to the customer, sales effectiveness drops rapidly and then levels out as the remaining customers are those who particularly want this specific product and are unwilling to change to competitive suppliers unless delivery delay becomes too long.

The switch at SEDS in Figure 5 permits opening of the market loop in the simulation runs. The sales effectiveness, SE, is given by multiplying the sales effectiveness from delay multiplier SEDM by the value of sales effectiveness maximum SEM. SEM represents the sales effectiveness when delivery delay is zero, assuming some particular and constant set of conditions with respect to price, quality, competence of salesmen, and other influences on the selling process. In Figures 5 and 6, one can see that, as the order backlog increases (assuming some constant production capability and therefore a limited delivery rate), the delivery delay indicated will increase. After a delay, the delivery delay recognized by the company DDRC increases, and

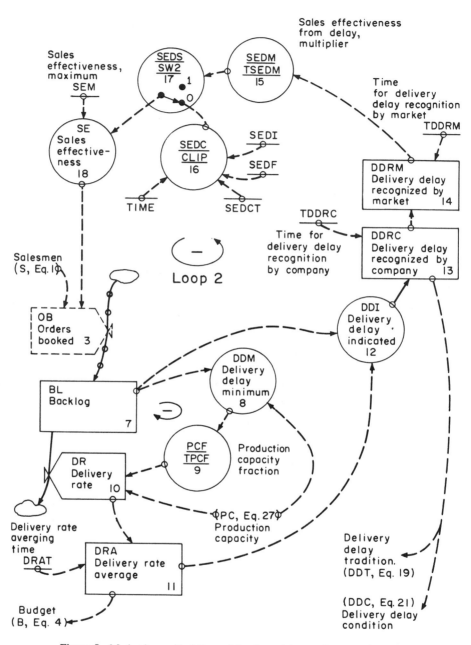

Figure 5   Market loop with delivery delay determining product attractiveness

after a further delay the delivery delay recognized by the market DDRM increases. This causes the sales effectiveness multiplier SEDM to decrease as shown in Figure 6, which causes sales effectiveness SE to decline and thereby reduces orders booked OB until the order backlog BL no longer rises.

In Figure 5 the small lower negative loop determines delivery rates in terms of

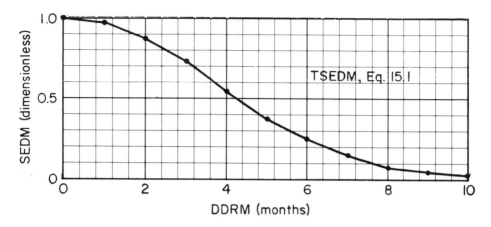

Figure 6   Table for sales effectiveness from delay multiplier as it depends on DDRM

backlog and production capacity. These relationships have two objectives. First, for a given production capacity they should properly relate delivery delay to backlog. When the backlog is low, the delivery rate should be such that the delivery delay is the minimum order filling and manufacturing time, taken here as two months. As the backlog rises, the delivery rate increases but gradually levels off as it approaches the production capacity. As the second objective, the relationships should permit changing the level of production capacity while retaining a proper relationship between backlog and delivery rate. This is done by first generating the concept of delivery delay minimum DDM, which is the ratio of backlog to the maximum production capacity. DDM then enters a table as given in Figure 7, which yields the fraction of the production capacity actually utilized. The rising slope of the curve in Figure 7 determines the minimum delivery delay caused by order handling and minimum manufactur-

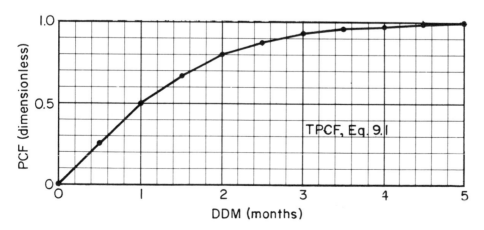

Figure 7   Table for production capacity fraction as it depends on delivery delay minimum

ing time. The curve is for a delivery delay of two months when capacity is lightly loaded. To see the effect, assume that backlog divided by maximum production capacity would yield an implied one-month delivery for DDM. The value of one month enters on the horizontal axis of Figure 7 and yields a production capacity fraction of 0.5. In other words, only half of the production capacity will be utilized. A delivery rate which is half the production capacity will work its way through the backlog in two months. Likewise, smaller backlogs yielding smaller values of delivery delay minimum will produce still smaller values of the production capacity fraction. Going in the other direction, as the backlog increases, the fraction of capacity utilization increases but not as rapidly as the increase in backlog. As shown in Figure 7 the delivery delay minimum must increase to five months before the theoretical maximum capacity is achieved. This extra time permits scheduling, ordering of materials, rearrangement of work load, and backlogging items in front of each machine so that it can be fully utilized.

A negative feedback loop, as in Loop 2 of Figure 5, is goal seeking. Here the loop tends to adjust the rate of order booking to equal the delivery rate. If order booking is too high, the backlog rises and decreases the rate of order booking and vice versa. But such adjustment does not necessarily progress smoothly to the equilibrium conditions. Because of the three delays around the loop—in the order backlog, in the company recognition of delivery delay, and in the market recognition of delivery delay—the adjustments may occur too late and cause a fluctuating condition in the system. Such is shown in Figure 8, which illustrates the behavior of Loop 2 when the number of salesmen is constant and the production capacity is constant (although delivery rate still depends on order backlog in the region below maximum production capacity). Figure 8 starts with a backlog and a delivery rate below their equilibrium values for the number of salesmen and the production capacity which have been used. The rate of order booking is initially too high because of the low backlog and the low delivery delay. But the order rate in excess of delivery rate causes backlog to rise and causes the delivery delay recognized by the market to rise. Sales effectiveness and orders booked fall. The rate of order booking declines below the delivery rate, thereby causing a decline in the order backlog. Fluctuations of decreasing amplitude continue over the period of 100 months shown in the figure.

This fluctuating condition is often found in actual market situations. Many factors enter to create the behavior in addition to those identified in Figure 5. When delivery delays become long, not only are the customers unwilling to order but previously placed orders are likely to be delivered later than had been promised and salesmen spend time explaining late orders rather than obtaining new orders. Salesmen become demoralized and feel there is no point in trying to sell a product which is not available. These factors reinforce one another to cause a downturn in orders. But orders must fall below the delivery capability before there is a reduction in the order backlog. One then finds a reverse situation. Backlog is falling, inventories are rising, deliveries are improving, pressure is put on salesmen to sell the product, the product becomes more attractive, and the order rate rises.

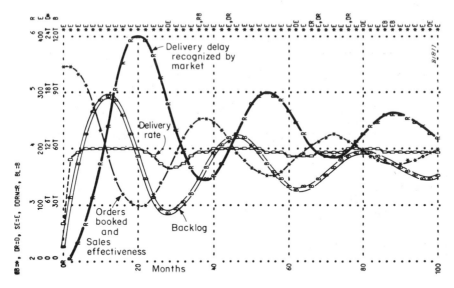

Figure 8 Fluctuation caused by delayed responses within Loop 2

COMBINED SALESMEN AND MARKET LOOPS

If Loops 1 and 2 of Figure 1, as detailed in Figures 2 and 5, are combined, system performance is as shown in Figure 9. Here a constant production capacity is assumed. The system starts with an initial number of salesmen but the number can change. The capacity is greater than needed to produce what the salesmen can sell. In Figure 9 exponential growth occurs until about the 30th month. But at that time delivery delay recognized by the market begins to increase. Sales effectiveness begins to decrease, order rates begin to level off, and revenue no longer supports the rapid expansion of the sales force. The righthand section of Figure 9 shows generally the kind of behavior already seen in Figure 8: sales overshoot and then return toward production capacity. The number of salesmen continue to increase for a time as the sales effectiveness continues to fall toward a value low enough that the salesmen generate only sufficient sales budget to maintain themselves.

The combined system consisting of Loops 1 and 2, as illustrated in Figure 9, can serve to show one of the broad classes of hazards in the changing of policies. Very often the symptoms of a difficulty superficially suggest a policy change which the system itself will defeat. Suppose that in the preceding system one were not aware of the importance of delivery delay in limiting sales. Such lack of awareness is found repeatedly on the industrial scene. As illustrated in a later figure, the lack of appreciation of the influence of delivery delay can arise simply from becoming accustomed to a particular level of order backlog. Or the lack of awareness can occur because the industrial system is so complex that few people see all of its manifestations at one time and are unaware of the implications on one section, such as the marketing effort, of conditions that exist elsewhere, as in production. Suppose, therefore, that the leveling

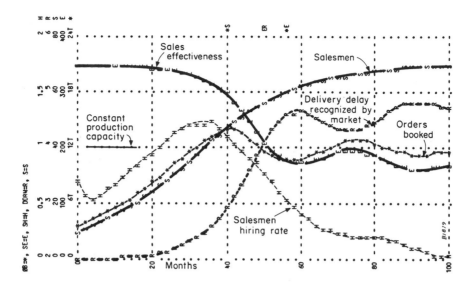

Figure 9   Sales growth and stagnation caused by interaction of Loops 1 and 2

off and stagnation of sales in Figure 9 were interpreted as a signal to increase the marketing effort. Such would be represented in this model by increasing the fraction of revenue going to sales RS in Figure 2. The particular numbers used here are incidental but, for the sake of the example, RS in Figure 9 represented a $12 contribution from revenue to sales for each unit of product sold where the unit selling price is $50. Suppose that this revenue to sales is raised from $12 to $13.60. One then finds the behavior shown in Figure 10. Here again the constant production capacity is 12,000 units per month. However, production capacity is often not clear and evident when one product is immersed in a manufacturing organization involving a multitude of products. The effect in Figure 10 is to increase slightly the early rate of product growth. The peak in orders booked is somewhat higher and occurs at 36 months instead of 42 months. However, in the long run, the effect of the higher budget allocation to sales is to increase the total number of salesmen and to decrease the sales effectiveness in exactly the right proportions so that the average orders booked continue to equal the available production capacity. The higher sales effort increases the selling pressure on the market, increases the order backlog, increases the product delivery delay, decreases the sales effectiveness, and results in the same level of sales. Profitability is, however, reduced because of the greater expenditure to support sales and may also be reduced because of the higher order backlog, the greater likelihood of factory confusion caused by rearranging schedules to expedite priority orders, and a less than optimum use of production equipment.

The differences between Figure 9 and Figure 10 illustrate a very common characteristic of multiple-loop, nonlinear systems. A change in policy can have quite unexpected equilibrium effects as well as unexpected dynamic effects. The change in policy may be aimed at a specific point in the system, here to increase the rate of order

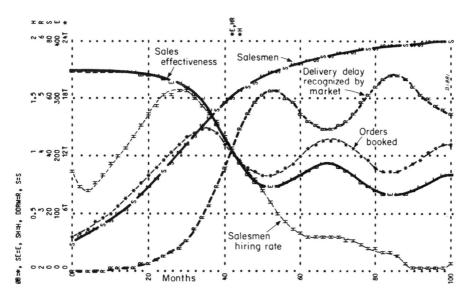

Figure 10 Higher budget to sales effort

booking. The consequence, however, may be an indirect warping of the system to defeat the intended result. Here the number of salesmen does indeed go up but the sales effectiveness goes down correspondingly.

CAPITAL INVESTMENT

Clearly, the fixed production capacity of Figures 9 and 10 is not typical. One should then explore capital investment policies. For the sake of illustration, one of these has been incorporated into the present example to show how capital investment policy can couple to market variables.

Figure 11 shows a basic part of the decision-making process for addition of production capacity. The addition of capacity is of course contingent on many factors such as projection of sales trends, financial condition, and product profitability. However, all of these tend to produce variations on a basic capacity addition rate which depends on the adequacy of the present capacity in terms of market demand. One of the most persuasive indicators of the adequacy of existing capacity is the size of the order backlog and the length of time the customer must wait for delivery. As the delivery delay rises above the company's goal, the pressure increases for expanding capacity. Figure 11 relates delivery delay to production capacity. In an earlier section of this paper it was suggested that a policy (rate equation) contains a statement of the decision-making goal and a detection of the related system state. In Figure 11, the delivery delay operating goal DDOG is generated in Equations 19, 20, and 20.1. Here the goal can be a fixed goal determined by management and adhered to rigidly as a constant goal. Or, at the other extreme, the goal can be the goal of matching the traditional delivery delay. Or any intermediate weighting factor can be used to blend

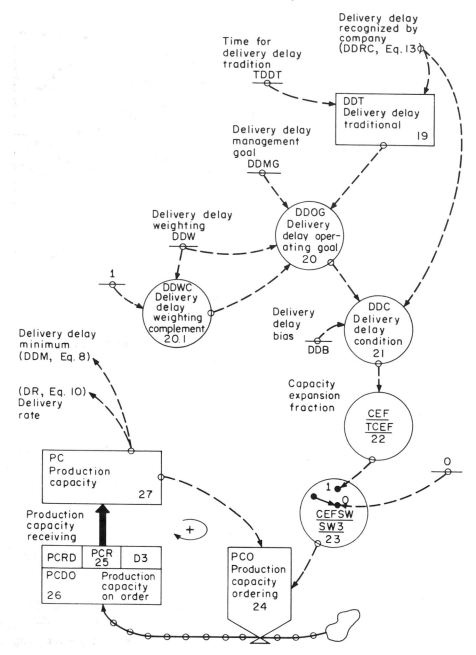

Figure 11   Capacity expansion loop

these two extremes of goals. Consider first a fixed delivery delay goal given by the constant DDMG which is here taken as two months and equals the minimum order processing and manufacturing time. The delivery delay condition DDC in Equation 21 is the ratio of the delivery delay recognized by the company DDRC to the delivery delay goal DDOG. From this ratio is subtracted a delivery delay bias DDB, which simply represents the competition for resources throughout the company and represents the deviation between goal and performance that is necessary to sustain any given level of resource allocation. A company under great pressure on resources would fall further behind its goals than a company not under pressure. The coefficient DDB would, in a more complete model, be a variable generated by such things as financial pressure within the organization and by the extent to which other operating goals were not being met. Once the ratio of performance to goal has been established and offset by the bias created by other pressures, the resulting delivery delay condition DDC is conceived to operate through a relationship similar to that in Figure 12. Here, as DDC rises above 1.0, capacity expansion occurs. When DDC falls, pressure on production capacity is reduced and resources are diverted to other areas. The vertical scale is given in terms of the fraction of existing capacity which is ordered each month. Again, the switch at CEFSW exists not in the real system but in the model to permit deactivating the capacity expansion loop. A minor positive feedback loop exists in the figure where capacity ordering adds to capacity, which adds to the capacity ordering rate because the variable coming in from CEF is in terms of the fraction per month of the existing capacity. The effect is to make capacity ordering a function of the operating scale that the system has currently achieved.

Consider first the case of a constant goal of management to hold a two-month delivery delay. The effect of delivery delay tradition is not active. The coefficient DDW in Equation 20.1 is zero. Figure 13 shows the consequence and should be compared with Figure 9. Production capacity starts at 12,000 units per month, which is

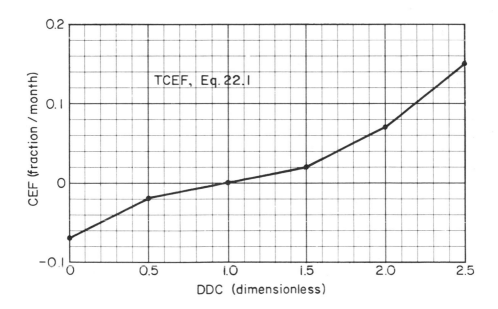

Figure 12   Table for capacity expansion fraction as it depends on delivery delay condition

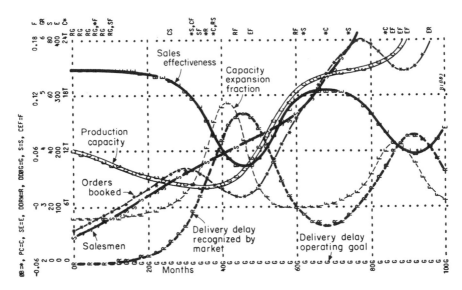

Figure 13   Capital expansion Loop 3 responds to delivery delay and restores growth

well above the initial rate of sales. As a consequence, production capacity is diverted to bring capacity more in line with the rate of order booking. For this reason the initial increase in sales is somewhat slower because sales reach capacity and delivery delay rises sooner than in Figure 9. The rate of order booking rises above the production capacity at about the 24th week. At this time order backlog is rising rapidly, capacity is falling slowly, and the delivery delay is climbing steeply. As delivery delay rises above the two-month goal, the capacity expansion fraction moves from a small negative value to a large positive value. As a result of the capacity ordering, the production capacity rises steeply after the 40th week. It overtakes the orders booked, which have fallen because of the earlier poor deliveries; delivery delay as recognized by the market again falls; this signals a reduction in the rate of capacity expansion; and production capacity levels off around the 70th week. Because delivery delay is low and sales effectiveness is high, the order rate again climbs and exceeds production capability. Production capacity continues to climb but with a repeating fluctuation of capacity and order rate crossing one another. One sees here a classic form of growth instability. High delivery delay simultaneously causes the expansion of capacity and the suppression of orders. Very sharp crossovers of capacity and orders occur, which at the 84th week are almost in a right angle relationship to one another.

But Figure 13 is based on management consistently adhering to its delivery delay goal of two months even under circumstances where actual delivery delays have fluctuated between 2.5 and 4.5 months. An organization which has experienced sales growth and periods in which capacity exceeded sales would be inclined to shift its goal structure. The shift would be to compare present performance with historical or traditional performance. The historical performance simply means the average perception of past performance. In Figure 11 this average is generated in Equation 19 for the delivery delay traditional DDT. Suppose that this tradition is initially set at two months and the weighting factor, DDW, is set at 1, meaning that full weight is given to tradition and none to the delivery delay management goal DDMG. Here a rather short averaging time of 12 months has been taken for the time to establish delivery delay tradition TDDT. The goal structure of the organization is now floating. It simply strives to achieve its historical accomplishments. For the more subtle goals in an organization, this striving to equal the past, and conversely being satisfied if one equals the past, is a strong influence.

The result of changing the goal structure from a fixed goal to a goal set by tradition is shown in Figure 14, which should be compared with Figure 13. The delivery delay recognized by the market DDRM and the delivery delay operating goal DDOG of the company are shown. After delivery delay rises, the operating goal rises after a time delay. (The goal is responsive to DDRC , not plotted, which is six months earlier than DDRM, which is plotted as the symbol R.) This means that delivery delay does not produce the degree of concern that it did when the goal was fixed and low. As a consequence, expansion does not seem so justified or so important. In Figure 14 the goal structure continues to collapse. Delivery delay continues to rise, the traditional goal rises after it, the discrepancy is never great enough to produce active expansion of capacity, and there is a constant erosion of capacity. As capacity goes down, the rate of order booking declines to correspond because, in the long run, average orders can not exceed capacity. Sales effectiveness declines, the revenue to sales declines, and the revenue becomes insufficient to support the existing number of salesmen. After about the 70th week the number of salesmen begins to decrease and stagnation has turned into decay.

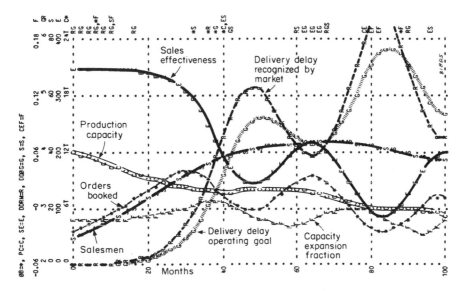

Figure 14 Delivery delay goal based on past performance

IMPLICATIONS FOR MARKETING

Marketing is not an activity limited to one corporate subdivision. Marketing interacts with research to guide product design. Marketing interacts with price policy to determine profitability. Marketing interacts with production to determine product availability and quality. Marketing interacts with personnel policy and training to determine skill in the marketing activities. Marketing interacts with the corporate information system in determining how market information guides resource allocation within the company. The relationship of marketing policy to the market, to the other corporate functions, and to competition is particularly intimate. There are many interacting feedback loops. These loops are capable of producing product growth or stagnation and decline. How the loops are balanced determines product profitability. Misplaced emphasis can raise costs, as illustrated by the increased marketing cost in Figure 10, whereas the solution to product growth lies in the capital investment policies.

Numerous feedback loops of importance exist in the market complex beyond those illustrated here. The preceding example assumes a market of unlimited extent. Although the market responds to delivery delay, for a fixed delay the rate of order booking is proportional to the number of salesmen. This assumption of an unlimited market is true for a much wider range of market situations than normally believed. But given a specific product, there is an upper limit to demand, and the demand-limiting process within the market represents additional important loops in the market system. As an example, one of the most important market loops concerns the kind of product where the product inventory in the hands of the customer generates customer satisfaction rather than the rate of product consumption. Customer satisfaction is obtained from the size of the customer inventory in capital items such as automobiles and household appliances. Here the sale of a new product fills an inventory, and sales then decline to a replacement level. The recent steep rise and decline in the sale of pin-setting machines for bowling alleys illustrates a situation where customer inventory can dominate the dynamic behavior.

Market interactions are so complex that they cannot be intuitively appreciated. One must have a concept of feedback system structure for organizing his knowledge about the system. Such a structure has been suggested at the beginning of this paper. The structure can be used for arranging the parts of a system so that behavior can be simulated as shown in the preceding examples. Market research should be directed toward identifying the structures that can cause the many dynamic modes that exist in actual market situations. Emphasis should be reduced on numerical data gathering in market research and should be increased on conceptualizing the structures which produce typical classes of market behavior.

APPENDIX

The following equations were used for the system simulation in this paper. Knowledge of the system structure described in *Industrial Dynamics* [2] and the *DYNAMO User's Manual* [3] is assumed. To understand fully the equation format and structure, the reader will need to be familiar with those books. These equations are included primarily for those who may want to experiment further with the model herein described. They represent the full set of equations as they appear in the model. The basic system structure extends through Equation 27.2. Control cards follow and then the variations of coefficients used to produce the different computer runs in this paper for Figures 3, 4, 8, 9, 10, 13, and 14.

```
0.1              MARKET LOOPS
0.2     RUN      STD
0.3     NOTE     U. OF ILL.--CONVERSE AWARDS SYMPOSIUM, APRIL 13, 1967
0.4     NOTE
0.5     NOTE     POSITIVE LOOP--SALESMEN
0.6     NOTE
1       1L       S.K=S.J+(DT)(SH.JK+0)
1.1     6N       S=10
2       49A      SSW.K=SWITCH(SCT,S.K,SW1)
2.1     C        SCT=60
2.2     C        SW1=0
3       12R      OB.KL=(SSW.K)(SE.K)
4       12A      B.K=(DRA.K)(RS)
4.1     C        RS=12
5       20A      IS.K=B.K/SS
5.1     C        SS=2000
6       21R      SH.KL=(1/SAT)(IS.K-S.K)
6.1     C        SAT=20
6.4     NOTE
6.5     NOTE     NEGATIVE LOOP--MARKET
6.6     NOTE
7       1L       BL.K=BL.J+(DT)(OB.JK-DR.JK)
7.1     6N       BL=8000
8       20A      DDM.K=BL.K/PC.K
9       58A      PCF.K=TABHL(TPCF,DDM.K,0,5,.5)
9.1     C        TPCF*=0/.25/.5/.67/.8/.87/.93/.95/.97/.98/1
10      12R      DR.KL=(PC.K)(PCF.K)
11      3L       DRA.K=DRA.J+(DT)(1/DRAT)(DR.JK-DRA.J)
11.1    6N       DRA=DR
11.2    C        DRAT=1
12      20A      DDI.K=BL.K/DRA.K
13      3L       DDRC.K=DDRC.J+(DT)(1/TDDRC)(DDI.J-DDRC.J)
13.1    6N       DDRC=DDI
13.2    C        TDDRC=4
14      3L       DDRM.K=DDRM.J+(DT)(1/TDDRM)(DDRC.J-DDRM.J)
14.1    6N       DDRM=DDRC
14.2    C        TDDRM=6
15      58A      SEDM.K=TABHL(TSEDM,DDRM.K,0,10,1)
15.1    C        TSEDM*=1/.97/.87/.73/.53/.38/.25/.15/.08/.03/.02
16      51A      SEDC.K=CLIP(SEDF,SEDI,TIME.K,SEDCT)
16.1    C        SEDF=1
16.2    C        SEDI=1
16.3    C        SEDCT=36
17      49A      SEDS.K=SWITCH(SEDC.K,SEDM.K,SW2)
17.1    C        SW2=0
18      12A      SE.K=(SEDS.K)(SEM)
18.1    C        SEM=400
18.4    NOTE
18.5    NOTE     CAPITAL INVESTMENT
18.6    NOTE
19      3L       DDT.K=DDT.J+(DT)(1/TDDT)(DDRC.J-DDT.J)
19.1    6N       DDT=DDRC
19.2    C        TDDT=12
20      15A      DDOG.K=(DDT.K)(DDW)+(DDMG)(DDWC)
20.1    7N       DDWC=1-DDW
20.2    C        DDW=0
20.3    C        DDMG=2
21      27A      DDC.K=(DDRC.K/DDOG.K)-DDB
```

```
21.1    C      DDB=.3
22      58A    CEF.K=TABHL(TCEF,DDC.K,0,2.5,.5)
22.1    C      TCEF*=-.07/-.02/0/.02/.07/.15
23      49A    CEFSW.K=SWITCH(0,CEF.K,SW3)
23.1    C      SW3=0
24      12R    PCO.KL=(PC.K)(CEFSW.K)
25      39R    PCR.KL=DELAY3(PCO.JK,PCRD)
25.1    C      PCRD=12
26      1L     PCOO.K=PCOO.J+(DT)(PCO.JK-PCR.JK)
26.1    12N    PCOO=(PCO)(PCRD)
27      1L     PC.K=PC.J+(DT)(PCR.JK+0)
27.1    6N     PC=PCI
27.2    C      PCI=12000
27.5    NOTE
27.6    NOTE   CONTROL CARDS
27.7    NOTE
27.8    PLOT   OB=*,PC=C(0,24000)/SE=E(0,400)/S=S(0,80)
27.9    NOTE   B42, RERUNS OF B41
28      NOTE
28.1    RUN    A
28.2    NOTE   UNLIMITED EXPONENTIAL GROWTH
28.3    SPEC   DT=.5/LENGTH=100/PRTPER=100/PLTPER=2
28.4    PRINT  1)S
29      C      SW1=1
29.1    C      PCI=100000
29.4    PLOT   OB=*(0,24000)/SE=E(0,400)/BL=B(0,120000)/S=S(0,80)
29.5    RUN    B
29.6    NOTE   GROWTH AND DECLINE
30      C      SW1=1
30.1    C      SEDF=.25
30.2    C      PCI=100000
30.5    RUN    C
30.6    NOTE   NEGATIVE LOOP OSCILLATION
31      C      SW2=1
31.3    PLOT   OB=*,DR=D(0,24000)/SE=E(0,400)/DDRM=R(2,6)/BL=B(0,120000)
31.4    RUN    D
31.5    NOTE   SALES STAGNATION
32      C      SW1=1
32.1    C      SW2=1
32.4    PLOT   OB=*(0,24000)/SE=E(0,400)/SH=H(0,2)/DDRM=R(2,6)/S=S(0,80)
32.5    RUN    E
32.6    NOTE   INCREASED SALES BUDGET ALLOCATION
33      C      SW1=1
33.1    C      SW2=1
33.2    C      RS=13.6
33.5    RUN    F
33.6    NOTE   CAPACITY EXPANSION
34      C      SW1=1
34.1    C      SW2=1
34.2    C      SW3=1
34.5    PLOT   OB=*,PC=C(0,24000)/SE=E(0,400)/DDRM=R,DDOG=G(2,6)/S=S(0,80)/CEF=F(
34.6    X1     -.06,.18)
34.7    RUN    G
34.8    NOTE   GOAL=TRADITION WITH DELIVERY DELAY BIAS PRESSURE
35      C      SW1=1
35.1    C      SW2=1
35.2    C      SW3=1
35.3    C      DDW=1
```

References

1. Forrester, Jay W. "Industrial Dynamics After the First Decade." *Management Science* 14, no. 7, (March 1968), pp. 398–415.

2. _____. *Industrial Dynamics*. Cambridge, Mass.: The MIT Press, 1961.

3. Pugh, Alexander L., III. *DYNAMO User's Manual*, 2nd ed. Cambridge, Mass.: The MIT Press, 1963.

13

Systems Analysis of Apparel Company Problems

Edward B. Roberts

This chapter illustrates the effectiveness of industrial dynamics in treating apparel industry problems. It is based on a case study of a cooperating apparel manufacturer. The study was one part of a several year effort by my consulting firm, Pugh-Roberts Associates Inc., sponsored by the Textile and Apparel Technology Center of the Department of Commerce under the direction of Dr. Cecil Brenner. The contracts developed systems analyses of a broad variety of textile and apparel industry problems and have produced trial applications of the techniques to one major textile company and one medium-sized apparel firm.

In conducting the case study of the cooperating apparel company we began with a general familiarization phase, including interviews with company personnel and the study of operating data over a several year period. During this first phase ideas were formulated as to how individual management practices might be related structurally to produce the company trends observed. As certain aspects of the firm began to appear influential on the firm's overall performance, they were translated into an industrial dynamics computer model. The resulting computer model was then tested using computer simulation to see if the hypothesized model structure produced the same type of behavior that was actually observed in the firm's history. In particular, the case study model was tested against the company's performance over the previous five years. Once the model produced the basic underlying trends and changes that were apparent in the real situation, it became a useful tool with which to understand the problems of the apparel firm.

Historical Perspective

The apparel company that had been selected for study is identified here as the Everdry Company. It is a rainwear manufacturer and is one of the older firms in the

This is a revised version of a paper presented by the author at the Apparel Research Foundation Conference, November 30, 1967, Washington, D.C. It has been published in *DYNAMICA*, vol. 3, part 3 (Summer 1977). The study described in this paper was supported by National Bureau of Standards Contract CST-240 to Pugh-Roberts Associates, Inc. Opinions and conclusions expressed in this paper do not necessarily represent the views of the supporting agency. Equations for the model are listed in Appendix C of this book.

industry, having been in business for over fifty years. Considering its current sales volume, it is a medium-sized manufacturer, larger firms having developed only recently due to some basic changes in the nature of the industry. Like many apparel firms, it is held and operated primarily by the family of the founder, who in this case only recently passed away.

The analysis of Everdry has come up with a number of problem symptoms that suggest the need for management systems analysis. Despite the firm's success in the long run, its most recent performance has been disappointing compared to the potential indicated by other firms and by the economy in general. Although sales doubled in the period from 1955–60, dollar volume in the last five years has been approximately constant. Moreover, the fact that the firm is now selling a product with a higher average price somewhat disguises the fact that unit sales have actually been declining.

Everdry has also been plagued recently by difficulties in meeting delivery commitments. Outside problems have contributed to the situation but plant control seems to be more difficult with the increased number of products in the line. This was indicated also by the fact that the plant recently encountered a period with record work-in-process inventories, despite the fact that unit sales were below those of earlier years. Other difficulties have been encountered with quality control recently—the introduction of the new products places a strain on the system in terms of training workers to perform several different jobs.

Labor turnover has been a general problem in this part of the country in that the apparel industry has fared relatively poorly in competing with some of the alternative job opportunities available. This has been particularly true during the recent economic boom. Fluctuations in the work available at Everdry have also had an effect on turnover in the plant.

The decline in sales in recent years has also had a detrimental effect on turnover among the company salesmen. Other companies in the industry that have been expanding have attracted some salesmen and other salesmen apparently have not been able to maintain sales high enough to satisfy their income requirements. In addition to salesmen difficulties, the firm also has changed advertising agencies several times because of management's apparent dissatisfaction with the results.

Model Description

One way to better understand the situation in a company is to build a representation of what has taken place that has resulted in the symptoms described previously. This representation is called a model and industrial dynamics provides us with a way to build a model that provides a concise and lucid description of what may have been the important factors in this case. The model is best described by considering the cause-and-effect relationships between small groups of factors at a time. The overall effect of the factors on the company's performance will be considered after we have examined several individual sectors of the model.

Promotional Market Sector.   Figure 1 illustrates the major relationships in the environment in which the company sells its product. The factors have been aggregated to a great extent to allow an overview of the relationships and later of the effects of this

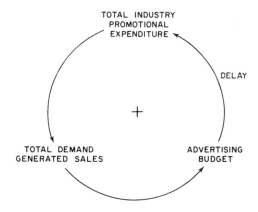

Figure 1   Industry promotional feedback

sector on other portions of the apparel company model. The key relationship is the way in which total industry promotional expenditures result in sales for the entire apparel industry. This includes promotional efforts of all the companies, although in the case of the Everdry Company's market, one company had dominated the industry's promotional effort until recently. Sales, in turn, have an effect on the promotional budget in that next year's plans depend very much on this year's sales. Thus a company that is growing due to its promotional efforts tends to reinforce its growth by expanding its budget for the next year each time its sales improve. This positive feedback effect is an important structural factor that appears to have been the cause of one company dominating the rainwear market for the higher priced coats.

Everdry's share of these "demand-generated" sales is based on its own promotional efforts and how they compare to that of the total industry. In addition, the company's market share is also affected by product innovation where early introduction of a new product gives the firm an extra advantage in promotional benefits. As in the industry case, the sales generated by the firm's promotional efforts create the revenues necessary to produce next year's promotional budget. Figure 2 illustrates these relationships along with the industry market structure shown in Figure 1.

Sales Sector.   In addition to the sales created by promotional efforts, the original market for Everdry's products consisted of customers who purchased the coats because of their apparent physical characteristics when seen at a retail store or because of the retailer's reputation. This basic market can be considered to be relatively constant, changing primarily only with population growth. The number of coats that represent the company's sales in this market are equivalent to the exposure they get to the public through the retailers. Therefore, the company's share of the basic market is shown in Figure 3 as that proportion of the total market that is covered by the retail outlets that carry the company line.

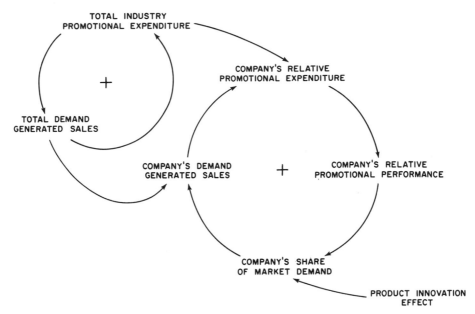

Figure 2   Company promotional feedback

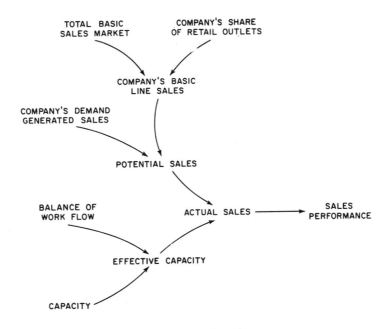

Figure 3   Company sales determinants

The sales from the basic market and the demand-generated sales combine to represent the total sales that might be sold by the apparel company. If this is in fact within the production capability of the firm, this total will become actual sales. The sales rate will be the capacity of the firm, however, if production becomes a limiting

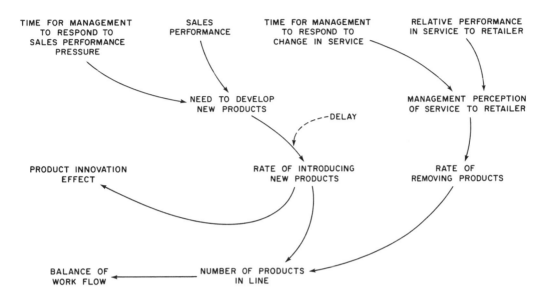

Figure 4   Product line influences

factor. Management has an idea of what type of growth is possible from the conditions in the industry in general and compares the current rate to the perceived industry trend.

Product Line Sector.   One of the effects of low sales performance, that is, not achieving the growth rate that management feels is attainable, is for serious doubts to be raised about the suitability of the company's product line for the market conditions. In this case, it appears that after mediocre performance has persisted for some period of time, management responds by planning the introduction of new products. The time it takes management to respond to the pressure caused by poor sales performance is not an exact figure and in this situation appears to have been one to two years. If a period of low sales performance persists, management will, after the initial delay, introduce new lines on a continual basis. As the new apparel products are offered to the market, there is usually a season or two of market enthusiasm and good sales volume, then a gradual falling off in interest occurs. The initial boost might result from several factors—the novelty of the product, the salesmen's initial enthusiasm for a new item, or the retailers' estimates of the product's potential combined with inventory filling by retailers. After this initial phase, however, it appears that the product's performance falls back on the same factors that affect all of Everdry's products: promotional effort, reputation, number of retailers, effectiveness of the company salesmen, etc. These factors are illustrated in Figure 4.

The rate at which new products are introduced together with the rate at which Everdry management decides to prune out some of the old products causes variations over time in the number of products in the company's line. In recent years the trend of product lines for the apparel company studied has been very definitely upward, particularly when one considers all the color-pattern combinations offered within any one

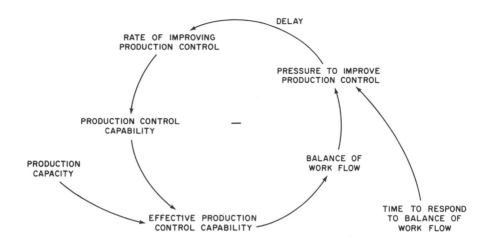

Figure 5   Production control loop

basic style. The effect of this upward trend has been to put more of a load on the plant in terms of problems of controlling the production and distribution end of the business. More product items imply more production runs with fewer items in each run. More time is spent on set-up effort, on changing an operator from one type of stitching job to another. Balancing Everdry's plant so that all work sections have enough to do becomes a very difficult problem. Also, storing the goods before they are shipped, picking the orders just prior to shipment, and knowing what is on hand that can be shipped all become more difficult requirements. More items in the line also increase the likelihood of running out of a particular size and being forced to delay the shipment of an order. All these effects have been included in what is called balance of work flow. In its simplest form, an increase in the number of products in the line results in a corresponding decrease in the balance of work flow.

Production Control Sector.   The production control sector of the model describes how management reacts to improve the balance of work flow described in the previous sector. When work flow is seriously impaired and it becomes apparent that it is more than just a temporary problem, steps are taken to improve production control. Usually some portion of the plant is studied for potential improvements. Occasionally changes are made that affect work flow throughout the firm, such as a new application on the company's data processing system. In either case, the delay before improvements begin to affect the system is on the order of 48 months. If Everdry's capacity were increasing at the same rate as the firm's ability to control the plant, effective production control would remain constant. As improvements in control capability come on line without corresponding increases in capacity, the effective production control capability of the firm increases and directly affects the balance of work flow, improving the situation. This sector, as shown in Figure 5, is an example of a single negative feedback loop in which a problem situation creates management actions which work to improve a problem situation and bring it back to a more normal level. Note that significant time passes, however, before the results of these actions can be felt. It is possible that the initial problem might grow worse in the interim. In a situation where factors continually depress the balance of work flow, management's efforts to improve can continually lag behind, sometimes resulting in production control barely holding its own at a relatively poor level.

Labor Sector.   Because of the piece-rate payment system used in the apparel industry, the balance of work flow situation in the Everdry plant can have a serious effect on employment stability in the firm. A worker receives wages only for the number of bundles on which she has actually worked. The union agreement provides that management must pay a minimum wage equivalent to four hours work each time a worker is called in. But when work is not available, management either tells her not to come in or sends her home half-way through the day, resulting in a corresponding cut in her wages.

Because of this basic practice in the apparel industry, poor balance of work flow in the plant can directly affect the weekly wages received by the workers. When the balance is low, some work stations run out of work, resulting in situations where workers only work half-days. This lack of employment stability results in increased labor turnover. Workers who need the wages look for work at other apparel firms in the area and, once started, will work for the new firm as long as the work is stable. This turnover of the apparel company's work force has an additional degrading effect on the balance of work flow. The worker who has left for another firm has to be replaced and the delays in hiring and getting a new worker adjusted to her new environment add to the problems of controlling the plant. Thus the labor turnover caused by the poor balance of work flow worsens the work flow situation. This is particularly true during times of strong economic conditions when other firms nearby are in need of more help. These relationships are indicated in Figure 6, as are those aspects discussed below.

Another factor which becomes important is the generally depressing effect high labor turnover has on the quality of the apparel company's labor force. If other nearby industries offer stable employment they are often able to attract some of the apparel industry's better skilled workers. Thus, labor turnover causes a decline in the average skill level of the apparel labor force as the less qualified workers are left behind and the new ones that can be hired have fewer skills yet. One can discover a trend in the makeup of the company's work force over time in that it is derived more and more from the lower cultural groups in the community. The effect of this trend is additional reinforcement of the labor turnover problem as worker absenteeism is higher, work skills are not developed, and good work attitudes are frequently nonexistent. These factors act through these two sets of relationships to reinforce poor balance of work flow, although at a very gradual rate.

Retailers Sector.   The retailers who sell Everdry's product line see the company from two points of view, directly in the way they order and receive their goods, and indirectly when they resell the company's goods to the general public. In the first case,

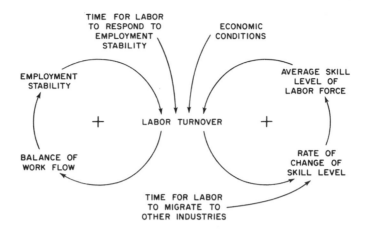

Figure 6 Labor interactions

the retailer knows the company salesman and he sees the garments as they arrive from the plant. If sales performance for the Everdry Company has been poor, however, its salesmen turnover tends to be high. The average salesman can accept a slump for a short period but if it persists he decides to work elsewhere, particularly if other portions of the industry appear to be doing well. An increase in salesmen turnover has a detrimental effect on the company's relative performance in service to the retailers. A new man, even after the time required to find him, takes some time to get to know the retailers and to build strong relationships that ensure regular orders each season. Sometimes, a loyal retailer takes the opportunity presented when a salesman changes to experiment with competitive lines. The other company factor that directly affects the retailer is the way in which the orders are processed and fulfilled. If the balance of work flow at the apparel company is poor, deliveries are often delayed, items sometimes are missing, and occasionally entire orders can be misplaced. Another serious problem that can arise is a fall-off in the average quality of the garments themselves due to the confusion and pressures in the plant. The combination of the salesman's performance and the way in which the company delivers the goods results in the company's performance in service to its customers. This in turn has a direct bearing on a retailer's decision to continue carrying the company line. Figure 7 illustrates these causes and effects.

The other factor that affects the attitudes of retailers is the way the product is received by the public. Each retailer has an idea of what volume of business he can expect to do with a type of product. He sees reports of industry volume in the trade papers and he is actively aware of his competitive position in the local community in which he does business. If his year to year figures for an item decline when it does not appear justified by other factors, he tends to blame the particular brand of the product

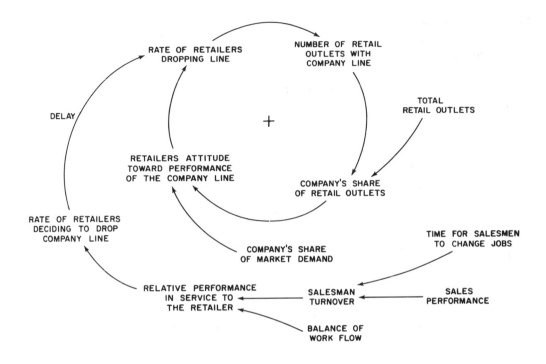

Figure 7 Influences on retailers dropping company lines

he is carrying. This is confirmed if his floor salesmen report difficulty in selling the merchandise, a situation that appears to have been prevalent in the rainwear industry in recent years as the promotional images of some brands have become strong enough to have customers ask for them by name. The retailer soon begins to develop an idea of the company's relative performance with the public. If he feels that it is not sufficient to give him the amount of business that is warranted by the size of his retail outlet, he begins to plan to change lines. This is not something that is done quickly, however. Sometimes the goods in inventory have to be worked down, or delays arise in getting a new line on board, or possibly just plain inertia affects the retailer's actions. On the average it appears that a retailer takes at least two years to closeout one line and take on a replacement. When such a change occurs, the number of retail outlets carrying the Everdry Company's goods are correspondingly decreased, as is Everdry's share of the total number of retail outlets available. This, in turn, has an effect of reducing the sales the firm makes in the basic market, that portion of the market where customers are not particularly brand conscious, but where purchases of the garment occur because of its physical characteristics or because of the retailer's reputation.

Thus we have closed the full circle of relationships by which the various portions of Everdry and its market are related. Next we shall examine the effect of these interactions on the overall performance of the firm during recent years.

Model Simulation

The completed company model was simulated on a large-scale computer using time rented from a local computer service bureau. The total computer rental costs in the study amounted to approximately $1000, making these costs insignificant to the total effort. Some of the computer results for a five-year test run are shown in the next several figures.

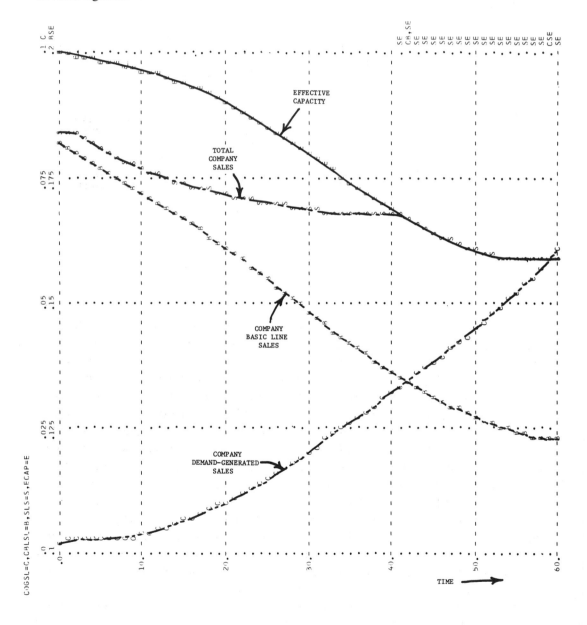

Figure 8   Company sales determinants

Total Company Sales.   Figure 8 illustrates the basic Everdry Company situation of declining sales over the period of the simulation run. Sales (S in Figure 8) represents the total sales of the firm, the sum of both the company's demand-generated sales (C) and the company's basic line sales (B). The increase in demand-generated sales is not enough to compensate for the rapid decline in the basic line sales, the company's original business. It does slow the decline, however, so that the decline in total sales in the first three years is approximately 16,000 units as compared to a decline of 40,000 units in basic line sales. The difference is the growth in sales of the new higher priced coats.

In the 41st month a new factor comes into play. The effective capacity of the plant (E) has been declining throughout the simulation run and at this point it becomes the limiting factor. Despite the growth in sales of the higher priced coats, the company cannot deliver primarily due to problems in plant control. The balance of work flow has deteriorated to a point where enough orders are cancelled due to delivery delays that the plant is not producing (and delivering) its normal capacity. Normal capacity has been set at 200,000 units per year. Effective capacity continues to limit sales during the remaining months of the simulation resulting in a total sales rate of 160,000 units per year. The decline in effective capacity that was caused by production control problems has levelled out by the end of the run, however, and it appears it will turn up in the near future.

Product Line.   In Figure 9, management's decision to introduce new products (D) represents a response to the pressure to do something about the poor sales performance situation. It builds up to a steady flow of product plans by the end of the second year, masking the fluctuations in sales performance because of its slow response to changes. The rate of introducing new products (A) follows from this directly, although an average delay of one year is required to design and select the items for the new line. The product innovation effect is directly dependent on this rate and generates an increase in the company's share of the promotional market.

Management is also removing products from the line (R) both due to obsolescence and to pressures on the plant because there are too many product varieties. As shown in the simulation, this was a small product outflow compared to those that were being added. The number of products in the line (N) at any point in time is simply the accumulation of the new products being added less those that are being removed. It has been on a dramatic climb throughout the five year period, resulting in a detrimental effect on a key plant variable, the balance of work flow (B). As was explained in the model description, an increase in the number of styles or even items in the product line makes it difficult to keep all sections of the plant balanced, to keep plant throughput time down, and to keep track of the outstanding orders in all parts of the system. Balance of work flow declines throughout the simulation run, although near the end it has begun to stabilize at a low level.

Labor Sector.   The decline in balance of work flow shown in Figure 9 also has effects on labor conditions that are not readily recognized in an apparel firm. These are

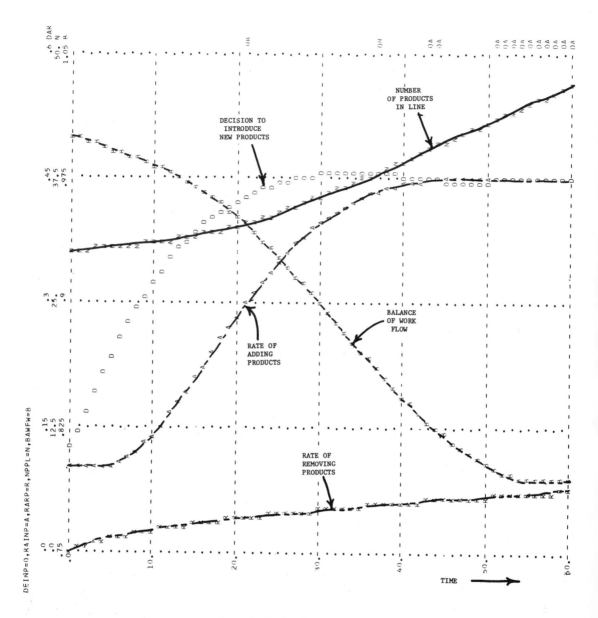

Figure 9   Product line management

indicated in Figure 11. As the workers are paid on a piece rate basis, problems in keeping the work flow balanced result in a decline in employment stability (E). As the employees find their incomes are becoming more and more uncertain, they tend to look for other work and, after the time it takes to find new jobs, leave. The resulting labor turnover (T) reinforces the decline in balance of work flow. It also has a depressing effect on the quality of the work force in the plant. If labor turnover persists, better workers are attracted to other industries and others, less skilled, will be hired to replace them. The resulting decline in the average skill level (S) also, after it has been taking

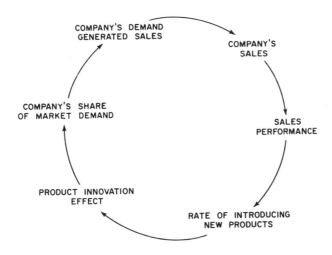

Figure 10 Structure providing short-term correction of the sales decline

place for a period of time, begins to have its own effect on labor turnover. The lower skilled workers tend to come from lower cultural groups with poorer work habits and less suitability for job training. Thus a process that reinforces itself is triggered by an initial decline in the balance of work flow. And it in turn further reinforces the decline of balance of work flow. Note also that although balance of work flow is being corrected by improvements in production control, the changes in the labor sector tend to be irreversible and, at best, hold steady at their new low levels.

Implications for the Firm

It is apparent, both in the real situation and in the model, that the Everdry Company is suffering a serious sales decline, despite its efforts to improve its manufacturing plant, its warehousing, and its data processing. Its facilities are among the most modern in the industry, yet its business performance does not rank accordingly. As has been shown, the company's basic response of introducing new products at a rate sufficient to keep sales in their new higher-priced line of coats growing has had depressing effects on other parts of the firm's operation. The continual introduction of new products has resulted in such a number and variety of items being manufactured at the same time that it has become very difficult to produce efficiently and on schedule. This, in turn, has had a depressing effect on total sales both directly, in that all the coats ordered simply cannot be delivered on time, and indirectly through the gradual loss of retailers who are handling the company line. The decline of sales further reinforces management's response of introducing new products which, after a delay required for the additions to be made, worsens the situation even more.

With the computer model accepted as representative of the company's situation, it becomes possible to test alternative policies, using the computer as the testing ground instead of trying the new policies directly on the company itself.

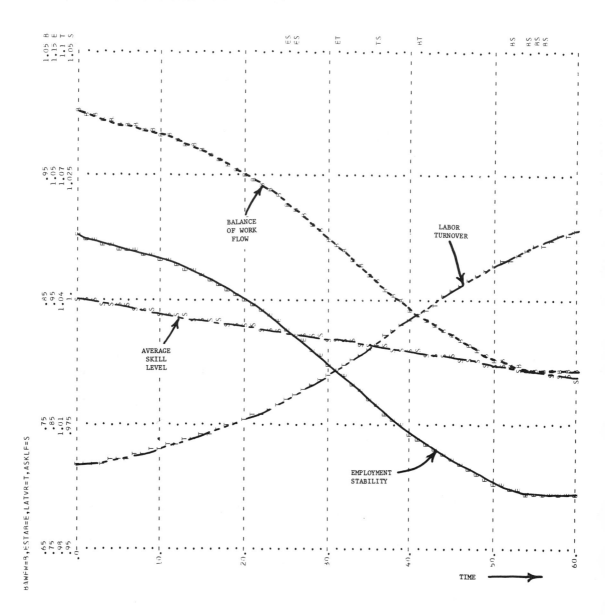

Figure 11   Work flow problems

One such policy change that has been tested on the computer is that management becomes more sensitive to the decline in its service to retailers and reacts strongly by cutting products out of its line. Figures 13 and 14 show the changes in sales and other pertinent company variables under these new conditions. Demand-generated sales are about the same as they were in the original run but the decline in the company's basic line sales is held to a fraction of what it was before. Total sales recovers from the decline very quickly and in the last three years climbs to a new high for the company.

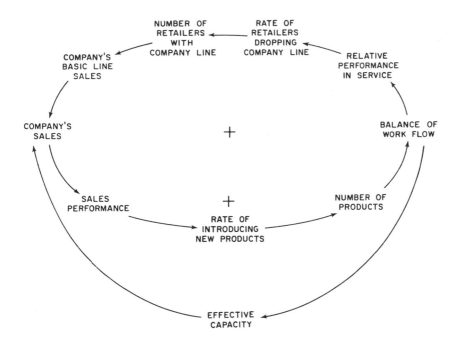

Figure 12   Structure reinforcing the sales decline

Effective capacity does not become a limiting factor as it did in the original simulation. Figure 14 shows the change in management's policy on removing products, resulting in as many being taken away from the product line as are being added. Thus, the total number of items on the line remains quite stable and the balance of work flow shows only small variations about its normal value. The resulting improvement in sales performance in the latter part of the run also affects management's need to develop new products, resulting in the decline shown in Figure 14 in the last two years. This policy change is of course but one of many alternatives that might be explored using the company model. And such models can be developed for any medium- to large-sized apparel company at readily absorbable expense.

The Need for Better Management Tools

A key point that has emerged from this chapter is that apparel management problems are indeed system problems of great complexity. The interplay among company, market, competitors, suppliers and labor force is subtle but crucial in its dynamic implications. Despite managerial attempts to reorient its view toward new market conditions or to keep abreast of changing materials and manufacturing technologies, the overall managerial burden is great, perhaps overwhelming to the small firm in particular.

In this environment, apparel management needs to develop and/or avail itself of

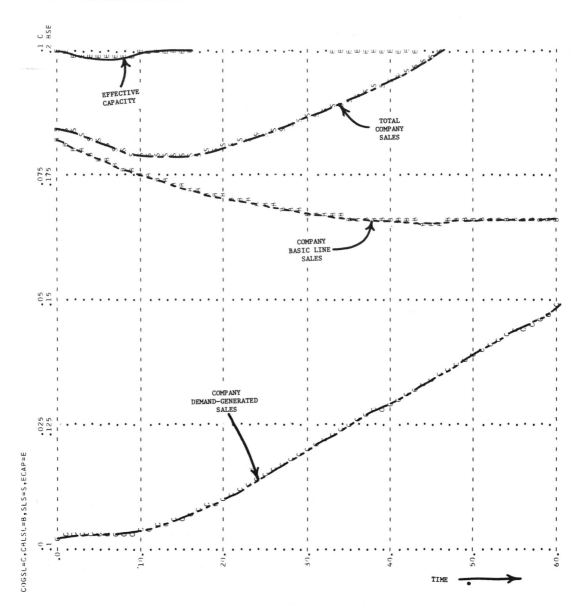

Figure 13   New policies: sales impact

existing tools for improving managerial insight and control. Computer data processing methods are but one form of management improvement opportunity that needs further exploitation by progressive apparel companies. Yet such utilization of the computer is but a meager tapping of the new capabilities provided in recent years. New approaches to management systems analysis, such as outlined in application in this chapter, offer

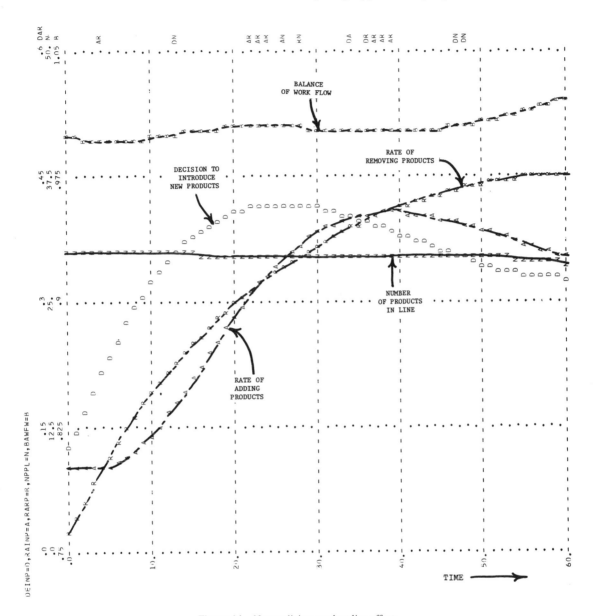

Figure 14 New policies: product line effects

wholly new managerial concepts and analysis possibilities.* In the realization of these potentials lies significant performance improvement for the apparel industry.

*NOTE: The DYNAMO equations for the Everdry Company model are listed in Appendix C of this book.

14

Growth Strategies for a Trucking Firm

Richard D. Wright

Introduction

Strategies for profitable growth are a major concern of most businesses. The size and intricacy of management systems, the multiple conflicting goals within the organization, and the interface between the firm and its market all work to make successful policy design difficult. The firm's own strategies for controlling resources, marketing, and trading off immediate expense for long-term results may interact to define growth in spite of potential market demand. This paper reports a simple and inexpensive industrial dynamics study that suggested profitable policy changes for a trucking company. A management group with limited exposure to industrial dynamics used this methodology to design successful policies and to monitor an effective implementation.

The management of the trucking company was interested in uncovering strategies to improve growth. Several techniques, including multivariate statistical methods and dynamic programming, had been used in an attempt to isolate key factors for profitable growth. None of these efforts showed clear cut, useful results; all were too complicated to be accepted with confidence by the firm's operating management.

Discovering effective management controls requires understanding of the causal mechanisms which underlie corporate system behavior.[1] The industrial dynamics methodology takes the view that complex, non-linear feedback processes form the important structure of socio-economic systems. To design control policies for dynamic socio-economic problems, an industrial dynamics practitioner builds a model that explicates this essential structure. The field is grounded in the state-space

---

[1] See Roberts [6].

This article was first published in the *Sloan Management Review* 12, no. 1 (Fall 1971), pp. 71–86, under the title "An Industrial Dynamics Implementation: Growth Strategies for a Trucking Firm."

approach of modern control theory; its techniques include feedback systems analysis and computer simulation of complex models.[2] Many applications of industrial dynamics have been directed toward enterprise design and the development of control policies for continuous monitoring of corporate activity.[3]

The industrial dynamics approach was selected for two reasons.

1   A substantial body of theory of corporate growth had been developed.[4] Some of the research suggested a new way of addressing this firm's problem. It was believed that the processes which encouraged or constrained growth were part of a non-linear, closed loop, feedback system.

2   The approach was straightforward enough so that management could take active part in the course of the project.

To build an industrial dynamics model, it is necessary to focus on specific questions, to find a system boundary which includes all important causal mechanisms needed to answer the questions, to specify the feedback loops within this system boundary, and to estimate the values of system constants. The paper will outline these steps and their application to the company involved.

Model Formulation

The company studied was a medium-sized trucking firm that carried general freight between Worcester-Boston, Massachusetts and the Washington-Baltimore area. When this study was originated, the firm had two major terminals, 40 competitors, and three million dollars in yearly revenues.

Three topics guided the formulation of the model of the company's activities.

1   The trade-off between the results of long-term efforts to maintain customer satisfaction and the company's immediate out-of-pocket cost for good service. Was the firm's traditional policy optimal?

2   Mechanisms for capacity control. How did the firm's resource acquisition strategy affect growth?

3   Company response to sales uncertainty. To what extent did company policies account for sales fluctuations?

Many significant constraints on the operation and profitability of the firm lay beyond the control of management. These factors included general economic conditions, total area freight, Interstate Commerce Commission and Teamsters' Union work rules, most freight rates, and wage levels. But because they were not affected

---

[2] See Forrester [2].

[3] See Fey [1], Roberts [7], and Gorry [5].

[4] See Forrester [3], Forrester [4], Swanson [8], Swanson [9], and Swanson and Thorsten [10].

by the firm's operations, these factors were not included in the closed system boundary.

Management had effective control of intracity freight collection and distribution, intercity line-hauling, and administrative functions. Small "city trucks" picked up freight shipments during daily rounds in the metropolitan areas. At the originating terminal, the freight was batched into large (60 foot) over-the-road van loads for night shipment to the destination city by special intercity tractor-trailers. At the other end, van loads were sorted into deliveries to consignees and sent out during the day. Intercity drivers, arriving at the destination terminal, slept during the day and drove a tractor-trailer back to their home city the next night. The origin terminal was responsible for generating bills and records. The central office handled billing, damage claims, salesmen, staffing and accounting.

Capacity utilization and customer satisfaction were key issues in the list of problems the model investigated. All potential customers did not have the same needs and criteria. Some worried about thefts and damaged freight; others wanted special schedules for pick-ups and deliveries; a few wanted to use trailers for temporary warehouse space. The essential competitive variable, however, was found to be speed of delivery. The firm, therefore, promised its customers one-day, door-to-door service between Boston and Baltimore; meeting this schedule dominated all other service criteria.

It appeared that once freight was received at the destination terminal, delivery the same day to the consignee could be assumed. Loss of one-day service resulted only from holding freight at its originating terminal. Given the random nature of customer freight inputs and a limited intercity fleet, a terminal manager sometimes had more filled vans ready to ship than tractors to pull them. Maintaining a superior service level depended on rapidly clearing such freight backlogs. The measure of service that was used was the smoothed percentage of freight held overnight (or longer) at its originating terminal before being sent over the road. This measure was generated by the model.

While intercity tractors were limited and expensive, small "city trucks" and tractor vans were relatively inexpensive and easy to procure. It was assumed that terminal capacity would not be a constraint. The important capacity measure was the average-usage of over-the-road tractors.

As major factors that affected customer service, resource control, and sales fluctuations occurred only in the over-the-road sector, the model boundary included that sector alone (see Figure 1). Within the system boundary, four interacting feedback mechanisms were identified. These mechanisms were concerned with (1) the effect of service reputation on sales, (2) policies for capacity acquisition, (3) special sales efforts, and (4) daily operations. Their interactions are shown in Figure 2 and described below.

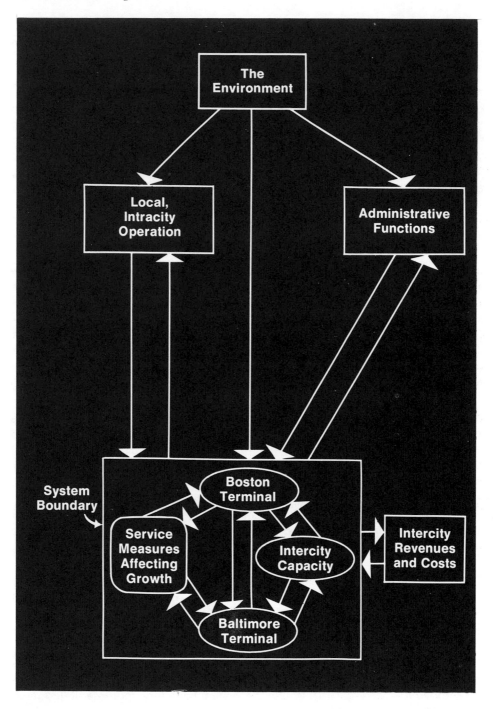

Figure 1   System Boundary

1   Reputation-Sales Loops: A major hypothesis in the model was that each terminal's sales rate was affected by market perception of the firm's service. The measure of reputation was the smoothed ratio of late loads times number of days late to total freight loads. Smoothing daily service was necessary as it takes time for the market to perceive changes in the firm's service pattern. One day's good or bad service directly affected only a small subset of the potential market.

2   Capacity Acquisition Loops: When to purchase new trucks was a decision made by top management. Tractors were almost always bought in pairs, one tractor to be based at each terminal. This purchasing policy followed from the firm's expectation of long-run balance between mean sales rate in Boston and mean sales rate in Baltimore. New truck purchasing was controlled by capacity pressure and profitability. When profits were satisfactory, acceptable chattel mortgages could be easily negotiated. There were no direct cash constraints on the truck purchasing. Capacity pressure was defined by smoothed tractor utilization. Utilization beyond a desired level signaled the need for new equipment. There was a substantial delay between the indication that new trucks were needed and their delivery.

3   Special Sales Effort Loops: Sales fluctuations caused occasional freight backlogs at one or the other terminal. A short-term, expensive sales effort at the terminal without the freight backlog was suggested to help control these backlogs. The extra business would result in more trucks being sent to the clogged terminal; with an increased number of available trucks, the backlog could be reduced. The special sales effort might include calls and visits by salesmen to inactive customers, soliciting and accepting marginal freight, and gifts to customer shipping managers.

4   Daily Operations: The boxes marked "daily over-the-road operation" in Figure 2 were the core of the system. Measures of customer satisfaction and capacity use were generated by these loops and all other feedback loops were connected to them. Figure 3 shows the over-the-road operation in detail. Shipments from individual customers were brought to the origin terminal and grouped into loads, a load being one long-haul trailer filled with freight. "Holds" were defined as filled trailers, not shipped the day received, but held overnight in the terminal yard. In either terminal there were two groups of men and trucks: men and trucks whose home base was that terminal and those based in the opposite city.

The company's shipping policy contained the following restrictions:

1   No men from one terminal could be kept at the other terminal over the weekend.

2   Freight was first assigned to out-of-town men and trucks because layovers, the holding of out-of-town men an extra night, were expensive and bad for morale.

3   Loads which had already been held one night (holds) were given priority for shipment.

4   Empty trucks were never sent.

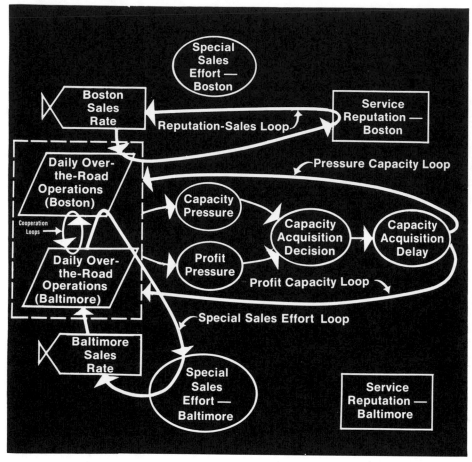

Figure 2   Feedback Loops of the Model*

This traditional policy allowed for no real feedback between the two terminals. There was no mechanism by which one terminal could help the other when an abnormal backlog of freight developed. Despite the claims of management, it was clear that the "no empties" policy could not be maintained in all circumstances. With a random variation in sales rate and a limited supply of tractors, there was certain to be a large number of delayed shipment loads at one of the two terminals sooner or later. After pressing company personnel on the "no empties" policy, it was found that serious backlogs did develop. When this happened, top management acceded to the terminal managers' request for help by authorizing shipment of empty trucks. There were, in fact, "cooperation loops" which connected the shipping policies (see Figure 3).

---

* Special sales effort loop is shown for Baltimore only; reputation-sales growth loop for Boston only.

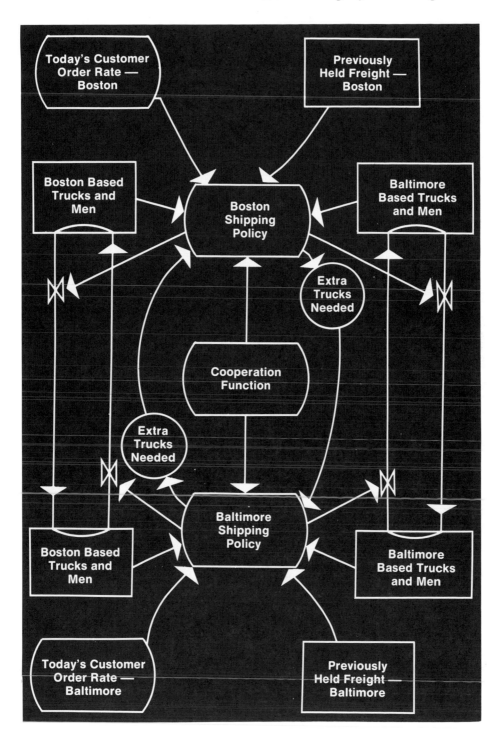

Figure 3 The Over-the-Road Sector

Estimating the Parameters of the Model

With company data and estimates published by the Interstate Commerce Commission and the American Trucking Association, selecting values for most model parameters was straightforward. But finding the constants for cooperating loops, the reputation sales effect, and capacity acquisition delays required some investigation. The cooperation loops reflected the willingness of the terminals to revise their normal shipping policies. The company's traditional cooperation policy was that as long as five or fewer trailer loads were backlogged in a terminal, no special action was to be taken to clear them out; that is, empty trucks were not sent from the opposite terminal. If more than seven or eight loads were backlogged, the full number of empty trucks was dispatched. Examining alternative formulations of this function was an important part of the study.

Two questions were raised in determining the effect of reputation on sales rate: how long did it take the market to perceive a change in the firm's service, and how powerful was the effect of good or bad service on growth of sales rate? To estimate these factors, three sources were used. The first was the firm's top management, salesmen, and terminal managers. Active customers were the second source; 20 major customers were asked their opinion of the effect of service on potential growth in sales. Finally, at an American Management Association distribution meeting, estimates were solicited from logistics executives of many large national firms. From these sources, the market's perception of service was estimated to follow a three- to six-month smoothing of the firm's daily holds to orders ratio. The range of realistic estimates for the service level-sales rate relationship is shown in Figure 4. While it was not certain where the true line lay, we were confident that it was bounded by the optimistic and pessimistic estimates. It was generally agreed that a perfect service record would result in 10 to 12 percent yearly growth. Very poor service, on the other hand, might cause the firm to lose a third of its business in a year.

The sales generators (one for each terminal) were of the form:

SALES = (Average Sales) (Growth Factor) (1 + Noise)

where average sales was a momentum component, growth factor was taken from Figure 4, and noise represented the daily fluctuations of sales, derived from a probability distribution with a mean value of zero.

Capacity acquisition was controlled by profit and capacity utilization pressure. If the firm's operating ratio (yearly expenses/revenue) exceeded 96 percent, no new trucks could be purchased. Otherwise there were no financial constraints on obtaining new trucks.

When the firm's smoothed (over a three- to four-month period) capacity utilization ratio reached 70 to 75 percent, new trucks were ordered. The firm had experienced

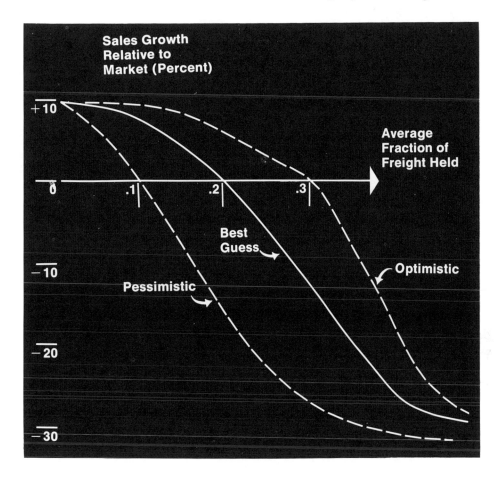

Figure 4   Service-Reputation Effect on Sales Growth

a four- to six-month delay (a two- to three-month delay in placing the order and a two- to three-month wait for delivery), between recognizing a need for new capacity and putting the new tractors into service.

Having carefully chosen and justified the model boundary, feedback loops, and parameter values, the model was coded and debugged.[5] A test run was used to check the reasonableness of the complete model. This validation test used initial values from company records, historical policies for service commitment, and the best estimate of the service-reputation to sales-growth relationship. The result of this test is shown in Figure 5. The trend line for sales growth for the six year simulation and the long period cycles on the sales rate proved consistent with the firm's actual experience. The nodes of actual sales rate oscillations occurred at points in

---

[5] Once the model components are specified, writing the computer code is straightforward. The DYNAMO language was used to code the 70 equations of the model. For details of model formulation, see Wright [12].

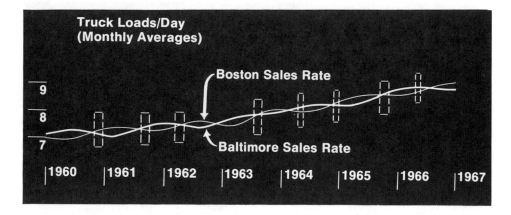

Figure 5   Validation of Simulation

time between the dashed lines in Figure 5. If the model were perfect, and the random components of the order rates exactly matched company history, the nodes produced by the simulation would also fall between the dashed lines.

Although a poor point estimator, the validation run did generate a time series that reflected important patterns in real data. A particularly interesting point was the low frequency oscillations on sales rates. The model showed a pattern of shifting terminal sales rate dominance, with 32-week cycles. Although not noticed before building the model, the same phenomenon was found in company records. The ability of the model to point out an unsuspected pattern in real data did a great deal to build confidence in the formulation.

As the system boundary, causal mechanism, and the parameter choices were defendable and since the complete model's behavior accurately reflected the important components of the firm's real experience, the model appeared to be a valid tool for policy design analysis.[6]

Policy Change Analysis

By examining system structure and model behavior and by testing alternative suggestions, new operating policies were developed for reputation-induced growth, capacity acquisition, and control of imbalance in order-rate between the two terminals.

---

[6] The verification of dynamic models is a problem that has generated much debate. The ability of a model to provide point predictions is not an appropriate validation criterion, given the nature of stochastic differential systems. The fact that model sales oscillations do not match up with actual sales oscillations is expected, and unimportant. For a discussion of the problems and methods of verifying dynamic models, see Wright [11].

With respect to reputation-induced growth, management had two alternatives to consider. The first was to increase the use of empty trucks and encourage long-term growth with good service, but degrade immediate profits. The second was to restrict the use of empty trucks, thus improving or maintaining present profits but reducing long-term growth potential. Increasingly larger costs resulted from increasing commitment to customer satisfaction. The optimal trade-off point was not obvious.

The control policy here was a direct result of the form of the cooperation function. System behavior was examined for a broad range of possible cooperation policies and assumptions about the values of the reputation-growth multiplier. The simulation runs showed that over the range of assumptions about the effect of service on sales rate, increasing the service commitment of the firm would result in increased and profitable growth. Shipping empties would pay back immediate cost in long-term growth. Table 1 summarizes the results of the runs. Profit indices for a 10-year growth period are shown for nine simulations. The reputation-growth assumption estimates are based on the plots of Figure 4. The "ship half needed" option clearly dominated the traditional company policy.

Model behavior was insensitive to reasonable changes in the capacity measure that signals new truck acquisition. In a period of rapid growth, however, the long delay in the firm's original acquisition policy could temporarily constrain growth. Reducing the acquisition delay was practical; management had never seen a need for expediting the ordering process.

The simulation runs for a special, short-term sales effort showed poor results. By the time a small surge in sales appeared, a week or so after initiating the policy, unbalanced sales rates had often corrected themselves or even reversed. Further, management was suspicious of the practicality of such a policy. Investigation of this policy resulted in an analysis of the effect of order rate patterns on total system performance.

In a period when the mean order rates differed at the two terminals, profit was destroyed and growth inhibited. Simulations showed that a 10 percent difference in order rates for four months could cost the firm 30 to 50 percent of the year's potential profits. Growth would thereby be precluded; and it would be impossible to maintain a good service pattern. Substantial noise on the order rates at either terminal also caused a large reduction in profits. The model indicated that a 10 percent standard deviation on order rates could cost 15 to 25 percent of annual potential profits. Such a high daily sales variability made it difficult to ship enough empties to maintain a superior service record. Although everyone knew that imbalance and noise on sales were unprofitable, no one had previously seen exactly how balance between the terminals, and daily sales fluctuations affected profits or how they were tied to growth and customer satisfaction. Quantitative estimates of the significance of these factors and illustration of how they were affected by the firm's operating policies were major results of this study.

	Service Commitment Policy		
Reputation-Growth Assumption	Ship No Empty Trucks	Ship Half Needed Extra Trucks	Ship All Needed Extra Trucks
Optimistic	130	210	140
Best Estimate	100	160	80
Pessimistic	96	120	20

Table 1   Simulation Results Showing Profit Indices Under Various Assumptions

The results indicated that if a situation of imbalance could be anticipated, the firm should add business, profitable or not, at the light terminal and turn away prospective customers at the heavy terminal. Once the system became unbalanced, its internal structure would propagate sustained, unprofitable sales rate oscillations like those shown in Figure 5. Also, to minimize daily sales fluctuations, the firm should seek out shippers who are not concerned with one-day service, even if their freight provides only enough revenue to cover out-of-pocket costs. Such freight could be used as an inventory for smoothing daily operations.[7]

It is important to stress that these policy suggestions were not transparent at the beginning of the study. They made sense only when evaluated with respect to the complete corporate system. A policy of sending empty trucks to smooth daily operations alone was not reasonable, but if they could also be used to encourage growth and to increase overall capacity utilization, the policy made sense. While the direction of possible new policies could probably have been found without dynamic simulation, the simulation analysis was necessary to investigate the interdependence of these policies, to set specific parameter values (as for sending empties), and to demonstrate these improvements to management.

Implementation and Results of Policy Changes

A good deal of time was spent in cultivating support from operating managers for the suggested changes, especially for increased effort for high customer satisfaction. The executive vice-president finally responded to the service campaign with, "I know what you're trying to get me to say. You want me to say we should ship empties. I'll never ship empties." This statement epitomized the failure of the first attempt at implementation. Trying to sell results proved insufficient. It was neces-

---

[7] Several other alternatives for variable control were tested and rejected. These included increasing fleet size and renting trucks. Devices to control for sales uncertainty are discussed in Swanson [8].

sary to provide the operating managers with a conceptual framework for judging the model for themselves so that they could confidently accept the model-based proposals.

A great virtue of industrial dynamics is its simplicity. It was possible to explain to operating executives who were high school graduates enough about feedback systems to teach them the model and sell the model's suggestions. It is fair to point out that the second pass removed misconceptions and dead ends that were present in the initial model formulation. In any case, management bought the model. Convincing the prospective users of policy suggestions that the model structure and behavior were reasonable was the real validation test.

New policies were adopted in the four important areas of balance control, daily sales fluctuations, customer service, and capacity acquisition.

1   Balance Control: The weekly computer-generated accounting reports were expanded to include listings of smoothed sales rates and estimates of potential imbalance. The sales force and terminal managers, now aware of the importance of maintaining system balance, agreed to try to predict major changes in sales patterns in their areas. To correct imbalance, marginally profitable customers were to be solicited at the light terminal and marginally profitable business at the heavy terminal was to be eliminated. There was resistance to the idea of turning away sales, but it was clear from analyzing the model that unless the firm itself took this step, the market would inevitably do so. There was no real choice.

2   Daily Sales Fluctuation: More freight would be solicited, even if only marginally profitable, from customers indifferent to one-day service. Federal, state, and local governments were identified as major sources of such buffer stock; their freight rates are set by bids and not by law. Other possible sources were certain large shippers for whom special rates might be established with Interstate Commerce Commission permission.

3   Commitment to Customer Service: To increase growth, management agreed to improve service levels. The terminal managers were instructed to send one-half of the needed empty trucks to the opposite terminal. If an empty truck could be filled with marginal smoothing freight, so much the better. The firm kept careful count of empties, holds, and average revenue per truckload. The bonus compensation program for terminal managers and salesmen was revised to take account of soliciting and using marginal smoothing freight.

4   Capacity Acquisition: The simulation runs showed that reducing delay in acquiring new tractors meant average utilization could be increased without constraining service and growth. Management, therefore, took steps to expedite ordering decisions.

The policy changes described above were successful. First, imbalance between the two terminals was reduced. Twice during the implementation period the firm took action to mitigate developing imbalance. Thus, when the firm's largest Boston customer, a paperbox factory, was burned to the ground, management regretfully refused several large Baltimore contracts. The computer-generated estimate of imbalance was not, however, useful as a warning signal. Informal information sources such as salesmen, terminal managers, the business press, and trucking industry meetings and publications, turned out to be better forecasting devices.

The new policy appeared to have caused a small improvement in overall system balance. In the two and a half years of active implementation, the balance measure averaged 3.5 unmatched loads per week whereas before implementation, the average was 4.4 loads per week. After adjusting this number for the reduction in daily order balance, a small improvement remained. The firm used marginally profitable service-insensitive freight to help control the effects of daily sales fluctuations. These fluctuations were reduced by 25 percent. Before implementation, average variance on daily shipments was 12 percent; afterward, the variance averaged nine percent.[8] These new policies also reduced over-the-road costs. During the implementation period, the fraction of total expense in the over-the-road sector fell from .115 to .105, a 10 percent reduction. Expenses were cut despite a policy of sending empties when needed. There was, in fact, sufficient smoothing "junk" freight to reduce the number of physical empties. On the other hand, the number of disappointed customers was substantially reduced.

The combination of policies to increase customer service caused substantially improved growth. The firm improved its service measure by reducing the held freight ratio from 20 percent to two percent (not counting deliberate holding of smoothing freight). Growth in sales increased from two percent to eight percent.

Adaptation to New Circumstances

The policy for increased cooperation and service and resulting growth was not maintained. The model boundary had originally been justified with the argument that the intracity operation would never constrain the ability to give good service. A year and a half after implementation, this assumption was invalidated. When the project began, a new terminal was under construction for the Baltimore-Washington area. Zoning, labor, and financing problems delayed completion. In the meantime, rapid growth was taxing the capacity of the old terminal. Terminal freight handling capacity began to dominate the ability to give good service.

The industrial dynamics approach and the model itself were clear and simple enough to be easily adapted to this new situation. Revised simulations showed that steeply rising overtime expenses would absorb any further growth in revenue. As maintaining good service and growth would require substantial and costly overtime operations, the growth strategy was discontinued. The intention was that

---

[8] The standard deviation of daily orders input into the system remained as it had been.

growth inducing strategies would be re-started as soon as the new terminal came on line. Unfortunately, the combination of long construction delays and serious labor problems precluded the reestablishment of an aggressive growth strategy.

The major impact of the model, however, was helping to evaluate a proposed merger and developing control policies for an enlarged operation. When the firm had an opportunity to purchase a small, unprofitable carrier with complementary routes (between Boston and Buffalo), the model was adapted to assist policy design for the proposed three-terminal operation. While the basic ideas of the original model could be directly extended by duplicating sector equations for Buffalo, some revisions were required.

Two interesting constraints had to be considered with respect to shipping policy. First, the expanded firm could not carry freight between Buffalo and Baltimore; the new route pattern was two legs of a triangle, not a closed loop. Second, for the original Boston-Baltimore route, state laws restricted the firm to using a tractor with 60-foot trailers. But for the Boston-Buffalo route, a single truck was allowed to haul two 45-foot trailers. While the driver of such a "double bottom" leviathan did receive premium pay, it was still profitable to haul double loads. There were different opportunity costs, risks, and payoffs for variance smoothing and service strategies. Furthermore, the competition on the Buffalo-Boston route was less keen than on the Boston-Baltimore route. Industry service standards were lower. The potential for service-induced growth was greater on the new route than for the original operation.

New shipping policies were tested; the extended model indicated that the smaller carrier could be profitably integrated into the firm. The acquisition was made and in the next two and a half years revenues for the Buffalo-Boston operation more than doubled. The subsidiary operation showed a substantial profit in place of loss. While part of the growth resulted from increased capitalization and general economies of scale, objective measures of capacity utilization (nearly 90 percent), smoothing of daily sales fluctuations (variance eight to nine percent), service levels (holds of prime freight less than seven percent), and low road sector costs suggested that the operating strategies indicated by the model were an important factor in this substantial, profitable growth.

In summary, the industrial dynamics application provided a substantial return to the firm. It suggested successful policies for the problems to which it was addressed. In addition, it proved highly adaptable to a changing environment. Direct benefits far outweighed total project expenses.

References

[1] Fey, W.R. "An Industrial Dynamics Case Study," *Industrial Management Review,* Vol. 4, no. 1 (Fall 1962).

[2] Forrester, J.W. *Industrial Dynamics.* Cambridge, Mass., MIT Press, 1961.

[3]   Forrester, J.W. "Market Growth as Influenced by Capital Investment," *Industrial Management Review,* Vol. 9, no. 2 (Winter 1968).

[4]   Forrester, J.W. "Modeling the Dynamic Processes of Corporate Growth," *Proceedings of the IBM Scientific Computing Symposium on Simulation Models and Gaming,* December 1964.

[5]   Gorry, G.A. "The Development of Managerial Models," *Sloan Management Review,* Vol. 12, no. 2 (Winter 1971).

[6]   Roberts, E.B. "Industrial Dynamics and the Design of Management Control Systems," *Management Technology* (December 1963).

[7]   Roberts, E.B., Abrams, D.I., and Weil, H.B., "A System Study of Policy Formulation in a Vertically Integrated Firm," *Management Science,* Vol. 14, no. 12 (August 1968).

[8]   Swanson, C.V. "Information and Control for Corporate Growth," *Sloan Management Review,* Vol. 12, no. 3 (Spring 1971).

[9]   Swanson, C.V. "Resource Control and Mar'.eting Policies Using Industrial Dynamics," *Industrial Management Review,* Vol. 10, no. 3 (Spring 1969).

[10]   Swanson, C.V., and Thorsten, A.C. "A System Dynamics Design and Implementation of Inventory Policies." Sloan School of Management Working Paper 539-71; Cambridge, Mass., MIT, 1971.

[11]   Wright, R.D. "On Validating Dynamic Models." Sloan School of Management Working Paper 553-71; Cambridge, Mass., MIT, 1971.

[12]   Wright, R.D. "Scannell Transportation, An Industrial Dynamics Implementation." Unpublished M.S. thesis; Cambridge, Mass., MIT. 1969.

15

The United States Plywood Industry:
A Systems Study

Thomas J. Manetsch

Introduction

This paper takes a rather broad view of a national industry and describes a study which was directed at determining a set of causal relationships which relate the behavior of macroscopic variables, such as aggregate industry output and an aggregate price index, to the structure of the industry and to certain exogenous variables. The general methodology employed is not new, being along the lines of the *industrial dynamics* approach introduced by Forrester.[1] The unique characteristics of particular real-world environments make for a rich diversity in the application of the basic methodology; in this case, an industry which is nearly competitive (in the classical economic sense) provides an interesting problem environment within which the basic methodology is employed.

General Industry Description

Though the production of plywood is heavily concentrated in the Pacific northwestern United States, plywood is a national industry. In excess of 160 mills ship plywood to approximately 1000 distribution warehouses located throughout the country. The industry or *system* studied includes producers, wholesalers, and tens of thousands of retailers, industrial users, and individual customers. Not included in the system definition are related industries, such as lumber, paper and paper products, and the timber industry. This exclusion is based upon evidence that the interrelationships with these industries are *weak* ones. Thus, the assumption of *near complete decomposability*[2] is made with respect to the larger system within which the plywood industry is embedded.

The objective of the study was to construct and test a model which would relate the behavior of major industry variables, in particular price and output, to relevant

The work reported in this article was supported by the Electrical Engineering Dept. and the Agricultural Experiment Station at Oregon State University and the Dept. of Engineering at the University of California. The article was previously published in *IEEE Transactions on Systems Science and Cybernetics* SSC–3, no. 2 (November 1967), pp. 92–101.

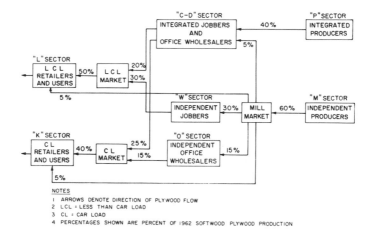

Figure 1   General system model.

industry structure—corporate policies, technology, time lags, etc. Of particular interest were feasible changes in industry structure which would result in more stable market price behavior. One cause of industry price instability, to be discussed in some detail, is a seasonal fluctuation in demand for plywood due to yearly variations in construction activity.[3]

Due to the basic complexity of such a system it was necessary to aggregate system microvariables and analyze the system in terms of a relatively small number of macro or aggregate variables. Loosely speaking, aggregation took place by grouping together those firms in the industry, which, due to similar corporate structure and technology, tend to behave alike economically. The model then approximates the interactions of the thousands of industry firms by the interactions of a small number of groups of firms or *sectors*.

The *general system model* of Figure 1 depicts seven sectors into which firms of the industry were placed for purposes of aggregation. It should be stressed that no one general model can correctly aggregate every firm in the industry. Due to the wide diversity of organizational patterns that were found to exist, some firms, of necessity, did not fall into the sectors defined. Since aggregation, for the present at least, is essential from the practical standpoint, the problem is one of defining the sectors of the general model so that 1) as many firms as possible are correctly aggregated, 2) the resulting model is tractable. In what follows, the sectors which make up the general system model will be described.

Producing Sectors.   The two producing sectors are designated as the M and P sectors in Figure 1. Firms included in the M sector are *independent producers* in the sense that they are not tied organizationally to wholesaling organizations—they are in business primarily to produce plywood. On the other hand, the producers of P sector are tied organizationally to the plywood distributors of C–D sector and are hence termed *integrated producers.* The integrated producers are typically the giants of the industry and small independent producers bound to larger firms by contractual agreements. In 1962, independent mills, about 100 in number out of a total of 165, were responsible for 60 percent of industry production, with the remainder produced by integrated mills and mills that *act like* integrated mills because of contractual ties.

This sectoral breakdown of plywood producers was based upon two considerations. First, as seen in Figure 1, the output of the independent producers of M sector is offered for sale on a competitive market designated the *mill market*, while that of the integrated producers of P sector, for the most part, bypasses the mill market and is transferred intrafirm to the distribution outlets of C–D sector. Second, due to the organizational difference cited, the independent and integrated producers have markedly different price and production policies. Independent mills are subject to the direct competitive forces of the market which strongly influence their price and production decisions. Integrated mills on the other hand are buffered from these market forces by the large distribution warehouses to which they are organizationally tied.

Retailer-User Sectors.   The retail-user sectors are designated L and K in Figure 1. These sectors include not only plywood retailers but also users of plywood who buy from the same sources as do the retailers. Included among such users are building contractors and industrial users who, due to the volume of their utilization, can purchase from wholesale outlets.

In Figure 1 the L sector represents the aggregation of retailers and users who buy plywood in less than boxcar load lots from distribution warehouses. They are called LCL *Retailers and Users* where LCL is a mnemonic abbreviation of *L*ess-than-*C*ar-*L*oad. On the other hand, K sector represents users and retailers who buy plywood in boxcar load lots. They are hence called CL retailers and users where CL stands for *carload*.

The distinction between the two types of retailers and users is the following. While less-than-carload purchases usually are made out of distribution warehouses, boxcar-sized lots are normally shipped directly from the mill to save unloading, warehousing, and reloading costs at the wholesale level. There are therefore the two distinct wholesale markets for plywood shown in Figure 1. Prices in the LCL market are higher than those prevailing in the CL market because of increased costs in selling out of warehouse. In 1962 it was estimated that 50 percent of production was sold through the LCL market, 40 percent through the CL market, and 10 percent bypassed wholesale markets.

Wholesale Sectors.   As shown in Figure 1, three sectors have been defined at the wholesale level. The three sectors represent firms that are distinctly different in terms of policies and behavior. The C–D sector has been mentioned in connection with the integrated producers of P sector. The C–D sector is an aggregation of jobbers and office wholesalers who are organizationally integrated with firms in P sector.[4] As seen in Figure 1, this sector obtains the major portion of its plywood on intrafirm transfer from integrated producers. In the aggregate, however, the C–D sector is able to sell more plywood than P sector can produce. The C–D sector is, therefore, a net buyer in the mill market and, in 1962, obtained about 10 percent of its input by buying from independent mills in the mill market. On the selling side, the C–D sector sells out of warehouse into the LCL wholesale market and arranges for direct shipments from mills to customers through the CL wholesale market. The sector therefore represents the aggregation of firms which perform both jobbing and office wholesaling functions. This dual role is the reason for the dual nomenclature in the sector designation C–D. Large integrated firms spanning the P–C–D sectors make profit by producing as well as by selling plywood and *overall* profit is of primary importance to these firms. Production as well as selling policies are therefore influenced by the integrated nature of firm organization.

In Figure 1, the O sector represents an aggregation of distributors who act as independent office wholesalers. The firms of O sector buy plywood in carload lots from mills (mainly independent ones) and sell with a markup of approximately three percent to the retailers and users of K sector. Though these firms legally own the plywood for a time, the physical flow of plywood is from mill to customer. Some firms of this sector take advantage of the seasonal variation in plywood price and sell short, and engage in position buying to increase their normal three-percent markup. In 1962 it was estimated that 15 percent of industry production was handled through independent office wholesalers.

The last of the three sectors at the wholesale level is W sector, an aggregation of independent jobbers. These firms are not integrated with producers and make their profit by selling plywood and other building materials out of inventory. As shown in Figure 1 these firms buy from independent mills and sell out of inventory in less-than-carload-lots to retailers and users of L sector. Independent jobbers also perform an office wholesaling function but since this part of their operation is essentially the same as that of the office wholesalers of O sector, it has been lumped together with the firms of O sector. Independent jobbers also take advantage of seasonal plywood price variation. They tend, as a group, to increase buying when prices are low and decrease buying when prices are high and are largely responsible for the negatively-sloped demand curve which has been measured by econometric methods.[5] Independent jobbers handled 30 percent of 1962 production.

Salient Features of the Simulation Model

In this section the structure of the simulation model is discussed in some detail. Due to the large scope of a model of this nature it is necessary to omit many structural details of the model; this discussion centers around a 2-sector model which is the first step in the construction of the larger 7-sector model of Figure 1. The 2-sector model, essentially M and W sectors, is interesting in its own right as it incorporates some of the major industry interactions and in significant respects exhibits behavior characteristic of the industry. In what follows, then, major aspects of M and W sectors are discussed along with the mechanism which generates market price.

Independent Mills of M Sector.   The typical independent plywood mill is a production-oriented firm that relies upon efficient production techniques for survival in an intensely competitive market. A major problem of the industry has historically been overproduction with attendant low market prices. It was learned that the nature of independent mill costs, which makes it rational for an individual mill to produce at capacity until low market prices make such a policy unprofitable, is a major cause of overproduction. Independent mill production policies are therefore of major importance in determining mill market price and are discussed in some detail here. Because independent mills hold little finished inventory, inventory control policies are not a major factor influencing market price and industry output, and will not be treated in detail here. Independent mills of M sector were found to play a key role in mill market price determination and for this reason the simulation of the market price mechanism is discussed in this section.

Production Process.   Before describing in detail independent mill production policies as incorporated in the simulation model of M sector, it should be emphasized that the output of an individual plywood mill is not just *plywood* but in general a varied mix of different sizes, thicknesses, and grades of the product. An individual mill must therefore make decisions as to how its output is best allocated among the various product alternatives. Though of vital interest to a particular firm, these decisions do not appear to have a major influence upon production rate and *mill market price*,[6] and are not considered in the simulation model. This simplification is possible because the prices of the many variations of the product tend to move together (except perhaps in the very short run) in response to aggregate supply and demand. The simulation model, then, seeks to represent the process whereby an individual independent mill, and hence the M sector as a whole, adjusts its overall production rate.

According to the classical (static) theory of firm behavior,[7] a firm maximizes profits in the short run[8] by producing at the rate for which the marginal cost of producing a unit of output is equal to the price of a unit of output in the market. This policy, modified by a number of practical constraints, appears, on the basis of industry data and interviews with industry managers, to be followed among independent producers of the industry.

A cost function which is typical of independent producers is that of (1). From this cost function, the production rate for maximum profit will be derived.

$$C = C_0 + nWh + MQ \ (h \leq s)$$
$$C = C_0 + nWs + MQ + nW_0(h\text{-}s) \ (h > s) \tag{1}$$

where

C—total cost (dollars/week)

C_0—fixed cost (dollars/week)

n—number of men required to operate mill

W—wage rate (dollars/man-hour)

W_0—overtime wage rate (dollars/man-hour)

h—total hours operated per week

s—hours worked per week on *straight time* (non-overtime)
M—material cost (logs, glue, etc.) dollars/ft²
Q—total production (ft²/week).

The first part of (1) represents cost when there is no overtime production while the second is valid for the case of overtime production. Total production Q is related to hours worked per week h by (2)

$$Q = qh \qquad (2)$$

where q is the plant capacity (ft²/hr).
    Combining (1) and (2):

$$C = C_0 + (nWQ/q) + MQ \ (h \le s)$$
$$C = C_0 + nWs + MQ + nW_0(Q/q - s) \ (h > s). \qquad (3)$$

The optimum production rate Q is derived from the following expression for profit rate

$$\text{II} = PQ - C \qquad (4)$$

where

II—profit, dollars/week
P—price, dollars/ft².

To maximize profit with respect to production rate Q, (4) is normally differentiated partially with respect to Q, set equal to zero, and solved for optimum Q. In this case, the procedure breaks down since the resulting expression is independent of Q

$$\partial\text{II}/\partial Q = P - (nW/q + M) = 0 \ (h \le s)$$
$$\partial\text{II}/\partial Q = P - (nW_0/q + M) = 0 \ (h > s) \qquad (5)$$

In spite of this difficulty (5) still tells the mill manager what he must do to maximize profit with respect to production rate Q. Since profit is an increasing function of Q as long as the right side of (5) is positive, the manager maximizes profit by increasing Q as much as possible without causing (5) to be negative.
    These results are summarized by the independent mill supply curve of Figure 2 from which three cases of interest arise. If the market price is greater than $(nW/q + M)$ (the marginal cost on a straight time basis) but less than $(nW_0/q + M)$ (the overtime marginal cost), a mill maximizes profit by producing as much as possible without going to overtime production. Operation in this case takes place s hours per week and output is qs as shown in the figure. The second case is that of market price in excess of $(nW_0/q + M)$. In this case, profit is maximized by producing at the maximum production rate

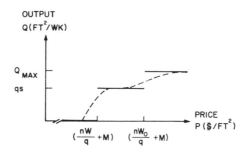

OUTPUT
$Q(FT^2/WK)$

Q_{MAX}

qs

PRICE
$P(\$/FT^2)$

$(\frac{nW}{q}+M)$ $(\frac{nW_0}{q}+M)$

Figure 2   Independent mill supply function.

possible, Q_{max} in Figure 2. Case three is that of market price less than $n(W/Q + M)$. If this situation prevails, $\partial\Pi/\partial Q$ is negative from (5) and in the long run a mill would be forced to cease operation. Due to shut down and start-up costs, mills tend to operate for limited periods of time at reduced output in this case.

These three cases define the theoretical supply curve for an individual mill shown in heavy lines in Figure 2. The actual curve for an individual mill is probably more like the smoothed curve shown in the figure. The aggregate supply curve for the M sector as a whole is obtained by adding individual firm supply curves and has the general shape of an individual firm curve.

It is generally accepted in the industry that the nature of this supply curve is a cause of a major industry problem—overproduction with attendant low market prices. As seen from the figure, a mill maximizes profit by producing at normal (straight time) capacity until low prices force a cut in production. This phenomenon is not just theoretical; it is a very real part of the behavior of independent mills.

The nonlinear supply function discussed is readily incorporated into the simulation model by means of table functions. In the chosen simulation language DYNAMO,[9] such functions are included in the model with two programming statements. Since the dynamic behavior of the system is of interest here, the simulation model must also include relevant time lags as they occur in the real world. In the case of mill production decisions, significant lags occur in the decision-making process which must be included in the simulation model. The nature of these lags is illustrated by the block diagram of Figure 3. Variables in the figure are shown as functions of the Laplace transform variable s.

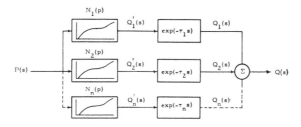

Figure 3   M sector production process.

The figure shows n mills with supply functions $N_1, N_2, \ldots N_n$ with common input variable (of transform) $P(s)$ where $P(s)$ is a function of market price and its first time derivative. The $Q_1'(s), Q_2'(s), \ldots Q_n'(s)$ in Figure 3 are the desired production rates (for maximum profit) and the $Q_1(s), Q_2(s), \ldots Q_n(s)$ are the actual production rates. The transfer functions $\exp(-\tau_1 s), \exp(-\tau_2 s), \ldots \exp(-\tau_n s)$ are the Laplace transform transfer-functions for discrete time lags $\tau_1, \tau_2, \ldots, \tau_n$, where $(\tau_1, \tau_2, \ldots, \tau_n)$ is assumed to be a random sample from a probability distribution with density function $f(\tau)$. These discrete time lags arise from the nature of the human decision process and the plywood production process. $Q(s)$ in the figure is the aggregate or sector production rate.

Direct simulation of the production process of Figure 3, with n equal to 100 in this case, is computationally inefficient and an onerous programming task. A simplified representation of Figure 3 is therefore of interest. Fortunately the process of Figure 3 can be approximated by a vastly simpler one. The development of this simplified production process is described in what follows.

From Figure 3 the sector output $Q(s)$ can be written as

$$Q(s) = \sum_{i=1}^{n} Q_i'(s)e^{-\tau_i s} \tag{6}$$

on taking the expected value $E [\ \ ]$ of (6), (7) results

$$E[Q(s)] = nE[Q_i'e^{-\tau_i s}]. \tag{7}$$

Assuming statistical independence between the supply functions N_i and the discrete time lags τ_i, (7) becomes

$$E[Q(s)] = nE[Q_i']E[e^{-\tau_i s}] \tag{8}$$

where

$$E[e^{-\tau_i s}] = \int_0^\infty e^{-\tau s}f(\tau)d\tau$$
$$= L[f(\tau)]$$
$$= F(s)$$

and

$$E[Q_i'] \approx \bar{Q}_i = \frac{Q_1' + Q_2' + \ldots + Q_n'}{n}$$

since the sample mean $\bar{Q}'$ is an estimate of the population mean. Since

$$Q_i' = N_i(P)$$

$$E[Q_i'] \approx \frac{N_1(P) + N_2(P) + \ldots + N_n(P)}{n} = \bar{N}(P).$$

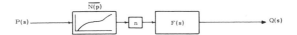

Figure 4   M sector production process-aggregate representation.

The aggregate supply curve $\overline{N}$ is obtained by arithmetically averaging the ordinates of the individual functions $N_1, N_2, \ldots, N_n$.

On inserting these results into (8), (9) results which verifies the simplified aggregate representation of Figure 4.

$$E[Q(s)] = n\overline{N}(P)F(s). \tag{9}$$

It is thus clear that the Laplace transform $F(s)$ of the density function $f(\tau)$ is an unbiased estimate of the more complex delay process of Figure 3.

In the simulation model it was assumed that $f(\tau)$ is a member of the Erlang family[10] and thus

$$f(\tau) = \frac{(\alpha k)(\alpha k \tau)^{k-1} \exp(-k\alpha\tau)}{(k-1)!} \tag{10}$$

where $E[\tau] = 1/\alpha$.

The approximating transfer function $F(s)$ in Figure 5 is, therefore

$$F(s) = \frac{1}{(s/k\alpha + 1)^k}. \tag{11}$$

The transfer function of (11) is readily simulated by the **DYNAMO** simulation language used in this study.

As would be expected, the quality of the approximate representation improves with increasing n. Though discussion of the error involved in the approximation is not possible here, the subject is treated elsewhere.[11] The approximation is *good* in this case where n is of the order of 100.

The technique described for obtaining an aggregate representation for many discrete time lags was used a number of times in the simulation model, including the aggregate representation of discrete information and material handling lags. A significant point here is that aggregate economic phenomena, such as those discussed here, can rationally be analyzed in terms of transfer functions, time domain methods, and other tools of engineering system theory.

Simulation of the independent mill production process also included certain production constraints that are not discussed in detail. One of these is an annual curtailment of production during summer months caused by employee vacations.

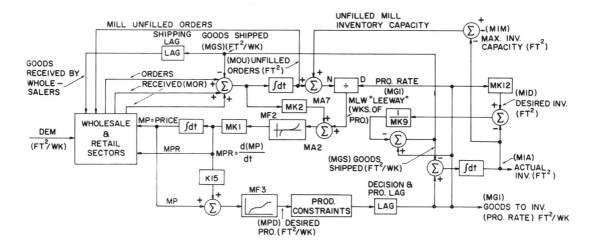

Figure 5 Block diagram of M sector and price mechanism.

Mill Market Price Mechanism. The mill price mechanism is discussed here in connection with the independent mills of M sector because of the great influence of independent mill behavior upon market price. All sectors in the industry influence market price to some extent but, due to the production policy previously discussed, independent mills have disproportionately large influence upon the market. As has been seen, the nature of costs induces independent mills to produce at or in excess of normal capacity for all market prices for which profit rate is non-negative. To maintain this production rate when net industry supply is in excess of demand, mills are forced to cut price to maintain the order backlog necessary to continue production at the desired level (small mill inventory capacities and inadequate capitalization make it impractical to store large quantities of excess production). The result of this behavior pattern is a low market price during times of excess supply that forces less efficient plants to curtail production. During times of excess demand, price rises until sufficient production is induced to equate supply and demand.

This discussion of price behavior is embodied in Figure 5 which illustrates the price mechanism of the simulation model embedded in the structure of M sector. A number of details necessary in the simulation model have been omitted from Figure 5 for clarity. Figure 5 also indicates the interactions between the independent mills of M sector and the rest of the plywood industry.

The variable MGI[12] in Figure 5 is the sector production rate (Q in the preceding discussion of M sector production policies). The variable MGS is the rate at which M sector ships goods to other sectors and is the production rate plus or minus a small quantity to adjust inventory. The variable MGS is necessary in the model to calculate M sector unfilled orders MOU which is of key importance in the price mechanism:[13]

$$\text{MOU}(t) = \text{MOU}(0) + \int_0^t [\text{MOR}(x) - \text{MGS}(x)]dx \qquad (12)$$

where

MOU—*M* sector *O*rders *U*nfilled, ft²
MGS—*M* sector *G*oods *S*hipped, ft²/week
MOR—*M* sector *O*rders *R*eceived from other sectors, ft²/week.

Orders received by M sector, MOR, is in turn a function of market price and its rate of change as indicated by Figure 5. The origin of this variable is discussed further in connection with the independent jobbers of W sector.

The variable MLW in Figure 5, closely related to unfilled orders MOU, is given by

$$\text{MLW}(t) = \frac{\text{MOU}(t) + [\text{MIM} - \text{MIA}(t)]}{\text{MGI}(t)} \tag{13}$$

where

MLW(t)—*M* sector *leeway*, weeks of production
MIM—*M* sector *I*nventory capacity *M*aximum, ft²
MIA(t)—*M* sector *I*nventory *A*ctual, ft²
MGI(t)—*M* sector *G*oods to *I*nventory, ft²/week (production rate).

M sector *leeway* MLW is from (13) the number of weeks the sector could operate at the production rate MGI with no incoming orders and without curtailing production. The concept of *leeway* is an important one in the minds of independent producers. A certain minimum amount, in the order of 2–3 weeks, is necessary to plan production runs in an efficient manner. When *leeway* falls much below what is considered desirable, mills cut price in an attempt to increase it to an acceptable level. For *leeway* in excess of that desired, mills increasingly refuse to accept orders and market price tends to rise. This behavior is represented in the simulation model by the function MF2 in Figure 5 which relates the time derivative of market price to M sector leeway–MLW:

$$\text{MPR}(t) = (\text{MK1})[\text{MF2}(\text{MA2}(t))] \tag{14}$$

where

MPR(t)—*M*ill market *P*rice *R*ate, dollars/ft²·week
MK1—model parameter
MF2( )—nonlinear function of MA2(t)

and

$$\text{MA2}(t) = \text{MIW}(t) + \text{MK2}(d\text{MOU}/dt) \tag{15}$$

where

MA2(t)—*expected* leeway, ft²
MIW(t)—M sector leeway, ft²
MOU(t)—M sector Orders Unfilled, ft²
MK2—model parameter.

The introduction of the rate of change of unfilled orders into (15) and hence into (14) is necessary because mill managers use available information on the trend of unfilled orders to estimate the *expected* leeway of (15). It can be shown by application of control theory that the inclusion of the rate of change of unfilled orders in (15) is necessary for stable market equilibria.

To summarize the operation of the market mechanisms, if expected leeway MA2 is in some normal or desired range (the flat portion of MF2 in Figure 5) the rate of change of market price is zero. For values of MA2 less than or greater than this normal range, the rate of change of price is respectively negative or positive as determined by the function MF2. Market price is determined by integrating the variable MPR:

$$MP(t) = MP(0) + \int_0^t MPR(x)dx \tag{16}$$

where

> MP(t)—*M*arket *P*rice, dollars/ft^2
> MPR(t)—*M*arket *P*rice *R*ate, dollars/ft^2·week.

Independent Jobbers of W Sector.   As discussed, the independent mills of M sector and the independent jobbers of W sector play a key role in the determination of mill market price and output. In this section the more important aspects of the simulation model of the independent jobber sector are discussed. In particular, the policies underlying the sector order rate, which strongly influence demand in the mill market, are discussed.

In industry interviews it was learned that three major factors dominantly determine the rate at which independent jobbers order plywood in the mill market. These are: expected future sales, current price and its rate of change, and the status of inventory levels with respect to a *desired* value. Equation (17), the order-rate decision rule incorporated into the simulation model, contains these three basic components:

$$WOIM(t) = WSFL(t) + \frac{1}{WK3} [WIF(t) - WIA(t) + WPD(t) - WPA(t) +$$
$$WOU(t) - WON(t)] + (WK4) \times [MPR(t)] +$$
$$(WK5)[MPM(t) - MP(t)] \tag{17}$$

where

> WOIM(t)—*W* sectors *O*rders *I*mpending to *M* sector, ft^2/week. (WOIM differs from the actual order-rate, WOSM, by an ordering lag. This lag is simulated in the same manner as the M sector production lag previously discussed.)
> WSFL(t) —*W* sector *S*ales *F*orecast (to *L* sector), ft^2/week. (This variable is generated in the model by seasonally averaging past sales.)
> WK3   —model parameter which determines speed of inventory adjustment
> WIF(t)   —*W* sector *I*nventory *F*orecast, ft^2 (future desired inventory)

WIA(t)   —W sector *I*nventory *A*ctual, ft^2

WPD(t)   —W sector *P*ipeline inventory[14] *D*esired, ft^2

WPA(t)   —W sector *P*ipeline inventory *A*ctual, ft^2

WOU(t)   —W sector *O*rders *U*nfilled,[15] ft^2

WON(t)   —W sector unfilled *O*rder *N*ormal, ft^2

MPR(t)   —mill *M*arket *P*rice *R*ate, dollars/ft ·week

WK4   —parameter that determines the strength of speculative ordering based upon the rate of change of price

MPM(t)   —mill *M*arket *P*rices *S*moothed, dollars/ft^2 (This is a *normal* or average price obtained by exponentially smoothing past prices.)

MP(t)   —mill *M*arket *P*rice, dollars/ft^2 (as determined by the market mechanism previously discussed)

WK5   —parameter that determines the amount of speculative buying due to excursions of price away from what is considered *normal*.

From tests of the simulation model it became evident that the parameter K5, which determines the amount of speculative ordering which is based upon excursions of price from what is considered *normal*, has a great deal of influence upon mill market price and industry output. For example, the magnitude of seasonal price variations over a year was strongly affected by the magnitude of WK5, with price oscillations diverging toward instability as WK5 approached zero. From physical reasoning it can be seen that, with independent mill production policies as they are, such must be the case. If jobbers are not willing to absorb excess production through speculative buying, price tends to decrease to a very low level. Jobbers do, in fact, absorb excess production—at the right price—and hence act as a buffer to match seasonally fluctuating end user demand to relatively constant supply.

It will be noted that the independent jobber order rate as determined by (17) is a linear equation. The model was so constructed because initially the formulation of a more appropriate nonlinear relationship was uncertain and because a linear approximation is known to be valid in some region of state space. As is seen later, a model incorporating the linearized equation (17) behaves like the actual industry in a number of significant respects. Model tests provided insight into refinements of model structure and in this case suggest a more appropriate nonlinear form for (17) which emphasizes speculation when inventory lies within certain acceptable limits and inventory control only when inventory excursions become intolerable.

Though they are not discussed in detail here, the simulations of user-retailer sectors, L and K in Figure 1, are quite similar to that of W sector. The simulation model of C–D sector is different from that of W sector in a number of respects, due to their organizational integration with the producers of P sector. The simulation model of O sector also differs rather markedly from the W sector model, due to the fact that the office wholesalers of O sector do not physically hold inventory.

Simulation Model Tests

In the course of model tests, three successively more complex models were programmed and simulated using the simulation language DYNAMO.[16] The philosophy underlying model building was to begin with a relatively simple model which embodied those aspects of the system which appeared to be of major importance in determining market behavior and to add refinements in discrete steps. This approach made possible some evaluation of the model complexity necessary to describe system behavior. In accordance with this philosophy, a 2-sector model composed of sectors M and W was constructed which was followed respectively by a 5-sector model composed of sectors M, W, C–D, P, L, and a 7-sector model incorporating sectors M, W, C–D, P, L, O, and K. Results of tests of the 2-sector model are presented here because this relatively simple model behaves in a number of interesting respects like the actual industry, and because tests of the more sophisticated models are inconclusive due to time and computational restrictions imposed upon the study.

The model tests to be described simulate the response of the industry to a cyclic variation in end user demand for plywood. Such a variation arises due to seasonal fluctuations in construction activity caused by winter weather in the northern parts of the country. Accordingly, end user demand (closely related to the variable DEM in Figure 5) is taken to be of the form of (18).

$$\text{DEM}(t) = \text{DEM}_0 - \text{DEM}_1[\cos(2\Pi t/52)] \qquad\qquad (18)$$

where

DEM(t)—end user demand for plywood, ft^2/week
DEM$_0$, DEM$_1$—constants
t—time.

The cosine function of (18) approximates the cyclical variation in demand rather well if $t = 0, 2\Pi, \ldots, n\Pi$ (n even) is considered to be the start of a given year. An assumption implicit in (18) is that of end user demand independent of plywood price.[17]

With end user demand specified by (18), the simulation model generated the time paths of major variables such as price, production rate, profit, mill unfilled orders and wholesale inventory. Typical model data are shown in Figure 6. Figure 6 illustrates one year of simulated industry behavior with time in weeks plotted along the horizontal axis. The curves labeled D, P, Q, S, and U in the figure are defined as follows:

D—end user demand, millions of ft^2/week
P—mill market price[18], dollars/thousand ft^2
Q—production rate, millions of ft^2/week
S—wholesale inventory, millions of ft^2
U—mill unfilled orders, ft^2.

The vertical scales for these variables appear at the left of the figure.

Since the model tests described represented a typical year of industry behavior and not a particular year, it was not possible to compare model results with industry behavior directly. It was possible, however, to compare these results with average

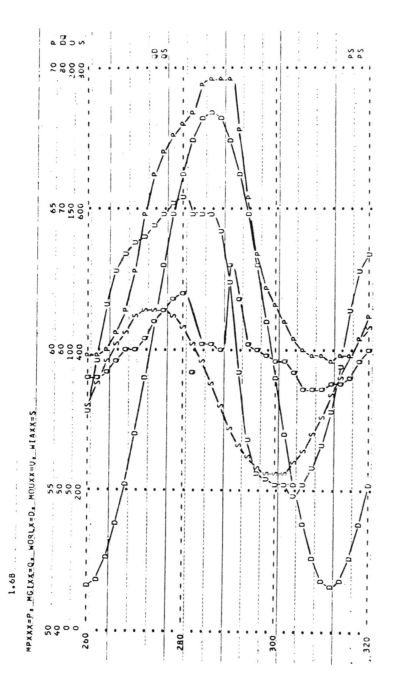

Figure 6 One year of simulated industry behavior (2-sector model).

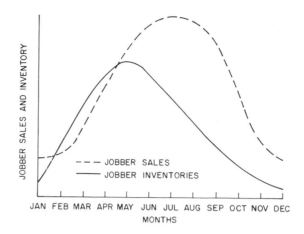

Figure 7 Industry data—jobbers and sales inventory.

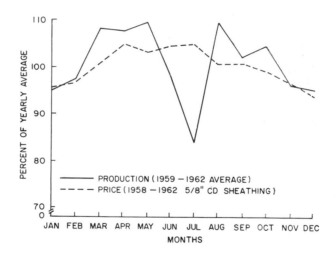

Figure 8 Industry data—price and production.

industry behavior over a number of years. These data are shown in Figures 7 and 8. Figure 8 depicts the average seasonal behavior of wholesale sales and inventory. The dashed curve of Figure 7 depicts the seasonal behavior of jobber sales and corresponds to the end user demand (curve labeled *D*) of Figure 7. The solid curve in Figure 7 illustrates the seasonal variation of jobber inventories. The peak in jobber inventory is seen to precede the peak in jobber sales by about nine weeks. In the simulation run depicted this time lead was about 12 weeks. In model tests of parameter sensitivity this time interval was found to vary from 8–12 weeks as critical model parameters were varied over wide limits. Unfortunately, the data source for Figure 7 did not provide a quantitative measure of jobber sales and inventory oscillations with time.

Figure 8 depicts the average seasonal variation of plywood production and price over three and four year intervals respectively. These curves correspond to the Q and P curves of the model data in Figure 6. The irregular nature of these data is due to the fact that monthly averages were plotted. The large production decrease in summer months is due to employee vacations.

To obtain an objective assessment of the model, data similar to the model results of Figure 6 were discussed with plywood industry managers well-acquainted with the industry and its market behavior. The general reaction was that the model exhibited behavior typical of the industry itself.

The model tests described are with respect to a 2-sector model of the industry. A basic assumption underlying this 2-sector model is that *all* producing firms act like the independent producers of Figure 1 and that all wholesalers act like independent jobbers. From earlier discussion this is obviously not the case. The more complex 5-sector and 7-sector simulation models would be expected to better represent the industry and its more subtle interactions. Further work is attempting to apply the study to particular problems of the plywood industry.[19]

Acknowledgment

The author is indebted to Z. B. Orzech and A. N. Halter of Oregon State University for their collaboration during industry interviews and valuable discussions throughout the research program.

Notes

1. J. W. Forrester, *Industrial Dynamics*. Cambridge, Mass.: The MIT Press, 1961

2. A. Ando, F. M. Fisher, and H. A. Simon, *Essays on the Structure of Social Science Models*. Cambridge, Mass.: The MIT Press, 1963, pp. 64-112.

3. Residential and industrial construction accounts for over 50 percent of the total demand for plywood. National construction falls markedly during the winter months.

4. The term *jobber* here will be taken to mean a middleman who physically stocks plywood and sells out of his inventory. An *office wholesaler* will be defined as a middleman who buys and sells plywood without taking physical possession of the product.

5. R. S. Simpson, "An econometric analysis of demand and supply relationships in the Douglas Fir plywood industry," Master's thesis, Oregon State University, Corvallis, Oregon, 1963.

6. The industry standard and that used here is the price of 1,000 square feet of 1/4 inch 3-ply AD grade.

7. J. M. Henderson and R. E. Quandt, *Microeconomic Theory—A Mathematical Approach*. New York: McGraw-Hill, 1958.

8. The *short run* here is a time short enough to preclude the expansion of production through investment in capital equipment.

9. A. L. Pugh III, *DYNAMO User's Manual*. Cambridge, Mass.: The MIT Press, 1963.

10. For $k = 1$ the Erlang density function is the familiar exponential distribution, and, for increasing k, $f(\tau)$ approaches the normal density function with mean $1/\alpha$. By properly selecting k a wide range of physical delay processes can be simulated.

11. T. J. Manetsch, "Transfer function representation of the aggregate behavior of a class of economic processes," *IEEE Transactions on Automatic Control*, vol. AC-11, pp. 693-698, October 1966.

12. Variable nomenclature is essentially that of the computer simulation program.

13. It will be noted that simulation model equations are explicitly represented by the diagram of Figure 6.

14. *Pipeline* inventory refers to goods in the supply pipeline from producer to customer. To maintain control of warehouse inventory (WIA), pipeline inventory must also be adjusted as sales rate varies.

15. Unfilled orders *act like* negative physical inventory and must be adjusted as sales rate varies.

16. See no. 9.

17. *End user* demand should not be confused with retailer or wholesaler demand which definitely does vary with price due to speculative activities. *End user* demand is generated by a demand for products which utilize plywood such as buildings and industrial products.

18. The price of 1/4 inch AD grade plywood was used as a price index.

19. This work is being done through the Agricultural Experiment Station at Oregon State University, Corvallis, Oregon.

Part Four:
Research and Development System Dynamics

As soon as system dynamics work was initiated at M.I.T., students began to see potential applications in the areas of technical organizations and research and development (R&D) activities. To a great extent this was a natural consequence of the engineering background of system dynamics and of its initial practitioners. The technical approach, the feedback view, and the use of continuous-process models similar to analog computer work all helped to make system dynamics logical and communicable to the technical man and manager.

In addition, the M.I.T. student body quickly showed inclinations to apply dynamic systems analysis and modeling to the industrial area they knew best, i.e. R&D. About one-third of the Sloan Fellows Executive Development Program enter M.I.T. from technical management positions; 80 percent of the Sloan School graduate students were formerly undergraduate majors in science or engineering; and open registration policies encourage many students from the M.I.T. Schools of Science and Engineering to register for the system dynamics courses. These factors have produced a heavy concentration of M.I.T. theses on research and development management problems, with spin-off applications in industry and government.

The work can be divided into three main areas: (1) the dynamics associated with research and development projects; (2) phenomena associated with the whole R&D organization, especially resource allocation among projects or areas; (3) interrelations between the R&D effort and the total corporation (or government agency). Part 4 of this volume is organized along these lines.

The first system dynamics thesis on R&D management issues was written by Abraham Katz in 1958 as a member of the M.I.T. Sloan Fellows Program [2]. Katz desired to formulate a systems analysis of the systems engineering process. Because of lack of formal equation-writing techniques and simulation tools in that initial year of industrial dynamics teaching, Katz' effort was restricted to the development of an intriguing conceptual framework. The editor, working then as a research assistant in the industrial dynamics area, had been assigned to monitor Katz' thesis progress and provide assistance as needed. The editor became fascinated with Katz' ideas and with the entire R&D management area, followed up on the thesis with his own Ph.D. dissertation, and concentrated his M.I.T. activities in related areas. The editor's Ph.D. dissertation on the life cycle of R&D projects resulted in two publications: a comprehensive book on the subject and the article reprinted as Chapter 16 [5].

The project model included in that book consisted of about 400 DYNAMO equations. For classroom teaching purposes a much more simplified model was required, and was prepared by the editor. Chapter 17 captures many of the essential features of single R&D projects, though it omits the effects of interaction between project sponsor and performer.

Not much more has been published on the application of system dynamics to single R&D projects, although Chapter 23 contains some additional discussion, and the Company C case study in Chapter 8 is an application of the major model described in Chapter 16.

Chapter 18 examines one of the major problems of R&D organizations, the technical obsolescence and declining vitality that can result from aging of the professional staff, especially when induced by fixed or reduced organizational size. The article describes a feedback loop representation without a corresponding set of model equations. This kind of ''structural modeling,'' without computer simulation, is now in increased use as an organizational consultation approach for facilitating task force problem-solving processes [6]. The model structuring identifies critical cause-effect relationships in an organization, indicates interdependencies among organizational parts, and suggests likely consequences of inaction and possible outcomes of proposed actions. All this is achievable while focusing group conflict upon model structure rather than upon traditional interpersonal or interorganizational issues, thereby permitting constructive progress toward implementing problem solutions.

Another critical R&D organization management problem is the appropriate timing and allocation of funding/staffing resources. This problem is the essence of the Chapter 19 discussion of the model structure and simulation results from a system dynamics consulting effort undertaken for the entire R&D activity of a major equipment producer. That article, by Henry Weil, Thomas Bergan and the editor, focuses on the phenomenon of ''workflow bunching'' that occurs as a major system project moves downstream through a multi-stage, research-design-development-production engineering-field trouble shooting technical organization. The policy analyses in that chapter indicate R&D resource allocation alternatives that might alleviate the workflow bunching problem.

Similar considerations of multi-stage R&D resource management dominate Robert Spencer's Chapter 20 paper, in which he describes work he carried out in the Bioproducts Division of Dow Chemical Company. Spencer's model, however, clearly goes beyond R&D itself, interconnecting both inputs and outputs of the research process to the marketing and financial aspects of the rest of the division. Private communications as well as several years' notes published in the M.I.T. *System Dynamics Newsletter* indicate the long-term impact that Spencer's system dynamics modeling achieved at Dow on problems related to R&D management as well as to overall corporate planning.

Chapter 21 shifts the emphasis from resource allocation to the overall R&D organization. Wade Blackman learned system dynamics as an M.I.T. Sloan Fellow, applied it "back home" at the United Aircraft Research Laboratories, and continues its advocacy in his present position in the U.S. Energy Research and Development Administration. Space constraints prevent including in this book other works showing the uses of system dynamics in the aerospace R&D area. One industry publication, for which the editor developed the model analysis, focuses on the near-impossibility of converting airframe producers into aerospace R&D organizations, a conversion that was deemed necessary in the mid-'60s [4].

Another paper included in this Part (Chapter 22) is the editor's critical review of technological forecasting. One objective of this paper is to place system dynamics in the context of the methodological requirements for technological change modeling. Of special note is that paper's citation of Ralph Lenz' M.I.T. Sloan Fellow system dynamics thesis as one of the classics in the field of technological forecasting [3]. Blackman has also contributed system dynamics works in the area of technological forecasting [1].

Because of the large number of technically qualified people available in R&D organizations, with in-house experience in computer simulation and model development, most system dynamics models in the R&D area have been carried out without outside consulting assistance. Consequently the public awareness of these models has also been restricted. However, published reports in various annual editions of the M.I.T. *System Dynamics Newsletter* indicate that R&D project models based on the Roberts project model [5] have been undertaken by Sony Labs, Raytheon, FMC Inorganic Chemicals Division, Motorola Military Electronics, and General Dynamics/Fort Worth. More advanced but related work has been performed by Grumman and IBM among others. Pugh-Roberts Associates, Inc. carried out a project modeling effort showing the application of system dynamics to foreign development project activities of the U.S. Agency for International Development. In addition, Pugh-Roberts Associates has developed a huge model for Litton Industries of the entire design, development and engineering phases of the DD and LHA shipbuilding programs.This model was intended to identify responsibility for the major cost overruns and schedule slippages in those programs. R&D organization level models have been developed by Raytheon, Battelle Memorial Institute, and General Dynamics. The editor also initiated work at Hughes Aircraft which was continued in-house over many years in a number of R&D related applications.

References

1. Blackman, A. W. "Forecasting through Dynamic Modelling," *Technological Forecasting and Social Change*, vol. 3, 1972, pp. 291–307.

2. Katz, Abraham. *An Operations Analysis of an Electronic Systems Firm* (unpublished M.I.T. S.M. thesis, 1958).

3. Lenz, Ralph C., Jr. *A Development of Explicit Methods in Technological Forecasting* (unpublished M.I.T. S.M. thesis, 1959), later reprinted as U.S. Air Force Report ASD-TDR-62-414.

4. Miller, Thomas G., Jr., and Leo P. Kane. "Strategies for Survival in the Aerospace Industry", *Industrial Management Review*, Fall 1965.

5. Roberts, Edward B. *The Dynamics of Research and Development*. New York: Harper and Row, 1964.

6. Stearns, Norman S., et al. "Systems Intervention: New Help for Hospitals," *Health Care Management Review*, Fall 1976.

16

Research and Development Policy-Making

Edward B. Roberts

The potential impact of research and development policies necessitates the development of a new approach to the design and testing of managerial ideas. In engineering and scientific laboratories, wind tunnels, ship-towing tanks, scale models, pilot plants, analog and digital simulators are used to check plans and ideas for flaws before any mistake can produce serious consequences. Can similar techniques be found for improving the management of research and development?

To erect a new building, one needs a plan, the tools and materials, and skilled artisans to carry through the construction. In an analogous fashion, the development of a management policy laboratory for R&D requires a conceptual framework, tools and materials for filling in that frame, and able and interested R&D managers and researchers.

The industrial dynamics research program started at the M.I.T. Sloan School of Management seven years ago by Professor Jay W. Forrester, '45, has provided the basis for a plan of attack. Industrial dynamics emphasizes the information-feedback characteristics of all industrial and economic activities. Its students consider the ways in which a business is affected by its structural aspects, including the sources of amplification in decisions and the time lags throughout the organization. The industrial dynamics program is based on the belief that top-level management problems are best viewed from a framework of the dynamic system in which the time-varying interactions of the industrial (or governmental) organization are manifested. Hence an industrial dynamics analysis takes into account the underlying basic flows of men, money, materials, orders, and capital equipment, and the information flows and decision-making network which tie the others together.[1]

An industrial dynamics study requires a specific dynamic theory of cause-and-effect interaction which encompasses the problem of interest. Such an hypothesis is now available for describing the life cycles of research and development projects. A research and development project consists of a set of underlying activities which

This article was previously published in *Technology Review* 66, no. 8 (June 1964), pp. 3–7.

continuously interact to produce the project history. The resulting actions continuously feed back upon the other decision areas of the project to induce further changes. This closed-loop system of activities is pictured in Figure 1.

The changing world situation continuously alters the need for new products (military, industrial, and consumer). Technological capabilities for obtaining them change, too. Both the potential customers and the firms that develop new products are continuously engaged (consciously or unconsciously) in activities aimed at foreseeing the market for them, and the technological feasibility of the product development effort. The manpower, materials, facilities, and equipment that will be needed must be estimated, and an attempt made to judge the total cost of the program.

The research organization then has two choices: it can submit a request to its potential customer for financial support, or invest its own money in the project. If a customer reacts favorably to a request for support, he may commit funds to the project, but not until after a long delay. The alternative involves risk to the R&D group should it elect to commit its own funds before the customer makes such a commitment.

When the project group obtains funds, it begins to hire or reassign engineers and supporting manpower. Their rate of progress then reflects, among other factors, the magnitude of the manpower effort, the technological state of the art, managerial influences on productivity, engineering experience on the project, and inefficiencies resulting from organizational growth. Both the customer and the firm continuously attempt to assess the progress. These measures lead to new estimates of the work yet to be done, which feed back into the closed-loop process. New evaluations are continuously made by the R&D organization, as to its appropriate investment rate in the project, and by the customer, as to possible modifications of the project programming and support.

This continuing cycle of activities goes on until the job is completed or canceled.

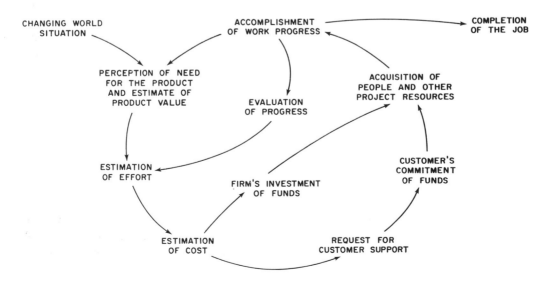

Figure 1   Feedback relationships in project management

Changed estimates and evaluations may appear formally only in periodic reports, but the increments of progress and change, real and observed, take place continuously. On-time or late completion, customer stretch-out or acceleration of the project schedule, satisfactory performance or job cancellation, can all result from the system interactions. These various results, and the system which underlies them, are observable both in government-sponsored research and development projects and in programs to develop new commercial products. Thus the dynamic system structure shown in Figure 1 can be applied to investigation of managerial policies in all forms of R&D.

With this framework, an R&D management laboratory can represent research and development organizations effectively and modify the represented structure and policies experimentally. The industrial dynamics program has developed the methods for describing such structures and policies in a management-oriented language suitable for computer interpretation.

Once represented, the effects of alteration of the parameters and policies can be studied with the DYNAMO digital computer simulation system.[2] DYNAMO is an automatic compiler and simulator for the IBM 704, 709, 7090, and 7094 computers which makes easy and inexpensive the multiple simulation runs that are required. The computer system permits valuable payoff by making the feedback of theory-test-results-theory more immediately available, thus allowing redesign of hypotheses and gradual synthesis of the findings.

Our management laboratory approach to the design of more effective R&D policies now has a framework and the tools and materials to put on the frame, but craftsmen to carry out the job are still needed. Some farsighted R&D managers have begun preparing themselves for this new managerial role, and several members of the M.I.T. Sloan School of Management's Program in Executive Development have taken first steps to develop capabilities in this approach. The researchers in these areas have come from responsible management positions in such companies as RCA, Boeing, IBM, Hughes, and Chrysler, as well as government agencies such as the Air Force and the Navy.

R&D managers whose engineering backgrounds include servomechanisms, chemical process controls, or electronic information-feedback systems are ideally suited to undertake industrial dynamics studies. Their engineering experiences have given them strong intuitive grasps of the nature of system behavior and of principles of systems design. Many of these men have carried out simulation studies with physical systems and are aware of the insights to be gained from carefully thought-out and executed model simulations. As managers they also have tackled (and often been confounded by) the complexities of R&D management. Thus they come prepared with an understanding of both the methodology and the problems. What they require is the encouragement of a top management willing to exercise the same patience with managerial policy design as with physical product design.

Some Model Tests

To demonstrate how the proposed laboratory approach might work, we have added a set of specific hypotheses to the initial dynamic systems framework (Figure 1), and from these have developed a policy-oriented model for studying project management problems. It is not really important at this point whether or not every hypothesis is completely validated by data collection and analysis. Alternatives based upon a particular set of experiences might be offered to any of our hypotheses. What is important is that the general usefulness of the laboratory approach to policy design be demonstrated. The assumptions made in the model are based on the literature, personal experience in research and development organizations, and discussions with many managers.[3] Each organization would need only to change the model to make it descriptive of its own experiences and problems.

The completed model of research and development that we have simulated on a digital computer contains about 250 variable equations and an additional 135 constants and initial conditions. These describe the causes of both the customer's and the firm's actions as well as the characteristics of the product. Calculation of the values of these equations at successive time intervals produces the life cycle of the project simulated. Alteration of any system parameter or policy produces changes in the project life cycle which can be detected in a simulation study.

A typical project history simulated in the M.I.T. Computation Center is one requiring from 600 to 3000 man-years of engineering effort, depending on the state-of-the-art advances which can be utilized and the overall ability of the firm's management and engineers. The cost is expected to be between 18 and 90 million dollars, a range covering such projects as an air-to-air missile for the Air Force, a scientific satellite system for NASA, an airport traffic radar-control center for the Federal Aviation Agency, or a new type of nuclear power station for a western utility. It is a project of the type in which the relevant technology is rapidly advancing, the need for the product is changing, and both the firms and customers involved have earlier experiences with each other and with similar kinds of undertakings.

The project history is pictured from several points of view in Figure 2. The curves are outputs of the computer simulation, generated by the interactions of the modeled policies of the customer and firm. The graphed data correspond to our general notions about the dynamic behavior of research and development projects. For example, the cycle of the product value phenomenon is clearly visible: the intrinsic product value, which is the principal input to the model run, grows, levels off, then falls gradually to zero; in partial response to this, the recognized current value of the project lags the real value throughout the life cycle; the estimated future product value lags at first, then rapidly advances, overshooting the real value by a large factor, finally falling back toward zero. This relationship between the behaviors of real and believed product values is an important characteristic of many projects.

Another vital phenomenon is the changing curve of estimated project cost. Starting very high relative to product worth at that time (lack of technical feasibility implies infinite costs), the estimated effort and cost on the project gradually fall with the rising state of the art. As expected costs fall, and perceived product value rises, the firm hires (or assigns) more engineers to the project. When the cost estimate is sufficiently low relative to anticipated value to attract the customer's support, the project moves into a full-scale development program. The resulting increase in engineering effort tends to

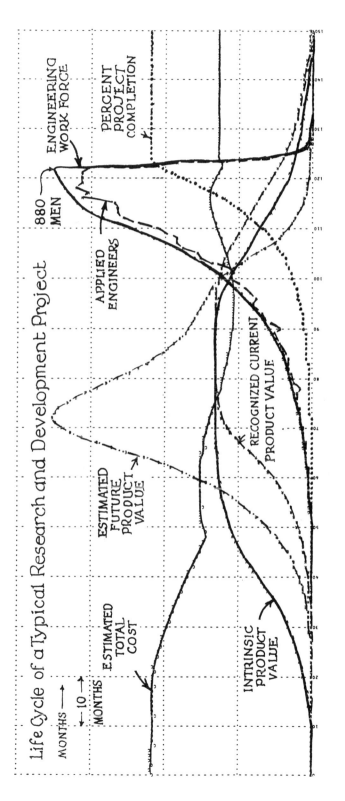

Figure 2 Life cycle of a typical research and development project

stabilize the earlier decline in estimated cost as the firm begins to form a more realistic impression of the magnitude of the job and the effectiveness of the engineers. Cost estimates gradually rise during the rest of the project's life, with final costs about 20 percent greater than those expected during the early growth phase of the project.

The curve of engineering employment is also interesting. For a long time only a single engineer is working in the product area. Then the curve rises gradually as the firm invests more of its own funds. When the project receives customer support, the staff grows steadily and ever more rapidly until it nears completion. The more jagged curve of applied engineering effort takes into account the usual holidays, vacations, and absenteeism. This closely resembles the fluctuating curves of engineering effort well known to R&D project managers.

As you would expect, the curve of real cumulative percent completion is hardly visible for many months. Only as the project activities enter their early growth phase does project accomplishment begin to appear on the graph. In part, this is misleading. For much had already been accomplished prior to the period charted. The engineering staff had been increased to form a nucleus for the project expansion; cost estimation on the project had been firmed up; and funds had been allocated by the customer. These achievements were all vital to the project, but none of them can be directly related to the elements of engineering needed to finish the product development. They took place before the large expenditures of effort or funds which characterized the "formal" beginnings of the project. Managers and researchers who ignore the existence of this earlier phase of a life cycle are forgetting the very sources of the entire project concept and execution.

From month 100, the project engineering tasks were gradually accomplished, and the percent completion rises correspondingly. About 80 percent of the effective work was done in the last 18 months of the project. The work was actually completed in month 122 and some extras added while the engineers were being transferred from the project.

Prior to month 100, by which time full-scale activities were under way, only about 300 cumulative man-years of engineering effort had been invested out of the 1,395 man-years ultimately needed for completion. From that time, an additional two years were needed to finish the project work. When the job was finally completed, the customer was dissatisfied, feeling that the costs had exceeded the product value and that the product was no longer particularly useful. Such has often been the case in both military and commercial research and development undertakings.

The computer results demonstrate the plausibility of the hypothesized model. More important they indicate that with such a model (or with an alternate model, if preferred), R&D managers can begin to determine experimentally the effects of changes in characteristics of the product, customer, or firm, or in the policies of the customer or firm. Some results of such simulation experiments with the model will now be described.

Conservatism and Low Bidding

Disappointments in R&D often are blamed on the complexities of the product, rapid changes in technology, the competitive situation, or faults in customer planning or decision-making. Such factors are significant. However, the policies and practices of organizations actually doing the research and development work also vitally influence the success or failure of a project. For example, the firm's relative optimism or pessimism, its speculativeness or conservatism, biases its estimates of future product value, technological progress, and engineering effectiveness, and influences the firm's investment of its own funds.

The firm involved in the project pictured in Figure 2 had a high risk-taking propensity. To illustrate the effects of conservatism on project dynamics, the basic simulation was rerun, with the hypothesis that the modeled firm was conservative instead of speculative. The new results are shown in Figure 3 (with the same set of scales as in Figure 2) and the changes are obvious. This firm's estimate of the future value of the product was much lower. This made the project less attractive: the conservative firm was unwilling to risk as much of even these expected profits, and waited instead for the customer to provide financial support. This policy retarded the acquisition of an engineering team, contributed additional delay to the customer's funding, and significantly slowed progress. By month 122, the project had been completed in the case simulated in Figure 2; by month 122 in this case, however, the customer had become so dissatisfied that he cut back on funding, and by month 130 the engineering on the job came to a halt with only 75 percent of the task completed.

Thus in this particular case the firm's policy of conservatism actually caused the failure of the job and the waste of the 34 million dollars that the customer spent on the effort. Under other project circumstances, of course, the conservative approach may be the more advisable policy for the firm to adopt. The power of the industrial dynamics approach is that it permits study of the likely results of various policies.

At times company "optimism" is so extreme, particularly with respect to cost and effort estimates, that R&D proposals really reflect intentional low bidding. Many companies are led to underestimate project costs in their attempts to get R&D contracts. Under traditional Cost Plus Fixed Fee (CPFF) contracts, the firm is not directly penalized for the resulting overruns on project costs. However, as Figure 4 illustrates, the firm's policy of intentional cost underestimation has significant effects on project dynamics, and through them on the firm and customer, too. The simulated project life cycle pictured in Figure 4 evolved from the basic situation portrayed in Figure 2, the only change being in the degree of integrity of the firm, affecting the cost estimates it submitted to the customer.

The smaller initial contract size induced by the low bid caused a rate of engineering effort much lower than really needed. This led to a considerable stretch-out of the project, with attendant fluctuations in the size of the engineering effort. The project finally was completed at month 145, about two years after the completion date of the project simulated in Figure 2. Though less money was spent by the customer in this case (the slower growth was more efficient and the engineers took advantage of later

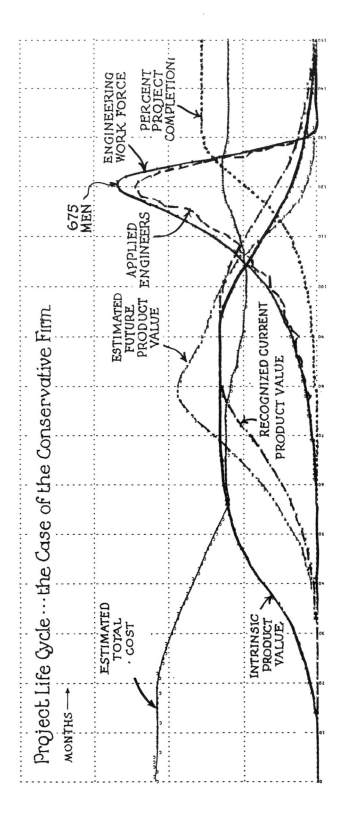

Figure 3   Project life cycle: the case of the conservative firm

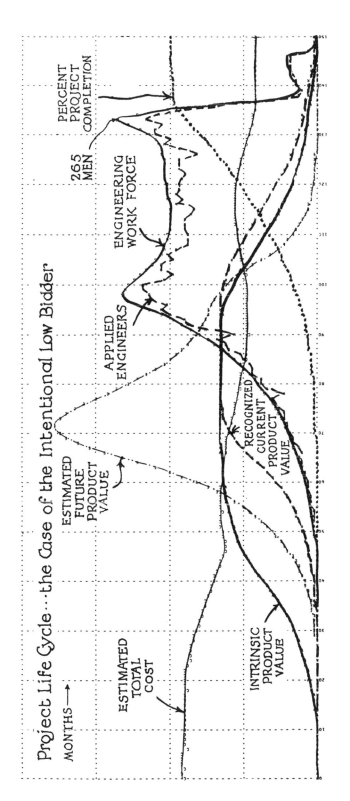

Figure 4 Project life cycle: the case of the intentional low bidder

developments in the state of the art), the customer was dissatisfied because of its delayed completion.

The firm suffered, too: its reputation and relationships with the customer worsened, and its profits were slightly lower than in the case studied in Figure 2. In many projects, however, the company with low-bidding integrity does increase its profits by following this policy. Again, these results highlight the need for more extensive management laboratory studies of R&D policies in different company-customer-product situations.

The computer results demonstrate that a high risk-taking propensity as well as a high degree of integrity by the firm very favorably affect the outcomes of research and development projects, i.e., from the customer's point of view. Greater company willingness to assume risk and invest in potential projects, for example, gets jobs finished sooner and pushes progress to a further point even for projects which are eventually canceled. Under existing government contracting practices, however, neither high risk-taking nor high integrity is directly profitable to the firm. The company assuming greater risks almost always suffers, at least in the short run; the company exercising greater honesty in bidding reduces its individual project profits as often as it gains.

Still unpublished empirical data collected by the author on a number of R&D projects support this theoretical finding. Thus the policies followed by the government seem to influence companies to adopt practices which are counter to the government's best interests. A changed philosophy, matched by revised procurement policies, could benefit both the R&D companies and the government.

A management systems laboratory offers great potential as a means of studying the design of improved R&D policies. Even a small gain in effectiveness so achieved would mean annual cost savings or performance improvements on the order of hundreds of millions of dollars.

Notes

1. See Jay W. Forrester, *Industrial Dynamics* (The MIT Press, 1961) and Roberts, "Industrial Dynamics and the Design of Management Control Systems," *Management Technology* (December, 1963).

2. Alexander L. Pugh III, *DYNAMO User's Manual*, second edition (The MIT Press, 1963).

3. Full development of the model, the theory underlying it, and the results of extensive simulation investigations are provided in Roberts, *The Dynamics of Research and Development* (Harper and Row, 1964).

17

A Simple Model of R&D Project Dynamics

Edward B. Roberts

Introduction

Management techniques for planning and control of research and development often seem based incorrectly on the single-loop system shown in Figure 1. Here the difference between the scheduled completion date and the forecast completion date is seen as causing decisions to change the magnitude or allocation of project resources (manpower, facilities, equipment, priorities). As these resources are employed, they are assumed to produce the progress that is reported during the project. These reports cumulate and are processed to create the forecast completion time. Adding complexity to this scheme might entail paralleling the single loop based on schedule response with two others based on budget and technical objectives control, respectively.

The above description, however, is clearly inadequate, since some of the most vital aspects of the real R&D system have been excluded from the underlying analysis. For example, the real system of an R&D project lacks tangible, precise measurement sources. This lack produces much of the error between the *real* situation in the project (its true scope and actual progress to date) and that which is *apparent* to those doing the scientific and engineering work.

Another part of the real system that appears to be ignored by the R&D system outline of Figure 1 is the human element in the project actions and decisions. The attitudes and motivations of the technical performers and their managers, their knowledge of the schedules and current estimates in the project, the believed penalty-reward structure of the organization all affect the real progress that is achieved, as well as the progress and problems that are reported upward in the organization. All systems of measurement and evaluation (in R&D, manufacturing, government, universities, or what-have-you) create incentives and pressures that encourage specific responses. These incentives interact with the goals and character of individuals and institutions to produce decisions, actions, and their results.

This chapter was originally published in *R&D Management*, vol. 5, no. 1 (October 1974), and is reprinted here with the permission of the publishers.

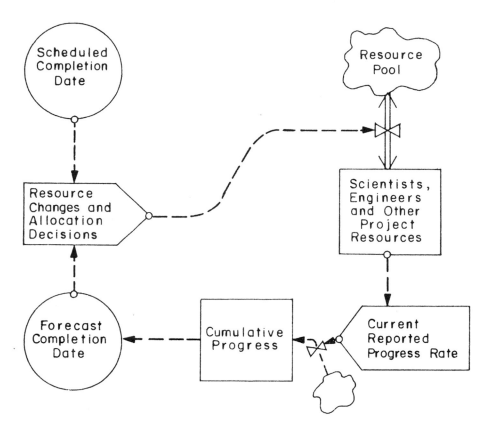

Figure 1   Assumed R and D project control system

Addition of the omitted aspects of progress intangibility and scientist/engineer motivations to the system diagrammed in Figure 1 produces the more complete representation shown in Figure 2. This diagram is more-or-less a minimum structure for studying research and development project dynamics. It omits explicit consideration of many factors which have been treated in other more extensive or differently focused R&D models by the author.[1, 2, 3] The purposes of this representation, however, are illustration and education, for which goals a simple model is preferable.

The Model

The model to be presented consists of thirty equations, plus associated initial conditions and constants. The format of level and rate equations is that used in the industrial dynamics methodology of Forrester and his associates[4] (now called system dynamics), and the equations are presented in the manner called for by the DYNAMO compiler-simulator.[5]

The initial equations are those for the real progress rate and the level of cumulative real progress. The progress rate is represented as the product of the average level of manpower recently at work on the project and their average productivity in job units per man per month. This rate of real progress integrates continuously to form the cumulative progress.

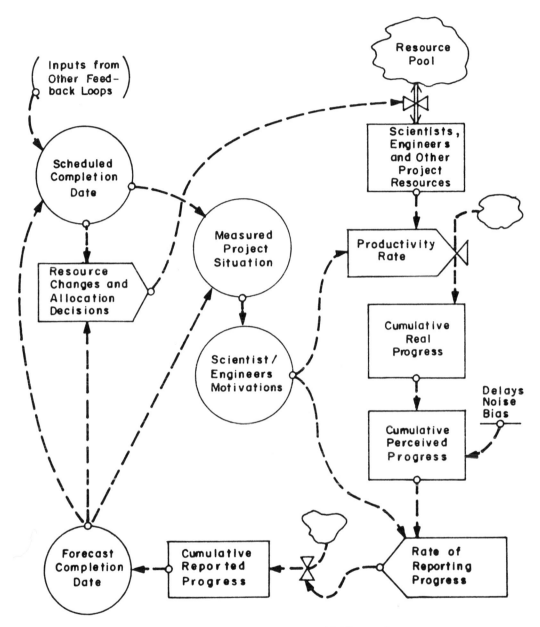

Figure 2 More complete representation of R&D control system

PR.KL=(AMEN.K) (PROD.K)   1,R

CRP.K=CRP.J + (DT) (PR.JK)   2,L

CRP=0   2,N

PR—Progress Rate (job units/month)
AMEN—Average MEN on Project (men)

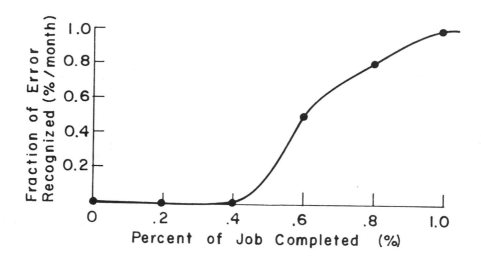

Figure 3   Tangibility effect on error detection

PROD—PRODuctivity (job units/man-month)
CRP—Cumulative Real Progress (job units)
DT—Delta Time, DYNAMO time interval between computer
    calculations (months)

However, the real progress is not the basis of action in the project, except as it is perceived. Anyone who has worked in R&D knows that there may be a significant difference between the real achievement and the perceived progress on a job. We thus now formulate a level of perceived progress which sums the perceived progress rate as well as perceived errors in earlier progress perceptions.

$$PCP.K = PCP.J + (DT)(PPR.JK + PECR.JK) \hspace{3cm} 3,L$$

$$PCP = 0 \hspace{6cm} 3,N$$

PCP—Perceived Cumulative Progress (job units)
PPR—Perceived Progress Rate (job units/month)
PECR—Perceived Error Correction Rate (job units/month)

The current progress rate that is perceived is the product of the manpower cur-rently employed on the project and their perceived average productivity.

$$PPR.KL = (MEN.K)(PPROD.K) \hspace{4cm} 4,R$$

PPR—Perceived Progress Rate (job units/month)
MEN—MEN on project (men)
PPROD—Perceived PRODuctivity (job units/man-month)

To the extent that the perceived progress rate differs from the real progress rate, an error in perceived cumulative progress will gradually accumulate. Here one of the important characteristics of research and development, the usual relative intangibility of the project progress, has its effect. The further the project is along, the greater the likelihood that product assembly and/or test will reveal errors in earlier progress estimates. We therefore model the organization's rate of correcting perception errors as being a fractional part of the error, where the fraction of the error that is perceived increases significantly as real project progress approaches job completion.

$$PECR.KL=(FER.K)(CRP.K-PCP.K) \hspace{4cm} 5,R$$

$$FER.K=TABLE(TFER,PJC.K,0,1,.2) \hspace{3.5cm} 6,A$$

$$TFER=0/0/0/.5/.8/1 \hspace{5cm} 6,C$$

$$PJC.K=CRP.K/ER \hspace{5.3cm} 7,A$$

$$ER=1200 \hspace{6.6cm} 7,C$$

      PECR—Perceived Error Correction Rate (job units/month)
      FER—Fraction of Error Recognized (percent/month)
      CRP—Cumulative Real Progress (job units)
      PCP—Perceived Cumulative Progress (job units)
      TABLE—DYNAMO special TABLE lookup function, for data tables
      TFER—Table, Fraction of Error Recognized (percent/month)
      PJC—Percent of Job Completed (percent)
      ER—Effort Required (job units)

The fractional error perceived as a function of the cumulative real job progress is shown in Figure 3. Values for the curve are given by 6, C. Each job is represented by an effort requirement of a number of job units. For the initial model simulations, the job size has been designated as 1200 job units. At a productivity rate of 2 job units per man per month, this job size indicates a requirement of 600 man-months of scientific/engineering effort.

The actual productivity of the average scientist/engineer working on the job is represented simply by his normal productivity and a multiplier that reflects motivational aspects. Given no particular pressures from scheduling considerations, scientist/engineers are usually self-motivated to turn out well-engineered products that incorporate additional reliability, desirable but not necessary special features, perhaps more aesthetic appearance, etc. At an extreme such activities constitute unnecessary (sometimes dysfunctional) gold-plating. Thus with low schedule pressure some of the R&D work does not really contribute to principal project objectives, and only a fractional part of the technical effort is counted as being real progress on the job. Conversely, as pressure for more productivity gradually builds, the scientists and engineers respond relatively quickly by a greater concentration on the essential tasks. With greater pressure the technical effectiveness grows further, accelerated by the

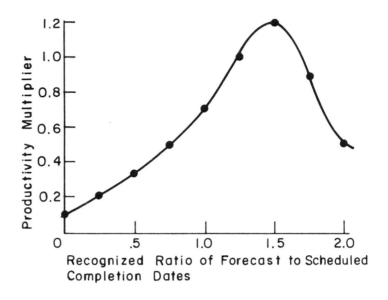

Figure 4   Motivational effects on productivity

tendency of the engineers to put in longer hours at work. An excess of pressures stemming from a large forecast schedule slippage, however, tends to demoralize the R&D team and has effects of decreasing its productivity. These facets of motivational effects on technical productivity are pictured in the Productivity Multiplier curve, Figure 4.

PROD.K=(PM.K)(PRODN)   8,A

PRODN=2   8,C

PM.K=TABLE(TPM,RRFSC.K,0,2,0.25)   9,A

TPM=.1/.2/.35/.5/.7/1/1.2/.9/.5   9,C

    PROD—PRODuctivity (job units/man-months)
    PM—Productivity Multiplier (dimensionless)
    PRODN—PRODuctivity, Normal (job units/man-months)
    TPM—Table, Productivity Multiplier (dimensionless)
    RRFSC—Recognized Ratio of Forecast to Scheduled Completion dates
        (dimensionless)

The above productivity formulation represents a response to the recognized ratio of the currently forecast completion date to that currently scheduled. A short interval of time is usually required before the actual ratio is recognized. This delay is modeled as an exponential lag in Equation 10 below.

RRFSC.K=RRFSC.J+(DT)(1/DRSS)(RFSC.J−RRFSC.J)   10,L

RRFSC=RFSC   10,N

DRSS=1   10,C

RFSC.K=FCD.K/SCOM.K   11,A

    RRFSC—Recognized Ratio of Forecast to Scheduled Completion dates
        (dimensionless)
    DRSS—Delay in Recognizing Schedule Situation (months)
    RFSC—Ratio of Forecast to Scheduled Completion dates (dimensionless)
    FCD—Forecast Completion Date (months)
    SCOM—Scheduled COMpletion date (months)

The forecast date of project completion is found by adding to the current date the indicated time remaining on the job. This additional time in turn reflects the believed effort remaining to be performed, the level of manpower working on the project, and their perceived productivity. Formulation of the effort believed remaining on the project has two noteworthy aspects. First, the total project effort requirement is used in the equation without error or modication; this obvious simplification is justifiable only as a convenience and can be replaced in any model extensions. Second, the effort required is contrasted to that reported complete; this indicates that the managers responsible for resource change decisions are not restricted to having the same knowledge as the engineers performing the work, with the progress reported to management here treated as potentially different from the progress perceived by the engineers. This organizational situation represents the typical R&D case.

FCD.K=TIME.K+ITR.K   12,A

ITR.K=EBR.K/(PPROD.K*MEN.K)   13,A

EBR.K=ER−RCP.K   14,A

    FCD—Forecast Completion Date (months)
    TIME—TIME provided by DYNAMO simulation (months)
    ITR—Indicated Time Remaining (months)
    EBR—Effort Believed Remaining (job units)
    PPROD—Perceived PRODuctivity (job units/man-month)
    MEN—MEN on project (men)
    ER—Effort Required (job units)
    RCP—Reported Cumulative Progress (job units)

Schedules in research and development projects tend to shift to reflect the forecast ability to complete the job. However, a lag exists before the schedules are adjusted, its length indicative of the organization's (firm and/or customer) reluctance to permit schedule slippage. Initially, the schedule and forecast are here viewed as coinciding, and the delay in schedule change shows some resistance to schedule slippage.

SCOM.K=SCOM.J+(DT)(1/DCS)(FCD.J−SCOM.J)   15,L

SCOM=FCD   15,N

DCS=6   15,C

> SCOM—Scheduled COMpletion date (months)
> DCS—Delay in Changing Schedule (months)
> FCD—Forecast Completion Date (months)

The level of technical manpower employed on the project is initially established in this model at the number that constantly would be needed throughout the desired project duration, provided that initial job size and technical productivity estimates are correct and unchanging. This initialization excludes from model behavior the initial transient build-up of the R&D staff. This simplication can also be relaxed in future model extensions.

MEN.K=MEN.J+(DT)(MENCH.JK)   16,L

MEN=ER/(DCOMI*PPROD)   16,N

DCOMI=30   16,C

> MEN—MEN on project (men)
> MENCH—MEN CHange rate (men/month)
> ER—Effort Required (job units)
> DCOMI—Desired COMpletion date Initially (months)
> PPROD—Perceived PRODuctivity (job units/man-month)

As management recognizes it is falling behind in meeting its current schedule, additional scientist/engineers will be hired or reassigned to the project. The fractional change in the work force is a function of how far behind management perceives the schedule to be as well as the managerial response policy. This is pictured in Figure 5. The policy does not handle the transfer of the scientist/engineers from the project as the job nears completion. This can also be added in other later models.

MENCH.KL=(FCHM.K)(MEN.K)   17,R

FCHM.K=TABLE(TFCHM,RRFSC.K,0,2,.25)   18,A

TFCHM=−.65/−.40/−.2/−.1/0/.1/.2/.4/.65   18,C

> MENCH—MEN CHange rate (men/month)
> FCHM—Fractional CHange in Manpower (percent/month)
> MEN—MEN on project (men)

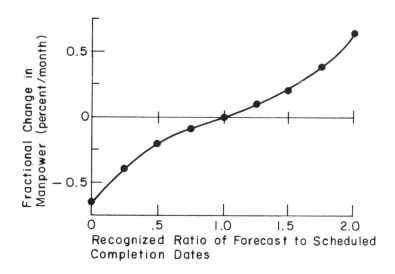

Figure 5   Manpower change policy

TFCHM—Table, Fractional CHange in Manpower (percent/month)
RRFSC—Recognized Ratio of Forecast to Scheduled Completion dates
             (dimensionless)

The average number of men employed on the job is merely a short-term smoothing of the manpower level.

AMEN.K = AMEN.J + (DT)(1/DAMEN)(MEN.J − AMEN.J)   19, L

AMEN = MEN   19, N

DAMEN = 1   19, C

AMEN—Average MEN on project (men)
DAMEN—Delay in Averaging MEN on project (months)
MEN—MEN on project (men)

The reported cumulative progress on the job represents the summation of the
reported progress rate. In this initial model formulation, the reporting rate by the
engineers is viewed as being identical to their complete perception rate, except as they
hesitate to report too much of the job as complete too soon. For example, they will not
report the last remaining project work as completed until that completion is factually
established. Here is a point in the model where the organization's character could have
been represented in a more important fashion. In many organizations, for example,
there is a strong tendency to report the scheduled completion as the actual completion,
until the gap between reported progress and apparent progress becomes too large to

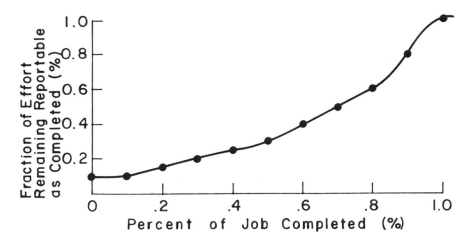

Figure 6   Realized limit on reporting progress rate

sustain this fantasy. Such a practice can be substituted in later versions of the model. The maximum fraction of effort believed remaining that is considered reportable as completed during any given month is shown in Figure 6.

$$RCP.K = RCP.J + (DT)(RRP.JK) \qquad\qquad 20,L$$

$$RCP = 0 \qquad\qquad 20,N$$

$$RRP.KL = MIN(TPRP.K, RLRPR.K) \qquad\qquad 21,R$$

$$TPPR.K = PPR.JK + PECR.JK \qquad\qquad 22,A$$

$$RLRPR.K = (FERRC.K)(EBR.K)/DT \qquad\qquad 23,A$$

$$FERRC.K = TABLE(TFERR, PJC.K, 0, 1, .1) \qquad\qquad 24,A$$

$$TFERR = .1/.1/.15/.2/.25/.3/.4/.5/.6/.8/1 \qquad\qquad 24,C$$

    RCP—Reported Cumulative Progress (job units)
    RRP—Rate of Reporting Progress (job units/month)
    MIN—DYNAMO special MINimum function, for finding the lesser of
        two variables
    TPPR—Total Perceived Progress Rate (job units/month)
    RLRPR—Realized Limit on Reportable Progress Rate (job units/month)
    PPR—Perceived Progress Rate (job units/month)
    PECR—Perceived Error Correction Rate (job units/month)
    FERRC—Fraction of Effort Remaining Reportable as Completed (percent)
    EBR—Effort Believed Remaining (job units)
    TFERR—Table, Fraction of Effort Remaining Reportable as completed
        (percent)
    PJC—Percent of Job Completed (percent)

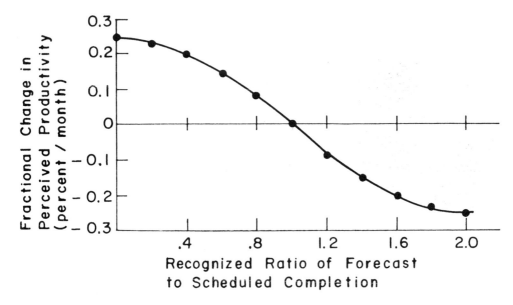

Figure 7   Changes in perceived productivity

The final variable grouping needed in the model defines the average productivity perceived by management. Changes in the perceived level arise from expected schedule slippages; when the job seems to fall behind schedule, the firm tends to lower its estimate of technical productivity. In a more complex model, effects might alternately be seen in the estimate of total job size and complexity, not considered in this simple model. The perceived productivity is initially set equal to the normal productivity by Equation 25, N. The responsiveness in changing perceived productivity as a function of the schedule situation is shown in Figure 7.

PPROD.K = PPROD.J + (DT)(CPPR.JK)   25,L
PPROD = PRODN   25,N
CPPR.KL = (FCPP.K)(PPROD.K)   26,R
FCPP.K = TABLE(TFCPP,RRFSC.K,0,2,0.2)   27,A
TFCPP = .25/.23/.20/.15/.08/0/−.08/−.15/−.20/−.23/−.25 27,C

  PPROD—Perceived PRODuctivity (job units/man-month)
  CPPR—Change in Perceived PRoductivity (job units/man-month/month)
  PRODN—PRODuctivity, Normal (job units/man-month)
  FCPP—Fractional Change in Perceived Productivity (percent/month)
  TFCPP—Table, Fractional Change in Perceived Productivity (percent/month)
  RRFSC—Recognized Ratio of Forecast to Scheduled Completion dates
        (dimensionless)

The preceding equations are the only ones needed for simulation and study of the simple R&D project system originally indicated in Figure 2. Three additional variables, however, shall be specified for providing supplementary policy evaluation information. These three are the perceived percent of job completed, the reported percent of job completed, and the cumulative manpower effort on the project.[6]

$$PPJC.K = PCP.K/ER \qquad\qquad 28,A$$

$$RPJC.K = RCP.K/ER \qquad\qquad 29,A$$

$$CMEN.K = CMEN.J + (DT)(MEN.J) \qquad\qquad 30,L$$

$$CMEN = 0 \qquad\qquad 30,N$$

PPJC—Perceived Percent of Job Completed (percent)
PCP—Perceived Cumulative Progress (job units)
ER—Effort Required (job units)
RPJC—Reported Percent of Job Completed (percent)
RCP—Reported Cumulative Progress (job units)
CMEN—Cumulative MEN on the project (man-months)
MEN—MEN on project (men)

System Behavior

To be sure, the model developed thus far is only a first-order approximation of the complex system of research and development projects. Yet the system characteristics contained are sufficiently broad that they deserve study based upon DYNAMO simulation results.

Basic Model Behavior.   Some of the key dynamic variables during the project life are shown in Figure 8. The project starts at time zero with a desired completion date of month 30. At a believed normal productivity of 2 job units per man-month, the project effort seems to require 600 man-months of R&D work. Spreading this effort evenly over the 30-month schedule demands 20 scientist/engineers on the project, the initial condition of the manpower level.

Under this initial condition of coincident scheduled and forecast completion time, however, group motivation is not particularly high, and the usual self-motivated goals of the scientist/engineers tend to produce over-engineering on the early tasks. The average effective productivity of the R&D staff—that is, their work contributing directly to project objectives—is therefore only 1.4 job units per man-month instead of the initially assumed 2 value. A basic problem source in research and development, however, is the relative intangibility of much of the work, particularly during the early phases of a project. Because of this intangibility, the perceived (and scheduled) progress, based on the 2 job units per man-month, cumulates at a faster rate than the actual progress (shown by the ''A'' curve in the figure, beneath the Perceived Cumulative Progress curve). The gap is not detected until simulated month 17, from which date changes begin in the observable project behavior.

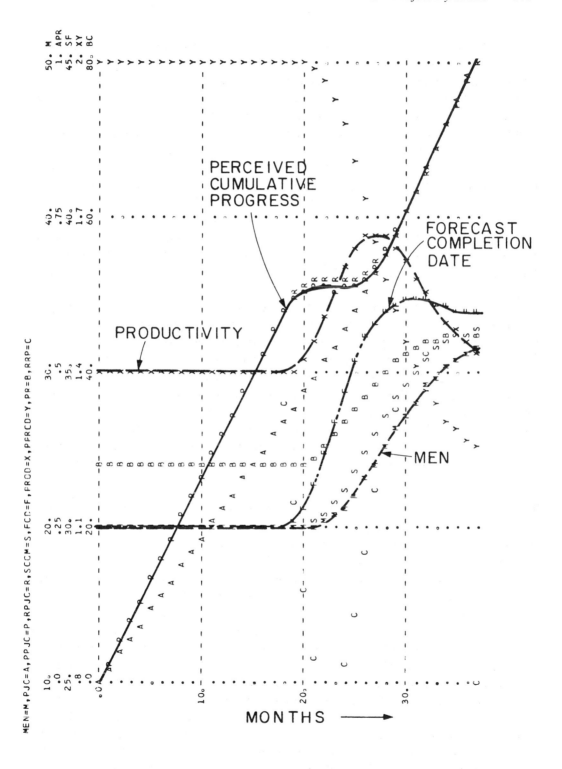

Figure 8   Basic model simulation

As the scientists and engineers and management sense the errors in their earlier perceptions of job progress, the cumulative progress flattens out with current progress rate estimates tending to just counterbalance corrections of earlier cumulative estimates. The forecast completion date for the project begins to climb, based on the new indications of work remaining and the assumed lower technical productivity, tapering eventually at month 37, a 7-month slippage from the original schedule. With this change in forecast, three observable changes also occur. First, under pressure because of the deviation of forecast completion from schedule, technical productivity begins to rise, peaking at 1.65 job units per man-month, an increase of about 20 percent above the earlier productivity. This productivity gradually drops back as the forecast and schedule come into line. The second change is that the company assigns more men to the project, going from its initial level of 20 men to 31 men by the end of the job. Finally, the schedule is slowly adjusted to take account of new forecast expectations, tending to reduce the pressure on the technical staff as it begins to become more aligned with the forecast.

These changes result in job completion during month 37, a 23 percent slippage of the original schedule. The total effort required is 822 man-months, in contrast to the "ideal" case (i.e., steady productivity of 2 job units per man-month) of 600 man-months. However, the increased productivity that exists from about month 18 of the project does benefit the project. Had productivity remained at its initial 1.4 job units per man-month throughout the project, the cumulative effort required would be about 860 man-months. The productivity change thus produces approximately 5 percent savings of total effort (hence, total cost) in the project. It is interesting to note that productivity can thus be recognized as a dynamic buffer, decoupling manpower change from perceived job scope change, just as inventory can decouple production rate from sales rate.

Accurate Progress Perception.   One of the important problems noted in the preceding discussion is that lack of tangible results causes delay until month 17 in the recognition of project problems. An interesting experiment, illustrated in Figure 9, is a project simulation in which any error in perceived progress is immediately detected and corrected.[7] Under this assumption, as Figure 9 shows, perceived and actual progress remain together throughout the project. From the beginning of the project, this corrected perception causes changes in perceived technical productivity, which is soon reflected in the forecast completion date. The gap between forecast and schedule has some beneficial influences on productivity. However, the effect at no time is very great, and it soon diminishes toward its initial value. Cumulative required effort is 831 man-months, slightly more than in the basic model simulation, but other benefits do result from the accurate progress perception. The project is completed during month 35, 5 months behind initial schedule but 2 months ahead of the basic project. Furthermore, peak manpower is 28 scientist/engineers instead of the 31 of the basic run, thus indicating a small improvement in stability of the organization. These results, however, are not significantly different from the earlier base case. They imply that more tangible progress measures in research and development might not suffice to change the character of project management problems.

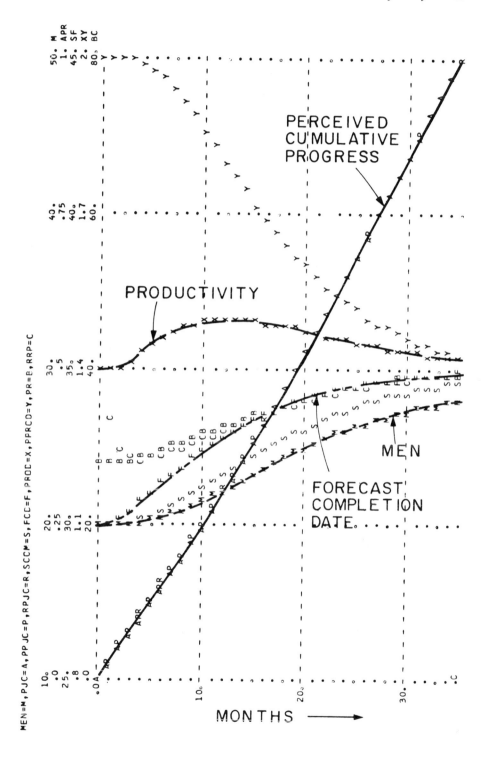

Figure 9 Accurate progress perception

Immediate Schedule Adjustment.   Policies for managing research and development projects can have significant impact on results. The next three simulations describe various aspects of these policies as related to schedule and technical work-force changes. Figure 10 pictures the results of a policy in which schedules are immediately adjusted to correspond with changed forecasts of project completion time.[8] Such a practice may result from project funding of a "level of effort" nature, in which only a certain number of men can be employed on the job. Alternately, it may arise from lack of availability of additional scientist/engineers to assign to the project. In either case, as soon as detected problems result in a later forecast completion date, the schedule is adjusted to agree with the forecast. One effect that is obvious in the graph is that this situation generates little additional pressure or motivation to change the nature or rate of technical productivity. The organization size is maintained at a stable level, rising only by one person during the project life. The brunt of the policy is seen to be schedule slippage, with the project reaching completion during the early part of month 42, a slippage of 40 percent of the original schedule. A penalty is also paid in a slightly higher total effort (cost) due to the lack of productivity gains during the project, with 853 man-months utilized on the job.

Fixed-Schedule Policy.   In contrast to the above case, Figure 11 presents the situation in which the initial schedule is treated as more or less fixed.[9] This kind of situation is true in "crash" projects and in many other R&D programs in which the time of product availability is given high priority. The curves demonstrate that as the forecast completion date rises in response to recognition of errors in progress perception, the scheduled completion date is held nearly fixed at its initial value. Two principal changes result: (1) productivity is stimulated to rise significantly, peaking at 1.88 job units per man-month during month 29, an increase of 35 percent over initial technical productivity; (2) the manpower level on the project is greatly increased, rising up to a value of 44 scientist/engineers from the initial group of 20. The project is completed by the end of month 34, cutting the slippage encountered in the basic model simulation by almost half. Also significant is that the total manpower effort on the project is reduced to 783 man-months because of the higher technical productivity, saving 5 percent of the effort of the basic model run.

Contrasting Figures 10 and 11 provides illuminating demonstration of the tradeoff between completion time and organization stability. The crash project gets completed in 20 percent less time than the ultra-stable project, but employs at its peak twice as many scientist/engineers. The high pressure project requires about 10 percent less total effort than the low pressure case. Generalization beyond these specific computer runs would be dangerous because of the many aspects of increased realism omitted from the model.

Dead-Zone Manpower Change Policy.   The final simulation of the model to be reported is one in which company policy toward technical work force change is made wholly unresponsive to small changes in the schedule situation.[10] The results, as

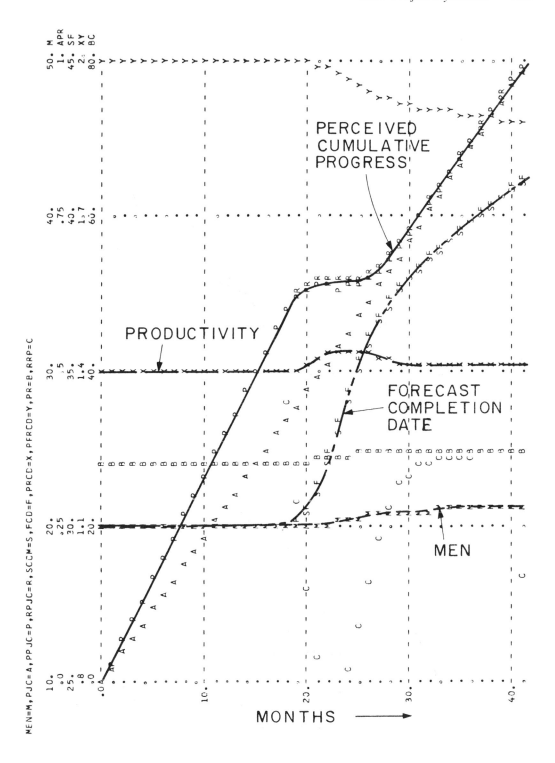

Figure 10 Immediate schedule adjustment

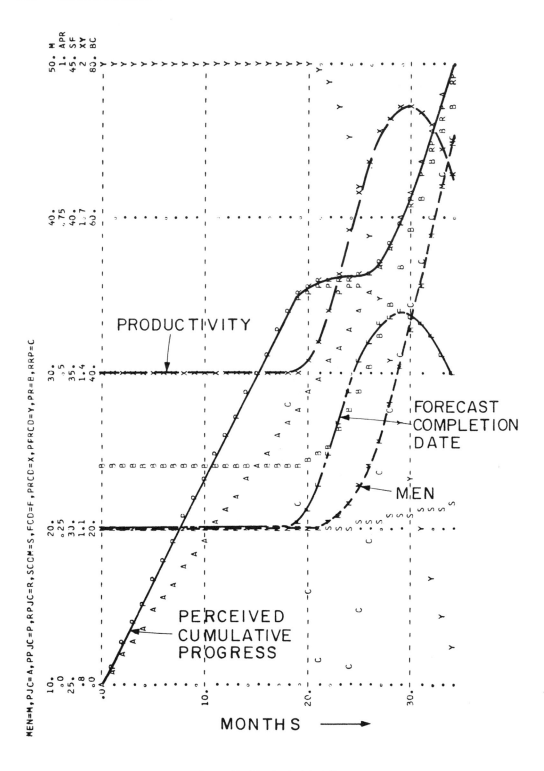

Figure 11   Fixed-schedule policy

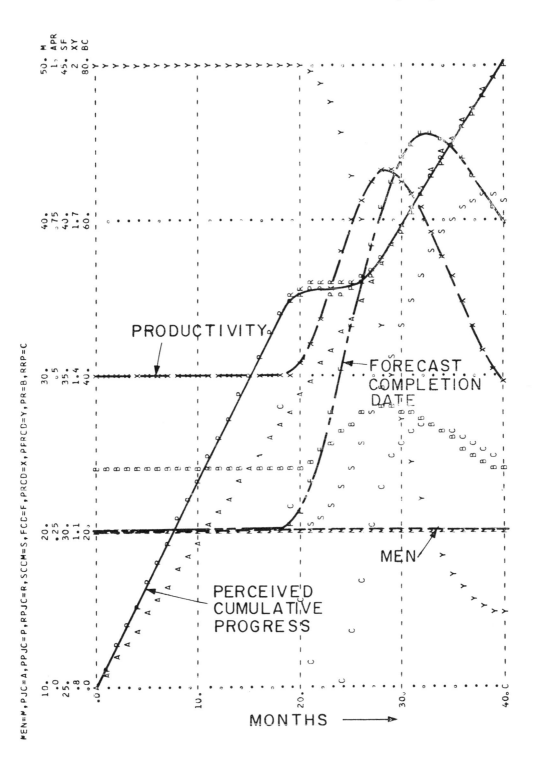

Figure 12 Dead-zone manpower change policy

shown in Figure 12, indicate that no changes in the level of manpower are made during the entire project. Significant effects on productivity push this variable to a peak of 1.78 job units per man-month during month 29, declining rapidly, however, as schedule adjustments alleviate the pressure. The project is completed by the end of month 40, a 10-month slippage of the original schedule. Total effort required is 793 man-months, reflecting the benefits of the higher productivity. Although the manpower stability under this policy is equivalent to that shown in Figure 10, the current case is completed sooner with a lower total effort expended. Both benefits result from the differences in technical productivity generated between the two projects.

Further Model Development and Exploration

The simple model developed in this paper seems to demonstrate important aspects of research and development project behavior. Despite the obvious simplifications made, new insights can be gained from model study. Other simulations of the basic model, not reported here, seem to justify a belief that further extensions of the effort should be made, particularly along the lines suggested earlier in the model description section of this paper.

Notes

1. Edward B. Roberts, *The Dynamics of Research and Development* (New York: Harper & Row, 1964).

2. Edward B. Roberts, "The Problem of Aging Organizations," *Business Horizons*, Winter 1967. (See also chapter 18 in this volume.)

3. Henry B. Weil, Thomas B. Bergan, and Edward B. Roberts, "The Dynamics of R&D Strategy," *Proceedings of the 1973 Summer Simulation Conference*. (See also chapter 19 in this volume.)

4. Jay W. Forrester, *Industrial Dynamics* (Cambridge: The MIT Press, 1961).

5. Alexander L. Pugh III, *DYNAMO II User's Manual* (Cambridge: The MIT Press, 1973). L represents a level equation, R = rate equation, A = auxiliary equation, N = initial condition, C = constant term(s).

6. For the purpose of stopping the project run as soon as the job is complete, a simple mechanism was also provided. An equation was written that determined the length of the computer simulation as 0 or 50 weeks, dependent upon whether or not the job was perceived as yet completed. Thus, if PPJC > 1, LENGTH would be set equal to 0 and further computer simulation stopped.

$$\text{LENGTH.K} = \text{CLIP}(0, 50, \text{PPJC.K}, 1)$$

7. This was accomplished by changing the TFER table to:

$$\text{TFER} = 1/1/1/1/1/1$$

8. DCS was set equal to 0.5 months.

9. DCS was set equal to 96 months.

10. This was accomplished by changing the TFCHM table to:

$$\text{TFCHM} = -.65/-.4/-.2/0/0/0/.2/.4/.65$$

APPENDIX A
CAUSAL FEEDBACK SYSTEM DIAGRAM OF R AND D PROJECT MODEL

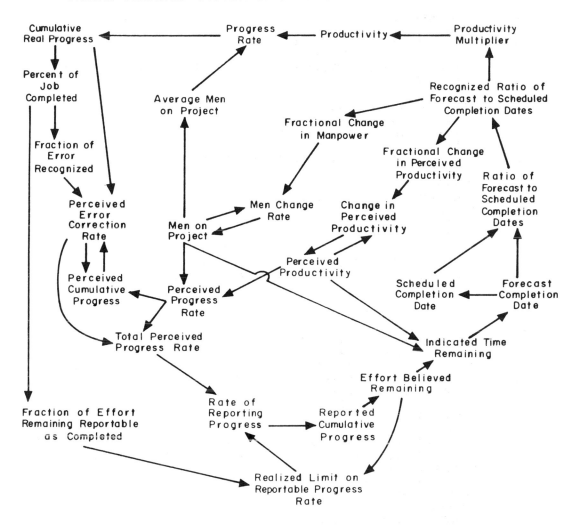

APPENDIX B

R AND D PROJECT MODEL   5/1C/74

```
*       R AND D PROJECT MCDEL
R       PR.KL=(AMEN.K)(PRCD.K)
L       CRP.K=CRP.J+(DT)(PR.JK)
N       CRP=0
L       PCP.K=PCP.J+(DT)(PPR.JK+PECR.JK)
N       PCP=0
R       PPR.KL=(MEN.K)(PPROD.K)
R       PECR.KL=(FER.K)(CRP.K-PCP.K)
A       FER.K=TABLE(TFER,PJC.K,C,1,.2)
```

```
T       TFER=0/0/0/.5/.8/1
A       PJC.K=CRP.K/ER
C       ER=1200
A       PROD.K=(PM.K)(PRCDN)
C       PROCN=2
A       PM.K=TABLE(TPM,RRFSC.K,0,2,.25)
T       TPM=.1/.2/.35/.5/.7/1/1.2/.9/.5
L       RRFSC.K=RRFSC.J+(DT)(1/DRSS)(RFSC.J-RRFSC.J)
N       RRFSC=RFSC
C       DRSS=1
A       RFSC.K=FCD.K/SCOM.K
A       FCD.K=TIME.K+ITR.K
A       ITR.K=EBR.K/(PPROD.K*MEN.K)
A       EBR.K=ER-RCP.K
L       SCOM.K=SCOM.J+(DT)(1/DCS)(FCD.J-SCOM.J)
N       SCOM=FCD
C       DCS=6
L       MEN.K=MEN.J+(DT)(MENCH.JK)
N       MEN=ER/(DCOMI*PPRCD)
C       DCOMI=30
R       MENCH.KL=(FCHM.K)(MEN.K)
A       FCHM.K=TABLE(TFCHM,RRFSC.K,0,2,.25)
T       TFCHM=-.65/-.40/-.2/-.1/0/.1/.2/.4/.65
L       AMEN.K=AMEN.J+(DT)(1/DAMEN)(MEN.J-AMEN.J)
N       AMEN=MEN
C       DAMEN=1
L       RCP.K=RCP.J+(DT)(RRP.JK)
N       RCP=0
R       RRP.KL=MIN(TPPR.K,RLRPR.K)
A       TPPR.K=PPR.JK+PECR.JK
A       RLRPR.K=(FERRC.K)(EER.K)/DT
A       FERRC.K=TABLE(TFERR,PJC.K,0,1,.1)
T       TFERR=.1/.1/.15/.2/.25/.3/.4/.5/.6/.8/1
L       PPROD.K=PPROD.J+(DT)(CPPR.JK)
N       PPROD=PRODN
R       CPPR.KL=(FCPP.K)(PPROD.K)
A       FCPP.K=TABLE(TFCPP,RRFSC.K,0,2,.2)
T       TFCPP=.25/.23/.20/.15/.08/0/-.08/-.15/-.20/-.23/-.25
A       PPJC.K=PCP.K/ER
A       RPJC.K=RCP.K/ER
L       CMEN.K=CMEN.J+(DT)(MEN.J)
N       CMEN=0
A       LENGTH.K=CLIP(0,50,PPJC.K,1)
NOTE
PLOT    MEN=M(10,50)/PJC=A,PPJC=P,RPJC=R(0,1)/SCOM=S,FCD=F(25,45)/
X1      PROD=Y(.8,2)/PR=B,RRP=C(0,80)                    PROD=X,P
SPEC    DT=.5/PLTPER=1/PRTPER=0
RUN     SIMPLE MODEL
```

18

The Problem of Aging Organizations

Edward B. Roberts

In recent years, research and development organizations have had their own kind of "population explosion." Like the human equivalent, such growth has presented management problems. Not the least of these difficulties is the discovery that there is no automatic harvest of benefits just because a growing R&D organization becomes established. Moreover, "fertilizing" an R&D group with top people does not ensure a bumper crop of technical productivity. Even the less naïve companies are finding that such organizations inexplicably grow and decline—that productivity enigmatically waxes and wanes. Like all groups of people working together, R&D organizations can and must be effectively managed.

Managing such creative professional groups requires, first of all, an understanding of the R&D organization dynamics that underlie the technical effectiveness of the group. Effective management requires not only learning what makes an R&D organization tick, but also knowledge of what gives the organization viability.

Wheels Within Wheels

To aid in such understanding, I have developed a "wheels within wheels" theory of R&D dynamics that describes the cyclic nature, both short- and long-term, of such organizations. This theory, based on several years of study, applies to all exploratory groups from manufacturing R&D to basic scientific research. It has as much relevance to industrial R&D groups as to those in government or universities. Generally, the larger the organization, the more valid the theory.

This theory is based on the industrial dynamics approach, which assumes that the problems affecting an organization are the natural outgrowths of the organization's own activities and structure. The theory further asserts that the problems arise from interrelated causes and effects that operate as a series of upward or downward spiraling

This paper is based on a study supported in part by Contract Nonr–3963 (30) from the Office of Naval Research to the Sloan School of Management, M.I.T. Opinions contained in the article are the author's and do not necessarily reflect those of the sponsoring agency. The article was previously published in *Business Horizons,* Winter 1967, pp. 51–58.

positive and negative feedback loops. The industrial dynamics approach is described in depth in Jay W. Forrester, *Industrial Dynamics* (Cambridge: The M.I.T. Press, 1961). For its application to R&D project management see Edward B. Roberts, *The Dynamics of Research and Development* (New York: Harper & Row, 1964). Within these self-contained loops are numerous variables that interact with one another. For R&D organizations these key variables include a varied group: the kind of work performed by the organization; limitations imposed on the organization's growth; the organization's attractiveness to outsiders; its technical effectiveness or productivity; the average age of its personnel; the ''corporate'' evaluation process (how top management rates and responds to the organization); the R&D organization's ''marketing'' activities; and the size of the organization's budget. Many other variables also affect organizational dynamics.

In the context of industrial dynamics, the various facets of R&D organizations are delicately balanced. A change in any of the variables can alter the unit's life cycle. However, the corporate evaluation process—what top management in the company, government agency, university, or the customer thinks of the unit's capabilities and mission and how top management acts in response to evaluation—appears to be the most important. This process has the power of rescuing a technical organization from stagnation or a fatal decline.

As the organization is composed of a series of interlocking closed loops, management attitudes toward an R&D group seriously affect the organization's dynamics. For example, the amount of useful information in the pool of technical knowledge that an organization can bring to bear on its work determines the kind of jobs received and how well they are performed. What the parent organization thinks of the R&D group and its ability to do these jobs is based on the work performance. The information pool is deepened by the expertise accumulated from past work and by the addition of new employees who frequently bring in new skills and knowledge. In like manner, this pool is made more shallow by the obsolescence of technical information and the departure of employees from the organization.

The organization's different R&D activities determine when its accumulated knowledge becomes most useful and when it becomes obsolete. In some types of projects, the knowledge picked up ''yesterday'' is the most useful to the unit today. This often occurs in solving manufacturing engineering problems. And in a year or two this information may be obsolete as far as the unit's then-current work is concerned. But with other project types, the greatest use of the knowledge gained yesterday may be applied, not today or in the near future, but in several years hence, and it may not be out of date for five to ten years. Such a knowledge life-span is more characteristic of the outputs of applied research activities. The varying usefulness over time of technical information derived from the organization's work should be remembered when assigning goals to R&D organizations.

Management can influence the generation of the R&D organization's pool of knowledge and its effective use by determining the laboratory's mission or goals. An organization with a low level of technical skill can still perform in an effective manner

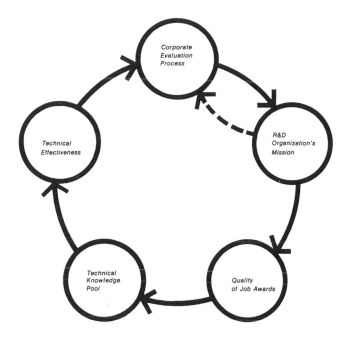

Figure 1   The evaluation process and R&D performance

if management carefully tailors the organization's mission to its capabilities, based on available manpower and technical know-how. Alternately, by assigning more advanced work to the group, management can help the organization "learn" its way to a higher level of technical effectiveness.

Corporate Evaluation

The foregoing relationships—knowledge, technical effectiveness, evaluation, mission-designation, job awards—constitute a single feedback loop (Figure 1). Under usual management policies as one factor moves upward or downward, the whole loop begins to turn in that direction. The movement not only continues in the same direction, but it increases momentum as the cycle continues. For example, an increase in the pool of knowledge increases technical effectiveness relative to the present R&D mission. This raises the R&D organization's esteem in the eyes of management. Management, in turn, usually tends toward a "natural response" of raising the laboratory's mission requirements or goals, which results in better jobs being assigned, thereby improving the pool of knowledge, which further increases the organization's technical effectiveness. This response tendency creates a positive feedback loop affecting organizational performance.

Unfortunately, the same positive feedback loop process holds true in the opposite direction. Should the organization's technical effectiveness drop for any reason—for example, due to a major breakthrough by competition in an area of technology unfamiliar to the R&D team—the corporate evaluation would decline. In these circumstances the natural response of the corporate group is to decrease the goal expectation of the

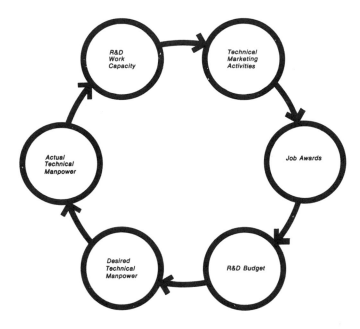

Figure 2   Technical marketing and organizational growth

R&D organization. Management often assumes that it must turn to outsiders for the advanced technology or that a new advanced research organization must be established elsewhere. In this way, the organization's mission is altered, and the jobs assigned to it are changed correspondingly. The new simpler jobs contribute less to the group's pool of technical knowledge; technical effectiveness diminishes further; and the downward spiral continues.

On the other hand, the corporate evaluation process can work differently. Instead of readjusting the technical objectives to match the evaluated organizational effectiveness, corporate management might hold the laboratory's objectives firm or even enlarge them to match the new technical demands. New jobs assigned to the organization would include greater opportunities to learn. And although technical effectiveness may remain low for several years, such a "corrective" managerial policy eventually can turn the declining R&D group into an improving organization. Seldom, however, does top management show the foresight to adopt this corrective negative feedback policy instead of the natural response described previously.

Other Variables

Another feedback loop that affects the R&D organization's life cycle encompasses the variables of desired and actual technical manpower, work capacity, marketing activities, job awards, and the organization's budget (Figure 2). The larger the R&D work force, the more extensive its capacity for undertaking technical work. Special equipment as well as special skills become more available as the organization grows, permitting the group to tackle a broader range of jobs.

As the organization grows its technical marketing activities accelerate. It may seem strange to refer to the marketing efforts of a manufacturing R&D group or industrial laboratory. But "selling," by means of technical discussions and proposals, is an integral part of an R&D organization's life. The scientists and engineers usually sell indirectly through their contacts with their present customers, but sometimes more directly by seeking new potential customers among company product managers and manufacturing plant personnel. The larger the R&D team, the greater its marketing activities. Also, as the organization grows its visibility improves, thereby enhancing its implicit marketing activities.

The technical selling brings in more work for the unit, both requiring and providing for a larger budget. This in turn generates a need for more employees. Eventually the greater number of desired staff leads to a buildup in the size of the R&D group, which further increases the group's total technical capabilities. Thus the upward cycle begins anew. This positive feedback loop can also perform its accelerating function in either an upward or downward direction. If, for example, management were to cut back on the actual manpower level for any reason, this action would tend to decrease the R&D organization's technical capability, which would then lessen the marketing effort; decreased marketing activities would produce a drop in the number of new projects assigned, resulting in a budget cut, and imposing another round of cuts in manpower.

Increasing or decreasing the technical effectiveness of R&D fits into a third feedback loop affecting the organization's attractiveness, that is, what others believe the organization's capabilities to be (Figure 3). An organization that has superior technical effectiveness in the performance of its work tends to draw more desirable projects. As shown in Figure 3, a higher level of job assignments produces significant additions to the pool of effective technical knowledge, which increases the technical capabilities of the people in the unit, boosting technical effectiveness and adding to the organization's attractiveness. Thus, jobs of better quality are assigned to the unit, further helping to maintain or improve the level of work. If, on the other hand, the organization loses its attractiveness for any reason, the system begins a downward spiral. Although not shown in Figure 3, the organization's attractiveness also affects the volume of job assignments the R&D group receives, as well as their quality.

The positive feedback loop affecting the quality of employed people and the nature of the jobs they perform interlocks with a manpower feedback loop that is similar to the phenomenon described in Figure 3. Here, organizational attractiveness is viewed as a factor that stimulates the inflow of new people (Figure 4). The more attractive the R&D organization is to outsiders, the greater the organization's recruiting ability and selectivity of staff. An injection of higher caliber employees into the group boosts its technical effectiveness, which increases attractiveness and further enhances the group's recruiting ability.

Conversely, an organization that loses its attractiveness minimizes its chances to hire top graduates and people from competitor organizations. As a result, the quality of the people hired falls, and the loop begins to move downward as the organization's technical effectiveness drops. Consequently, recruiting ability falls even more.

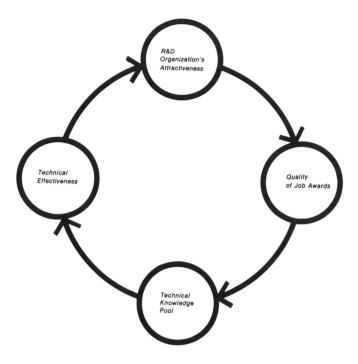

Figure 3   Organizational attractiveness and job quality

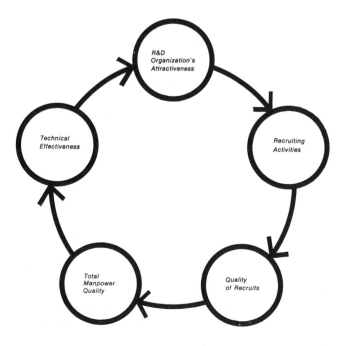

Figure 4   Organizational attractiveness and manpower quality

Personnel and Growth Limitations

Once recruiting is considered, we can consider what are probably the two most important feedback loops describing the R&D organization. These bring into play the aging of technical personnel (with its effects on turnover and productivity) and the impact of growth limitations on the organization (Figure 5). As recruiting activities increase the growth rate of the unit, the average age of the technical staff decreases. This increases the group's technical effectiveness by the addition of both new ideas and vitality, adding more boost to the organization's growth potential. An organization showing signs of stagnation usually is staffed with personnel whose average age is increasing or is already high. Most studies of technical organizations bear out this premise; the exceptions emphasize the rule.

These organizational studies indicate that new Ph.D. scientists make their major contributions shortly after joining an organization. Thereafter, their technical effectiveness declines. On the other hand, a young engineer's productivity is greatest five to ten years after joining the R&D organization; after that time his creative contributions are fewer. On this basis, the technical effectiveness of the R&D group depends on a continual inflow of new people.

Also indicated in Figure 5 is the fact that, as an organization's average age increases, its staff turnover declines. The older engineers and scientists are less likely to leave the organization to seek new opportunities. A small turnover diminishes the number of jobs opening up in the group, reducing recruiting activities and restricting the number of new younger people moving into the organization. This causes intensification of the organizational aging phenomenon.

At times this aging problem is somewhat artificially created for the group by the imposition of limitations on its growth. Corporate management, and more often the government in running its own laboratories, frequently restricts the size of R&D organizations "to keep them from getting out of hand." But such growth limits often produce more than what was bargained for.

A recent comparative analysis of two government-oriented laboratories pointed out the correlation between the trend in the average age of the technical staff, and the resulting personnel turnover and overall productivity. One organization in which growth had been restricted by fiat had an aging technical staff and a low turnover. It had slowed down considerably in its production of new ideas and practicable developments for the outside world. By comparison, the R&D unit that was allowed to keep growing, and where average age remained the same, continued to generate its "products" at an unbounded rate.

These observations suggest that growth limitations, whether by directly restricting the budget or by setting a "head count limit" on the number of employees, can be critical factors in R&D organization dynamics. Although implemented for apparently sound management control reasons, the growth restrictions, once they take effect, can force the upward moving spirals of progress to slow down, stop, and then begin to retrace their paths. First, recruiting slows, then manpower stabilizes, aging sets in, and the organization's technical effectiveness loses its edge. The laboratory's attractiveness

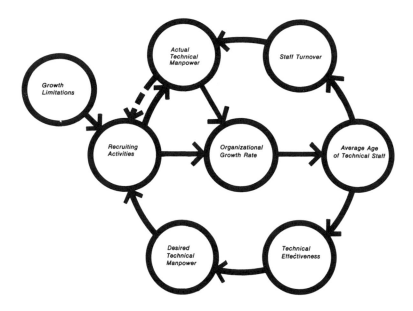

Figure 5   Organizational aging and growth

begins to tarnish, marketing efforts become less successful, and the quality level of projects is not quite what it had been. The pool of effective technical knowledge dries up a little, and technical effectiveness dulls even more, creating a backlash through the whole set of interlocking loops. In short, growth limitations become a reversal factor that changes advance into decline.

Though it may take some time for this decline to become evident to top management, management by its own actions can hasten the decline and fall of the R&D effort. As was discussed earlier in reference to Figure 1, confronted with a faltering group, management usually makes things worse (often without realizing it) by realigning the R&D goals to coincide with the organization's apparent reduced capability. The group is, in effect, down-rated, and the new work assigned to it is poorer in quality. This adversely affects the pool of R&D knowledge and causes a further decline in technical effectiveness. The upshot of these events is that management seems to have confirmed its original evaluation of the situation.

The downward momentum of a declining R&D organization can be slowed, but probably not halted, by the use of several stop-gap policies, all of which contribute to a reduction in the average age of the technical staff. Among these techniques are allowing attrition to reduce the average age and reassigning aging members to other departments. It should be noted here that a program of continuing employee education, while helpful to the organization's overall effectiveness, does not by itself revitalize the technical organization, although it does alter the duration of the organization's change cycle.

Another way of averting the effects of externally imposed growth limits is changing the ratio of engineer-scientists to technician-support personnel from, say, 60–40 to

90–10. This can be done where the head count restrictions limit the maximum number of employees available to the organization, but where funds available exceed direct manpower requirements. This approach has been used by some government R&D centers where everything but in-house scientific and engineering activities has been jobbed to outside contractors—technician services, computer programming, even secretarial and janitorial services. This practice has allowed the government center to continue expanding its professional staff with good results. Of course, when the organization's manpower begins to approach 100 per cent technical staff, the growth limitation begins to have its usual effect.

Revitalize the Organization

Unfortunately, few of the countermeasures to imposed size limits have worked effectively. Unless the restraint on growth is temporary, the restrictions eventually set off a decline that almost inevitably results in the technical death of the organization. If the organization is to be regenerated, management must recognize what has to be done and responsibly carry out the needed actions.

Instead of automatically downgrading the R&D organization's mission in line with what appears to be its faltering technical effectiveness, management must see in the initial decline a warning signal that the organization needs an infusion of revitalizing influences. Rather than downgrade the R&D group, management should readjust its goals sideways or even upward. This positive reshaping of mission, even without added funds or personnel, will likely produce new assignments that eventually regenerate the organization's technical effectiveness. But managerial patience is required to see such a change through to its eventual beneficial outcome.

The mission change can take many forms. Instead of studying speed and feed rates on conventional machining processes, for example, the group can attack metalworking problems from another angle—by studying nontraditional machining techniques, such as electrical discharge machining, electrochemical grinding or laser welding. Another way would be to switch the group from projects involving manufacturing processes to those concerned with engineering design and development. In this way a fixed-size group can maintain and even rebuild technical effectiveness by the infusion of new demands and challenges. The spirit of innovation can be used as a substitute for the flow of new people that revitalizes a growing organization.

Not all R&D groups are worth preserving. In some cases, the wisest course may be to let the organization die—even to encourage its demise—and start over. This is essentially what some aerospace companies do when they set up competing R&D project teams to explore two or more approaches to a problem. When the problem is solved, the "loser" organization is then disbanded.

Attempting to design policies for improving the level of usefulness of an R&D organization raises more questions than we can presently answer. I am now trying to employ computer simulation, using mathematical models of R&D organizations, to provide new insights to the kinds of questions that ordinarily depend on intuition: what policy should management adopt in attempting to save an organization once it gets into trouble; does a corrective policy have to be followed in a dramatic manner, or is it enough to follow such a policy in moderation; how long should a corrective policy be maintained to set in motion the organization's recovery—six months or six years; are the best intended and pursued policies doomed to failure merely because good engineers and scientists are reluctant to join an organization that has a bad technical reputation?

It is apparent from our description of the feedback loop theory of R&D organizational dynamics that the organization's short-term and long-term cycles are largely self-induced by a complex process. Adding more meat to the bare bones theory presented means adding still more complications. For corporate and R&D management to cope with the dynamics of technical organizations we need both more elaboration of the theoretical structures and more development of tools like computer simulation for understanding the implications of the theory. Both improvements are likely to be forthcoming during the next several years of continuing R&D growth.

19

The Dynamics of R&D Strategy

Henry B. Weil, Thomas A. Bergan,
and Edward B. Roberts

Introduction

The myth persists that R&D organizations are concerned with the long-term. It is re-enforced by statements like: "our future depends on the success of our R&D," "R&D is a long-term investment," and "it takes years, sometimes a decade, for an idea to move from the lab to the marketplace."

Our experience with many of the world's leading R&D organizations suggests a rather different reality—a most alarming case of corporate schizophrenia. While the activities which comprise R&D occur over lengthy periods of time and can have a profound impact (one way or the other) on overall corporate performance in many industries, most R&D managers are almost totally preoccupied with short-term concerns. What preoccupies them are the problems of individual projects, the battle for next year's budget, immediate staffing and organization problems, and playing company politics.

All of those things are critically important. An R&D organization's day-to-day survival depends on them. But they all pertain to R&D management at the *tactical* level.

There is a second, higher level of R&D management issues that are largely overlooked, even in the most progressive and sophisticated R&D organizations. These are the issues of R&D *strategy*. They are more general and longer-term than the tactical problems. They focus on the policies by which an organization is managed, not on particular decisions that need to be made. And, much more than the tactical issues, they determine the overall effectiveness, credibility, and viability of an R&D organization. As any good historian will tell you, one can win many skirmishes and still lose the war.

This paper is about the formulation of R&D strategy. It begins by noting what some of the key strategy issues are. Next we discuss strategy formulation as a "systems

This chapter was originally presented at the 1973 Summer Simulation Conference and is reprinted here with the permission of the authors.

problem'' and a computer simulation model that can serve as an analysis tool to help R&D managers decide on strategy. Use of this model is then described in terms of the principal change options through which R&D strategies can be implemented. The last major section presents a simulation-based analysis of workflow bunching: a common pattern of oscillating and badly-distributed workload experienced by many R&D organizations. That example is intended to illustrate how a much broader range of strategic issues can be approached.

Key Strategy Issues

Many important R&D strategy issues pertain to the policies that govern the acquisition and allocation of resources. The predominant resource in an R&D organization is people. Even when the overall size of an R&D organization is limited by a headcount or budgetary ceiling, skills mix and quality of human resources require continuing careful attention.

The allocation issues concern the assignment of resources to the various R&D activities: research into new technologies; refinement and mastery of the technologies underlying current products; new product conceptualization; engineering design and testing of new products; refinement of products already being manufactured and sold; technical troubleshooting and problem solving on projects; etc. They pertain to the ways in which the various pressures and direction from corporate management should affect the disposition of R&D resources.

Resource acquisition and allocation issues are intimately interwoven with aspects of technology strategy. Technology strategy deals with questions like advancedness of products, technological risk taking, mastery of technologies used, nature of new technology programs, obsolescence, the role of back-room support for new ideas, and the priority (with respect to resources) accorded technology-oriented activities. Technology strategy can have a critical impact on R&D (and overall corporate) performance.

The following list is intended to be illustrative of what we mean by ''R&D strategy issues''; it is not intended to be exhaustive:

The appropriate allocation of resources among technology programs, exploratory new product activities, and major new product development and design programs.

The appropriate technological lead that technology programs should maintain over exploratory new product activities, and that the latter should maintain over new product development and design programs.

The rate at which R&D can respond to corporate management's desires to diversify away from historical product areas (how do R&D policies and corporate management pressures affect this).

How well mastered a technology should be before it is incorporated in a significant way in a new product concept being seriously explored,. . .in a major new product development and design program (what are the interrelationships between technology mastery and R&D productivity).

The extent to which technologies and product concepts can be ''stockpiled'' (what is the ''shelflife''; the likelihood they will ever be used).

The breadth of potential candidates for major new product development and design programs that should be maintained (how do technology programs and exploratory new product activities constrain management's ability to initiate new product development and design programs).

The rate at which R&D can respond to a big new product push designed by corporate management.

The appropriate hierarchy of responses to problems like falling behind schedule and inability to meet a product's technical performance objectives.

The impact of R&D being significantly overoptimistic about feasible schedule and/or attainable technical performance of products as part of its "selling" tactics.

The appropriate mix of human resources for the R&D organization as a whole, and for each area of activity (what is the appropriate degree of assignment flexibility that should be maintained).

The relative priorities of performance with respect to budgetary, schedule, and technical product objectives (how should conflict among these goals be resolved).

The priorities for assigning human resources to each area of R&D activity and for "stealing" people for reassignment to higher priority activities (appropriate constraints on reassignment; how should priorities shift in response to changes in the situation and problems of the R&D organization).

The best response to corporate management pressures for diversification, increased level of new product development and design problems, meeting schedule and/or budget objectives, meeting technical product performance objectives, or over-optimism in order to "sell" programs.

Avoiding "workflow bunching"—a common pattern of oscillating and maldistributed workload experienced by many R&D organizations.

The implications of moving into markets where technology is harder to master and/or technology obsolesces more rapidly (what are the implications of various reactions to "technology gaps").

The implications of speeding up the R&D process (what would be the impact of moving into markets characterized by a much shorter R&D cycle).

All of the preceding examples combine aspects of resource allocation strategy and technology strategy. In these terms, a "strategy" is a particular combination of management policies that will guide R&D activities in the desired direction. These policies take the form of priorities (e.g., for resource allocation), constraints (e.g., minimum levels of effort that must be maintained), targets (e.g., desired mastery of technologies used in new products), and decision rules (e.g., the proportion of new hires that should have particular skills). As we will discuss below, R&D strategies can be very complicated, involving the careful design of multiple interdependent policies.

A Strategy-Oriented R&D Model

R&D strategy formulation is a complex "systems" problem. An enormous web of inter-related factors must be considered: how technology-oriented activities and product-oriented activities affect one another; sequential inter-dependencies between phases of R&D; the trade-offs among different aspects of R&D performance (e.g., budgetary, schedule, technical); the implications of having to take resources away from some activities in order to apply them somewhere else; the relationships between how R&D "sells" its programs and its subsequent problems; the effect of a short-run problem-solving behavior on long-run R&D performance. Not only are there a large number of factors to consider, but they all interact with one another over time. Thus, one must deal with a high degree of dynamic complexity, characterized by multiple chains of cause and effect that close on themselves to form self-reinforcing and self-correcting "feedback" loops.

Given this situation, it is clear that intuitive analysis is likely to lead the R&D manager astray. Perhaps this is why so few have ventured into the realm of strategy issues.

To provide R&D managers with a powerful tool for formulating and evaluating new policies and strategies, we developed a computer simulation model of an R&D organization. This model builds on earlier work by Roberts (1) and Weil (2). It should be noted however, that while Roberts' original R&D model focussed on the management of an individual project, this model represents the functioning of an *entire organization* with many different categories of on-going activities.

The model focusses on the dynamic behavior of an R&D organization as it responds to various pressures and direction from corporate management. All important behavior-influencing policies, decisions, and activities internal to the R&D organization have been included in the model. The corporate-level decision-making process, however, is not represented in the model. Rather, it is treated as an exogenous input.

The R&D model consists of five interrelated sectors:

1. *Technology programs*—research into new technologies and efforts directed toward the refinement and greater mastery of the technologies underlying current products.
2. *New product exploration*—the early stages of new product development, i.e., conceptualization and feasibility analysis.
3. *Product programs*—major new product efforts in the advanced development, engineering design, testing, and initial production stages.
4. *Performance measurement and control*—measurement of progress versus schedule and technical performance commitments; determination of desires for additional people through hiring and/or reallocation from other areas within the R&D organization and desired slippages of schedule and technical performance commitments.
5. *Human resources allocation*—reallocation of human resources among resource uses; hiring and firing.

These five sectors deal with the flow of information, projects, and people.

The model represents technology programs, new product exploration and product program activities along two dimensions: "magnitude" of the effort and "degree of technical advancedness" of the effort. Technology programs, new product exploration and product programs are inter-related in such a way that innovations in technology enable innovations in exploratory new product activities and in major product pro-

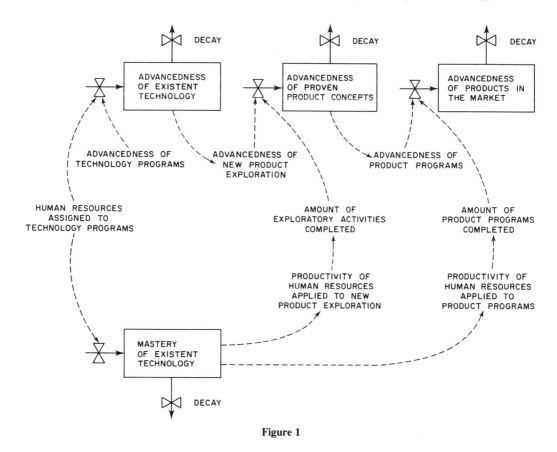

Figure 1

grams. Thus, technological advancements can have a cascading effect through the system, leading ultimately to the introduction of more advanced products in the market. The approval of exploratory activities and product programs that are not adequately supported by technology, though possible, results in reduced productivity due to the emergence of formidable technical barriers. These relationships are displayed in Figure 1.

An R&D organization is limited in the approval of product programs to select from among the available candidates. The field of candidates, called proven product concepts in the model, consists of successfully completed exploratory activities that have not been approved as product programs. Proven product concepts are described in the model by their quantity and by their distribution in terms of technical innovativeness.

The quantity or level of proven product concepts is increased by the completion of new product exploration projects and decreased by the approval of these projects as product programs. The level of proven product concepts is also decreased by decaying over time, representing the decreasing probability that older candidates will be approved without further concept or feasibility work. These sequential interdependencies between new product exploration, proven product concepts, and product programs are shown in Figure 2.

The performance measurement and control sector of the model deals with the setting of schedule and technical product performance commitments, recognition of

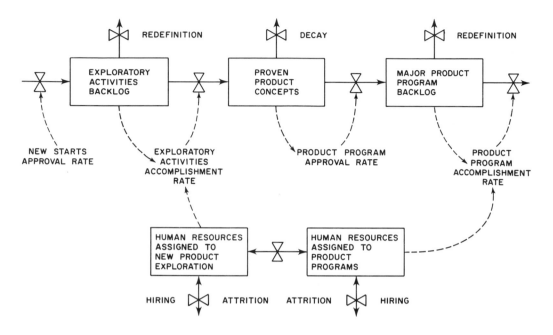

Figure 2

schedule and performance problems, and the initiation of corrective action. Schedule commitments and problems are dealt with for both exploratory activities and major product programs. Technical performance commitments and problems, however, are only represented in product programs since firm product performance commitments are not usually made until a project passes beyond the early exploratory stages.

Technical product performance problems reduce the rate at which the product program workload can be accomplished, due to critical path effects. That is, the overall productivity of human resources applied to the product program workload decreases. Thus, product performance problems lead to schedule problems both through an increase in the total work (in man-months) to be accomplished; and a decrease in the rate of accomplishment of the work dependent on the particular solution to the performance problems.

The human resource allocation sector deals with the hiring and firing of people, and with the allocation of people among resource uses. More specifically, this sector is responsible for the allocation of two types of people to six resource uses. The two types of human resources are technical people (researchers & applied technologists) and engineers. These two types of people are allocated in certain proportions to the following resource uses:

   product performance problems

   major product programs

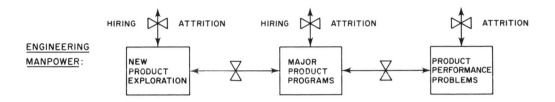

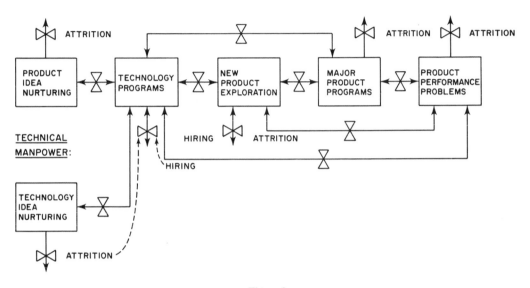

Figure 3

new product exploration

technology programs

technology idea nurturing

product idea nurturing

When an area of activity desires additional people, this need may be satisfied through hiring or through reallocation of men from one resource use to another. Reallocation of human resources between resource uses is permitted, however, only via the paths shown in Figure 3. A priority is associated with each resource use. Higher priority resource uses may "steal" people from lower priority resource uses subject to a number of constraints.

Two types of constraints limit the extent to which reallocation does occur. First, skill-related constraints limit the reallocation of people between resource uses. For example, a skills-related constraint limits the reallocation of engineers from new product exploration to product programs, reflecting the differences in skills between development engineers and design engineers. Similarly, a constraint limits the reallocation of some technical people from technology programs to other resource uses, representing skill differences between scientist-researchers and applied technologists. Secondly, the reallocation of men among resource uses may be limited by managerial policy. Specifically, the R&D model represents policies which establish a minimum number of people (i.e., "manpower floor") that will be assigned to each resource use, regardless of the needs of other resource uses.

These flows of information, projects, and men are represented in the R&D model by approximately 650 equations and nearly 100 feedback loops. The model was developed using the techniques of system dynamics (3) and implemented in the DYNAMO simulation language (4).

It is important to remember that this is an aggregate model of an R&D organization—not a model of individual R&D projects. It is a high-level model designed to assist in the development strategies—not to tell management what to do about a particular short-term operational difficulty.

Use of the R&D Model

The model has been used to evaluate the impact of various changes in strategy and policy on an R&D organization. The possible changes in the R&D model represent opportunities to affect the organization's behavior. These changes can be divided into three categories: key managerial control decisions; key behavioral variables; and key characteristics of the organization's management system. Examples of each category are listed below. The results of various combinations of changes in these factors have been analyzed through series of simulation runs with the model.

Key managerial control decisions:

R&D management's preferences for the "advancedness" of technology programs, new product exploration activities, and product programs.

Rate of addition to new product exploration and product program backlogs.

Desired rates of accomplishment for technology programs, exploratory activities and product programs.

Allocation of human resources to product programs, technology programs, new product exploration, product idea nurturing and technology idea nurturing.

Priorities of each resource use, affecting the reallocation of resources to solve schedule and technical performance problems.

The extent to which resources in the various uses are protected from competing demands.

Rate at which corrections for schedule and performance problems are attempted via various policy routes.

Priorities of various alternative policies aimed at solution of the problem: adding human resources, slipping schedule, redefining scope of project, lowering technical performance targets.

The magnitude of corrective actions attempted.

The phasing over time of various alternative policies aimed at solution of the problem.

Hiring rate (and type of skills acquired).

The commitments made with respect to schedule and technical product performance.

The priorities attached to performance with respect to schedule vs. performance with respect to technical product performance targets.

Key behavioral variables:

The R&D organization's response to conflicting pressures from corporate management.

The R&D organization's response to pressure to be over-optimistic with respect to feasible schedules and technical performance of products.

The extent to which the R&D organization conforms to corporate management's preferences for the nature of product programs.

Effect of perceived R&D management preferences on the nature of ideas generated.

Composition of experience-based biases for technology and product programs and the rate at which they change.

The extent to which experience-based biases dominate idea generation and program selection.

The willingness to admit to unattainable commitments; how bad things have to get before a revision in targets is sought.

Key characteristics of the organization's management system:

Delays in perception of performance variances, productivity of resources, management preferences.

Delays in obtaining approvals for new projects and programs, resource allocations, changes in schedule and technical performance targets, redefinition of work load.

The method by which the effect of remedial actions is projected.

The degree of flexibility or inflexibility built into commitments; whether these can be modified at any time or only at fixed periodic reviews (e.g., every 6 or 12 months).

The accuracy with which performance, progress, productivity, management preferences can be determined.

The extent to which information regarding what is going on in one area (e.g., exploratory activities) is inputted into decisions affecting a different, but interrelated area (e.g., product programs).

When policy or behavioral changes in the above three areas are examined through simulation analyses, some criteria must be used to determine which simulations produce better results than others. In extreme cases, visual examination of the model's output alone can lead to conclusions as to the desirability of a given change. In many cases, however, the question of which behavior is actually better for the organization remains. Therefore, a set of criteria has been added to the model to assist in the comparison of various simulation runs. These measures are listed below:

Total R&D cost;

Total output (or accomplishment) of product programs;

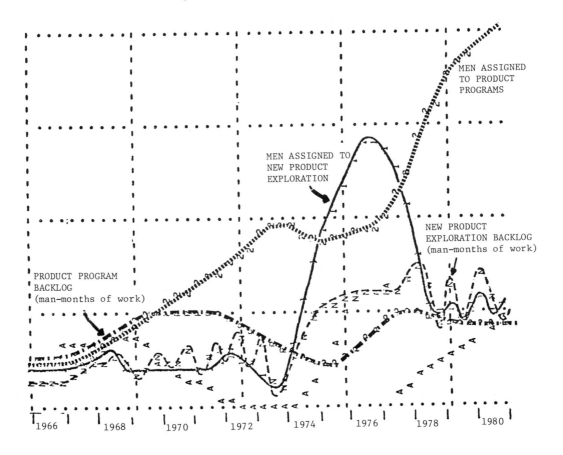

Figure 4

Output of product programs per dollar;
Cumulative slippages in product program schedule commitments;
Cumulative slippages in technical product performance commitments;
Average productivity of human resources applied to product programs; and
Average mastery of technology.

A typical simulation run with the R&D model is presented in Figures 4 and 5. The model was initialized with 1966 data.

Pressure from corporate management to increase the product program effort results in an increased new product exploration effort to produce the desired candidates for approval as major product programs, and in an increase in the approval of product programs as these candidates are completed. This leads to the hiring of additional people and to the reallocation of some people within the R&D organization: as the product program effort increased, resources are reallocated from new product exploration and technology programs to support the increased product program effort. By 1968 the technology effort is reduced to a low level. Early in 1969, new product exploration activities also decline. The high level of product program effort and low level of new

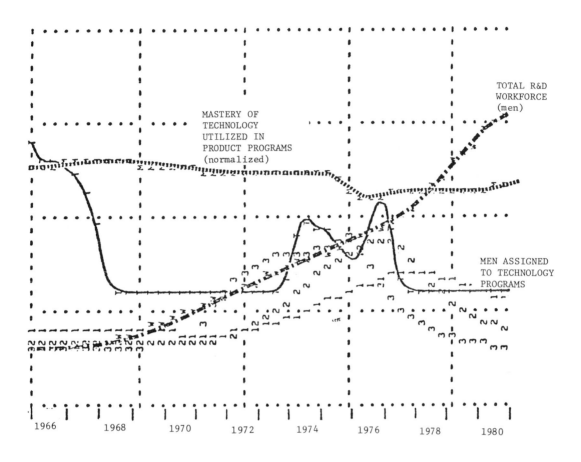

TOTAL R&D
WORKFORCE
(men)

MASTERY OF
TECHNOLOGY
UTILIZED IN
PRODUCT PROGRAMS
(normalized)

MEN ASSIGNED
TO TECHNOLOGY
PROGRAMS

1966   1968   1970   1972   1974   1976   1978   1980

Figure 5

product exploration effort inhibit the approval of additional product programs. Because of over-optimistic schedule and performance commitments, the major product programs initiated in the later 1960's encounter problems in meeting performance targets within the approved schedule. Eventually performance commitments, and, to a lesser extent, schedule commitments are redefined.

In 1971, the pressures from corporate management change. There is now high pressure to diversify into new market areas and high pressure to meet technical product performance commitments. As the product programs of the late 60's are completed, the new product exploration increases, to develop the next generation of products. Due to the diversification pressure, these exploratory activities are more technically advanced than previous ones. Thus, the time to complete these more innovative new product explorations is also increased. During this period of time, the organization is characterized by (a) the existence of underutilized engineers in the product program area and (b) absence of program product concepts constraining the approval of major product programs below the desired approval rate. This situation starts to improve in mid-1974, however, as some of the new product exploration activities initiated in response to the diversification pressure are completed. The approval of this generation of product programs is delayed until that time due to problems encountered in the first generation programs (those started in the late 60's) which caused extensive reallocation away from new product exploration and advanced technology efforts. As this next generation of product programs is approved and begins to require additional resources, the new product exploration workload levels off.

The feedback loops which are most important in determining the behavior of the model in this simulation are the loops concerning the sequential interdependencies between new product exploration and major product programs shown earlier in Figures 1 and 2. Response to pressures to expand the product program effort initiated the first "bulge" in the R&D workload. This bulge was accentuated by over-optimistic schedule and technical product performance commitments. Resources were stolen from new product exploration and technology programs to assist in solving product program crises. Furthermore, hiring activities during this first bulge emphasized the hiring of design engineers to work on product programs rather than the hiring of technologists to replace those stolen from new product exploration and technology programs. These factors combine to generate the forces which produce a second major bulge in the R&D workload.

Workflow Bunching—An Example of Strategic Analysis

The workload bulges produced in the simulation run described above are indicative of a generic problem that plagues many R&D organizations. We call this problem "workflow bunching." Because it is an important strategic problem with complex causes and no clear cure (R&D managers have been wrestling with the problem for years), it provides a good illustration of how the R&D model can aid in strategy formulation and evaluation. Our general approach is to: (a) determine which feedback loops dominate the behavior associated with the problem; (b) find the leverage points in these crucial feedback loops which can be affected by changes in managerial policy; and (c) evaluate alternative policies through comparison of simulation results.

What is Workflow Bunching?   To begin with, the term "workflow bunching" refers to a pattern of oscillating and maldistributed workload in an R&D organization. For a while, parts of the organization will experience a very high workload at the same time that other parts are lightly loaded. Then the situation will reverse itself, and still later, it will reverse itself again. More specifically, the organization goes through periods of high product program workload and low workload in the new product exploration area, followed by a high exploratory workload and a low one for major product programs.

The behavior described above, plus skills-related constraints which limit the reallocation of human resources, produce a second aspect of workflow bunching: a condition of needing more human resources in one part of the organization (e.g., new product exploration) and having a surplus somewhere else (e.g., major product programs), but not being able to transfer many people from one place to the other. The problem of matching skills with the workload to be accomplished can lead to a situation in which people are being hired into one area of an R&D organization while an excess of people with different skills exists in another part of the organization. To pursue the example begun earlier in this paragraph, the organization would be hiring into new product exploration groups, while living with underemployed human resources in product development and design groups that would decline over time through attrition. Thus, workflow bunching is also characterized by oscillations between "under-capacity" and "over-capacity" in different parts of the organization.

Periods of under-capacity (i.e., too few usable resources compared to the work-load in a part of the organization) lead to rising backlogs of work to be accomplished, the stretching out of schedules, and instances where sequentially dependent "down-stream" activities are severely constrained. Thus, a third aspect of workflow bunching is the existence of periods in which the approval of product programs is limited by an insufficiency of candidates (proven product concepts) of the type preferred by R&D management. This situation can occur when either an insufficient number of new product exploration projects has been completed, or few of the existent candidates conform with management's current preferences for product programs.

Looking at the output of the R&D process, the result of workflow bunching appears as "bursts" of product programs followed by "lulls." Within the R&D organization, it looks like a series of waves, surging down the product development pipeline.

What Combinations of Factors Produce Workflow Bunching?   Workflow bunching is not typically caused by one policy or constraining factor. Rather it is produced by the complex interactions of many related factors. The feedback relationships which are most crucial in producing or eliminating workflow bunching are:

1. the sequential interdependencies between the magnitude of the new product explo-ration and product program efforts;
2. the feedback loops determining the nature of technology programs, exploration activities, and product programs;
3. the interrelationships between technology and productivity, and the emerging solution of performance problems; and
4. the human resource allocation policies which determine the allocation of people to each of the resource activities, thus, affecting the behavior within each of the above feedback loops.

These important feedback loops are reviewed briefly below, as they relate specifically to the issue of workflow bunching.

An increase in the rate of product program approval results in the need for additional resources for product programs. Additional human resources can be ac-quired through hiring and through "stealing" people from other resource uses. The greater the reallocation of men from new product exploration activities and technology programs to product programs, the greater is the tendency for initiating workflow bunching. Conversely, if less reallocation is permitted by managerial policy, the ten-dency to produce workflow bunching declines (at the expense of making the solution of the product program crises more difficult, since skilled technologists are more effective problem solvers than design engineers). The required reallocation of human resources to product programs is highly dependent on the rate of growth of the approved R&D manpower ceiling. That is, as the manpower ceiling increases, additional men can be hired to ease crises. The smaller the rate of growth in the manpower ceiling, the more product program crises must be solved through stealing resources from other R&D activities, or through redefinition of commitments. If the organization is allowed to grow fast enough, the crises are eventually handled by the larger workforce. Alternatively, the stress will be relieved before substantial bunching builds up if targets and commitments are easily redefinable.

If over-optimistic commitments are made at the same time that the total R&D effort is increased, hiring must be done to accommodate both the increase in the approved workload and the additional real workload resulting from over-optimistic commitments. This situation is more severe than the one described above. It has a greater potential for producing workflow bunching, since more reallocation of resources is required. The effects of various rates of growth in the manpower ceiling, and of policies limiting the reallocation of human resources, apply here as discussed in the preceding paragraphs.

The tendency to produce workflow bunching is further increased by changes in diversification pressure, which produce changes in R&D management's preferences for the nature of projects (by definition, away from historical product areas). After a change in preferences for the nature of product programs, management's ability to approve major product programs in keeping with its new preferences depends on the existence of ready candidates of the newly desired type. If the new product exploration effort had encompassed a broad range of projects, the organization will most likely be able to respond initially with the approval of some product programs of the desired nature. After this initial approval, few or none of the proven product concepts will be of the type now desired. In this case, R&D management must either approve product programs which are significantly different from its preferences, or mount a major new product exploration effort to provide a generation of product program candidates which are more consistent with management's preferences. Corporate pressures usually cause the organization to favor the latter. The more this is favored over the former, however, the greater is the tendency to generate workflow bunching.

The existence of a technology base which can support desired product activities also relates closely to the issue of workflow bunching. If short-term pressures and problems cause technology efforts to be directed primarily towards today's problems, it is unlikely that new technologies will be developed to support the next generation of new products. New product exploration and product program completion times are greatly lengthened when enabling technologies do not exist, or are not sufficiently mastered. Productivity of human resources is lower and technical performance problems are more likely. These stresses increase workflow bunching.

Workflow Bunching Policy Evaluation.   Given the three causes of workflow bunching, it is still not at all clear what policies, if any, an R&D organization should change

Summary Data — Workflow Bunching

(All numbers represent the percentage change from the base.)	Total Cost	Total Output of Product Programs	Output of Product Programs per Dollar	Cumulative Schedule Slippages	Cumulative Performance Target Slippages	Productivity of Human Resources Assigned to Product Program	Average Mastery of Technology Base
1. Base-run	0.0	0.0	0.0	0.0	0.0	0.0	0.0
2. Increase in priority of new product exploration effort when the approval of product programs is limited	7.9	32.1	22.2	102.2	−7.8	16.0	−1.0
3. Protected new product exploration effort	7.3	24.3	15.9	149.4	−15.3	11.1	−1.1
4. Protected technology effort	−13.9	−5.9	9.2	−50.8	−.8	11.4	10.7
5. Protected technology effort & increase in priority of new product exploration	1.6	44.4	41.9	80.8	−15.6	32.8	11.0
6. Protected technology effort & protected new product exploration effort	3.9	41.9	36.4	134.4	−20.5	28.7	10.9
7. Hiring priority favoring technologists	−2.3	33.0	36.1	83.3	−30.1	33.8	16.1
8. New product exploration higher priority than product programs	7.2	36.7	27.4	249.1	−39.4	27.8	3.0
9. Longer shelf-life for proven product concepts	5.0	7.1	1.9	21.1	−.5	.6	−1.1
10. Protected technology, increase in priority of new product exploration & hiring priority favoring technologists	−1.6	41.3	43.7	100.5	−35.3	40.1	16.1
11. Protected technology efforts, protected new product exploration effort & hiring priority favoring technologists	−.7	43.7	44.9	126.3	−51.8	42.2	16.5
12. Growing minimum technology and new product exploration efforts, hiring priority favoring technologists	−24.1	−20.4	4.7	440.0	−86.3	45.6	35.2

Figure 6

to reduce workflow bunching, or how much workflow bunching really costs. Each of the policies which could be changed to reduce this problem has some implications with respect to other problems. For example, the reallocation of technologists from technology programs and new exploration to product programs greatly assists in the solution of short-term product performance problems, while increasing future workflow bunching. Should this reallocation of men be limited or stopped? If this policy is not altered, what other changes in managerial policy can reduce the future detrimental effects of this reallocation? Simulation analyses can be used to answer these types of questions. With respect to workflow bunching, the effect of various policy changes was evaluated using the R&D model. The results of these simulations are summarized in Figure 6.

Conclusion

The simulation results regarding workflow bunching do not purport to yield the "correct" set of policies for dealing with the problem. Several combinations of policies substantially stabilize the R&D workload. Each of these produces fairly significant improvements in organizational performance along one or more dimensions, usually accompanied by little or no improvement along some other dimensions. Because there is inherent conflict among the set of criterial variables used to evaluate alternative policies, there is no clear cut optimum strategy. It is a matter of preference.

This, of course, is precisely the case in the real world. Due to conflicting performance objectives (e.g., budgetary, schedule, and technical; short-run and long-term), trade-offs are always required. That is where enlightened managerial judgment comes in.

The workflow bunching example was intended to illustrate how a broad range of R&D issues can be approached. The R&D model has been used to explore a rich set of resource allocation and technology problems: diversification; acceleration of the R&D process; technological obsolescence; technologies that are more difficult to master; highly constrained growth in R&D resources. Much more could be done. The real challenge is causing R&D managers to more seriously address the strategic issues on which the longer-term effectiveness, credibility, and viability of their organizations depend. This is a problem of consciousness raising.

References

1. Roberts, E. B., *The Dynamics of Research and Development*, Harper & Row, New York, 1964.

2. Weil, H. B.,"Industrial Dynamics and MIS, " *Proceedings of the 1971 Summer Simulation Conference*, Boston, July, 1971. (See also chapter 27 of this volume.)

3. Forrester, J. W., *Industrial Dynamics*, The MIT Press, Cambridge, 1961.

4. Pugh, A. L., III, *Dynamo II Users Manual*, (fourth edition) The MIT Press, Cambridge, 1973.

20

Modelling Strategies for Corporate Growth

Robert S. Spencer

The necessary steps to be taken in constructing a business model are the following:

1. defining the objectives of the study;
2. formulating the structure of the model;
3. determining the values to be assigned to the parameters, and the initial values of the variables;
4. validating the model by comparison with experience, when that is possible;
5. using the model to answer the questions set forth in the objectives.

These steps will be illustrated in terms of constructing a model of a relatively self-contained division of the Dow Chemical Company. This is a relatively simple model of the industrial dynamics type,[1] which produced some rather interesting results.

"Simulation of a social system involves building and operating a model designed to represent those features of a system which are deemed to be significant in view of the objectives behind the simulation."[2] Thus, our first step is to ask, "What is the purpose of the study? What questions do we want answered?" Definition of objectives must come first, because there is no such thing as *the* model of a system. Several models may be built to answer several questions. For example, a wing-loading model, a wind tunnel model, a Link trainer, and a production prototype are all models of an airplane and each is useful. But each is different in terms of its purpose, and consequently in what features are included or omitted.

In the division model the primary concern was with the dynamics of growth—growth of sales and growth of profits. We wanted to know the relative importance of various factors in determining rate of growth, the probable results of certain policy changes, the influence of organizational style, and the effect of combining some of these changes into strategies. Time does not permit a comprehensive discussion of results but I will try to present illustrations from each of these four areas.

This paper was presented at the Society for General Systems Research session of the conference of the American Association for the Advancement of Science, Washington, D.C., December 26, 1966.

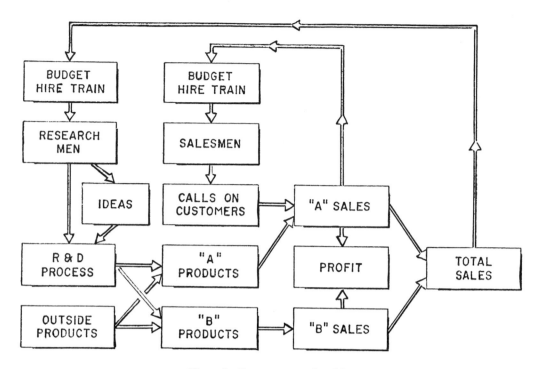

Figure 1   Gross structure of model

The gross structure of the model is shown in Figure 1, comprising two major feedback loops. Preliminary analysis showed that the rate of growth of mature products was much less than the overall rate desired. Therefore the new product development process is represented in the model in some detail. From total sales an R&D budget is derived, and new men are gradually hired and trained as called for by the budget. Trained research men have ideas and work on them. Ultimately, new products emerge from the R&D process to create new sales, thereby closing the research loop of the model. In addition, a new product may occasionally enter the system from outside the R&D process. It was necessary to separate the products into two types, differentiated both as to market area and marketing and distribution channels. "B" type products require only a modest selling effort and have typically realized close to their full market potential. "A" type products require a very considerable selling effort and historically this selling effort has been directed at only a fraction of the total market. This implies that the future marketing effort *could* be quite different from the past, and therefore this part of the model is also structured in some detail, giving the second major loop.

Figure 2 shows some details of the R&D process. Projects are recognized as being in one of three stages of development. Stage 1 work consists of exploratory and testing activities before project definition. There is a maximum rate at which projects leave a stage, which is the ratio of the number of projects in that stage to the average dwell time of projects through the stage. The actual rate of completing projects cannot exceed this maximum, and is otherwise determined by the number of men assigned to that stage of work and their productivity. At the conclusion of each stage there is a given probability

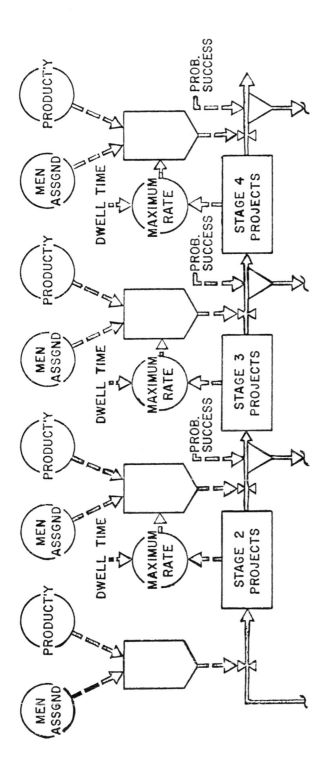

Figure 2   Research & development process

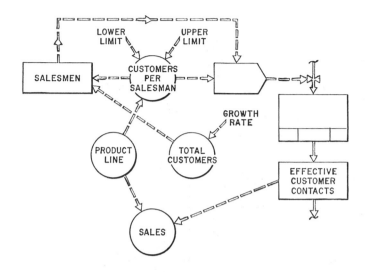

Figure 3   Selling operation

that the project will be promoted to the following stage rather than be discontinued. Projects which successfully complete stage 4 become new products.

Figure 3 illustrates the operation of selling "A" type products. The number of customers per salesmen must fall within a range defined by the nature of the selling process in this market area. Within that range, the value of customers-per-salesmen is determined inversely by the extent of the product line. The total number of salesmen is not permitted to exceed that required to service the total number of customers. The number of salesmen times the customers-per-salesman is passed through a suitable delay to give effective customer contacts, which then gives "sales" when multiplied by "product line."

In order to operate the model, initial values must be assigned to the variables and to the parameters or constants in the equations which relate the variables to one another. These numbers are arrived at by analyzing records, looking at plans, talking to informed individuals, comparing with similar systems, or just plain guessing. This step in model construction gets my vote as consuming the most time and calling for the greatest ingenuity.

A point should be emphasized. This kind of glimpse into the future is based upon the past, but is not *bound* by the past. This is not like a statistical forecast which extrapolates past trends. The past only provides a foundation. We can assume any deviations from the past that we choose, and use the model to look at the probable results of such a deviation. However, we are forced to recognize explicitly and justify to ourselves our assumptions about improvements or other deviations.

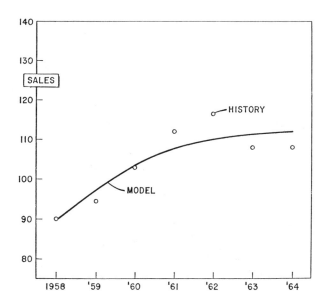

Figure 4   Validation curve

The first thing usually done with a model is to compare its behavior with recent history to see if it gives reasonable or plausible results. The validation curve for the division model is shown in Figure 4, in which the points represent historical data and the solid line represents the behavior of the model, which would seem to be producing a fairly good trend.

Figures 5 through 9 illustrate what happens when certain factors are changed from the historical pattern. This kind of sensitivity analysis has two important results: it suggests where to center efforts toward improvement, and it indicates critical areas for better measurement and control. As a secondary benefit, it can also point out the need for refining certain data inputs.

For reasons of expediency, the figures show responses in terms of sales only, but the behavior of profits was also examined in every case. These represent forecasts, in a sense, but perhaps they are better described as "differential forecasts." That is, attention should not be focussed on a single curve or growth rate, but rather on the difference resulting from the particular change being studied. The question being answered is not so much "What is going to happen?" as it is "How much difference would this change make?"

One of the more significant parameters is the average growth rate of products after reaching maturity (which might take 10 years after introduction). Historically, this rate was − 2.8 percent per year. Figure 5 shows that any actions which could improve this situation would have important consequences for the future. It was mentioned earlier that "A" products have reached only a portion of the available market. The discontinuity in slope in the upper curve marks the point at which complete market coverage is achieved.

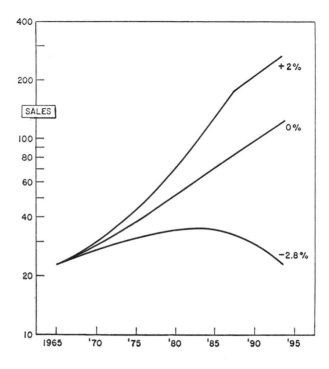

Figure 5   Growth rate of mature products

Figure 6 points out the extreme importance of the priorities given to different kinds of projects in allocating research effort. ''A'' products contribute much more to growth than do ''B'' products, but historically the output of R&D has contained only 27 percent of ''A's.'' This figure also indicates the time required for any change in the R&D area to have perceptible impact on sales.

Figure 7 also represents the research area, showing the effect of increasing productivity. A slow, steady rate of improvement does not have much impact, except very long range. The upper curve represents a more interesting situation. About half of the entire R&D effort is devoted to exploratory and testing work. If somehow the productivity of this activity could be significantly raised, the result could be very worthwhile. Needless to say, this area is now receiving careful attention.

The effect of the overall level of R&D effort is illustrated in Figure 8, with 100 percent representing the recent historical level. In order to emphasize differences, another change was also made so as to create some growth potential. This figure suggests that much reduction in R&D would be disadvantageous. However, general conclusions cannot be drawn from this family of curves. The optimum R&D level can be determined with a model such as was used here, but the proper procedure is rather more complicated.

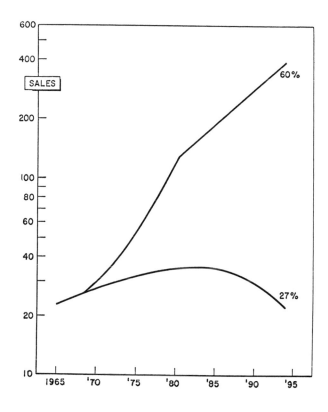

Figure 6 "A" products in new product mix

Figure 9 demonstrates the consequences of adding new products to the line, ready for marketing, without expenditure of R&D effort. This is taken as a one-shot event, occurring at the beginning of the time span shown. There is an initial displacement corresponding to the new products added. This is followed by an incubation period or time lag for additional sales to create a larger marketing budget, hiring and training additional salesmen, and contacting and influencing customers. After this incubation period, the effect of the change becomes apparent.

Now we will look at a couple of examples involving matters of policy. One of the sensitive areas in the model turned out to be the policy which determines the sales budget for "A" products. At the time the model was constructed, the historical pattern had been to maintain a sales force of a constant size. Since market coverage is incomplete, one possible change would be simply to increase the sales force, with probable results as shown in Figure 10. It should be noted that this is a linear scale, for contrast, rather than the logarithmic scale used heretofor. Another approach might be to tie the sales budget to the level of sales, as is done for the R&D budget. None of these alternatives seem promising, and the profit situation is even more dismal than Figure 10 shows for sales.

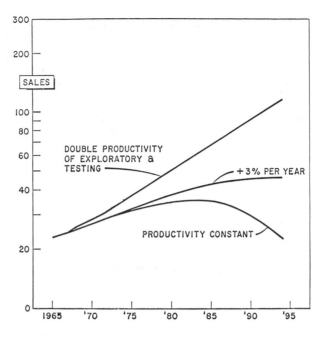

Figure 7   Increasing research productivity

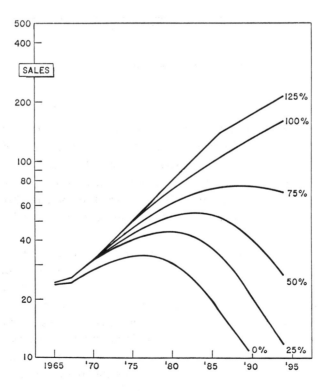

Figure 8   R&D level

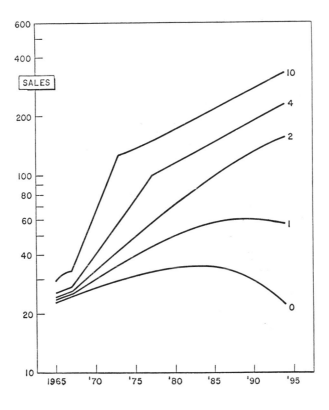

Figure 9 "Buying" new products

The picture changes, however, when we add another factor, as in Figure 11, where we have "bought" a few new products to create a growth situation. In this case we find that the constant sales force cannot take advantage of the opportunity, whereas a budget tied to sales is more favorable. In all fairness, it should be added that the constant sales force will defer collapse as well as inhibit growth. This figure is typical of many similar situations which were observed.

In Figure 12, we have changed nothing but the structure of the policy. Here we see what happens when the sales force is expanded at a constant rate until it is adequate to cover the market. It appears that an aggressive sales budget policy can of itself create a potential for growth.

Another example in the policy area attempts to answer the question: "If we can reduce our marketing and distribution costs, what is the best thing to do with the savings?" As presented in Figure 13, the measure used to compare alternatives is the net present value of profit before tax for 20 years, discounted at 8 percent.[3] This is the kind of question that is difficult to answer in the absence of a model because of the complex interactions present in the system. It appears that the best investment is to put the savings into broadening the market coverage and the poorest one is to devote it to additional R&D. Just taking the savings as profit occupies an intermediate position.

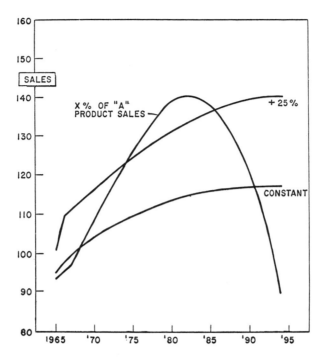

Figure 10   Salesmen manning policy

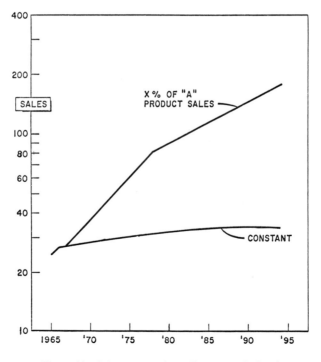

Figure 11   Salesman manning policy—growth situation

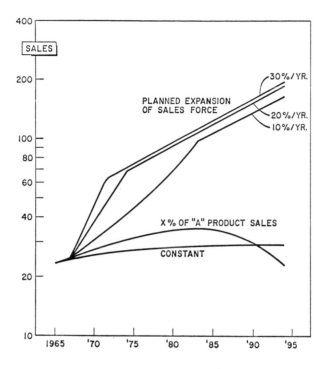

Figure 12   Salesman manning policy

At about this point in the study I was asked to compare the growth of the division under two alternative organizational arrangements. One was to be the monolithic structure heretofor assumed, and the other a somewhat more decentralized structure arranged to provide more specialized services to various segments of the market. This decentralization would commence at a late stage of new product development and carry through marketing.

This problem was approached by focussing attention on differences—principal advantages and disadvantages of specialized vs. monolithic structure. In the specialized structure, products tailored for each market segment would be developed from the basic products available, and salesmen would work within a single, coherent market segment. These two factors should result in an increase in average sales per customer per product family, as compared with a monolithic unspecialized structure. This ratio was called the sales improvement factor. On the other hand, two factors would tend to restrain profit growth. The multiplicity of specialized products would increase the development costs for each product family, and hence less of the R&D dollar would be available for creating new basic products. This would tend to reduce the sales growth rate. Along with this, the decentralized structure would require an increase in administrative costs. Sales growth would not be affected, but profits would be reduced.

Two kinds of situations were explored, as probably representing extremes on either side of what is likely to occur in fact. In the one case, it was assumed that the

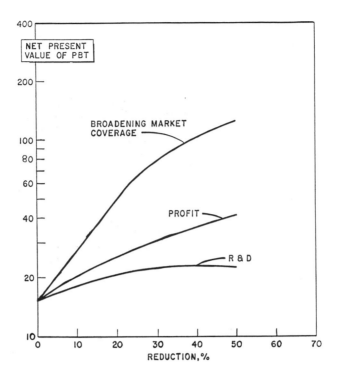

Figure 13   Disposition of reduction in unit marketing cost

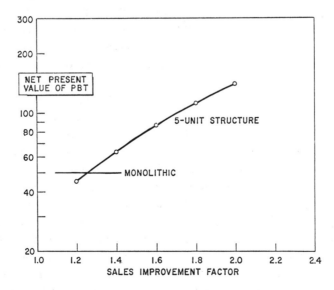

Figure 14   Different marketing organizations

	Internal Growth	**Acquisition**
5-unit structure	1.55	1.25
Same + 25% greater conversion cost	1.75	——
8-unit structure	1.90	1.44

Figure 15 Indifference point—sales improvement factor

business would evolve by growth from its present position. In the second case, it was assumed that several comparable organizations might be acquired and either integrated into a monolithic structure or maintained as separate marketing organizations. In all cases a range of sales improvement factors was studied, as in Figure 14, and an attempt made to decide what value of this factor was needed to tip the balance in favor of the specialized approach. This figure shows the net present value of discounted profit before tax for the case of acquisitions, both monolithic and as a 5-unit structure. The point of indifference comes at a sales improvement factor of about 1.25.

Figure 15 summarizes the indifference points for the various cases studied. It was left to management to assess the probability of realizing sales improvement factors in excess of these values.

Up to this point, with some minor exceptions, we have discussed single changes and their effects. Considerable time was spent in looking at the combination of feasible and favorable changes into strategies. This becomes important when it is realized that considerable synergism may be formed in a system like this one. An example is shown in Figure 16. Here we see three changes which separately produce improvements adding up to only 54 percent of what the combination gives. As a further interesting point, the productivity improvement, which has a separate value of only 12.9, has an incremental value of 75.7 when added to the other two changes.

You have seen a few of the results obtained in just one of a number of studies carried out at Dow using models of business systems. Perhaps this brief exposure is not really adequate to lead you to any conclusions, so let me share with you my own

	Net Present Value of P. B. T.	**Improvement**
Base	100.0	——
(1) Productivity Improvement	112.9	12.9
(2) "Buying" New Products	258.6	158.6
(3) Aggressive Manpower Policy	305.7	205.7
		(377.2)
(1) + (2) + (3)	804.3	704.3
(2) + (3)	728.6	——
Incremental Value of (1)	——	75.7

Figure 16 Synergism in combined changes

opinions. Business modelling is not the answer to every management problem. It does, however, provide a fruitful approach to many questions in the area of long-range planning. Of equal or greater importance is the improvement in understanding the system, which typically results from such a study. One of our top managers has commented that modelling provides a very useful diagnostic tool. More and more companies are becoming interested in this kind of tool and are starting to apply it to their problems.

Notes

(1) Forrester, Jay W., *Industrial Dynamics*, The MIT Press, 1961.

(2) "Views on Simulation and Models of Social Systems," Guy H. Orcutt, in "Symposium on Simulation Models: Methodology and Applications to the Behavioral Sciences," ed. A. C. Hoggatt and F. E. Balderston, South-Western Publishing Co., Cincinnati, 1963.

(3) "Find What Money Costs Your Company," by Peter D. Moskovits, *Hydrocarbon Processing*, vol. 43, p. 129 (Aug. 1964).

21

The Use of Dynamic Modeling for Conditional Forecasts of Resource Allocation Policies

A. Wade Blackman

Introduction

One of the most difficult as well as one of the most important tasks associated with the management of many industrial research laboratories is the optimization of resource allocation strategies to achieve the dual objectives of (1) obtaining smooth growth and (2) obtaining a research output that is relevant to corporate needs. Often these two objectives are in conflict. For example, a laboratory which is highly dependent on government funding for growth must allocate its discretionary funds to support those research areas where government funding exists in order to compete effectively for government funds and thereby achieve growth. Although such a resource allocation policy may result in growth of the laboratory, the laboratory may produce an output more closely related to the needs of government sponsoring agencies than the needs of the corporation which owns and partially supports the laboratory. The problem of resource allocation for research is further complicated by the long lag times (as high as approximately 30 years in some cases) that exist between investment in research and the eventual return which the investment may yield. These long lag times often preclude an accurate evaluation of the relevance of research programs because of difficulty in assessing future needs for technology.

In the past, most research resource allocation decisions have been made primarily on the basis of intuition, with relatively little support from analytical models, and a need exists for better, more extensive analytical models which can lead to a better understanding of the resource allocation process and the various interactions which affect it.

The emerging field of system dynamics, pioneered by Professor J. W. Forrester and his associates at MIT [1] provides new capabilities far exceeding those used in the past for investigating resource allocation policies. System dynamics has been defined as "a body of knowledge, a theory of representation, and a methodology for analyzing and designing complex feedback systems and their dynamic behavior." These techniques allow com-

Parts of this paper were originally presented at a Conference on Technology Forecasting sponsored by the Industrial Management Center and held at Castine, Maine, June 10–15, 1973. The paper was published in *Technological Forecasting and Social Change* 6, (1974), pp.191–208.

puter models to be constructed which replicate a laboratory's operations and allow simulation of the effects of various resource allocation policies on the laboratory's operations in the future.

Reference 2 describes the application of these techniques in developing, for a representative industrial research laboratory, a dynamic simulation model to indicate the effect on future laboratory operations of matching an exploratory forecast of the laboratory's output to an exogenous goal schedule set by normative forecasts of future requirements. In [3], a dynamic simulation model is described which was used to investigate the effect of various R&D resource allocation policies on long-term sales and earnings performance.

In the resource allocation models described in [2, 3], the level of aggregation considered was on the basis of the overall laboratory or firm. However, many resource allocation decisions must also be considered at lower levels of aggregation (e.g., at the program level) if good overall performance of a laboratory or firm is to be obtained.

The objective of the work described herein was to develop a system dynamics resource allocation model applicable to the resource allocation decision-making processes which occur at the program level of aggregation in a typical industrial research laboratory and to employ the model to produce conditional forecasts of various resource allocation policy options.

Method of Approach

System dynamics is based on servomechanism theory and other techniques of systems analysis and is predicated on the ability of high-speed digital computers to solve large numbers (hundreds) of equations in short periods of time. The equations are mathematical descriptions of the operation of the system being simulated and are in the form of expressions for levels of various types which change at rates controlled by decision functions. The level equations represent accumulations within the system of such variables as dollars, personnel, facilities, etc., and the rate equations govern the change of the levels with time. The decision functions represent either implicit or explicit policies established for the system operation.

Mathematical simulation of a system can only represent a real system to the extent that the equations describing the operation of the components of the system accurately describe the operations of the real system components. It is usually impossible to include equations for all of the myriad components of a real system, because the simulation rapidly becomes too complex. It is, therefore, necessary to obtain an abstraction of the real system based on judgment and assumptions regarding which components of the real system are those which control overall system operation.

Application of the system dynamics approach involves three steps [4]. First, it is necessary to identify the dynamic behavior of interest and to hypothesize the interactions that create the behavior: the problem definition step. Secondly, a computer simulation model must be developed which replicates the essential elements of the interactions which create the behavior under investigation. Thirdly, the model is then used to understand the cause of existing behavior and to test new policy design in an effort to improve behavior.

The approach followed in implementing these three steps is illustrated in Fig. 1. In developing the resource allocation model, an iterative process was followed wherein assumptions regarding laboratory performance were transformed into equations which constituted a dynamic model of the research resource allocation process. The model

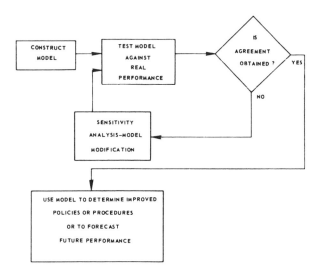

FIG. 1. System dynamics model–building procedure.

performance predictions were then checked against historical performance data, and the model was changed until the real performance was replicated satisfactorily. The model was then used to investigate the effects of various resource allocation strategies on future laboratory performance.

Analysis

Resource allocation decisions within industrial research laboratories generally relate to a number of separate, fairly independent research areas. In formulating the resource allocation model described herein, one such research area was selected as the primary area of interest. The model which has been formulated is general, however, and should apply to the other research areas, provided the appropriate model parameters are changed.

The assumed model of the interaction between the industrial research laboratory and the market for external research support (i.e., primarily government support) is similar to those discussed in [5, 6] and is illustrated in Fig. 2. In this model, resource allocation decisions are made within the laboratory which affect the value of competitive variables, which go to make up the laboratory's competitive posture. The value of the competitive variables perceived by the government, along with the overall government demand for research, affects the rate at which research contracts are awarded the laboratory. The number of contracts awarded affects the laboratory's contract backlog, and the effect of the contract backlog on resource allocation closes the loop.

Although the resources shown in Fig. 2 consist of funds, sales force, facilities, and personnel, it was assumed that the primary resource affecting government funding was that of internal (laboratory-sponsored) discretionary research funding. Such funding

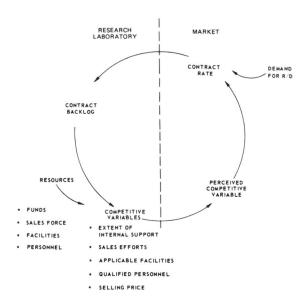

FIG. 2. Relationship between research laboratory and contract research market.

provides ideas for new research, allows new experimental and analytical techniques to be developed, and provides a source of experienced personnel and would, therefore, be expected to exert the strongest influence on government funding decisions. For similar reasons, the extent of internal support was the only competitive variable considered in the model.

Figure 3 presents a simplified diagram of the model as applied to the selected research area. It can be seen that two primary feedback loops exist. The upper loop is a positive loop, because an increase in the government funding budget increases the laboratory's research experience, which increases its competitive posture and tends to further increase its government funding budget. The lower feedback loop can be positive or negative, depending upon the laboratory's resource allocation decisions.

A detailed description of the resource allocation model is presented in the Appendix, and the flow diagram of the completed model is shown in Fig. 4. The symbology used in the diagram and the types of equations represented are discussed in [1] and in the Appendix. The numbers in Fig. 4 refer to the equation numbers given in the Appendix.

Results and Discussion

The approach used in developing the system dynamics model of the research resource allocation process is illustrated in Fig. 1 and has been discussed previously. After developing an initial formulation of the equations in the model describing the resource allocation process, the results predicted by the solution of the equations were compared with historical data, and changes were then made in the model formulation as required until satisfactory agreement between model predictions and historical data were obtained.

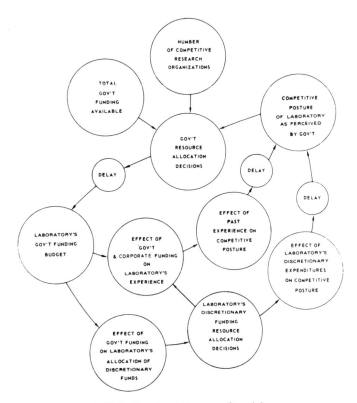

FIG. 3. Simplified diagram of model.

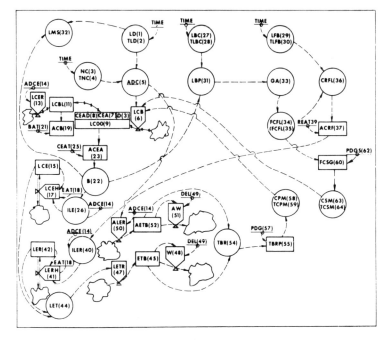

FIG. 4. Flow diagram of resource allocation model.

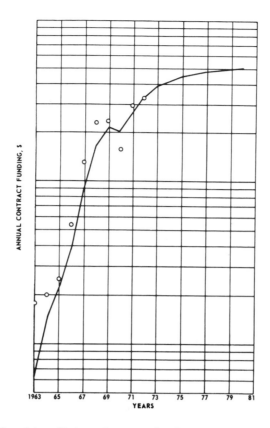

FIG. 5. Comparison of model predictions of contract funding with historical data; − − − − −Computed from Model; o Historical data.

Figures 5 and 6 show the agreement obtained between the predictions of the model (in its final form) and historical data. Figure 5 compares model predictions of laboratory contract funding for the selected research area with historical data for the time period 1963–1972. The numerical scale on the ordinate has been removed because of proprietary reasons; however, it can be seen that there is good agreement between the data and the model predictions. The model was used to forecast future contract funding for the 1972–1980 period as indicated.

Figure 6 presents the resource allocation schedule of the laboratory's discretionary funds (in the selected research area), which corresponded to the contract funding shown in Fig. 6. Again, good agreement was obtained between the model predictions and historical data. The forecast of contract funding shown in Fig. 5 is conditional and is predicated upon the resource allocation policy for discretionary funds given by eqs. 33–36 in the Appendix.

For the calculations shown in Figs. 5 and 6, a discretionary funding resource allocation policy was used which assumed that the percentage of all laboratory funds allocated to the selected research area was a function of the percentage of the total laboratory contracts received in the research area. The relationship assumed is shown in Fig. 7. When

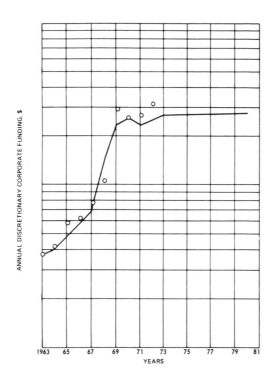

FIG. 6. Comparison of model predictions of discretionary funding with historical data;————
Computed from Model; o Historical data.

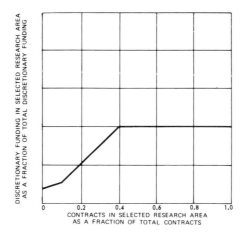

FIG. 7. Assumed relationship between contract research funding and discretionary research funding.

contracts in the selected research area exceeded a specified 40 percent of all of the laboratory contract funding, it was assumed that internal sponsorship for the research area would saturate and would remain a constant percentage of total internal funding.

Figure 8 presents a plot which indicates the laboratory's share of the contract market in the selected research area as a function of time. These results correspond to the

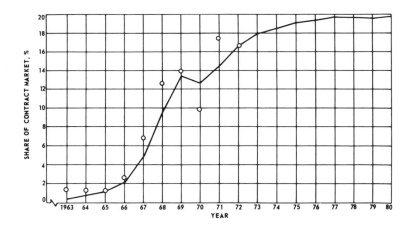

FIG. 8. Laboratory's share of government contract expenditures in selected research area vs. time; ----Computed from model; o Historical data.

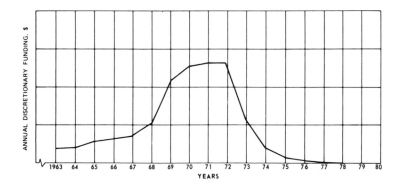

FIG. 9. Discretionary expenditures for research vs. time assumed in revised resource allocation policy.

resource allocation policy indicated in Fig. 7. This curve indicates that this policy would lead to approximately a 20-percent market share in the long run.

It was desired to use the model to investigate the effects on future laboratory contract funding (in the selected research area) of a resource allocation policy which differed significantly from the one shown in Fig. 7. A revised version of the model (described in the Appendix) was used to exogenously input the schedule of discretionary research funding shown in Fig. 9. This funding schedule corresponds to the actual laboratory discretionary funding which was allocated to the selected research area during the 1963–1972 time period. This funding was arbitrarily reduced during the 1973–1980 time period to investigate the effects on government contract funding of a reduced funding schedule.

Figure 10 shows model predictions of the effects of the revised (Fig. 9) resource allocation policy on projected market share in the selected research area. By comparing Fig. 8 with Fig. 10, it can be seen that the projected effect of the reduced resource

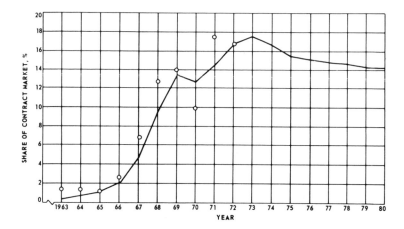

FIG. 10. Effect of reduced discretionary research expenditures on projected share of government contract market;—————Computed from model; o Historical data.

allocation policy would lower the laboratory's share of the government research market from approximately 20 percent to approximately 14 percent in 1980.

The model predictions indicate that future contract funding would be reduced, if internal discretionary funding is reduced, as might be expected. The model assumptions indicate that the elasticity of the government research market to a reduction in internal discretionary funding is not as catastrophic as it might be in the absence of a large backlog of accumulated experience in the selected research area.

A policy of reduced discretionary funding would be desirable in the future if investment opportunities exist in other research areas which offer a research output deemed more relevant to future corporate research needs or if greater growth in total contract support can be achieved by diverting some discretionary funding to other areas. By systematically using the model developed herein to investigate and compare potential future contract growth in each of the laboratory's areas of research, it should be possible to better arrive at the optimum amount of funds which should be allocated to each of the areas and to maximize overall government contract support.

This optimization can be accomplished by applying the system dynamics model to each of the research areas of interest within the laboratory and developing curves which indicate the magnitude of government contract dollars which can be expected within a selected planning period as a function of the level of investment of discretionary funds. Dynamic programming procedures, such as those described in [7], can then be applied to determine the discretionary funding levels in each research area, which will tend to maximize total government contract support over the planning period.

If it is desired to spend discretionary funds to maximize government support, the model would tend to indicate that discretionary funds would be most effectively allocated to those research areas which are relatively new (i.e., where the backlog of total laboratory experience in the research area is low) and in which the future level of government support is projected to be high.

The fundamental difficulty in following a policy of maximizing government support lies in creating the possibility that the research produced will not be very highly related to future corporate needs, although it may be highly relevant to future government research needs. To preclude this possibility, it is necessary to seek government support only in those areas which are deemed relevant to future corporate needs.

Concluding Remarks

System dynamics models of the type developed herein can be a valuable aid to decision-making in the area of resource allocation for research programs. The greatest usefulness of these models lies in providing answers to "what-if" type questions, which are often impossible to address on the basis of intuition alone.

The process of model-building can also lead to greatly improved communications among those involved in resource allocation decision-making, because the construction of a model requires explicit statements of those assumptions (regarding the resource allocation process), which generally are different in the minds of different people and which often lead to misunderstanding because they are never explicitly stated.

It is believed that systematic use of models of the type described herein can provide a better understanding of the long-term implications of resource allocation decisions and can thereby lead to improvements in the decision-making process and enhance the achievement of long-term research growth objectives.

REFERENCES

1. J. W. Forrester, *Industrial Dynamics.* The MIT Press, Cambridge, Massachusetts (1961).
2. A. W. Blackman, Forecasting through dynamic modeling *Technology Forecasting and Social Change* **3**, 291–307 (1972). This paper also appears as a chapter in *A Guide to Practical Technological Forecasting.* (J. R. Bright and M. E. F. Schoeman (Eds.) Prentice-Hall, Englewood Cliffs, N. J., 257–275 (1973).
3. A. W. Blackman, New venture planning: the role of technological forecasting, *Technological Forecasting and Social Change* **5**, No. 1, 25–49 (1973).
4. C. V. Swanson, Design of resource control and marketing policies using industrial dynamics, *Industrial Management Rev.* **10**, No. 3 (Spring 1969).
5. C. V. Swanson, Information and control for corporate growth, *Sloan Management Rev.* **12**, No. 3 (Spring 1971).
6. J. W. Forrester, Market growth as influenced by capital investment, *Industrial Management Rev.* **9**, No. 2 (Winter, 1968).
7. C. E. Kepler, and A. W. Blackman, The use of dynamic programming techniques for determining resource allocations among R/D projects: an example, *IEEE Trans. Engin. Management* **EM−20**, No. 1 (February, 1973).
8. A. L. Pugh, III, *Dynamo II User's Manual,* The MIT Press, Cambridge, Massachusetts (1970).

Appendix

MODEL FORMULATION

A detailed formulation of the equations used in the system dynamics resource allocation model is presented in the following section. All equations appear in the format required by the DYNAMO compiler simulator program [8]. The DYNAMO program uses a time notation as follows:

.K denotes the present time

.J denotes the preceding time

.L denotes the next time

.JK denotes a rate of flow between times J and K

.KL denotes a rate of flow between times K and L

DT denotes the computation interval, Delta Time, that separates time steps.

Three equation types are used: levels, rates, and auxiliaries. Level equations express accumulations of physical quantities or averages of information, and rates express flows between levels. Auxiliary equations are used in the information channels between levels and rates to facilitate formulation of the rate equations. Letters preceding the equation (L, R, or A) denote the equation type. Equations defining constants are indicated by C, and those equations defining initial conditions are denoted by N. Tables are denoted by T.

The total expected external demand for contract research in a selected research area is an input to the model in the form of a table in which the expected external contract demand is projected for each year of the simulation.

A   LD.K=TABHL(TLD,TIME.K,O,216,12)   (1)

T   TLD=———   (2)

      LD   = Total expected external contract demand, \$/mo

      TLD = Table of expected external contract demand, \$/mo.

Similarly, a projection of the number of research firms expected to compete for the available external contract support in the selected research area is an input to the model for each year of the simulation.

A   NC.K=TABHL(TNC,TIME.K,O,216,12)   (3)

T   TNC=———   (4)

      NC   = Expected number of competitors for contracts

      TNC = Table of expected number of competitors for contracts.

The average value of contracts in the selected research area funded during a period of the simulation is given for an average competitor as

A   ACD.K=LD.K/NC.K   (5)

ACD   = Average contract dollars received, $/mo.

It is assumed that two factors will influence the amount of external (government) support received by the simulated firm; viz., (1) the amount of past experience the firm has in the research area under consideration and (2) the extent to which the firm is currently supporting work in the research area with its own internal funding. The rate at which the government books contracts with the simulated firm is the amount received by an average competitor modified by these two factors.

R $LCB.KL=(ACD.K)(CPM.K)(CSM.K)$ (6)

LCB   = Contract booking rate at government, $/mo

CPM   = Laboratory's past experience multiplier

CSM   = Laboratory's internal sponsorship multiplier.

A delay will exist between the time that a decision is made by the government to fund contract research at the firm being simulated and the time at which the firm is authorized to initiate expenditures at the firm. The rate at which contract expenditure authorizations are received at the firm is expressed by third-order delay equations [1] as follows:

R $CEA.KL=DELAY3(LCB.JK,CEAD)$ (7)
C $CEAD=3$ (8)

CEA   = Contract expenditure authorizations received
    at firm, $/mo
CEAD   = Delay in receiving expenditure authorization from
    government, mos

L $LCOO.K=LCOO.J+(DT)(LCB.JK-CEA.JK)$ (9)

N $LCOO=O$ (10)

LCOO   = Contracts on order by government, $.

The contract backlog level at the simulated firm in the selected research area is given by the following equations:

L $LCBL.K=LCBL.J+(DT)(CEA.JK-LCER.JK)$ (11)

N $LCBL=O$ (12)

LCBL   = Contract backlog at firm, $

LCER   = Contract expenditure rate, $/mo.

The contract expenditure rate is expressed by the product of the number of engineers working in the contract area under consideration and the average expenditure rate per engineer.

R $LCER.KL=(LCE.K)(ADCE)$ (13)

LCE   = Number of contract engineers employed

ADCE   = Average dollars spent per contract engineer
    per month, $/man-mo

C   ADCE=---   (14)

The level of engineers working under external contract support in the selected research area is given by

L $LCE.K = LCE.J + (DT)(LCEH.JK + 0)$ (15)

       LCEH   = Contract engineers hiring rate, men/mo

N $LCE = O.$ (16)

The rate at which new engineers are hired is expressed by the difference between the number of engineers desired (as indicated by the contract research budget) and the number of engineers available divided by the time required to find and train engineers for the research area.

R $LCEH.KL = (1/EAT)(ILE.K - LCE.K)$ (17)

C $EAT = 2$ (18)

       EAT   = Engineers' adjustment time, months required to find and train engineers, mos

       ILE   = Indicated number of contract supported engineers required.

To damp out possible short term effects, the average contract backlog is expressed as an exponential average (see Ref. 1) of the contract backlog.

L $ACB.K = ACB.J + (DT)(1/BAT)(LCBL.J - ACB.J)$ (19)

N $ACB = LCBL$ (20)

C $BAT = 12$ (21)

       ACB   = Average contract backlog, $

       BAT   = Contract backlog averaging time, mos.

Similarly, the budget for contract research (which controls the desired number of contract supported engineers) is expressed as an exponential average given by

A $B.K = ACEA.K$ (22)

       B   = Budget for contract research for period K, $

       ACEA   = Average contract expenditure authorizations for period K, $

L $ACEA.K = ACEA.J + (DT)(1/CEAT)(CEA.JK - ACEA.J)$ (23)

N $ACEA = O$ (24)

C $CEAT = 12$ (25)

       CEAT   = Contract expenditure averaging time, mos

A $ILE.K = B.K/ADCE$ (26)

ILE = Indicated number of engineers required for
contract work, men.

Projections of the laboratory's budget for contract work in all areas of research activity is an input to model for each period of the simulation and is given by the following table:

A   LBC.K=TABHL(TLBC,TIME.K,O,216,12)   (27)

T   TLBC=———   (28)

LBC   = Laboratory's budget for all contract work for
period K, $

TLBC   = Table of laboratory's budget for all contract work.

Similarly, projections of the laboratory's budget for all internally sponsored work in all areas of research activity is input for each period of the simulation as

A   LFB.K=TABHL(TLFB,TIME.K,O,216,12)   (29)

T   TLFB=———   (30)

LFB   = Laboratory-funded budget for all research areas for
period, K

TLFB   = Table of laboratory-funded budget for all research
areas.

The contract budget in the particular research area under consideration in the simulation can be expressed as a fraction of the total contract budget for all research areas of activity as

$$\text{LBP}$$

A   LBP.K=(B.K)/LBC.K   (31)

LBP   = Contract budget in selected research area as fraction
of laboratory's budget for all contracts in all
areas of research activity.

The fractional share of the total government contract support received by the laboratory in the selected research area can be expressed by

A   LMS.K=B.K/LD.K   (32)

LMS   = Laboratory's share of contract market in selected
research area.

The managerial resource allocation policy which governs the extent to which internal, discretionary research funds are allocated to the selected research area is assumed to be a function of the extent of government support in the selected research area relative to government support in all other areas of research activity at the laboratory. This policy can be expressed as

A   GA.K=LBP.K   (33)

   GA = Management goal auxiliary for contract funding in
      selected research area as percent of total contract
      funding

A   FCFL.K=TABHL(TFCFL,GA.K,O,1,O.1)   (34)

T   TFCFL=———   (35)

   FCFL   = Fraction of Corporate research funds allocated
       to research in selected research area

   TFCFL = Table of fraction of internal research funds
       allocated to selected research area

A   CRFL.K=(FCFL.K)(LFB.K)   (36)

   CRFL   = Internal, discretionary research funds budget allocated
       to selected research area. $.

The average internal, discretionary funding allocated to the selected research area is expressed as an exponential average as

L   ACRF.K=ACRF.J+(DT)(1/REAT)(CRFL.J−ACRF.J)   (37)

N   ACRF=CRFL   (38)

C   REAT=12   (39)

   ACRF   = Average internal, discretionary research
       funds budget allocated to selected research area

   REAT   = Corporate expenditure averaging time, mos.

The number of engineers working in the selected area of research activity under internal, discretionary funding is developed in a manner similar to the previously discussed development of the equations for the number of engineers working under government funding (see eqs. 15–18) and is given by the following:

A   ILER.K=ACRF.K/ADCE   (40)

   ILER   = Indicated number of engineers required for
       internally funded work in the selected
       research area, men

R   LERH.KL=(1/EAT)(ILER.K−LER.K)   (41)

   LERH   = Hiring rate for engineers working on internally-
       sponsored work in the selected research area,
       men/mo

   LER   = Number of engineers working on internally-
       sponsored work in the selected research area,
       men

L   LER.K=LER.J+(DT)(LERH.JK+O)   (42)

N   LER=10.   (43)

The total of all engineers working in the selected area of research activity can be expressed as

A   LET.K=LCE.K+LER.K   (44)

> LET   = Sum of all engineers working in the selected research
> area of activity, men.

The past experience at the simulated laboratory in the selected research area of activity is assumed to produce a bank of technology which can be drawn on in the future to solve future research problems in the selected area of activity. The technology in the bank is assumed to be related to the engineering man-months devoted to the research area; however, the technology in the bank has a finite lifetime because of technological obsolescence. The level of the technology bank can be expressed by the following equations.

L   ETB.K=ETB.J+(DT)(LET R.JK−W.JK)   (45)

N   ETB=114   (46)

> ETB   = Engineering man-mos in technology bank, man-mos
>
> LETR   = Engineering man-mos added in period JK, man-mos
>
> W   = Rate of man-mos flow from bank due to
> obsolescence, man-mos/mo

R   LETR.KL=LET.K   (47)

R   W.KL=ETB.K/DEL   (48)

C   DEL=72   (49)

> DEL   = Delay in man-mos becoming obsolete, mos.

It can be shown that the form of eq. (45) is equivalent to the form of an exponential average (or smoothing) equation [1] in which data are given progressively less weight in determining the average as they become older. The weighting of past values is exponential; the importance of each successive past value falls by the same ratio, and the greatest weight is given to the most recent value.

It is assumed that the simulated laboratory's past experience in the selected research area will affect its competitive position and the extent of government sponsorship in the research area (see eq. 6). The laboratory's past experience relative to an average competitor which relies solely on government support is used as a measure of the laboratory's competitive posture. The technology bank level of an average competitor relying solely on government support can be expressed by

R   ALER.KL=ACD.K/ADCE   (50)

> ALER   = Average engineering man-mos in technology bank
> for an average competitor using only Government
> funding man-mos/mo

R   AW.KL=AETB.K/DEL   (51)

> AW   = Average rate of man-mos flow from technology
>   bank due to obsolescence, man-mos/mo
>
> AETB   = Engineering man-mos in technology bank for
>   an average competitor using only Government funding,
>   man-mos

L   AETB.K=AETB.J+(DT)(ALER.JK−AW.JK)   (52)

N   AETB=114.   (53)

A measure of the laboratory's competitive position is expressed by the ratio of the two technology bank levels given by

A   TBR.K=ETB.K/AETB.K   (54)

> TBR   = Technology bank ratio.

A finite time is required for the government to become aware of the relative competitive positions of competitors. A first-order delay [1] can be used to model this effect, and it is expressed as

L   TBRP.K=TBRP.J+(DT)(1/PDG)(TBR.J−TBRP.J)   (55)

N   TBRP=1.0   (56)

C   PDG=6   (57)

> TBRP   = Technology bank ratio perceived by government
>
> PDG   = Time delay for government to recognize tech-
>   nology bank ratio.

The past experience multiplier used in eq. 6 to determine the extent of government funding is expressed as

A   CPM.K=TABHL(TCPM,TBRP.K,.8,1.7,.1)   (58)

T   TCPM=.8/.9/.95/1./1.02/1.04/1.06/1.08/1.1/1.12   (59)

> TCPM   = Table of values of past experience multiplier.

In addition to the effect of past experience (which is determined both by past government sponsorship and past internal, discretionary sponsorship) in the research area on competitive position, it is assumed that the extent of internal, discretionary sponsorship in the research area of interest relative to discretionary sponsorship in other areas of interest also affects the extent of government contracts received; that is, the laboratory commitment to the research area of interest as perceived by the government affects sponsorship. This effect is modeled by the following equations.

L   FCSG.K=FCSG.J+(DT)(1/PDGS)(FCFL.J−FCSG.J)   (60)

N   FCSG=0.05   (61)

C   PDGS=6   (62)

FCSG   = Fraction of total discretionary funding allocated to selected research area as perceived by government

PDGS   = Time delay for government to recognize fraction of discretionary funds allocated to selected research area, mos

A   CSM.K=TABHL(TCSM,FCSG.K,O,.5,.1)   (63)

T   TCSM=.85/1./1.04/1.06/1.08/1.1   (64)

TCSM   = Table of values of discretionary sponsorship multiplier

PRINT   LD,NC,ACD,LCB,LCBL,LCE,ACB,B,LBP,LMS,CRFL,ACRF,LER,LET,TBR,
X   TBRP,FCSG,LFB,CPM,CSM

PLOT   LD=L/B=B/LFB=F/LBP=P/LMS=M/CRFL=C/LET=E/LCE=*

SPEC   DT=1/LENGTH=216/PRTPER=6/PLTPER=6

RUN   BASIC.

A second version of the model was formulated in order to show the effects of a resource allocation policy which did not allocate discretionary research funds in a research area as a function of the contributions of that research area to the laboratory's total government contract funding. In this version of the model, eq. 35 was eliminated, eqs. 34 and 36 were modified, and eq. 36.1 was added as shown below.

A   FCFL.K=CRFL.K/LFB.K   (34)

FCFL   = Fraction of discretionary research funds allocated to research in selected research area

CRFL   = Internal, discretionary research funds budget allocated to selected research area, $

LFB   = Discretionary funds budget for all research areas for period, K

A   CRFL.K=TABHL(TCRFL,TIME.K,O,216,12)   (36)

T   TCRFL=———   (36.1)

TCRFL   = Table of internal, discretionary research funds allocated to selected research area, $.

The effect of these changes is to allow the discretionary funding allocated in each time period to the selected research area to be an exogenous input to the model, rather than having the model determine the allocation for a particular resource allocation policy.

22

Exploratory and Normative Technological Forecasting: A Critical Appraisal

Edward B. Roberts

Abstract

Comparison of the still evolving approaches to "exploratory" and "normative" technological forecasting yields marked contrasts. In particular the simple schemes used by those trying to *predict* the technology of the future look pallid when matched against the intricate techniques designed by those who are allocating the resources that will *create* the future. Exploratory technological forecasts are largely based either on aggregates of "genius" forecasts (e.g., the Delphi technique) or on the use of leading indicators and other simple trend-line approaches. The practitioners of economic forecasting, in contrast, long ago recognized the need for multivariate systems analysis and cause-effect models to develop reliable predictions.

So-called "normative" forecasting is at the opposite extreme on the sophistication scale, fully utilizing Bayesian statistics, linear and dynamic programming, and other operations research tools. Here, despite the uniqueness, uncertainty, and lack of uniformity of research and development activities, the typical designer of a normative technique has proposed a single-format wholly quantitative method for resource allocation. Along the dimensions of unjustified standardization and needless complexity, for example, the proposed R & D allocation methods far exceed the general cost-effectiveness approach used by the Department of Defense in its program and system reviews.

For both exploratory and normative purposes, dynamic models of broad technological areas seem worthy of further pursuit. In attempting to develop "pure predictions" the explicit recognition of causal mechanisms offered by this modeling approach seems highly desirable. This feature also has normative utility, provided that the dynamic models are limited in their application to the level of aggregate technological resource allocation and are not carried down to the level of detailed R & D project funding.

I. On Technological Forecasting

Increased recognition during the present decade of the importance of science and technology to corporate and national existence has produced an intensive search for new

This paper was originally presented at the NATO Defense Research Group Seminar on Technological Forecasting and its Application to Defense Research, Teddington, Middlesex, England on November 12, 1968. It was supported in part by funds from the M.I.T. Center for Space Research under a grant from the National Aeronautics and Space Administration (NsG-496). The article was first published in *Technological Forecasting* 1, no. 2 (Fall 1969), pp. 113–127. (© 1969 by American Elsevier Publishing Company, Inc.)

methods for managing research and development. The attention being devoted to so-called "technological forecasting" is one manifestation of this concern.

"Technological forecasting," as defined by those claiming to be its practitioners, is actually two fields, joined more by a vision than a reality. On the one hand is "exploratory forecasting," the attempt to predict the technological state-of-the-art that will or might be in the future, or as Cetron puts it, ". . . a prediction with a level of confidence of a technical achievement in a given time frame with a specified level of support [1]." Most laymen assume that all of "forecasting" is this kind of forecasting. The second aspect has been called "normative forecasting [2]" and includes the organized attempts to allocate on a rational basis the money, manpower, and other resources that might effect the creation of tomorrow's technological state-of-the-art. Normative forecasting presumably provides aids to budgetary decisions in the technological area. Still more broadly defined by some of its leading exponents, normative forecasting applies to a wide variety of attempts to determine policies and decisions that will influence the effective growth of science and technology, in the corporation, the government agency, or the nation as a whole.

No doubt both kinds of forecasting are necessary contributors to the technical planning process. And for the military as well as for most corporations, this technical input is a critical ingredient of an overall business plan. Yet only in theory but not in fact have these two components, the exploratory and the normative, been integrated adequately. In his milestone book on the subject, Erich Jantsch expresses the logic of and the need for this integration: "*Exploratory technological forecasting* starts from today's assured basis of knowledge and is oriented towards the future, while *normative technological forecasting* first assesses future goals, needs, desires, missions, etc., and works backward to the present. . . . The full potential of technological forecasting is realized only where *exploratory and normative components* are joined in an iterative or, ultimately, in a feedback cycle [3]."

This paper presents a critical appraisal of the field of technological forecasting. The central theme is that the two phases of exploratory and normative approaches are out of step with each other. Exploratory techniques are too naive and do not take advantage of what has been learned about forecasting in non-technical areas. Nor do the exploratory techniques reflect what is known about the influences upon the generation of future technology. Normative techniques in contrast are too complex and mathematically intricate and cannot justify their complexity on substantive grounds.

If "the full potential of technological forecasting" is to be realized, a more harmonious relationship must be established between the exploratory and normative parts. Dynamic systems models of broad technological areas, stressing the feedback relations that affect the growth of science and technology, demonstrate promise of providing a basis for that harmony. Such models have already been developed in prototype form, addressed to a number of problems of interest to technological forecasters. Their further development is dependent upon the availability of skilled manpower and necessary funding.

II. An Appraisal of Exploratory Technological Forecasting

Exploratory technological forecasting includes a variety of techniques for predicting the future state of science and technology. Unfortunately most of the methods are really only variants on simple trend extrapolation procedures, broadly defined, that have limited utility in today's rapidly shifting technological environment. The principal exploratory methods are:

1. so-called "genius" forecasting, based either on individual wisdom or on a group "genius" forecasting process known as the Delphi technique; and
2. formal trend extrapolation to either a straight-line fit or an S-shaped expectation [4].

The formal trend methods include single-curve projections as well as estimations based on the envelope encompassed by the projection of a family of related curves. They also include both the extrapolation of a single time series as well as the projection of lead-lag relationships between two time series, the latter known as "precursive event" forecasting.

Intuitive Trend Forecasts

In theory technological forecasting is not supposed to be able to foretell the "major breakthrough." In fact this is one of few ways in which intuitive hunches or guesses might provide services. Occasionally, but unpredictably, the brilliant scientist (or the perceptive marketeer, or the starry-eyed science fiction writer) may predict the future as different from a mere extension of the past. But more usually individual wisdom-based forecasting works on the rule that "past is prologue." Trend extrapolation thus becomes the simple kind of model that the unaided mind can manipulate intuitively.

In one well-publicized approach, the hunches of individual "experts" have been coaxed and guided in an iterative group forecasting procedure known as the "Delphi method [5]." This procedure assumes that collective (and normalized) wisdom is better than individual "guesstimates," although recent behavioral research raises questions about this assumption. In using the Delphi approach numerous experts are solicited for their opinions on the future technology in a specified area. Assembled opinions thus gathered are redistributed to the panel for a series of reassessments during which criticisms and defenses of extreme forecasts are also obtained and communicated. The end result tends to be a more polarized and justified range of future estimates than were originally gathered. Thus the collective "ballpark guesses" of the experts are refined and legitimized. It is interesting to speculate whether a Delphic sampling of the appropriate whiz kids would have predicted an effective intercontinental ballistic missile when Vannevar Bush failed in his prophecy! Would Delphi have done better than Lindemann in his lack of foreseeing the German V-2 rockets? Remember that large group consensus (as in Delphi) overruled Watson-Watt's correct forecast on radar! Is there sufficient evidence to believe that the Delphic search for consensus produces more "truthful" forecasts than a comparable assemblage of individual genius forecasts?

Formal Trend Forecasts

Those who lack the wisdom demanded by genius forecasting (perhaps in reality they possess the wisdom needed to appreciate the weaknesses of the intuitive methods!) have adopted formal procedures for translating the events of the past into the predictions of the future. Data on the time-history of some parameter of technological progress (e.g., tensile strength of materials, engine thrust per pound of fuel) are plotted against time on linear or logarithmic scales. Using "eyeball" extrapolation, or statistical "best fit" procedures, a growth-of-technology line is drawn through the data points and extended into the future. An assumption of technology saturation effects produces the biological growth pattern with its S-shaped curves; an assumption of no saturation leads merely to longer straight lines. Poor fit of the data to a single line suggests the need for alternative technological projections and often leads to a forecast of an envelope of possible technological states. When two sets of these progress parameter curves appear to be correlated, with one curve consistently leading the other in time (e.g., the speed of bombers versus commercial transports), similar trend extrapolations are applied. In this case, the process is referred to as "forecasting by the analysis of precursive events."

The trend extrapolations, both intuitive and formal, fail to state explicitly their underlying assumptions. As Jantsch points out, ". . . the simple extrapolation of secular trends does contain one analytical element—the intuitive expectation that the combined effect of internal and external factors which produced a trend over a past period will remain the same during a future period, or that it will undergo an estimated gradual change [6]." Yet the changes occurring in numerous areas of technology deny the validity of these stability-oriented assumptions.

The Experiences of Economic Forecasting

Rather than continue to berate the undeveloped state of exploratory forecasting it appears wiser to apply the forecasters' own tools. The development of exploratory forecasting techniques seems to be following the path previously taken by economic forecasting (in a precursive event relationship). A review of the parallels involved indicates that exploratory forecasting can advance more rapidly by skipping some of the development that occurred in economic forecasting.

Economic forecasting is now beginning its fifth stage of development, with an obvious sixth stage just over the horizon. These stages of evolution are:
1. wisdom, expert, or genius forecasting;
2. "naive" models;
3. simple correlative forecasting models;
4. complex multivariate econometric forecasts;
5. dynamic causally-oriented models; and
6. learning models.

Expert forecasts. The first stage of development of economic forecasting was the intuitive judgmental expert forecast. Perceptive economists, applying their mental models to analyses of economic factors, predicted future economic performance, often with excellent foresight. This nonquantitative "genius" stage has been (and still is being) paralleled in the technological field.

"Naive" forecasting models. As economists began applying quantitative techniques to economic forecasting, so-called "naive" models came to the front. The most naive kinds of forecasts are the "same level" and the "same trend" predictions. The "same level" model assumes that next year will be the same, economically, as this year. The "same trend" forecast says that the economic trend from this year to next will be the same as from last year to this one. Economists themselves have labelled these approaches as "naive," yet technological forecasters are using them almost exclusively. (The use of S-shaped curves and log scales by technical forecasters merely reflects their higher mathematical training relative to their earlier economic counterparts.)

Simple correlative models. In the third stage of development of economic forecasting two or three variables were interrelated by statistical correlation (or just by charts) to forecast economic behavior. The use of "leading" economic indicators is the simplest representation of this phase of forecasting and is replicated in technological forecasting by precursive event forecasts. Recent work by Mansfield in predicting the rate of diffusion of technological innovations indicates that exploratory technological forecasting is now in this third stage [7].

Complex multivariate econometric forecasting. The great growth of quantitative economics accompanied its movement into large-scale multivariate statistical models for explaining and predicting economic performance. No longer were the models simple or naive, and the computer quickly found an important role in implementing the needed calculations. (Input-output models of the economy can be associated with this fourth stage of evolution.) But the models were not usually causally-oriented; rather the "best fit" criterion, applied to tests on past data, was the primary measure of acceptability. It is not surprising, therefore, that these complex but non-causal forecasting models usually performed no more accurately than did simpler models and naive forecasts; nor have they even consistently outperformed the "expert" forecasts of the business economists. Although technological forecasting has not yet moved openly into this fourth phase, it is likely to do so soon unless effectively urged in other directions.

Dynamic causally-oriented forecasting. Recently a change has begun to show up in the style and structure of economic forecasting models. The model-builders have attempted to include more *a priori* causal structuring, mixed linear and nonlinear relationships are being represented, feedback phenomena are included in the models, and dynamic computer simulation is being used to project economic forecasts [8].

Moreover, this new type of economic forecasting model has the unique feature of coupling exploratory and normative purposes in a consistent manner. Not only can the models be initialized with present and historical inputs to project the future economy, but simulated tests can be run using proposed normative changes in policies and parameters. Contemplated resource allocations, for example, are thus fed into the "exploratory" model to project anticipated consequences, and these in turn suggest alternatives to the proposed allocations. This type of iteration between exploratory forecasts and normative recommendations has been proposed as the ultimate for technological forecasting [9].

As shall be pointed out in the last section of this paper, much work has already been done along similar lines in technology-related areas. But the review literature recognizes only the contributions of Lenz to the dynamic modelling phase of exploratory forecasting and views his work, unfortunately, as "hardly useful for any practical purpose [10]." Until this work and related dynamic models are indeed recognized for their potential, exploratory forecasting will stall in its third stage of development or waste itself needlessly in the unproductive fourth stage it seems about to enter.

Learning models. The next logical stage of development for economic forecasting is the creation of learning models. These would be structured similar to those used in stage five, but they would be paired with real-time data collection and data interpretation systems. The combination, monitored by computer routines for analyzing model adequacy, would permit parameter and possibly even structural changes in the forecasting model based upon experienced model and economy performance. However, no serious activity is yet underway in this stage in either the economic or the technological forecasting area.

This review of exploratory forecasting has concluded that pathetically simple methods are being used to predict what technology will be in the future. The techniques parallel an earlier stage of growth of economic forecasting and as yet have not recognized the importance of causal dynamic models. Jantsch seems to agree with this condemnation of exploratory forecasting's underdevelopment: ". . . no model has so far succeeded in taking into account more than a limited number of influencing factors by assuming relationships that are generally unproved or not known in detail, and mathematical formulations do not yet include even all of these recognized factors [11]."

The empirical "research on research" of the past decade has now produced an impressive basis of understandings of the influences on scientific and technological progress [12]. Surely it is important to begin embodying these findings into the development of improved exploratory models.

III. An Appraisal of Normative Technological Forecasting

Normative technological forecasting activities attempt to provide a basis for allocating technology-generating resources so as to maximize attainment of organizational goals. The effectiveness of any normative method depends upon:

1. the meaningfulness of its treatment of goals;
2. the correctness of its assumed relationships between allocated resources and generated technology;
3. the adequacy of its balancing of the resources-to-technology considerations against the worth of goal fulfillment; and
4. the implementability of the method, including the ability to acquire reasonable inputs at reasonable costs as well as the ability to persuade organizational decision-makers to use the generated outputs.

Most of the effort in the development of normative forecasting techniques has gone into items 1 and 3 above. The expression of goals, the establishment of values for them, the accounting for the conflicting interests of various groups, are primary questions debated by the designers of normative forecasting methods. The techniques for manipulating the resources being allocated against these assumed values are also many and varied, ranging from simple linear and dynamic programming to elaborate embodiments of Bayesian analyses and Monte Carlo techniques. And these techniques are under continuing refinement, with accompanying developments of the computer software needed for the desired calculations. These areas can be left to others to criticize.

Yet items 2 and 4 above have been largely ignored. Little effort has been devoted to making the forecasting techniques practicable or believable by the manager. The most sophisticated, perhaps even the best, normative approach requires thousands of estimate inputs for every use. Moreover, the assumed relationships between allocated resources and generated technological outputs are seldom even explicitly identified in the normative techniques. Usually, the forecasts receive as inputs the estimates of the technical outputs that would be produced by various funding levels. In other words, in most cases no exploratory forecasting techniques are used to generate the basis for normative manipulations! The assumed technical outputs are guesses only. In other cases (see Sections III, *PATTERN* and III, *PROBE*), only the simplest exploratory methods are applied.

Technical Output Generation

Let me treat first the question of how technical outputs are handled in normative forecasting. If resources are to be deployed wisely by a company, a government agency, or a nation, that deployment should be based upon the best understandings available of the likely results of the use of those resources. The area of exploratory forecasting is devoted to a search for and an expression of these understandings. But the exploratory forecasters have made little impact on their normative brethren. An examination of the most widely publicized normative forecasting techniques demonstrates this failing.

Perhaps other better methods exist which have been less extensively promoted and adopted. This review is limited, however, to the dominant normative approaches being advocated and somewhat attempted.

PROFILE. PROFILE (Programmed Functional Indices for Laboratory Evaluation), developed by Marvin J. Cetron for the U.S. Navy, is among the better known methods for resource allocation in R & D [13]. PROFILE uses three basic criteria—Military Utility, Technical Feasibility, and Application of Resources—plus a fourth criterion, Intrinsic Value to the Laboratory, which acts as a "fudge factor" to influence the final weighted index that is developed.

In his PROFILE paper Cetron asserts, "Research and development tasks become more technically feasible if they are being executed by personnel who have the necessary expertise, have confidence in the successful completion of the task and recognize the benefits to other applications [14]." This statement seems obvious albeit there is little empirical substantiation of the relative roles and relationships of these and other factors to the technology generation process. The theory is interpreted in PROFILE by criteria for Applicability to Long Range Plan and Mission, Probability for Achieving Task Objective, and Technological Transfer. Of the three only the "probability of achievement" estimate is related to a forecast of anticipated technological output, and that is a single-valued "genius" forecast, produced generally by a "non-genius." The fact that the man who must do the work is usually the estimator as well raises further questions as to the meaningfulness of the input. The "applicability" measure assesses *value* of the output's contribution to lab objectives generally, while "technological transfer" identifies output *value* in terms of possible contributions to other technical tasks. These estimates are hardly related to the likelihood of future technology being generated, yet PROFILE misuses them in this fashion.

PROFILE's Application of Resources sector treats availability of manpower, facilities, and funding for the R & D project being contemplated. Yet this treatment mixes considerations of factors that might be included in a model of technology generation with project cost considerations. And, of course, all of these are weighted in PROFILE as if they are measures of value and added in a linear combination of factors. The failure to appreciate the difference between worth of an outcome, the influences upon the attainment of that outcome, and the cost of the outcome thus characterizes the PROFILE approach. Most critical is that the explicit "exploratory" forecast is limited to a "hunch" probability estimate by the staff members filling out the PROFILE forms.

QUEST. What PROFILE is designed to do for an individual laboratory, the QUEST system (Quantitative Utility Estimates for Science and Technology), developed by Cetron, is supposed to do for the entire Navy R & D program [15]. The complexity of QUEST's matrices of Value of Technology to Missions and Relevance of Science to Technology illustrates the heavy emphasis placed upon the valuing procedure. The technology generation procedure, however, is largely ignored by QUEST. In its examination of the contribution of a technical effort to a given mission, "the assumption is that the objective of the technical effort will be accomplished [16]." In its evaluation of the relevance of each science area to each technology area, a subjective single-valued estimate is assigned by the forms-filling engineer and researcher to describe the essentiality of the science to the technology. These estimates range from 0, "the technology does not draw on this science at all," to 10, "no progress is possible in this technology without vigorously pursuing this science." This estimate is hardly what would be described as an elaborate exploratory forecasting method.

PATTERN. PATTERN (Planning Assistance Through Technical Evaluation of Relevance Numbers), developed by Honeywell's Military and Space Sciences Department, is perhaps the most extensive and expensive normative forecasting technique in use [17]. Yet PATTERN's sophistication is largely concentrated in its allocation methodology, as opposed to its generation of exploratory forecasts. Primarily "genius" forecasting, trend extrapolation, and envelope curves are employed to predict the possible technical state of the art, and resource allocations are not fed back to affect technological developments. In particular, the key exploratory forecast embodied in PATTERN is someone's estimate of the number of years that a system in question will remain in each of several sequential stages of advancement. The stages considered are: research, exploratory development, advanced development, product design, and availability. This series of timing estimates is a rather modest recognition of exploratory forecasting capabilities.

PROBE. Finally, an examination of TRW's Probe II approach further indicates the conflict between simple exploratory forecasting and elaborate normative procedures [18]. Based on a modified Delphi technique, TRW determines Desirability, Feasibility, and Timing of each forecast event. Then to determine appropriate corporate response, SOON (Sequence Of Opportunities and Negatives) charts, similar to PERT networks, are prepared to demonstrate the details of specific accomplishments that will be needed to realize the forecast event. Apparently no one is concerned (at least, not in print) that collective wisdom alone produces the exploratory forecasts whereas detailed R & D planning is the basis of the normative reaction.

Investigation of other well-known normative forecasting techniques (e.g., TORQUE) provides further evidences to support the point already established. Very ponderous methods of valuing technology and allocating resources are being combined with very trivial methods of forecasting technical outputs. The methods appear to be aimed at producing five decimal-place accuracy outputs from one decimal-place accuracy input, a task comparable to acquiring silk purses from sow's ears. The inconsistency of this practice, and the obvious notion that a chain is only as strong as its weakest link, have not yet shifted enough attention to the needed improvement of exploratory forecasting methodology.

Implementability of Normative Forecasts

If the problem just cited were corrected, if the normative allocations were indeed based on legitimate and respectable efforts at exploratory forecasting, a number of problems would still exist in gaining effective implementation of the normative techniques. Some of the observed problem areas are:

1. the costliness of the inputs;
2. the dubious accuracy of the estimates;
3. the inflexibility of the methods; and
4. the probable limited impact upon managerial decisions.

Costliness. Each of the primary normative methods described above is a heavy user of resources. Jantsch estimates the original setup cost for a PATTERN scheme at $250,000 to $300,000 with annual "maintenance" costs of roughly $50,000 [19]. QUEST requires estimates for a "value of technology to missions" matrix that may be of the order of 30 by 50 and for a "relevance of science to technology" matrix of approximately 50 by 130 size. Each of these QUEST inputs may have to be provided for the three time frames of now, five years from now, and ten years from now, as well as for several sets of assumed funding levels [20]. Probe II required inputs from 140 experts [21]. Many organizations, including those already cited, may find the expenditure of these resources to be an awesome consideration, especially as the techniques require resubmittal of all the inputs on a reasonably regular basis. To be sure, learning no doubt takes place which reduces these input acquisition costs, but each estimator is still needed to regenerate on a regular basis his inputs to the forecasting systems.

Dubious accuracy. A second problem is the questionable believability of the inputs submitted. The scientific-technological expert is a doer who understands the state of knowledge in his field and the process employed for advancing that state. Instead of asking the expert to assess that state or to describe that process, the normative methods principally call upon him to become a crystal-ball gazer and to leap inferentially to a conclusion (usually probabilistic) as to what will occur in the future. Little objective evidence exists to defend this kind of expert testimony.

Perhaps even more harmful to the accuracy of the normative systems is that many of the required data inputs cannot be known until it is too late to really affect R & D programs. Jantsch points out that present techniques, such as relevance trees, demand a clear recognition of items on each of the following levels: goals, missions, primary systems, sub-systems, components, technology deficiencies, etc. Because of the need to know with confidence how each of these levels integrates with the other levels, Jantsch feels that the full normative schemes may be feasible frequently only at a point where specific strategies may already be "frozen."[1]

The problem of input accuracy and adequacy is worsened by the likelihood that the estimator providing the inputs will be affected by the conclusions derived from his inputs. The scientist entering data into a normative forecast has to guard against "signing his own death warrant." This participative role in what are likely to be self-fulfilling or self-defeating forecasts almost assures that the inputs will be biased consciously or unconsciously and surely not in any systematic manner.

Inflexibility. In many areas of critical decision-making, resource allocators evaluate their alternatives using quantitative techniques such as, for example, the cost-effectiveness analyses used by the DOD in selecting weapons systems. These cost-effectiveness evaluations permit wide latitude in the mode of costing adopted, as well as in the method for value assessment. Top level Defense management reviews each analysis for its soundness in order to qualify the adequacy and acceptability of the derived recommendations. Following these formal reviews the overall resources allocation is still subject to a balancing against other usually nonquantified social, economic, and political considerations.

Of the managerial areas being subjected to quantitative resource allocation techniques, research and development consists of more unique programs, with more uncertain outcomes, and less uniformity of types of results than any other area. Yet the new types of normative forecasting techniques discussed herein, which have been proposed and occasionally adopted for selecting and funding R & D programs, are supposed to be applied uniformly to all programs, regardless of scope, phase, duration, criticality, technology, or what-have-you. This degree of unjustified standardization is not matched

---

[1] Private communication from E. Jantsch.

by the flexible view taken for DOD weapons system tradeoffs. Nor is it matched by many more traditional approaches taken for normative analyses which have not been dignified by labels or publicity. Moreover, the complexity and mathematical sophistication of the normative technological forecasting methods again exceeds by far the relatively simple formats and seldom-more-than-arithmetic computation procedures used in DOD cost-effectiveness determinations. Is it possible that the current style of proposed normative technological forecasting is an overreaction to the difficulties of managing research and development?

Limited impact. The characteristics of normative forecasting just described, as well as the characteristics of the decision-making process, combine to suggest that the present generation of techniques is likely to have only limited impact on specific managerial decisions. The costliness, dubious accuracy, and inflexibility of approach will naturally tend to limit the use of these methods. But more important is that experience in other related areas has shown that comparable techniques are seldom truly responsible for selection decisions.

In their excellent review of formal project selection methods, Baker and Pound found that few organizations of the 50 studied were employing the formal selection processes that were described in published papers by their employees [22]. Perhaps this is indicative only of the low state of managerial decision-making generally, but other evidences suggest that the problem is more fundamental.

In a study by the author of about 100 R & D contractor selection decisions, informal person-to-person factors were found to influence the awards far more than did formal evaluation procedures [23]. In fact, six to eight months prior to formal award announcements, long before the formal proposal evaluations, all but 10 percent of the awards of R & D contracts up to several millions of dollars in magnitude were predictable from the available data.

When major decisions are to be made it appears that management needs to consider factors other than those generally included in formal complex evaluation procedures. Investigation of 51 of the largest contracts awarded by the National Aeronautics and Space Administration revealed that NASA headquarters did not follow the suggestions of its Source Evaluation Boards in 25 percent of the cases [24]. But these 25 percent accounted for 67 percent of the total funds contracted on the 51 awards. It is possible that formal evaluation methods are followed only when the outcome is not regarded as vital to the organization.

Previously this paper pointed out that the PROFILE technique contains a "fudge factor" criterion, Intrinsic Value to the Laboratory, that permits managerial "overrides" of otherwise elaborate evaluations. More recently Cetron has indicated that consideration of so-called "sacred cows" in another technique under investigation by the Navy also permits the rest of a complex evaluation procedure to be scrapped in favor of explicit management preferences [25]. Is it not reasonable that in the important cases such "sacred cow" factors would limit the impact of formal evaluations oriented against a top manager's desires?

Evidence gathered in a series of other studies also argues that real decisions are not made in the manner suggested by the formal, complex decision-aiding systems in R & D [26]. These data do not suggest that the formal evaluation systems are without value. Indeed these methods seem to stimulate a more thoughtful and more orderly planning process that enhances management effectiveness. But the data do indicate that the present type of normative forecasting techniques is likely to have only limited impact on managerial resource allocation for R & D.[2]

Of course, other factors are also at work that would tend to restrain the impact of any form of forecasting system, regardless of formality or complexity. "Top management finds it very difficult to force R & D into certain channels on the basis of these forecasts. Middle management all too frequently is impervious to such recommendations and resistant to change. The larger the organization, the more difficult it is to force such changes. Scientists and engineers often would rather change positions than implement an R & D shift in the organization."[3] Organizational inertia and reluctance to accept the risks of program change based upon technological forecasts will also generally restrict the effectiveness of the normative methods.

IV. Integrating Exploratory and Normative Forecasting with Dynamic System Models

Throughout this paper the inconsistencies between the developments of exploratory and normative forecasting techniques have been highlighted. In mathematical sophistication and level of detail the simple schemes used by those trying to predict the technology of the future look pallid when matched against the techniques employed by those who are allocating the resources that will create the future. The examination of exploratory forecasting methods indicates that what is known about the process that generates future technology is not presently included in the forecasting models. This lack shows up further as a critical weakness of the normative techniques, which are attempting to select and budget R & D projects based on meager schemes for forecasting future technological possibilities.

An earlier section of the paper pointed out the potential of dynamic models that are oriented toward the inclusion of those cause-and-effect relationships that are likely to alter future technological developments. These models are being utilized in economic analysis, forecasting, and policy design, i.e., in both exploratory and normative modes. Jantsch has realized how much these dynamic system models might contribute to technological forecasting. However, he has seriously underestimated the degree of their present development.

Rigid computer models are on the threshold of becoming useful for technological forecasting. In particular, "dynamic forecasting" is serving as a guideline in a number of serious attempts; this term, introduced by Lenz to denote the modelling of all significant cause-effect relationships which influence the growth of technology in general or a functional capability, may be extended here so as to include technology transfer in general. The hope, of course, is to achieve adequate results with a limited dynamic model. The "Industrial Dynamics" concept of Forrester for complex business decision-making provides the background to many attempts in this area [27].

---

[2] One reviewer went further to suggest that the real underlying purpose of the normative techniques is awareness of the logical structure underlying the forecast, and not the proposed resource allocations produced by the techniques! If true, more direct and less expensive approaches to structural awareness should be adopted.

[3] Private communication from Harold A. Linstone, Lockheed Aircraft Corporation.

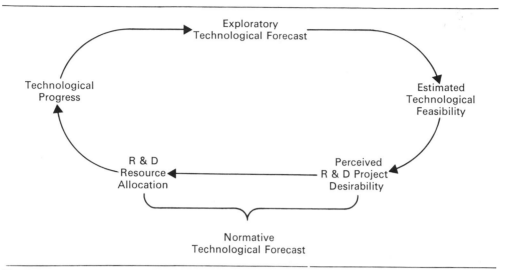

Fig. 1. Feedback relationship between exploratory and normative technological forecasts.

The "Industrial Dynamics" concept that Jantsch refers to emphasizes the importance of feedback relationships in influencing the dynamic evolution of a situation [28]. For example, the connections between exploratory and normative forecasting form the kind of feedback loops that significantly affect future behavior, as shown in Figure 1. An exploratory forecast generates a prediction that a desired outcome is highly feasible within a reasonable time period; this leads to a high value index established for the related R & D project in the normalized forecast, which in turn influences increased funding for the project. The resultant strengthened research support enhances the likelihood of timely completion of the project, and this status improvement is reflected in the exploratory forecast. This type of feedback relationship is critical to the technological growth process and it demands the integration of the exploratory and normative phases. Dynamic feedback system models are the most likely candidates for accomplishing this integration.

Dynamic System Models in Technology-Related Areas

Though generally unrecognized by Jantsch and other reviewers of the technological forecasting field, dynamic models of technology-related feedback systems have been under development for ten years. A brief review of these models will demonstrate their present availability for broader exploitation in technological forecasting and their traditional integration of exploratory and normative considerations.

R & D projects. As the primary present use of technological forecasting is in the area of R & D project selection and budget allocation, it seems appropriate to mention the dynamic systems models oriented towards examining these projects. The major effort here is the author's book on the factors affecting R & D project life cycles [29]. The mathematical model of the project process follows the scheme illustrated in simplified form in Figure 2. Indeed the model treats both the exploratory and normative sides of the project process and contains a detailed sector that represents the technology-generating process.

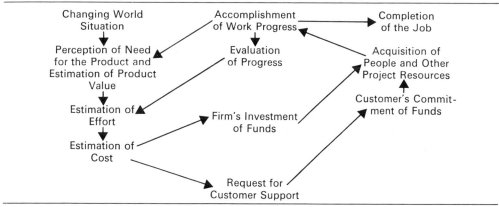

Fig. 2. Dynamic system underlying project life cycles.

Initially this model was intended as a conceptual tool only, but it has already been applied to specific technological forecasting in the United States and Japan, resulting in publications in both countries [30].

Multi-project and multi-phase allocations. Beyond looking at projects singly, technological forecasters are concerned with the problems of beneficial and conflicting "cross support" between multiple projects. This problem has been treated in dynamic feedback system models aimed at two subtopics—the cross-support between projects and the cross-support between various phases of R & D activity in a technical organization. The former area has been the subject of one excellent graduate thesis [31], while the latter has been covered by a variety of high quality thesis efforts [32].

Technical organization forecasting. Several dynamic system models have been developed as attempts at analyzing and causally predicting the growth (or decline) of a technical organization (exploratory style) and the effect of various policies on that growth (normative style). Two papers and an array of good quality graduate theses document this area of activity [33]. The paper listed by Robert Spencer describes ventures undertaken at the Dow Chemical Company to better plan and allocate resources for one of its major divisions.

Technological growth forecasts. A number of dynamic system models emphasizing feedback effects have tackled the question of the growth of a new technology. Lenz and Reisman have concerned themselves with the training and employment of the professional people who cause a new technological area to develop [34]. Nord has focused on the growth process for a new product, while Forrester has written on the growth of a new technology-based firm [35].

Many other papers, theses, and unpublished studies have also dealt with exploratory and normative aspects of scientific and technological developments. The wide variety of models identified here does indicate that "rigid computer models," as Jantsch refers to them, or, preferably, "dynamic feedback system models" are part of the presently available state-of-the-art of technological forecasting.

Towards Effective Use of Dynamic System Models

It is clear that the large-scale dynamic simulation models described herein have the capacity to include realistically the cause-and-effect relationships believed to generate technological advances. What is not clear is how to use these models most effectively.

A focus on the previously asserted need for consistency between exploratory and normative forecasting seems to provide a clue toward effective use. Although many of the general factors influencing growth of a technological area are understood, this understanding does not extend down to rather minute details or up to any high degree of accuracy. The uncertainties of research and development, the uniqueness of the programs, the intangibility of the progress, and the long time delays in the feedback of results constrain the possible accuracy of understanding to a marked extent. Thus, exploratory forecasting models are similarly limited in the accuracy and detail that can be demanded of them. And, consistently, attempted normative forecasts must be confined to the same range of uses. To attempt to use normative technological forecasting to select and allocate funds to hundreds or thousands of individual projects is obviously beyond the effective capacity of the models that can or should be built. Much more knowledge is needed, not about allocation techniques but rather about the technological development process, before such a high degree of disaggregation becomes meaningful.

It seems reasonable that dynamic feedback system models can be developed to help answer a number of fundamental resource allocation questions. Should more money in total be expended on research and development activities? How should the R & D budget be split between its research and its developmental components? How should the budget treat new potentially important areas of science and technology as opposed to the older on-going activities? How should funds be allocated in support of various broad missions or goals? These and other key questions are now largely being ignored in the mistaken rush to decide quantitatively but unjustifiedly the selection and funding of each and every R & D project. But it is in the realm of these policy issues that integrated exploratory and normative technological forecasting, enriched by the use of dynamic feedback systems models, will make its most potent contribution.

References

1 Cetron, M. J., *et al.*, *A Proposal for a Navy Technological Forecast* (Washington, D.C.: Naval Material Command, May 1966, AD 659–199 and 560–200).

2 Gabor, D., *Inventing the Future* (London: Seckery Warburg, 1963).

3 Jantsch, E., *Technological Forecasting in Perspective* (Paris: Organisation for Economic Cooperation and Development, 1967), pp. 15, 17.

4 Another exploratory approach, called "morphological forecasting," seems so unwieldy in use as not to merit detailed review in this paper. See Zwicky, F., *Morphological Astronomy* (Berlin: Springer Verlag, 1957), for a more complete reference to this method.

5 Gordon, T. J. and Helmer, O., *Report on a Long-Range Forecasting Study* (Santa Monica, Calif.: The RAND Corporation, September 1964, Paper P-2982).

6 Jantsch, p. 156.

7 Mansfield, E., Technical change and the rate of imitation, *Econometrica*, October 1961, Vol. 29, No. 4, pp. 741–766.

8 Examples of this "new" type of economic forecasting model are: Duesenberry, J. S., *et al.* (eds.), *The Brookings Quarterly Econometric Model of the United States* (New York: Rand McNally, 1965); Fromm, G., and Taubman, P., *Policy Simulations with an Econometric Model* (Washington, D.C.: The Brookings Institution, 1968); Hamilton, H. R., *et al.*, *Systems Simulation for Regional Analysis* (Cambridge: The M.I.T. Press, 1968); Weymar, F. H., *The Dynamics of the World Cocoa Market* (Cambridge: The M.I.T. Press, 1968).

9 Jantsch, p. 17.

10 Lenz, R. C., Jr., *Technological Forecasting*, 2nd ed. (Wright-Patterson Air Force Base: U.S. Air Force Aeronautical Systems Division, June 1962, Report ASD-TDR-62-414), as cited in Jantsch, p. 241.

11 Jantsch, p. 155.

12 Among the recent summaries of aspects of this research are: Gruber, W. H. and Marquis, D. G. (eds.), *Factors in the Transfer of Technology* (Cambridge: The M.I.T. Press, 1969); Isenson, R. D., "Factors Affecting the Growth of Technology--As Seen through Hindsight," unpublished paper presented at the NATO Defense Research Group Seminar, Teddington, England, November 1968; and Marquis, D. G. (ed.), *Second Report of the M.I.T. Research Program on the Management of Science and Technology* (Cambridge: Sloan School of Management, M.I.T., October 1967).

13 Cetron, M. J., "Programmed Functional Indices for Laboratory Evaluation (PROFILE)," presented at the 16th Military Operations Research Symposium, Seattle, Washington, October 1966.

14 *Ibid.*, p. 5.

15 Cetron, M. J., QUEST Status Report, *IEEE Transactions on Engineering Management*, Vol. EM-14, No. 1, March 1967.

16 *Ibid.*, p. 62.

17 Jestice, A. L., *Project PATTERN—Planning Assistance Through Technical Evaluation of Relevance Numbers* (Washington, D.C.: Honeywell, Inc., 1964).

18 North, H. A., "Technological Forecasting in Industry," presented at the NATO Defense Research Group Seminar, Teddington, England, November 12, 1968.

19 Jantsch, p. 226.

20 Cetron, *ibid.*

21 North, p. 9.

22 Baker, M. R. and Pound, W. H., R and D Project Selection: Where We Stand, *IEEE Transactions on Engineering Management*, Vol. EM-11, No. 4, December 1964.

23 Roberts, E. B., "Questioning the Cost/Effectiveness of the R & D Procurement Process," in Yovits, M. C., *et al.* (eds.), *Research Program Effectiveness* (New York: Gordon and Breach, 1966).

24 Bergsteinsson, P., "The Evaluation and Selection of Sources for Major NASA Contracts" unpublished Master of Science thesis, M.I.T. Sloan School of Management, 1967).

25 Cetron, M. J., Technological Forecasting: A Prescription for the Military R & D Manager, *Naval War College Review*, Vol. 21, No. 8, April 1969, p. 31.

26 Roberts, E. B., Facts and Folklore in Research and Development Management, *Industrial Management Review*, Vol. 8, No. 2, Spring 1967.

27 Jantsch, p. 202.

28 Forrester, J. W., *Industrial Dynamics* (Cambridge: The M.I.T. Press, 1961).

29 Roberts, E. B., *The Dynamics of Research and Development* (New York: Harper & Row, 1964).

30 Schlager, K. J., How Managers Use Industrial Dynamics, *Industrial Management Review*, Vol. 6, No. 1, 1964. Reference to the Japanese application is contained in a private communication to the author from S. Sakakura.

31 Nay, J. N., "Choice and Allocation in Multiple Markets: A Research and Developments Systems Analysis," unpublished Master of Science thesis, M.I.T. Department of Electrical Engineering, 1966. Interested readers can purchase copies of M.I.T. graduate theses in Xerox or microfilm form by ordering directly from the M.I.T. Microreproduction Service, Hayden Library, M.I.T., Cambridge, Massachusetts 02139.

32 D. C. Beaumariage (1960), P. W. Lett (1961), G. R. Wachold (1963), and G. Welles III (1963) produced thesis studies at the M.I.T. Sloan School of Management on the allocation of funds and effort among several series-related phases of work.

33 Roberts, E. B., Problems of Aging Organizations, *Business Horizons*, Vol. 10, No. 4, Winter 1967; Spencer, R. W., "Modelling Strategies for Corporate Growth," presented at the Society for General Systems Research Conference, Washington, D.C., 1966; and M.I.T. Sloan School of Management theses by L. Salba (1967), C. H. Perrine (1968), and J. Troutner (1968).

34 Lenz, *ibid.*; Reisman, A., Higher Education: A Population Flow Feedback Model, *Science*, Vol. 153, July 1, 1966.

35 Nord, O. C., *Growth of a New Product* (Cambridge: The M.I.T. Press, 1963); Forrester, J. W., "Modelling the Dynamic Processes of Corporate Growth," presented at the IBM Scientific Computing Symposium, Yorktown Heights, New York, December 1964.

Part Five:
Management Control and Financial Applications

Management systems can be better understood, better designed, and better controlled through the feedback structure approach used in system dynamics modeling. The concepts of system goals, measurement of performance relative to the goals, and reaction to deviations from those goals underlie inventory or financial control systems just as much as they underlie physiological or thermostatic controls.

The editor's first attempt to apply system dynamics philosophy to design requirements for management control systems was in a paper prepared for the Stanford University Graduate School of Business Conference on Basic Research in Management Controls in February, 1963. Republished here as Chapter 23, that paper develops three different examples of management controls — production-inventory control, R&D project planning and control, and industrial quality control — to illustrate a range of analysis and synthesis applications.

Carl Swanson, while a doctoral student and faculty member at the M.I.T. Sloan School, focused his interests primarily on management control system design. Chapter 24 is a synopsis of Swanson's Ph.D. dissertation, completed in 1969.

Chapter 25 examines the workings of several intended and unintended management control systems in a large vertically-integrated Canadian food producer and retailer. At the retail store level the chapter illustrates the conflicting dynamics of the managerial behavior systems controlling gross margin and sales. The manufacturing division's system for controlling return-on-investment is shown to be in conflict with the merchandising division's objectives. Top-level corporate growth goals were left unfulfilled by the overall suboptimal orientation of mid-level management controls. The model described in Chapter 25 was developed by Dan Abrams, Henry Weil and the editor from detailed data gathered during a consulting project by Pugh-Roberts Associates in the Canadian company. The model was validated in part by comparison of its simulation results with five-year company historical data, as shown in Figure 8 of that chapter. Detailed equations for the model are presented in Appendix D of this volume.

The same management control concepts apply to organizational change as well as to operations, as is illustrated in Chapter 26 by Fillmore McPherson. McPherson was a research assistant in the M.I.T. System Dynamics Group and worked on early staff efforts to model group dynamics and organizational behavior. McPherson did the computer simulation work in a collaborative project by Jay Forrester and Douglas McGregor to model the development process of sensitivity training groups, better known as T-groups. Chapter 26 is a synopsis of McPherson's Sloan School Master of Science thesis. More recent related works on the dynamics of organizational change include Pugh-Roberts Associates efforts for Polaroid Corporation (see Chapter 32) and unpublished work for the U.S. Agency for International Development.

Henry Weil, the author of Chapter 27 (also co-author of Chapters 19 and 25), began working on system dynamics projects as an M.I.T. undergraduate, intensified his efforts during his graduate work at M.I.T., and further expanded his contributions to the field in his full-time professional capacity in Pugh-Roberts Associates. Weil goes beyond management control system design to the related management information system problems. His several real-world examples include the Canadian food chain discussed in Chapter 25, a plant engineering information system for a major world-wide manufacturer, and a new venture evaluation system for a large bank holding company.

The last four chapters in Part 5 reflect other applications of system dynamics to financial systems. Daniel Hickson, then Senior Vice President for Forward Planning of Bankers Trust Company, provides some insights into his bank's experiences with system dynamics. In Chapter 28 note Hickson's strong crediting of the system dynamics activities as supporting major reorganizational and refinancing decisions of Bankers Trust.

James Lyneis, now an Assistant Professor teaching system dynamics courses at M.I.T., completed his Ph.D. at the University of Michigan. His dissertation, which applied system dynamics to corporate financial planning problems, is summarized in Chapter 29.

The introduction to Part 3 of this volume described the numerous commodity market models that have been developed using system dynamics techniques. Chapter 30, however, is the only publication known to the editor that illustrates system dynamics use for stock market modeling. Toshiro Shimada developed his model while on sabbatical leave at M.I.T. and continued his system dynamics interests following his return to Japan. The editor knows of several other stock market-oriented models created by system dynamics practitioners, but all of these have been carried out as proprietary activities.

The last chapter in the section, by Kenneth Veit, Vice President in charge of AEtna Insurance Company's Variable Annuity division, focuses on a strategic planning model carried out for a major financial institution. Chapter 31 provides some details of the AEtna model, but is concerned more with the processes of realistic model development and implementation. Veit's main points support arguments posed previously in Chapters 3, 4 and 9 and deserve careful note. The reader should be interested to know that following his preparation of the Chapter 31 manuscript, Veit directed additional system dynamics projects, both for AEtna in the area of strategic planning, and for the Jockey Club of New York, reflecting Veit's extra-curricular interests in thoroughbred horse breeding and racing.

Review of the annual M.I.T. *System Dynamics Newsletters* indicates several other system dynamics applications in the area of management control and finance. Lockheed Missiles and Space Company reported modeling the information and work flows associated with the production of critical reports. Toa Nenryo Kogyo K. K. (Tonen) undertook cash accounting and inventory control models. Two other banks, First National Bank of Boston and National Shawmut Bank, publicly reported on system dynamics projects, and the editor knows of several other banks, in New York and Boston, which did similar modeling. As an indirect result of the Bankers Trust project described in Chapter 28, a banking-oriented model of the U.S. economy was developed by Alexander Pugh for the U.S. Federal Deposit Insurance Corporation, but no publication is available on that effort.

Corporate financial planning models have also been developed by a number of companies in the U.S., Europe and Japan, but few companies have publicly mentioned these efforts. In addition to the AEtna effort described in Chapter 31, E.G.&G., Inc. has described a large financial forecasting system model, and both Boeing and Japan Air Lines have developed world airlines financial planning models.

23

The Design of Management Control Systems

Edward B. Roberts

I. The Organization as a Control System

Every organization is a control system. Each has direction and objectives, whether explicit or implied. Each has beliefs as to its current status. Each has policies and procedures whereby it reaches decisions and takes actions to attain its goals more closely. Every organization actually contains a myriad of smaller control systems, each characterized by the same goal-striving, but not necessarily goal-attaining, behavior.

The organization as a whole or any one of its component subsystems can be represented by the feedback process shown in Figure 1. Four characteristics of this diagram are noteworthy. First, the transformation of decisions into results takes place through a complex process which includes a basic structure of organizational, human, and market relationships; this structure is sometimes not apparent because of its numerous sources of noise or random behavior and due to its often lengthy time delays between cause and effect.

The second aspect to be noted is the distinction between the achievements that are apparent in the organization and those which are real. The real situation is translated into the apparent through information and communication channels which contain delays, noise, and bias. These sources of error may be the inadvertent features of an organization's communication system, or they may result from the chosen characteristics of a data-processing system which sacrifices accuracy for compactness. In any event, however, the bases of actual decisions in an organization may be assumptions which bear but little relation to fact.

The third feature of the diagram is that the decision-making process is viewed as a response to the gap between objectives of the organization and its apparent progress toward those objectives. Although both the objectives and achievements

This article is based on studies supported by grants of the Ford Foundation and the National Aeronautics and Space Administration. The computer simulations were carried out at the M.I.T. Computation Center. The paper was first presented at the Stanford University Seminar on Basic Research in Management Controls, February 20, 1963. It has been previously published in *Management Technology* 3, no. 2 (December 1963), pp. 100–108, under the title "Industrial Dynamics and the Design of Management Control Systems."

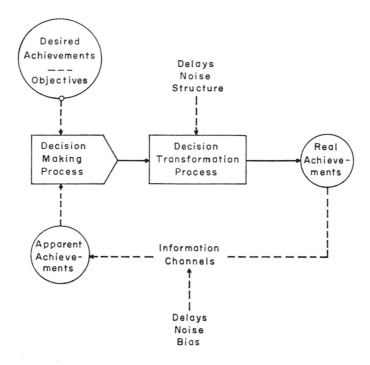

Figure I.   Control System Structure of Organizations

may be difficult to define precisely and measure accurately, such a goal-seeking behavior is nonetheless present in all organizations and in every subsystem of the organizations. At any level of an organization, many similar decisions are being made. The real problem of the management control system designer is to recognize these multiple decision loops and their interrelationships, and to develop policies and an organizational structure that will tie these activities into progress toward total organization objectives.

The fourth characteristic of Figure 1 is the continuous feedback path of decision-results-measurement-evaluation-decision. It is vital to effective system design that each element of this feedback path be properly treated and that its continuous nature be recognized. Whether the decision in the system is made by the irrational actions or logical deductions of a manager or by the programmed response of a computer, the system consequences will eventually have further effects on the decision itself.

II. Industrial Dynamics—Philosophy and Methodology for Control System Design

Industrial Dynamics is a philosophy which asserts that organizations are most effectively viewed (and managed) from this control system perspective. It is also a methodology for designing organizational policy. This two-pronged approach is the result of a research program that was initiated and directed at

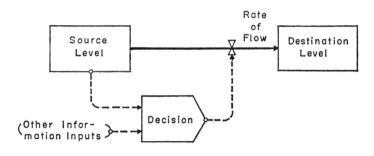

Figure 2. The Decision as a Controller

the M.I.T. School of Industrial Management by Professor Jay W. Forrester The results of the first five years of this program are described in Professor Forrester's book, *Industrial Dynamics*, which also discusses a variety of potential applications to key management problems.[1]

Industrial Dynamics recognizes a common systems base in the flow structure of all social-economic-industrial-political organizations. This perspective ties the segmented functional aspects of formal organizations into an integrated structure of varying rates of flow and responsively changing levels of accumulation. The flow paths involve all facets of organizational resources—men, money, materials, orders, and capital equipment—and the information and decision-making network that links the other flows.

Industrial Dynamics views decisions as the controllers of these organization flows. Such decisions regulate the rate of change of levels from which the flows originate and to which they are sent. In the flow diagrams drawn as part of an Industrial Dynamics study, decisions are even represented by the traditional control valve symbol of the engineer. Figure 2 shows such a decision, based in part on information about the contents of the source level, controlling the rate of flow to the destination level.

The system structures and behavioral phenomena that are studied by the Industrial Dynamics methodology are present at all levels of the corporation. The top management of the firm is involved in a system that can be studied and aided in the same manner as the middle management of the organization, and again in the same fashion as the physical operating system of the plant. The potential payoff from changes derived from system studies increases greatly, however, as the study is focused higher up in the organization. For all studies the pattern of forming a dynamic verbal theory, developing mathematical equations, computer simulation of the model, and derivation of improved policies is followed. The problems encountered in these phases do not significantly change as we move from the bottom to the top of an organization. Only during the final stage of implementation of system change does the problem complexity get significantly greater the higher the level of organization involved. But the impact of

[1] Jay W. Forrester, Industrial Dynamics (Cambridge, The M.I.T. Press, 1961).

improved corporate-level policy on company growth, stability, and profitability can readily justify this added effort to renovate top management policy making.

III. Problems of Management Control Systems

The preceding discussion has focused on the nature of organizational problems as management control system problems, and on the intended applicability of Industrial Dynamics to these problems. Observation of several different types of management control systems and a survey of the literature in this field lead to a belief that a new attack on control system design is needed. The traditional approaches to management control systems have mushroomed in number and sophistication of applications as operations research and electronic data processing have developed during the post-war era. Although these systems have made significant and successful inroads, many fail to cure the problems for which they were designed; other management control systems even amplify the initial difficulties or create more significant new problems. All this is taking place even as we derive enhanced but misplaced confidence in the systems.

Several examples will help to illustrate these problems and lead us to some findings about the design of management control systems.

Systems Inadequate for Their Problems

Sometimes the management control system is inadequately designed for the problem situation. In such a case the control system may improve performance in the trouble area, but be far short of the potential gains. At times the limited effectiveness may transform a potentially major benefit to the company into but a marginal application.

The Control of Research and Development Projects

One example of an area in which the traditional approach to control system design has proven inadequate is the management of research and development projects. The intangibility, lack of precise measurements, and uncertain character of R and D results are partly responsible for this failure. But a more basic lack of system understanding has implications of even greater significance. All systems of schedule and/or budget controls that have been tried till now have failed to achieve success in R and D usage. These techniques have included Gantt charts, milestone schedules, and computerized systems of budgetary and manpower control.

The latest approaches to control of research and development projects are based on PERT (Program Evaluation Review Technique) or PERT/COST. The management control systems implied by the methods used can be represented by the diagram of Figure 3. As shown here, the basis of the current sophisticated methods is a single-loop system in which the difference between desired completion date and forecast completion date causes decisions to change the magnitude or allocation of project resources (manpower, facilities, equipment, priorities). As these resources are employed, they are assumed to produce the progress that is reported during the project. These reports are processed through a PERT-type evaluation and forecasting system to create the forecast completion time.

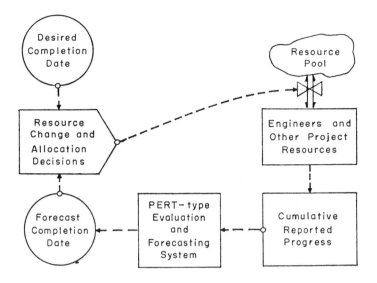

Figure 3. Assumed Basis of Current R and D Project Controls

But the design of a management control system based on such a set of assumptions is doomed to failure, since some of the most vital aspects of the real system have been excluded from the underlying analysis. For example, the lack of tangible, precise measurement sources is entirely ignored. Yet these factors contribute much of the error between the *real* situation in the project (its true scope and actual progress to date) and that which is *apparent* to those doing the engineering work.

Another part of the real system which appears to be ignored by current R and D control system designers is the human element in the project actions and decisions. The attitudes and motivations of the engineers and managers, their knowledge of the schedules and current estimates in the project, the believed penalty-reward structure of the organization—all affect the progress and problems that are reported upward in the organization. Furthermore, these same factors even affect the rate of real progress toward project objectives. All systems of measurement and evaluation (in R and D, manufacturing, government, universities, or what-have-you) create incentives and pressures for certain actions. These interact with the goals and character of individuals and institutions to produce decisions, actions, and their results. For example, a system which compares "actual to budgeted expenditures" creates an incentive to increase budgets, regardless of progress; one which checks "proportion of budget spent" creates pressures on the manager or engineer to be sure he spends the money, whether or not on something useful. The presence of such factors in research and development ought to be recognized in the design of systems for R and D control.

Adding these two additional sources of system behavior to the earlier diagram produces the more complete representation of a research and development system that is pictured in Figure 4. But even this is an incomplete representation

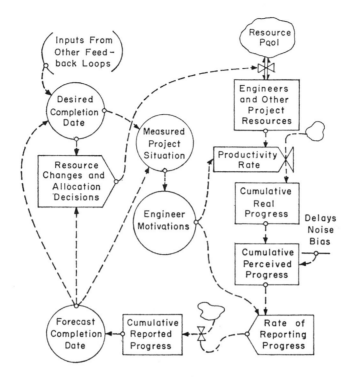

Figure 4.   More Complete Representation of R and D System

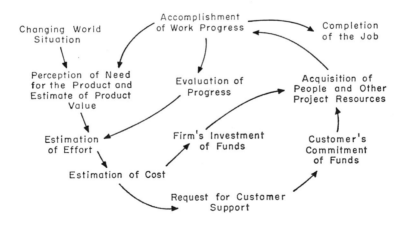

Figure 5. Dynamic System Underlying R and D Projects

of the complex system which interrelates the characteristics of the product, the customer, and the R and D organization. A proper characterization of research and development projects must take into account the continuous dynamic system of activities that creates project life cycles. Such a system will include not just the schedule and accumulated effort, costs, and accomplishments.

Rather, it will encompass the full range of policies and parameters that carry a research and development project from initial perception of potential need for the product to final completion of the development program. The fundamental R and D project system is shown in Figure 5, from which we have developed an Industrial Dynamics model of research and development project dynamics.

Some of the results of simulation studies of this model are of particular interest to designers of management control systems. They demonstrate the importance of taking cognizance of the complete system structure in attempting to create and implement methods of system control. For example, one series of simulations of the general project model was conducted in which only the scheduled project duration was changed in the various runs. Within the model the effort allocation process *attempts* to complete the project during this scheduled period. However, the actual completion dates of the projects seem only remotely responsive to the changes in desired completion time.

Figure 6 demonstrates the nature of this response, using the outputs of four model simulations. The horizontal axis is an index of the scheduled project duration as a percentage of the maximum schedule used; the vertical axis shows actual completion time in a similar percentile manner. If changes in schedule produced corresponding changes in actual completion dates, the curve of results would have followed the diagonal "perfect response" line; that is, a 50 percent reduction in scheduled duration should produce a 50 percent reduction in actual duration, if control is *perfect*. But the actual response is far from perfect; a 50 percent schedule change effects only a 25 percent actual change. And at the extreme, the actual change is even in the opposite direction, taking longer to complete the urgent crash project because of the resulting organizational confusion and inefficiencies. Of course, this response curve does not present the simulation data on the manpower instability, total project cost, and customer satisfaction changes that also accompany shifts in the project schedule.

Some of the implications of Figure 6 are more clearly presented in the next curve. Here the slippage in project schedule is plotted as a function of the scheduled duration, the points on the curve coming from the project model simulations. A completion time slippage of 242 percent of schedule was incurred in the crash project, with a rapid decrease in this percentage completion date overrun as the schedule is dragged out. When the project is slowed too much, the slippage increases again as lack of enthusiasm induces further stretch-out during the project life.

The principal point made by these two illustrations is that many factors other than desired schedule determine the resultant actual schedule of research and development projects. *Control systems for R and D which resort to schedule and effort rate control without full understanding of the system structure of projects are bound to be ineffective.* The current PERT-based project control systems seem guilty of this error in design philosophy. In fact, many aspects of our government contracting program suffer similar faults of inadequate system understanding, producing ill-conceived policies with attendant poor results. For example, increased risk-taking (i.e., greater willingness to invest company funds prior to contract receipt) and higher bidding integrity by R and D companies would act in the best interests of the government customer of research

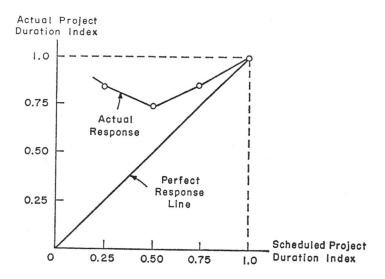

Figure 6. Scheduled vs. Actual Project Durations

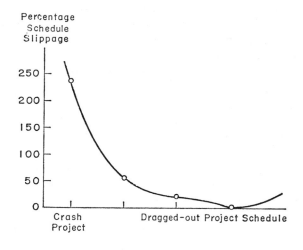

Figure 7. Schedule Slippage as a Function of Schedule

and development. However, our simulation studies show that neither policy is in the short-term best interests of the R and D companies, under existing government regulations and practices. Thus the contracting policies, a government control system for R and D procurement, act to the detriment of national objectives by inducing company behavior which produces unsatisfactory project outcomes.[2]

---

[2] A general theory of research and development project behavior, a model of the theory, and extensive simulation studies of parameters and policies influencing R and D outcomes are reported in the author's book, *The Dynamics of Research and Development* (New York: Harper and Row, in press).

The proper design of research and development control systems, for both company and customer, should take into account three things: (1) the source of internal action, information, and control in a project is the individual engineer; measurement and evaluation schemes and the internal penalty-reward structure must be designed with him in mind; (2) the total results of research and development projects are created by a complex dynamic system of activities, which interrelates the characteristics of the product, the customer, and the R and D firm; control systems which ignore vital aspects of these flows cannot succeed; (3) institutional objectives of R and D companies (profits, growth, stability) can be aligned with the objectives of government customers; procurement policies constitute the system of control which can effect or destroy this alignment.

A Production-Inventory-Employment Control System

As another example, let us take the case of an industrial components manufacturer who initially has no formal production-inventory-employment control systems. Such a firm operates by its response to current problems. It follows the example of the firemen trying to use a leaky hose—as soon as one hole is patched up, another leak occurs elsewhere. A company operating in this manner does not keep sufficiently close tabs on changes in sales, inventories, backlogs, delivery delays, etc. Rather, when customer compaints build up on company delivery performance, people will be hired to increase production rate and repair the inventory position. Similarly, when a periodic financial report (or the warehouse manager's difficulties) shows a great excess in inventory, workers will be laid off to reduce the inventory position. Despite the obvious faults, the majority of our manufacturing firms have these problems. The dynamic behavior of such a firm (as here illustrated by simulation results of an Industrial Dynamics model) has the appearance of Figure 8, with wide swings in sales, inventories, employment, order backlog, and correspondingly in profitability. The potential for a well-designed management control system in such a firm is enormous.

The traditional approach (some may prefer calling it the "modern approach") to the design of a control system for such an organization will recognize that: (1) better information on sales is necessary; (2) such information should properly be smoothed to eliminate possibilities of factory response to chance order-rate variations; (3) inventories should be periodically (perhaps even continuously) checked, and reorders generated when needed to bring stocks into line with target inventories; (4) order backlogs should not be allowed to drift too far from the normal levels; and (5) work force should be adjusted to meet the desired production rate that stems from consideration of current sales volume and the manufacturing backlog situation. Using our earlier company model, we can readily build into the model a management control system that incorporates all these features. The modeled company would then be a leader in its use of management control techniques. And, as Figure 9 illustrates, the company would have benefited by this approach. With the new control systems installed, fluctuations in the business have in general been reduced in magnitude as well as periodicity. Yet the basic dynamic pattern observed in the earlier diagram is still present— periodic fluctuations in sales, larger ones in inventories, and corresponding

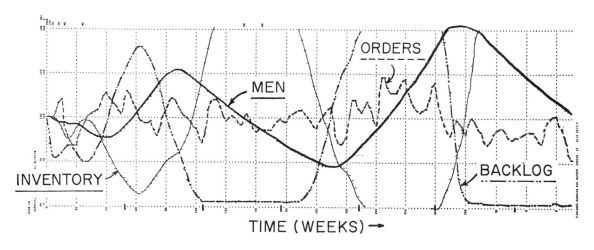

Figure 8.   Management by Crisis

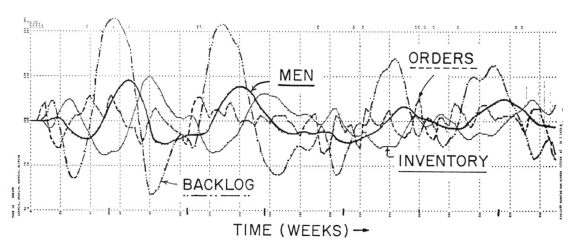

Figure 9.   Effects of Management Control Systems.

variations in production rate and work force. The latter situation is similar in character to that which we encountered at the Sprague Electric Company, at the beginning of our Industrial Dynamics study program with them several years ago.

Let us briefly review their case. The Sprague Electric Company is a major producer of electrical components, with an annual sales volume of approximately 75 million dollars. The particular product line which was selected for Industrial Dynamics research is a relatively mature industrial component, developed by Sprague several years ago and now past its market introduction and major growth phases. The principal customers of the product are manufacturers of military and high-grade consumer electronic systems. The industry competition is not price-based, but is rather dependent on product reliability and delivery time.

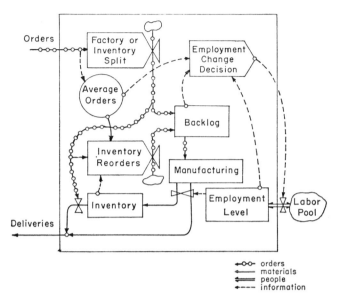

Figure 10. The Manufacturer's Organization Structure

The work structure of the company, including its inventory and manufacturing control aspects, is diagrammed in Figure 10. Orders arrive from the customers, and a determination is made as to whether or not they can be filled from existing inventories. Orders for those catalogue items not ordinarily stocked, or for those which are currently out of stock, enter into the backlog of manufacturing orders. The customer orders for which inventory is in stock are processed and shipped from inventory.

The inventory control system of the company attempts to maintain a proper inventory position for the product line. Target inventories are adjusted to take into account average sales, and inventory reorders are generated to reflect the shipping rate from inventory and the desired inventory corrections. The orders for inventory replacements enter into the manufacturing backlog.

Production rate in the company is determined by the level of employment, with manufacturing output being sent to the customers or to inventory in reflection of the relative production order backlogs. Control of both backlog size and employment level is attempted by means of the employment change decision of the company.

As the curves of Figure 9 demonstrated, inventory, backlog, and employment all had sizable fluctuations, despite the existing controls in these areas. They seem to reflect, with some amplification, the variability in incoming orders. Given this situation of fluctuating sales, the traditional management control designer would either express satisfaction with the system performance or perhaps seek additional improvement by parameter adjustment. Neither approach would get at the source of the difficulties, and this source is not the fluctuations in incoming customer orders.

To determine the real system problem, let us examine our next diagram. Here we have duplicated the manufacturer's organization of Figure 10 and

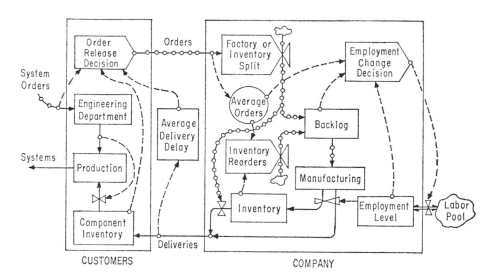

Figure 11.   Company – Customers System

added a representation of the customer sector of the industry. The customers receive orders for military and commercial electronic systems. These are processed through the engineering departments, resulting in requirements for components. Customer orders for components are prepared and released as demanded by the delivery lead time of the component manufacturers. Delivered components enter into the system manufacturers' component inventories and are used up during production of the systems.

Having added this sector to our diagram, we now discover the presence of another feedback loop in the total company-customer system: changes in the company delivery delay will affect the customer release rate of new orders, which in turn will influence the company delivery delay. This loop amplifies the system problems of the company, being able to transform slight variations in system orders into sustained oscillations in company order rate, producing related fluctuations in company inventories, backlog, employment, and profits.

Let us follow through a possible dynamic sequence that will illustrate the full system interactions. If, for any reason, system orders received by the customers temporarily increase, the customers will soon pass this along to the component supplier as an order increase. Since, even under ordinary circumstances, weekly fluctuations in order rate to the component manufacturer are sizable, some time will elapse before this order rate change is noticed. In the meantime, the component manufacturer's inventory will be somewhat reduced, and the order backlog will be increased. Both of these changes tend to increase the delivery delay. The smaller inventory allows fewer incoming orders to be filled immediately; the larger backlog causes a longer delay for the now increased fraction of orders that must await manufacture. As the customers become aware of the longer lead time, they begin to order further ahead, thus maintaining a higher order rate and accentuating the previous trend in sales.

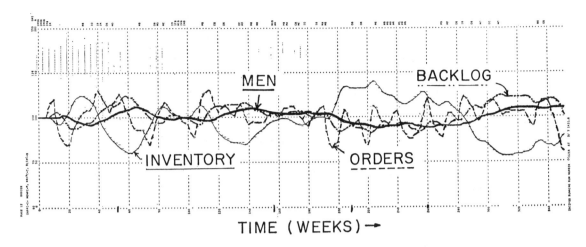

TIME (WEEKS) →

Figure 12. Effects of Industrial Dynamics Policies.

Eventually, the component manufacturer notes the higher sales, larger backlog, and lower inventory, and begins hiring to increase his factory employment. The employment level is set higher than that needed to handle the current customer order rate, so that backlog and inventory can be brought into line. As the increased work force has its gradual effect on inventory and backlog, the changes tend to reduce the delivery time. The information is gradually fed back to the customers, lowering the order rate even below the initial value. This set of system interactions can produce order rate fluctuations unrelated to the basic demand pattern for the customer products.

To dampen the fluctuations in customer order rate, the component manufacturer must control not inventory or backlog or employment, but rather he must stabilize the factory lead time for deliveries. This can readily be accomplished once the nature of the need is recognized. System behavior can also be improved to a great extent when the component manufacturer becomes aware that his inventory control system does not really control inventory, but it does contribute to production overshoots of any change in orders received.

The details of the Sprague case, the model for its study, and the new policies now being implemented at Sprague are discussed fully in Chapters 17 and 18 of *Industrial Dynamics*. It is sufficient for our purposes to show the effects of the new policies applied to the same situation shown earlier in Figure 9. The curves shown on the next graph demonstrate a higher degree of stability achieved in all variables except inventory, which is now being used to absorb random changes in sales. In particular, the employment swings have been dampened significantly. The simulation results forecast significant benefits to the company deriving from the application of this new approach to management policy design. Our experiences during the past year of system usage at Sprague seem to support the initial hypotheses, and the product line is currently benefiting from higher productivity, improved employment stability, higher and smoother sales, and lower inventories.

Systems Creating New Management Problems

The two control system areas discussed above were intended to demonstrate that many management control systems are designed in a manner that makes them inadequate to cope with the underlying problems. In each example, however, certain aspects of the systems were described which actually aggravated the existing problems. Our discussion of research and development project control indicated that government contracting policies often create resulting behavior that is contrary to the government's own interests. In the Sprague case, the inventory control system amplified sales changes to create wider swings in production and employment than actually existed in orders received from the customers. Other examples can be presented which have similar effects: the attempt to achieve management control leads to situations in which initial difficulties are amplified or significant new problems are created.

Problems of Logistics Control

One apparent instance of this type occurs in the Air Force Hi-Value Logistic System. This inventory control system was developed over a long period of time at great government expense by some of the nation's most sophisticated control system designers. The Hi-Value System is intended to provide conservative initial procurement and meticulous individual item management during the complete logistic cycle of all high-cost Air Force material. Yet an Industrial Dynamics study of this system by a member of the M.I.T. Executive Development Program concluded that the system behavior can result in periodic overstatement of requirements, excess procurement and/or unnecessary repair of material, followed by reactions at the opposite extreme.[3] These fluctuations produce undesirable oscillations in the repair and procurement work loads and in the required manpower at Air Force installations, supply and repair depots. The study recommended changes in policy and information usage that tend to stabilize the procurement system behavior.

Quality Control Systems

A commonly utilized management control system has as its purpose the control of manufacturing output quality. The feedback system apparent to the designers of such quality control systems is pictured in Figure 13. Component parts are produced by a process that has a certain expected quality or reliability characteristic. The parts are inspected for flaws and rejects discarded or reworked. Statistically-designed control charts determine when the production process is out of control, and reports are fed back to production to correct the problem sources.

The effectiveness of such quality control systems becomes questionable when we view the performance curves generated by a typical system. Figure 14 plots

---

[3] Max K. Kennedy, "An Analysis of the Air Force Hi-Valu Logistic System; An Industrial Dynamics Study" (unpublished S.M. thesis, M.I.T. School of Industrial Management, 1962).

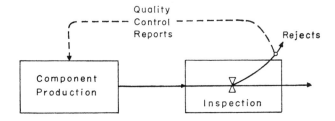

Figure 13. Theoretical Quality Control System

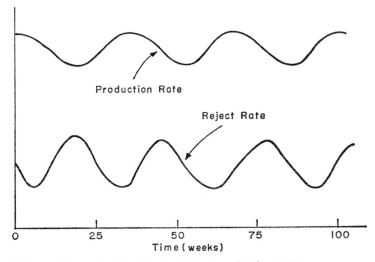

Figure 14.   Quality Control System Performance

component production rate and inspection reject rate over a period of two years. Wide periodic swings in reject rate produce violations of the control system tolerance limits which cause machine adjustments in production and temporarily lower production rates. But what causes the oscillations in the reject rate? Its periodic nature suggests seasonal fluctuations in production quality, often strangely encountered in many manufacturing plants. The manager has almost no way of checking the validity of such an assumption. Therefore, since the explanation seems reasonable, it would probably be accepted under most circumstances.

This situation illustrates one of the key problems in quality control—the lack of an objective confirming source of information. We are in a more favorable position to understand the phenomenon, however, since the results were produced by a computer simulation. The surprising fact is that the actual production quality was held constant, without even random variations, throughout the two years of the run. This means that the oscillations of reject rate and production shown in Figure 14 are not responses to outside changes, but rather are internally created by the behavioral system.

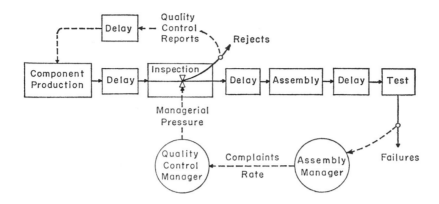

Figure 15.   More Complete Representation of Quality Control System

Let us examine a more complete picture of the total factory system, as shown in the next diagram. Components are produced, then inspected, rejects being discarded. The accepted components are forwarded to an assembly operation, where they enter into the manufacture of complete units. In an electronics plant, for example, the component production and inspection might correspond to a grid manufacturing operation, with the assembly operation putting together complete electronic tubes. When the tube is put through a life test, tube failure and the source of failure are far more obvious than are the grid imperfections during the component inspection. Should too many imperfections get through component inspection, eventual tube failure rate will produce complaints by the assembly manager to the quality control manager. As these complaints continue to build, the quality control manager puts pressure on his inspectors to be more careful and detect more of the poor grids. In response to this pressure, the inspectors reject far more grids. Without an objective measure of grid quality, the reject rate tends to be a function of subjective standards and inspection care. Under pressure from the manager, the inspectors will reject any grid which seems at all dubious, including many which are actually of acceptable quality. As the rejects rise, fewer poor grids enter the assembly process, thus causing fewer tube failures in test. The assembly manager's complaints drop off and, in fact, soon switch to a concern for getting more grids for his assembly operation. Without pressure from the quality control manager and with counterpressure to get more grids to the assembly operation, the grid inspectors tend to slacken gradually their care and their reject standards. Eventually, the number of rejectable grids getting into the tube assembly creates the problem of tube failures again, and the cycle repeats. Given normal delays in such a process, the entire cycle takes on a seasonal appearance. Thus, a system intended to assure control of product quality actually creates serious fluctuations of rejects, component production, and tube failures, all attributed to unknown factors "out of our control".

The consequences of such a situation are even more serious when the inspection output is distributed to eventual customers through the normal multi-stage

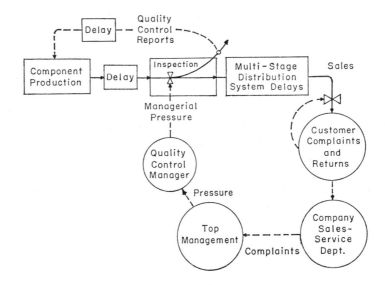

Figure 16. Total Quality Control System

distribution system. In this case the customer complaints and store returns also affect sales. These influences combine after a long delay to produce significant top management pressure on the quality control manager in reflection of a situation which existed many months before. In both Figures 15 and 16, the quality control manager's response is a key to system behavior. Here the manager of the formal quality control system is himself the most important aspect of the total system of quality and production control.

IV. Some Principles of Management Control System Design

The examples discussed represent a wide range of management control systems. Study of these applications produces some general principles of management control system design.

A. The key to effective control often lies outside the boundaries of *conventional* operational control systems; in fact, it is sometimes outside the *formal* boundaries of the company organization.

Too many organizations give up altogether too soon the battle for mastering a management problem caused by factors apparently "out of our control". Government changes in project funding of research and development, the cyclic swings in customer orders in the production-inventory case, seasonal variations of product reject rate in the quality control problem are all examples of such factors. Yet in each case successful control system management rests within the access of company policy.

Project success in R and D is strongly influenced by company integrity and risk-taking. Yet the customer can affect these results by redesigning his own policies to achieve more desirable company behavior. Again, in the Sprague case the system requiring control included the ordering decisions of the customer, certainly not part of Sprague's formal organization. But the basis for system control exists in the stabilization of the input to the customer decision, the component delivery delay. And the key to quality control involves recognition of the total system of product flow to assembly (or to customers) and the resulting feedback of complaints and pressures.

The boundaries of a management control system design study must not be drawn to conform with organizational structure merely because of that structure. System boundaries cannot ignore vital feedback channels for information and action if the system is to be effective.

B. The proper design of management control systems often requires inclusion of the effects of intangibles; in particular, the role of decision makers who are part of the total system of control must be treated carefully.

Control system designers who are working with computers often have as their end product a computer model for calculating (or searching for) an optimal control decision. Yet while being willing to model a decision for a machine, they seem unwilling to include in their studies any models of man—of human decision-making within the control loops. Our initial example emphasized that a properly designed R and D control system should be based on models of engineer and manager decision-making in both the company and customer organizations. In the production-inventory control case, the modeling of aggregate customer decision-makers is a vital part of the system. Finally, we observed that the decision-making and responses of both managers and inspectors are crucial aspects of the quality control case.

These illustrations emphasize the usual failure to recognize and cope with the nature of human response in organizations. The decision-makers, single or aggregated—their motivations, attitudes, pressures, models of response—must be included in management control system design. *The man (and manager) is part of the system of control, and management control system design must be viewed as a form of man-machine system design.*

C. A true understanding of total system basis and system behavior can permit effective design of both operational control systems and top management policy, without differences in philosophy or methodology of approach. In fact, most significant control system applications inherently require supra-functional or multi-departmental organization.

In the Sprague case, for example, successful control involved consideration of such aspects as customer service (marketing), inventory and production rate (manufacturing), and employment policies (personnel). Thus what often gets treated as a middle-management problem becomes resolvable only at the top policy-making level of the firm. The important elements in research and development tend not to be middle-management concerns for schedules, but rather top management policy affecting investment planning, customer relations, and company-wide attitudes. Management control systems can therefore seek to achieve the major goals of the organization as a whole, and not just the sub-optimizing aims of individual segments. A great present hazard, in fact, is the common planning and programming of control systems at the wrong level of the company, by people who lack total system perspectives and the authority to achieve broad system integration.

The Industrial Dynamics program has demonstrated the possibilities of examining and treating system problems of great variety and scope of complexity. We have dealt with many situations in which stabilization was needed and more recently with other cases in which balanced growth was the objective of the policy design efforts. The potential advantages to companies who pioneer in this work are significant and may become the basis of our future industrial competition. In this regard, it seems fitting to close with the implied advice of the Japanese scholar who said: "When your opponent is at the point of striking you, let your mind be fixed on his sword and you are no longer free to master your own movements, for you are then controlled by him."[4]

---

[4] Takawan, as quoted by Charles H. Townes, "Useful Knowledge", *Technology Review*, January, 1963, p. 36.

24
Design of Resource Control
and Marketing Policies

Carl V. Swanson

Introduction

The marketing policies and resource controls of a firm can have more impact on its growth than market demand. In the same market, one set of resource control and marketing policies can produce smooth, rapid growth; another set can yield slow, fluctuating growth; a third can result in stagnation; and a fourth can produce decay. Management is initially interested in analyzing how its resource control and marketing policies are affecting growth. In addition, management needs to design marketing and resource control policies that give rapid, profitable growth. The purpose of this paper is to illustrate, by an application to gas transmission companies, the use of industrial dynamics for the analysis and design of resource control and marketing policies.

Industrial dynamics is a body of knowledge, a theory of representation, and a methodology for analyzing and designing complex feedback systems and their dynamic behavior.[1] It has been used to develop a theory of how a firm's policies control its growth,[2] which in turn has been applied to the design of resource and marketing management policies in a trucking company.[3]

The Problem

Long distance gas transmission companies perform a transportation service. They buy natural gas through long-term contracts from gas producers and then transport the gas to consumer areas. There it is sold, also largely through long-term contracts, to large users of gas such as electric power companies, large manufacturing companies, and gas distribution companies. Since the gas industry is capital intensive, both the customers and the transmission companies want assurance of a long-term supply of gas in order to amortize their investments.

[1] See Forrester [1] and [2] for background material on industrial dynamics.

[2] For the more recent theoretical work, see Forrester [3] and Swanson [8].

This paper is adapted from an earlier paper delivered to the American Gas Association's Transmission Conference in New Orleans on May 26, 1969. It originally appeared in the *Industrial Management Review* (currently published as the *Sloan Management Review*) 10, no. 3 (Spring 1969), pp. 61–76. (© 1969 by the Industrial Management Review Association; all rights reserved.) The author thanks Mr. Henry I. Meyer, at whose invitation this paper was written, and Mr. Glen Sanders, both of Penzoil United, Inc., for their support and encouragement, and the time they spent describing the gas transmission business. The author also wishes to thank Dr. Dennis L. Meadows for his considerable help with the earlier version of this paper.

Gas transmission companies are utilities regulated by the Federal Power Commission. In its role as a protector of consumer interests, the Federal Power Commission is also concerned that gas transmission companies have a long-term supply of gas. The commonly used measure of the long-term supply of gas is the "reserve life index." The reserve life index (RLI) is the ratio of the transmission company's proven gas reserves to its sales in the previous year. Stated another way, it is the number of years that the company's proven reserves will last at the last year's sales rate.

The difficulties that many gas transmission companies face are fluctuations in the reserve life index, in sales, and in gas reserves acquisition. The cycle time of these fluctuations ranges from eight to 15 years. The fluctuations are accompanied by slow growth. During some periods, a company may find that its RLI is high (perhaps 16), which means that it has contracted for more gas reserves than it needs for its current sales. Since many gas purchase contracts stipulate a minimum annual payment whether or not gas is taken from the ground, the transmission company with a high RLI finds itself paying for more gas than it is prepared to sell. As a result, the company may experience serious cash flow problems as it builds up assets of prepaid gas. During such periods, the transmission company stops buying gas reserves, the resource upon which its long-term growth depends, and may even sell some of its reserves to other transmission companies. When faced with surplus gas reserves, the company markets gas aggressively, perhaps by giving price concessions or other favorable terms to customers. A few years later, however, the company may find itself with a low RLI (eight is a common low reserve life index). With such a reserve position, the Federal Power Commission will prevent sales to new customers, and some expiring contracts may not be renewed. Thus, gas deliveries and revenues may decrease even though the demand for gas may be rising. At such times, the firm regrets not having acquired gas reserves earlier as it sees its sales growth halted by the lack of gas reserves.

One hypothesis that is often used to explain fluctuations in the reserve life index, in sales, and in the rate of gas reserves acquisition, is that these fluctuations are merely a normal and expected response to the random nature of gas field discoveries. The implication of this argument is that management should passively accept the fluctuations and lost sales opportunities since they are caused by unmanageable, random events. We propose an alternative explanation by demonstrating that typical policies by which transmission companies acquire gas reserves and sell gas to customers interact to create the fluctuations and to slow the growth of the firm.

The first step in any industrial dynamics study is to identify the dynamic behavior of interest and then to hypothesize the interactions that create the behavior. This is the problem definition stage. The second step is to represent in a computer simulation model the essential elements of the interactions which create the behavior under study. The model is then used to understand the cause of the existing behavior and to test new policy design in an effort to improve behavior. Underlying these steps, and fundamental to all industrial dynamics applications, is an understanding of how feedback processes create dynamic behavior. The final step is implementation of the new policy design.

The initial hypothesis of the causal behavior is fundamental to a successful study. Theory of feedback processes, as found in the interaction between a firm and its market, reveals that the interaction of the control of resources and marketing policies can produce the kind of fluctuations and the retarded growth observed in some gas transmission companies.[4] Thus, we would hypothesize that the interaction of the gas reserves acquisition policy and the gas marketing policies does produce the slow growth and fluctuations.

---

[4] See Swanson [8]

The Model

The computer simulation model is designed with two decision points: the acquisition of gas reserves and the marketing of new long-term gas sales contracts. The actual gas reserve acquisition rate depends on the rate at which management desires to acquire gas reserves and on the availability of reserves from producers. Reasonably priced gas reserves appear to become available randomly, as new gas fields are discovered. In the model, a randomly generated time series represents the availability of reserves. This time series is multiplied by the desired reserve acquisition rate to calculate the actual gas reserve acquisition rate. When the number representing gas reserve availability is one, the company acquires gas reserves at its desired rate. When the number is greater than one, the price for gas reserves is low, and the actual rate of acquisition is greater than would normally be desired. When the number representing reserves availability is less than one, the actual gas reserves acquisition rate is lower than desired, either because the price is too high or because there are too few gas reserves available. The time series of gas reserve availability in the model ranges between 0.4 and 2.0.

The company determines its gas acquisition rate by (1) seeking to replace gas delivered to customers, (2) attempting to increase reserves five per cent per year in order to follow the expected rate of growth in demand, and (3) adjusting its acquisition of reserves to bring the amount of reserves on hand to a level equal to 12 times last year's sales within two years. Thus, the firm controls the acquisition of reserves in an attempt to maintain a RLI of 12.

The model assumes a delay of one year between the decision to acquire new reserves and addition of the reserves to the pool of reserves from which gas can be shipped. The delay represents the average time it takes to negotiate purchase contracts and to link the new gas fields to the pipeline.

The second decision point concerns the marketing of gas sales contracts. The rate at which new gas sales contracts are made is a function of both demand and the level of corporate gas reserves. Normal demand for new contracts at any time is assumed in this model to be equal to the sum of contract expirations and a five per cent annual growth in demand for gas. The actual rate of signing new sales contracts, however, will depend on the ratio of gas reserves to last year's sales (i.e., the reserve life index). Whenever the RLI is at its normal value of 12, 80 per cent of the normal demand will result in new contracts. Whenever the RLI falls as low as 10, government pressures will prevent the company from signing any additional contracts. When the reserve life index rises to around 15, a shortage of cash due to prepayments for gas reserves generates sufficient pressure that sales of new contracts are 50 per cent higher than normal as concessions are made to sell gas. After a contract has been negotiated, it takes one year to extend the transmission system to the customer. The average life of a contract is assumed to be 10 years.

Figure 1 presents a flow diagram of the model. The rectangles in the figure represent important system stocks: gas reserves and sales contracts. The dashed lines are flows of information; solid lines represent flows of reserves and orders. The decision points in the system are shown by valves.[5]

The dynamic behavior of any system is caused principally by its feedback loop structure. A feedback loop is a closed circle of causal linkages. There are three feedback

---

[5] The parameter values in the model are approximations. Although they may not be accurate for all companies, such errors would not alter the fact that managerial policies can cause fluctuations and stagnation.

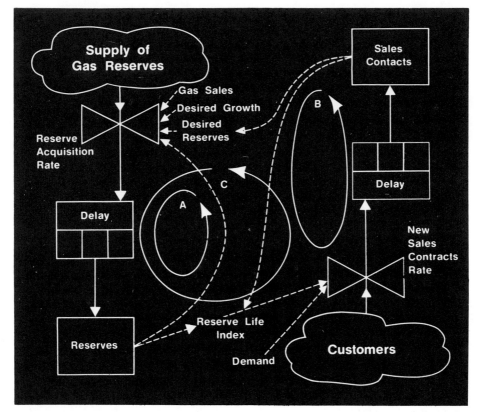

1 Flow Diagram of the Model

loops in the model, labeled A, B, and C in Figure 1. Loop A is composed of two variables: the acquisition rate of gas reserves and the stock of gas reserves. This feedback loop attempts to keep the gas reserves near the desired level of 12 times the average sales rate of the previous year. Whenever gas reserves exceed 12 times last year's sales, loop A acts to reduce the acquisition of gas reserves. Whenever gas reserves fall below 12 times last year's sales, it increases the acquisition of gas reserves, which raises the ratio of reserves to last year's sales.

Feedback loop B connects the reserve life index, the stock of sales contracts, and the rate of making new sales contracts. Loop B attempts to control sales contracts in such a fashion that the reserve life index is 12. If sales contracts rise rapidly, forcing the reserve life index below 12, the signing of new contracts is stopped. The normal expiration of contracts reduces the sales of gas, which boosts the RLI. On the other hand, an increase in the reserve life index causes an increase in the marketing of new sales contracts, which increases the sales of gas and lowers the RLI.

Feedback loop C connects the stock of sales contracts, the reserve acquisition rate, the actual reserves, the reserve life index, and the marketing of new sales contracts. Loop C is responsible for growth. Whenever actual reserves are smaller than desired reserves, the rate of acquisition is increased, if reserves are available. The RLI increases as gas reserves are added. A higher index spurs the search for new customers and ultimately results in new sales contracts. The growth in sales contracts increases the amount of gas reserves desired, which results in the need for additional reserves to maintain the growth. Loop C will produce growth only if the investment and sales decisions are properly integrated. When they are not, these policies can produce stagnation even in the face of growing demand.

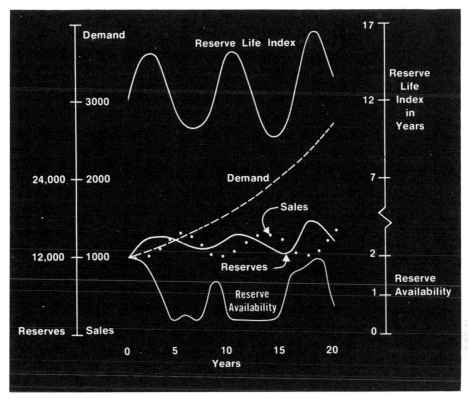

2   Current Policies

Analysis of Current Policies

Having completed a model that represents the current operating policies of the firm, the next step is to simulate the policies by running the model on a computer (see Appendix A). Figure 2 presents the plotted output of the computer simulation of the model just described. It shows the dynamic behavior of the firm over a period of 20 years resulting from the current gas reserve acquisition and marketing policies described above. The variables plotted in the figure are the reserve life index, demand, the annual rate of selling gas as determined by the sales contracts (sales), and the stock of reserves. The scales for demand, sales, and reserves are shown at the left of the plot and the scale for the reserve life index is to the right. The other variable plotted is reserve availability, which shows the ease with which the company can acquire new gas reserves. This scale is also to the right of the plot.

Two aspects of the behavior of the company are significant. First, sales, reserves, and the reserve life index all fluctuate. The fluctuations peak about every eight years. Second, sales stagnate in the face of rising demand. After 20 years, sales have grown only 32.5 per cent while demand grew 171 per cent. The demand curve in Figure 2 represents the sales which the company could have achieved had it grown five per cent per year, the normal growth in demand assumed in this model. However, this curve shows only what sales might have been. It does not include the customers who are currently willing to buy gas. It is assumed that these customers find other suppliers if the modeled firm does not meet their needs. In this model, the actual demand which the gas transmission company can exploit at any time is five per cent greater than its current sales contracts.

Let us now examine the causes of this behavior. Initially, at time zero, the gas reserves are 12 times sales, and reserves are readily available from producers. The firm acquires additional reserves until, by year two, the reserve life index has increased to 15. At that point, operating through feedback loop A, the gas reserves acquisition policy calls for a halt in the buying of additional reserves, even though reserves are still readily available. A high RLI creates an outflow of cash to pay for gas which is not sold. This cash shortage causes the company to stop buying gas.

Meanwhile, as the reserve life index increases, the marketing of new sales contracts picks up from year two to year five, as feedback loop B tries to lower the reserve life index. By year four, the cessation of gas purchases and the increased marketing of sales contracts achieve the desired result, an RLI of 12. But these activities go too far, because neither the gas reserve acquisition policy nor the marketing policy takes account of the one-year delay between purchasing gas reserves and connecting them to the company's supply or the one-year delay in extending a transmission pipeline to a new customer. At the same time that the reserve life index overshoots, available reserves are no longer plentiful, and the RLI falls to 10. Marketing activity ceases and total sales contracts decline as expired contracts are not renewed. Earlier sales gains are lost, contributing to long-run stagnation. As sales decrease, the reserve life index begins to increase slowly. Suddenly, reserves again become available, around year eight, and the cycle just described begins anew. Some reserves are purchased, but not many, since sales are still low and it takes only a small increase in reserves to bring the reserve life index up to 12. However, more reserves than are immediately needed are added and a sales campaign is started at about the time the reserves availability drops. The result is a drastic fall in the reserve life index and a subsequent decrease in sales contracts. Thus, the policies continue the pattern of fluctuation and stagnation.

Stagnation sets in because every time reserves are available, the firm is unwilling to acquire a sufficient amount to keep up with demand when reserves become scarce. Then. when reserves are scarce, the firm is obliged to reduce sales. Neither reserves nor sales grow as rapidly as possible.

From the simulation run shown in Figure 2, it is not clear whether the fluctuations are caused by managerial policy or by the random availability of gas reserves. To test whether managerial policy can produce fluctuation, we assumed a constant availability of gas reserves, thus eliminating random availability as a cause of fluctuation. Figure 3 is the output of a simulation run identical to that of Figure 2 except that the gas reserve availability is constant at a normal availability of one. A fluctuation with about a nine-year cycle is revealed. The relevant measure of this tendency to fluctuate is called "damping." Damping is the fraction change in adjacent peaks (or valleys) of a cycle. In Figure 3, the height of the peaks in the reserve life index decreases by 50 per cent from cycle to cycle. This is low damping, which indicates that the managerial control policies make a significant contribution to the fluctuations observed in Figure 2.

Design of New Policies

The goals of policy design in this case are to reduce fluctuations and to speed the growth of the gas transmission company. To attain these goals, new policies must respond gracefully and effectively to the random variations in gas reserves availability. Typical industrial dynamics studies involve extensive investigation of alternative policies. In this example, we examine only one alternative to the policies previously described. Four changes are made in the information flow and decision systems to create the new policies.

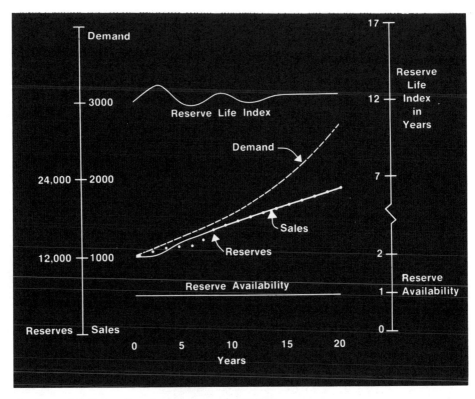

3   Current Policies: Constant Reserves Availability

1   In the reserve acquisition policy, the desired reserve life index is increased by 25 per cent, from 12 to 15.

2   The amount of reserves purchased but not yet putting gas into the system is accounted for in the reserves acquisition policy.

3   Sales of new long-term contracts are limited to normal demand. No special sales efforts or price concessions will be made to increase sales of long-term contracts when reserve life index is high.

4   A new short-term, flexible market for gas is created. Customers in this market will accept or relinquish gas with one-year's notice. It is assumed that this market is no more than 15 per cent of the long-term sales. The short-term market should ease cash flow problems when reserves begin to increase relative to sales.

These four changes were incorporated into the computer simulation model (see Appendix B). Figure 4 shows the improved behavior resulting from these changes. With the new policies, long-term sales have increased 65 per cent, compared to 35 per cent under the current (old) policies. If short-term sales are also included, the total sales increase is 88 per cent. The increase in reserves is even more dramatic. Under the old policies, reserves grew 23 per cent in 20 years; with the new policies, they have grown 96 per cent. In addition, the new policies have reduced the fluctuations in sales and reserves. Surprisingly, the reserve life index, when calculated with long-term sales contracts only, has a peak of 15 with the new policies, compared to a peak of 16.5 under the old policies. Even without inclusion of the short-term market, the new policies reduce fluctuations and the peaks in the reserve life index. When the short-term

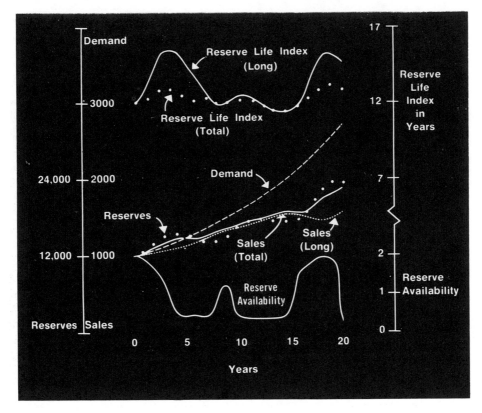

4   New Policies

market is included in the calculation, the RLI fluctuates within a narrow range, 11.0 to 13.5.

The necessity for a quantitative approach to the design of management policy is illustrated by the counter-intuitive response of the system to the new policies. Even while raising the level of desired reserves, the new policies resulted in lower peaks of the RLI. The fact that these lower peaks occurred without inclusion of the short-term, flexible market indicates that although this market does contribute significantly to a reduction in fluctuations, it is not necessary for such a reduction. The other counter-intuitive response of the system is that restricting the rate at which new contracts may be negotiated helped to create a faster rate of growth of long-term sales contracts.

Intuition would seldom indicate that this new policy set would improve behavior. Management would probably have rejected the new policies in the belief that peaks in reserves would be higher and growth slower. Yet the mathematical simulation model and the subsequent analysis show the opposite to be true. The policies yield smaller peaks of reserves and faster growth.

Decreased fluctuations and increased growth result from three changes. First, the decision to acquire additional reserves takes account of gas reserves acquired but not yet producing. Thus, the purchase of gas reserves does not overreact to a low condition and turn it into a high reserve state. Second, the firm does not attempt to increase sales contracts at a rate faster than normal demand. That is, when reserves are ample, the firm does not make concessions in order to get extra business, except on short-term contracts. Thus, by limiting the increase in long-term sales when the re-

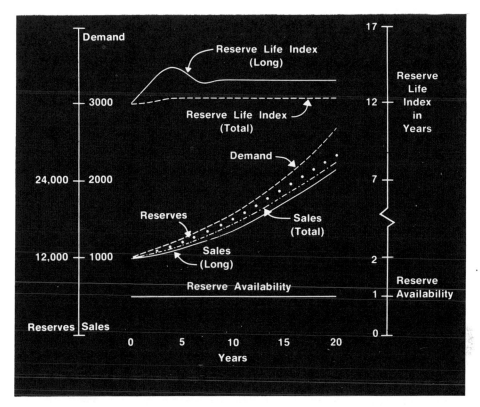

5 New Policies: Constant Reserves Availability

serve life index is high, the firm does not find itself in a position of having to diminish long-term sales when reserves begin to run out. Third, under the new policies, desired reserves are 15 years of the average long-term sales: the desired reserve life index is 15. Thus, when reserves are available, they are stockpiled against years of scarce reserves, and growth can continue even when reserves are difficult to acquire. Also, when the RLI begins to drop below 15, there is pressure to add to reserves. Consequently, even when gas reserves are scarce, reserves are acquired to replace gas sold. In this way, long-term gas contracts can be renewed and sales of gas do not decline. To test the stability of the new policies and compare them with the current policies, a simulation run was made with the new policies, but with a constant availability of gas reserves. The plotted output of this simulation run is shown in Figure 5.

In the presence of an identical pattern of reserves availability (Figures 2 and 4), the greater stability of operations shown in Figure 4 indicates that the new policies are themselves more stable than the current policies. It also illustrates the point that managerial policies can foster fluctuations. To confirm this assertion, Figure 5 can be compared with Figure 3. In both cases, the reserves availability is constant at one. The fraction height reduction from peak to peak in the reserve life index is 95 per cent in Figure 5, compared with 50 per cent in Figure 3. The greater damping in Figure 5 confirms the much greater stability of the new policies.

Conclusions

We have illustrated the use of industrial dynamics for the design of gas reserves acquisition and marketing policies. This brief example is not a complete policy analysis and design. Analysis of the reserve cycle for purposes of new policy design would include study of other policy alternatives, more precise evaluation of the contribution to improvement of each change, and more careful attention to specifying the structure and parameter values of the model. Measures of profitability with which to judge alternative policies should be included. A thorough risk analysis would also be necessary to evaluate the effectiveness of the policies under a wide range of market conditions. The risk analysis should insure that the policies will operate effectively in the face of error, bias, and delay in information flow and decision making.

A complete study can be performed at a reasonable cost. The study reported here required less than three man-weeks of effort. Two days were needed to program and debug the model, and each computer run took 12 seconds on an IBM 7094.

The inadvertent fostering of fluctuations and growth retardation is a common problem. For example, in some companies, an unwillingness or inability to acquire productive capacity results in a long delivery delay that keeps the order rate equal to the production capacity of the firm but far below demand. Unfortunately, it is too easy to interpret the equality of order rate and production capacity as proof of the wisdom of the firm's planning rather than as the poor exploitation of demand which it may be. A bank that is unwilling to add loan officers may find itself growing slowly as its loan officers become so busy handling current business that they lack the time to promote the new business necessary for growth. Finally, in the case of a trucking company, the scheduling of trucks between terminals created fluctuations in loads upon different terminals. An industrial dynamics study was undertaken to evaluate the existing managerial policies and to test changes in those policies.[6] The adoption of the new policies developed through the study eliminated the fluctuations.

As we have demonstrated in the case of gas transmission companies, industrial dynamics can be used for the effective analysis and design of resource control and marketing policies.

---

[6] See Wright [9].

Appendix A

Current (Old) Policies — DYNAMO Simulation Model of Gas Reserves Acquisition*

```
*        GAS RESERVE ACQUISITION MODEL
NOTE
NOTE     *******  GAS RESERVE SECTOR   *******
NOTE
L   RES.K=RES.J+(DT)(RESD.JK-SALES.JK)         GAS RESERVES
N   RES=NRES
C   NRES=12000    INITIAL GAS RESERVES
R   RESD.KL=DELAY3(RESA.JK,TDR)     GAS RESERVE DEVELOPMENT RATE
C   TDR=1  YEAR       TIME TO DEVELOP GAS RESERVES FOR PRODUCTION
R   SALES.KL=CONT.K    SALES RATE
NOTE
NOTE     *******  GAS RESERVES ACQUISITION POLICY  *******
NOTE
R   RESA.KL=CLIP(TRESA.K,DRESA.K,DRESA.K,0)  GAS RESERVE ACQUISITION RATE
A   TRESA.K=(DRESA.K)(TEST1.K)   TRIAL RESERVE ACQUISITION RATE
A   DRESA.K=NRESA.K+RESADJ.K   DESIRED RESERVE ACQUISITION RATE
A   NRESA.K=ASALES.K+(DGRES)(RES.K)   NORMAL RESERVES ACQUISITION RATE
C   DGRES=.05
A   RESADJ.K=(DRES.K-RES.K)(FAR.K)    RESERVES ADJUSTMENT RATE
A   DRES.K=(DRLI)(ASALES.K)    DESIRED RESERVES
C   DRLI=12  YEARS    DESIRED RESERVE LIFE INDEX
L   ASALES.K=ASALES.J+(DT)(1/TAS)(SALES.JK-ASALES.J)  AVERAGE SALES RATE
N   ASALES=SALES
C   TAS=1  YEARS     TIME TO AVERAGE SALES
NOTE
NOTE     *******  SALES CONTRACTS  *******
NOTE
L   CONT.K=CONT.J+(DT)(CONTC.JK-CONTEX.JK)      CONTRACTS BEING SUPPLIED
N   CONT=NCONT
C   NCONT=1000
R   CONTEX.KL=DELAY3(CONTC.JK,ALC)    CONTRACT EXPIRATION RATE
C   ALC=10  YEARS      AVERAGE LIFE OF A CONTRACT
R   CONTC.KL=DELAY3(CONTS.JK,TCC)     CONTRACT CONNECTION RATE
C   TCC=1  YEARS     TIME TO CONNECT A CONTRACT
N   CONTS=CONT/ALC
NOTE
NOTE     *******  GAS CONTRACT SALES  *******
NOTE
R   CONTS.KL=(NDNC.K)(FDC.K)  GAS CONTRACT SALES RATE
A   NDNC.K=(CONT.K)(DGR.K)+ACEX.K NORMAL DEMAND FOR NEW CONTRACTS
A   FDC.K=TABHL(TFDC,RLI.K/FPCRLI,0.9,1.3,0.1)  FRACTION OF DEMAND CONTRACTED
C   TFDC*=0/.8/1.2/1.35/1.5
L   ACEX.K=ACEX.J+(DT)(1/TACEX)(CONTEX.JK-ACEX.J)  AVERAGE CONTRACT EXPIRATIONS
N   ACEX=CONTEX
C   TACEX=1 YEARS    TIME TO AVERAGE CONTRACT EXPIRATIONS
A   RLI.K=RES.K/ASALES.K  RESERVE LIFE INDEX
C   FPCRLI=12  YEARS  FEDERAL POWER COMMISSION RESERVE LIFE INDEX
NOTE
NOTE     *******  EXOGENOUS DEMAND GROWTH  *******
NOTE
A   DGR.K=(NDGR)(TEST2.K)    DEMAND GROWTH RATE
C   NDGR=0.05  FRACTION / YEAR   NORMAL DEMAND GROWTH RATE
NOTE
NOTE     *******  TEST INPUTS  *******
NOTE
```

* See Pugh |7|.

```
A    TEST1.K=1+(Z1)(MAX(LFN1.K,-.6))   TEST INPUT FOR GAS ACQUISITION
C    Z1=1
A    LFN1.K=DELAY3(SN1.K,DN1)
A    SN1.K=SAMPLE(N1.K,STN1,1)
A    N1.K=(RN1)NOISE()
C    RN1=3
C    STN1=1
C    DN1=1
L    CT1.K=CT1.J+(DT)(TEST1.J)
N    CT1=0
A    AT1.K=CT1.K/(TIME.K+.001)
A    TEST2.K=1
NOTE
NOTE       *******  OUTPUT EQUATIONS  *******
L    D.K=D.J+(DT)(ND.JK)  DEMAND POSSIBLE
N    D=NCONT
R    ND.KL=DELAY3(ND1.JK,TCC)  NEW DEMAND
R    ND1.KL=(D.K)(DGR.K)  NEW DEMAND 1
N    ND1=D/ALC  INITIAL NEW DEMAND 1
L    CNCONT.K=CNCONT.J+(DT)(CONTS.JK)  CUMMULATIVE NEW CONTRACTS
N    CNCONT=0
NOTE
NOTE       *******  OUTPUT REQUEST  *******
NOTE
PRINT   1)RES,DRES,CNCONT/2)SALES,RESD/3)DRESA,RESA
PRINT   4)CONT,D/5)CONTEX,CONTC/6)RLI,CONTS
PRINT   7)FDC,NDNC
PRINT   8)AT1
PLOT   RES=R(0,48000)/RLI=I(-3,17)/SALES=S,RESA=A,D=2(0,4000)/CONTS=M(0,400)/
X1   FDC=F(-6,2)/TEST1=*(0,8)
SPEC  DT=.1/LENGTH=20/PRTPER=5/PLTPER=.5
RUN   TEST
```

Appendix B

New Policies — DYNAMO Simulation Model of Gas Reserves Acquisition

```
*       GAS RESERVE ACQUISITION MODEL
NOTE
NOTE            ******  NEW POLICIES  ******
NOTE
NOTE
NOTE
NOTE       *******  GAS RESERVE SECTOR  *******
NOTE

L    RES.K=RES.J+(DT)(RESD.JK-SALES.JK)       GAS RESERVES
N    RES=NRES
C    NRES=12000    INITIAL GAS RESERVES
R    RESD.KL=DELAY3(RESA.JK,TDR)    GAS RESERVE DEVELOPMENT RATE
C    TDR=1  YEAR      TIME TO DEVELOP GAS RESERVES FOR PRODUCTION
N    RESA=RESUD/TDR
L    RESUD.K=RESUD.J+(DT)(RESA.JK-RESD.JK)  RESERVES UNDER DEVELOPMENT
N    RESUD=(NRESA)(TDR)    INITIAL RESERVES UNDER DEVELOPMENT
R    SALES.KL=CONT.K    SALES RATE
NOTE
,NOTE      *******  GAS RESERVES ACQUISITION POLICY  *******
NOTE
R    RESA.KL=CLIP(TRESA.K,DRESA.K,DRESA.K,0)  GAS RESERVE ACQUISITION RATE
A    TRESA.K=(DRESA.K)(TEST1.K)  TRIAL RESERVE ACQUISITION RATE
A    DRESA.K=NRESA.K+RESADJ.K  DESIRED RESERVE ACQUISITION RATE
A    NRESA.K=ASALES.K+(DGRES)(RES.K)  NORMAL RESERVES ACQUISITION RATE
C    DGRES=.05
```

```
A   RESADJ.K=(DRES.K-RES.K-RESUD.K)(FAR.K)     RESERVES ADJUSTMENT RATE
A   FAR.K=.5  FRACTION ADJUSTMENT OF RESERVES
A·  DRES.K=(DRLI)(ASALES.K)      DESIRED RESERVES
C   DRLI=15  YEARS   DESIRED RESERVE LIFE INDEX
L   ASALES.K=ASALES.J+(DT)(1/.TAS)(SALES.JK-ASALES.J)  AVERAGE SALES RATE
N   ASALES=SALES
C   TAS=1  YEARS    TIME TO AVERAGE SALES
NOTE
NOTE      ******* SALES CONTRACTS  *******
NOTE
L   CONT.K=CONT.J+(DT)(CONTC.JK-CONTEX.JK)    CONTRACTS BEING SUPPLIED
N   CONT=NCONT
C   NCONT=1000
R   CONTEX.KL=DELAY3(CONTC.JK,ALC)  CONTRACT EXPIRATION RATE
C   ALC=10  YEARS     AVERAGE LIFE OF A CONTRACT
R   CONTC.KL=DELAY3(CONTS.JK,TCC)    CONTRACT CONNECTION RATE
C   TCC=1  YEARS      TIME TO CONNECT A CONTRACT
N   CONTS=CONT/ALC
L   NCBC.K=NCBC.J+(DT)(CONTS.JK-CONTC.JK)  NEW CONTRACTS BEING CONNECTED
N   NCBC=(CONTS)(TCC)
NOTE
NOTE      ******* GAS CONTRACT SALES  *******
NOTE
R   CONTS.KL=(NDNC.K)(FDC.K)  GAS CONTRACT SALES RATE
A   NDNC.K=(CONT.K)(DGR.K)+ACEX.K NORMAL DEMAND FOR NEW CONTRACTS
A   FDC.K=TABHL(TFDC,RLI.K/FPCRLI,0.9,1.3,0.1)  FRACTION OF DEMAND CONTRACTED
C   TFDC*=0/.8/1/1/1
L   ACEX.K=ACEX.J+(DT)(1/TACEX)(CONTEX.JK-ACEX.J)  AVERAGE CONTRACT EXPIRATIONS
N   ACEX=CONTEX
C   TACEX=1 YEARS    TIME TO AVERAGE CONTRACT EXPIRATIONS
A   RLI.K=RES.K/ASALES.K  RESERVE LIFE INDEX
C   FPCRLI=12  YEARS  FEDERAL POWER COMMISSION RESERVE LIFE INDEX
NOTE
NOTE      ******* SHORT TERM SALES ACCOUNTING  *******
NOTE
A   STS.K=MIN(MXSTS.K,ARSTS.K)  SHORT TERM SALES
A   MXSTS.K=(FSTSMX)(ASALES.K)  MAXIMUM SHORT TERM SALES
A   ARSTS.K=MAX(0,(RES.K/FPCRLI)-CONT.K)  AVAILABLE RESERVES FOR SHORT TERM SALES
C   FSTSMX=0.15  FRACTION OF SHORT TERM SALES MAXIMUM
A   TS.K=SALES.JK+STS.K  TOTAL SALES RATE
NOTE
NOTE      ******* EXOGENOUS DEMAND GROWTH  *******
NOTE
A   DGR.K=(NDGR)(TEST2.K)   DEMAND GROWTH RATE
C   NDGR=0.05  FRACTION / YEAR   NORMAL DEMAND GROWTH RATE
NOTE
NOTE      ******* TEST INPUTS  *******
NOTE
A   TEST1.K=1+(Z1)(MAX(LFN1.K,-.6))  TEST INPUT FOR GAS ACQUISITION
C   Z1=1
A   LFN1.K=DELAY3(SN1.K,DN1)
A   SN1.K=SAMPLE(N1.K,STN1,1)
A   N1.K=(RN1)NOISE()
C   RN1=3
C   STN1=1
C   DN1=1
L   CT1.K=CT1.J+(DT)(TEST1.J)
N   CT1=0
A   AT1.K=CT1.K/(TIME.K+.001)
A   TEST2.K=1
NOTE
NOTE      ******* OUTPUT EQUATIONS  *******
L   D.K=D.J+(DT)(ND.JK)  DEMAND POSSIBLE
N   D=NCONT
R   ND.KL=DELAY3(ND1.JK,TCC)  NEW DEMAND
R   ND1.KL=(D.K)(DGR.K)  NEW DEMAND 1
```

```
N    ND1=D/ALC   INITIAL NEW DEMAND 1
A    RLIT.K=RES.K/(ASALES.K+STS.K)   RESERVE LIFE INDEX FOR TOTAL SALES
L    CNCONT.K=CNCONT.J+(DT)(CONTS.JK)   CUMMULATIVE NEW CONTRACTS
N    CNCONT=0
A    FTSST.K=STS.K/CONT.K   FRACTION OF SALES SHORT TERM
L    CFSTS.K=CFSTS.J+(DT)(FTSST.J)   CUMMULATIVE FRACTION OF SHORT TERM SALES
A    AFSST.K=CFSTS.K/(TIME.K+.001)   AVERAGE FRACTION OF SALES ARE SHORT TERM
N    CFSTS=0
NOTE
NOTE       *******   OUTPUT REQUEST   *******
NOTE
PRINT    1)RES,DRES,CNCONT/2)SALES,RESD,TS/3)DRESA,RESA,AFSST
PRINT    4)CONT,D,TS/5)RLIT,CONTEX,CONTC/6)RLI,CONTS
PRINT    7)FDC,NDNC
PRINT    8)AT1
PLOT     RES=R(0,48000)/RLI=I,RLIT=T(-3.17)/SALES=S,RESA=A,TS=8,D=2(0,4000)/
X1       CONTS=M(0,400)/FDC=F(-3,2)/TEST1=*(0,8)
SPEC     DT=.1/LENGTH=20/PRTPER=5/PLTPER=.5
RUN      TEST
```

References

[1]   Forrester, J.W. *Industrial Dynamics*. Cambridge, Mass., MIT Press, 1961.

[2]   Forrester, J.W. "Industrial Dynamics — After the First Decade," *Management Science* (March 1968).

[3]   Forrester, J.W. "Market Growth as Influenced by Capital Investment," *Industrial Management Review*, Vol. 9, no. 2 (Winter 1968), pp. 83-105.

[4]   Forrester, J.W. "Modeling the Dynamic Processes of Corporate Growth," *IBM Scientific Computing Symposium on Simulation Models and Gaming* (December 1964).

[5]   Nord, O.C. *Growth of a New Product*. Cambridge, Mass., MIT Press, 1963.

[6]   Packer, D.W. *Resource Acquisition in Corporate Growth*. Cambridge, Mass., MIT Press, 1963.

[7]   Pugh, A.L., III. *DYNAMO User's Manual*, 2d ed. Cambridge, Mass., MIT Press, 1963.

[8]   Swanson, C.V. "Resource Control in Growth Dynamics." Unpublished Ph.D. dissertation; Cambridge, Mass., Massachusetts Institute of Technology, 1969.

[9]   Wright, R.D. "Scannell Transportation: An Industrial Dynamics Implementation." Unpublished M.S. thesis; Cambridge, Mass., Massachusetts Institute of Technology, 1969.

25

Policy Formulation in a Vertically-Integrated Firm

Edward B. Roberts, Dan I. Abrams, and Henry B. Weil

Organizations formulate policies, make decisions, and undertake various activities as responses to gaps between their objectives and their measured performance. As a firm's objectives shift relatively slowly, changes in its performance gaps, hence in its behavior, can be created simply by changes in the measures used to monitor the firm's performance. Thus one of top management's more important tasks is the selection of a set of performance measures that will lead to behavior consistent with achievement of company goals.

This is not an easy task. The typical business enterprise has multiple goals that are changing in relative importance over time. Organizational responses to different types of performance measurement and reward schemes are not immediately obvious, especially when multiple (and often conflicting) measures are applied simultaneously.

The opportunity for conflict among performance measures, and therefore the lack of clarity as to how the measures mold behavior, is probably greatest in vertically-integrated companies. Not only do these firms offer the usual possibility of individual measures conflicting to some extent (e.g., sales and profits), but also the opportunity exists for interdivisional conflict as a result of the measurement process (e.g., the frequent outcome of applying the profit center concept).

This paper describes the use of Industrial Dynamics for investigating, understanding, and experimenting with the process of goal achievement in a vertically-integrated firm. Industrial Dynamics is a feedback systems-oriented approach to dynamic socio-economic problems. Its techniques include feedback systems analysis and computer simulation of complex models.[1] Based on the study of a vertically-integrated manufacturer and retailer of food products,

---

[1] The basic background text in the field is Forrester [1]. An early general discussion of the principles of the approach is Roberts [2].

This paper first appeared in *Management Science* 14, no. 12 (August 1968), pp. B-674–B-694 under the title "A Systems Study of Policy Formulation in a Vertically-Integrated Firm." (© by The Institute of Management Sciences.)

the paper will discuss the desirability of interdivisional competition, the effect of pressure on performance, and the relative merits of a number of alternative performance measures.

Methodology

Although other approaches might have been adopted, Industrial Dynamics was considered appropriate for this study for several reasons.

1. As shall be indicated, the interaction of different levels in the vertical organization forms a closed-loop feedback-type system of relationships.

2. With Industrial Dynamics techniques it is relatively easy to model qualitative behavioral relationships such as reactions to organizational pressures and incentives.

3. Empirical data were not available sufficiently to permit use of statistical techniques for deriving some critical market relationships (e.g., retail price elasticity, consumer response to advertising). The Industrial Dynamics methodology does not insist upon such data availability, although added confidence in the model formulation does result when derivation of relationships can be enhanced by statistical analysis methods. Given these data unknowns, however, Industrial Dynamics does offer the advantage of providing an easy vehicle for testing the sensitivity of company performance to deviations from the initial estimates made of the relationships. (Any other approach that utilizes efficient simulation techniques would also provide this benefit.)

4. The relatively low mathematical sophistication required by the Industrial Dynamics approach enhances (but does not assure) the chances of management understanding of the system analysis effort. In the area of policy formulation it is likely that such enhanced understanding will for long be the principal direct and immediate result of a system study. Much more time than is consumed by the study will usually be required before any change in managerial understanding is reflected clearly in company policy and performance.

The Company Studied

The company studied is a large diversified corporation with activities in the supermarket, department store, food manufacturing and restaurant fields. The findings presented resulted from a several months' study conducted within the vertically-integrated retail food and manufacturing divisions accounting for sales of several hundred million dollars.

Retail Food Division

The company owns and operates a large chain of supermarkets in North America, enjoying an excellent growth record. The number of outlets has been expanded ten-fold since 1945, while retail food sales have grown by a factor of about 25 in the same period.

This division is characterized by two rather dissimilar activities:

1. operation and control of the supermarkets, each of which is a profit center; and

2. performance of a centralized merchandising, procurement, and distribution function.

Included in the latter activity is responsibility for promotion and retail pricing, as well as the planning of each week's program of featured special merchandise items.

For certain classes of products, corporate policy dictates that most or all of the goods sold by Retail be "bought" from the company's Manufacturing Division. Under current company practices this means that the negotiation of transfer prices for these items is also an important activity.

The Retail Division's performance is measured in terms of both sales volume and profitability. More specifically, performance is compared with a monthly dollar sales budget and a desired retail gross margin percentage. The Division's performance is monitored quite closely by the company president.

Manufacturing Division

Within the past five years, the company has become heavily engaged in the manufacture of private label products for sale primarily in its stores. Although the manufacturing activities were first operated by the Retail Division, they soon grew to such proportions that financial control considerations dictated the establishment of a separate division.

As the Retail Division is Manufacturing's sole customer for most of its output, and because Manufacturing is capital-intensive, performance of the Manufacturing Division is measured almost exclusively in terms of profitability. Specifically, the Division's income contribution (i.e., its accounted profits before allocation of corporate overhead charges) has been used as its principal performance measure.

The Product

A new bakery facility, requiring substantial capital investment, had recently been added to Manufacturing. In light of this it was decided to limit the scope of the study to the manufacture, distribution, and sale of one class of product—bakery goods. The major portion of the company's manufacturing investment is contained in this area.

Bakery products are characterized by high perishability (i.e., they must be sold within one to two days of production), impulse sales, and high substitutability within commodity groups (e.g., cakes). The latter characteristics of impulse sales and substitutions are prevalent in many consumer goods (e.g., detergents, apparel, gasoline). The perishable nature of these products precludes extensive use of inventories as buffers to uncouple either production from orders by the supermarkets (for the company) or demand from actual product availability (for consumers). Thus, management is faced with the classic "Christmas tree" or "newspaper" problem.

A Production-Sales Model of an Integrated Firm

The development of a model of a complex organization is usually a task of moderate-to-significant difficulty. In addition to overcoming the problems involved in finding a purposeful focal point for the organizational model, the model builder must effectively conceptualize the model's overall structure and carefully define the model's functional relationships. A variety of data gathering and analysis approaches are employed in these several stages of organization model development. But regardless of the care exercised by the model builder the resulting model can always be subjected to question on the grounds of model validity.

In developing the model of the production and sales activities of the company described in this paper, several different data sources were used. Most important among them were the personal observations of the several active participants in the model development, the plentiful information gained through extensive interviewing, and the results of analyses of a variety of company reports covering a several year period. Despite the concerns of the model builders, the resulting model is admittedly still a simplification of reality, but does represent the authors' best conceptualization of the major behavior-determining decisions and the ways in which they interact. When completed the model included equations for 110 variables written in the DYNAMO compiler language.

A model of this scope is far from "intuitively obvious," particularly to the manager not experienced in management science endeavors. Thus special attention was given throughout the model development to the gaining of managerial acceptance of the model. Although it was not possible to derive every equation rigorously from empirical evidences, the assumptions underlying each relationship were documented and discussed with participating managers. One satisfying measure of model validity is that the model was wholly accepted by company management as being sufficiently realistic for policy testing before actual computer simulations began.

Presentation of the model centers around a discussion of two related flow streams: the flow of orders and goods, and the flow of cash. Continual reference will be made to the accompanying diagrams of these flows.

The Flow of Goods and Orders

Figure 1 shows the flow of goods to the market place in response to orders generated at two points within the system. The discussion begins at the top of the figure and follows the flows downward.

One set of orders for bakery goods originates at the store level; these are orders for non-special items. "Non-specials" are items that during a particular week are not being featured at special low prices or with bonus stamp offerings. The specials are changed each week. In placing these orders, the person in charge of each store's bakery department relies quite heavily on historical data. This individual is called "the dairyman," as in addition to bakery department he is responsible for the store's dairy and frozen foods sections.

Orders for items to be featured as weekly specials are generated by the Merchandising Group based on its decisions on how much to allocate to the stores. Historical data again form the basis for ordering, but Merchandising deviates from the amounts so indicated in response to pressures from higher up in the Retail Division. A substantial body of evidence supports the existence of these pressures, including monthly Merchandising Meeting minutes and statements by Retail Division managers. When under pressure to increase sales, Merchandising tends to order more than is indicated by past data. Based on interviews,

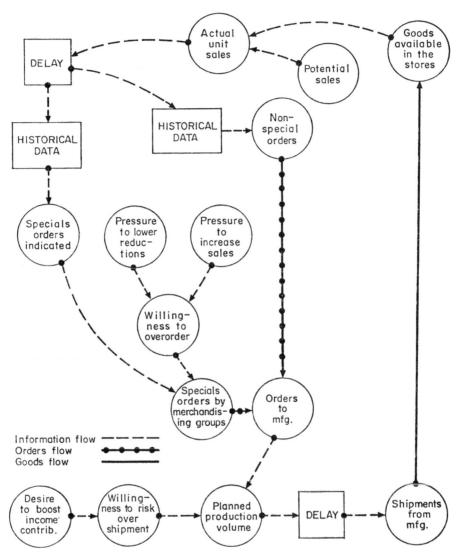

FIGURE 1. The flow of goods and orders

it was conservatively estimated that increased allocations of up to 10% might occasionally occur. This behavior is motivated by a desire to make certain that there are sufficient goods in the stores to capitalize on the increased market potential created by sales-boosting efforts. It represents an attempt by Merchandising to increase sales by pushing goods into the stores. On the other hand, Merchandising is under pressure to be very conservative in its store allocations of special items whenever gross margin percentage is low. In such situations Retail's top management gets concerned about the problem of "reductions," i.e., those sales at $\frac{1}{3}$ off that are necessitated when the perishable goods remain unsold at the expiration date marked on the merchandise.

Thus, two sets of orders flow into the Bakery manufacturing organization and serve as a basis for production planning. But this does not mean that the amount produced and shipped exactly equals the amount ordered. Rather, Manufacturing has the option to modify orders, and both the magnitude and direction of these modifications are affected by the desire to increase Manufacturing's accounted income contribution. Specifically, Manufacturing has tended to overship in an effort to improve its income contribution through increased volume. Interviews disclosed that 10% overshipment occurred infrequently, but that 5% was not uncommon. After lead-time and production delays, Manufacturing ships its goods to the stores.

Referring to the upper left-hand corner of Figure 1, one sees that the flows of goods and orders really form a closed loop. Orders based on historical data determine production, which in turn limits sales, as Retail cannot sell more than Manufacturing has produced and shipped. Today's sales, of course, become part of tomorrow's historical data base.

Potential Sales

Figure 2 shows the six major determinants of potential retail unit sales:
(a) the amount of effort devoted by dairymen to bakery products;
(b) dollars spent on advertising and in-store promotion;
(c) retail prices;
(d) the number of bakery specials;
(e) the price elasticity of bakery items, especially of the specials;
(f) total market size.

It is hypothesized that a dairyman has a definite effect on sales through his ordering and by his handling of displays and in-store promotion. Interviews disclosed an opinion among Retail and store operations personnel that the difference between a bad dairyman and one doing an outstanding job can be as much as 25–30% in unit sales.

It is the opinion of several of the company's executives that bakery items are often bought on impulse, and as a result unit sales are very responsive to increased advertising expenditures. For example, market reactions to "blockbuster" (or key feature, hard-sell approach) advertising supports this. Given the fact that there is some (but unfortunately an unknown) degree of responsiveness to advertising expenditures, several alternative linear market response curves were used in model simulation experiments.

Experience with specials has provided ample evidence that unit sales rise when prices are cut. Again, the exact shape of the response curve was unknown, but our assumption (Alternative A in Figure 3) appears to be quite reasonable in light of Retail's experience with specials. As examples, one variety of bread at half price sells three times the normal amount; a popular pie at sixty percent of its regular price sells over five times the normal amount, but partially at the expense of other items.

Normally five bakery products are selected as specials each week, and past records indicate that these consistently contribute a substantial portion of total

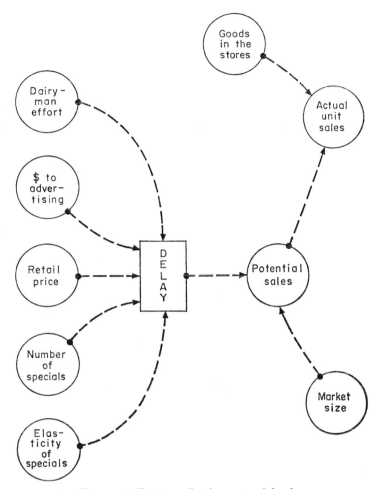

FIGURE 2. Factors affecting potential sales

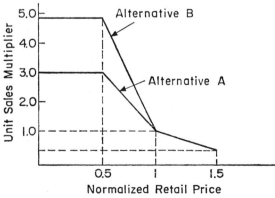

FIGURE 3. Effects of retail price

bakery goods sales. From the data available, it seems reasonable to assume that a sixth special might boost sales 10 % if it were a normal one and 20 % if Retail offers a "super-special." In supporting this formulation Bakery Merchandisers gave several examples of how "super-specials," such as 29 cents apple pie (regularly 49 cents), have been effective in the past.

The last sales multiplier under management's direct control is the price elasticity of items featured as specials. The model includes an estimated 50 % difference between maximum and minimum elasticities which seems quite conservative in the context of the data.

Cash Flows

Starting near the upper left-hand corner of Figure 4, the diagram indicates that dollar sales are merely unit sales (see the flow of goods and orders, Figure 1) times average retail price. When dollar sales compare unfavorably with the budgeted level, the interviews and Merchandising Meeting minutes indicate that pressure built up within the Retail Division to take corrective action. It should be recognized that this desire to remove an unfavorable sales variance can be amplified by a general pressure for the whole company to boost sales.

Under pressure to increase sales, Retail Division's management responds through the five sales multipliers discussed in the preceding section. These responses, as evidenced in the company records, are:

(a) through personal contact and by its weekly newsletter, the Merchandising Group exerts pressure on the dairymen to stimulate a higher level of attention to bakery products;

(b) expenditures on advertising and in-store promotion are increased, and one or more "blockbuster" ads may be featured;

(c) the Merchandising Group selectively lowers retail prices, through lower pricing of new products or greater price cuts for specials;

(d) the number of weekly specials may temporarily rise to six;

(e) items with large price elasticities are chosen as specials.

After lead-time delays in achieving their effects, the impacts of these stimuli are felt in the market place. After reporting delays, an improvement in sales becomes apparent; the unfavorable variance is reduced. Thus, sales performance and the management decisions that control it form a definite closed loop.

Referring again to Figure 4, there is a second control loop involving Retail gross margin percentage (center of the diagram). Under pressure to improve an unsatisfactory gross margin, Retail is quite unwilling to lower prices. Prices are cut only when there exists simultaneously a significant desire to boost sales. On the other hand, the interviews showed that Retail rarely increased regular prices, even to improve gross margin. Further, Retail top management becomes quite concerned about the problem of reductions on "expired date" merchandise when gross margin is low. The Merchandising Meeting minutes clearly show that these concerns encourage the Merchandising Group to be conservative in its allocations to the stores.

It is apparent that management's efforts to boost sales conflict with its efforts to increase gross margin, especially in the areas of pricing and production

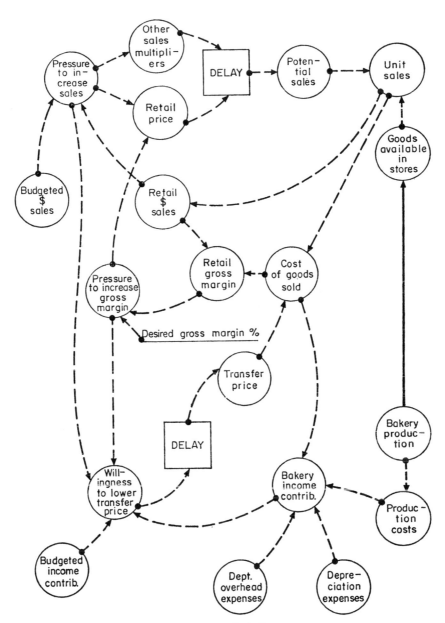

FIGURE 4. Cash flows

policies. To increase sales, one lowers prices (among other things) to create expanded market potential and ships more to the stores to capitalize on the additional demand. To improve gross margin, however, management does the opposite. There are no price cuts and Merchandising is under pressure to be quite conservative in its allocations to the stores so as to avoid excessive reductions. In the section on the system's dynamic behavior, it will be shown that this conflict (and its resolution) is a critical determinant of how well this part of the company performs.

Turning now to the last of the three performance measures, Manufacturing income contribution equals dollar sales (at transfer prices) to Retail minus production costs, depreciation, and departmental overhead. When income contribution is low, Manufacturing takes the initiative by offering lower transfer prices to Retail in exchange for expected (but not guaranteed) larger volume. Further (as indicated earlier in this section), Manufacturing ships more than is ordered to increase its volume even more. So long as transfer prices are not reduced too much, the increased volume so generated improves Manufacturing's income contribution position.

The System's Dynamic Behavior

The System's Control Loops

The preceding section describes a production and distribution system in terms of its structure and the rationale behind it. Now, let us turn to the ways in which Manufacturing, the centralized Retail activities and the stores interact through the system's three major control loops (Figure 5).

It is apparent from this diagram that the interactions among the three performance measures (i.e., manufacturing income contribution, retail dollar sales, and retail gross margin percentage) form a complex feedback system that determines company behavior.

The first control loop represents performance measurement of the Manufacturing Division. In response to pressure to correct an unfavorable income contribution variance, Manufacturing attempts corrective action. It ships more to the stores than was ordered and endeavors to stimulate more aggressive sales promotion at Retail by offering lower transfer prices. The longer lead time required for stimulating increased retail sales suggests that the effects of the overshipment are felt first. Overshipments result in increased "reductions" caused by quantities above historical levels being shipped to the stores without attendent sales-boosting efforts by the Retail Division. The immediate result of this, at worst, is a drop in the gross margin percentage that causes Retail to be more conservative in its allocations to the stores. This causes manufacturing income contribution to decline even further than before (because of the lower transfer prices). At best, Retail uses the lower transfer prices to maintain an acceptable gross margin percentage at the same sales level as before the concerted overshipping began, leaving Manufacturing with about the same income contribution variance as it faced prior to lowering transfer prices and overshipping.

Turning now to the second control loop, consider an instance in which sales have fallen below their budgeted level. Retail's response is a relaxing of prices, an increase in advertising expenditures, and the possible offering of more specials. Pressure increases on the manufacturing group for more sales results in specials with larger price elasticities, allocation and ordering in excess of historical amounts, and pressure on the dairymen. A diagram of this process is shown in Figure 6.

However, none of these actions has an immediate impact on sales because all require many weeks of lead-time. In fact, the unfavorable variance becomes

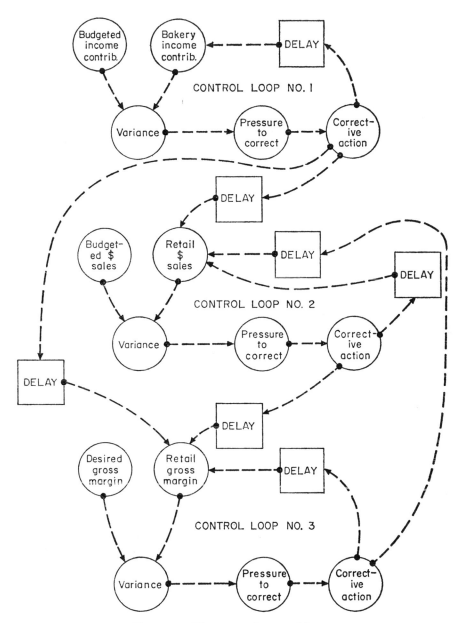

FIGURE 5. The system's control loops

worse as built-in growth in the budget causes the budget targets to rise each week. Especially when under pressure from the President, Retail intensifies its corrective measures. This is to be expected, since for many weeks management does not have an opportunity to measure the success of its first attempts.

After some weeks the first effects of Retail's efforts are apparent as sales begin to recover. The market-place's full response follows shortly, and everyone seems much happier.

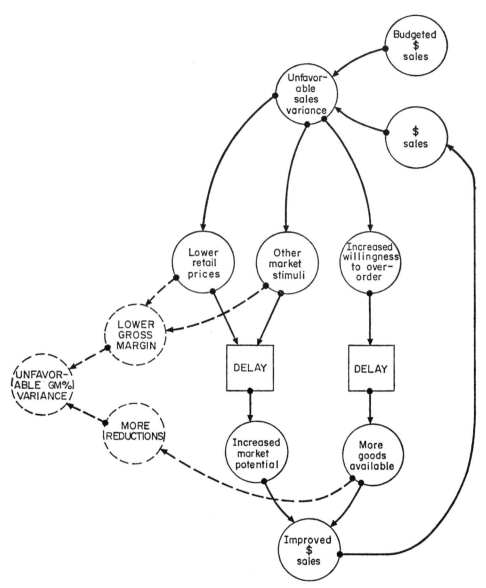

FIGURE 6. Correcting an unfavorable sales variance

Sales are rising, but lower prices and over-ordering already have had a depressing effect on gross margin. Thus, with sales in relatively good shape, Retail's top management naturally turns its attention to this second area, improvement of profits, shown as Loop No. 3 in Figure 5.

Retail's natural reaction to a low gross margin is unwillingness to lower prices below their normal level. In addition, pressure is exerted on the Merchandising Group to boost gross margin and cut reductions. Thus, Merchandising responds by being quite conservative in its choice of specials and its allocations of merchandise to the stores. Figure 7 shows this in diagram form.

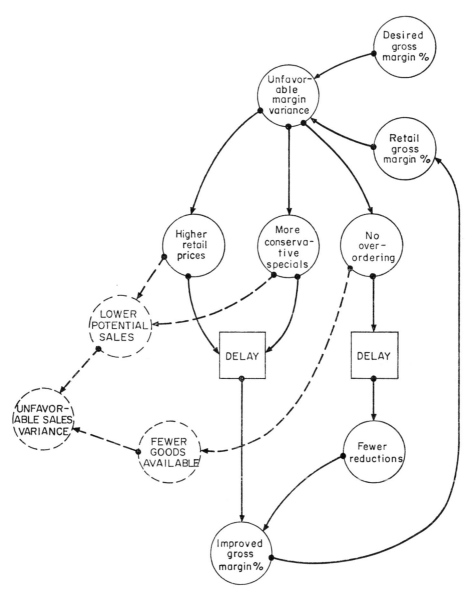

FIGURE 7. Correcting an unfavorable gross margin variance

The tendency to continue in this pattern of behavior is intensified by Manufacturing income contribution's close relation to dollar sales, both of them being functions of unit sales. Manufacturing's usual corrective action in this area has a definite multiplier effect on Retail's efforts to raise sales. Manufacturing tends to over-ship, puts pressure on Retail for increased sales, and often lowers transfer prices as an incentive.

A Simulation Run of the Basic Model

In this section of the paper a simulation run is used to illustrate the results

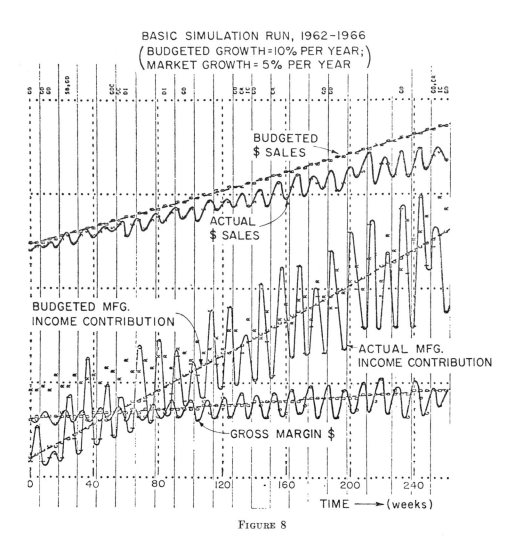

BASIC SIMULATION RUN, 1962–1966
(BUDGETED GROWTH = 10% PER YEAR;
MARKET GROWTH = 5% PER YEAR

FIGURE 8

of the behavior described previously. For the purpose of the simulation, budgeted growth was set at 10% per year and annual growth of the potential market was set at 5%. In addition, there was no new investment over the 5 year simulated period. Initial conditions of the model were set to correspond with 1962 company data.

From examination of the graphical computer output in Figure 8, two general observations can be made. First, there are definite short-term fluctuations in dollar sales, retail gross margin dollars and manufacturing income contribution. Second, none of these performance measures attains its budgeted level, but all are able to grow at a rate in excess of the market's 5% growth. These five year results were compared with the actual company performance during the 1962–1966 period. Management's satisfaction with this comparative test provided further validation of the company model.

The short-term oscillations result from the conflict in behavior caused by employing dollar sales and gross margin percentage as performance measures as discussed in the previous section (see Figures 6 and 7). Therefore, let us now turn to the second phenomenon. Why is it impossible to grow at the budgeted rate when this rate is faster than the growth of the market? Again, the cause is the conflict between dollar sales and gross margin percentage as Retail performance measures.

Assuming that prices, advertising expenditures, and the other sales multipliers (Figure 2) stay at their normal levels, sales cannot grow faster than the market. In the model these "normal" levels are, by definition, those which are just sufficient to maintain constant market share. Thus, growth faster than the market can only be achieved with lower than normal prices, greater than normal advertising, or a combination of these and other stimuli.

In the simulations, the market is responding to price much more than it is responding to advertising. This is in line with the disclosure from the interviews that Retail seemed much more willing to use price as a stimulus than to increase advertising expenditures. The latter variable remains relatively fixed in current practice. Hence, if gross margin were ignored, Retail could progressively lower prices to keep up with its sales budget.

One cannot, however, ignore gross margin. After all, sales volume would grow amazingly if goods were given away. Thus, there must be—and is—a compromise: prices are cut to a point where pressure to raise them as a help to gross margin exactly equals pressure to lower them as a stimulus to sales. The result of such a compromise is growth faster than the market, but slower than the budgeted rate.

Summary

From the preceding discussion, one concludes that performance measures are important determinants of behavior within the system. If there is inherent conflict between performance measures, then organization behavior reflects that conflict. While the resulting overall performance may be "satisfactory", it falls short of the firm's potential.

Finally, it is important to review exactly how growth is achieved. Lowering prices, as well as using other stimuli (Figure 2), increases the potential market for bakery goods. However, no manufacturer can sell more than he produces. Thus, the key to growth is simultaneous market stimulation and increased output to capture the newly-created demand.

In the company studied, production is based on orders from Retail. These orders, however, seem often to be intuitive straight-line extrapolation of historical growth.

There must be more to it than that, however, or the company could never grow out of a stagnation period. The keys to accelerated growth in production are the pressures within the system that cause the Merchandising group to abandon historical guidelines and allocate more goods to the stores and the pressures that cause the Manufacturing Division to ship more than is ordered. Thus, perhaps unfortunately, only the violations of present formal company policy enable the company to break out of the trap of past performance and to produce enough to capitalize on a more rapidly growing future potential. It seems worth noting that similar breaking of corporate internal rules, such as by "bootlegging" research projects, have in other companies also provided the key to achieving growth objectives.

Comparative Simulation Results

In addition to utilizing the model to understand and investigate system behavior, it was employed to investigate alternative policies in a number of areas. These policy areas include:

(a) transfer pricing;
(b) retail pricing;
(c) promotional expenditures;
(d) performance measuring;
(e) pressures within the organization;
(f) budgeting.

Rather than discussing each simulation run individually, this section summarizes the general points concerning policy formulation and goal achievement.

Interdivisional Competition

The principal way in which the Retail and Manufacturing Divisions compete is for shares of the total profit that results from making and selling an item. The split is, to a large extent, determined by transfer prices.

Three possible transfer pricing policies were investigated:

(a) negotiated transfer prices;
(b) costs + % of costs;
(c) costs + constant $ mark-up.

The percentage and constant mark-ups were chosen so that they agreed with the initial negotiated price, thereby making the simulations directly comparable.

Despite its aura of randomness and disconnection with costs, the policy of negotiated transfer prices proved to be superior in both 5 year cumulative $ sales and 5 year cumulative total profits (see Table 1). This is true even though Costs + Constant Mark-up (the next best policy) produced higher unit sales.

Both of the alternatives to negotiated transfer prices give Retail an increasingly larger share of total company profits as unit sales grow. The reason for this is that Bakery's mark-up is a constant while manufacturing costs per unit fall. Thus, transfer price drops as unit volume grows, causing Retail costs to decline substantially. This is not unlike the effects produced by a quantity discounting scheme. However, under these alternatives Retail receives an amazingly high gross margin, which (in both cases) it proceeds to "give away" by cutting prices.

In periods of stagnation, these three policies are virtually identical, but under conditions of rapid growth, negotiated transfer prices make more money for the company. With a fixed or nearly fixed mark-up, the Manufacturing Division has little trouble meeting its income contribution budget. Thus, it has no reason to over-produce, and production tends to lag the market potential created by Retail's low prices.

In this context, interdivisional competition is not the ogre conjured by those who believe that attempts to optimize on the Divisional level inevitably lead to

TABLE 1

Effects of Alternative Transfer Pricing Policies

	Normalized Cumulative 5 year SALES \$	Normalized Cumulative 5 year PROFIT \$*	Normalized % of 5th Year Profit to Retail
Negotiated Transfer Prices	1.00	1.00	1.00
Costs + Constant Mark-up	0.98	0.96	1.31
Costs + % of Costs	0.97	0.93	1.39

* Profit = Retail Gross Margin \$ + Bakery Income Contribution

sub-optimization of corporate achievement. On the contrary, in this type of vertically-integrated organization, interdivisional competition for profits stimulates volume-consciousness in Manufacturing and prevents excessive promotional price cutting by the Retail Division.

Performance Measures

The introduction to this paper contained the assertion that performance measures strongly influence behavior. The computer simulations provide excellent illustrations of this phenomenon.

Three basic performance measures are currently being used in the system:
(a) retail dollar sales;
(b) retail gross margin percentage;
(c) manufacturing income contribution.

Two of these, sales and income contribution, are accounting quantities that reflect the level of the company's activities. They are dynamic, growing as the company grows.

Gross margin percentage, on the other hand, gives only a very incomplete picture of Retail's profit performance. One can only spend gross margin dollars, not gross margin percentage. By concentrating on gross margin percentage, management does not take advantage of the possibility of reducing gross margin but realizing higher total profit through greatly increased sales.

In addition, Retail gross margin percentage has evolved into something more than just a performance measure. It is a tradition, an institution, not only in the company studied but throughout the retailing industry. While budgeted sales and income contribution are accepted as products of the accounting system, the expected gross margin percentage is different. It is a magic number (or sacred cow). As a result, it takes years to change people's idea of what a proper gross margin should be.

In the simulated replacement of negotiated transfer prices with costs plus a fixed percent mark-up, it was shown that at one point Retail realized a gross margin considerably in excess of its traditional performance. Yet, slowly, this increased profit was lost because Retail lowered prices. Gross margin in excess of the historic target was spent in attempts to boost sales.

Similarly, simulated price reductions of 10–20% created a vastly greater potential market for bakery goods. However, the potential went unrealized because Retail, disturbed by gross margins below traditional levels, was too conservative.

The simulation runs demonstrated that the use of a performance measure that was decoupled from sales volume had a definitely negative effect on both sales and profit growth. Thus, it was recommended to the company management that gross margin dollars be substituted as a measure of Retail profitability.

Effects of Pressures on Goal Achievement

Two types of pressures affect behavior within the bakery goods manufacture and sales system:

(a) internally generated pressures arising from management's desire to perform well in terms of sales, gross margin, and income contribution;

(b) pressures generated by sources outside the bakery products system (the President, for example).

The objective of this portion of the paper is to show that these pressures are an important determinant of corporate growth.

The first series of simulations concentrated on the impact of pressures on the Merchandising Group. As shown in Table 2, the amount of pressure has a definite effect on both five-year sales and five-year profits. While the initial differences are not huge, they do grow and the correlation is inescapable between pressure and profits.

These results are strong argument against any form of automated merchandising that eliminates the Merchandising Group's ability to feel and respond to pressures.

The Merchandising Group's willingness to allocate more to the stores and its willingness to choose high-elasticity specials are the most direct ways by which it contributes to accelerated growth in the simulation runs. While increasing pressures by 100% to 300% is quite drastic, additional simulations showed that the same improvements can be realized if incentives of some sort make the Merchandisers more responsive to current pressures.

A second set of simulations investigated the effects of Manufacturing overshipment. Despite wide-spread feelings in the Retail Division that Manufacturing should merely produce what is ordered, simulations show that over-shipment is a significant growth stimulus. It permits the company to take advantage of the market potential created by advertising and low prices, and its elimination reduces five-year profits by about 10%.

TABLE 2

Effects of Various Forms of Pressure

	Normalized Cumulative 5 Year SALES $	Normalized Cumulative 5 Year PROFIT $
No Pressure	0.98	0.98
Normal Level of Pressure	1.00	1.00
Sales Pressure Increased by 100%	1.05	1.08
Sales Pressure Increased by 300%	1.11	1.17
Profit Pressure Increased by 100%	1.02	1.07

NOTE: Negotiated transfer prices were used in all of the above simulations.

TABLE 3

Impacts of Pressures are Additive

	Normalized Cumulative 5 Year SALES $	Normalized Cumulative 5 Year PROFIT $
Negotiated Transfer Prices; Other Pressures Normal	1.00	1.00
Constant Mark-up; Other Pressures Normal	0.98	0.96
Constant Mark-up; No Manufacturing Over-shipment	0.93	0.86

TABLE 4

Budgets as Stimuli to Performance

Budgeted Annual Growth Rate	Normalized Cumulative 5 Year SALES $	Normalized Cumulative 5 Year PROFIT $
15%	1.00	1.00
23%	1.08	1.09
30%	1.19	1.20

NOTE: Negotiated Transfer Prices; Gross Margin $ used.

An earlier part of this section discussed how negotiated transfer prices led to better performance than a fixed mark-up above costs. This, too, was traced to pressures. The fixed mark-up made it easy for Manufacturing to achieve its budgeted income contribution and, thereby, removed from Manufacturing its incentive to increase volume.

The simulation results in Table 3 highlight the effects of pressure as a stimulus to growth:

It can be seen that as each pressure is eliminated, five-year performance grows worse. Under conditions of constant mark-up, no Manufacturing overshipment, and no pressure on the Merchandising Group, it becomes impossible for sales to grow faster than the market.

In the same way that removal of pressures has a detrimental effect on performance, the application of more pressure through higher budgeted rates of growth leads to significant improvements. With the market growing at 5% per annum, the budgeted growth rates in Table 4 were used.

In every case, higher budgeted growth leads to higher actual growth. Although these very high growth-rate budgets were never achieved, they stimulated growth several times faster than the market.

As a result of these findings, incentive schemes were recommended to make critical areas of the system more pressure-sensitive.

Results to Date

At various points during the study several meetings were conducted with key company executives. These sessions covered several topics: (1) the feedback systems conceptualization of the company, shown earlier as Figures 1 and 4; (2) the detailed assumptions, including parameter values, that were included in the model equations; (3) the principal simulation results, emphasizing those covered in Tables 1 through 4; and (4) the implications of the results with accompanying recommendations for policy. It is reasonable to point out that some aspects of the study effort, in particular some parts of the system conceptualization, were not accepted immediately by all the affected management personnel. However, an encouraging fact is that by the end of the study general agreement did exist (among the company president and the vice presidents of retailing, manufacturing, and finance) that the feedback concepts and the model did embody the essential characteristics of the organization.

The response to the study's completion (at least, temporary completion) has not been a rush to implement the specific recommendations derived from the computer results. This appears to be too much to hope for from an initial use in a company of management science tools aimed at policy formulation problems. Longer familiarity with the concepts, tools, and analysts is probably needed before specific policy changes will directly follow simulation outcomes.

However, the study has resulted in an ongoing series of meetings, both formal and informal, in which the company's basic operating practices and performance pressures have been reexamined. Furthermore, in addition to encouraging this new dialogue, the systems study described in this paper has supplied a new conceptual framework within which to conduct the examination. The study apparently has contributed significantly to a greater understanding of the complexities and interdependencies of the firm's activities in this vertically integrated sector. Finally the study has underlined the need for divisional executives to consider the company-wide effect of decisions previously regarded as of divisional importance only.

The experiences encountered in this study reemphasize the challenge to management scientists posed by the policy formulation (and other) problems of top management. They also point a way by which eventual success may be attained. If management science is to alter the way by which the corporation is directed, early efforts must be launched at issues critical to top management. But the objectives of these early studies in a firm need not be immediate policy change—such an objective is probably unrealistic in most organizations. Rather the effort should be aimed at top management education in the management science process and possibilities via exposure to studies of real company problem areas. Direct impact on managerial attitudes and understandings will pave the way to later policy change.

References

1. FORRESTER, J. W., *Industrial Dynamics*, The M.I.T. Press, Cambridge, 1961.
2. ROBERTS, E. B., "Industrial Dynamics and the Design of Management Control Systems," *Management Technology*, Vol. 3, No. 2 (December 1963).

26

Organizational Change:
An Industrial Dynamics Approach

L. Fillmore McPherson III

The investigation of psychological variables in organizations is a new direction in recent industrial dynamics activity[1] as the sociologist and the businessman have become increasingly aware of particular behavioral phenomena in organizations.[2] Relating these phenomena in an organic approach to significant problems, however, demands an insight beyond that normally obtained from observing isolated events. The difficulty in relating phenomena to problems results from: (a) the "systems" nature of most problems—diverse and apparently unrelated happenings bear on the problem, and (b) time delays as they affect the development of the problem's history. Industrial dynamics philosophy and techniques[3] can surmount these difficulties, providing a deeper understanding of major problems.

The Implementation Problem

Both sociologists and businessmen are confronted with the problem of implementing new policies and programs. Since the Western Electric studies in the 1920's, evidence has established the importance of human organizational factors in the effective production of goods and services. Despite such evidence, there have been disappointingly few cases of successful implementation of policies and practices based on the findings. Part of the failure undoubtedly results from imperfect knowledge of the findings: some people know nothing of the evidence; others are familiar with both the evidence and the suggested new policies but doubt their applicability. In today's world of professional managers, management training programs, and consultants, such an excuse cannot possibly be accepted as the complete answer.

An alternate reason for the lack of successful implementation is that a new policy cannot be introduced in a vacuum, but must be introduced in a continuing organization. Such an organization, composed of individuals and informal groupings of individuals, can exhibit many of the phenomena associated with group behavior. Of particular relevance to the implementation problem are group characteristics pertaining to the adoption of goals and ways of fulfilling goals. An organization operates under commitments to goals. Through practice, ways of meeting these commitments have been established. A new policy disrupts these methods and poses a threat to the fulfillment of goal commitments. The organization meets commitments, therefore, in a way which experience proves will suc-

This article is based on studies supported by a grant of the Ford Foundation. The computer simulations were carried out using the facilities at the M.I.T. Computation Center and Project MAC. The paper first appeared in the *Industrial Management Review* (currently published as the *Sloan Management Review*) 6, no. 2 (Spring 1965), pp. 51–63. (© 1965 by the Industrial Management Review Association; all rights reserved.)

ceed. The tried and true method gains reinforcement and the new policy falls short of successful implementation.

The dismissal of an idea because it contains something new and different is a familiar part of our experience. Familiar also is the idea which can be entertained with minimal cost or threat; as soon as trouble looms, the untried idea gives way to that method which we know will weather the approaching storm. So it is with a new policy introduced in an organization. Action will be taken in order to reduce a perceived threat to goal commitments. Since the perceived threat may result from the disruptions and inefficiencies of the policy introduction itself, the abandonment of the new policy can be related to pressures generated by its introduction and the new policy can cause its own destruction.

The Systems Viewpoint

When an organization attempts to implement a new policy, the attempt itself generates pressures which discourage or encourage the implementation. Pressures arising from perceived threats to goal fulfillment have been previously mentioned. Since the goals usually relate to the organization's task, the designation "task pressures" serves to identify them. A second source of pressure develops from the perception that the new policy can either aid or hinder goal attainment. These pressures directly associated with the new policy are termed "association pressures." The systems viewpoint of the implementation problem delineates causal linkages connecting the introduction of the new policy to the task and association pressures. Proper consideration of time delays constitutes an important part of the resulting system of interactions.

Task pressures arise because the new policy typically disturbs the established method of operation yet does not have an immediate payoff. The combined effect decreases ability to meet task goals, which triggers, in turn, a shift toward greater organizational effort to meet the goals. Such a shift favors the proven methods of meeting the goals and therefore tends to operate to the disadvantage of effort directed toward the new policy; this forces the new policy's abandonment because the organization lacks the extra time and effort to devote to its implementation. This process does not necessarily imply a repudiation of the new policy, only its implicit abandonment because of the necessity of fulfilling goals.

The task pressures indirectly defeat the new policy because the overt action is taken for the task goals, not against the new policy. The new policy dies because the organization must allocate its limited resources among numerous activities and has only a small amount to devote to the new policy. The association pressures, however, produce action aimed directly at the new policy. If the organization associates desirable results with the new policy, the new policy receives support and the task pressures may be effectively countered. As this acceptance or internalization occurs, the new policy has less to fear from the older established methods of meeting the goal because the new policy loses some of its newness and becomes a part of the established methods. Working against the new policy is its necessarily slow start. Because of displeasure with the slow pace, the new policy is not internalized and the task pressures work unhindered by opposing association pressures. The association pressures can therefore work for the new policy or not, depending on the success or failure associated with the new policy.

The System Model of the Implementation Problem

The structural interworkings of the new policy and the task and association pressures are the focus of attention. Figure 1 shows how the key system variables relate to one another in a complex, feedback manner. Tracing the successive cause and effect relationships should provide an understanding of the system.

The first step in implementation occurs when the organization decides to make a new policy effort allocation. Any new policy requires thought on formulation and feasibility, development of actual procedures, and dissemination of information—in short, any new policy requires some effort and normally it comes at the expense of task effort allocation.

The amount of new policy effort allocation determines the rates of new policy growth and new policy decay, which control the degree of new policy implementation. The degree of new policy implementation is a level, or state variable, and as such, responds to new policy effort allocation only as this effort is able to produce new policy growth. A new policy effort allocation normally means that planning, informing, consultation, and introduction receive attention, causing a new policy growth rate and an increase in the degree of new policy implementation.

An important element in determining how the new policy effort allocation affects the rate of new policy growth is the amount of effort needed for maintenance. Whatever an organization does, some effort must be spent in maintaining an activity or program at its current level: communication channels must be kept open, interests and attitudes must not deteriorate. A new policy is not excepted from this need. If the new policy effort allocation equals the effort needed for maintenance, only the housekeeping items pertaining to the new policy will be accomplished and the degree of new policy implementation will remain at its present level. If the new policy effort allocation fails to satisfy the effort needed for maintenance, then even these housekeeping chores will be neglected—conferences will be postponed, reports will be unheeded, and actions will be deferred—thus allowing the new policy decay rate to dissipate the degree of new policy implementation. A new policy effort which exceeds the effort needed for maintenance, on the other hand, allows for the additional thought and work necessary to advance the degree of new policy implementation. The amount of effort needed for maintenance depends on the degree of new policy implementation, some policies requiring a larger amount as the degree of new policy implementation increases, and some requiring less.

The major reason for introducing the new policy appears in the next cause-effect linkage. As the degree of new policy implementation increases, presumably the task effort efficiency also increases. A feasible new policy should aim at some change, such as increased morale or a closer alignment of the individual's and the organization's goals, which will allow a more efficient use of the task effort allocation. The task effort efficiency and the task effort allocation determine the organization's results.

The structure relating results to goal satisfaction forms an important part of the system. First, the results produced by the organization are not readily perceived. An explicit action may be quickly observed, but its results—profits or personal growth, for example—become perceived only after a time delay. Furthermore, in a changing situation, incoming data tend to be discounted if they differ markedly from previous impressions, and thus repeated inputs of the new data are necessary before results can be perceived. For both these reasons, substantial time delays may differentiate results and perceived results.

Secondly, the organization builds up a level of traditional results, based on its history of perceived results, which indicate what the organization has accomplished in the past and, therefore, what may reasonably be expected in the future. Thus, traditional results along with relatively constant goal standards determine the goal under which the group operates. A corporate annual report with its comparisons of current to previous results illustrates a goal composed of both traditional results and constant goal standards. A comparison of perceived results and the goal indicates the amount of goal satisfaction—the amount that perceived results exceed or fall short of the goal.

The meaning of the word "goal" needs some amplification. The organization's goal and the formal, written goal need not coincide, and the former probably defies explicit measurement. The organization's goal is the result which, if equalled, will cause the organization to be just satisfied—not elated and not disappointed. The organization's goal may be ninety per cent or one hundred ten per cent of the explicit, formal goal, or it may have no relation at all to the formal goal. Perhaps the best definition of the organization's goal is an operational one. If the organization's goal is not fulfilled, a sense of urgency arises causing an increase in task pressure, which in turn causes a shift from new policy effort allocation to task effort allocation.

A new policy effort allocation serves as the organization's major indication that a new policy exists and a positive goal satisfaction signifies a desirable orientation or operation. The coupling of these two—new policy effort allocation and positive goal satisfaction—causes the internalization of the new policy. On the other hand, a negative goal satisfaction coupled with a new policy effort allocation detracts from the internalization of the new policy. A high internalization of the new policy causes favorable association pressure which acts to shift allocation of effort to new policy effort allocation; this will not occur with an unfavorable association pressure resulting from a low internalization of the new policy.

The model shown in Figure 1 contains eleven closed feedback loops. One of the simplest ones shows that as the new policy growth rate increases, the degree of new policy implementation also increases. The effort needed for maintenance might then increase, causing a decrease in the new policy growth rate, thus closing the ring. A more complicated feedback loop relates an increase in internalization of the new policy with an increase in association pressures, a decrease in task effort allocation, a decrease in results, a decrease in perceived results, a decrease in goal satisfaction, and a decrease in internalization of the new

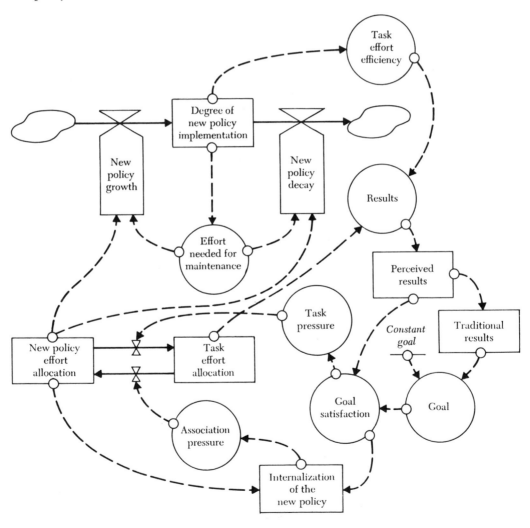

Figure 1   Structure of Key Variables

policy. Keeping track of the interaction of eleven such loops can fortunately, for purposes of analysis, be delegated to a large digital computer.

Model Simulation

The systems model of the implementation problem is closed and self-contained. The simulated behavior reflects behavioral assumptions underlying the model structure; this behavior follows automatically once the new policy is introduced. Freed from random influences, the system produces basic behavior patterns. A great number of simulations are possible, representing the wide range of new policy and organization characteristics. The three simulations shown here illustrate important behavior patterns.

The model needs some numeric frame of reference for proper operation. New policy effort allocation NPEA,* task effort allocation TEA, degree of new policy implementation DNPI, and internalization of the new policy INP can vary from zero to 100 per cent, as shown on the plot scales on the simulations. All three simulations begin prior to the new policy introduction, so task effort allocation TEA starts at 100 per cent and the other three above variables at zero. With task effort allocation TEA at 100 per cent and before a new policy distorts task effort efficiency, normal results RES is set at unity. GOAL has the same dimensions and scale as results RES. GOAL satisfaction GS has the same dimensions as results RES and GOAL, but, being the difference between the two, has a different scale centered about the zero position. A final illustrated variable has not previously been described. The comparison of actual to needed effort CANE shows the difference between new policy effort allocation NPEA and effort needed for maintenance, and is also centered at zero.

In the first simulation, the new policy has been given the characteristics shown in Figures 2 and 3. Figure 2 illustrates the relationship between task effort efficiency and degree of new policy implementation DNPI. When degree of new policy implementation DNPI reaches a full 100 per cent, this particular policy increases task effort efficiency from one hundred to 150 per

---

* For those variables exhibited in the simulation plots, pneumonic designations will be included in the text.

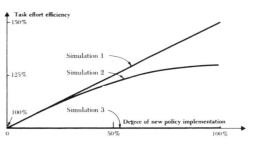

Figure 2   Task Effort Efficiency vs. Degree of New Policy Implementation

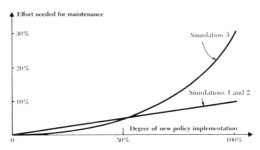

Figure 3   Effort Needed for Maintenance vs. Degree of New Policy Implementation

cent. Figure 3 shows the relationship between effort needed for maintenance and degree of new policy implementation DNPI. When the degree of new policy implementation DNPI reaches a full 100 per cent, the effort needed for maintenance rises from zero to demand 10 per cent of the organization's effort.

A third important characteristic in the first simulation concerns GOAL. The constant goal has a value of 1.1, which is greater than the value of results initially attainable. Results RES, and traditional results, have an initial value of 1.0. Since GOAL reflects both the constant goal and traditional results, GOAL starts the first simulation run with a value of 1.05.

At time 5, in the first simulation, the organization initiates the new policy. It shifts ten per cent of its task effort allocation TEA to new policy effort allocation NPEA. This transfer immediately detracts from the organization's ability to produce results RES. Consequently results RES decline sharply. Goal satisfaction GS, already negative because results RES cannot meet the high GOAL, dips lower as results RES decline. Task

Simulation 1

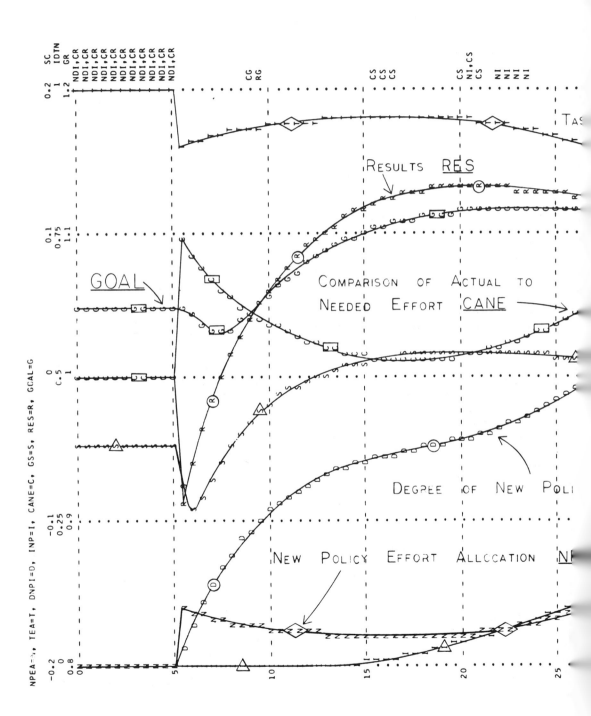

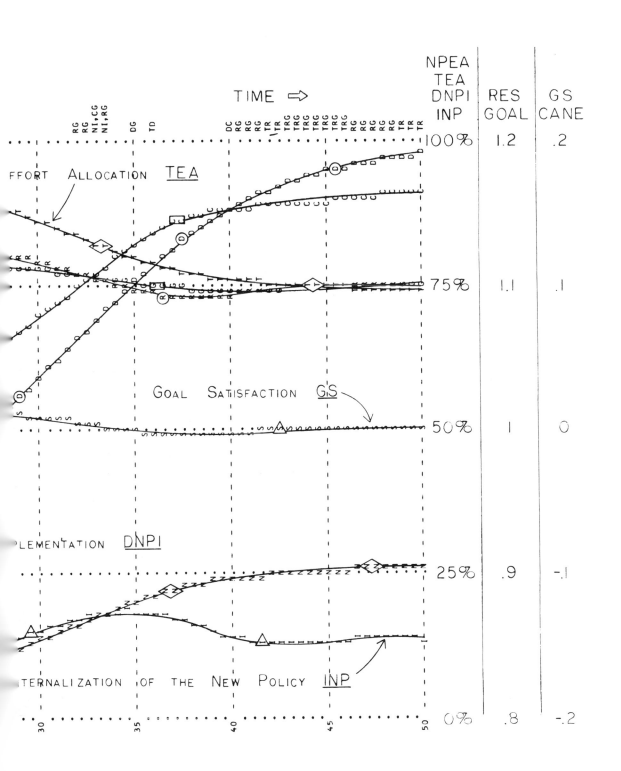

Simulation 2

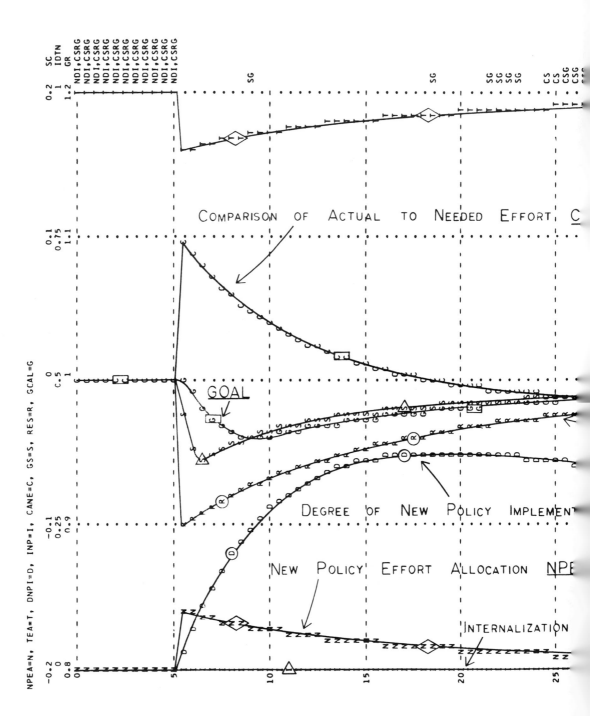

TIME ⇨

	NPEA TEA DNPI INP	RES GOAL	GS CANE
	100%	1.2	.2
	75%	1.1	.1
	50%	1	0
	25%	.9	-.1
	0%	.8	-.2

Task Effort Allocation TEA

Goal Satisfaction GS

Results RES

DNPI

New Policy INP

Simulation 3

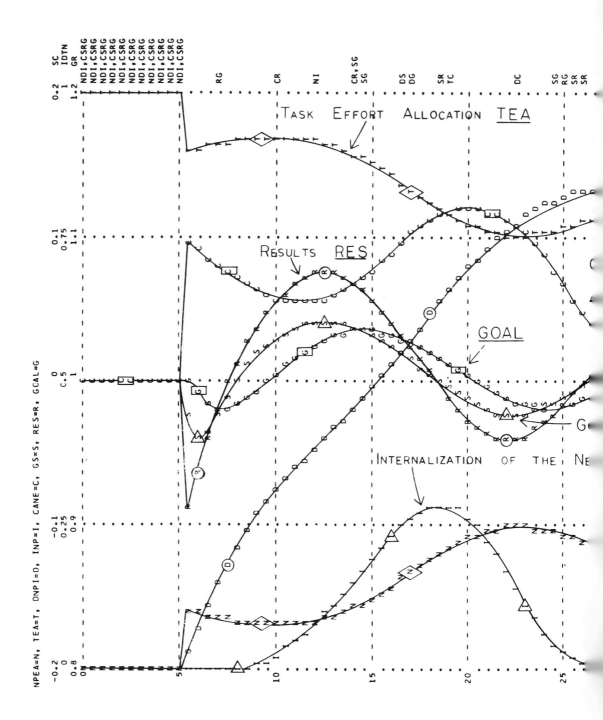

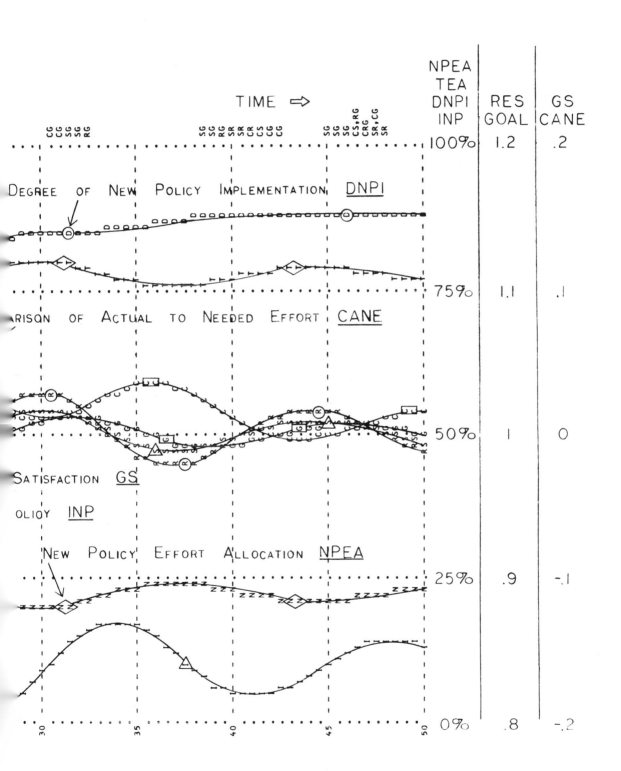

pressures arising from the negative goal satisfaction GS exist from the start, but now become greater. The increasing pressures force some of the new policy effort allocation NPEA back to task effort allocation TEA in an attempt to fulfill the goal commitments.

The degree of new policy implementation DNPI, meanwhile, has been rising because of initial new policy effort allocation NPEA. The effort needed for maintenance now absorbs a greater per cent of new policy effort allocation NPEA. The comparison of actual to needed effort CANE falls toward zero, reflecting the combined effect of lessened new policy effort allocation NPEA plus greater effort needed for maintenance. Little effort is available to advance the new policy. The degree of new policy implementation DNPI grows only slightly. The organization's ability to produce results RES, however, has risen because of two simultaneous effects: (1) the slight recovery of task effort allocation TEA, and (2) the increased task effort efficiency resulting from the degree of new policy implementation DNPI. Results RES rise enough, therefore, to cause a positive goal satisfaction GS, thereby removing the task pressures.

The combination of positive goal satisfaction GS and new policy effort allocation NPEA signals the start of internalization of the new policy INP. With internalization comes association pressure, which shifts task effort allocation TEA to new policy effort allocation NPEA. This shift causes the comparison of actual to needed effort CANE to rise, renewing growth in the degree of new policy implementation DNPI. The resulting increase in task effort efficiency nearly cancels the effect upon results RES of a falling task effort allocation TEA. Results RES hover around 1.1, and goal satisfaction GS steadies to zero.

Two features of this simulation deserve mention. The first is the two-stage advance of the degree of new policy implementation DNPI: the initial advance levels off and strength is marshalled for a renewed advance to full implementation. The second feature concerns the satisfying, rather than optimizing nature of the system. Given the particular assumptions concerning task effort efficiency and effort needed for maintenance, results RES could have stabilized at

1.35 instead of 1.1. The system instead selected a mode of operation which just satisfied the GOAL, allowing the untapped potential to be wasted in an unnecessarily high new policy effort allocation NPEA. The high value of comparison of actual to needed effort CANE indicates the magnitude of waste.

The second simulation differs from the first in both behavior pattern and in new policy and organization characteristics. A different new policy assumption eliminates the large gain in task effort efficiency as degree of new policy implementation DNPI rises. As shown in Figure 2, the new policy does not affect task effort efficiency. A different organization assumption reduces the constant goal from 1.1 to 1, causing initial results RES to equal GOAL, and causing initial goal satisfaction GS to equal zero. As in the first simulation, the behavior pattern develops when the organization shifts ten per cent of its task effort allocation TEA to new policy effort allocation NPEA at time 5.

Some of the early behavior in this simulation is reminiscent of the previous one: results RES and goal satisfaction GS decline sharply, task pressure begins to shift some of the new policy effort allocation NPEA back to task effort allocation TEA, and the degree of new policy implementation DNPI grows in response to the new policy effort allocation NPEA. Because the task effort efficiency remains constant, however, results RES reflect only the task effort allocation TEA and remain below GOAL. The negative goal satisfaction GS causes continuing task pressure without any counterbalancing internalization of the new policy INP and attendant association pressure. Thus, the new policy effort allocation NPEA continues its decline, effecting a negative comparison of actual to needed effort CANE. The negative comparison of actual to needed effort CANE reverses the trend in degree of new policy implementation DNPI and causes it to die out.

It seems reasonable that a nonproductive new policy should fail. The surprising part of this simulation lies in the length of time necessary to dispose of a worthless new policy. The task pressure mechanism indirectly and with great inefficiency affects the disposal because it operates in response to the goal structure, not through a direct evaluation of the new policy.

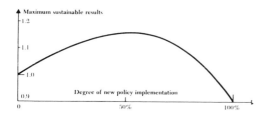

Figure 4   Maximum Sustainable Results

The third simulation contains some unusual but not wholly unrealistic assumptions regarding the new policy characteristics. The constant goal characteristics remain the same as in the second simulation. Figure 2 shows the relationship between degree of new policy implementation DNPI and task effort efficiency. The initial gain is substantial, but as degree of new policy implementation DNPI approaches 100 per cent, the task effort efficiency flattens out to a maximum of 130 per cent.

In Figure 3, the effort needed for maintenance rises slowly at first, and then very rapidly as degree of new policy implementation DNPI increases. Figure 4 shows how task effort efficiency and effort needed for maintenance combine to produce maximum sustainable results RES.

These non-linear relationships introduce some oscillation in the variables. The degree of new policy implementation DNPI does not reach 100 per cent because, as Figure 4 makes clear, that point is very unproductive. The system does settle, however, at a point far removed from the broad area of near maximization. The system has again chosen merely to satisfy its GOAL. The sharply rising demands of effort needed for maintenance ensure that there is no excess new policy effort allocation NPEA. The system's selection processes, however, still exhibit inefficiency in terms of what could be obtained.

Advantages of the Industrial Dynamics Approach

The industrial dynamics approach to the implementation problem contains two distinct advantages over non-system, non-dynamic approaches. First, the investigator's understanding of the complex interactions surrounding the implementation process in-

creases greatly. As an example, this study clearly demonstrates that the organization embodying these pressure responses is inefficient in selecting worthwhile new policies, in implementating them, and in rejecting worthless new policies.

With this greater understanding as a foundation, the investigator may now become a problem solver. He is more able to suggest improvements, both in crucial parameters and relationships and in system redesign. The simulation model provides a ready testing ground for these suggestions. Without resorting to the expensive and time-consuming method of actual trial, he may find out whether his suggestions would alleviate the basic problem. The advantages relating to suggested changes in the system have not been exploited here, leaving a fertile area for future work.

References
1 Roberts, Edward B., "New Directions in Industrial Dynamics," *Industrial Management Review*, Fall, 1964, pp. 5-13.

2 Berelson, Bernard, and Gary A. Steiner, *Human Behavior: An Inventory of Scientific Findings*, New York and Burlingame, Harcourt, Brace, and World, Inc., 1964.

3 Forrester, Jay W., *Industrial Dynamics*, New York and Cambridge, M.I.T. Press and John Wiley and Sons, Inc., 1961.

4 Pugh, Alexander L., III, *Dynamo User's Manual*, Second Edition, Cambridge, Mass., M.I.T. Press, 1963.

5 Schein, Edgar H., and Warren G. Bennis, *Personal and Organizational Change Through Group Methods: The Lab Approach*, New York, John Wiley and Sons, Inc., To be published.

27

Industrial Dynamics
and Management Information Systems

Henry B. Weil

Designing management information and control systems has all too often been a hit-or-miss proposition. What has been missing is a framework for identifying fundamental systems requirements and assessing the broad impact of alternative designs on organizational performance. A series of examples illustrates how industrial dynamics can provide the needed conceptual and analytical framework.

Introduction

What causes a large organization to be successful? Numerous factors enter into it including plain, ordinary luck. But in the final analysis, it's people. Many people, at different levels, making many decisions about what activities will be undertaken and how, and taking actions based on these decisions.

The decisions they make and the actions they choose to take are significantly influenced by the incentives, pressures, and perceptions existing in the organization. Research and study over the past few years have clearly shown that:

1. the organization's planning, performance measurement, and control systems are the major source of these influences;
2. as a result, the characteristics of those systems have a critical impact on organizational success; and, additionally
3. one can deliberately select a set of systems characteristics to steer an organization efficiently toward a given set of goals.

The relationships involved are very complex. One must assess the effect of systems characteristics—e.g., the specific performance measures employed, the frequency at which performance is measured, the bases for performance evaluation, the time period over which variances are corrected—singly and in various combinations on overall organizational performance. And one must do this within the context of an environment that is in a continual state of flux. It is well beyond the ability of intuition, experience, or ordinary analysis to deal with such a degree of dynamic complexity. The only practical approach has proven to be computer simulation.

To tackle design issues of this kind, we have employed the modelling, simulation, and systems analysis techniques of industrial dynamics. The basic analytical techniques were first conceived within the engineering disciplines to design complex feedback control systems like automatic pilots. It became apparent, however, that these techniques could also be applied to the study of any business, social, or economic system whose behavior is caused by the feedback nature of its intrinsic structure. In so doing, the original engineering approach has been modified to place more emphasis on analysis through simulation and less on calculating mathematical "solutions." The result is a methodology for analyzing the behavior of complex systems through: the development of structure-dominated *causal* models; feedback systems analysis; and computer simulation. The basic reference is Forrester [1].

The practitioner of industrial dynamics sees a firm, an industry, or the economy as a system of flows (e.g., funds, orders, goods) and levels (investment, deposits, employment, etc.) controlled by an interrelated set of decisions. The behavior of such systems depends importantly on its *structure* — that is, the levels and flows that constitute the system and the factors (e.g., information flows and decisions) upon which these depend. With industrial dynamics, it is relatively easy to model qualitative behavioral relationships such as attitudes or reaction to pressures and incentives. The methodology does not insist on the availability of empirical data, although added confidence obviously results when important relationships can be derived from statistical analyses.

This paper discusses how industrial dynamics can be used to design more effective management information and control systems. A general conceptual approach will first be presented, followed by several specific examples of how we have practiced what we preach.

Systems Analysis for Systems Design

The Usual Way.   An organization develops planning, performance measurement, and control systems to help it attain its objectives. Such systems provide management at many levels with information to steer portions of the firm's activities. This information typically includes:

1. operating targets (e.g., sales quotas, desired inventory levels, profit contribution goals);
2. plans for achieving these targets (e.g., budgets, staffing plans, sequences of required activities or events);
3. priorities for use in dealing with competing or conflicting alternatives;
4. policy guidelines or constraints within which plans must be developed and executed (e.g., the "approved list" and other guidelines for trust portfolios);
5. actual accomplishments;

6. variances between actual accomplishments and the various targets and plans;

7. linkages between performance and rewards.

From one organization to another, various portions of this information will be explicit in formal systems and reports, while the rest is implicitly understood. But in all cases, it produces incentives, pressures, and perceptions (of situations, of performance, of priorities, etc.) that influence decisions and lead managers to take actions. To the extent that these decisions and actions lead to effective accomplishment of overall organizational objectives, the systems are a success.

How is the process of system design usually approached? For one thing, managers commonly underestimate the impact of systems characteristics on organizational success. Often, they limit their thinking to the question: are our systems adequate for carrying out present and planned future activities? While this is a question of critical operational importance, stopping there ignores entirely a broad spectrum of policy-level issues. This incomplete conceptualization views planning, performance measurement, and control systems *too passively*. It suggests that systems inadequacies must stem from either improper anticipation of future activities (and, hence, systems requirements) or poor execution of indicated changes and developments.

Underestimation of broad systems impact has several consequences. First, it leads both managers and technical systems people to draw their conceptual boundaries too narrowly. This usually produces a functional compartmentalization of perceived systems requirements and of systems themselves. One typically finds production control systems, financial control systems, marketing information systems, inventory control systems, manpower information systems, corporate planning systems, capital budgeting systems, etc. which were developed without full recognition of their mutual interdependencies or collective impact.

A second consequence is that important policy decisions inherent in information and control systems design are not recognized for what they are. Selection of what turn out to be key systems characteristics are not treated as policy issues, by policy makers. Too frequently, they are subsumed into the design process to be decided by technicians.

A further weakness of the usual approach to systems design stems from the way in which requirements are generated. The ''problems'' that a given information or control system is intended to deal with are most often just manifestations of a more subtle and pervasive underlying fault. So long as this underlying malaise is not diagnosed, one is doing nothing more than symptom suppression. And until the real problem is solved, it will continue to manifest itself in one way or another no matter how many systems are developed.

As a result of the factors I have outlined above, the design and operation of management information and control systems has, all too often, become a hit-or-miss proposition. Much money has been wasted on systems that failed to produce the expected benefits or, in achieving their objectives, produced major unanticipated negative side-effects. What has been missing is a framework for identifying fundamental systems requirements and assessing the broad impact of alternative designs on organizational performance.

A More Inclusive Framework for Analysis.   What management information and control systems are really needed? How will this particular set of designs affect overall organizational performance? These are the key questions. And we have found that industrial dynamics provides a very powerful conceptual framework for dealing with them.

Anyone who designs an information or control system has a ''model''—a model that categorizes the problem, relates symptoms with causes, suggests problem-solving approaches, and relates that system to the corporate environment in which it will function. Usually, this model is in the designer's head. It is implicit and intuitive, based on his experience and a presumption that the situation is not too dissimilar from others he has encountered. Unfortunately, it is also usually incomplete, internally inconsistent, at least partially incorrect, and conflicting with the models of others who view the problem from different perspectives. Yet, despite these weaknesses, people have proven to be considerably better at specifying the structure of their environment than predicting the impact of that structure (or changes therein) on organizational performance. In this latter regard, the record is particularly dismal. Models that are incorrect and misinterpreted can easily lead to unproductive or counterproductive conclusions. Thus, few implicit models provide a confident and correct basis for systems design.

To get around those difficulties, we start by developing an *explicit* model of how a management information and control system relates to its ''environment.'' Employing computer simulation techniques, we then use this model to explore the likely effects of various systems characteristics on organizational performance.

This approach forces those involved in systems design to make explicit, and thoroughly test the assumptions that underlie their design decisions: the nature of problems; their causes; the consequences of alternative actions; and how various human, managerial, economic and operational factors interrelate. Our experience has shown that this is a very valuable process—that people are really quite surprised when it turns up things no one had thought of before, incorrect assumptions and differences of opinion about cause and effect. The analytical power and efficiency of simulation lets you pose extensive ''what if?'' questions. And furthermore, this approach leads to and facilitates a very close working relationship between the technical systems experts and their management ''customers.'' The modelling process serves as an important communications link between the two and makes it easier for their different expertise and experience to make the maximum contribution toward successful system design.

Now what, exactly, do we mean by ''. . . a model of how a management information and control system relates to its environment?'' I'll try to answer that first in conceptual terms and then follow it with a series of specific examples. Let me begin by going back to an earlier discussion—i.e., how many managers limit their thinking to the question of whether systems will be adequate to support future operations. As I said, that is only a part of the story. Yes, the nature of future activities does affect the adequacy of systems. What's more significant, however, is that the nature of planning, performance measurement, and control systems *determines what activities will be undertaken in the future and the adequacy with which they are performed.*

This is a very important point. It goes much further than merely saying these systems provide a procedural framework for planning and carrying out plans. It says that the variety of systems employed and the characteristics of each system determine what pressures, incentives and perceptions are produced at various points in the organization. And that the pressures, incentives and perceptions created by these systems *cause* the outcome of the planning process to be what it is, *cause* some alternatives to appear more desirable than others, *cause* an organization to emphasize some aspects of performance over others, and *cause* people at all levels to behave the way they do in managing their activities.

Some of these causal relationships are illustrated in a general way in Figure 1. This diagram depicts some important, but less obvious ways in which an organization's success in achieving its goals (growth, diversification, profitability, etc.) is dependent on the characteristics of its management systems. Specifically, the diagram portrays a sequence of cause-and-effect relationships, with the arrows indicating the direction of dependence or causality. Systems characteristics directly affect an organization's perception of its achievements. Indirectly (through the pressures, incentives, biases, etc. they create), they affect the action priorities and decision criteria existant within the

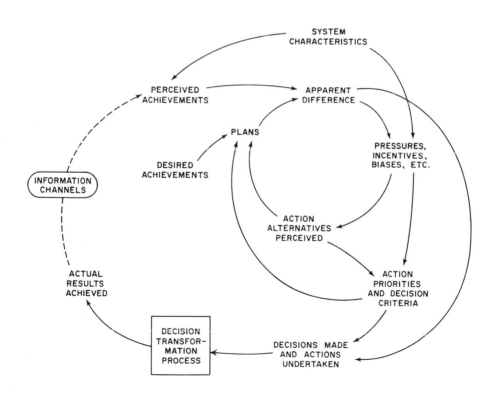

Figure 1   Impact of systems characteristics on decision making

organization and the action alternatives that are perceived. All of these influence plans, decisions, and actions taken which, in turn, produce whatever results are actually achieved.

This conceptual "model" is based on the study of many organizations. It has several noteworthy features. First, the transformation of plans and decisions into results takes place through a complex process which includes a basic structure of organizational, human, and market relationships. This structure is often obscured by its numerous sources of "noise" and random behavior, by the typically lengthy delays between cause and effect, and by its very complexity. A second aspect to be noted is the distinction between the achievements that are apparent in the organization and those that are real. The real situation is translated into the apparent through information and communication channels which contain delays, noise and bias. A third feature of the diagram is that the planning/decision-making process is viewed as a response to the gap between objectives of the organization and its apparent progress toward those objectives. Although both the objectives and achievements may be difficult to define precisely, and measure accurately, such goal-seeking behavior is nonetheless present in all organizations and in every subsystem of the organization. The fourth important characteristic of Figure 1 is the continuous feedback path of planning-decisions-actions-results-measurement-evaluation-planning. It is vital to effective systems design that each element of this feedback path be properly treated and that its continuous nature be recognized.

This very general model can be detailed and tailored to a wide variety of situations. In doing so, the "decision transformation process" and the relevant "information channels" would be modelled as they actually exist. Systems characteristics themselves would be represented at a macro level: e.g., the information impinging at various decision points; its timeliness and accuracy; the processes by which targets are set and performance against them evaluated; and the time horizons employed by decision makers.

In the following paragraphs I'll illustrate our approach with several examples of its application. Several other examples can be found in Roberts [2].

How We Practice What We Preach

Design of a Financial Information and Control System.   Vertical integration in a firm often produces conflict among performance measures and among the component organizations whose performance is being evaluated. This arises out of the vertical interdependencies that exist in terms of product flows, plus the need to establish separate performance objectives for the various component organizations despite those interdependencies. The extent to which the firm benefits from or is hurt by these conflicts depends on the factors previously discussed : i.e., precisely what structure of pressures, incentives, and perceptions they produce.

We have used industrial dynamics to analyze this kind of situation and to facilitate design of an improved system of financial controls. The setting was a large manufacturer-retailer of perishable food products. The apparent problem was growing discord between the firm's principal manufacturing department (which happened to produce bakery goods) and the Retail Food Division (which sold them to the public).

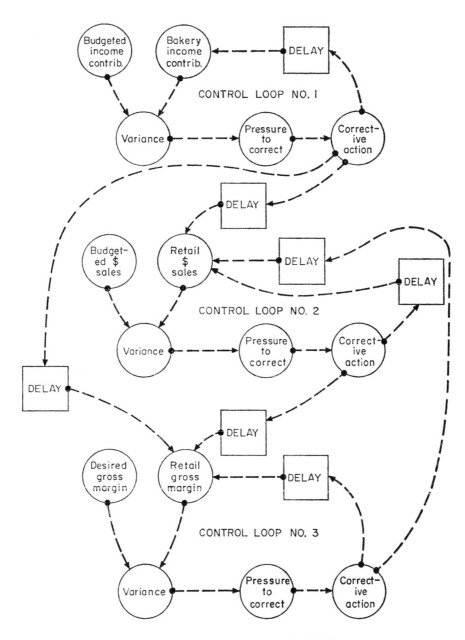

Figure 2 Major control loops in the production/sales system
Source: Roberts et al. [3]

An industrial dynamics model of the production and sale of bakery goods was developed. A complete description of this model can be found in Roberts, et al. [3]. In brief, the model had two major sectors, one that described the flow of orders and goods and another that described cash flows and the flow of financial performance information. From preliminary simulation analyses with this model, it became apparent that the interactions among three performance measures (i.e., manufacturing income contribution, retail dollar sales, and retail gross margin percentage) formed a complex feedback

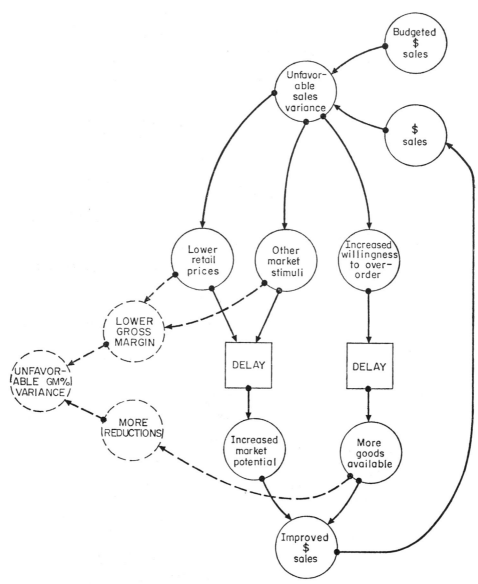

Figure 3   Correcting an unfavorable sales variance
Source: Roberts et al. [3]

system which determined company behavior. These relationships are depicted in Figure 2.

It further became clear that there were some significant built-in conflicts which were producing short-term fluctuations in company performance and were at the heart of the intra-organizational discord. Look at the second "control loop" in Figure 2. Consider an instance in which sales have fallen below their budgeted level. Retail's response was relaxing of prices, an increase in advertising expenses, and the offering of more specials. Pressure in the merchandising group for more sales resulted in specials with larger price elasticities, allocation to the stores and ordering from manufacturing in excess of historical amounts, and pressure on responsible individuals (known as "dairymen") in the stores. A diagram of this process is shown as Figure 3.

However, none of these actions had an immediate impact on sales because all required many weeks of lead-time. In fact, the unfavorable variance would become worse as built-in growth in the budget caused sales targets to rise each week. Especially when under pressure from the President, Retail intensified its corrective measures. This was to be expected, since for many weeks management was unable to measure the success of its first attempts.

After some weeks, the first effects of Retail's efforts would become apparent as sales began to recover. The marketplace's full response followed shortly, and everyone would seem much happier. At this point, sales would be rising back to and, in fact, past the budgeted level. But lowered prices and over-ordering (tactics used to stimulate sluggish sales) had a depressing effect on gross margin. Thus, with sales in relatively good shape, Retail's top management naturally turned its attention to this second area—improvement of profits—shown as "Loop 3."

Again, management's tactics for dealing with one type of performance problem would cause another problem to occur. Specifically, Retail's natural reaction to low gross margin was to turn conservative: resisting price reductions (and, in some cases, actually raising prices) and becoming quite cautious in its choice of specials and its allocation of merchandise to the store. Inevitably, these moves would hurt sales volume—and the whole cycle would be reinitiated. This pattern was amplified by the behavior of the Manufacturing group, as it attempted to produce budgeted income contribution.

Having diagnosed the original situation, we then used the simulation model as a "test bed" to develop an improved financial control system. We explored a number of alternative approaches to performance measurement, transfer pricing, and budgeting. And we studied the impact of various levels of performance pressure within the company. In this last regard, we found that interdivisional competition was not the ogre conjured by those who believe that attempts to optimize at the Division level inevitably lead to sub-optimization of corporate achievement. On the contrary, in this type of vertically-integrated organization, interdivisional competition for profits (and other forms of performance pressure) turn out to be the principal stimuli for company growth.

Design of an Engineering Information System. In response to the growing inability of its Engineering Department to service the demands placed upon it, a major world-wide manufacturing corporation undertook development of an on-line engineering information and design system. This might appear to be a rather straightforward, though demanding, technical endeavor. In fact, it involved many subtle "systems" issues (e.g., performance appraisal, financial controls, capital budgeting, sales estimation) not too dissimilar to the ones discussed in the preceeding example. The answers to questions like: "How might the firm's sales forecasting method and the speed with which it can add new capacity interact to produce short-term capacity cycles?" are difficult to obtain. Yet it is essential to consider them when one is designing an information system that may, among other things, significantly increase the speed with which capacity can be added. The industrial dynamicist is both aware of the need to investigate these more subtle aspects of information system design and equipped with the analytical tools to do so.

To explore issues of this type, we developed a series of industrial dynamics models that addressed both the corporate level and intradepartmental implications of the new information system. At the corporate level, the principal issues had to do with the proposed system's impact on overall growth and stability. Figure 4 represents the way in which the company attempted to match its production capacity to demand or potential sales. In Loop 1, the difference between existing capacity and projected sales generates new capacity requirements which, after planning and approval delays, become capacity under construction. Loop 2 corrects the estimate of new capacity requirements by taking into account capacity already under construction. In Loop 3, an increase in sales leads to new plant construction which, if potential sales are above capacity, leads to further increases in sales.

These relationships are, in many industries and companies, the cause of "capacity cycles." They can occur when the "gain" (i.e., the force or vigor with which action is taken in response to changes in information) is high at any decision point in Loops 1 or 2, a situation we might characterize as over-reaction. It was possible that a significant reduction in capacity planning and approval delays might have caused the company to over-react to short-term variations in the market. This would have produced cycles of

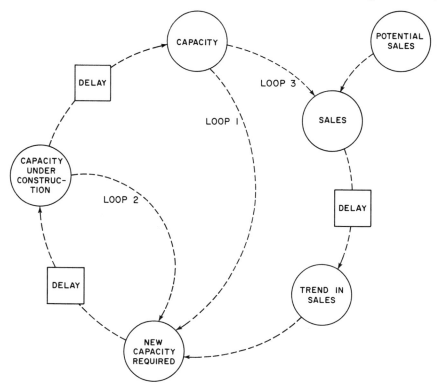

Figure 4   Sales forecasting and capacity acquisition

under- and over-capacity. Hence, it was crucial that the forecasting techniques being used to generate potential sales and estimated capacity requirements contain adequate "smoothing" to avoid unstable behavior. Here is a good example of how a characteristic of an information system can importantly affect overall organizational performance.

Within the Engineering Department, it became quite clear that a well-organized and structured method of presenting historical and current data to the design engineer was necessary if learning from experience were to occur effectively. This was defined as one of the prime tasks of the new information system. However, it also became evident that there were factors which might conflict with our attempts to strengthen the system's heuristics. These are shown in Figure 5.

The evaluation of engineering performance took place on the basis of variances in purchase orders from the budget and on the basis of problems in construction and operation of a facility that were attributed to poor planning or design. These forms of performance information — budget variances and other problems — must be compared against some standard in order to provide evaluation. The standards themselves are, as shown in Figure 5, the result of past performance. This is especially true in the absence of outside, independently determined performance standards.

The relationships as they then stood discouraged change and innovation. This was so because the engineers knew they were being measured against their own past

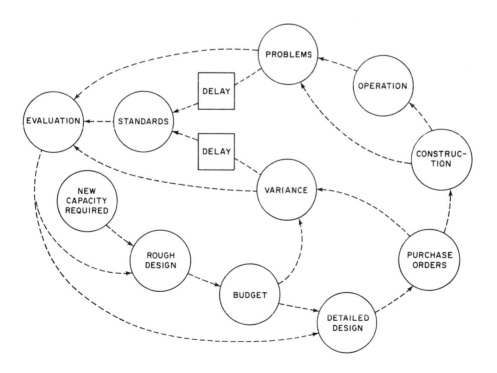

Figure 5   Performance evaluation

performance. The easiest way to avoid negative evaluation in this case was to simply do the same things that were done in the past. Any departure from the past risked an evaluation indicating poor performance.

Thus, in designing the engineering information system, the company had to deal with two interrelated problems. First, they had to decouple current evaluation standards from past performance, so that the structure of pressures and incentives encouraged, rather than discouraged, change and improvement. Second, they had to deal directly with the conflict between evaluation of *present* performance and the engineers' willingness to learn from and improve on *past* performance — i.e., encourage them to "risk" innovation.

In addition to the issues discussed above, interrelationships between the new information system and both the company's capital budgeting and engineering resource allocation practices were investigated. Out of all these analyses came a series of design criteria the engineering information system had to meet, and a series of concurrent enabling changes which were required elsewhere in the company to make the new system work.

Planning at a Large Commercial Bank.   The impression of future conditions portrayed in the Bank's longterm plans (especially the future availability of funds) sets the tone for considering new undertakings. If the outlook is optimistic, more new projects are initiated; the Bank is more venturesome in taking risks and entering new areas. Thus, in these regards, there are incentives to be unrealistically optimistic about the future, particularly if you have a proposed new venture coming up for consideration. To maintain objectivity, there must be counterbalancing pressures to be realistic in long-range planning. Typically, these are produced by having long-range plans closely integrated with short-term budgets and targets (e.g., by having a "rolling" five-year financial plan, the first year of which becomes the basis for current budgets) *and* by explicitly measuring performance against the near-term portions of these plans. The latter step, in particular, produces pressures for conservatism because if you plan recklessly and then can't make it, you are in trouble.

However, evidence suggests that at this particular Bank long-range planning is not closely linked to annual budgeting, etc., nor has performance relative to long-range plans been an important basis for managerial control. This imbalance of pressures has biased long-range plans toward over-optimism. Some short-term actions taken on the basis of these plans have turned out to be unrealistic. And unless a balance of pressures is attained, the more this information is used for near-term decision making, the more mistakes will be made. This year, for example, required levels of computer services were formulated from volume data in the long-range plans. They turned out to be excessive. When the volume planned by other Divisions failed to materialize, the Computer Services Division had to cut back. But additional reductions could have been made (or some increases never initiated) if more realistic estimates of volume had been prepared last year.

The relationships being discussed here are shown in Figure 6. In a somewhat expanded form, this diagram could be the basis of an industrial dynamics model. That

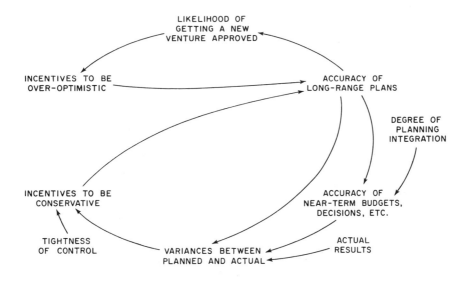

Figure 6   Factors causing bias in long-range plans

model, in turn, would help us design a more balanced long-range planning system. We would use simulation to explore questions such as:

1. What balance of incentives will maximize orderly progress toward the Bank's objectives (profitability, growth, diversification, etc.)?
2. How can overall Bank performance be made less sensitive to inaccuracies (which, to some degree, are inevitable) in long-range plans and forecasts?
3. What degree of "control tightness" is best?
4. What would be the effect of employing different decision criteria for approving proposed new ventures?

The same problems of pressure balance and bias exist in the decision process by which new ventures are considered and approved. Evidence suggests that this is responsible for the Bank's present difficulties in two areas of recent expansion. Any proponent of a new venture is tempted to make his opportunity look as good as possible. If he is biased toward over-optimism in order to sell top management, and if in addition everyone is working with a future outlook that itself is overly optimistic, you get a compounding of errors. After a brief honeymoon, the result is a manager struggling desperately to live up to unrealistic projections. The natural reactions are to promise more than you can deliver, to take on marginal customers, to skimp in ways that ultimately lower the quality of service, and to churn people and strategies in hope of stumbling on "the right combination."

All of these things happened to some extent at the Bank in question. Salesmen oversold the new services. The Bank solicited and accepted the business of marginal customers. At first, people couldn't be hired into these areas fast enough; now they

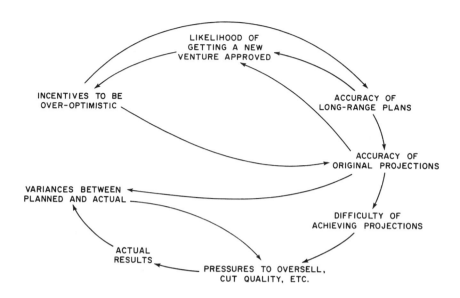

Figure 7   Factors causing new ventures to get into trouble

appear to be over-staffed. Services are being redesigned to make them more economical to provide. Almost inevitably, this will lower their quality. There are still many unanswered questions about customer acceptance of these changes. But as the pressure for performance increases, the risks are reassessed.

So here is a second example of how systems characteristics produce biases, pressures, incentives, and unrealistic perceptions that, in turn, caused problems for the Bank. It is summarized in Figure 7. Again, this simple model could be expanded (e.g., to include the relationships shown in Figure 6) and used to design a refined approach to planning.

Now, what would happen in the above situation if the Bank instituted a negotiated transfer pricing system for computer services? In all likelihood, a division in trouble would be very aggressive in seeking price reductions from the Computer Services Division. It might threaten to drastically cut its consumption of services, and might actually carry out some reductions as part of cost cutting. Alternatively, the division might attempt to procure the desired services outside the Bank. And the whole commotion over computer costs might just be a smokescreen to obscure other problems. What would be the impact of all of this on the Computer Services Division's performance, and on what it would have to charge other "customers" to meet the profit contribution target it would have under such a system? What would be the effect on other divisions' performance as Computer Services tried to raise the prices it charged them? And how much deeper in trouble would the problem division get as a result of all of this?

There are no fast and easy answers to those questions. Just to diagram all of the relationships involved takes several pages and ends up looking like a plate of spaghetti. But the questions and a hundred others like them cannot be ignored. This Bank is in the midst of rapid change in its systems, its business, and its environment. Everything is changing at once, yet at the same time the Bank is considering and implementing new concepts of cost allocation, transfer pricing, performance measurement, incentive compensation, planning, and asset management.

So much change in a complex structure defies intuition, experience, or ordinary analysis. However, in all of the cases discussed in this section, the payoffs are enormous to a management that can understand these complicated cause and effect relationships and architect the systems structure that most effectively leads to desired accomplishments. In both engineering and management, a simulation modelling approach has repeatedly proven to be the best way to handle this type of analytical problem.

Conclusion

Most organizations of any size have an elaborate structure of planning, performance measurement, and control systems. And the activities which these systems impact are quite extensive. With such a complex set of interrelationships, it is *very* difficult to determine exactly what incentives, pressures, and perceptions are being created at any given point in the organization, and, thus, what impact all of these systems *as a group* are having on decisions and actions. In fact with a structure of more than moderate complexity, it is completely impossible to make those determinations based on observation, experience, or conventional forms of analysis. But it is important to do so, because the very difficulties being discussed keep most managements from manipulating systems characteristics to control organizational performance. And they tend to produce systems structures that don't deliver their full potential benefits or, sometimes, create problems more significant than those they resolve. This is why we have employed industrial dynamics to assist in designing management information and control systems.

References

1. Forrester, J. W. *Industrial Dynamics*. Cambridge, Mass.: The M.I.T. Press, 1961.

2. Roberts, E. B. "Industrial Dynamics and the Design of Management Control Systems," *Management Technology*, vol. 3, no. 2 (December 1963).

3. Roberts, E. B., D. I. Abrams, and H. B. Weil. "A Systems Study of Policy Formulation in a Vertically-Integrated Firm," *Management Science*, vol. 14, no. 12 (August 1968).

28
A Banker's Appreciation
of Systems Considerations

Daniel C. Hickson

Awareness of the existence of basic ideas comes with the recognition of similarities. Such similarities are more often found in the relationship of parts than in the parts themselves. In your field, the application of this kind of thinking has opened new approaches to the learning process. In my field, that of business, a parallel line of thinking is going on. Where you seek basic ideas in different subjects such as biology, history, physics, and mathematics, we seek basic ideas in different departments such as accounting, production, marketing, and finance. We also are discovering more similarities in interactions than in components.

In the field of business we have borrowed from you—even your language. We speak of systems engineering as though we originated it. But a banker never forgets a loan, so accept my thanks. I am going to tell you a little about the application in business of the systems approach. I shall be personal in that I shall outline things I have seen, endeavors in which I played a role. In these accounts I hope you will see that attempts are being made to study the business enterprise as a whole—to recognize its structure, to understand its behavior.

Six summers ago I attended a special program in Advanced Industrial Dynamics at M.I.T. This was conducted by Professor Jay W. Forrester whose excellent first textbook on the subject had just been published.[1] In hindsight I realize that my reasons for taking the course were unique. I awoke to this in part as I became acquainted with my fellow students; a few were from the academic world, primarily curious about this new subject; most of them were bright young men from industry, sent by their companies as part of their management training. But I was there for a more explicit reason: I was seeking a new approach to a specific problem which I had identified in my industry and in my company. To make that meaningful, I must tell you that my field is planning, my industry is banking, and my company is Bankers Trust Company, one of the ten largest banks in the country.

This is an edited version of a paper presented by the author to the annual meeting of the American Society for Engineering Education, June 17–20, 1968, at the University of California at Los Angeles. The author was then Vice President of Forward Planning, Bankers Trust Company, New York. The paper is reprinted here with the author's permission.

As I have said, I chose to expose myself to industrial dynamics for a particular purpose. I can say to you with great sincerity that for me, for my purpose, and for my company, it was a very wise choice. Before you turn off this seeming commercial, I add that I am not saying this might be true for anyone else or in any other circumstances. In fact, I am not offering my pills to anyone.

As business grows, it tends to become more complex. The company which expands by vertical or horizontal integration finds itself involved with complexity. So also does the company which seeks diversification. Six years ago when I took Forrester's course, I was seeking a new approach to increasingly complex problems in the growing banking business. Possibly my long-ago engineering education was evidencing itself. In any event, the systems approach appealed to me—and the inclusion of the concepts of feedback was particularly attractive. What were the banking problems to which a new approach was needed?

Money flows into a bank for a number of reasons and flows out for other reasons. But a great deal of it seemingly stays right there. People are using it for various purposes and it does change hands a lot, but often the man who takes some money out gives it to someone else who puts it in.

Today, Bankers Trust's balance sheet shows in excess of six billion dollars in assets. Most of these are in various types of loans. Some are loans to the Federal Government of short maturity—government bills. Others are loans to the Federal Government of longer maturity—government bonds. Then there are loans to states and municipalities with wide ranges of maturities and with so-called tax-free status. Even greater are the loans to commerce and industry with different interest rates, varying maturities, and considerable ranges of credit-worthiness.

On the other side of our balance sheet are our six billion dollars of liabilities. Here we see our deposits, both demand and time. Here also is reflected what we owe our bondholders and the equity of our shareholders.

Whether they be assets or liabilities, the characteristic common to all is that they are constantly changing. Every minute of every day deposits are made and deposits are withdrawn; loans are made and loans are paid; government bills are purchased and government bonds mature; municipal bonds are purchased and state bonds are sold.

The traffic is intense. The rules of the regulatory bodies are many and the probes of the bank examiners go deep. Obviously our Chief Executive is not receiving every deposit, buying every bond, or making every loan. These actions are taken by many different people.

Before I lose you in the seeming confusion of this traffic, let me be sure I have not scared you too much. We big banks do a good job of managing our assets. One simple fact makes my point: no large American bank has had a loss year in the last quarter of a century.

But being an average bank in our industry is not consistent with the goal of my institution. We call this mediocrity. We are not satisfied to judge ourselves only by analysis of our results compared to our competition. We know this will not cause us to innovate. Frankly, we are not striving to be the largest bank—but we constantly try to grow. We have a young management—by intent. We welcome challenge. We seek the virility of growth and the stimulation of competition.

Since we do a good job in managing our assets, why are we not content to let it go at that? Because we know there may be different and better ways—ways which our competitors and we have not explored.

Now you can see why I became interested in the industrial dynamics approach. Could not the flows of money into the bank and out of it be subjected to systems analysis? Are not the tax laws typical constraints? Are not the regulations typical parameters? Why would we loan a million dollars to our customer at 5½% during a tight money period when we could buy a municipal bond that would yield us 7%? We answer this last question today by saying: because of loan-deposit feedback. Sounds good, and we mean it even though we have a great deal more to investigate in this particular feedback loop.

For the past five years we have been applying many of Forrester's methods of systems analysis to our operations at Bankers Trust. Let me hasten to add we are also applying methods other than Forrester's. In fact, I do not agree with his downgrading of operations research approaches. We have been using a linear programming model to aid in our asset management decisions for several years.

Our systems investigation strived to recognize structure in order to understand behavior. Our attempts to date have been limited to considerations of the interactions between flows of materials and information. Our materials in a financial institution are dollars. We have made no attempt to date to add the other flows of the industrial dynamics approach, that is orders, personnel, capital equipment, and money in the usual sense.

Many effective business studies start with the collection of large quantities of factual data as to past performance. These are subjected to searching analysis. Valuable conclusions may result. Better ways of generating, storing, retrieving, communicating, and using factual data may be found. By this approach, or some other one, the so-called Management Information Systems are developed. Harnessing the power and speed of modern computers makes such endeavors fascinating tasks. We are doing a lot of this at Bankers Trust but, I hasten to advise you, before I proceed, that this is not what I am talking about today. I am telling you the story of our asset management studies.

First of all, we did not collect quantities of factual data. We were aware that in our complex system there were many small decisions made under decision rules somewhat quantitative in their expression. A maximum or a minimum was involved. Somewhat greater decision rules were based on two variables—ratios like loans-to-deposits. To us these seemed like orderly controls.

Our asset management study was concerned with the why behind such decision rules. We recognized that we were traveling over well established roads; many people had been there before us and the road signs were in place, readable and being used. You will be correct if you imply that we were challenging some of these.

We adhered to systems concepts including the closed boundary and the feedback loops. Within feedback loops we organized our approach into the substructures of levels and rates. Possibly because we are a financial institution, we found that the system structure organized in such a way was quite natural. Level of loans and level of deposits seemed acceptable to us and quite in keeping with our traditional accounting system. These were merely new labels for accumulations shown on our balance sheet at any particular instant.

In a bank the idea of a new balance sheet each day is not a drastic one. The difference between the level of deposits on June 18th and June 19th is the result of rates or flows. To call them rate of making deposits and rate of withdrawing deposits was easy. In turn, the rate of making loans and the rate of paying loans certainly changes the level of loans. Information about the level of loans affected the rate of making loans, so it seemed quite proper to consider the rate of making loans a decision point.

We have built a mathematical model of our asset management system. It is a dynamic model.

We carefully organized our model building team. Three young men from our Management Science group were assigned by their boss. These men were quite recent employees. Since they did not work for me, the superior-subordinate discipline was avoided. Each man was encouraged to make his individual contribution. This was helped by the addition to the team of two outside consultants who did not know each other before the project started. One consultant was Dr. Kalman J. Cohen, Head of the Economics Department of the Graduate School of Carnegie-Mellon. He had acted as a consultant to Bankers Trust for about five years and was partly familiar with our bank operations and problems. The other consultant was Alexander L. Pugh III, from Forrester's teaching staff at M.I.T. He was one of the creators of DYNAMO, the special-purpose compiler for generating the running code for industrial dynamics models. He had no particular familiarity with banking when the project started. I acted more or less as the godfather of the project and as the voice of experience.

Our joint work sessions lasted three consecutive days at monthly intervals. Assignments were suggested and accepted at these sessions for work between sessions. One of the young men undertook the project housekeeping tasks. For the most part, we went out of town for three days and two nights. Our work days were long and uninterrupted. We found dialogues on conceptual matters required prolonged concentration periods. On a number of occasions we invited different top officials of the bank to participate for the middle day of such three-day meetings, never more than one official at a time.

This helped all of us to keep in touch with the real world we were trying to model. It also gave us the point of view of the manager as to that world. Several other desirable features were by-products of this idea. Frank exposure to the intensity of our wranglings with concepts developed strong building blocks of confidence for our conclusions. Our willingness, in fact our invitation, to have our efforts monitored helped prevent clouds of mystery from forming around our project. Our humility was interpreted as a tribute to the importance of the endeavor. Most important, we developed a feeling of involvement on the part of potential beneficiaries of our effort.

As I look back upon the work we did, several milestones of progress stand out. One was when we resolved to discipline ourselves to keep working on our beliefs as to the nature of the existing system rather than give in to temptations to improve parts of it as we went along. This was not easy. I must admit that at times the drudgery of detective work threatened to dampen the creative fires. But we unearthed enough artifacts to challenge our imaginations and keep going forward. We kept reminding ourselves that a system did exist—for the management of the bank's assets was going on every minute of every day and every night that we were at work on our project.

Another milestone of progress was erected after we had been working a long time. With the clarity of hindsight I now know that we should have arrived at it sooner. After spending much time trying to find the best way to take each forward step, we resolved to stop trying to be so perfect and to push forward to get a crude model working. We evolved a practical way to do this—or maybe we were just lucky. We agreed that one of us (Alexander Pugh) would act as a scout and move out ahead of the pioneering task force. He went forward alone hacking his way through the underbrush and swimming the rivers. We followed and later went back to build our roads and our bridges. Our strategy was built on the hypothesis, or hope, that a crude working model would be a powerful tool for model building. It was a successful strategy!

I shall now identify for you several of the systems approaches of industrial dynamics which we found particularly valuable in our model building.

High on the list is the simplicity of the mathematics. Time was taken to arrange to express procedures in mathematical terms far simpler than those required to design such procedures. I think this is one of Forrester's most important contributions and marks him as a modern educator.

The simplicity of the mathematics allowed me to participate in the model building—and for this thrilling experience my debt of gratitude to Forrester is a personal one. I like to think that my "voice of experience" role was important in the model building—but here I may be subjective rather than objective. However, putting my own ego aside, I can report that we were able to enlist the help of many people in my bank. Often we found that we could test our understanding of what was told to us by writing a simple difference equation on a blackboard in the presence of the person interviewed. Some people picked up quite easily our references to levels and rates. They found the mnemonic representation of quantities rather fascinating. These preliminary peeks at our model helped build empathy which contributed to our success.

Another of the approaches of industrial dynamics which was important to us was the capability to cope with nonlinearity. Most of the real-world conditions which we were attempting to portray were not linear. In banking we are very conscious of the money market. We know that price is an information link between supply and demand which has to be tempered in the heat of the busy market place. For example: anticipation of money scarcity causes pressure in the money market. The reflection of this pressure is more seeming scarcity. The seeming scarcity translates back into more anticipation. Feedback circuits exist and the amplification may be great. To treat the pressures of such real world conditions as linear is as ridiculous as to assume they are static.

Part of the capability of dealing with nonlinearity was developed as Forrester's first textbook was being published. Here I use "capability" to include the thought of "compatible with the simple mathematics." A nonlinear functional relationship between two variables can be brought into use. The relationship can be expressed by a graph. A table corresponding to it can be made by considering one of the variables as independent and expressing its value at equally spaced steps. Opposite each such value is placed the value of the other variable. The DYNAMO Compiler, for use with industrial dynamics models, can bring this so-called TABLE function into use.

Another feature of industrial dynamics which had high value to us was the empirical nature of it. Exhaustive studies by elegant mathematics have their place but were not compatible with the way in which we planned to use our model. Business opportunity often will not wait for the one best answer to be found, communicated to, and accepted by the decision-making executive. I observe that today black boxes are looked upon with considerable suspicion—too many of them have Pandora labels under their black paint and turn out to be booby traps for budgets. But, the experimental approach is understandable to business managers and progress can be monitored by them. This characteristic appeals to the business decision maker who prides himself on his practicality, a quality he has found desirable in dealing with customers, employees, and shareholders.

My account of our asset management studies will be incomplete if I fail to give you a partial report on the benefits derived. At Bankers Trust in the past two years we have had to make a number of changes in personnel at quite high levels. Almost all of these were occasioned by our age 65 retirement rule. However, two of the changes were something other than orderly changes in people. We established a marketing department, something new in our organization, and we hired an executive from outside the bank to run it—a man new to banking. Also, we created a specific new job at top level—that of asset management—and transferred to that job one of our most valuable line department managers.

In 1964 we successfully sold to the public 100 million dollars of debentures at a 4½% rate. At that time, for a large bank to issue debentures was a very daring thing to do. No other large bank in New York did it for two years; then almost every one did. Two years later the effective rates they paid were much higher than ours. Our early model building efforts had given us the confidence to be courageous.

According to the financial publication, Forbes, reporting on 1967 performance, Bankers Trust was at the top of the growth list of large banks. Also among New York banks it was at the top as to average profitability over a five-year period. Certainly some of the credit for such achievements can be attributed to the better understanding of our business and the systems approach used to gain it. Our model building was a most revealing task. Star shells of insight burst around us and we have been busy doing things as a result of what we saw revealed. I wish to emphasize that these insights came out of the building of models rather than the operation of them.

We are engaged in further work in building better models, knowing we will continue to get a large return on the small investment involved. How much added benefits we shall receive from operations of models remains to be seen.

Notes

1. The textbook referred to is Jay W. Forrester's *Industrial Dynamics*, (Cambridge, Mass.: The MIT Press, 1961).

29

Designing Financial Policies to Deal with Limited Financial Resources

James M. Lyneis

Introduction

Managers of growth firms often encounter a situation in which available cash resources are not sufficient to finance investment in productive assets. Investment in productive resources generally requires a relatively large initial cash expenditure. The cash return on the investment, however, tends to be spread out over many years in the future. By exhausting both internal and external sources of funds, the cycle of cash expenditure and cash return may strain a firm's ability to make the necessary investment.

One accepted solution to a cash shortage is limiting investment to a level which can be supported by available funds. Models of capital budgeting under conditions of capital rationing illustrate the limited-investment solution. However, managers can take other actions besides control of investment expenditures to alleviate a shortage of cash. Alternative actions, including increasing price or restricting credit to customers, have not been adequately evaluated in the financial literature. Instead, managers have had to rely on intuition and experience to estimate the possible consequences of their actions.

Unfortunately, two factors greatly complicate the design of financial policies through intuition and experience: (1) the multiplicity of factors and interrelationships influencing cash flow, and (2) the manner in which long-run effects of policy change differ from short-run effects. The multiplicity of influences on a firm's cash flow greatly complicate a calculation of the total impact of a policy change. Many complex interactions are inherent in a firm's accounting structure, debt-maturity structure, and tax and dividend payments. Moreover, a policy change often produces opposing effects on cash flow. For example, an increase in price increases the cash flow from a unit sale but also reduces the number of unit sales. The price increase thereby also lowers the investment in productive assets necessary to support the new rate of sales. As another

This chapter originally appeared as M.I.T. System Dynamics Memorandum D-2155-2. An edited version of this paper appears in *Financial Management*, Vol. 4, No. 1, Spring 1975. The paper is reprinted here with the permission of the author.

example, a reduction in credit period may not only decrease the delay between the time of a sale and the cash flow from that sale, but also lower the volume of unit sales. Interactions between sales and cash flow are further complicated because a firm's level of sales is determined not only by the price of its product or its credit terms, but also by the availability of its product relative to the availability of competing products. Consequently, the net effect of a change in price (or credit period) also depends on the change in relative product availability following the initial increase or decrease in unit sales caused by the price change.

The long-run effects of a policy change often differ from the short-run effects. For example, a decrease in new investment reduces the current outflow of cash, thereby alleviating any cash shortage. In the long run, however, product availability is lower than it would be if the investment were undertaken. As a result, unit sales and the cash flow from sales are reduced. As another example, a price increase, even though it reduces unit sales, may so improve cash flow that more investment in productive assets can be undertaken. The firm thereby achieves an improvement in long-run product availability and sales, in exchange for a short-run decline in sales.

Design of financial policies can be facilitated through the use of a computer simulation model. A simulation model is superior to a manager's intuition and experience in that all of the interactions within the firm can be individually estimated and precisely (although perhaps not accurately) stated, and both the long-run and short-run effects of a policy change can be calculated. The manager's intuition and experience, however, are extremely important in determining the variables and interactions within the financial system and in evaluating simulation results.

A computer simulation model based on the system dynamics methodology[3] has been developed. The model incorporates the major determinants of the flow of funds within the financial sector of a firm, and between the financial sector and, respectively, the production sector of the firm and the financial markets. The model assumes that the objective of financial management is the design of financial policies to maintain an acceptable balance among profitability, risk, and growth pattern. Therefore, the model includes measures of profitability, risk, and growth pattern with which firms can establish the "best" set of financial policies for that firm. Explicit optimization, however, is avoided for two reasons. First, the criteria for a "best" set of financial policies (an objective function) may vary from firm to firm. Second, optimization of a nonlinear dynamic model is extremely difficult, if not impossible.

The model developed in this research differs in two important aspects from traditional cash flow models.[4,9] First, the model explicitly describes the effects of financial policies both on the firm's short-run and long-run sales and on the future ability of the firm to internally generate funds and/or obtain funds from the financial markets. Second, the model includes all the decision-making mechanisms which bring about change in the financial system. The model describes the manner in which information about the current and past state of the system is converted by decision-makers into actions altering the future state of the system. The model, therefore, is dynamic rather than static.

The remainder of the paper describes the overall structure of the model and illustrates the type of policy simulation experiments which can be conducted with the model. Three important policies for dealing with limited financial resources are compared—reducing investment, raising price, and restricting trade credit.

Introduction to System Dynamics

System dynamics is a theory of the structure of dynamic systems, a methodology for analyzing the behavior of such systems, and a vehicle for evaluating alternative policies designed to improve system behavior. A dynamic system is any system which changes over time as a result of conditions within the system. Examples of dynamic systems include the system regulating temperature in a house, the system balancing supply and demand in commodity markets, and the system governing the growth of a firm. According to the system dynamics theory of structure, a dynamic system consists of a set of interconnected feedback loops within a closed system boundary. A feedback loop exists whenever action A affects variable B, and variable B in turn affects subsequent action A.

Two types of feedback loops can be distinguished on the basis of the polarity of influence around the loop. In the positive feedback loop a change in system condition leads to actions which produce still further changes in the same direction. Positive feedback loops, therefore, are the sources of growth in a system. In the negative feedback loop the polarity of action is such as to counteract any deviation from a desired condition. If the value of a variable is too great, the system acts negatively to reduce the value, while, if the value is too small, the influence is in the opposite direction to increase the value. Negative feedback loops are the sources of goal-seeking behavior in a system.

System dynamics models attempt to describe the causal forces which produce change in a system. One type of causal force is the process of accumulation or integration. For example, the level of debt on a firm's balance sheet is increased by debt financing and decreased by debt repayment. Therefore, a system dynamics model of a firm's financial system might contain the following equation:

$$\text{DEBT (t)} = \text{DEBT (t} - 1) + (\text{DEBTFIN (t} - 1) - \text{DEBTPAY (t} - 1)) \qquad (1)$$

Equation 1 states that the level of debt (DEBT) at time t equals the level of debt at time $t - 1$ plus debt financing (DEBTFIN) over the interval from $t - 1$ to t (here assumed to be the value determined at time $t - 1$), minus debt repayments (DEBTPAY) over the interval from $t - 1$ to t. Further equations would then describe debt financing and debt repayment. Integrations are largely responsible for the dynamic behavior of real systems and for the dynamic behavior of system dynamics models of such systems.

A second type of causal force represents a static relationship between two variables. For example, Equation 2 below states that sales in period t is a function of price in the same period. In the model the normal rate of sales would be adjusted downward in response to an increase in price.

$$\text{SALES (t)} = \text{F (PRICE (t))} \qquad (2)$$

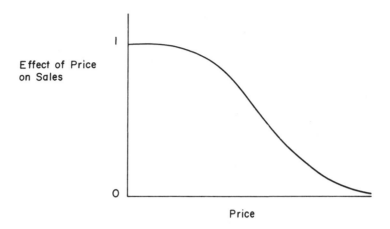

Figure 1 Effect of price on sales

Figure 1 illustrates one possible function. For low and high values of price, the function states that price changes have little marginal effect on sales. For a middle range of price, sales decline sharply with increases in price. The exact shape of such a function would of course depend on the nature of the product market.

Not all static relationships between variables are nonlinear. For example, labor costs might simply be total employment multiplied by the wage rate. System dynamics models, however, are capable of handling nonlinear relationships between variables when appropriate.

System dynamics models can also explicitly represent any delays occuring within a feedback loop. For example, the effect of price on sales defined by Equation 2 would realistically depend on a delayed value or the trend of price rather than the current price. Such a delay might reflect the time necessary to perceive and act on a price change. The length of the delay would depend on the nature of the product. (Technically, system dynamics models represent delays as exponential averages with a time constant equal to the average delay.)

In summary, a system dynamics model consists of a set of equations defining various static causal relationships between variables and integrations of variables. System dynamics models can be written as a set of first-order difference equations. The variables are embedded within positive and negative feedback loops.

The feedback loop structure of a model (and of the corresponding system) is the primary determinant of the model's (and system's) behavior. Behavior of a system dynamics model is determined by simulating recursively on a digital computer the set of equations comprising the model. Alternative policies are evaluated by observing the effect of changes in model parameters (inputs) and model structure (equations) on the simulated behavior of model variables (outputs). From such policy experiments, inferences concerning decision making in the real system can be made.

A policy in this context is a statement of how decisions are made. For example, a policy might state that if the demand for funds exceeds the supply, reduce investment expenditures. A manager would make operating decisions based on this policy.

A Model of the Financial System

Pricing, credit, and investment decisions are imbedded in many separate but interrelated feedback loops within a firm. These feedback loops connect the firm's financial system to the firm's production sector and to the financial markets. Feedback loops also connect the firm's production sector to the product market. The model developed in this research explicitly represents the feedback loops surrounding the firm's pricing, credit, and investment decisions as well as the firm's debt-maturity, equity issue, and dividend decisions; thereby, the model embodies a theory of the determinants of the flow of funds within, to, and from the firm.

The feedback loops described below are responsible for the multiplicity of interactions, opposing forces, and differing long-run and short-run effects associated with financing policy options. The accompanying simulation experiments show how the model can be used to evaluate the effect of alternative policies on financial system behavior.

Production Sector of the Firm.   In order to determine the short- and long-run effects of financial policies on the firm's sales, the model contains a representation of the production sector of a firm. The production sector contains one positive feedback loop and one negative feedback loop as shown in Figure 2. In the positive feedback loop, an increase in sales leads to an increase in forecast sales which, other things staying equal, causes an increase in investment. The increased investment eventually results in an increase in plant and equipment acquisitions and therefore in production capacity. A higher level of production capacity means increased production and, other things staying equal, greater product availability. The improved product availability increases sales by increasing the market share attained by the firm. Consequently, through the feedback loop just described, the initial increase in sales leads to a further increase or growth in sales.

Figure 2 shows one major negative feedback loop connecting sales and product availability. An increase in product availability increases market share and sales. The increased sales, however, tend to decrease product availability by either increasing order backlog or by decreasing inventory. Reduced product availability would be manifested in a lengthened delivery delay for the firm's product. The decreased product availability then acts to depress further sales through reduced market share. Thus an initial increase in product availability leads to a later decrease in product availability. The feedback loop is a negative loop whose effect is to equate sales to the firm's production capacity. An increase in sales above production capacity lowers product availability, thereby decreasing future sales. Similarly, a decrease in sales below production capacity improves product availability, thereby stimulating future sales. The feedback loop is in equilibrium when sales equal production capacity.

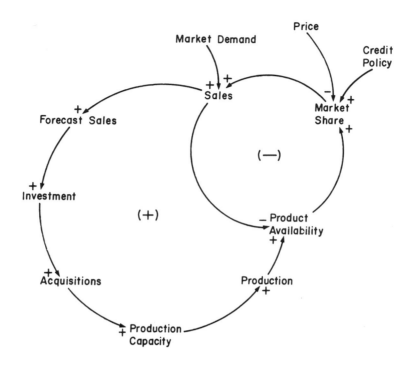

Figure 2   Feedback loops in the production sector of the firm

The arrows indicate the direction of causality with the sign at the end of the arrow showing the polarity of the influence. A positive sign indicates that an increase (decrease) in the variable at the beginning of the arrow causes an increase (decrease) in the variable at the end of the arrow; a negative sign indicates that an increase (decrease) in the variable at the beginning of the arrow causes a decrease (increase) in the variable at the end of the arrow. For example, an increase in production increases product availability, while an increase in sales decreases product availability. The signs in the center of each of the two feedback loops denote the polarity of the whole loop. In general, loop polarity can be determined by counting the number of negative influences around the loop. If the number of negative influences is zero or even, the loop is positive; if the number is odd, the loop is negative.

Figure 2 indicates that sales are determined by market demand, price, credit policy, and product availability. Market demand is defined as the rate of unit sales for all firms in the market. Market demand is specified exogenously. In the simulation runs which follow, market demand follows the growth pattern of a typical product life cycle: an introductory period of slow growth, followed by a period of rapid growth, and then a gradual leveling off to constant demand. In a specific situation, the model builder would determine, with the aid of market research and past company data, likely future patterns for market demand for the product in question.

The competitive variables price, credit policy (as measured here by credit period), and product availability jointly determine a firm's market share. The exact manner in which these competitive variables determine market share would depend on the particular product market being modeled. For illustrative purposes, in the simulation runs which follow, the hypothetical firm attains 100 percent market share if its competitive variables are at the industry minimum (or maximum). As price increases from the industry minimum or credit period or product availability decreases from the industry maximum, market share decreases and the firm's sales rate no longer equals market demand. In a specific situation, a firm's "maximum" market share would likely be less than 100 percent because of differences in other competitive variables such as product quality and sales effort not included in the model.

Within the simulation model curves of the type shown in Figure 1 specify the elasticity of sales to price, credit period, and product availability. Because the simulation runs which follow are included only to illustrate the system dynamics approach to designing financial policies, the exact curves used are not given. Briefly, market share decreases with increases in price, decreases in credit period, or decreases in product availability. Furthermore, the competitive variables interact to determine sales. An increase in price causes a decrease in unit sales. The decrease in sales, however, improves product availability thereby tending to increase unit sales. Therefore, the effects of price changes on sales are mitigated by the interaction of price and product availability in determining sales.

Each interaction and causal force in the feedback loop just described is represented by one or more model equations of the type discussed in the previous section. Additionally, equations describe the firm's accounting and cash flow structure. Variables on the balance sheet and other accumulations such as production capacity are modeled as integrations. Items on the income statement and such variables as sales and investment are modeled as static functions of other variables, including the integrations. (Further model equations represent the interactions in feedback loops described in the remainder of the paper). Detailed equations are not presented here, but can be found elsewhere.[5, 6]

Figure 3 shows the simulated behavior of several important system variables from the model. The complete output of a simulation run would also include balance sheets, income statements, and cash flow statements for any desired time interval over the length of the simulation, as well as time plots of any system variables. For illustrative purposes, the parameters determining asset, liability, and cost structure were derived from data in Robert Morris Associates' *Annual Statement Studies*[7] and were meant to be representative of manufacturing firms. In the simulation run used to generate the data in Figure 3, the firm has no debt limit; retained earnings and debt are used to finance investment. In this "base" case, the firm's investment is not constrained by financial considerations because external debt financing is always available; also, price and credit period remain at the industry norm as a result of the available financing. Sales grow rapidly in years 2 through 5, although sales growth is somewhat below market demand because the delay in acquiring resources causes product availability to fall below the industry maximum (2.0). Earnings per share also increases rapidly during the same period.

Throughout the rapid growth phase, internal cash flow (defined as collections of accounts receivable minus payments on accounts payable for operating expenses, in-

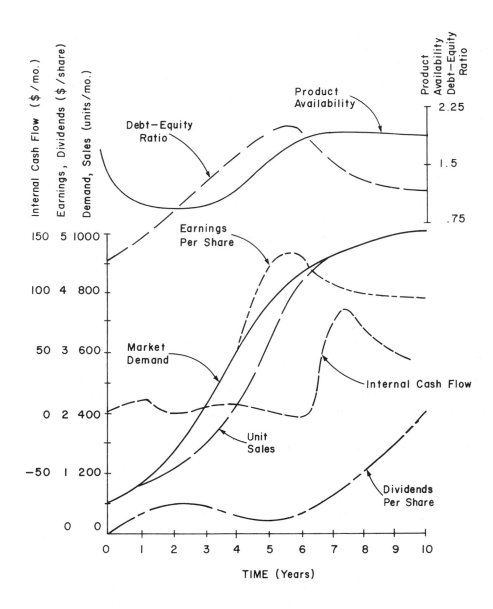

Figure 3 "Base" case—retained earnings and debt finance growth

terest, taxes, and dividends) remains fairly constant. A large portion of the revenues from sales is stored in the accumulation of accounts receivable (not shown) associated with growth. Production costs (not shown) to build inventory and deplete order backlog increase operating expenses. Interest payments (not shown) on the large debt level necessary to finance growth further increase cash outflow. Consequently the firm experiences a low internal cash flow.

The fall in the sales growth rate beginning in year 5, coupled with the increase in production capacity (not shown), allows the firm to increase production (not shown) above sales. As a result, inventories rise and order backlog falls; product availability improves. Improved product availability allows the firm to cut back on the capacity utilization rate (not shown) and, therefore, on production.

With the continued flow of accounts receivable accumulated during the growth phase and the decrease in interest expenses as debt levels fall, the decrease in production expenses associated with a lower utilization rate brings about a dramatic rise in internal cash flow. Earnings per share, on the other hand, peaks, then declines and stabilizes as the rise in fixed charges associated with growth in firm size overcomes the increase in income generated by the growth in sales. As growth ends around year 9, earnings per share and internal cash flow also stabilize.

The low internal cash flow in years 1 through 6, combined with the investment in productive assets necessary to meet growth in market demand, create a great demand for external funds. Demand for funds is high even though, simultaneously, the return on assets and the return on equity are both very high. Return on assets peaks at 17 percent; return on equity at 38 percent. The primary problems facing the firm are raising the money to finance investment during the rapid growth phase, and then determining the amount and timing of payments to owners from excess cash flow as growth slows. With the financing policy in the base run, heavy debt financing produces a peak debt-equity ratio of 1.67 in year six before falling to .9 in year ten. When sales level off, investment needs also decline. Internal cash flow continues to rise, however, as the return on previous investment is realized. Consequently, the firm generates a large excess of funds and dividends per share rise.

The base case simulation assumes that the firm has access to an unlimited supply of external debt. With a more realistic assumption of limited financial resources, the firm will encounter a cash shortage during the rapid growth phase. The balance of this paper is devoted to exploring alternative financial policies for achieving growth near market demand under conditions of limited financial resources.

Capital Rationing Response To Limited Financial Resources.   One common method for dealing with limited financial resources is to restrict investment expenditures. Both a negative feedback loop (Figure 4) and a positive feedback loop (Figure 5) influence the investment process. The negative loop acts to keep the cash expenditure for investment equal to the supply of funds. The positive loop generates increased cash flow from investment and therefore an increased supply of funds for future investment.

The dashed rectangle in Figure 4 surrounds a simplified representation of the production sector shown in Figure 2. An increase in investment leads to an increase in plant and equipment acquisitions and therefore an increase in cash expenditure. The increased cash expenditure causes the firm to increase debt financing. Increased debt financing increases the level of debt outstanding, and in turn reduces the firm's unused debt capacity. The lower unused debt capacity means that a lower supply of funds is available for future investment. The lower supply of funds constrains future investment, thereby completing the feedback loop.

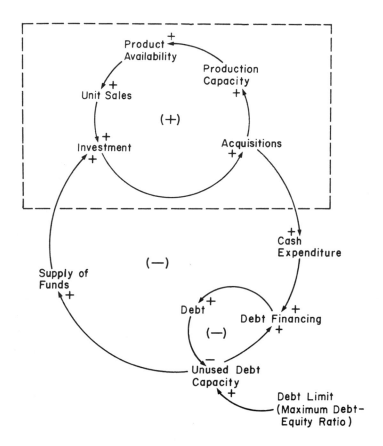

Figure 4   Negative feedback loop through investment

The existence of overall debt and equity limits is widely documented in the descriptive financial literature.[1,2,8] The inability to obtain additional debt or new equity may be imposed on a firm by the financial markets. In addition, some firms impose such limits on themselves. In the model described here, a debt limit is specified by a maximum (or target if internally imposed) debt-equity ratio. Multiplying the maximum debt-equity ratio by total equity gives the firm's debt limit or debt capacity. Unused debt capacity then equals debt capacity minus outstanding debt. As unused debt capacity approaches zero, debt financing also approaches zero. The inability to issue equity is represented in the model simply by not allowing the firm to issue any new equity.

Figure 5 shows the positive feedback loop associated with investment. An increase in investment increases sales through improvement in product availability. An increase in sales increases both internal cash flow and earnings. An increase in internal cash flow lowers the amount of debt financing required to meet cash expenditures for plant and equipment acquisitions (see Figure 4). As a result, less debt accumulates and

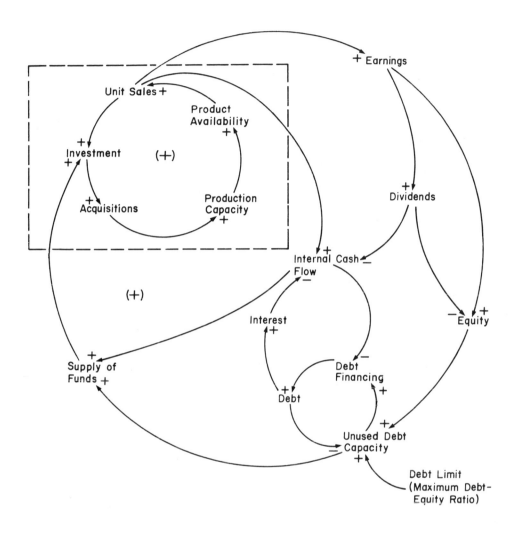

Figure 5 Positive feedback loop through investment

the firm has a larger reserve of unused debt capacity for future investment. Moreover, increased internal cash flow indicates a larger supply of funds for investment. The increase in the firm's earnings brings about an increase in equity and a larger supply of unused debt capacity. However a negative effect is also associated with increases in earnings. Dividends may also increase, thereby lowering both internal cash flow and additions to equity; interest expenses also decrease cash flow. An increase in investment, working through the feedback loops shown in Figure 5 has a net effect of generating an increased supply of funds for future investment.

The impact of the positive feedback loop on the supply of funds is weaker and more spread out in time than the impact of the negative feedback loop. The acquisition of assets represents a current cash expenditure; the flow of cash returns from these assets may be spread out over many years. Therefore, during the firm's growth phase when investment is high, the demand for cash is likely to substantially exceed internal cash flow. As growth slows, returns from past investment should continue while the demand for cash drops.

Capital rationing policies limit the demand for cash by controlling the acquisition of productive assets. As a result, growth is constrained by deterioration in the firm's product availability. Through a capital rationing policy, growth is constrained to approximately the level supportable by the growth in internal cash flow and unused debt capacity. The demand for cash generated by the negative feedback loops illustrated in Figure 4 equals the supply of cash provided by the positive feedback loops illustrated in Figure 5.

Figure 6 shows the behavior of several system variables when capital rationing is used to balance demand for funds with a limited supply of funds. Limitations on financial resources are accomplished in the model by the imposition of three restrictions: (1) the firm cannot issue new equity; (2) the firm has a total debt limit expressed as a maximum debt-equity ratio (equal to approximately 60 percent of the value attained in the base case); and (3) the firm has a short-term debt limit expressed as a maximum ratio of short-term liabilities to total assets. The capital rationing policy results in production capacity below market demand. Consequently, low product availability reduces sales well below the level attained in the base case. Earnings per share also remain significantly lower.

Capital rationing policies can lead to growth patterns which range from the "retarded" growth shown in Figure 6 to "stagnation" (where sales are essentially flat). The type of pattern depends on the internal cash flow and unused debt capacity available for investment in productive assets. Two factors affect the level of available funds: (1) the firm's debt limit; and (2) the internal cash flow as determined by the firm's price-cost structure, credit policy, and dividend policy. The debt limit has an obvious effect. The effects of pricing and credit policy on internal cash flow will be discussed later. Dividend policy can change both internal cash flow and the firm's debt limit through additions (or lack of additions) to the firm's equity position.

Another aspect of a firm's growth pattern is the existence of cyclical fluctuations or, in some situations, "crises" during which sales drop off dramatically. These cycles and crises are predominantly a function of the type of information used as a measure of the supply of funds. These issues have been treated elsewhere.[5]

In summary, capital rationing designed to deal with limited financial resources generate growth in unit sales well below market demand. While reductions in investment expenditures limit cash expenditures in the short-run, the reductions also limit future cash flow by keeping product availability below what product availability would be if the investment were undertaken.

Alternative Responses to Limited Financial Resources.   Reduction of investment is only one action available to the firm for dealing with a limited supply of funds. As alternatives, a firm might raise price or reduce credit period to balance the supply and

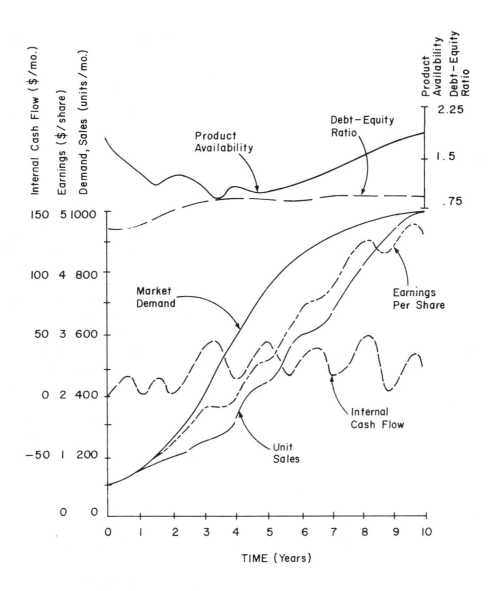

Figure 6 Debt limit: capital rationing

demand for funds. Space limitations prohibit a detailed examination of the feedback loops surrounding price and credit period decisions. Only the general nature of the influences and simulation results are presented below.

Associated with price and credit period policies are both positive and negative feedback loops. In the negative loops associated with price, an initial increase in price increases with the firm's cash flow and earnings per unit sale. The price increase also reduces unit sales and, consequently, lowers the amount of investment required. Therefore, other things staying equal, the supply of funds tends to improve (through the financial sector mechanisms described previously) and price tends to decrease. As with all negative feedback loops, an initial increase in price stimulates reactions which tend to reduce price. Similarly, an initial decrease in credit period improves cash flow by (1) increasing the speed with which receivables are paid, and (2) reducing the investment required as unit sales decreases. Improved cash flow allows the firm to increase credit period.

In the positive feedback loops associated with price and credit period policies, an increase in price or decrease in credit period lowers unit sales and reduces internal cash flow and earnings. Therefore, the supply of funds decreases, inducing a further increase in price or decrease in credit period.

When the positive and negative loops are combined, the net result of price or credit period policies depends on the relative strengths of the positive and negative loops. The relative strength of these loops depends primarily on the relationship defining the effect of price (or credit period) on sales. The effect of price on sales is determined not only by the direct relationship between price and sales, but also by the interaction between price and product availability in determining sales. A decrease in price causes a short-run decline in sales. The drop in sales, however, improves the firm's product availability (see Figure 2), thereby increasing sales. Therefore, the strength of the direct effect of price on sales is reduced by the interaction of product availability and price in determining sales. As a result, for all but very large elasticities of sales with respect to price, pricing policies can improve the balance between the supply and demand for funds. A similar argument applies to credit period.

The feedback loops discussed above indicate the relatively short-run effects of price and credit period policy. Longer-run effects of these policies manifest themselves through investment. The feedback loops through pricing and credit period tie into the feedback loops through investment policy via the effect of the supply of funds on investment. As a result, for example, an increase in price which results in an increased supply of funds may allow the firm to undertake investment for which previously there was no financing. Therefore, long-run product availability may be improved and sales increased. The price increase may have opposite short-run and long-run effects on sales.

As an illustration of the potential benefits of price or credit period policies, Figure 7 compares the results of the capital rationing policy of Figure 6 to the results of a simulation run in which pricing policy is used to balance the supply and demand for funds. The growth in unit sales is much closer to growth in market demand and earnings per share is much higher with the pricing policy. When the firm raises price to balance the supply and demand for funds, price rather than product availability becomes the competitive variable limiting sales. Figure 7 shows that product availability is improved with pricing policy. As a result, unit sales are nearly identical for both policies in the first 3 years of the simulation. But because of the higher price, cash flow and earnings are higher with the pricing policy. This allows increased investment which dramatically improves product availability beginning around year 4.

For a particular firm, the benefits of price and credit period policies relative to capital rationing policies would depend on the elasticities of sales to price, credit

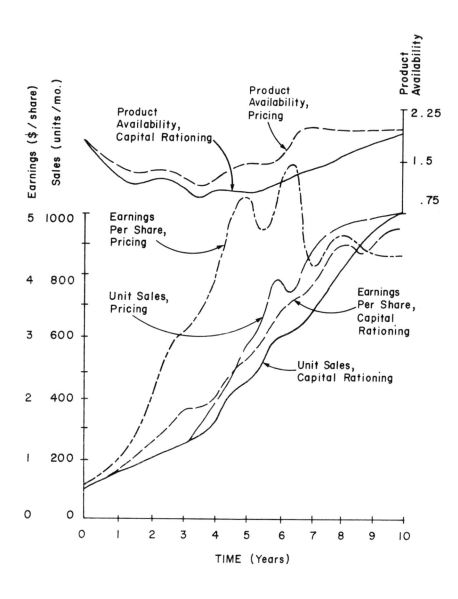

Figure 7 Debt limit: comparison of capital rationing and pricing policies

period, and product availability. A simulation model of the type presented here would allow the firm to investigate the possible benefits under a variety of assumptions concerning elasticity (or parameters or market demand) by simply resimulating the model with the changed elasticity (parameter or demand). In general, however, for a product whose sales are limited by product availability, some benefits can be attained by raising price so as to shift the burden of limiting sales from product availability to price.

System Dynamics as a Tool for Policy Design

The model developed in this research and the system dynamics methodology on which the model is based are powerful tools for designing financial policies to deal with conditions of limited financial resources. The model can aid the manager in several ways.

First, the multiplicity of interactions, opposing forces, and differing short-run and long-run effects greatly complicates the manager's task of determining appropriate actions in response to a limited supply of funds. Intuition and experience are capable of perceiving and identifying these forces individually. A system dynamics model can be used to structure and trace out the cumulative consequences of interactions within the financial system.

Second, the manager can use a system dynamics model to explore a wide range of policy alternatives and to choose the best policies for his situation. This paper has considered each policy option in isolation. In practice, the firm might consider, for example, both restricting investment *and* raising price. In addition to investment, price, and credit period policies, the model can also be used to explore the effects on cash flow of a wide range of other financial policies, including dividend policy, debt-maturity structure, and new equity-issue.[5] Furthermore, the model can be used to test the sensitivity of the simulation results to any changes in parameters, elasticities, or exogenous inputs.

Third, the manager can obtain from a system dynamics model the necessary information on which to evaluate the policy alternatives. Important considerations include profitability, growth pattern, and risk. The ability to evaluate policies on the basis of growth pattern, as carried out in this paper, reflects the dynamic character of system dynamics models. System dynamics models capture the causal forces which produce change in a system. Furthermore, the simulation output potentially provides much additional information about profitability and risk. Measures such as profit margin, return on investment, debt-equity ratio, and interest coverage are easily obtained. Equations defining the cost of capital can be specified, and, as a result, present value per share of a dividend stream can be calculated.

Finally, the model provides a means for investigating and communicating to other managers the short- and long-run effects of different policies. When the impact of financial policies on value, risk, and growth pattern is viewed over the total growth period, the policy recommendations offered in this paper are not easily disregarded. Yet, many managers would be reluctant to follow these prescriptions in practice. Their reluctance is, for the most part, a function of the separation in time and space between managerial decision and its long-run effects. The problem which the financial manager faces is an actual or projected shortage of funds and an inability to raise further funds through traditional channels—the equity, long-term debt, and short-term debt markets. A reduction in investment expenditures is the obvious, and probably traditional, response to the shortage. In the short run, reduced investment expenditure alleviates the problem. The longer term results which run in the opposite direction can easily be viewed as a problem for another department such as sales. The reduction in investment, after an acquisition delay, begins to affect the delivery delay position of the firm. As a result, the competitive position of the firm deteriorates and begins to affect the firm's sales. The separation between the initial decision and its ultimate effect on sales may take several years. Furthermore, the loss of sales due to long delivery delay may not even be perceived in many firms. The negative effects may not be recognized for several reasons: (1) production capacity is equal to or near the order rate due to adjustments by the market in the firm's delivery delay; (2) high order backlogs and long delivery delays are often viewed as desirable; (3) the production capacity for a given product may not be clear if the capacity is buried in production capacity for many products.

Pricing and credit period responses have a short run negative effect on sales. The negative effect is directly attributable to financial policies. Improved cash flow may not result until some time later, and the long-run effects on sales growth may never be fully appreciated.

The differences between the short- and long-run effects of financial policies often impel managers to take the safest way out and fall back on such traditional policies as cutting investment. A model of the type discussed here can provide the means for investigating these short- and long-run effects. Policy design which considers the value, risk, and growth pattern of the firm over the total growth period is one potentially beneficial consequence of such an investigation.

Notes

1. Gordon Donaldson, *Corporate Debt Capacity* (Homewood, Ill.: Richard D. Irwin, 1961).

2. Gordon Donaldson, *Strategy for Financial Mobility* (Homewood, Ill.: Richard D. Irwin, 1969).

3. Jay W. Forrester, *Industrial Dynamics* (Cambridge, Mass.: MIT Press, 1961).

4. George W. Gershefski, "Building A Corporate Financial Model," *Harvard Business Review*, (July–August 1969).

5. James M. Lyneis, "The Impact of Corporate Financial Policies on Corporate Growth and Profitability." Ph.D. Dissertation, University of Michigan, 1974. (Available from University Microfilms, Ann Arbor, Mich.).

6. James M. Lyneis, "A Model For Designing Financial Policies To Deal With Limited Financial Resources."

7. Robert Morris Associates, *Annual Statement Studies* (Philadelphia: Robert Morris Associates, 1973).

8. Roland Robinson, *Financing The Dynamic Small Firm* (Belmont, Calif.: Wadsworth Publishing Co., Inc., 1966).

9. James M. Warren and John P. Shelton, "A Simultaneous Equation Approach To Financial Planning," *Journal of Finance* (December 1971).

30
Industrial Dynamics Model
of Weekly Stock Prices: A Case Study

Toshiro Shimada

Introduction

Stock price has been studied by many investment analysts, who have investigated mostly the relations between stock prices and earnings or dividends.[1] This means that the stock price theories formulated until now fundamentally depend upon investors' behavior. However, the stock market includes various speculative behaviors and interactions between the actions of speculators and investors.

Speculative behavior has been rarely studied and moreover, the interactions between these two groups have hardly ever been treated by analysts.

Another type of study is usually done by mathematical economists, who have focused on the random character of stock prices.[2] These studies are more recent than the former group of studies and are now in an early stage, but are quickly developing.

Thus, there have been many studies made about stock prices and yet we know little about by what mechanism the stock price is decided.

In this paper, we will treat speculative behavior and investors' behavior separately and then combine them in one model. These behaviors of two groups contain several feedback loops described later.

Industrial dynamics[3] seems to be most useful to treat these feedback loops and the dynamic movement of the stock price.

Objectives

The first objective of this model is to simulate stock price movement. For this simulation we assume that stock price change is mainly due to the excess demand and

This work was done at Harvard University under a grant from Meiji University. The author wishes to express sincere gratitude to Professor Hendrick S. Houthakker for his advice during his stay at Harvard University. The writer wishes to thank Professor Edward B. Roberts and Dr. Carl V. Swanson, of M.I.T., and Professors Chris A. Theodore and H. K. Wu of Boston University for their careful reading of the manuscript and for kind suggestions. The author must also thank Dr. Leon T. Kendall of the New York Stock Exchange and Blair S. Williams & Co., who helped to collect necessary data. This chapter is an edited version of an article which appeared in the *Bulletin of the Izumi Laboratory of Meiji University*, no. 42, 1968, and is reprinted with permission of the author.

this excess demand depends on the stock price change indirectly, so there are feedback systems in the stock market.

The second objective is to study the influence of random shocks added to the primary model. Several studies have demonstrated that changes of weekly stock prices are random.[4] So we would like to study a model which contains random variables.

The third objective is to investigate the effects of sudden large stock price changes occurring at some time points which correspond to various situations of the fluctuations of stock prices. In the actual stock market, changes often occur which influence the future price movement. These influences may differ from each other according to the situation of the price cycle when the changes take place.

Model Description

We will deal with fluctuations of the stock price of a major U.S. corporation. It has various kinds of stockholders. We divide them into two categories. One is the speculator and the other is the investor. Indeed, it is difficult to distinguish between a speculator and an investor actually, but we here define an investor as one who buys and sells securities on the basis of dividend income while a speculator buys and sells securities to obtain a profit from anticipated changes in the market price.

Now, we will treat the behavior of the above two groups and their flow diagrams separately.

Speculator Sector.   Suppose that the market is at the beginning of a bull market. Then many speculators will want to buy shares of the company, because they believe that the stock price will rise and they will get gains from price changes. On the other hand, some may think there will be a small possibility for the stock price to go down, so there may be a few speculators who are willing to place sell orders. Here we will name the difference between buy orders and sell orders, ''Excess Demand, ''which will include buy orders and sell orders from investors also. In the above case, the excess demand will be positive and large, and this will push up the stock price. Then buying speculators will place orders to buy more shares; on the other hand, sell orders from selling speculators will not increase so much. Therefore stock prices will go up more.

However, the stock price cannot rise without limit, because as the price rises apprehension of its descent will appear, then sell orders will increase and buy orders will decrease. Thus the excess demand will turn negative, and consequently a negative stock price change will appear, and the stock price will begin to go down.

In this stock price movement, we may see two feedback loops, the buying speculator loop and the selling speculator loop. In the upswing, both loops are positive while in the downswing the reverse is the case.

As we see above, the stock price change may be considered to depend on excess demand, so we assume a functional relation between them. In this model we assume the simplest relation, in which the price change is proportional to the excess demand value, which means the stock price times the excess demand. We will call the inverse of the proportionality constant in this relation ''floating shares,''[5] which mean shares floating in the market to be bought or sold easily and will be expressed as a certain assumed fraction of total shares. A large amount of floating shares, as is often the case for large companies, will cause only a small stock price change, while a small number of floating shares will generate a large stock price change as a result of the same amount of excess demand.

In other words, the stock price change is assumed to be proportional to the excess demand value and inversely proportional to floating shares.

$$\text{Stock price change} = \frac{\text{Excess demand value}}{\text{Floating shares}}$$

Floating shares will actually fluctuate weekly, but floating shares are defined here to mean the maximum value of weekly changing floating shares. In this case the percentage of floating shares to total shares is assumed to be a constant value of 2 percent.

The excess demand is assumed to be the difference between buy orders and sell orders, and of course contain speculators' orders and investors' orders, although in this section we consider mainly speculators.

Now we will consider how speculators' buy orders and sell orders will increase or decrease. At the beginning of a market upswing, only few people understand that the upswing begins, so both buy orders and sell orders will be small. Shortly after the start, some speculators know of the upswing, then buy orders will gradually increase, but sell orders will be left as small as before, therefore the excess demand will increase and the stock price goes up. However, when the stock price reaches a certain high level, speculators who have bought already will place sell orders, so these sell orders will be added to other sell orders from selling speculators, who have no stocks and yet are willing to place sell orders. Then speculators' buy orders will decrease and sell orders increase, so the peak of sell orders will appear a while after the peak of buy orders. At this point the stock price will be, in general, already turning.

Thus, we may think that speculators' buy orders and sell orders depend on the situation of the stock price cycle, and the degree of this relation may be measured by the change of stock price level. Therefore, we assume that speculators' buy orders and sell orders are functions of the deviation between stock prices and the trough price at which the upswing starts.

The trough price will be determined in the model by the following method. When we get the lower turning points of 5 weeks' moving average of simulated stock prices, we will choose the stock prices corresponding to the above turning points of moving averages as trough prices.

The percentage deviation between the stock price and the trough price does not contain any growth effect of this company, so we include this growth effect as follows.

$$\text{PDSAG} = \frac{(\text{SP} - \text{SPDVC}) - \text{TRP}}{\text{TRP}}$$

where

PDSAG—Percentage Deviation between the Stock price And the trough price
with Growth effects

SP   —Stock Price

TRP   —TRough Price

SPDVC—Stock Price corresponding to future DiVidend Change.

We assume that if the gross profit and the dividend level are increasing, the stock price
may be evaluated lower by the amount corresponding to the growth effects. To measure this amount, we use the quantity

$$SPDVC = (const) \frac{ADIVC}{TS} / DIVYG$$

where

ADIVC—Assumed future DIVidend Change

TS   —Total Shares

DIVYG—the DIVidend Yield with Growth effects.

ADIVC/TS is assumed future dividend change/share (described later in the investor
sector), so (ADIVC/TS)/DIVYG means the stock price due to the assumed dividend
change. Thus we consider that the growth effects which have influences upon the stock
price will be estimated by the values calculated from the assumed dividend changes and
the dividend yields with growth effects.

Now we will discuss the excess demand change due to the second difference of the
stock price. We defined before that if the stock price change is assumed proportional to
the excess demand value, then we may consider the change of the stock price change
CSPC (the second difference of the stock price) as a function of the excess demand
change. Here we assume a simple relation for this functional form, in which the excess
demand change is proportional to floating shares and the second difference of the stock
price, CSPC, while it is inversely proportional to the stock price. In other words, it is
assumed that if floating shares and stock prices are fixed, large excess demand changes
generate large CSPC, and if CSPC and stock prices are constant, large floating shares
cause large excess demand changes, while if floating shares and CSPC are fixed and
stock prices are high or low, excess demand changes may be small or large respectively. The relation is

$$\text{Excess demand change} = (const) \frac{\text{(floating shares) x (CSPC)}}{\text{stock price}}$$

Actually the price change and CSPC become larger near the turning points of the
stock price cycle. This characteristic may be seen in the outputs of this model and is
partially caused by the relation between the excess demand change and CSPC.

Figure 1 shows the flow diagram of the speculator sector.

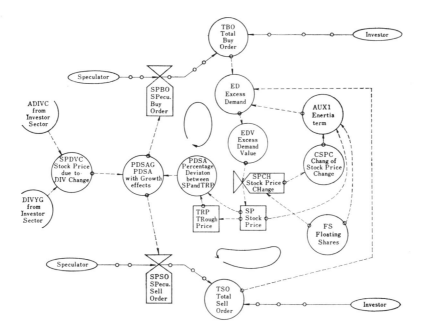

Figure 1   Flow diagram for speculator sector

Mathematical Model

Now, we will explain the equations in the mathematical model which correspond to the verbal description already mentioned.

$$SP.K = SP.J + (DT)(SPCH.JK) \tag{1, L}$$

SP — Stock Price (dollars/share)
DT — Delta Time, the time interval between calculations of the equations (week)
SPCH — Stock Price CHange (dollars/share/week)

This is the equation of stock price. All equations in this article are in a form required by the **DYNAMO** compiler and simulator program.[6] The equation says that the stock price at the present time, K, equals the price at the previous time, J, plus the change in stock price that has taken place between time J and K. (The postscripts .K and .J correspond respectively to the subscripts t and t − 1 in the traditional difference notation.) The designation (1, L) at the extreme right of the equation shows that it is equation 1 and that it is a Level type.

$$SP = 55 \tag{2, N}$$
$$SPCH = 0 \tag{3, N}$$

N in the parentheses means the initial equations which provide initial values for stock prices or stock price changes. We are beginning from the above initial values. [Note: DYNAMO does not require Eq. 3,N.]

$$\text{SPCH.KL} = \text{SPCH1.K} + \text{SPCH2.K} + \text{SPCH3.K} \qquad (4,R)$$

$$\text{SPCH1.K} = \frac{\text{EDV.K}}{\text{FS.K}} \qquad (5,A)$$

$$\text{SPCH2.K} = \text{PULSE(PULH,20,50)} \qquad (6,A)$$

$$\text{SPCH3.K} = \text{(RNC)NORMRN(MEAN,DEV)} \qquad (7,A)$$

SPCH —Stock Price CHange (dollars/share/week)
EDV —Excess Demand Value (thousand dollars/week)
FS —Floating Shares (thousand shares)
RNC —Random Number Constant
MEAN—MEAN of random numbers
DEV —standard DEViation of random numbers.

Equation 4 shows that the stock price change consists of SPCH1, SPCH2, and SPCH3. R in the parentheses means that the equation is a Rate type. SPCH1 in the equation 5 is the main part of stock price change and is proportional to the excess demand value, EDV, and inversely proportional to Floating Shares, FS. A in (5, A) shows that this is an Auxiliary equation.

SPCH2 is a pulse train in which the pulses are of height PULH. The first pulse appears at time 20, and subsequent pulses appear at Time $= 20 + 50, 20 + 100$, and so on. SPCH2 is used as a pulse input.

The equation 7 gives SPCH3 as a product of (RNC) times random numbers normally distributed with mean MEAN and standard deviation DEV. SPCH3 is used later as random variable input. At first we are beginning from SPCH2 = 0 and SPCH3 = 0.

$$\text{FS.K} = \text{(TDAY) (PCFS) (TS.K)} \qquad (8, A)$$

FS —Floating Shares (thousand shares)
TDAY—Trading DAYs in a week (unitless)
PCFS —decimal PerCentage of Floating Shares to total shares (decimal percentage)
TS —Total Shares

We assume that floating shares are proportional to total shares, so they are expressed as the number of trading days in a week times daily floating shares, which is a decimal percentage of floating shares to total shares times total shares. This decimal percentage is assumed to be a constant value of 0.02 at first, so

$$\text{PCFS} = 0.02$$

and trading days in a week are 5 days.

TDAY = 5 (unitless)
$$\text{EDV.K} = \text{(SP.K) (ED.K)} \qquad (9, A)$$

EDV—Excess Demand Value (thousand dollars/week)
SP   —Stock Price (dollars/shares)
ED   —Excess Demand (thousand shares/week)
Excess demand value is the stock price times the excess demand.

$$ED.K = ED1.K + EDC2.JK \qquad (10, A)$$

ED   —Excess Demand (thousand shares/week)
ED1   —Excess Demand due to the difference between total buy orders and
          total sell orders (thousand shares/week)
EDC2—Excess Demand Change due to the second difference of stock price
          (thousand shares/week)

We assume that excess demand consists of two parts. The main part ED1 is the difference between total buy orders and total sell orders. The second part EDC2 is the excess demand change due to the second difference of the stock price, which may be considered as an inertial term.

$$ED1.K = TBO.K - TSO.K \qquad (11, A)$$

ED1—Excess Demand due to the difference between total buy orders and total
          sell orders (thousand shares/week)
TBO—Total Buy Orders (thousand shares/week)
TSO—Total Sell Orders (thousand shares/week)

This equation is self-evident.

$$EDC2.KL = \frac{(CEDC2)\,(FS.K)\,(CSPC.K)}{(SP.K)} \qquad (12, R)$$

EDC2   —Excess Demand Change due to the second difference of stock price
            (thousand shares/week)
FS   —Floating Shares (thousand shares)
CSPC   —Change of Stock Price Change (the second difference of stock price)
            (dollars/share/week/week)
SP   —Stock Price (dollars/share)
CEDC2—proportionality constant (= .25) (week)

The inertial term EDC2 is assumed proportional to the floating shares and the change of stock price change (the second difference of stock price), while it is inversely proportional to stock price, as mentioned earlier.

$$TBO.K = SPBO.JK + IBO.JK \qquad (13, A)$$
$$TSO.K = SPSO.JK + ISO.JK \qquad (14, A)$$

TBO   —Total Buy Orders (thousand shares/week)
TSO   —Total Sell Orders (thousand shares/week)

SPBO—SPeculator Buy Order rate (thousand shares/week)
IBO   —Investor Buy Order rate (thousand shares/week)
SPSO—SPeculator Sell Order rate (thousand shares/week)
ISO   —Investor Sell Order rate (thousand shares/week)

Total buy orders (or sell orders) are the sum of speculator buy orders (or sell orders) and investor buy orders (or sell orders).

Excess demand change EDC2 has to be contained in total buy orders or total sell orders in accordance with its positive or negative sign, but for convenience we added this change to the excess demand ED as shown in equation 10. These two methods to treat the inertial term EDC2 are essentially equivalent.

Now we will treat the trough price. At first, we will compute a 5 weeks moving average of the simulated stock prices. (See note 6 for reference.)

$$SPB = BOXLIN\ (5,1) \tag{15,B}$$

$$SPB = BOXLOAD\ (55,1) \tag{16,N}$$

$$SPB*1.K = SP.K \tag{17,A}$$

$$SSP.\ K = SPB*1.K + SPB*2.K + SPB*3.K + SPB*4.K$$
$$+ SPB*5.K + 0 \tag{18,A}$$

$$MASP.K = \frac{SSP.K}{5} \tag{19,A}$$

SPB   —Stock Prices in the linear Boxcar train (dollars/share)
BOXLIN   —specifies a linear progression with discard of last box
5   —number of boxes in the train
1   —stepping interval (week)
BOXLOAD—this equation type specifies that each car in SPB will be given the
              initial value of the product of 55 and 1, in which 55 is the initial
              value of the stock price
SPB*i —the ith boxcar in the train SPB (dollars/share)
SP   —Stock Price (dollars/share)
SSP   —Sum of Stock Prices in the boxcar train (dollars/share)
MASP   —5 weeks Moving Averages of Stock Prices (dollars/share)
Then, we will use the next boxcar train.

$$MASPB = BOXLIN\ (5,1) \tag{20, B}$$
$$MASPB = BOXLOAD\ (55,1) \tag{21, N}$$
$$MASPB*1.K = MASP.K \tag{22, A}$$

MASPB   —Moving Averages of Stock Prices in the linear Boxcar
            train (dollars/share)
MASPB*1—the first boxcar in the train MASP (dollars/share)
MASP   —5 weeks Moving Averages of Stock Prices (dollars/share)

Next, we will compute the trough value of 5 weeks moving averages, which must correspond to the stock price 2 weeks ago given as the third boxcar in the train SPB. We will choose this price as the trough price at which the upswing will start.

$$\text{CMASP.KL} = \text{MASP.K} - \text{MASPB}*2.\text{K} \tag{23,R}$$

$$\text{AUX1.KL} = \text{CMASP.JK} \tag{24,R}$$

$$\text{TRP1.K} = \begin{array}{l} \text{TRPB}*2.\text{K if (AUX1.JK) (CMASP.JK)} \geqq 0 \\ \text{SPB}*3.\text{K if (AUX1.JK) (CMASP.JK)} < 0 \end{array} \tag{25,A}$$

$$\text{TRP.K} = \begin{array}{l} \text{TRP1.K if CMASP.JK} \geqq 0 \\ \text{TRPB}*2.\text{K if CMASP.JK} < 0 \end{array} \tag{26,A}$$

$$\text{TRPB} = \text{BOXLIN (5,1)} \tag{27,B}$$

$$\text{TRPB} = \text{BOXLOAD (55,1)} \tag{28,N}$$

$\text{TRPB}*1.\text{K} = \text{TRP.K}$

    CMASP—Changes of Moving Averages of Stock Prices (dollars/share/week)
    AUX1 —CMASP during the previous time interval (dollars/share/week)
    TRP1 —auxiliary function of the TRough Price
    TRPB*i —the ith boxcar in the train TRPB (dollars/share)
    SPB*3 —the third boxcar in the train SPB
    TRP   —TRough Price (dollars/share)
    TRPB —TRough Price in the linear Boxcar train (dollars/share)

At the trough value of 5 weeks moving averages, the moving average curve will turn from the downswing to the upswing. This value will correspond to the trough of stock prices, which will be given in the boxcar train SPB. Equations 25 and 26 describe this process.

The next stage is to deal with the percentage deviation between stock prices and trough prices.

$$\text{PDSA.K} = \frac{\text{SP.K} - \text{TRP.K}}{\text{TRP.K}} \tag{29,A}$$

    PDSA—decimal Percentage Deviation between Stock prices And trough prices
            (decimal percentage)
    SP   —Stock Price (dollars/share)
    TRP —TRough Price (dollars/share)

PDSA does not contain the growth effects of the company, so we will consider these effects in the following manner.

$$\text{PDSAG.K} = \text{PDSA.K} - \text{PDSAD.K} \tag{30,A}$$

$$PDSAD.K = \frac{SPDVC.K}{TRP.K} \qquad (31,A)$$

$$SPDVC.K = (CSPDC) \frac{ADIVC.JK}{(DIVYG.K)(TS.K)} \qquad (32,A)$$

> PDSAG—decimal Percentage Deviation between Stock prices And trough prices with Growth effects (decimal percentage)
> SPDVC—Stock Price corresponding to future DiVidend Change (dollars/share)
> PDSAD—Percentage Deviation between SPDVC AnD trough prices (decimal percentage)
> CSPDC—proportionality Constant for the equation SPDVC (unitless)
> ADIVC—Assumed future DIVidend Change (dollars)
> DIVYG—DIVidend Yield with Growth effects (decimal percentage)
> TS   —Total Shares (thousand shares)

ADIVC is assumed future dividend change, which will be due to the change of the gross profit and the dividend level (mentioned later in the investor sector). ADIVC/TS is the dividend change per share. Dividend yield is the ratio of dividend per share to stock prices, so (ADIVC/TS)/DIVYG may be considered to be proportional to the stock price due to the assumed dividend change. This price is SPDVC in equation 32, and the proportionality constant is set equal to 0.20. The percentage deviation between stock prices and trough prices is assumed to decrease by the amount PDSAD, which is the ratio of SPDVC to trough prices.

Next we will treat speculator buy orders.

$$SPBO.KL = (TDAY)(MSBO)(SBRC.K) \qquad (33, R)$$

> SPBO —SPeculator Buy Order rate (thousand shares/week)
> TDAY—Trading DAYs in a week (days/week)
> SBRC —Speculator Buy order Reaction Coefficient for percentage deviation between stock prices and trough prices with growth effects (unitless)
> MSBO—Maximum Speculator Buy Order rate per day (thousand shares/day)

Speculator buy order rate SPBO between the time K and the time L equals trading days in a week times average speculator buy order rate per day in the Kth week, which is expressed as maximum speculator buy order rate per day MSBO times speculator buy order reaction coefficient SBRC. K in the week.

Before we discuss SBRC, we will treat speculator sell orders, which equation is quite similar to speculator buy orders.

$$SPSO.KL = (TDAY)(MSSO)(SSRC.K) \qquad (34, R)$$

> SPSO — SPeculator Sell Order rate (thousand shares/week)
> TDAY — Trading DAYs in a week (days/week)

SSRC — Speculator Sell order Reaction Coefficient for percentage deviation between stock prices and trough prices with growth effects (unitless)

MSSO — Maximum Speculator Sell Order rate per day (thousand shares/day)

Equation 34 may be self-explanatory, compared with equation 33.

We begin with the values MSBO = MSSO = 200 (thousand shares).

Now we will treat the reaction coefficients SBRC and SSRC. The word (reaction) means speculators' reaction for the percentage deviation between the stock price and the trough price with growth effects, PDSAG. These coefficients are given in Figure 2 and Figure 3, both of which contain 2 figures: the figures for the upswing, SBR1, SSR1 and the figures for the downswing, SBR2 and SSR2, because the characteristics of speculator buy orders (sell orders) in the upswing will be different from those of the downswing.

First, we examine the curves for the upswing, SBR1 and SSR1. When PDSAG is 0, in other words, at the beginning of the upswing, the speculator buy order reaction coefficient is 0.4 (SBR1 = 0.4) and the sell order reaction coefficient is 0.3 (SSR1 = 0.3), so the difference between the speculator buy orders and the speculator sell orders equals 100,000 shares, which are the excess demand due to the speculator orders at the beginning of the upswing. This value is positive and small.

As PDSAG increases, both SBR1 and SSR1 gradually go up, but SBR1 increases more rapidly than SSR1, so the difference increases and reaches the maximum at PDSAG = 0.1. We assume that speculator buy orders concentrate at PDSAG = 0.1, because most speculators will place buy orders for a while after the upswing begins and they will expect about 20 percent or 25 percent ascent of the stock price. In order to obtain a 10 percent return, buy orders may be considered to concentrate at PDSAG = 0.1, which means a 10 percent rise of the stock price. When PDSAG is larger than 0.1 and less than 0.25, SBR1 decreases and SSR1 increases, so the gap between buy orders and sell orders is negative and its absolute value gradually increases to the maximum at PDSAG = 0.25.

The curves for the downswing are SBR2 and SSR2. In this case, buying speculators will await the recovery of stock price, and will place their buy orders at considerably low stock prices, so the curve SBR2 may be shifted to the left, compared with SBR1, while selling speculators will expect the descent of stock price and intend to increase their sell orders, but sell orders from buying speculators will decrease, so the curve may be shifted to the left.

SBR1 and SSR1 for PDSAG < − 0.04 are set equal to SBR2 and SSR2 respectively, because, in the case when the price goes down far beyond the previous trough price and passes the lower turning point, the number of buy orders will remain large at the beginning of the upswing. Soon after the price turns, this model will choose a new trough price and at this point PDSAG will become nearly equal to 0. Therefore we set the changing point from SBR2(SSR2) to SBR1(SSR1) at PDSAG = − 0.04, where SBR1 = SSR1 = 0.25.

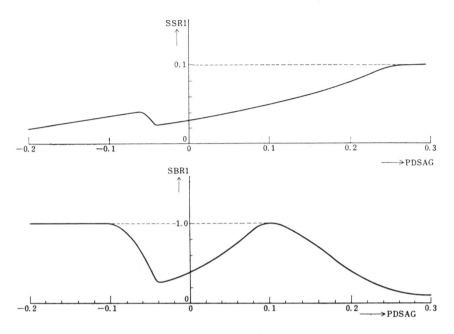

Figure 2   SBR1 and SSR1 for the upswing

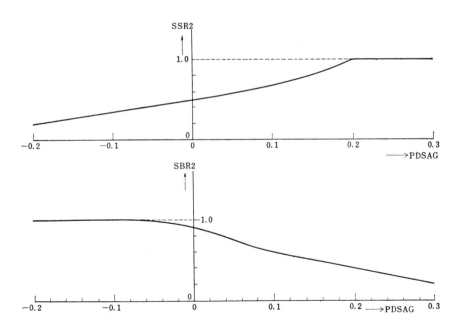

Figure 3   SBR2 and SSR2 for the downswing

$$SPBRC.K = \begin{matrix} SBR1.K \text{ if } SPCH.JK \geqq 0 \\ SBR2.K \text{ if } SPCH.JK < 0 \end{matrix} \qquad (35,A)$$

$$SBR1.K = TABHL(TSBR1, PDSAG.K, -0.2, 0.3, 0.02) \qquad (36,A)$$

$$TSBR1* = \begin{aligned} &1/1/1/1/1/1/.86/.6/.25/.32/.4/.5/.6/.76/.92 \\ &/1/.94/.84/.7/.64/.4/.3/.2/.13/.11/.1 \end{aligned}$$

$$SBR2.K = TABHL (TSBR2, PDSAG.K, -0.2, 0.3, 0.02) \qquad (37,A)$$

$$TSBR2* = \begin{aligned} &1/1/1/1/1/1/1/1/.98/.95/.9/.84/.77/.71/.65/ \\ &.6/.56/.52/.48/.44/.4/.36/.32/.28/.24/.2 \end{aligned}$$

$$SSRC.K = \begin{matrix} SSR1.K \text{ if } SPCH.JK \geq 0 \\ SSR2.K \text{ if } SPCH.JK < 0 \end{matrix} \qquad (38,A)$$

$$SSR1.K = TABHL (TSSR1, PDSAG.K, -0.2, 0.3, 0.02) \qquad (39,A)$$

$$TSSR1* = \begin{aligned} &.2/.23/.26/.29/.32/.35/.38/.4/.25/.27/.3/.33/ \\ &.36/.4/.45/.5/.55/..6/.68/.73/.8/.88/.96/1/1/1 \end{aligned}$$

$$SSR2.K = TABHL (TSSR2, PDSAG.K, -0.2, 0.3, 0.02) \qquad (40,A)$$

$$TSSR2* = \begin{aligned} &.2/.23/.26/.29/.32/.35/.38/.41/.44/.47/.5/.53/ \\ &.56/.6/.64/.68/.72/.77/.83/.92/1/1/1/1/1/1 \end{aligned}$$

SBRC   — Speculator Buy order Reaction Coefficient for percentage deviation between stock prices and trough prices with growth effects (unitless)

SBR1   — Speculator Buy order Reaction coefficient for the upswing (unitless)

TABHL — TABle, High-Low limits, a notation used by DYNAMO compiler to express SBR1 as an arbitrary function of PDSAG. The values of SBR1 are specified at regular intervals of PDSAG (0.02). These interval values are stored in the table TSBR1. For values between the regular intervals, DYNAMO interpolates linearly. Outside the range of values specified for PDSAG, the table's values at the indicated extremes of -0.2 and 0.3 will be used.

TSBR1   — Table, Speculator Buy order Reaction coefficient for the upswing, a table of numbers that gives an appropriate value of SBR1 for each value of PDSAG (unitless)

SBR2   — Speculator Buy order Reaction coefficient for the downswing (unitless)

TSBR2   — Table, Speculator Buy order Reaction coefficient for the downswing, tabular data indicating a value of SBR2 for each value of PDSAG (unitless)

SSRC   — Speculator Sell order Reaction coefficient (unitless)

SSR1   — Speculator Sell order Reaction coefficient for the upswing (unitless)

TSSR1   — Table, Speculator Sell order Reaction coefficient for the upswing (unitless)

SSR2   — Speculator Sell order Reaction coefficient for the downswing (unitless)

TSSR2   — Table, Speculator Sell order Reaction coefficient for the downswing (unitless)

Investor Sector.   Investors' orders will be considered to be mainly due to the expected dividend yield, which depends on the dividend income and the stock price, while speculators' orders are assumed to depend on the percentage deviation between stock prices and the trough price.

If prices rise with the constant dividend, dividend yields go down, so investors' buy orders will decrease and their sell orders increase. Then the excess demand that depends on investors' orders will decrease while remaining positive, so prices will rise more, but price changes will become smaller. Here we may see two feedback loops. One is the loop of buy orders and the other is that of sell orders. Both loops are negative.

With rising prices, the excess demand will become negative, so negative price changes will appear and prices will begin to go down. Then dividend yields begin to go up, so buy orders will increase and sell orders decrease. For a while this tendency will continue. At this stage both loops are positive.

Now, we have to treat the relation between investors' orders and the expected return. As long as prices approximate investment worths, which are to be measured in this model by a certain investment level of dividend yields, investors will be inclined to remain inert. If prices drop below investment worths and dividend yields rise above the investment level, the group tends to increase its buy orders and decrease its sell orders. If prices rise above investment worths and dividend yields drop below the investment level, the group will decrease its buy orders and increase its sell orders. In this model we will set the investment level equal to the 5 percent level.

This relation between investors' buy orders (sell orders) and dividend yields may be represented as a demand function (supply function) of dividend yields, although these demand and supply functions are different from ordinary demand and supply functions of prices. The functional forms will be discussed later in the mathematical model.

Now we will treat the growth effects. Suppose that the gross profit of the company is increasing and dividends may be expected to increase, then investors' buy orders will increase and sell orders decrease even at the same level of dividend yields as that of the case of no growth effect. This means that the demand and supply curves may be shifted to the left. We use the following quantity as the measure of this shift.

$$\frac{ADIVC}{(TS) \times (SP)}$$

Mathematical Model

GPR.K = (ICS) (RGPR.K)   (41, A)

  GPR   — Gross PRofit level at the company (thousand dollars)
  ICS   — Initial Common Stock (thousand dollars)
  RGPR — Ratio of Gross PRofit to initial common stock (unitless)

RGPR.K = TABLE(TRGPR, TIME.K, 0, 100, 5)   (42, A)

TRGPR* = 1.2/1.14/1.06/.92/.74/.7/.84/1.1/1.42/1.64/1.8/1.92/
              2/2.07/2.14/2.2/2.25/2.28/2.29/2.3/2.3

  TABLE — a notation used by the **DYNAMO** compiler to indicate that a set of
                 tabular values provides the specific number for the variable **RGPR**
  TRGPR — Table, Ratio of Gross PRofit to initial common stock, the name of
                 the table of input values for **RGPR**, in which values have been
                 inserted at 5 week intervals from **TIME** = 0 to **TIME** = 100 weeks
  TIME   — Simulated project time starting from **TIME** = 0 and proceeding until
                 the end of the computer run (weeks)

  Here, the gross profit means the profit before tax.

  Figure 5 shows the curve corresponding to the table function (42). We assume in
this model **RGPR** as shown in Figure 5, which is the ratio of the gross profit to the
initial common stock investment. The initial common stock investment is constant, so
the gross profit is to be given by this curve indirectly. In other words, the gross profit is
assumed to be given exogenously. (However, it is desirable to determine the gross
profit endogenously. If we formulate another model for the company growth, it may be
possible to obtain the gross profit value within the model. Then we will combine this

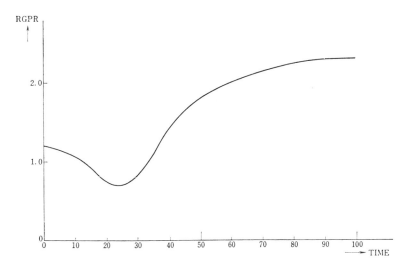

Figure 5   RGPR (Ratio of gross profit to initial common stock)

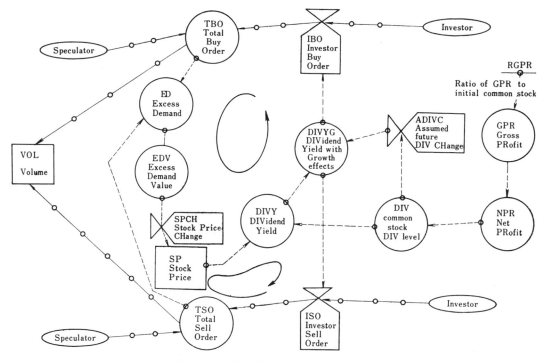

Figure 4   Flow diagram for investor sector

where

ADIVC—Assumed future DIVidend Change
TS   —Total Shares
SP   —Stock Price

ADIVC/TS is (assumed future dividend change/share), so the above term means the dividend yield for **ADIVC**. ADIVC is calculated here as the dividend change assumed at some future time point with the same slope of the current dividend level. In this case the future time point is chosen as 13 weeks later. The dividend level is calculated from the assumed input value of the gross profit before tax.

Up to this point, we supposed that the gross profit was increasing, but the other cases lead to the same conclusion.

As for the speculators' orders, investors' orders are the maximum investors' orders times **IBRD** (or **ISRD**) which is the investor buy (sell) order reaction coefficient for the dividend yield with growth effects **DIVYG**, expressed as

$$DIVYG = \frac{DIV + ADIVC}{(TS) \times (SP)}$$

where **DIV** is the dividend level.

The maximum investors' buy (sell) orders are set equal to 200,000 shares/week in this case.

Figure 4 shows the flow diagram of the investor sector.

company growth model with the stock model and we shall be able to treat the gross profit as an endogenous variable.)

$$NPR.K = (0.55) (GPR.K) \qquad (43, A)$$

    NPR—Net PRofit level at the company (thousand dollars)
    GPR—Gross PRofit level at the company (thousand dollars)

The net profit is the profit after tax, so we assume simply in this model that the ratio of the profit after tax to the gross profit equals 0.55.

$$PDIV.K = (POR) (NPR.K) \qquad (44, A)$$

    PDIV — Profit available to common stock DIVidends (thousand dollars)
    NPR   — Net PRofit level at the company (thousand dollars)
    POR   — Pay-Out Ratio

In this model we are beginning from the value POR = 0.7.

$$DIV.K = DIV.J + \frac{DT}{TDIV} (PDIV.J - DIV.J) \qquad (45, L)$$

    DIV   — common stock DIVidend level at the company (thousand dollars)
    PDIV — Profit available to common stock DIVidends (thousand dollars)
    DT   — Delta Time (week)
    TDIV — Time to adjust DIVidend level (weeks)

The common stock dividend level at the company, DIV, is given by the equation 45, which is an exponential averaging function (7) of PDIV.

The time to adjust dividend level, TDIV, is chosen as 13 weeks. This dividend level may be used to obtain the dividend yield.

$$DIVY.K = \frac{DIV.K}{(TS.K)(SP.K)} \qquad (46, A)$$

    DIVY — DIVidend Yield (decimal percentage)
    DIV   — DIVidend level (thousand dollars)
    TS   — Total Shares (thousand shares)
    SP   — Stock Price (dollars/share)

In this model TS is set equal to the constant value of 280 million shares, but in future we will treat the cases of new issues.

Equation (46) is self-evident. Equations 47, 48 and 49 correspond to the verbal descriptions of the dividend yield with growth effects.

$$DIVYG. K = DIVY.K + DIVYA.K \qquad (47, A)$$

$$DIVYA.K = \frac{ADIVC.JK}{(TS.K)(SP.K)} \qquad (48, A)$$

$$ADIVC.KL = \frac{(TADVC)(PDIV.K - DIV.K)}{TDIV} \tag{49, A}$$

DIVYG — DIVidend Yield with Growth effects (decimal percentage)

DIVYA — DIVidend Yield for Assumed future dividend change (decimal percentage)

ADIVC — Assumed future DIVidend Change (thousand dollars)

PDIV — Profit available to common stock DIVidends (thousand dollars)

TADVC— Time to Assumed DIVidend Change (weeks)

TDIV — Time to adjust DIVidend level (weeks)

Now we will treat investors' orders.

$$IBO.KL = (TDAY)\ (MIBO)\ (IBRD.K) \tag{50, R}$$

IBO   — Investor Buy Order rate (thousand shares/week)

TDAY— Trading DAYs in a week (days/week)

MIBO — Maximum Investor Buy Order rate per day (thousand shares/day)

IBRD — Investor Buy order Reaction coefficient for Dividend yields with growth effects (unitless)

This equation 50 is quite similar to equation 33 for the speculator buy order rate SPBO, so the explanation of the equation 50 may be abridged.

$$ISO.KL = (TDAY)\ (MISO)\ (ISRD.K) \tag{51, R}$$

ISO   — Investor Sell Order rate (thousand shares/week)

TDAY — Trading DAYs in a week (days/week)

MISO — Maximum Investor Sell Order rate per day (thousand shares/day)

ISRD — Investor Sell order Reaction coefficient for Dividend yields with growth effects (unitless)

We are beginning from the values MIBO = MISO = 200,000 shares, which equal MSBO and MSSO.

$$IBRD.K = TABHL\ (TIBRD,\ DIVYG.K,\ 0,\ 0.11,\ 0.01) \tag{52, A}$$
TIBRD* = 0/0/.02/.06/.11/.2/.35/.7/.95/.99/1
$$ISRD.K = TABLE\ (TISRD,\ DIVYG.K,\ 0,\ 0.1,\ 0.01) \tag{53, A}$$
TISRD* = 1/.99/.95/.7/.35/.2/.11/.06/.02/0/0

IBRD   — Investor Buy order Reaction coefficient for Dividend yields with growth effects (unitless)

TIBRD — Table, Investor Buy order Reaction coefficient for Dividend yields with growth effects, a table of values relating IBRD to DIVYG (unitless)

DIVYG — DIVidend Yields with Growth effects (decimal percentage)

ISRD   — Investor Sell order Reaction coefficient for Dividend yields with growth effects (unitless)

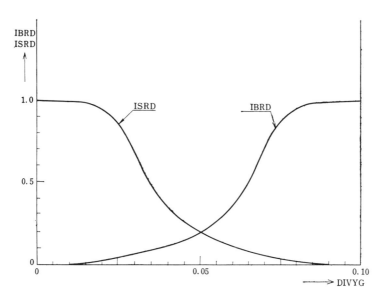

Figure 6   Investors' buy (sell) order reaction coefficient curve for dividend yields
with growth effects

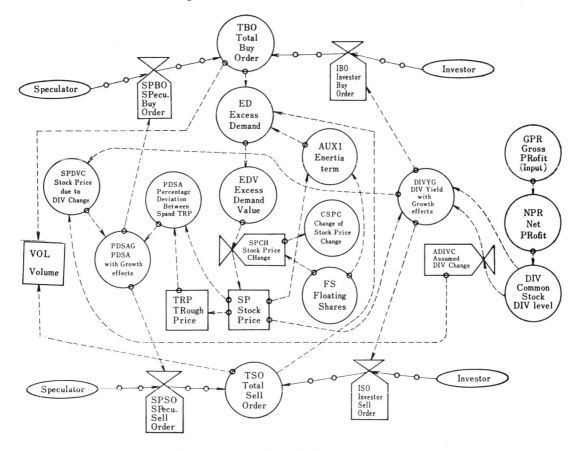

Figure 7   Flow diagram for the whole system

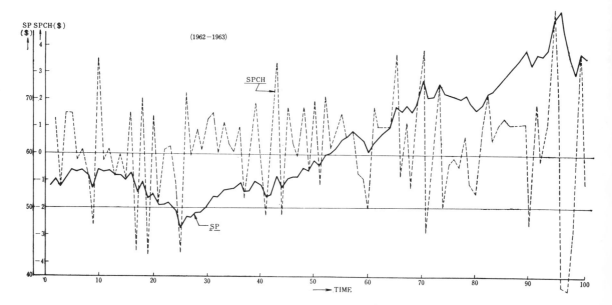

Figure 8 The actual movement of the stock price (SP) and the stock price change (SPCH)

TISRD — Table, Investor Sell order Reaction coefficient for Dividend yields with growth effects, a table of stored constants relating ISRD to DIVYG (unitless)

IBRD and ISRD are shown in Figure 6. The curves of IBRD and ISRD are the demand curve and supply curve respectively, which are different from ordinary demand and supply functions of prices, because DIVYG is inversely proportional to prices. These curves shall be inelastic near the investment level of dividend yields, while the demand (supply) curve must be very elastic far above (below) the investment level. In this model the investment level of dividend yields is set equal to the 5 percent level, where IBRD = ISRD = 0.2, so investors' buy orders equal investors' sell orders and the excess demand due to investors' orders is 0. With large values of DIVYG, IBRD rapidly increases, while with small values of DIVYG, ISRD rapidly rises. However, IBRD or ISRD cannot increase without limit, because funds of investors will be bounded, so the curves are assumed to tend to the upper limit of 1.0..

We have finished the whole description of the model. Figure 7 shows the flow diagram of this model, which contains the speculator sector and the investor sector.

Figure 8 shows the actual fluctuations of weekly stock prices and price changes of this company.

Simulation Results

The above mentioned relations were all written in the DYNAMO[7] language using the industrial dynamics method.

This model contains 37 variables, 12 constants and 5 parameters.

We obtained various results, of which 3 examples will be shown in this paper.

First Run. This run shown in Figure 9 and Figure 10 does not contain any pulse term or random variables. In Figure 9, for the downswing at the beginning and for the long upswing after the 50th week, calculated stock prices show good fit to actual 5 weeks moving averages of the simulated company stock. This fact may mean that the relations assumed in this model can explain the movement of the actual moving average of stock prices for the above mentioned period.

However, this model is unsuccessful for the time interval near the turning point of the 26th week from the depression to the long upswing. We used trough prices as starting prices of the upswing, but for long depressions it seems better to choose peak prices as starting prices of the downswing. We will improve this point in the next study. The square of the correlation coefficient between moving averages and simulated stock prices is 0.975.

In Figure 10 we may see that for the period before the 38th week investors' sell orders ISO are always more than their buy orders IBO, while speculators' buy orders SPBO are always more than their sell orders SPSO and both orders fluctuate. On the other hand, after the 40th week both of IBO and ISO fluctuate, but the differences of the orders are always positive, while SPBO and SPSO fluctuate very much and the former are more or less than the latter. Therefore, by this model the tendency of the price descent for nearly one-third of the time length and of the price rise for two-thirds of the same length mainly depends on investors' orders and is due to the assumed trend of the gross profit of the company. On the other hand, the short cycle is considered to be chiefly due to speculators' orders.

The fluctuation of price changes expands with the time and seems to become unstable, but for a longer period it continues to expand for the period of the long term upswing and when the price reaches the turning point of the long wave, it begins to contract, so we need not mind instability in this case.

Second Run. Sudden stock price changes of 4 dollars were added to the first run at T = 20 and T = 70 using the Pulse Input. Figure 11 shows this run.

The price change added at T = 20 has influences for 20 weeks, after which we cannot find much difference between this run and the original run.

However, the effect of the price change at T = 70 is remarkable and we may see that after T = 70 the wave is shifted to the left, compared with the original run. The price of the original run at T = 70 is near the peak, so the positive price change added at this point may shift the upper turning point to the left and have influences upon the price movement after the point, if there is no fundamental change in the economic conditions of the external world of the stock market.

Thus, we can see that these sudden price changes have certain influences upon the price movement and these influences will be different by their timing.

Third Run. Random stock price changes with mean 0 and standard deviation of 0.7 dollar were added to the first run. This run, Figure 12, is very different from the original run. The peaks and troughs were shifted to the left and downwards and the

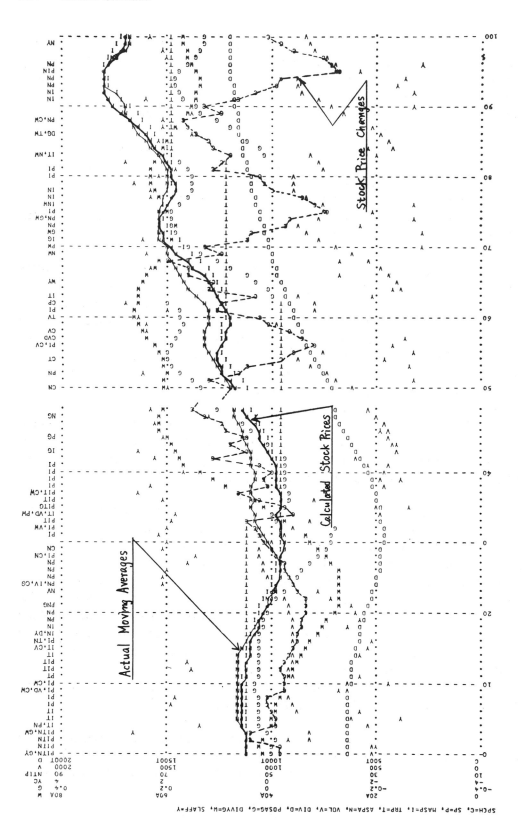

Figure 9   First run, stock prices and stock price changes

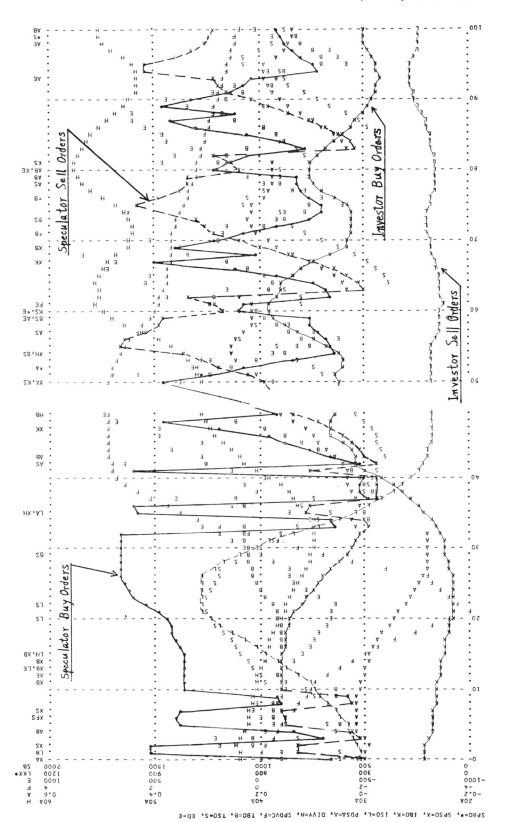

Figure 10   First run, buy orders and sell orders

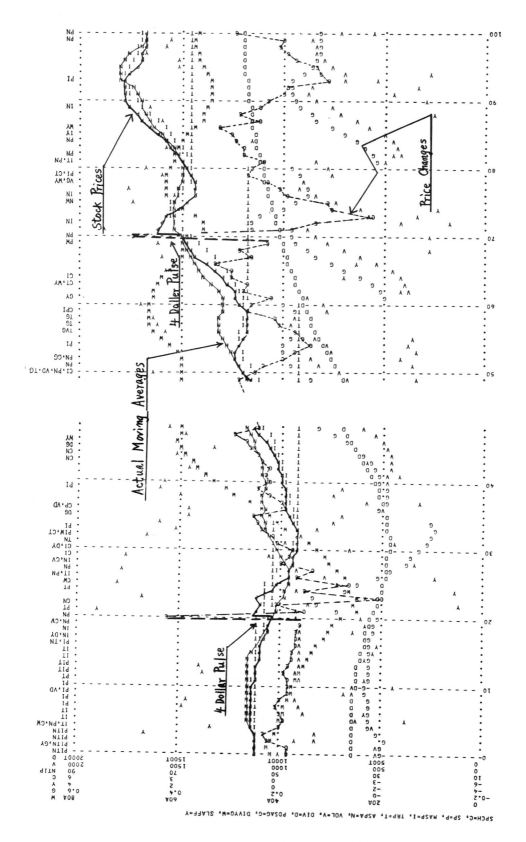

Figure 11 Pulse input

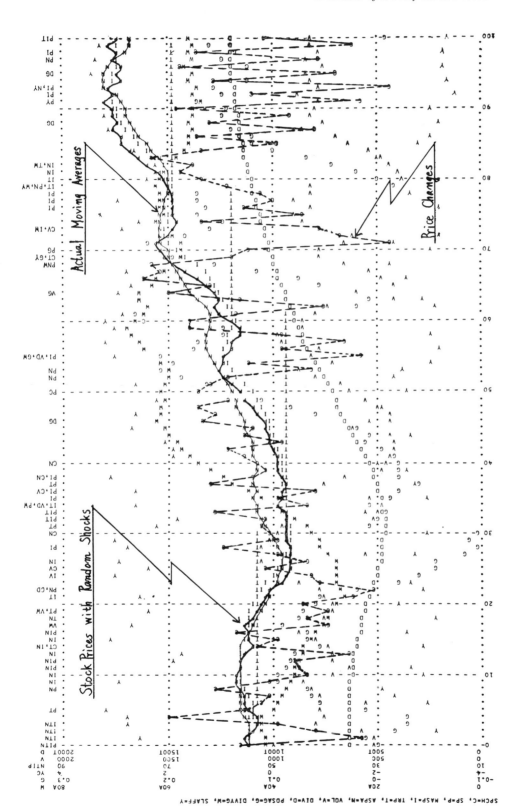

Figure 12 Random changes input

shape of the wave varied, so the short term wave was strongly influenced by these random changes added to the original run.

However, the long term trend seems not to have been much influenced in this time period, although the upper turning point of the long term trend may be shifted to a certain extent.

Random changes used in this run are a sequence of random numbers generated in DYNAMO. Using other sequences with the same mean and the same standard deviation we obtained other simulation runs, which are different from each other.

Conclusion

In this model we defined two groups, speculators and investors, and specified many special variables, of which the main terms are the excess demand, the excess demand change, floating shares, the deviation between the stock price and the trough price, assumed future dividend changes, and two measures of growth effects, one for stock prices and the other for dividends. We discussed two speculator feedback loops and two investor ones. As input data we used gross profits. Values of constants and parameters were chosen by the trial and error method in order that the simulated stock price might be close to the 5 weeks moving average of the actual stock price of the company studied.

Consequently, we obtained considerably good simulation results. Here we showed three runs.

The first run is the basic one and shows good fit with the actual moving average of the company's stock price, especially for the downswing and for the upswing, but it is not successful for the interval near the turning point from the depression to the long upswing.

The second run with sudden stock price changes shows that the price movement is influenced by these price changes, which effects will be different by the timing of their occurrence.

In the third run with random price changes the peaks and troughs were shifted to the left and the shape of the short term wave varied very much.

In consequence, we believe that it may be possible to simulate moving average of actual stock prices.

In the actual stock market, we cannot experiment with the effects of sudden price changes, but by this simulation method we may be able to study these problems.

However, this study is only a case study of one company for a period of two years, so we must note that the model must be changed for other companies and for longer periods. Moreover, it must be far more difficult to simulate the actual stock price movement itself, which will contain various random shocks.

Notes

1. Wilford J. Eiteman and others, *The Stock Market*, 4th ed. (New York: McGraw-Hill Book Company, 1966), and Benjamin Graham and others, *Security Analysis*, 4th ed. (New York: McGraw-Hill Book Company, 1962).

2. Paul H. Cootner, ed., *The Random Character of Stock Market Prices* (Cambridge, Mass.: The MIT Press, 1964).

3. Jay W. Forrester, *Industrial Dynamics* (Cambridge, Mass.: The MIT Press, 1961).

4. C. W. J. Granger and Oskar Morgenstern, "Spectral Analysis of New York Stock Market Prices," Princeton Econometric Research Program, Research Memorandum No. 66, June 8, 1964.

5. Floating shares defined here are different from the term "floating supply" used frequently by investment analysts. The latter will be defined as shares held by the speculative group. See Eiteman, p. 523.

6. Alexander L. Pugh III, *DYNAMO User's Manual*, 2nd ed. (Cambridge, Mass.: The MIT Press, 1963).

7. See note 6.

Appendix

Model Tabulation

M25-361489, DYN, TEST, 1, 1, 0, 0   SHIMADA
STOCK MARKET MODEL PROJECT
GEN MOTOR WEEKLY MODEL
PRICE CHANGE SECTOR

1 L	SP.K=SP.J+(DT) (SPCH.JK+0)	STOCK PRICE	1
6 N	SP=55		2
6 N	SPCH=0		3
8 R	SPCH.KL=SPCH1.K+SPCH2.K+SPCH3.K	STOCK PRICE CHANGE	4
20 A	SPCH1.K=EDV.K/FS.K	STOCK PRICE CHANGE DUE TO EDV	5
41 A	SPCH2.K=PULSE (PULH, PULS, PULW)	PULSE TO STOCK PRICE	6
C	PULH=0		
C	PULS=20		
C	PULW=50		
34 A	SPCH3.K=(SPCC)NORMRN(MEAN,DEV)	RANDOM SHOCKS TO STOCK PRICE	7
C	SPCC=1		
C	MEAN=0		
C	DEV=0		
13 A	FS.K=(TDAY) (PCFS) (TS.K)	FLOATING SHARES	8
C	TDAY=5	TRADING DAYS IN A WEEK	
C	PCFS=0. 02	DECIMAL % OF FS TO TS	
12 A	EDV.K=(ED.K) (SP.K)	EXCESS DEMAND VALUE	9
7 A	ED.K=ED1.K+EDC2.JK	EXCESS DEMAND	10
7 A	ED1.K=TBO.K−TSO.K	EXCESS DEMAND DUE TO ORDERS	11
46 R	EDC2.KL=(CEDC2) (FS.K) (CSPC.K)/((SP.K) (1) (1))	ENERTIA TERM	12
C	CEDC2=.25		
7 A	CSPC.K=SPCH.JK−AUX.JK	CHANGE OF STOCK PRICE CHANGE	
6 R	AUX.KL=SPCH.JK		
7 A	TBO.K=SPBO.JK+IBO.JK	TOTAL BUY ORDER	13
7 A	TSO.K=SPSO.JK+ISO.JK	TOTAL SELL ORDER	14
37 B	SPB=BOXLIN (5,1)	SP BOXCAR	15
36 N	SPB=BOXLOAD (55,1)		16
6 A	SPB*1.K=SP.K		17
10 A	SSP.K=SPB*1.K+SPB*2.K+SPB*3.K+SPB*4.K+SPB*5.K+0		18
20 A	MASP.K=SSP.K/5	MOVING AVERAGE OF SP	19
37 B	MASPB=BOXLIN (5,1)	BOXCAR OF MASP	20
36 N	MASPB=BOXLOAD (55,1)		21
6 A	MASPB*1.K=MASP.K		22
7 R	CMASP.KL=MASP.K−MASPB*2.K	CHANGE OF MASP	23

6 R	AUX1.KL=CMASP.JK		24
51 A	TRP1.K=CLIP (TRPB*2.K,SPB*3.K,AUX2.K,0)		25
12 A	AUX2.K=(AUX1.JK) (CMASP.JK)		
51 A	TRP.K=CLIP (TRP1.K,TRPB*2.K,CMASP.JK,0)	TROUGH PRICE	26
37 B	TRPB=BOXLIN (5,1)	TRP BOXCAR	27
36 N	TRPB=BOXLOAD (55,1)		28
6 A	TRPB*1.K=TRP.K		
21 A	PDSA.K=(1/TRP.K) (SP.K−TRP.K)	% DEVIATION BET SP AND TRP	29
7 A	PDSAG.K=PDSA.K−PDSAD.K	PDSA WITH GROWTH EFFECTS	30
20 A	PDSAD.K=SPDVC.K/TRP.K	PDSA BY SPDVC	31
46 A	SPDVC.K=(CSPDC) (ADIVC.JK) (1)/((DIVYG.K) (TS.K) (1))		

STOCK PRICE CORRESPONDING TO ASSUMED DIVIDEND CHANGE   32

C CSPDC=0.2

SPECULATOR SECTOR

13 R	SPBO.KL=(TDAY) (MSBO) (SBRC.K)	SPECULATOR BUY ORDER RATE	33
C	MSBO=200	MAXIMUM SPECULATOR BUY ORDER	
13 R	SPSO.KL=(TDAY) (MSSO) (SSRC.K)	SPECULATOR SELL ORDER RATE	34
C	MSSO=200	MAXIMUM SPECULATOR SELL ORDER	
51 A	SBRC.K=CLIP (SBR1.K,SBR2.K,SPCH.JK,0)		35

SPECULATOR BUY ORDER REACTION FOR PDSAG

58 A	SBR1.K=TABHL (TSBR1,PDSAG.K,−0.2,0.3,0.02)	SBRC TABLE FOR +SPCH	36
C	TSBR1*=1/1/1/1/1/1/.86/.6/.25/.32/.4/.5/.6/.76/.92/1/.94/.84/.7/.		
X1	64/.4/.3/.2/.13/.11/.1		
58 A	SBR2.K=TABHL (TSBR2,PDSAG.K,−0.2,0.3,0.02)	SBRC TABLE FOR −SPCH	37
C	TSBR2*=1/1/1/1/1/1/1/1/.98/.95/.9/.84/.77/.71/.65/.6/.56/.52/.48/.		
X1	44/.4/.36/.32/.28/.24/.2		
51 A	SSRC.K=CLIP (SSR1.K,SSR2.K,SPCH.JK,0)		38

SPECULATOR SELL ORDER REACTION FOR PDSAG

58 A	SSR1.K=TABHL (TSSR1,PDSAG.K,−0.2,0.3,0.02)	SSRC TABLE FOR +SPCH	39
C	TSSR1*=.2/.23/.26/.29/.32/.35/.38/.4/.25/.27/.3/.33/.36/.4/.45/.5/		
X1	.55/.6/.68/.73/.8/.88/.96/1/1/1		
58 A	SSR2.K=TABHL (TSSR2,PDSAG.K,−0.2,0.3,0.02)	SSRC TABLE FOR −SPCH	40
C	TSSR2*=.2/.23/.26/.29/.32/.35/.38/.41/.44/.47/.5/.53/.56/.6/.64/.6		
X1	8/.72/.77/.83/.92/1/1/1/1/1		

DIVIDEND SECTOR

12 A	GPR.K=(ICS) (RGPR.K)	GROSS PROFIT	41
12 N	ICS=(PAR) (CTS)	INITIAL COMMON STOCK	
C	PAR=5	PAR VALUE	
C	CTS=280000	CONSTANT TOTAL SHARES	
12 N	GPR=(ICS) (RGPR)		
59 A	RGPR.K=TABLE (TRGPR, TIME.K, 0, 100, 5)	RATIO OF GPR TO ICS	42

C   TRGPR*=1.2/1.14/1.06/.92/.74/.7/.84/1.1/1.42/1.64/1.8/1.92/2/2.07/

X1   2.14/2.2/2.25/2.28/2.29/2.3/2.3

12A   NPR.K=(CNPR) (GPR.K)   NET PROFIT   43

C   CNPR=.55

12A   PDIV.K=(POR) (NPR.K)   PROFIT FOR DIVIDEND   44

C   POR=.7   PAY—OUT RATIO

3L   DIV.K=DIV.J+(DT) (1/TDIV) (PDIV.J−DIV.J)   DIVIDEND LEVEL AT FACTORY   45

6N   DIV=PDIV

12N   PDIV=(POR) (NPR)

12N   NPR=(CNPR) (GPR)

C   TDIV=13

INVESTOR SECTOR

42A   DIVY.K=DIV.K/((TS.K) (SP.K))   DIVIDEND YIELD   46

6A   TS.K=CTS   TOTAL SHARES

7A   DIVYG.K=DIVY.K+DIVYA.K   DIVY WITH GROWTH EFFECTS   47

42A   DIVYA.K=ADIVC.JK/((TS.K) (SP.K))   DIVY FOR ASSUMED DIV CHANGE   48

22R   ADIVC.KL=(1/TDIV)((TADVC)(PDIV.K)+(−TADVC) (DIV.K))   49

ASSUMED FUTURE DIVIDEND CHANGE FOR TIME TADVC

C   TADVC=13

13R   IBO.KL=(TDAY) (MIBO) (IBRD.K)   INVESTOR BUY ORDER RATE   50

C   MIBO=200

13R   ISO.KL=(TDAY) (MISO) (ISRD.K)   INVESTOR SELL ORDER RATE   51

C   MISO=200

58A   IBRD.K=TABHL (TIBRD, DIVYG.K, 0, 0.1, 0.01)   52

INVESTOR BUY ORDER REACTION FOR DIVYG

C   TIBRD*=0/0/.02/.06/.11/.2/.35/.7/.95/.99/1

59A   ISRD.K=TABLE (TISRD, DIVYG.K, 0.1, 0.01)   53

INVESTOR SELL ORDER REACTION FOR DIVYG

C   TISRD*=1/.99/.95/.7/.35/.2/.11/.06/.02/0/0

PRINT   1)SP, SPCH, MASP/2)ED, EDV/3)SPBO, SBRC, PDSA/4)SPSO, SSRC

PRINT   5)DIVY, DIVYG, DIV/6)IBO, IBRD, ISRD/7)ISO, TBO, TSO/8)CSPC

PLOT   SPCH=C/SP=P, MASP=I, TRP=T/DIV=D/PDSAG=G/DIVYG=W

PLOT   SPBO=*, SPSO=X, IBO=K, ISO=L/PDSA=A/DIVY=H/SPDVC=F/TBO=B, TSO=S/

SPEC   DT=1/LENGTH=100/PRTPER=5/PLTPER=1   ED=E

31

System Dynamics in Corporate Long-Range Strategic Planning

Kenneth P. Veit

Introduction

Management decisions and the results flowing from those decisions are part of a logical process of interrelated events. This process or system is "dynamic" in that it takes place over time, with the unfolding of events causing changes in the system itself.

Figure 1 shows the key steps in the corporate decision-making process, with each arrow indicating the flow of events. The sequence is:

1. We start out with *objectives*.
2. From objectives flow *plans*.
3. Plans lead to *pressure for action*.
4. The pressure results in some immediate *decisions*, plus additional *consideration of alternatives*.
5. The consideration of alternatives leads to other decisions, and the deliberations are fed back into the planning process for the future.
6. As decisions are reached, there is *action*.
7. Action leads to *results*.
8. Results generate *information*.
9. Information causes *perceived results*.
10. Perceived results affect future objectives.
11. Perceived results, when compared with plans, generate *apparent differences*. This leads to pressure for action independent of the on-going planning process. In other words, pressure for action is caused both by the formal planning process and by developing events.

System Dynamics

System dynamics is a methodology which deals with the dynamic (time-varying) behavior of any type of "system" found in business or other organizations. A "management system" is simply a regularly interacting group of people, machines, etc.,

This chapter is a slightly reduced version of a paper prepared by the author for presentation at the 20th International Congress of Actuaries, Tokyo, Japan, October, 1976. It is published here by permission of the author.

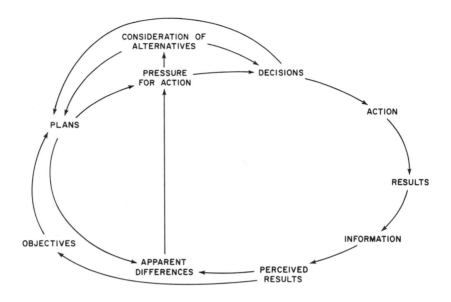

Figure 1   Decision making process

whose activities involve allocation and control of the resources of an organization. System dynamics simulation models can be constructed to study the information-feedback characteristics of management systems to show how organizational structure, response to information, and time delays (in decisions and actions) interrelate to influence results.

Traditional asset share models are the ones with which most North American actuaries are comfortable. They accept a large set of fixed assumptions about the levels and trends of many variables over the lifetime of a block of business and calculate what will be the actual or present value of emerging surplus at various key points. Similarly, standard profit models allow for the inclusion of values for a large number of variables. Given these constants, they do the laborious arithmetic needed to determine the balance between the income and expense streams over time.

These traditional models typically allow the values of some variables to be calculated as functions of the values of other variables, and the functional relationships may be different at different points of time. All of these must be specified precisely as input items. System dynamics models, however, have two important differences which are major advantages:

(1) They allow for far more complex multiple interrelationships of variables over time, and the outcomes of those relationships are calculated by the model rather than being done externally and inputed in advance. (As a simple example, one might wish to express some expense item as a percentage of sales. In a traditional model, you would be able to vary the percent used, depending on the volume of sales, but you would have to specify in advance what the percents to be used

would be and what volume of sales was being assumed. In a system dynamics model, on the other hand, you are able to specify a tabular relationship between the expense percent and the level of sales, and the model will select the appropriate percent to be used based on sales figures which themselves are projected and dynamically calculated, internally, from the current levels, trends, and *any number of variables modifying those trends*. Furthermore, the model can be instructed to modify the relationship between the expense percent and the sales volume based on the value of other variables, e.g., inflation, productivity levels, etc.)

(2) They can include the impact of variables which are not normally subject to quantification. This is done by arbitrarily assigning a value of 1.00 to a subjective variable, and allowing it to vary based on the management group's expectations of what would happen under certain conditions. For example, suppose we define a variable called "morale". A change in that variable from 1.00 to 1.20 would mean that morale had improved by 20 percent. To the extent that morale impacts efficiency, this is important in that it may help explain why a management decision which may affect morale can result in a change in other key variables, the values of which are a function of efficiency.

Admittedly, the assigning of assumed percentage changes in morale and efficiency sounds highly subjective. It is. But management itself involves many decisions based on relationships which can only be expressed subjectively. While the resulting numbers used may not be actuarially precise to three decimal places, they are generally accurate enough for use in strategy model-building.

A system dynamics model thus allows all variables to vary dynamically, whereas our more familiar static models can only handle changes indirectly, as described, or by conducting tests on several different bases (with respect to any variable whose behavior is being studied) and "holding everything else constant."

When is a System Dynamics Model Appropriate?

System dynamics models are basically strategy models. It is important that this be clearly understood. The purpose of these models is not to make precise quantitative predictions of the future, but rather to indicate the trends of key variables where many of them are interrelated in subtle and complex ways.

A recounting of our experience at AEtna may be useful in understanding where such a model may be useful. During the 1970 planning process AEtna's Life Division (which is responsible for individual life, health and equity products) embarked on an ambitious five-year plan (1971–1975) designed to dramatically increase our market share through an interconnected series of changes involving a substantial increase in our field force; increased specialization by product line and market area; and separate marketing through brokerage and career agencies. Our goal was to triple sales during that period and to lay the foundation for a much more profitable enterprise. The keystone of this growth plan was the variable annuity which had been experiencing phenomenal growth in the late '60s.

By 1974 it became apparent that we were going to achieve most of our objectives. However, while we were pleased with our results, we had not achieved them in precisely the manner we had anticipated. It was time to begin thinking about another five-year plan, and it was necessary to understand better the reasons for our past results (including some unanticipated problems which had surfaced) if we were to plan intelligently for the future.

For one thing, the economy in the United States of America was in bad shape, and this, of course, was reflected in the stock market which in turn created obvious difficulties for the equity-based variable annuity. A key question, therefore, became what should be the anticipated role of the variable annuity in the next 5-year period. Should we put more or less emphasis on it in the future?

Our product had an inherently unusual statuatory profit pattern, with a severe early strain followed by a very steep rise occurring in later years, as the result of its pricing and commission structure. The product was still relatively new, and no one had been selling it long enough, or in sufficient quantities through all kinds of economic conditions, to know whether the theoretical profits would actually emerge as anticipated. Furthermore, there were no company or industry historical data with respect to such key things as lapse rates and unit costs against which we could measure our progress. For example, it became apparent quite early that the patterns found in the various actuarial tables used to price traditional life insurance products were not going to be appropriate for the variable annuity.

Thus we were required to make an unusually high proportion of our decisions based largely on judgment and incomplete information. We had goals and objectives with respect to all of our critical cost factors. Each of these seemed attainable in isolation. But we had no idea whether they were reasonable as a package, or whether it was logically possible for all of them or any particular combination of them to be achieved simultaneously, since everything seemed to be affected by everything else. Add to this the constant change in products, markets, services, compensation programs, personnel, etc., and we found ourselves asking "what if" questions over and over.

Profit models were run over and over, and over again, on many different bases. But it became increasingly evident that the results had limited validity, because every time we would hold one set of variables constant in order to test variations in some other set, we would realize that in the real world everything was changing all of the time.

About this time I became interested in the work of the Club of Rome, an organization of international business leaders who were concerned about and investigating potential solutions to the world's complex social and economic problems. Based on the pioneering work of Jay W. Forrester of the Massachusetts Institute of Technology, a project team had been assembled to apply system dynamics techniques to the problems under study. A number of books were written including *World Dynamics*,[1] a technical tract on the subject, and a layman's summary of the project, entitled *The Limits to Growth*.[2]

Because of my interest in these problems, I read these books and became generally familiar with the concepts of system dynamics. I was particularly impressed by the fact that these models so often lead to what Forrester calls "counter-intuitive" results. In other words, when all of the experts expect that A will cause B, just the opposite often occurs because of multiple interrelationships, the indirect effects of which are not fully perceived. I certainly could relate that to our business environment and our planning process. Over and over the various written material on system dynamics impressed upon the reader the impossibility of intuiting the logical outcome of all of the interrelationships in any complex system of dynamically related variables over an extended period of time, in particular the difficulty of mentally compensating for delays between perception and decision; decision and action; and action and results.

After some discussion we decided to investigate building a simulation model based on these principles and techniques for ourselves. Since we had no inhouse expertise in this area, it was necessary to employ a consulting firm[3] composed of a number of Forrester's associates and former students.

Model Building Process

The process we followed is fairly typical and may be considered to be comprised of twelve steps.

(1) Agreement must be secured from the top executives in the company, division, or department being modeled for their participation in all stages of the model building. This is not a job to be delegated to staff personnel. The reason is that the model is a representation of how the senior decision-making executives view the environment in which they live and operate. It is a systematic linking together of all the variables that are considered to be critical to the business at hand, in the same way that its executives normally think about these variables and their relationships when making day-to-day decisions. The model, being driven by a computer, is simply more efficient than the human mind in following through to logical conclusions the implications of the many interactions and relationships between variables which are perceived as being critical. If these perceptions are those of staff personnel, rather than of the top executives themselves, then the decision-makers will be in the position of second-guessing the model, rather than using it as intended, as an extension of their own conceptions and mental decision-making processes. While this is a fairly "heavy" exercise for many senior executives, the effort pays handsome dividends in that the process significantly sharpens their understanding of how their organization really functions and of how their own decisions are made and carried through to results.

(2) Having made this commitment, the first question that the executives must ask themselves is: What problems are we looking to the model for answers? A laundry list of such questions provides a necessary starting point in determining the boundaries of the model. It is probably as important not to attempt to model too much as it is to avoid modeling too little. In our situation it was agreed upon after a series of exploratory talks that most of our questions concerned equity products. Therefore, we decided to model in detail the operations of AEtna Variable (our equity products subsidiary), and only

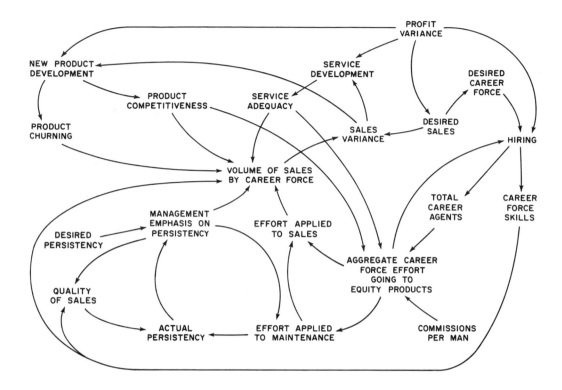

Figure 2 Overview of career force segment of sales sector

model those parts of Life & Health operations which were related to AEtna Variable in a critical way (e.g., expense allocations across lines).

(3) Next to be determined are the key factors/variables involved directly and indirectly in each of the problems to be addressed. This is an on-going process. Typically the number grows substantially as more and more relationships are identified and explored. Our model currently contains over 600 variables.

(4) Agreement must then be reached on the specific relationships between those variables. Which ones are related directly, which indirectly, and in what way? For example, do sales objectives determine profit objectives or vice versa? There are also two-way relationships (e.g., changes in price affect competitive position, and hence sales, but a change in sales volume also has an effect on pricing via its impact on unit costs. Many times in-depth discussion of questions like these leads to a new awareness of how an organization *really* functions, as opposed to the way in which people expect that it *ought* to be functioning).

(5) The next stage usually involves separating the several variables and relationships into different functional sectors for more detailed analysis. For example, in our model we have a sales sector, a service sector, accounting and policy inforce sectors, two agency manpower sectors (Career and Brokerage), a persistency sector, a profit control sector, and a management priority sector, among others. Each of these sectors

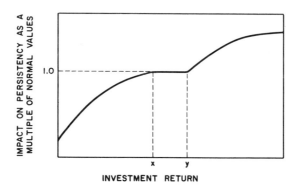

Figure 3 Assumed impact of investment return on persistency

is generally described through a ''word and arrow diagram'' (See Figure 2) where each of the variables is listed and an arrow drawn between any two variables that stand in cause and effect relationship, with the arrow going from the causal variable to the variable affected. It is particularly critical that all arrows be drawn where such relationships exist, so that all loops will be closed. Loops which reinforce or dilute relationships are the most critical in any system, yet they are often the ones most imperfectly understood.

(6) A timeframe is normally chosen over which the values of the variables will be examined. This can be any duration from months to decades. In our case, a four-year past history and ten-year future history were used. All of the variables are initialized at appropriate historical levels at time zero, and equations are defined which determine the rate of change of each variable, depending on its interrelationship with other variables. A particularly useful feature of a system dynamics model is its ability to allow for the same types of delays in cause/effect transactions as are present in the real world.

(7) Oversimplifying somewhat, each variable is then allowed to vary from one time period to another, with the ''normal'' progression of its values subject to modification depending on influences arising from the values of other variables. These modifications take the form of multipliers which change the value of a variable when the value of some other variable (with which it stands in a cause and effect relationship) becomes ''non-normal'' at any point in time.

In other words, we might feel (and have data to back up our subjective impressions) that as long as the rate of return credited to contracts in our variable annuity Separate Account is between x percent and y percent, investment performance will have negligible impact on persistency.[4] If our performance exceeds y percent, we might assume that it will have a positive effect up to a point, while performance worse than x percent will have a progressively worsening impact. This can be expressed graphically as in Figure 3.

Thus, any time investment performance, which is dynamically determined in the model, falls outside the range x, y, persistency will automatically be adjusted by the model.

(8) Once each of the sectors has been modeled and tested, and the executive group building the model is satisfied that all of the variables and relationships are reasonably representative of real world behavior, then each of the sectors is linked together. Now the model is generally rough but complete. All of the sectors are exerting influence over each other continuously during the period under consideration.

It is important to appreciate that with the large number of variables and relationships usually involved in a business model, not every relationship is going to be able to be precisely quantified. Some executives are skeptical of these models because they feel that without enormous amounts of precise data the model will produce results which are inaccurate or highly subjective. On the contrary, while precise data are naturally useful when available, most business decisions depend in great part on opinion, judgment, and intuition. If subjective data actually are built into the decision-making process which is used in the real world, then they also should be built into the model itself, since the model's purpose is to show the logical conclusions of the sum total of *all of our assumptions,* without regard to the correctness of those assumptions. However, to the extent that one's assumptions are invalid, the model usually is able to point out where some other explanation would more readily explain events in the past.

(9) While validation of assumptions for the most part must be done independent of the model, the model must validate itself. Generally speaking, if the model can reproduce the historical values of key variables within 10% then the structure of the model is probably sound. In other words, all of the variables and sectors are linked together in such a way that the model is a fair representation of the real world. Furthermore, this reproduction of the past is not just an exercise in curve-fitting. It is here that the uniqueness of the simulation technique stands out. Once all variables are initialized at their known or estimated values on some given date in the past, the model is turned on. If the *structure* of the model is correct, it will vary the values of the variables *at variable rates* over time in such a way that they reproduce historical data fairly closely.

If the model does not reproduce the past within an acceptable degree of tolerance, then one must ask why it does not. This usually leads to the uncovering of some very interesting relationships in the real world which might have been overlooked, ignored, or suppressed. Or, as indicated above, it may mean that some presumed relationships or other assumptions about the behavior of the organization have been wrong. This is not at all unusual. It is here that the skill of the model builder is most critical. The model is usually tested, refined and re-tested many times before it can be satisfactorily validated. A major reason for this is that many opinions are included in the model which, while initially expressed in fairly extreme statements of the form: ''If we could just improve x slightly, it would have a big impact on y,'' often turn out to involve a much more muted relationship in actual fact.

(10) Once the model is seen to reproduce the past satisfactorily, then it is common to make several ''base runs'', using the organization's latest long-range goals and one

or more sets of exogenous inputs with respect to things outside the company's control (e.g., inflation). Generally, the model contains only a few such independent variables; most of the variables in the system have values calculated internally based on their interactions with all the other variables included in the model. The set of base runs answers the fundamental question "What important trends will develop if we keep running the business the way we have been?" They also are a yardstick against which the effect of changes in the way the organization operates can be measured.

(11) The next step is to conduct a fairly exhaustive set of "sensitivity runs" to determine what are the critical areas where changes can significantly change the behavior of the model. For example, suppose that the company's long-range goals for sales growth, profit growth, or any other objectives over some time period are revised. How important are such established goals in the overall behavior of the model?

Or suppose that the response time to a change in some policy could be shortened. How fast would the total system respond, and in what way? Would all parts of the organization have to alter their response times to change? If this were not possible, what would be the consequence? For example, if sales goals are revised and the sales force responds with a rapid increase in sales, does this mean an increased need for administrative backup; can the service organization respond quickly enough, or will administrative support deteriorate to the point where the sales momentum cannot be maintained?

Obviously the important thing here is to determine what is critical to the behavior of the variables which management is really concerned about. There are often a number of surprises in that relationships which are thought to be incidental may have enormous impact down the road if they go through one or more reinforcing loops before they work themselves through the entire system. The true causes of bottlenecks often go unperceived by management.

(12) Once that key trends and critical control points in effecting changes have been determined, management is in a position to address the question: "What would we like to change?" The final step then is using the knowledge gained of where the sensitivity points are to try to introduce changes which will lead to more acceptable results. This is usually expressed by saying that a system dynamics model allows one to ask it questions of the type: "What if?" For example: "What if we invest more money in computer systems? How will their impact work through the company with varying effects on unit costs, service, efficiency, etc., and ultimately to the bottom line? Will spending more money now result in more profits over the entire timeframe under consideration? Is the short-term depression of profits acceptable in this light or not?"

AEtna Variable Model

These were the kinds of questions we wanted to and did ask. But before we could, endless discussions were held, including many debates on such controversial issues as: How much productivity improvement do data processing systems really generate (as opposed to providing the capability for doing things not done previously, or merely making it easier to do more where we used to settle for fewer)?

One of the more complicated areas we explored was management controls. How does management respond to crisis and influence change? In order to get this into the model we described what goes on by a highly idealized but not unrealistic set of variables and relationships.

We agreed that, in the broadest sense, the elements of profit which are most directly under management control are sales, expenses, and persistency. Almost everything else is either exogenous, the domain of specialists (e.g. investment performance), or can be considered as part of one of the three elements mentioned (e.g., the adequacy of service support which affects sales, persistency and unit expenses). We defined three variables:

(1)   Management Emphasis on Sales;
(2)   Management Emphasis on Persistency; and
(3)   Management Emphasis on Expenses

as the determinants of management's attention. Under normal circumstances, about half of management's attention is devoted to sales and the balance is split equally between persistency improvement (or maintenance) and controlling expenses.

When something goes wrong in any one of those three areas, emphasis shifts (but differently for each factor), and the time to correct the problem is a function of management's attention. We assumed that in any situation which is receiving 50 percent of management's attention, the average time to correct a perceived problem is six months. When attention rises above 50 percent, the time shortens; conversely, when the emphasis is less than 50 percent, the time period lengthens. While arbitrary, the following table seemed to represent reasonably what happens in the real world.

Management Attention	Delay Time (months)
.70	2
.60	4
.50	6
.40	9
.30	12
.25	14
.20	18

When a variance from current objectives arises in any of these three factors, management's emphasis on that variable naturally changes. If we assign a factor of 1.0 to "normal" emphasis, then the emphasis on each of the factors might vary according to the following table:

Sales		Persistency		Expenses	
Variance from Objectives	Management Emphasis on Sales	Actual/Expected Lapse Rates	Management Emphasis on Persistency	Variance from Unit Cost Objectives	Management Emphasis on Expenses
−20%	1.5	1.75	5.0	−10%	2.5
−15%	1.3	1.60	3.0	− 8%	2.0
−10%	1.2	1.45	2.0	− 6%	1.6
− 5%	1.1	1.30	1.5	− 4%	1.3
0	1.0	1.15	1.2	− 2%	1.1
+ 5%	1.0	1.00	1.0	0	1.0
+10%	.9	0.85	0.8	+ 2%	.9
+15%	.8	0.70	0.7	+ 4%	.7

We assumed that the 50–25–25 percent composition of management's total attention is altered as the emphasis on each of the factors independently varies from 1.0. The emphasis factors in the table were then used as multipliers to arrive at a changed distribution of management's attention. In other words, the standard percentages (50–25–25) of management's attention were multiplied by the appropriate factors from the table and the products were scaled up or down as appropriate to get back to a 100 percent sum. This is best understood by an example.

Suppose that (1) sales were off by 5 percent from objectives; (2) our lapse indicators rose to 145 percent of normal; and (3) unit costs showed a favorable variance of 2 percent. The following calculations would be made:

(1) *Sales*: The standard weight of .50 is multiplied by a factor of 1.1 to get a revised weight of .55.

(2) *Lapses*: .25 × 2.0 = .50 revised weight.

(3) *Unit Costs*: .25 × .9 = .225 revised weight

(4) The sum of these revised weights is 1.275

(5) Obviously, management cannot give 127.5 percent of its available time to these areas. Therefore, each of the revised weights must be scaled down. The revised sales emphasis weight is .55/1.275 = .43. Similarly, the revised emphasis on unit costs is .18 and the revised emphasis on lapses is .39. In other words, we would see a substantial shifting of management's attention away from sales and expenses, towards lapses, under this set of conditions. This would dramatically shorten the response time to the lapse problem, as is the case in the real world. If you go back to the table of response times, you will find that this shifting of management attention towards lapses from .25 to .39 is equivalent to about a 5-month reduction in the time that it takes to respond to the worsening situation with respect to persistency.

In the model at each point in time these variances are calculated, and a new set of management emphasis variables is computed, based on the shift in management attention resulting from the variances. These management emphasis variables determine corrective strategies, response times, etc. The model then determines what new variances will occur in the next period based on management's new strategies and all other internal and external factors.

Results

Having done all this analysis, equation-writing and validation testing, what did we learn? Probably most significantly we learned that there are powerful forces driving our business, the momentum of which is difficult to reverse. This, of course, can operate both positively and negatively. We are also in a goal-driven business, that is to say one in which results tend to follow fairly close to the objectives we set. This is so because of the momentum factor. Goals tend to be influenced by the trend of momentum. Of prime concern to us, therefore, is the maintenance of positive momentum.

In looking at things which could reverse momentum we found that bad stock market conditions can cause a pause in forward progress, but will not reverse long-term momentum except under the most disastrous scenarios. On the other hand, inadequate field support by Home Office administrative units can cause serious problems unless quickly reversed. This is an extremely important consideration in times of tight budget controls.

The important thing about the model was that it explained for the first time many of our past problems in terms of organizational structure, and showed when, how, and why they might recur in the future. We ended up calling our model "AVALANCHE" which is the acronym for *A* Etna *V* ariable *A* nalyzer of *L* ikelihoods *A* ctuaries *N* ever *C* ould *H* ope to *E* xplain.

The predicted trends in critical sales, costs and other factors were then used as inputs to our standard profit models, so the two types of models complement each other. We were able to ask "what if" questions of the AVALANCHE model with respect to changes under consideration to determine their dynamic impact on key variables, then use this information in profitability projections.

All in all it has been an interesting and valuable experience, both from the point of view of what we have learned about the inner workings of our organization and the important things we have decided about the possible future trends of our business. Actuaries who have not yet done so would do well to become familiar with the techniques of system dynamics.

Notes

1. Jay W. Forrester, *World Dynamics*, (Cambridge, Mass.: Wright-Allen Press, Inc., 1971).

2. Donella Meadows et al., *The Limits to Growth*, (New York: Universe Books, 1972).

3. Alexander L. Pugh III of Pugh-Roberts Associates, Inc. of Cambridge, Mass., was one of the principal developers of the DYNAMO compiler which is used to translate and run continuous models described by a set of differential equations such as the system dynamics model discussed in this paper. He acted as project leader for the development of the AEtna AVALANCHE model.

4. Issues such as variable impact on persistency at different durations, and the timeframe over which investment return should be measured, obviously must be considered, but are outside the scope of this paper.

Part Six:
Applications of System Dynamics
to Societal Problems

Ending this book with a section on applications to societal problems parallels the recent shift in the interests of system dynamics model-builders. Yet, even in the earliest years of the M.I.T. "industrial dynamics" activity, staff efforts were often directed toward social issues because they provided both challenge and an opportunity to demonstrate the breadth of feedback systems modeling. One early graduate research assistant developed an ecological model of the lynx-rabbit cycle in Northern Canada. Another graduate student created a model of the dynamics of yellow fever epidemics [11]. An ambitious project to model a developing economy was also undertaken but the project died in 1962 due to the lack of staff interest.

Although the field was still labelled "industrial dynamics", major works focusing upon social questions began to take shape in the mid-'60s. The first substantial non-industrial project was a large model of demographic and economic development in the Susquehanna River Basin. Beginning in 1963, a consortium of stockholder-owned utility companies sponsored this multi-phase regional model development. The effort was coordinated by Henry Hamilton of Battelle Memorial Institute, and the modeling and simulation work was done by Alexander Pugh and Edward Roberts as a consulting activity. The model also dealt with problems of water pollution and its interactions with regional growth. The model was disaggregated into nine subregions, and included specific representation of population subgroups as well as varied industrial sectors. Although detailed reports on the work were available as early as 1964, the book describing the model and its results was not published until 1969 [6]. In later years system dynamics applications to regional planning were expanded by Schlager's work for the Southeastern Wisconsin Regional Planning Commission and Environmental Impact Center's projects for the Federal Office of Water Resources Research and HUD-EPA.

The second major social area to be attacked from a system dynamics perspective was the management of the city. The publication of Forrester's *Urban Dynamics* [3] in 1969 created a controversial national dialogue on urban policy, as well as on the role of mathematical models for urban analysis. This conceptual effort led to a substantial practical application in the city of Lowell, Massachusetts by Walter Schroeder, and to a series of books [1,2,10,16] and journal articles on urban modeling.

Soon after the urban work began to capture attention, the M.I.T. group formally shifted its designation to the "System Dynamics Group" to more accurately reflect the scope of its interests. Projects began in the areas of mental health and health care delivery, and eventually led to system dynamics books on the social problem of heroin addiction [8] and on the delivery of human services [7]. System dynamics applications to the health field have grown dramatically during the past several years under the editor's direction [15].

More recently system dynamics attention has turned to the global issues of resource limitations and the interactions of population, economic development, and environmental pollution. Forrester's *World Dynamics* [4], followed by the Meadows' *The Limits to Growth* [13] generated international controversy, leading to many related books [12,14] and to ambitious modeling efforts throughout the world. This interest has spilled over into extensive natural resource and energy policy modeling by major corporations as well as by government agencies in numerous countries. Present efforts in societal applications of system dynamics also include economic modeling of the United States as well as other countries [5,9].

The articles chosen for Part 6 of the book are but a sampling of those available on social systems dynamics. As a bridge to the managerial applications in the preceding parts of the book, Chapter 32 treats an increasingly important corporate management issue and social problem, the introduction of minorities into management positions. The work described was carried out by Alan Frohman and Alexander Pugh, both of Pugh-Roberts Associates, Inc., collaborating as consultants with Henry Morgan, the Director of Human Resources of the Polaroid Corporation.

Chapter 33 by Boyce and Goldstone communicates an attempt by staff of Battelle Memorial Institute to show the applicability of the regional model described earlier [6] to urban transportation planning.

In Chapter 34 Levin, Hirsch and Roberts preview the issues and system analysis of heroin addiction that are described in greater depth in their book [8]. Dr. Levin is Associate Professor of Psychiatry at the Albert Einstein College of Medicine, while Gary Hirsch heads the health and social systems area in Pugh-Roberts Associates, Inc.

In her article reprinted as Chapter 35, Nancy Roberts shows the application of system dynamics to educational issues. That work is also embodied in a more general treatment of human service delivery systems — health, education, et al. — presented in book form [7]. Dr. Roberts is Assistant Professor at Lesley College in Cambridge, and is also working as a Research Associate with the M.I.T. System Dynamics Group on developing curricula for elementary and secondary schools.

Finally, Chapter 36 examines issues of natural resources as well as sociological questions, reflecting the breadth of societal policy problems now being addressed using system dynamics. The author, William Newell, is professor of management at the University of Washington, and received initial exposure to system dynamics while serving as a Sloan Faculty Fellow at M.I.T. in the early-'60s.

References

1. Alfeld, Louis Edward and Alan K. Graham. *Introduction to Urban Dynamics*. Cambridge, Mass.: Wright-Allen Press, Inc., 1976.

2. Coursey, R. W., editor. *System Dynamics Modeling in Urban and Regional Planning*. Newcastle-upon-Tyne, England: University of Newcastle-upon-Tyne, 1974.

3. Forrester, Jay W. *Urban Dynamics*. Cambridge, Mass.: The MIT Press, 1969.

4. Forrester, Jay W. *World Dynamics*. Cambridge, Mass.: Wright-Allen Press, Inc., 1971.

5. Forrester, Nathaniel B. *The Life Cycle of Economic Development*. Cambridge, Mass.: Wright-Allen Press, Inc., 1972.

6. Hamilton, H. R., S. E. Goldstone, J. W. Milliman, A. L. Pugh III, E. B. Roberts, and A. Zellner. *System Simulation for Regional Analysis: An Application to River Basin Planning*. Cambridge, Mass.: The MIT Press, 1969.

7. Levin, G. and E. B. Roberts, with G. B. Hirsch, D. S. Kligler, J. F. Wilder, and N. Roberts. *The Dynamics of Human Service Delivery*. Cambridge: Ballinger Publishing Company, 1976.

8. Levin, Gilbert, Edward B. Roberts, and Gary B. Hirsch. *The Persistent Poppy: A Computer-Aided Search for Heroin Policy*. Cambridge, Mass.: Ballinger Publishing Company, 1975.

9. Mass, Nathaniel J. *Economic Cycles: An Analysis of Underlying Causes*. Cambridge, Mass.: Wright-Allen Press, Inc., 1975.

10. Mass, Nathaniel J., editor. *Readings in Urban Dynamics: Volume 1*. Cambridge, Mass.: Wright-Allen Press, Inc., 1974.

11. McPherson, L. F. "Urban Yellow Fever: An Industrial Dynamics Study of Epidemiology," Cambridge, Mass.: M.I.T. Industrial Dynamics Memorandum D-572; March 28, 1963.

12. Meadows, Dennis L., William W. Behrens III, Donella H. Meadows, Roger F. Naill, Jørgen Randers, and Erich Zahn. *Dynamics of Growth in a Finite World*. Cambridge, Mass.: Wright-Allen Press, Inc., 1974.

13. Meadows, Donella H., Dennis L. Meadows, Jørgen Randers, and William W. Behrens III. *The Limits to Growth*. New York: Universe Books, 1972.

14. Meadows, Dennis L. and Donella H. Meadows, editors. *Toward Global Equilibrium: Collected Papers*. Cambridge, Mass.: Wright-Allen Press, Inc., 1973.

15. Roberts, Edward B. and Gary B. Hirsch, "Strategic Modelling for Health Care Managers." *Health Care Management Review*, vol. 1, no. 1 (Winter 1976), pp. 69–77.

16. Schroeder, Walter W. III, and Robert Sweeney, editors. *Readings in Urban Dynamics: Volume 2*. Cambridge, Mass.: Wright-Allen Press, Inc., 1975.

32

Introduction of Minorities into Management

Alan L. Frohman, Henry Morgan & Alexander L. Pugh III

The civil rights movement awakened the United States from slumber in the 1960's with the call that millions of citizens were being denied full participation in the American way of life. One of the many pressing issues identified was that of unemployment and underemployment among minorities, particularly blacks, and more particularly young black males. In response to the violence in the cities in the late 1960's, the Federal Government called on America's businesses to join them in an effort to combat the high rate of unemployment among these groups.

Initial efforts created the National Alliance for Businessmen, charged with the creation of programs to hire and train the "hardcore." The focus of this response to Watts, Detroit, and Newark was to get young blacks off the streets into meaningful jobs. The results were mixed. While many were hired off the streets, few were hired into meaningful jobs.

From 1968 to 1972, the attention of the cognizant governmental agencies has shifted from reducing unemployment—getting young blacks off the streets—to reducing underemployment—upward mobility. The current emphasis from both the Equal Employment Opportunity Commission and the Office of Federal Contract Compliance is on Affirmative Action Plans, which call for goals and timetables to achieve greater minority representation in more responsible and better paying positions. Since the issuance of Revised Order No. 4 by the OFCC, Affirmative Action Plans must also include goals and timetables for women.

The demands for goals and timetables for minorities and women are beginning to force a new role upon personnel departments. In the past, the separate and disjointed functions of personnel services could maintain their independence. Recruitment and selection filled open positions. Wage and salary administration tried to establish rational reward systems. Training programs were developed as needed for corporate

This chapter was originally presented at the 1973 Summer Simulation Conference and is reprinted here with the permission of the authors.

purposes. Employee counseling was done in reaction to problems, with little if any relation to other personnel activities. In those companies which recognized organization development activities, these programs were conducted by a new and separate department, generally operating at management levels, devoid of minorities and women. Each of the personnel activities was carried out by specialists with little interdisciplinary coordination.

Achieving equality for minorities and women, however, cannot be done in such a piecemeal manner. It requires looking at personnel as a total human resource system. Affirmative Action Plans require the integration of recruiting, training and promotion, compensation, organization development, and counseling. An effective Affirmative Action Plan means additional recruiting efforts and a search for new sources of employees. It means a renovation of training and upgrading programs. It means a tough look at compensation practices to see if they have been unintentionally discriminatory. Organization development activities in the nature of awareness programs and behavior change may be necessary to help provide a more receptive climate for equal employment activities. The personnel function must provide a leadership role as the coordinator of a total system in which the relationships between various parts affect each other and the performance of the total organization.

This system-view requirement is seen in the most vivid sense when a manager considers what must be done to achieve equal employment opportunities. If he plans to increase the number of minorities and women, he must look at his organization plans to see if and where new skills or new people are needed. He must consider if the appropriate people are in his labor supply and what he must do to attract them. He must consider the growth potential for both his jobs and the people he has and will hire. He must consider his ability to pay competitively to attract and hold highly-skilled minorities and women. He must consider the impact of a changed work force on the personal preferences and prejudices of its members. All of these factors must be integrated into a coherent whole before an Affirmative Action Plan can be effective.

To accomplish this a new approach must be used which can provide a system view and permit the development of a coordinated strategy. The approach must be able to integrate the functions of recruiting, training, promotion, compensation, counseling, etc. so that the impact of a policy and practice change can be evaluated in terms of the total system it affects. System dynamics, a computer simulation approach, has accomplished this in helping one industrial organization design its affirmative action strategies. This article describes system dynamics, how it was used and the results. Let us begin by discussing the events which led up to the application of system dynamics.

In the spring of 1971, a major employer in the Boston area was asked by a group of its black employees to look closely at its progress in minority employment over the three-year period, 1968–1970. During that period, the minority population had risen from 6 to 10%. However, the number of blacks in salaried positions had only risen from 1.5 to 4%. The data indicated that blacks were well represented in many entry level and semi-skilled jobs, under-represented in the skilled trades, practically absent in executive and higher-level professional positions, and totally absent from the Board

Room. The same situation seemed to exist in every major corporation in the country. Management responded with a new corporate goal:

> "Our goal for the five-year period through 1975 is to achieve a balance which includes 10% 'minority' members at all levels of responsibility throughout the company."

There are only two ways to have more blacks at higher levels of responsibility:

1. promotion from inside the company, and

2. hiring from outside the company.

The problems which these two simple alternatives produce are many. If strategy one is used exclusively, does this mean preferential promotion of unqualified people? Does it mean an abandonment of the company policy of competitive bidding in an open job posting system? Does it mean special and exclusive training programs? What resentment or "backlash" will develop among whites? On the other hand, if strategy two is used exclusively, does it mean abandonment of the company policy of promotion from within? Is there a supply of minorities with the required skills or will less than fully qualified applicants be hired? Will premium prices have to be paid? What resentment or "backlash" will develop among blacks already in the company?

It was obvious that a combination of both strategies was required, but at what rate of internal promotion and at what rate of and in what job level by external hiring? Could the stated goal be achieved at all within the projected growth of the company? These were some of the questions which prompted the search for an analytical method which could handle many variables and permit experimentation with alternative strategies.

System dynamics appeared to offer the tools necessary to analyze such problems. System dynamics specifically addresses complex, interrelated problems. It can be applied even when good data is lacking. It does not require huge resources to gain new insights and understanding.

System dynamics translates the mental models that managers normally use for decision-making into complete models. In the process, the missing portions of the mental models are identified and completed. The imprecise portions are made precise. The various parameters are identified and assigned tentative values.

Once the model has been constructed, it can be initialized to correspond to some real or hypothetical time and run to produce the time sequence of events that follow from its structure and parameters. Unreasonable results force one to review the assumptions that went into the model (the factors that were believed unimportant and left out, the specific structure of causes and effects, the timing relating effects and causes, and the magnitude of these relationships).

Once the results appear reasonable, the importance of various parameters can be explored by varying their magnitude. Once the team that is building the model has come this far, they have gained new insight into the situation being studied and can devise and test alternative strategies for coping with the problem. Through the whole process of computerizing their understanding of their problem, exploring and refining the resultant model, and designing and testing new strategies, they should come up with a far superior policy than would be possible based solely on their original mental model.

It was clear that no single person in the organization possessed all of the necessary background, insight or information to develop the system dynamics models which were required. Therefore, two steps were taken. First, an outside consultant, experienced in applying system dynamics to the formulation and solution of complex social problems, was brought in. Second, an internal task force of blacks and whites, with a spread of responsibilities in the Personnel Division, was assembled.

A task force approach was used for several reasons. By blending the skills and experience of the outside consultants with the specific knowledge and perceptions of the internal group, it was expected that the problems could be defined more completely and the answers could be tested by different perspectives. Secondly, the new skills and information brought by the consultants could be taught to the internal group for future problem-solving. A final reason was that each of the internal participants had a piece of the action in the implementation of the program. Thus, each had a need for the other's inputs and each a need to buy into the solution.

To facilitate the achievement of these dual objectives of education and decision making two models were built. The first was a conceptual model which was used to educate the members of the internal group about system dynamics and the consultants about the characteristics of the organization. The second model, built after the first one was complete, was for crisp problem definition and solution evaluation.

Construction of the conceptual model began with the task force sifting through the myriad of issues that surrounded the introduction of blacks into management. It assembled a rich catalogue of problem areas:

Black availability
Black recruitment
Black promotion
Black training
Black salary scales
Availability of housing for blacks
Sincerity of company in seeking blacks
Prejudice
White backlash
Black backlash
Sponsorship
Sensitivity training
Under-utilization of black skills
Promotion of blacks beyond their skill level.

Once the catalogue had been assembled, the task force began to look at interactions between these various factors. The behavior of complex systems cannot be anticipated from a simple examination of its various components, if these components are elements of chains of cause and effect that close upon themselves. For example,

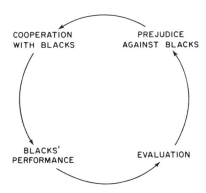

Figure 1

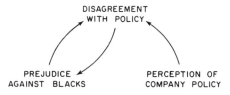

Figure 2

one cause of white prejudice toward blacks is the black's performance in his job. If prejudice should lead to poor cooperation with the black, the black's performance will, of necessity, fall. Poor performance in turn confirms and reinforces the prejudice that led to the poor cooperation. Even the company taking a positive position relative to blacks would be expected to provoke greater prejudice in those who were already prejudiced.

The system is already becoming complicated, so several diagrams will be used to explain the problem. In Figure 1, we see the first situation. Prejudice leads to poorer cooperation; poor cooperation leads to poor performance, which accentuates prejudice. Figure 2 shows prejudice dictating one's attitude toward company policies which in turn accentuates prejudice.

Should company policy be translated into a generous promotion policy? This too gets trapped in the prejudice loop, as is shown in Figure 3. Promotion, should it occur in response to the company's announced policy, would lead to poorer performance on the part of the blacks as they encounter more demanding jobs. Again, this increases prejudice which in turn will impede further promotion of blacks.

The set of relationships just described are sufficiently complex so that most people are unable to anticipate exactly how the system will behave without some sort of assistance. Capturing that system in a mathematical model permits one to explore the

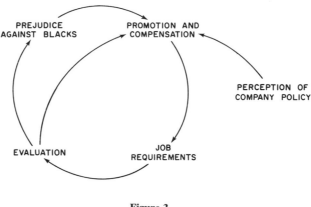

Figure 3

A GROUP

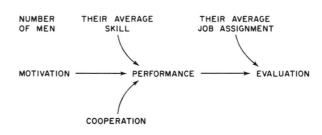

Figure 4

various sorts of behavior that might occur for a fairly wide range of assumptions about the specific character of each one of the links.

The task force actually went through this exercise as a means of learning about the construction of models. The model that was constructed was an interesting pedagogical tool, but not very convincing as a decision-making tool, as so many other elements had been left out.

To meet this requirement, another model was built that was about ten times the size. This model monitored two groups of people, the blacks and the whites, their course into the company up through the ranks and out through either retirement or turnover. It monitored their skill which was modified both by training and experience, and their average job which was altered through promotion.

As individuals joined the company, they brought with them certain average skills and accepted certain jobs. When they left, they took with them additional skills and left behind them more significant jobs. A diagram of one of the groups is shown in Figure 4. The relationships just described permit one to consider several other important relationships such as the average performance of the group by comparing its average skill level to its average job.

The complete model is constructed from two such "people" sectors, a set of interactions between them, and a set of company policies (see Figure 5). The interactions include prejudice and cooperation, discussed earlier, as well as turnover and motivation variables. Turnover for the whites goes up as the average promotion rate of blacks exceeds that of whites. The motivation of blacks is based on the prejudice shown by the whites. The task force agreed to make this particular relationship a rather complex one in which the black responded positively both to some encouragement from the whites (negative prejudice) and to small amounts of prejudice by attempting to prove their worth to the whites. As shown in Figure 6, extreme prejudice or extreme favoritism both resulted in low values of motivation.

Company action manifests itself in a number of important ways. First, was the issue of the number of blacks and whites recruited. Second, was the skill level at which they entered the company. Third, was the job to which they were assigned and, finally, once they were within the company, the amount of training they received.

The numbers were set up to implement the 10% policy. The percentage of new recruits that were black reflected the difference between the desired and actual percentage of blacks within the company at any point in time.

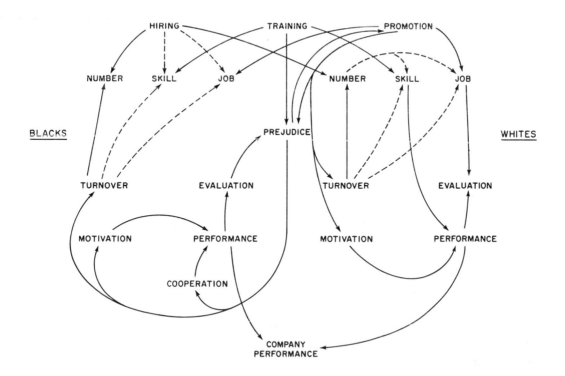

Figure 5

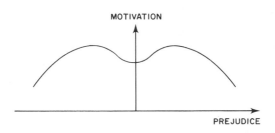

Figure 6

The area of the entering skill was one of the surprises that resulted from the construction of a mathematical model of the system. The task force had never given any particular consideration to this issue, but when the modelers were confronted with the data (the turnover rate of blacks is well in excess of that of whites) and the requirements that the average skill level of blacks was ultimately to equal that of whites, it was realized that the only way this goal could be achieved was either through recruiting blacks at a considerably higher level than that of entering whites or by a training and promotion program that moved blacks through the company at a much greater pace than that of whites. Consequently, the model reflected a policy of bringing in blacks with considerable experience.

Training was the last important dimension of company policy. If blacks were given preferential training, they could then be moved up through the company faster, as measured by contrasting abilities and job requirements. But preferential training was one of the important inputs into prejudice. Large amounts of preferential training resulted in greater prejudice and the consequential poorer cooperation, as well as the higher turnover rates of both whites and blacks.

Model Results

The first run reflects highly preferential treatment of blacks within the company. Starting at TIME = 0 the company attempts to double the number of blacks in management and to raise their average job to that of whites within a five-year period. The process of doubling the number of blacks means that 30% of all new hires must be black (see Figure 7). Additionally the entry skill of the new hires rises 3.5 pay grades.

The bias in hires is assumed to have negligible repercussions in comparison to the reaction to preferential training and promotion of blacks already in the company. In this run blacks individually receive about three times as much training as whites and are promoted about twice as frequently. This creates a major problem as prejudice rises to a high of 30 (on a scale of 0 to 100). Turnover (not plotted) of both blacks and whites rises sharply and productivity (also not plotted) of those who remain falls.

After the sixth year (when the goals are reached one year behind schedule) the preferential treatment is significantly reduced and the situation settles back to close to normal.

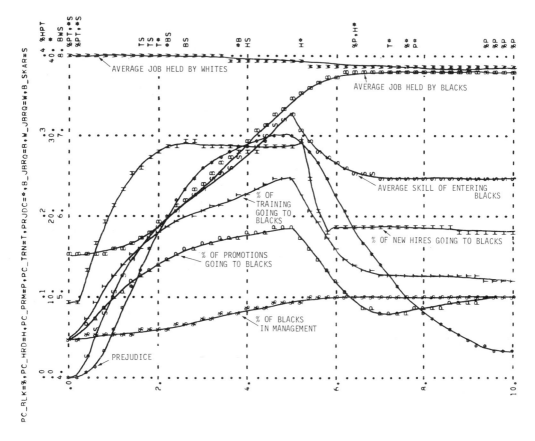

Figure 7

In the second run a policy of less preferential treatment of blacks within the company is followed (see Figure 8). To achieve the same goals in the same time frame, blacks with even greater skills are recruited. The more equal treatment means that prejudice rises only half as high. Turnover and productivity are more stable. The company suffers considerably less.

This run allows us to draw some important conclusions. The first is that the goal of 10% blacks at all levels can be reached with a reasonable expenditure of effort and resources. Second was that the goal could only be reached by recruiting blacks at high levels in the organization. Third was that a moderate amount of preferential training and promotion would have to be used but that they were secondary to an active-recruiting-at-all-levels policy. Finally, it was evident that there would be some cost to the company in terms of vacant slots, costs of recruiting and training and prejudice, but that they were within the company's tolerance level for a subset of the policies tested which permitted achievement of the 10% goals. In addition, other important results came from using this approach.

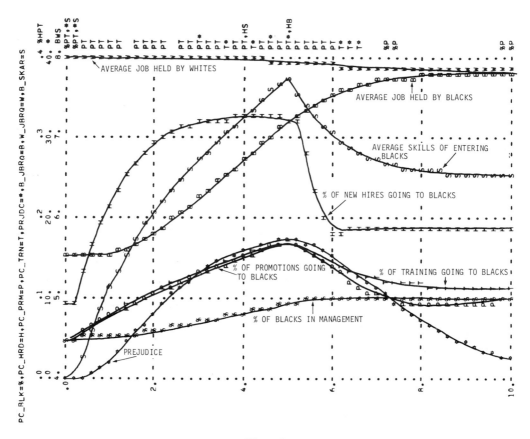

Figure 8

"How can a simulation ever tell us anything that we do not already know?" (H. A. Simon).   Throughout the development of the conceptual models, the descriptive equations and the trial runs, the task force was providing inputs and testing outputs. The model, its development and the results; came out of what the task force already knew, but at the start the group was unable to be as explicit about the formulation of the problem and the strategic solutions as they were at the end. Only after the computer printed the possible consequences of alternative strategies could anyone say, "Of course, we already knew that!" But did they? And, if so, what was gained in the process?

The first accomplishment was the creation of a work group with a wide range of inputs and insights. Without question, the old adage, "garbage in, garbage out" could be applied to this program. The time taken in the early stages of the consultation in seeking good inputs was critical. It is possible that an even broader range of inputs could have been sought. On the other hand, members of the task force had to have some faith in rational conceptualization in order to contribute the necessary degree of commitment. On reflection, there was an initial high degree of cynicism in the group which gradually disappeared as they saw the model refining their more nebulous thoughts.

The second accomplishment was the qualitative model itself. The process of refinement from the first clumsy attempts was a learning experience. A sharpening perception was achieved in the iterative steps leading to a model that everyone could accept as reasonably complete—simple enough to understand, but more complex than a simple mind could comfortably deal with.

The third accomplishment was the output data. More important than any single strategic result was the ability to test the sensitivity to alternative strategies. This is, in fact, the key to the whole program. One hope was that the tests could be made for high leverage actions and low leverage actions. What at first appeared to be a complex, interrelated set of problems was reduced to a set of simple alternative strategies. The hope was fulfilled.

The fourth accomplishment was the confirmation with hard data that it was indeed possible to achieve the goal stated by the company. In addition, there was a numerical plan by which to measure progress. It is possible to compare actual performance of the company against a strategic plan. Real data on hiring, promotion, training, turnover, etc. can be matched, quarter by quarter. Since no five-year plan should be left without modification, this model can continue to serve with updating of actual performance and be run again to prescribe future actions.

One of the major drawbacks has been the difficulty in convincing those not on the original task force of the validity of the approach and the model strategies. In some respects, the results make a very difficult and complex problem look too simple. There is also a resistance to accepting a cold, rational, numerical presentation of what is known to be a hot, irrational, human situation. The computer printout drops most of the value-laden negatives and coldly gives a solution.

Generality of Approach

The system dynamics approach clearly paid off for the task force. It helped them to find a common perception of the problem and to find the key leverage points for achievement of the company's equal employment goals. The major cost involved was the time internal personnel spent on task force meetings and related activities. (This came to about ten 1/2 day meetings over a six-month period.) The benefits in this case far outweighed the costs.

Under what circumstances might this approach be profitably employed in other companies for other problems? This experience and the experience of others with this approach provide ready guide lines.

First, the problem should contain a number of variables which interact with each other. The human mind is capable of handling only a few bits of data at a time (7 ± 2 is supposed to be the magic number). If the problem involves a number of variables, then the data load is probably too great for any one person. As a result, it is better to use computer models than it is to use the mental models in our heads to manipulate the data.

In this case, the variables included the number of people at each level in the organization, their promotion rate and turnover, training, promotion and hiring programs, prejudice, motivation and a general index of company performance.

Second, a number of alternative strategies should be available. A major strength of the system dynamics approach is that it allows a wide range of possible solutions to a problem to be "trial run" on a computer. The computer simulates the behavior of the system under each policy or set of policies and allows the user to evaluate the relative effectiveness of each. The development of the model also helps to point out other strategies or new combinations of strategies which may have gone unnoticed earlier. Personnel Departments can use hiring, training and promotion interchangeably in some instances. Each has very different types of implications for the resources expended, the supporting steps which need to be taken and the certainty and timing of goal achievement.

System dynamics allows a decision-maker to identify the leverage points in a system and determine the key ones to impact in order to affect the system's performance. In many cases, both multiple strategies and multiple points at which a system can be changed are available. For example, there were a number of job levels in the company discussed earlier. An important question was which level to start on with a given strategy? Should we start on top and work down with outside hiring, on the bottom and work up with hiring or promotion in the middle or start all at once?

If a number of variables are involved, a number of strategies can be used, or a number of leverage points are available, a system dynamics approach is likely to be worth the investment. Other areas where system dynamics has been employed are: the design of management control systems, the allocation of resources in an R&D division, the treatment of narcotics build-up in a community, the regional development of a river basin area, and the interaction between the staff and patients of a health center.

The task force process by which a system dynamics model can be built is also useful for the development of commitment to the solution and better understanding among the participants. Model development offers an excellent opportunity for the individuals involved to exchange their perceptions of how the system operates. Often those perceptions are colored by interesting assumptions which can then be explored. Differences in assumptions can be the underlying reasons for conflicting opinions. The rigor and discipline of the model building process forces the assumptions into the open where they can be examined and clarified on the intellectual level. Arguments over the interactions in a model are more readily subject to reason and observation than are arguments over the right or wrong way to handle something.

The model also provides a common framework for discussion and exploration. It is a commonly viewed schematic representation of abstract concepts and relationships. As such, it readily provides a starting point for discussion of the relationships, assumptions and possible solutions for the problem. Otherwise, each individual would use his own "mental model" of the problem which is probably unique to him as well as containing uncommunicated and untested perceptions. Consequently, system dynamics has a significant contribution in helping both to solve complex problems and to bring together the parties involved so that they are agreed upon as to the definition of the problem and what to do about it.

A Regional Economic Simulation Model for Urban Transportation Planning

David E. Boyce and Seymour E. Goldstone

A basic requirement for the preparation of land-use forecasts in urban transportation studies is a set of population and economic forecasts for the planning region. These regional forecasts provide control totals for the small analysis zone forecasts of land use, population, income, and employment. In addition, the regional population and economic analysis provides information on the economic vitality of the metropolitan region that bears directly on the region's need and capability for improving transportation facilities (2; 3, Chap. 2; 12, Chap. 2–3).

During the past 10 years regional forecasts in urban transportation studies have been based mainly on extrapolation of trends or on available forecasts that were adapted for the study. One recent study report (12) states that the land-use forecasting procedures are probably somewhat more refined than the regional population and economic forecasts, which are their basic inputs. As this report points out, most transportation studies have allocated much more effort to forecasting land use and urban travel models than to regional economic analysis. Two notable exceptions to this are the economic forecast prepared by Hoch (7) for the Chicago Area Transportation Study, and the forecasting model developed by Artle (1) for the Oahu Transportation Study.

Several reasons for this past underemphasis of the regional population and economic forecasts come to mind. First, the technical skills required to prepare economic analyses and forecasts have been extremely scarce, even more so than transportation planning skills. Second, the methodology required to produce reliable population and economic forecasts was being developed while transportation planning studies were being completed. Isard's work (9) is representative of the state of development of this methodology during this period. Methods available today are in many respects still unsatisfactory for the requirements of urban transportation planning.

This article was orginally published in *Highway Research Record*, no. 149 (1966), pp. 29–41. The paper was sponsored by the Committee on Economic Forecasting and presented at the 45th Annual Meeting.

This paper describes a regional population and economic forecasting model potentially useful in urban transportation planning. The model was developed as part of a water resources planning study for a large river basin in the eastern United States (6). The study was based on the philosophy that existing knowledge of causal forces should be fully exploited in preparing regional forecasts. The structure of the model is, therefore, based on theoretical concepts as well as empirically verified relationships. The relationships are assembled and integrated to achieve a fairly simple operational model of a regional economy. The model equations are solved in a recursive manner over the planning time horizon; the model is run on the IBM 7094 computer using the DYNAMO compiler developed by Forrester (5) and his associates in the Industrial Dynamics Group at M.I.T.

The model differs from previous population and economic forecasting procedures used in urban transportation studies in several important respects. First, and possibly most important, the model provides a framework for the planner to test readily the significance of alternative assumptions regarding growth rates and interaction of regional activities without significant model revisions. Second, the model forecasts the path of population and employment growth for the region through time. Most transportation studies have been concerned with a planning horizon 20 to 25 years in the future and have given little attention to the interim period. The model may thus help the transportation planner not only with the question of how much but also the question of when new facilities should be constructed.

Third, many procedures forecast population as a first step and then either reconcile this forecast with an independent employment forecast or base the employment forecast on the anticipated population level. This model treats population and employment growth as interacting processes (Figure 1). For example, the growth of employment opportunities will attract migrants to a region, in turn creating new job opportunities in the household-related businesses and services. These interactions between population and employment are an important part of the dynamics of regional economics. The manner in which they are treated can have a significant effect on forecasts.

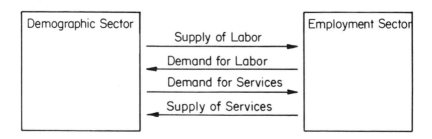

Figure 1   Overview of the model.

The Demographic Sector

The demographic sector of the model is designed to project the level of population and the supply of labor. Changes in population are the combined result of birth, death, and migration rates. Probably, the most important determinant of these rates, as well as the labor-force participation rate, is age. Thus, to trace these demographic variables through time, it is necessary to keep track of the distribution of age of the region's population.

An important question in modeling this sector is, therefore, what kind and how detailed an age breakdown to use. By examining the behavior of birth, death, migration, and labor-force participation rates by age, it is possible to define a set of age groups which is fairly homogeneous with respect to these age-dependent characteristics. Six age groups appear necessary to achieve effective simulation of the population dynamics: 0–13, 14–19, 20–24, 25–44, 45–64, and 65 years and older. Figure 2 shows the basic flows represented in the demographic sector of the model.

Birth and Death Rates.   Birth and death rates are fixed for each age group in the current formulation of the model and are based on 1960 regional data. For example, the birth rate for a given age group is estimated as the ratio of live births during 1960 for that age group to total population of the group. There are significant differences, especially for birth rates, among several regions examined. These differences may be explained to some extent by differences in the (a) urban-rural mix, (b) racial composition, and (c) ratio of males to females in the local populations.

Migration.   The demographic factor with the greatest potential for wide fluctuation in the short run is migration. In this model, the net migration rate (ratio of in-migration minus out-migration to regional population) for each adult age group is related to relative regional employment opportunities. The regional unemployment rate minus the national rate is used as an index of regional employment opportunities. The migration of children in the model is linked directly to migration of their adult parents.

Figure 3 shows the results of linear regression analyses on net migration between state economic areas in the period 1955–1960 (15). These results provide statistical

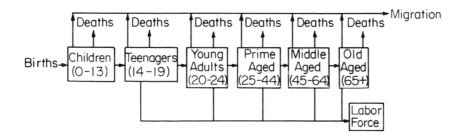

Figure 2   Structure of population flows.

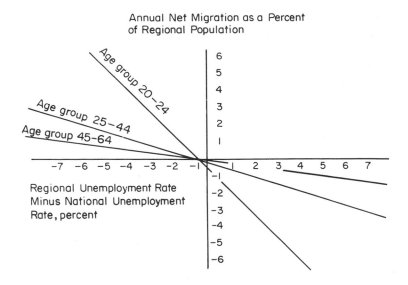

Figure 3   Net migration related to unemployment rate by age.

support for the thesis that the 20–24 age group is much more responsive to relative employment opportunities than the older age groups. However all age groups have a net out-migration when employment opportunities are equal.

Coefficients of determination (r^2) also show that relative employment opportunities are more strongly related to net migration for the 20–24 age group (0.52) and 24–44 age group (0.58) than for the older 45–64 age group (0.35). The results for the 15–19 age group (0.24) and the retired 65+ group (0.26) are considerably weaker.

Labor-Force Participation Rates.   The two important determinants of labor-force participation rates (i.e., ratios of labor force to population) are sex and age (17). Since the model does not break down the population by sex, it is assumed as a first approximation that the proportion of females in the population will tend to remain relatively constant. This being the case, participation rates are estimated by aggregating over sex tor a given age group. Data on participation rates show that age does not explain all the variation in participation rates. In some cases considerable differences exist for given age groups for selected regions. These differences may be attributable to such factors as degree of urbanization, average level of educational attainment, average earning levels, and employment opportunities.

The Employment Sector

Briefly, employment is of two types—provision of goods and services within the region and production for export out of the region. Locally-based employment is a function of demand for goods and services by households, local businesses, and manufacturing firms. Employment for export production is a function of the region's competitive advantage or disadvantage with respect to other locations for industry and is measured by comparative indices of wages and access to markets and raw materials outside the region. The employment sector is interrelated with the demographic sector through the regional unemployment rate and population level.

Definition of Employment Types.   Export employment is defined as production for sales primarily to nonlocal markets; export producers include both final producers and intermediate producers selling to firms that are producing for sales outside the region. The basis for the export employment forecast is a cost-oriented location model. Therefore, employment in noncost-oriented industries such as some installations of the Federal Government, higher education, and military service are forecast outside the model framework. Similarly, employment forecasts for resource-oriented industries such as mining and agriculture are prepared outside the model and entered as direct inputs to the model.

The second category of employment is designated "local serving" in the sense that goods and services produced are consumed within the region. This employment group serves both household demands for goods and services in the region and requirements of local firms for goods and services of a generalized type such as transportation, communication, and public utilities.

General knowledge of industry shipment patterns and results obtained in previous research (4, 10, 13) provide a basis for classifying industries into the two types. In general, production of goods and services for sales to the region's households and all types of firms in the region is the criterion used to distinguish local serving from export employment. This definition results in all 2-digit SIC manufacturing industries (Standard Industrial Classification Numbers 20 through 39) being classified as export, with several important exceptions. Those manufacturing industries whose products are produced entirely for local consumption, such as dairy products, newspapers, bakery products, commercial printing, public utilities, and construction materials, are removed from the export classification and designated as local serving employment. All other industries, including SIC Numbers 40 through 89, are classified as local serving.

The Export Employment Model.   The forecasting equations for location and growth of export employment in the region may be viewed as a simple adaptation of industrial location theory to the forecasting model. Industrial location theory, as formulated by Isard (8) for example, embodies the concepts of market area, source of raw materials, transportation costs, and local production costs including wages. The procedures for incorporating these concepts into the forecasting model are now described.

Consider a group of manufacturing industries with similar transportation costs, labor requirements, and market-area characteristics. The market area for these industries may be defined from data on shipping characteristics such as is available from the U.S. Census of Transportation (16). For example, a typical market area might be those states east of the Mississippi River for a metropolitan region located in the eastern United States. Industry growth rates for the total market area by 2-digit manufacturing industries are available from the national and state projections to 1976 by the National Planning Association (11).

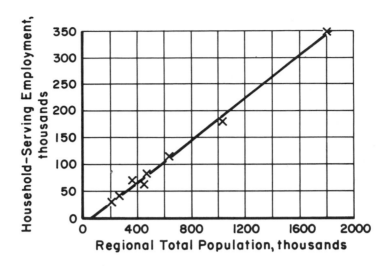

Figure 4   Household-serving employment vs. total population for selected regions in eastern United States, 1960.

This market area growth rate is used as a starting point for the computation of a regional growth rate. The region's industry growth rate, as contrasted with that of its market area, is determined by its relative advantage with respect to costs incurred in manufacturing and distributing the product. A cost index is formulated which compares the region's total costs with the costs of other regions serving the same market area. Costs that vary significantly between regions are wage costs and transportation costs for both raw materials and products. Wage costs are adjusted during the operation of the model in response to the local employment conditions. Transportation costs also may be varied during the model operation to incorporate major changes in the transportation system such as the construction of an interstate highway.

The cost index operates in the following manner. If the region offers lower cost characteristics than competing regions in the market area due to lower labor costs or better access to market and raw materials, then a regional industry growth rate greater than the corresponding market area growth rate is inferred. However, if the access characteristics of the region or its labor costs are higher than in competing areas resulting in a cost index greater than 1.0, then the industry growth rate is adjusted downward accordingly. A cost index equal to 1.0 means that the industry growth rate for the market area also applies to the region.

In the applications of the model to date, export employment is divided into four industry groups with similar labor and transportation cost characteristics; two of the groups are fabricating industries and two are processing industries. Market areas, wage costs, and transportation costs are defined and derived for each of these four industry groups, and regional growth rates are computed for each industry group.

Local Serving Employment.   Local serving employment is divided into two sub-categories, household serving and business serving. First, household-serving employment, which includes all employment primarily engaged in production of goods and

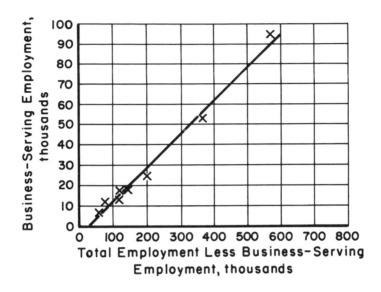

Figure 5   Business-serving employment vs. total employment less business-serving employment for selected regions in eastern United States, 1960.

services for sale to households, is forecast as a linear function of regional population. Analysis of the relation between total regional population and house hold-serving employment in several metropolitan regions in the eastern United States indicates a satisfactory relationship (Figure 4). Business-serving employment, which includes all employment engaged in the production of goods and services for sale to firms in the region, is related to all other employment in the region in a similar manner (Figure 5).

Interrelationships Between Employment and Demographic Sectors

The key variable in the interaction between the employment and demographic sectors is the local unemployment rate. Unemployment rate is determined by the combined forces of labor supply from the demographic sector and labor demand from the employment sector, and it in turn affects both these sectors. The path of causality is shown in Figure 6, depicting the main feedback loops of the model. A second important interrelationship (Figure 6) concerns the requirements for goods and services in the household-serving industries, which are related directly to population. Employment in this category in turn affects the demand for employment in the business-serving industries. With these interactions in mind, the next section describes how the regional economy evolves over time.

Model Dynamics: Sensitivity Analysis

One of the major advantages of using a computer model for making economic forecasts is that it is a very simple matter to test the effect of changing assumptions. This testing for sensitivity of various parts of the model is important during both the model formation and the model use stages. During the model formation period, various simplifying assumptions are invariably made. The planner will have less supporting

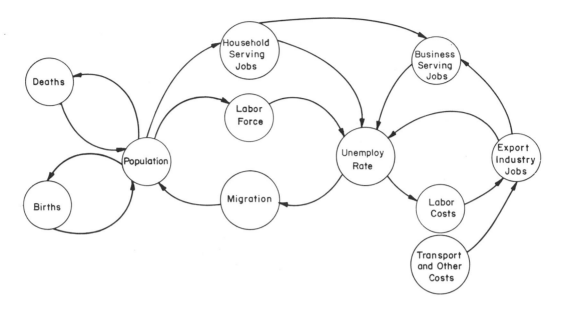

Figure 6   Main feedback loops of the regional economic model.

evidence for and less confidence in some of these assumptions than others. Therefore, he will vary these assumptions to see if the conclusions are sensitive to them. Sensitive and insensitive parts of models can thereby be pinpointed and the information used for guiding further model refinement.

In keeping with this research strategy, sensitivity experiments are made as a regular part of the research process. Two sets of these experiments, one on migration and the other on skills, are discussed. First, however, it will be helpful to examine several typical model runs. Figure 7 shows typical model output for population, migration, and unemployment rate for selected regions. These graphs show that the model is capable of producing different patterns for different regions. These different patterns arise from differences in initial imbalances between jobs and labor force, differences in the initial mix of export industries, and in enduring differences in competitive advantages due to different locations.

In Region B, because of a failure of jobs to grow fast enough, unemployment rate rises over the first decade. Because of the lack of job opportunities the model generates increased out-migration and reduces pressure for wage increases. This combination of forces results in a decline in labor force growth rate which coincides with increased growth in jobs (because of stable labor costs). A downward correction in the unemployment rate results, slowing out-migration and causing toward the end of the 25-year period, an increase in the rate of population growth. Examination of the patterns generated for the other regions represented in the diagram will reveal similar forces at work.

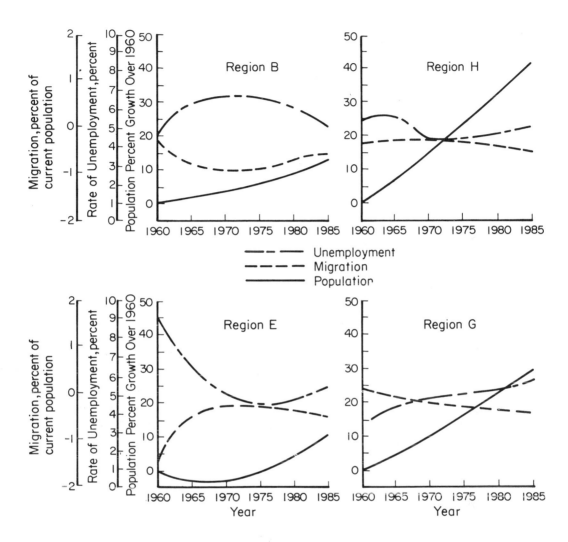

Figure 7 Selected percentage projections.

Sensitivity Experiments on Migration Formulation. One interesting set of sensitivity experiments concerns tests of various assumptions about the migration formulation. As discussed in the migration section, a statistically significant linear relationship exists between net migration and unemployment rate. We believed that additional research could improve on the accuracy of these results.

However, further expenditures on this part of the model could be justified only if it was sensitive. To determine this, several runs were made in which different relationships between migration and relative unemployment were tried. Figure 8 shows the migration line for the 20–24 age group for three of these runs. The relationships for the

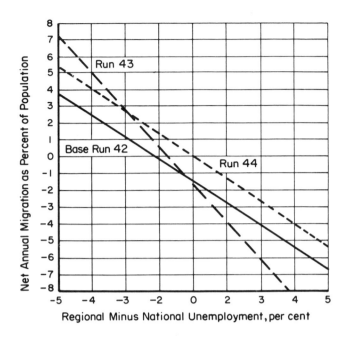

Figure 8   Migration functions assumed in sensitivity analyses (age group 20–24).

Simulation Run*	Characteristics of Migration Line	Population Growth Relative to Base Run After 25 Years
42	Migration line based on statistical analysis, so that region has out-migration even when local equals national unemployment	Base Run
43	Slope of migration line doubled	100.3%
44	Migration line shifted upward so that no out-migration occurs when local equals national unemployment	106.8%

*Numbers correspond to computer simulation identification system used internally by research group.

Figure 9   Results of sensitivity analyses of migration functions

other unemployment-dependent migrating groups (14–19, 25–44, 45–64) were changed in similar ways. Run 42 used the relationship drawn directly from the statistical results and thus serves as a basis for comparison against the other runs in this series.

In Run 43, the slope of the migration line was doubled (Figure 8). In this run, the initially high unemployment causes more out-migration from the area than in the base run. However, this reduces the labor force, thereby lowering the unemployment rate,

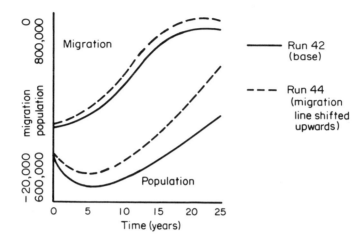

Figure 10 Run 44 superimposed on run 42.

resulting finally in less out-migration. Thus, despite doubling the slope of the migration line, population growth over the 25-year period in this run is almost the same as that in the base run.

Run 44 examined the effect of an upward shift in the migration line (Figure 8) such that no migration occurs when the local unemployment rate equals the national average. In this case the region grows somewhat more rapidly (Figure 9).

Figure 10, a graph of population and net migration of run 44 superimposed on the base run 42, illustrates what is happening here. Two factors in particular are combining to cause an increasing divergence in the population projections. First, the migration line is shifted upward, resulting in a reduced net outflow of people. Second, the upward shift in the 4 migration lines to pass through the origin mainly affects the young 20–24 age group (see Figure 3). Thus, in run 44 the area is not only losing fewer people but is losing fewer people in the age group which has the highest reproduction rate. Therefore, a higher natural rate of population increase is combined with a higher net migration rate, leading to an increasing divergence in the population projections.

The conclusion drawn from these sensitivity experiments is that the projections are insensitive to changes in the slope, but at the same time somewhat sensitive to changes in the intercept. As a consequence, additional statistical analysis has been undertaken on migration.

Sensitivity Experiments on Skill Level. There is a growing awareness and concern about the effects of education and skill level of labor on regional economic vitality. Unfortunately, in treating a variable such as skill level the investigator is confronted with measurement difficulties. Despite this lack of measurable cause and effect, we introduced several speculative hypotheses involving skill level. The purpose was to determine if regional growth is sensitive enough to this factor to justify the considerable additional exploration that may be needed to refine and test such hypotheses.

Years of School Completed	Migration Rate	
	25–44 Age Group	45–64 Age Group
0–7	5.2	2.9
8	5.7	2.3
9–11	5.8	2.6
12	5.2	3.0
13+	10.7	3.5

Figure 11   Relation between education level and migration rate by age

Source: U.S. Department of Commerce, Bureau of the Census, Current Population Reports, Series P–20, No. 127 (January 15, 1964): Mobility of the Population of the United States, April 1961 to April 1962, Table B, p. 4.

After considerable deliberation, despite the recognized limitations, we decided to use educational attainment as a measure of skill level. This is based on the idea that education increases the trainability and thus the potential skill a worker can achieve.

Available data also show that educational level affects the migration rate (Figure 11). The migration rate is substantially the same for people who have a high school diploma or less, whereas those with some college education migrate more frequently. The effect is particularly dramatic for the younger 25–44 age group.

Model Formulation of Skills.   In the model, the total skill level of the region's population is represented as the cumulative man-years of education and training of all people in the region in the age range of the labor force (14–64). To the cumulative man-years existing at the beginning of the forecast period are added those brought in by children growing up into the labor-force age group, by migrants into the region and by the continuing education and training of those over 14 years old. Lost from the region's cumulative skills are those withdrawn because of deaths and outward migrations among the "eligible" work group (age 14–64), and retirement of older people from the labor force. The factors modifying the overall cumulative skills level are shown in Figure 12.

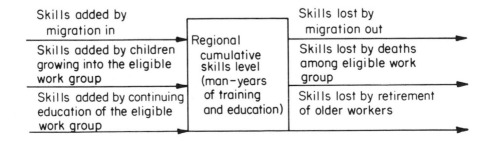

Figure 12   Influences on cumulative skills level.

Simulation Run*	Characteristics of Skills Effects on Relative Wage Costs	Population Growth Relative to Base Run After 25 Years
47	None	Base Run
62	Relative skills inversely related to relative wage costs	102.6%
63	Same as Run 62, except trend in national skills retarded relative to region	117.1%
76	Migration directly related to skill level	107.1%

*Numbers correspond to computer simulation identification system used internally by research group.

Figure 13   Sensitivity analyses of skills effects on relative wage costs and migration

In modeling the skills added by entry of the young into the eligible work group, the character of compulsory education is noted so that all youths becoming 14 years old are regarded as having completed 8 years of education. Education beyond the age of 14 is represented in 1960 as adding 3.6 years of education and training to every teenager and trended to 1985 to provide 4.8 years beyond the age of 14. Thus, it is assumed that the average 1960 teenager will receive 11.6 years of education and training, whereas the average 1985 teenager will receive 12.8 years. Such a trend appears reasonable. but variations of this trend have also been tested.

Sensitivity Experiments on Skills Formulation.   Three of the sensitivity experiments conducted on skills are reported here (Figure 13).

In run 76 a relationship between migration and skill level was hypothesized, roughly on the basis of Figure 11. According to this hypothesis, as the average skill level in an area increases, the migration rate is modified by an effect of skill index (ratio of regional migration rate to migration rates occurring at average national skill level, Figure 14). After 25 years this leads to a population projection 7 percent greater than the projection in the base run. This occurs because the region starts out with a relatively low skill level, resulting in a lower rate of out-migration and consequently a greater number of births than in the base run. These two effects combine to produce the higher population projection.

In run 62 a relationship between relative skills level and relative wage costs was hypothesized. According to this hypothesis, a region with higher average skills level has more productive labor and hence can supply more labor output per dollar wage, thereby cutting total wage costs (Figure 15). A very small but positive effect occurred due to the growth of skills in the region at a slightly higher rate than the national average.

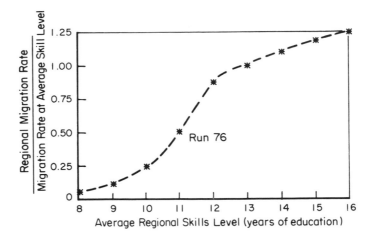

Figure 14   Migration related to average regional skills level.

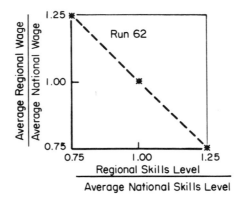

Figure 15   Relative skills level related to relative wage costs.

Run 63 shows the potential of increasing regional growth by accelerating skills development. In this run the region was allowed to outstrip the national average in the education and training of its population. The impact was quite large in 25 years (17%). Moreover, the effects of such skills buildup are cumulative and ever-increasing. These sensitivity experiments clearly indicate that skills level may have extremely important effects on regional economies. Assumptions made about skills do, therefore, significantly affect medium- and long-run projections.

Conclusions

The regional economic forecasting model described above has been successfully applied to develop 50-year forecasts for water-resources planning for 8 contiguous regions in a major eastern United States river basin. Although this forecasting technique has not yet been used in urban transportation studies, ongoing research indicates that the model can be adapted to this purpose in a straightforward manner. Several characteristics of the model indicate the utility of this approach for regional forecasting:

1. The explicit form of the forecasting methodology facilitates evaluation and use of the forecasts.
2. The use of a simulation compiler in the computer operation of the model essentially eliminates computer programming and facilitates experimentation with the model.
3. Low computer operating cost makes feasible the testing of alternative growth rates, parameters, and formulations so that an entire set of forecasts based on alternative assumptions and submodels may be prepared.
4. Updating the forecast as the model is revised or new data becomes available requires only a rerun of the model.

As with many operational forecasting techniques, model development is never entirely completed. Ongoing research studies are revising and extending the model described in this paper. Of particular importance for transportation planning is the incorporation of a regional income forecast into the model, from which may be derived the vehicle ownership forecast. The export employment sector is being reformulated in an attempt to incorporate recent research findings on the movement of investment capital among regions. The problems of migration rates and labor force participation rates are being restudied in light of recent developments in this research area. These model improvements may be expected to provide, over time, forecasting capability at least commensurate with the status of land use and trip forecasting models for urban transportation planning.

References

1. Artle, R. Planning and Growth—A Simple Model of an Island Economy: Honolulu, Hawaii. Papers, Regional Science Assoc., vol. 15, 1965.

2. CATS, Final Report. Vol. 1, Chicago Area Transportation Study, 1959.

3. CATS, Final Report. Vol. 2, Chicago Area Transportation Study, 1960.

4. Czamanski, S. A Model of Urban Growth. Papers, Regional Science Assoc., vol. 13, 1964.

5. Forrester, J. W. *Industrial Dynamics.* M.I.T. Press, Cambridge, 1961.

6. Hamilton, H. R. et al, *System Simulation for Regional Analysis,* M.I.T. Press, Cambridge, 1969.

7. Hoch, I. A Comparison of Alternative Inter-Industry Forecasts for the Chicago Region. Papers, Regional Science Assoc., vol. 5, 1959.

8. Isard, W. *Location and Space–Economy.* M.I.T. Press, Cambridge, 1956.

9. Isard, W. *Methods of Regional Analysis,* M.I.T. Press, Cambridge, 1960.

10. Lichtenberg, R. *One-Tenth of a Nation,* Harvard University Press, Cambridge, 1960.

11. National Planning Association. Regional Economy Projections Series, State Employment Trends to 1976, Report 1. Washington, D.C., 1962.

12. PJTS, PJ Reports. Vol. 2, Penn-Jersey Transportation Study, Philadelphia, 1964.

13. Pittsburgh Regional Planning Association. *Region with a Future.* Univ. of Pittsburgh Press, 1963.

14. U.S. Census of Population. State Economic Areas, Final Report. A (3)–1A, Washington, D.C., 1960.

15. U.S. Census of Population. Mobility of the Population of the United States, April 1961 to April 1962. Table B, p. 4, Current Population Reports, Series P–20, No. 127, Washington, D.C., 1964.

16. U.S. Census of Transportation. Commodity Transportation Survey. Series TC63 (a)—C1–1 to C1–25, Washington, D.C., 1963.

17. Wolfbein, S. L. *Employment and Unemployment in the United States.* Science Research Associates, Inc., Chicago, 1964.

34

Narcotics and the Community: A System Simulation

Gilbert Levin, Gary B. Hirsch, and Edward B. Roberts

We present here a summary of work still in progress after a year of effort devoted to the problem of narcotics addiction and its control. While the investigation has drawn substantially from consideration of a specific ethnically and economically heterogeneous geographic region in New York City, an area of eight square miles with a population of about 180,000 persons, the processes described are believed to apply substantially to a wide range of urban and suburban environments, excluding only those of exceptional wealth or exceptional poverty.

The computer model that has been developed describes the flow of numbers of people in a community through various drug use statuses: potential users, soft drug users, heroin users, addicts in the community, addicts in community care, addicts in custody, each of which is regulated by one or more associated rates of change. Other sectors of the model describe the important variables in the community that affect the rate at which people move through the various statuses. The model treats explicitly migration into and out of the community of addicts and other population subgroups, the consequences of community alarm versus inaction, crime and other visible manifestations of drug use, the attitude of the community toward addiction, attractiveness of the area to pushers, as well as other important, but often elusive, forces. Computer experiments assess the probable short- and long-range consequences of each of the programs and policies that have been advocated or tried. To our knowledge this constitutes the first attempt to integrate and systematically manipulate the large and unwieldy body of scientific knowledge and knowledgeable opinion relevant to this problem.

The information used in constructing the model has been gathered from a variety of sources including a critical review of the literature, an area study of an urban community, and interviews with treatment program directors, addicts, ex-addicts, research scientists, teachers, parole officers and other informant groups.[1] The purpose of

This article has been reprinted from the *American Journal of Public Health* 62, no. 6 (June 1972), pp. 861–873. The more complete work, including full model documentation, is Levin, Roberts, and Hirsch, *The Persistent Poppy: A Computer-Aided Search for Heroin Policy* (Cambridge: Mass.: Ballinger Publishing Co., 1975).

this investigation is to provide knowledge of use to a variety of groups responsible for making policy to control drug abuse.

While we will take a position on some issues, our intention in this paper is not primarily to advocate a particular policy, but to describe the work we have done and to show how it can contribute to the understanding and evaluation of any proposed policy.

Why Model?

Construction of a computer model begins with an effort to understand the system of forces that has created a problem and continues to sustain it. Relevant data are gathered from a variety of sources, including published literature, informed persons (experts, practitioners, victims, perpetrators, etc.) and specific quantitative studies. As soon as a rudimentary measure of understanding has been achieved a formal model is developed. This model is then exposed to criticism, revised, exposed again and so on in an iterative process that continues as long as it proves to be useful. Just as the model is improved as a result of successive exposures to people, a successively better understanding of the problem is achieved by the people who participate in the process. Their intuition about the probable consequences of proposed policies frequently proves to be less reliable than the model's meticulous arithmetical approach.

This is not as surprising as it may first appear. The behavior of any system in which as many as a hundred or more variables are known to be relevant and believed to be related to one another in various nonlinear fashions is complex far beyond the capacity of intuition and, incidentally, even further beyond the capacity of formal mathematical analysis. Simulation is one of the most effective means available for supplementing and correcting human intuition.

A computer simulation or model of the variety described here is a powerful conceptual device that can increase the role of reason at the expense of rhetoric in the determination of policy. A model is not, as sometimes supposed, a perfectly accurate representation of reality that can be trusted to make better decisions than people. It is a flexible tool that forces the people who use it to think hard and to confront one another, their common problems, and themselves directly and factually.

A computer model differs only in complexity, precision and explicitness from the informal subjective explanation or "mental model" that men ordinarily construct to guide their actions toward a goal. It is an account of the total set of forces that are believed to have caused and to sustain some problematic state of affairs. Like the informal mental model, it is derived from a variety of data sources including facts, theories, and educated guesses. Unlike the mental model it is comprehensive, unambiguous, flexible, and subject to rigorous logical manipulation and testing. The flexibility of a model is its least understood virtue. If you and I disagree about some aspect of the causal structure of a problem, we can usually in a matter of minutes run the model twice and observe its behavior under each set of assumptions. I may, on the basis of its behavior, be forced to admit you were correct. Very often, however, we will both discover that our argument was trifling, since the phenomenon of interest to us may be unchanged by a change in assumptions.

A computer model constructed and used by a policy-making group has these advantages: 1) It requires policy-makers to improve and complete fully the rough mental sketch of the causes of the problem that they inevitably have in their heads. 2) In the process of formal model building, the builders discover and resolve various self-contradictions and ambiguities among their implicit assumptions about the problem. 3) Once the model is running, even in a rudimentary fashion, logical "bootstrapping" becomes possible. The consequences of promising but tentative formulations are tested in the model. Observation of model behavior gives rise to new hypotheses about structure. 4) Once an acceptable standard of validity has been achieved formal policy experiments reveal quickly the probable outcomes of many policy alternatives; novel policies may be discovered. 5) An operating model is always complete, though in a sense never completed. Unlike many planning aids, which tend to be episodic and terminal (they provide assistance only at the moment the "report" is presented, not before or after), a model is organic and iterative. At any moment the model contains in readily-accessed form the present best understanding of the problem. 6) Sensitivity analysis of the model reveals the areas in which genuine debate (rather than caviling) is needed and guides empirical investigation to important questions. If the true value of many parameters is unknown (which is generally the case in social planning) the ones that maximally affect model behavior need to be investigated first. 7) An operating model can be used to communicate with people who were not involved in building the model. By experimenting with changes in policies and model parameters and observing the effects of these changes on behavior, these people can be helped to better understand the dynamic forces at work in the real-world system.

Counter-Intuitive Effects

An example illustrates the way in which logical analysis can correct dubious but intuitively appealing policies aimed at coping with the narcotics problem.[2]

Despite striking differences among policy advocates, there is general agreement that the social problem of heroin consists of the presence of too many addicts and of the crimes they commit to support their addiction. There is also agreement that the supply of heroin that enters this country illegally is a principal source of the problem. The implicit model may be shown as in Figure 1.[3] An increase (decrease) in the heroin supply increases (decreases) the number of addicts, thereby increasing (decreasing) addict-related crime.

Although there is agreement on this account of the problem, when it comes to potential corrective policy considerable disagreement exists. Let us consider two very different strategies which share this definition of the problem: 1) Eliminate the source of supply. The rationale is clear. If there is no heroin, there will be no heroin addicts and obviously, no addict related crime. 2) Provide a legal supply of heroin to all addicts. This policy accepts the continued presence of a population of addicts and aims at eliminating all addict-related crime.

While it is generally recognized that policy 1) would be difficult to implement and that policy 2) would solve only one aspect of the social problem, each of these policies has an additional deficit that is not initially obvious.

A.   Implicit Model of Addict Crime

B.   Price Considerations Added to Implicit Model

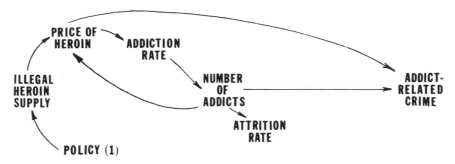

C.   Further Aspects for Policy Consideration

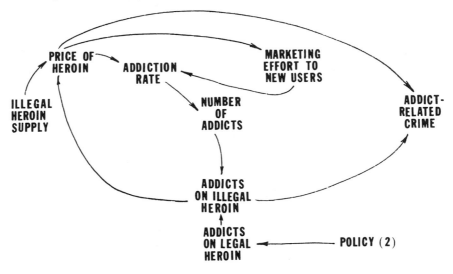

Figure 1   Several models of the narcotics problem

Let us consider first the policy of eliminating the source of illegal heroin. The long-run effects are as indicated. In the short run, however, a drastic reduction of the heroin supply would cause an increase in addict-related crime of unprecedented proportions. It is doubtful whether society would be willing to pay this short-term cost to gain the long-term advantage. A more complete and accurate model (Figure 1B) explains these consequences.

A reduction in the supply of heroin per addict would increase the price. The price of heroin plays two important mediating roles omitted from the previous account of the problem structure. First, it affects the rate at which potential addicts become addicted. When the price of heroin is low, it is more accessible to the discretionary (nonaddicted) user and vice versa. Secondly, the price of heroin determines the amount of crime each addict must commit to support his habit.

The causes of the differential short- and long-term consequences of a reduction in supply are implicit in the diagram. Significant time is required for the pool of addicts to change in size. Eventually, a high enough price would reduce the number of addicts and the amount of crime toward zero. The effects of a price increase on crime are much more immediate. Since a successful policy aimed at reducing supply would have a significant effect upon price long before the number of addicts was appreciably reduced, the total amount of addict-related crime would increase significantly.

The severity and duration of this increase cannot be stated precisely. What is made clear by our analysis is the need to acquire reliable information on this point if a policy of vigorous supply reduction is to be considered seriously.

The addition of another link in the causal chain, i.e., public resistance to policy, fills out the picture. The danger of not knowing and not disclosing fully the short-term negative effects of the policy is that public response to its actual implementation may be so negative as to force its abandonment before it has begun to work.

Turning to the policy of providing heroin legally to addicts, we observe another set of undesirable counter-intuitive consequences. The intention of this policy is to destroy the illegal production-distribution system through competition. If all addicts can obtain all the heroin they need through legal channels at zero or nominal cost, it is reasoned, illegal competitors will be driven out of business. There is a serious flaw in this policy.

The short-term effect of the introduction of a legal supply would be a vast increase of the total stockpile of heroin. Much of the heroin in the illegal pipeline at the time the policy went into effect would eventually reach the market place. Since addicted customers who in the past consumed the lion's share of the drug[4] would have turned to the legal supply, the market would be in a state of disarray. Many individual operators would be driven out of business because of falling prices, as intended. However, those remaining would be forced to seek buyers among nonaddicts. Low prices and more aggressive marketing would result in a significant increase in the number of new addicts.[5] The illegal supply of heroin, which was originally intended principally to satisfy the needs of existing addicts and only secondarily to increasing the total number of addicts, would be diverted entirely to the latter purpose. The shortcoming of this policy is that while it would reduce addict-related crime, it might significantly increase the total number of addicts. Figure 1C illustrates this causal structure. Policy (2) reduces crime by drawing addicts out of the market. It thereby also reduces at least temporarily the price of illegal heroin, thus increasing the addiction rate. This latter effect is amplified by an increase in marketing of heroin to new users, a response to falling prices. In the authors' opinion, zealous application of either policy (1) or (2) would probably worsen the problem. One or another of several "intermediate" policies appear to be more promising, as indicated later in the paper.

The principal intent of this extended example is to demonstrate how logical analysis of the general character permitted by computer simulation can reveal facets of the narcotics problem that are not immediately apparent to intuition. In an actual rather than an anecdotal simulation, the computer allows a vastly increased number of variables to be considered and provides a more accurate forecast of their behavior over time.

Model Structure

There is no way in ordinary language to describe a computer model precisely. The model consists of some 350 statements about the causal structure of the narcotics problem written in the DYNAMO compiler language.[6] This prose account of the model almost inevitably will obscure and oversimplify the very process of model representation that the special-purpose DYNAMO language was designed to clarify.

The best way to understand the model is to use it. DYNAMO is designed for use on a remote terminal. The user, seated at a teletypewriter terminal, engages in a responsive "conversation" with the model. Typically he will first summon and run the model in its most recently edited form. The printer then quickly produces a time plot, for any specified period, of the variables of interest to the user. The user inspects the time plot, discovering that some of the variables exhibit behavior he expected and that others do not. Why not? To answer this question he inspects the equations or "structure" of the model, searching for the assumptions that produced the surprising behavior. He may find a parameter that seems unrealistic or a linear relationship between two variables where a nonlinear function is more convincing to him. The user then shifts to the edit mode of the interactive computer language and quickly types in the desired changes. The model is run once more and its behavior compared to the earlier run. If its behavior is no longer surprising, the user gains confidence in his subjective account of the problem. However, if the surprising behavior is still present, the user may be forced to examine his own implicit assumptions and change them in the direction of greater accuracy. The user demonstrates his understanding of the system structure of the problem by his ability to conduct a series of runs that exhibit a variety of modes of behavior, all of which were expected by him. This is unlikely to occur except after a lengthy series of "conversations" between user and model. The model should be seen, therefore, less as a fixed account of the narcotics problem than as a structured but flexible vehicle that permits its user to test and increase his own understanding of the system being simulated.

The causal relationships of primary importance to the model behavior are described in this section. An overview of the major causal forces (Figure 2A) and a description of the population flows through the system (Figure 2B) are presented first. Discussions of the relationships underlying the key formulations including heroin addiction (Figure 3), community attitude shift (Figure 4) and community change (Figure 5) follow, and, within the limits stated above, give a fairly complete picture of the model's structure.

A. Macro Model of Drug Addiction and the Community

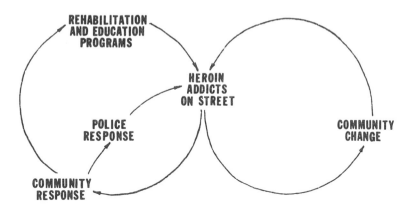

B. Total Person Flow

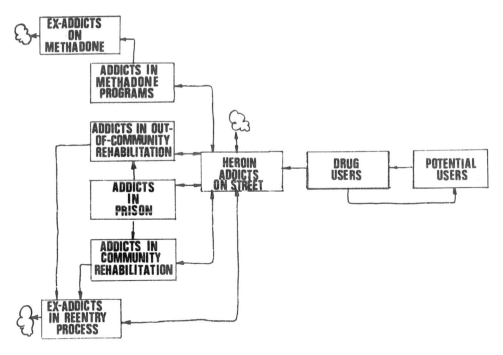

Figure 2 Overview of the narcotics problem

The model focuses on addicts who are functioning primarily in a community with a fixed geographic boundary. The addict population manifests itself in two major ways: creation of new addicts and commission of crimes. The addict population grows as addicts introduce their friends and acquaintances to heroin. This growth is enabled by the availability of heroin in the community required by the existing addict population, but also used to turn-on people, who later become new addicts. As the number of addicts in the community grows, more addicts are present to introduce new people to

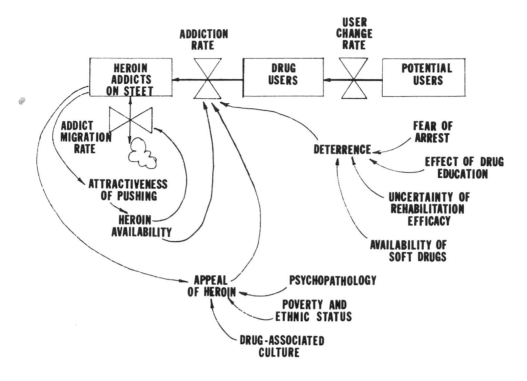

Figure 3   Heroin addiction

heroin and a larger heroin availability enables these introductions. The result is a more rapid growth of the addict population that accelerates as the number of addicts increases even further. This is a ''vicious circle'' or ''positive feedback'' phenomenon. In the absence of constraining forces the addict population would continue to grow without limits.

Some fraction of the addicts in the community will have to commit crime in order to support their habits. The impact of crime on the community has two major facets. The first of these is community change. A growing crime rate will reduce the attractiveness of the area. The residents of higher socioeconomic status and greater mobility will migrate out into areas they perceive to have a lower crime rate. Those with less mobility are forced to remain. The vacancies left by the people who migrated out are filled by people of lower socioeconomic status for whom the crime rate of the area is the lowest that they can afford. Ethnic and racial issues often complicate the process in this way: at first upwardly mobile middle-class blacks move into the community. Their presence amplifies the tendency of whites to leave. Rapid outmigration causes a temporary reduction in the price of housing, permitting successively poorer people to live in the area. Housing density then increases and public services are strained, thus facilitating the process of urban decay. In this way, as crime increases, the socioeconomic level of the community is driven down. Because people of a lower socioeconomic status have a higher incidence of social problems (including addiction) the in-migration brings an increasingly greater potential for new addicts that would eventually be realized in growth of the addict population. More addicts would produce more crime and the community would continue to deteriorate until its residents were of such a low socioeconomic status that they lacked the means to migrate out.

The second facet of the impact of addict crime, one that constrains the positive feedback loop, is the community's response. Its immediate reaction takes the form of police action against addict criminals and pushers. Attempts to establish rehabilitation programs in the community are blocked during this phase, because residents fear that the programs will only serve to concentrate addicts in the area. Addict crime is seen to be the problem, and it is assumed that enough police effort will solve it. Usually it is only after increased police effort fails to stem the rising tide of crime, and after addiction spreads to include the children of established families in the community, that the residents will realize that addiction is a social and medical problem. They will then allow programs to be established that attempt to cope with the causes of and that seek cures for addiction. Once the community accepts the social and medical aspect of the problem, it may also permit the operation of drug education programs that deal honestly with drug use, even if they require teaching ideas contrary to the community's values. It is assumed that the effectiveness of both education and rehabilitation is influenced by the community's definition of the problem. With rehabilitation programs aimed at the current addict population, and education programs to prevent new cases of addiction, the community can begin coping with the problem of addiction itself and effectively reduce the addict population.

Addict population growth, community change, and community response are the forces central to the creation of model behavior. Figure 2B shows the flow of people through the system created by the action of these forces.

Here, the category "potential users" refers to nearly all of the people in the community in a vulnerable age range, perhaps between the ages of ten and thirty, who are not currently involved in the illegal use of drugs. "Users" encompasses all people who indulge in the occasional illegal use of drugs up to, and including heroin, but are not addicted to heroin and do not take up the addict's life style. "Addicts on the street" refers to the group of people who live in the community and require at least daily shots of heroin to prevent withdrawal symptoms. This group includes addicts who live with their families and can buy heroin with money obtained from their families or from part-time jobs, without resorting to crime.[7] The arrow from "users" to "addicts" indicates that almost all heroin addicts were previously users of other drugs (such as marijuana) but is not intended to imply a causal relationship.

Addicts remain in the reference community or can migrate into or out of the community depending on the attractiveness of the area for an addict (the outside world being represented by the cloudlike symbol). They can also drop out of the addict population through death or by burning out, a process that occurs when an addict of many years standing simply becomes tired of all of the difficulties involved in being an addict and spontaneously stops taking heroin. Addicts who have been arrested and convicted spend time in prison and are released to the street or to rehabilitation programs if the programs have available capacity. Addicts also enter rehabilitation programs directly from the street. Community rehabilitation refers to therapeutic community programs, usually of a residential nature, that exist within the community itself. The Phoenix Houses in New York are an example of this kind of program. Out-of-community rehabilitation includes therapeutic community programs in nearby areas as well as remote programs, such as the federal narcotics hospital at Lexington, Kentucky. Out-of-community programs are available to treat addicts, even if the community does not regard addiction as a social and medical problem. However, this condition is necessary for the existence of in-community programs. The development of in-community programs must wait for a change in the residents' view of the problem.

Addicts in the re-entry process have been deemed "rehabilitated" by either an in-community or an out-of-community program, and will either successfully re-enter (remain heroin-free for a specified period of time) or return to being addicts. Addicts in methadone programs receive daily doses of methadone and are, for the most part, heroin-free. Those that remain in methadone programs for a specified period of time become ex-addicts on methadone. These people are assumed to remain indefinitely on maintenance doses of methadone. A large proportion of the addicts in the rehabilitation programs and a smaller proportion in the methadone programs will return to being active addicts before completion of the programs.

The principal forces responsible for the rate at which drug users become addicts are displayed in Figure 3.

There are a set of forces that promote the growth of the addict population and a set of forces that retard this growth. The number of potential heroin addicts in a community depends importantly on its socioeconomic level. The appeal of heroin is also a function of the drug associated culture previously discussed, and the number of addicts already in the community. If the addict life style is seen as appealing or at least not repulsive, and there are a number of addicts available to initiate new addicts, the addict population is likely to grow. "Psychopathology" is another causal factor implicit in the driving forces of the increase in addiction. This term refers to various individual aberrant personality patterns, such as negative identification. In this regard, a strongly negative reaction to addiction by the community will render it a more attractive outlet for antisocial tendencies.

Education can act as a deterrent to addiction if it is credible and stresses the dangers of addiction without making judgments about good versus bad life styles. The availability of soft drugs in an area may actually provide a deterrent to heroin use and addiction by making it easy to remain a soft drug user. The suppression of soft drug supplies could lead to an increase in addiction by depriving users of an alternative to heroin. Fear of arrest also deters some users from becoming addicts. Uncertainty of rehabilitation efficacy and its concomitant, fear of lifelong addiction, remain deterrents as long as rehabilitation programs are scarce and believed to be ineffective. The existence of successful programs mitigates against this effect.

The time required for users to become addicts is strongly dependent on drug availability. If heroin is abundant, addicts are more likely to share it with their friends than if the drug is scarce. When there is only a small addict population in an area, local

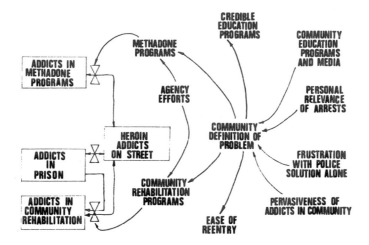

Figure 4 Community attitude

addicts will travel to other areas to get heroin and there will be very little excess heroin in the community of interest. As the addict population increases, so does the attractiveness of pushing to addicts as an alternative way of making money. Sales activities within the community necessitate inventories of drugs which increase the drug availability in the community and allow the growth of addiction to proceed more rapidly. More addicts will enhance the attractiveness of pushing, thereby increasing heroin availability and enabling the addict population to grow even more rapidly. The attractiveness of pushing is also affected by police action directed against heroin. Police action against addicts and hard drug availability are also responsible for migration of addicts into and out of the community.

Growth in the addict population has as a consequence the growth of the community's crime rate. Because crime is the primary direct impact that addiction has on the community, residents will usually define addiction initially as a crime problem and seek to combat it with a strong police response.

The forces responsible for changes in community attitude towards the drug problem and the effects of this attitude are shown in Figure 4.

The variable, "community definition of the problem," reflects the residents' perception of the nature of the narcotics problem. A low value indicates the belief that addiction is solely a criminal problem that needs to be, and can be, dealt with by sufficient police effort. A high value means that the community believes that the problem has a significant social and medical dimension, requiring treatment programs to cope with it.

The community definition is affected by exposure to media and to community education programs. This attitude change will not take place, however, until the residents realize several things. First, the police solution favored by the community's initial definition of the problem must fail to stem the increase in crime caused by a growing addict population. Frustration with the police solution alone will initiate a search for alternative methods of coping with addiction. As the number of arrests increases in response to growing addiction and crime, it becomes more likely that some of those youths arrested will be familiar to residents. When narcotics arrests become more personally relevant, members of the community cease blaming the problem on "other people". Recognition that "youths from good families" are involved in narcotics use forces people to discard an exclusively criminal view of addiction and accept some of its social and medical aspects. The pervasiveness of addiction in itself tends to persuade residents that the problem cannot be coped with by police methods alone.

As these realizations develop, media and community education begin having an impact on community attitude. Eventually, if attitude change continues, the community accepts addiction as a social and medical problem with criminal manifestations rather than one of a solely criminal nature.

Definition of the problem as one with a significant medical and social nature has several effects. One of these effects is the implementation of therapeutic community rehabilitation programs and methadone programs in the community. If residents feel that addiction is solely a criminal problem, attempts to establish treatment programs in the community will be vigorously opposed out of fear that the programs will merely concentrate dangerous sociopaths in the area with little benefit for the community itself. Only after the community develops a medical definition of the problem and drops the stereotype it has of the addict will it be willing to permit implementation of programs advocated by social agencies. Even when the community has a favorable attitude toward treatment, it may still make re-entry to "straight" society difficult by treating the ex-addict as a criminal and not trusting him with jobs or other rewarding social contact. An ex-addict facing this bleak prospect could easily find returning to addiction to be his most desirable alternative. In order for re-entry to be facilitated, the community must see the addict as a person who was formerly sick, but who has now been "cured."

A final effect of a favorable community attitude is the enabling of credible education programs. An education program in a community with a criminal definition of the problem is likely to be scare-oriented and therefore more likely to alienate youth than to dissuade them from addiction. A medical and social definition of the problem is assumed to be requisite for the acceptance of education programs that deal honestly with drugs, merely presenting the facts with a minimum of value judgments attached. The model assumes that if drug education programs are to be effective at all, they need to satisfy this condition of credibility, since most youths know too much about drugs to be fooled by scare techniques.

The other major impact of addict crime, community change, is depicted in Figure 5.

Some fraction of the addicts in the community will have to commit crime to be able to support their habits. As a result of the incidence of crime, some portion of its residents will decide to migrate out.[8] The fraction of the residents migrating is a function of the difference between the socioeconomic level compatible with the current

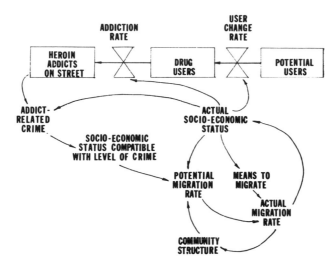

Figure 5 Community change

crime incidence and the current socioeconomic level. The concept of a compatible socioeconomic level is based on the premise that it is worth more to an individual to be in a neighborhood that is relatively free of crime. As crime increases, people living in the community no longer find their old neighborhood as attractive as it used to be, and some decide to move to an area with less crime. But outsiders who have been living in areas with a higher crime incidence would find the community of reference relatively crime-free and move in, filling the available housing. Since the new residents are of a lower socioeconomic level they are more vulnerable to the problems associated with a lower socioeconomic level. Among these social problems would be a higher vulnerability of their children to become addicts. This greater addict potential leads eventually to a larger addict population which will commit proportionally more crime. The increased crime will further drive down the compatible socioeconomic level. More migration will occur, aggravating the narcotics problem and bringing about further community deterioration.

As migration takes place, "community structure" is weakened. Structure is defined as the sum total of ties people have to a particular community and is assumed to be stronger among residents who have been living there for a long time. Strong community structure is assumed to retard migration. When migration is rapid, the average length of stay in the community decreases and community structure declines because residents have less time to establish ties before moving out. Deterioration of community structure permits even more rapid migration and further deterioration of structure.

Model Behavior and Preliminary Results

The structure described in the previous section based upon observation of an actual community in New York City has been represented in DYNAMO and subjected to a preliminary series of simulations, which are reported below. Even though this work is preliminary in nature and has been restricted to a particular community, results to date are so striking as to warrant two broad recommendations, applicable to a wide range of communities. 1) There is a need for a balanced set of programs to cope with a community narcotics problem. A total program for dealing with the problem should include sub-programs for rehabilitation, education, and police work directed at reducing heroin supply. Intensive application of any one of these programs will not be nearly as effective as the balanced use of all of them. 2) The community must perceive addiction at least in part as a social and medical problem in order for rehabilitation programs to be successfully implemented. Community education programs are required toward this end.

The following series of simulations support these recommendations.

The first computer simulation run shown is the symptomatic or base run against which we will compare behavior produced under the influence of remedial programs and policies. It represents the development of an extremely serious problem over a period of twenty-five years with police effort alone being used to combat the growth in addict population. The major computer outputs are shown in Figure 6.

The simulation begins with an initial addict group of 150 in a community with a population of 180,000 and a youth population (vulnerable to drug use) of 51,000. About 20 percent of these youths are occasional users of drugs. As the run begins, the number of addicts on the street (plotted by the computer using the letter A), is rising at a steady rate and total addicts on the street and in jail (T) is rising with it because police effort is not yet at a great enough intensity to arrest many addicts. The system structures of greatest importance during the first 100 months are the positive feedback loops that create the growth of addict and user populations due to the growth of the drug culture, exposure to addicts, and increasing availability of hard drugs. During this period, community problem definition (U) remains very low because there has not yet been a police response that could produce frustration, nor have there been enough arrests to make it probable that some of those arrested will be familiar to a large segment of the community. The low value of crime (C) reflects the relatively small addict population and the relatively high early socioeconomic level of the area. When socioeconomic level is high, it is assumed that addicts will be able to get a lot of money they need from their families and would have to commit a small number of crimes per addict. Because there is not a large amount of crime, not much migration takes place and socioeconomic level (L) remains near its initial value. Total program cost ($) remains small due to the small initial number of police, the only program element operating during this simulation run.

About 100 months after the beginning of the run, another important positive feedback loop comes into play. Crime becomes high enough to begin to cause outmigration and socioeconomic level starts to drop. As it falls, the futility-despair level associated with lower levels of income begins to increase and with it grows the potential number of addicts. This potential is eventually converted to a larger addict population that commits more crime causing more migration, and a further drop in

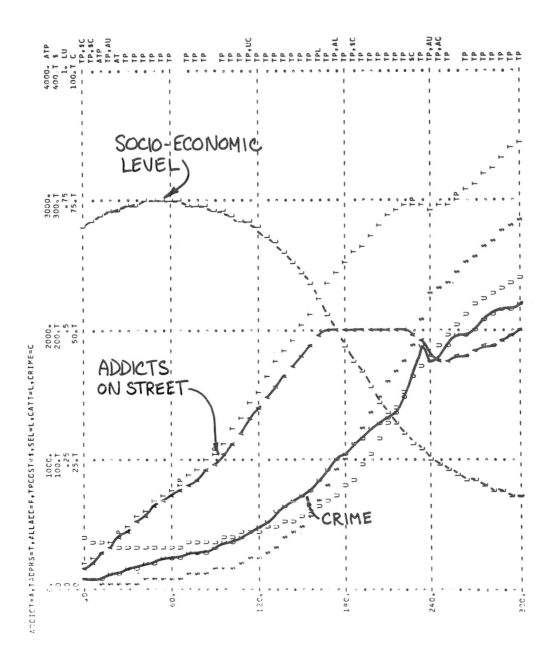

Figure 6 Base computer simulation results: Police used as only community response

socioeconomic level. Crime begins to grow more rapidly because of this and because crime per addict is greater at lower socioeconomic levels due to the unavailability of family funds. Figure 5 amply illustrates the system structure underlying this behavior. The more rapid growth of the addict population is enabled by the excess inventories of hard drugs in the community created in response to the increased attractiveness of pushing. Here, more rapid growth of the addict population makes pushing more attractive which brings more drugs into the community and enables even more rapid growth.

Another new mode of behavior arises at 170 months due to the action of the negative feedback loop embodying the police response. The police effort begins to grow in reaction to the rapidly increasing crime rate. This is reflected in the rapidly rising total program cost. It is also reflected in the rising community attitude that is produced by growing frustration with the results of the police efforts and increasing number of arrests relevant to community members. The number of addicts on the street reaches a plateau because, for a while, the police are able to make arrests at a rate equal to the rate at which new people become addicts. This, however, only amounts to transferring a growing part of the problem to jail as reflected in the total addict population in jail and on the street which continues to grow until 230 months. Growth of the total addict population peaks at that point, because the police effort has also decreased the drug supply. People who might potentially have become addicts lack the drug availability to do so and some addicts already in the area migrate to areas with more drugs and fewer police. As hard drug availability is reduced, the local price of drugs is driven up, forcing addicts to commit more crime to support their increasingly expensive habits.

Near the end of the run, from month 250 onward, addicts on the street and total addicts both begin to grow again. This marks the inability of police effort to deal ultimately with the problem. Here, the positive feedback loops producing the growth of the problem regain dominance and overpower even a very strong police effort. Crime increases with the number of addicts and the community problem definition shifts more toward a sociomedical view as the residents become more frustrated with the failure of police effort. Program cost continues to rise as more police are hired. Socioeconomic level bottoms out at a low value because the current residents no longer have the economic mobility to move out in response to increased crime rate. In all, the narcotics problem has grown completely out of control and the community has deteriorated into a slum.

Once a symptomatic behavior has been established in a base run, it is possible to do simulation experiments to determine the marginal benefit deriving from the use of various programs and policies. In the next run, police efforts have been supplemented by an additional program component: a methadone maintenance program has been added to the police response. Results are shown in Figure 7.

The behavior exhibited by the modeled community in this run is almost identical to that of the base run up to 108 months after the beginning of the run. At that point, the methadone program is able to begin accepting large numbers of addicts, as is represented in Figure 7 by the difference between total addicts—whether in programs,

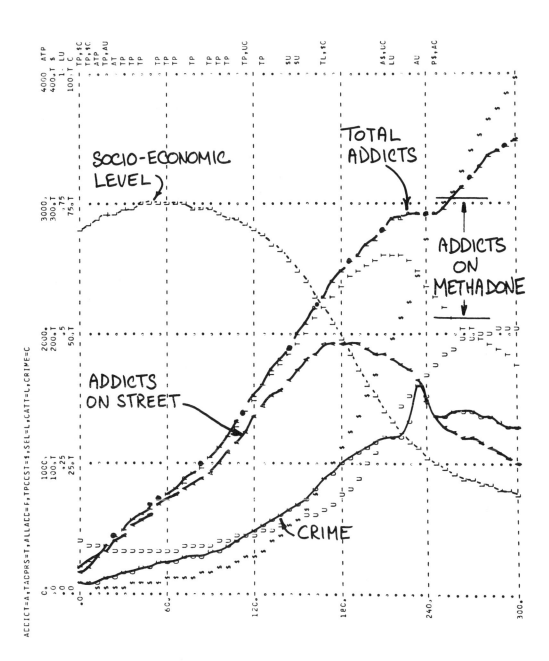

Figure 7   Computer simulation of police plus methadone

prison, or on the street (represented by P) and those addicts on the street and in prison only (T). The methadone program continues to accept addicts throughout the final 100 months of the run. At the end of the period simulated, total addicts in the community (P) is at the same level as was addicts on the street and in prison only (T) in the base run. However, almost half of these addicts are now in the methadone program and the number of addicts on the street and in prison is consequently reduced. Because there are fewer addicts on the street there is also significantly less crime. The presence of fewer addicts on the street decreases the requirement for (and cost of) police effort so that when rehabilitation cost is added, total program cost is only one-third greater than in the base run.

The methadone program does not represent a complete solution to the community's narcotics problem. Its existence enables a reduction in crime and permits many addicts to hold jobs and lead useful lives, but it does not affect a large segment of the addict population (mainly the younger addicts). The presence of a methadone program also has two other dysfunctional effects. First by reducing the market for heroin, excess hard drug availability is increased and addict population can grow more quickly. Second, uncertainty of rehabilitation efficacy is reduced by the perception of a successful methadone program and the deterrent value of this uncertainty is decreased.

The next simulation run illustrates the benefit that can be derived from using a comprehensive set of programs along with community education to speed their implementation. Three different types of rehabilitation programs, in-community, out-of-community, and methadone are employed. An educational program designed to dissuade potential addicts from becoming addicted to heroin has been added to the rehabilitation programs. A community education program is also employed to accelerate the change in the community's definition of the problem. The results of these additions can be seen in Figure 8.

The effects of using a comprehensive set of programs with community education are significant. Both the number of addicts on the street and the total number of addicts are far below the numbers of addicts in the previous run. Furthermore, the total number of addicts is not continuing to grow at the end as in the simulation with methadone and police alone. Crime rate is also down significantly and socioeconomic deterioration has been reduced as a result. Even though additional programs have been added, total program cost is slightly less than in the previous simulation, because the community has fewer addicts to cope with over time.

The education program aimed at youths who are potential addicts plays an important role in producing this result. Education had its effect by conveying information about the dangers of heroin use to potential and current occasional users of drugs. The number of potential and actual addicts was thereby decreased. Education programs aimed at potential addicts along with the set of rehabilitation programs are not able to produce the result shown in Figure 8 because they are ineffective until late in the run when the number of addicts is already great. This delay in effectiveness is due to the slowness of the community's definition of the problem to change. Community education accelerates the change in definition and this variable (U) rises much more quickly than in the previous runs. The community adopts a sociomedical outlook toward the

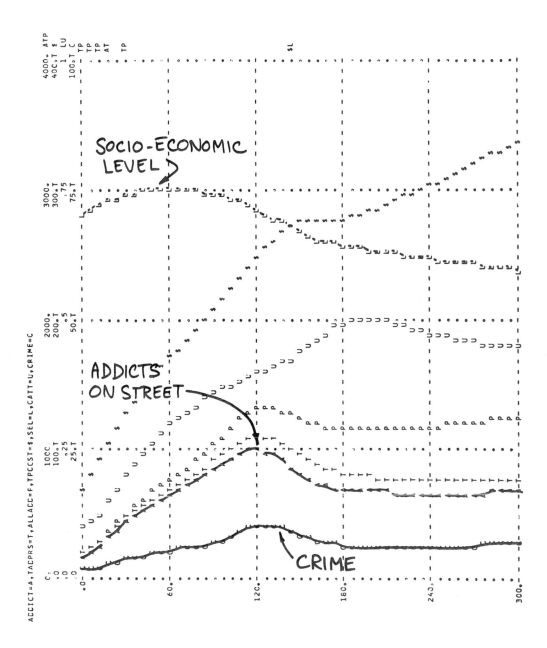

Figure 8 Computer simulation of three rehabilitation programs plus education plus community education

narcotics problem much sooner. Education can be made more credible at an earlier point in time and have a much larger impact. Rehabilitation has its impact 100 months earlier than in the previous run. The net effect of adding community education is the ability to control the spread of the addiction problem before it gets out of hand.

Summary

We have attempted to show how systems analysis and computer simulation can aid in the study of a complex social problem; to communicate our interim understanding of the system of forces that promotes and controls the growth of the narcotics problem; and to make several broad recommendations that may be useful to communities who have discovered their local problem and are seeking corrective policies.

The narcotics problem is a complex one. Too often policies advocated have been simplistic. For example, in our view, intensive efforts to eliminate importation of heroin, as well as legalization and delivery of heroin to addicts, have serious negative consequences that need to be faced before implementation of either policy should be considered. Within a specific community, a balanced program that includes a multiplicity of rehabilitation, education, and law enforcement efforts, each of which is known to be less than perfect, is more promising than one that is confined to a single modality.

The effectiveness of any program is enhanced if a community can persuade itself to define the problem at least in part as social and medical—rather than criminal in nature.

More specific recommendations depend upon further refinement of the model and its application to particular communities.

Notes

1. Especially we would like to thank Melvin Roman, Aaron Schmais, Erlene Collins, Deborah Kligler, Jack Wilder, Luis Diaz, David Laskowitz and John Langrod of Albert Einstein College of Medicine; Jerome Jaffee of the Special Office of Drug Abuse Prevention; Richard Brotman of New York Medical College; Albert Warner of Rockefeller University; Robert Lee of IBM; Fred Pomerantz, James Inciardi and Benjamin Lemon of the New York State Narcotics Addiction Control Commission. The authors assume full responsibility for this work, but acknowledge that it could not have been accomplished without the generous assistance of others.

2. This example is not based on actual computer runs. It is, however, similar in character to computer derived insights, more dramatic than most, and easier to describe briefly.

3. The authors are grateful to Elizabeth Levin, who contributed all of the drawings and system diagrams.

4. The dose required to maintain the habit of an individual who is dependent on heroin is many times greater than the dose required to produce a high in a non-addict.

5. Many authorities believe that there is a sensitive marketing mechanism in operation. For example, there are numerous reports that street pushers lowered the price of heroin in order to increase their market during the government's 1969 Operation Intercept in which the flow of marijuana and hashish was cut off at the Mexican border.

6. Full explanation of this language and its use is contained in A. L. Pugh III, *DYNAMO II User's Manual* (Cambridge: The M.I.T. Press, 1970).

7. The authors are aware that finer conceptual distinctions are usually made between types of drug users and have refrained from the practice because it would not have affected model behavior in a significant way.

8. Although people move for many reasons other than the incidence of addict related crime, the present discussion refers only to out-migration attributable to this source.

35

Student Performance in the Elementary Classroom: A System Simulation

Nancy H. Roberts

The academic performance of an elementary school student depends on several factors. A review of the literature indicates that one key in-school factor is the amount and quality of the teacher-student interaction. The most important out-of-school factor affecting student performance seems to be the family. This article presents a study of the interdependence of the variables affecting these factors as they in turn affect student performance. The tool used to examine the variables of concern to test their importance to the student-teacher system is the computer.

Until now, researchers, teachers, and parents have had to rely on mental models in an attempt to deal with the multifaceted dimensions of student performance. There now exists a computer compiler called DYNAMO (Pugh, 1973) that allows the model builder to incorporate into a mathematically precise computer model all the information which research has uncovered. The variables of this model can then be manipulated to test their impact on student performance.

The study of the effect of several variables on one another implies an underlying system. A system whose focus is student performance must be dynamic—that is, changing over time. Moreover, in order to have continuous change in the system elements of feedback must be present. "Feedback" indicates that output from one decision will influence a future decision.

Feedback systems concepts were first applied to managerial systems about fifteen years ago by Jay Forrester (1961) at M.I.T. and in recent years have spread to the social sciences, under the name "system dynamics." As early as 1959, a beginning was made to apply some of these ideas to education by C. Kyle Packer and Toni Packer (1968), but no published works have heretofore combined these educational feedback systems concepts with computer modeling.

This article is reprinted from *Simulation and Games* 5, no. 3 (September 1974), pp. 265–290, by permission of the publisher, Sage Publications, Inc. It was originally titled: "A Computer System Simulation of Student Performance in the Elementary Classroom."

Base Model

Using dynamic modeling as a research tool, rather than statistical analysis of empirical data, one is confronted with a number of interdependent variables rather than independent and dependent variables. The task of the model builder is to create a dynamic feedback model that expresses the relationships and effects these variables have on each other over time. When possible, the research literature should be used to justify the model design.

Figure 1 pictures the core of the model developed for this paper. The diagram is here presented in its simplest form to emphasize the perspective from which the base model was developed.

Figure 1 indicates that the academic performance of a student affects the amount of help he seeks. The child's request for help influences the amount of time a teacher allocates to him. This in turn determines the real help the teacher gives him, which affects his performance. If a student's performance falls, he seeks more help, which causes the teacher to allocate more of her time to him, which provides him with more help, which increases his performance, which causes him to seek *less* help, and so forth. (This, of course, assumes that the student's goals do not fall in the meantime—an assumption that will be waived below.)

The full base model of student-teacher interaction is presented in Figure 2. It can be divided into two parts: the teacher's side and the student's side. However, it must be recognized that this division is being made only as a means of organizing the following discussion. The two sides of the model have important overlapping variables. In addition, each aspect is part of the total system, and therefore the action in one area clearly has impact on the other area.

Student Goals.   A student comes to school at the beginning of the year with a preset but approximate notion as to where he would like to be academically. Since the year

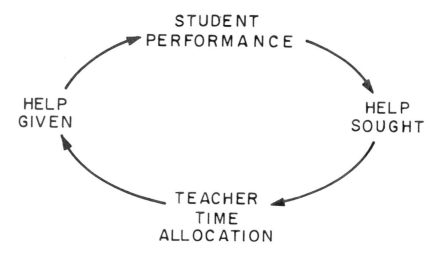

Figure 1 System overview

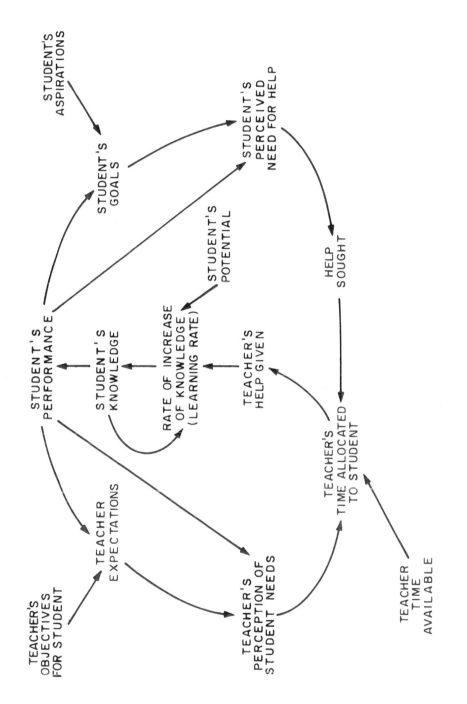

Figure 2 Systems diagram of student-teacher interaction as it affects classroom performance

has not yet started, his immediate goals are initially the same as the longer-term aspirations. As the education process gets under way, the student begins to sense and reflect upon his actual performance. The student judges himself in relation to his other classmates and absorbs the information about his performance that is conveyed by the teacher. As this process continues, the student gradually begins to believe that his actual performance represents what he will be able to attain. He slowly surrenders, confirms, or raises his prior aspirations and becomes more ''realistic'' about his goals.

The literature (LaBenne and Greene, 1969; Coopersmith, 1967; Trowbridge, 1972; Block, 1971; Kaufman and Lewis, 1968; Johnson, 1970) clearly supports this description of student goal-setting. Self-concept or self-esteem generally determines one's goals. If a student's academic self-concept or self-esteem is high, his goals are proportionally high.

Student Personality.   Further in the base model diagram, the model asserts that the dynamics of the classroom lead the student slowly to change his goals so that they are closer to his current performance. Even though his goals may be shifting, the student tends to get disappointed when his performance fails to live up to his present objectives. Sometimes he recognizes that he is in need of extra help if he is to attain his goals. The enthusiastic child makes a concerted attempt to get extra help from the teacher. If the student is unenthusiastic or turned off, he makes little or no effort to get extra help.

The little literature found in the area of student perseverance confirms the model assumptions just described (Barton et al., 1972; Combs, 1952; LaBenne and Greene, 1969). Brophy and Good (1972, p. 271) comment:

> Relaxed and active students who frequently initiate contact with teachers will get more attention and are more likely to correct any misconceptions that teachers may have about them. In contrast, quiet, withdrawn students who avoid teachers and do not say much when questioned leave the teachers more room for error in judging them.

At this point in the model, the student-teacher interaction begins to affect the student.

Teacher Help.   The model diagram conveys that the student's efforts to get more help from the teacher affect how much attention the teacher gives him. If the teacher finds a very enthusiastic and concerned student, she may give him even more help than she feels the child needs. However, if the child makes no effort at all to clarify his misunderstandings and shows no interest in learning, the teacher may be discouraged or even turned off by the child. Therefore, she may end up giving this student less help than she actually feels he needs.

If the teacher gives a child extra help, and this help is effective, the child's ability to absorb knowledge is increased. As the child improves his ability to learn, his body of knowledge grows. Moreover, additional follow-up help the teacher might give this child will then have a greater payoff, because the teacher will be working with a child with greater understanding and knowledge.

Several researchers have described this kind of phenomenon. Brophy and Good (1972, p. 277) found: ''The teachers were more likely to stay with highs [students the teachers expected to achieve well] after they failed to answer an initial question . . . In contrast, they tended to end the interaction by giving the answer or calling on someone else in parallel situations with lows.'' Brophy and Good also note that the teachers answered more of the highs' questions as well as praising the highs more often than the lows. Rosenthal and Jacobson (1968) and Kester and Letchworth (1972) report almost identical findings to Brophy and Good.

Student's Learning Rate.   Carroll, in his ''model of school learning,'' explains his theory that anyone, provided he has the aptitude, can master a learning task if he is given enough time by the teacher and if he is willing to spend the time necessary for mastery. Carroll (1971, p. 33) feels there are two variables important to learning: ''(1) the vitality of instruction and (2) the student's ability to understand and profit from instruction.''

Student Intelligence.   The model embodies Carroll's assumption that the child's learning rate is affected by his innate potential. This is described in the model in terms of IQ, the most easily understood and best scale available at present for measuring innate potential. The child with a high IQ has a fast learning rate. However, of two children with the same IQ, the child with more knowledge on the subject learns faster because level of knowledge also affects learning rate. The literature clearly supports the significant correlation between IQ and achievement (Arnoff, 1971; Baker et al., 1961; Barton et al., 1972; Harootunian, 1966; Kirsch, 1967; Klansmeier, 1965).

Thus, the base model reflects three factors affecting learning rate: innate potential, level of knowledge of the student, and extra help given by the teacher. In addition, the impact of family background on school performance is considered in a further development of the base model when parental influence is added.

The level of knowledge and understanding of a child manifests itself in the daily performance of that child. A child with a high level of understanding and knowledge does better work in school than a child with a low level of knowledge and understanding.

This completes the feedback loop of variables on the student's side of the student-teacher interaction. In review, during the course of a school year, a child adjusts his goals so they are in line with his performance. The gap between where a child is performing and where he would like to perform determines the amount of teacher help the child thinks he needs. This in turn influences the amount of help the student seeks, which affects the amount of time and help the teacher gives the student. This help, combined with the student's innate potential and current store of knowledge, influences his rate of learning. Learning rate increases as the student's knowledge base increases. This knowledge accumulation will then determine the student's performance.

Teacher's Expectations.   The teacher's side of the model parallels to some extent the student side. A teacher's objectives for a particular student are often set at the very beginning of the school year based on information obtained from the student's record as well as from other faculty members (Bloom, 1971; Good and Dembo, 1973; Johnson, 1970; LaBenne and Greene, 1969; Wellington and Wellington, 1970).

Initially, the teacher's expectations for a student are the same as her objectives. She has not yet received additional information that would lead her to expect otherwise. As the teacher becomes familiar with a student's classroom work, she gradually changes her expectations for that student so that they correspond more closely to the level of the student's actual performance. The process of a teacher setting her expectations for a student is therefore modeled in a manner similar to the process of a student setting his own goals.

Teacher's Help.   As the teacher recognizes that there is a difference between the level of work a student can do, and the level of work he is in fact doing, she makes an effort to give him extra help. The base model assumes that the teacher allots extra time to a student based primarily on her evaluation of that particular student's needs. The amount of time is limited by the amount of extra-help time a teacher can find during a school week. Given the typical tightness of a teacher's schedule, the amount of time a teacher spends with a student who does not seek help will no doubt be less than the teacher feels he needs. If the student occasionally asks for help, the teacher might be motivated to give him about what she feels he needs. The student who is constantly looking for extra help might sometimes pressure the teacher into giving him more time than she really feels he needs. However, there is a definite saturation point beyond which further pressure for attention and special consideration will have negative effects on the teacher.

The teacher side of the model and the student side now overlap. As the teacher gives the student more individual attention, she increases his learning rate and therefore his base of knowledge, which is reflected in better performance by the student. The student's increased knowledge then also makes the teacher's help more effective.

As the student's performance improves, the teacher gradually feels the student's needs are less and therefore gives him less extra help. Eventually this could cause a slow-down in the student's learning rate, slowing down his build-up of knowledge. The resulting gradual change in his rate of performance may cause the student no longer to meet the teacher's expectations. As this happens, the teacher then reassesses the student's needs, once again allocating more time to him.

As they have been described, each of the two main modeled feedback loops can lead to cyclic fluctuations in student performance, accompanied by fluctuations also in student goals and teacher objectives, in help-seeking and help-giving, and in student rate of learning. The student and teacher are clearly shown as affecting each other, with student performance being the joint product. Each modeled loop also reflects the processes whereby goals or objectives shift to accommodate short-term performance. Through these changes over time either the student or the teacher or both can turn off the help-seeking/help-giving interaction that so critically influences the dynamics of performance.

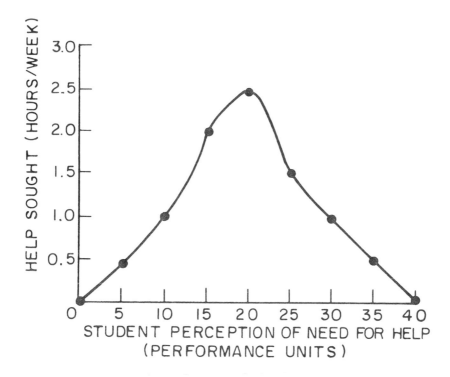

Figure 3   Help sought by student

The discussion presented here indicates that the base model just described has been developed to be consistent in general with available educational research. The next step is to translate this model into computer language.

The documentation and justification of the computer equations for the entire model is too lengthy a task for inclusion in this article.[1] However, as an example of the process of quantification, consider the student help-seeking process.

The computer model assumes that the amount of help (in terms of hours/week) a student will seek depends on the gap between his average performance and where he would like his performance to be (his goals). This is expressed in terms of a tabular relationship stored in the computer program, as shown in Figure 3. This graph shows the modeled assumption that when a student perceives a 5-point gap between his performance and his goals he will seek a half-hour of extra help per week. As he perceives a larger gap, he will seek more time per week. A gap of 20 points is the largest gap the modeled student can tolerate before getting discouraged and turned off. A student perceiving that his performance is 20 points below where he would like it can seek 2½ hours of extra help per week. After this point, the graph turns down again so that a student who perceives a 40-point gap between his goals and his performance is so discouraged he seeks no extra help at all. This modeled graphical function can easily be changed in the computer simulation runs.

All the other relationships shown in Figure 2 have been computer modeled in a similar manner, using empirical results from educational research whenever possible. By this process, a verbal and diagrammatic model is gradually translated into computer language. Once the verbal model becomes a computer model, the variables can then be manipulated to see in fact which factors of student performance are the most sensitive. These key sensitive areas can then be subjected to more data collection by researchers. Further, a more precise understanding by educators of the interdependence of the variables will then be possible.

Computer Simulations

This section describes a selection chosen from the large variety of computer simulation runs that were made with the base model. The first run indicated was made to test the reasonableness of the model. An average student (IQ 110) with moderate aspirations and a teacher expecting average work were used as the assumptions for the test case.

This run (Figure 4), showing a student with a moderate gap between performance and goals, indicates that initially he seeks a half-hour of extra help per week. But the teacher, perceiving no gap in her expectations for the student, feels little pressure for

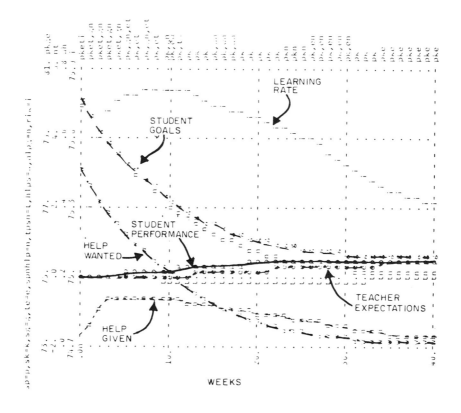

Figure 4 Run 1, base model test

help. Consequently, she gives the student very little help. The maximum this student receives is .10 hour or 6 minutes per week of extra help. Because of the small amount of extra help, this student's performance climbs very slowly from a grade point average of 75 toward, but not reaching, 76. Because his performance basically does not change, his goals (which started at 80) drop by the end of the year to meet his performance. As his goals drop, he seeks even less than his initial desire of a half-hour per week of help. Because the student does not want help and the teacher does not feel he needs it, the amount of help the student receives drops to virtually nothing. The student's learning rate shows the effect of even the small amount of help he gets at the beginning of the year by going from 75 to 75.8 at its peak. This boost in learning rate accounts for the small change in performance that the student does achieve.

This computer run illustrates what happens to the average student when everyone concerned is basically satisfied with things as they are. Nothing very much changes.[2]

In run 2 (Figure 5), three constants were changed to see what the effect would be on this student. The time for changing student knowledge was shortened from 25 to 4 weeks, teacher objectives were shifted from 75 to 80, and the amount of time the teacher had available was doubled (from 10 to 20 hours per week). In this simulation run, with both teacher and student starting the year feeling the student could do

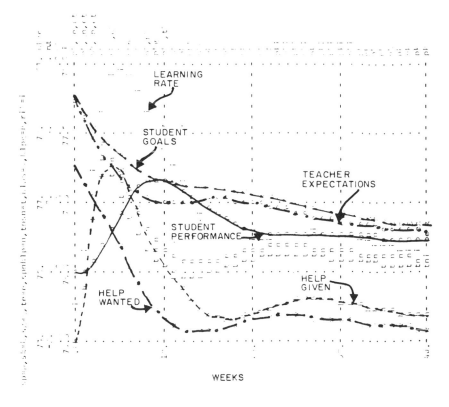

Figure 5 Run 2, increased teacher time and objectives, shortened time to affect knowledge

somewhat better, with more time available to the teacher, and with less time needed for effecting a change in cumulative knowledge, the student performance is only increased by one point. The only thing surprising about this run was the fact that the doubling of teacher time had really no effect. However, thinking about it again, if both student and teacher do not feel there is much of a need for help, help will not be given even with more time available.

Run 3 kept the changes made for the second run and added two more changes. Time for changing teacher expectations and time for changing student goals were both set at 1,000 weeks (from 8 and 12 weeks, respectively), basically so both teacher and student goals would be held essentially constant at 80 for the year. This, indeed, made some impact on student performance, which went from 75 initially to 78 at the end of the year, peaking at over 79 for weeks 11–13. This was due to the boost provided by about 40 minutes of extra help per week in the early part of the year. This run seems to show that when both teacher and student have constantly held but moderate goals for an average child, this child can make reasonable gains during a school year with some extra help.

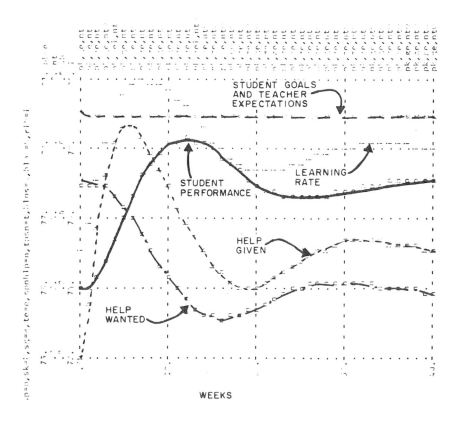

Figure 6 Run 3, run 2 plus teacher expectations and student goals essentially constant

The next several runs (4, 5, 6) are simulations of a student who would usually be classified as an underachiever. For run 4, the student's IQ is set equal to 130, his historic performance and his aspirations are low, at 80, but the teacher's objectives are high at 95. Teacher's time available was put back to 10 hours per week and time for change in student knowledge was also returned to 25 weeks.

In run 4, because the student perceives only a 5-point gap between his performance and his goals, he seeks only a half-hour of extra help per week. However, the teacher perceives a 20-point gap between performance and expectations. This situation results in the student getting, at the peak, over 40 minutes of help per week, only a bit more than the half-hour of help received in the previous set of runs (Figure 6) when the teacher perceived only a 5-point gap. The student's low goals contribute to shutting off the teacher from giving as much extra help as she might like. Furthermore, the teacher's perception tends to shut herself off, given the large, frustrating gap in student performance that she senses. Because the resulting amount of help the student is receiving is fairly small, his performance rises very slowly, causing the teacher's expectations to drop fairly rapidly (down from 95 to almost 80 by the middle of the

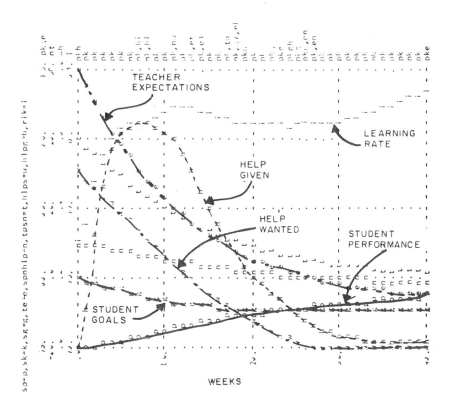

Figure 7   Run 4, underachiever—low student aspirations, high teacher objectives

year). Then, as both the teacher's expectations and the student's goals fall, the amount of extra help goes to only 12 minutes per week by mid-year. Nevertheless, because the student's IQ is high and learning rate increases, his performance increases to about 78 by the end of the year.

Run 5 reverses the above situation, setting student aspirations at 95 and teacher objectives at 80, with historic student performance at 75. The student initially seeks 2½ hours of help per week, but, at most, receives only one half-hour per week. Student goals drop down as teacher expectations had in run 4, because his performance rises very slowly. The student ends the year with the same 3-point gain as in run 4.

Run 6 has both the student aspirations and teacher objectives initially set at 95, with historic student performance at 75. The student again seeks 2½ hours of help per week. This time, because the teacher also perceives his need, he gets, by week 10, almost 2 hours of extra help per week. From week 4 to 14 he gets over an hour of extra help per week. Because of all this extra help, the student's performance climbs fairly rapidly and consistently. Student goals and teacher expectations come down as they did in the previous runs, but this time, because of good student performance, by the last quarter of the year, they have started to rise again. By the end of the year, the student had made a 10-point gain; his performance is just about at 85. This computer run

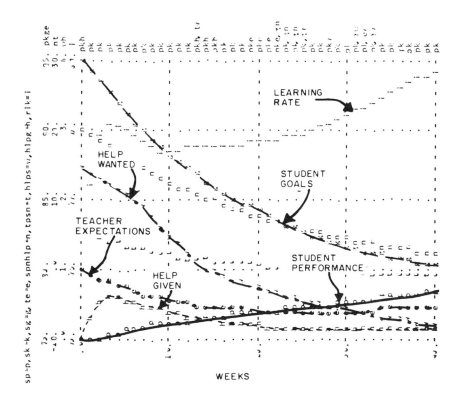

Figure 8   Run 5, underachiever—high student aspirations, low teacher objectives

suggests that if a student has the potential, and this is recognized by both teacher and student, therefore producing the help the student needs, a serious underachiever can be brought up to par in a couple of years.

In the last two runs to be reported here (Figures 10 and 11), the model was changed slightly to make the teacher directly responsive to student desires for help. This situation simulates a little more closely that which is theorized to occur in an open-type classroom. This is still an underachiever, with an IQ of 130. For run 7, the student aspirations were set at 95 percent so that the student recognizes the fact that he should be doing much better work. The teacher's objectives are set at only 80. Because he perceives a gap of 20 points, the student initially seeks 2½ hours of help per week. By week 6, he is getting over 2 hours of extra help per week from his assumed-to-be responsive teacher. This help starts increasing his performance. His goals, however, start dropping. They again turn up in the last quarter of the year, because of his consistently increased performance. The teacher's expectations start to rise also in the second half of the year. This student does very well over the course of the year, bringing his performance up to almost 87 by the year's end.

Run 8 reverses the above situation, setting student aspirations at 80 and teacher objectives at 95. Here the underachieving student initially seeks only a half-hour of

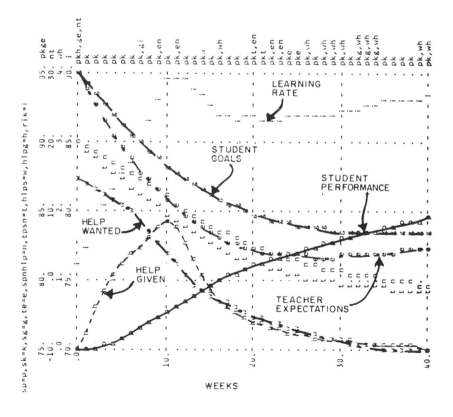

Figure 9   Run   6, underachiever—high student aspirations, high teacher objectives

help per week because of the small gap between his performance (of 75) and his goals. Given the assumed responsive teacher, the student gets almost that much help by the fifth week of school. As the student's goals come even closer to his performance, he seeks and gets even less help. The teacher's expectations for this student drop off sharply. By the end of the year, this student has made only about a 2-point gain in performance. For this student, the year was virtually wasted. These two runs illustrate that this type of open classroom can be marvelous for some students, really allowing them to work and be helped to their potential, while disastrous for other students who need closer attention by the teacher and might not receive it.

Conclusions

These computer simulations of student performance in an elementary classroom clearly point out the importance of three elements: student goals, teacher expectations, and the amount of extra help given. When both student and teacher recognize a problem exists and work together to overcome it, great gains can be made by the student. However, when either party fails to recognize a problem, much less is accomplished toward correcting it. The importance of teacher expectations alone has been shown in the studies by Rosenthal and Jacobson (1968) and Brophy and Good (1972).

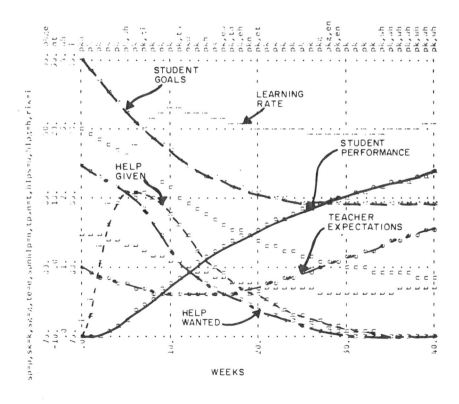

Figure 10 Run 7, underachiever—teacher directly responsive to student, high student aspirations, low teacher objectives

The education research literature does not, however, indicate substantial empirical results in the area of student goals, or in the situation of combined student and teacher goals. An experiment in which student goals as well as teacher expectations were the jointly manipulated subjects of the study would not only test the findings of the simulation results but would importantly extend the empirical boundaries of classroom research.

Teachers often blame the time they do not have available as a cause for poor pupil performance. These runs indicate that time (or class size) is not all that important. Figure 12, summarizing eight computer simulations, indicates that the doubling of teacher time is not the sensitive variable. Raising both teacher expectations and student goals causes a significant increase in student performance.

The enlarged model (Figure 13) suggests other areas that might influence student performance. Parents not only influence students directly by pressuring performance as well as objectives, but also indirectly by applying pressure (or not applying pressure) to both the principal and the teacher. The other children in the classroom are also a source of performance pressure for the student and might also be added to the modeled equations structure.

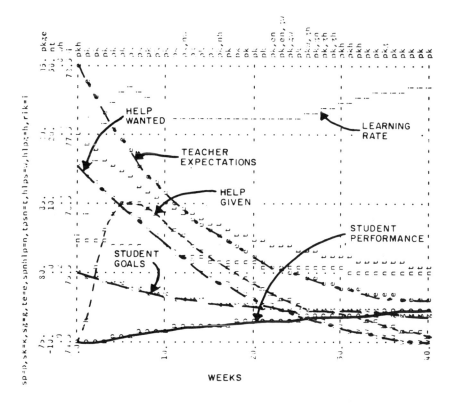

Figure 11 Run 8, underachiever—teacher directly responsive to student, low student aspirations, high teacher objectives

TEACHER EXPECTATIONS	STUDENT GOALS	STUDENT PERFORMANCE	
		10 HOURS/WEEK	20 HOURS/WEEK
75	80	75.5	76.2
75	95	76	77
95	80	76.8	78
95	95	82	84.8

Figure 12 Effect of doubling teacher time available for extra help on student performance

Moreover, the enlarged model indicates the possible addition of an evaluation process by both the teacher and the student, to assess and then affect the help given. As the teacher gives help to the student, this will increase his learning rate, causing the teacher to feel her help has been effective. As she evaluates her help positively, the model indicates that this would encourage her to give more time, and then more help, to the student. If the teacher encounters a reverse effect, where help given is not enough to increase noticeably a child's learning rate, this would probably cause the teacher to evaluate negatively her help and therefore decrease it. A perverse implication of this changed assumption is the possible outcome that the teacher will spend most time with those who respond best to her, leaving the worst students falling farther behind and harder to reach.

On the student's side of the suggested model expansion, if he feels the help he is getting has enabled him to learn more easily, he will positively evaluate the help and attempt to influence the teacher to give him still more help. The opposite effect can also take place here, with the student getting turned off by what he feels is ineffective help. The enlarged model therefore suggests other areas that obviously affect the dynamics of student performance. And there are even more dimensions that might be considered and added—for example, the quality implications and economic costs of various aspects of teacher-student interaction.

This base model, and the further implications of the enlarged model, indicate that model building and computer simulation can play an effective part in educational research. A model, first of all, is unlimited in the scope of the problem that can be considered. It is never complete, yet it can be used at any point when the model builders feel they have achieved some reasonable representation of the problem. If the builders have done thorough research on the problem, the model can contain all the present best understandings of the problem.[3]

The process of model building greatly deepens the educational understandings of those people involved. The model builders are forced to think through exactly what they feel happens in a given situation. They are forced to resolve all contradictions and come up with logical theories and explanations.

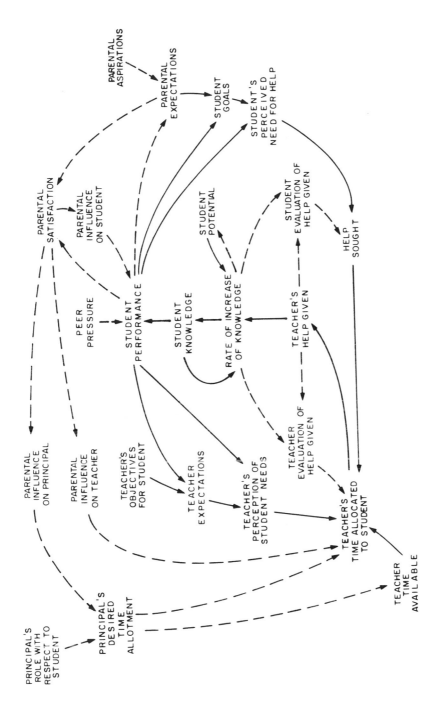

Figure 13 Enlarged model

When there are contradictory ideas or theories, the model can be changed at will. The impact and importance of these differences can be discovered almost immediately. The people involved will either discover that their differences have little impact on the problem being studied, or in fact they have hit upon a very sensitive area. If a sensitive area is found, this would indicate an important need for an empirical study to test the theories in question.

Other problem areas in education in which a model might prove very useful are drugs in the schools, school dropouts, or family dynamics. Actually, any problem area where a great many variables affect the problem and sustain the problem over time is very suitable for this kind of research study.

Notes

1. The listing and explanation of the equations for this model are available in Levin and Roberts et al., *The Dynamics of Human Service Delivery* (Cambridge, Mass.: Ballinger Publishing Co., 1976).

2. Obviously, if the teacher were assumed to be one who is generally more responsive to student help-seeking, the simulation results would show some moderate improvement in student performance. However, the general nature of results would be unchanged.

3. Further research might consider alternating expert Delphi forecasting interactions with multiple computer runs and model elaborations. This methodology would utilize both the data management capability of the computer and the intuitive power of the human groups' judgmental processes.

References

ARNOFF, M. (1971) "An investigation of factors related to the ability of children in grades two, three and four to comprehend concepts of government with an elementary social studies course on government," in R. Gross and L. de la Cruz, *Social Studies Dissertations 1963–1969*. Boulder, Colo. ERIC Clearinghouse for Social Studies/Social Science Education (ED054 999).

BAKER, R., R. SCHUTZ, and R. HINZE (1961) "The influence of mental ability on achievement when socio-economic status is controlled." *J. of Experimental Education* 30, pp. 255–258.

BARTON, K., T. E. DIELMAN, and R. CATTELL (1972) "Personality and I.Q. measures as predictors of school achievement." *J. of Educ. Psychology* 63, pp. 398–404.

BLOCK, J. (1971) *Mastery Learning: Theory and Practice*. New York: Holt, Rinehart & Winston.

BLOOM, B. (1971) "Affective consequences of school achievement," in J. Block, *Mastery Learning: Theory and Practice*. New York: Holt, Rinehart & Winston.

BROPHY, J. and T. GOOD (1972) "Teacher expectations: beyond the Pygmalion controversy." *Phi Delta Kappan* 54, pp. 267–277.

CARROLL, J. (1971) "Problems of measurement related to the concept of learning for mastery," in J. Block, *Mastery Learning: Theory and Practice*. New York: Holt, Rinehart & Winston.

COMBS, A. (1952) "Intelligence from a perceptual point of view." *J. of Abnormal and Social Psychology* 47, pp. 662–673.

COOPERSMITH, S. (1967) *The Antecedents of Self-Esteem*. San Francisco: W. H. Freeman.

FORRESTER, J. (1961) *Industrial Dynamics*. Cambridge, Mass.: MIT Press.

GOOD, T. and M. DEMBO (1973) "Teacher expectations: self-report data." *School Rev.* 81, pp. 247–253.

HAROOTUNIAN, B. (1966) "Intellectual abilities and reading achievement." *Elementary School J.* 66, pp. 386–392.

JOHNSON, D. (1970) *The Social Psychology of Education*. New York: Holt, Rinehart & Winston.

KAUFMAN, J. and M. LEWIS (1968) The school environment and programs for dropouts. Pennsylvania State University Institute for Human Resources.

KESTER, S. and G. LETCHWORTH (1972) "Teacher expectations and their effects on achievement and attitudes of secondary school students." *J. of Educ. Research* 66, pp. 51–55.

KIRSCH, B. (1967) "An evaluation of levels of cognitive learning in a unit of fifth grade social studies." Ph.D. dissertation. University of Southern California.

KLANSMEIER, H. (1965) "The effects of I.Q. level and sex on divergent thinking of seventh grade pupils of low, average and high I.Q." *J. of Educ. Research* 58, pp. 300–302.

LaBENNE, W. and B. GREENE (1969) *Educational Implications of Self-Concept Theory*. Pacific Palisades, Calif. Goodyear.

PACKER, C. and T. PACKER (1968) "Cybernetics information theory and the educative process," in R. Hyman (ed.) *Teaching: Vantage Points for Study*. New York: J. B. Lippincott.

PUGH, A. III (1973) *DYNAMO II User's Manual*. Cambridge, Mass.: MIT Press.

ROSENTHAL, R. and L. JACOBSON (1968) *Pygmalion in the Classroom*. New York: Holt, Rinehart & Winston.

TROWBRIDGE, N. (1972) "Self-concept and socio-economic status in elementary school children." *Amer. Educ. Research J.* 9, pp. 525–537.

WELLINGTON, J. and B. WELLINGTON (1970) "Should teachers see student records?" in H. Clarizio et al (eds.) *Contemporary Issues in Educational Psychology*. Boston: Allyn & Bacon.

36

Simulation of Natural Resource Management and Sociological Systems

William T. Newell

This paper discusses application of industrial dynamics feedback system analysis and DYNAMO simulation models to two "non-industrial" systems, ecological and sociological.[1] In the first area—natural resource management—several systems have been analyzed and modeled, but in the second area beginnings are just now underway. Two models are described in this paper, one of the regulation of fishing in a commercial salmon fishery, and the other of management policy changes in a prison system.

Salmon Fishery System Model

Problems of designing management systems and establishing fishing policies for proper exploitation of major fish populations have been under intensive study for several years. The College of Fisheries at the University of Washington has been engaged in the study of fish populations and fishing policies for such species as Pacific salmon, halibut, tuna, and hake.[2] In this paper is presented a description of a simulation model of an intraseasonal gantlet salmon fishery system.

A commercial salmon fishery operates within the context of dynamic interaction of many complex factors. These variables include the biological variables of the particular species which relate to growth, migratory behavior, and reproductive behavior; environmental variables; physical characteristics of fishing gear; and the factors affecting decisions of fishermen and fisheries managers. This latter group of factors includes economic, political, sociological and psychological variables. The complexity of these systems suggests simulation as a tool of analysis. A commercial salmon fishery system lends itself to continuous-flow simulation models because the fishery management agency functions as a regulator in a feedback control system.

The migratory behavior of salmon affects the operation and objectives of Pacific salmon fisheries. Mature salmon, after spending two or more years in the open sea, return to fresh water spawning grounds, lay their eggs, and die. Their progeny spend some time in the fresh water area and then migrate to the ocean feeding grounds. When they mature, they repeat the cycle by returning to their fresh water spawning grounds. There are physical limitations to the fresh water spawning and nursery areas, because of which there may be determined an annual optimum number of fish that should be allowed to spawn if long-run maximum food production is to be realized. The capacity of the spawning grounds to support eggs and young salmon fluctuates and causes a variation in optimum escapement to the spawning grounds.

Analysis of this system may be divided into interseasonal and intraseasonal phases. Interseasonal analysis is concerned with determining the optimum numbers of each species of fish which should be allowed to spawn. The interseasonal analysis has been the subject of a variety of analytic techniques, population dynamics models, and computer simulation models.

Intraseasonal Analysis

In the intraseasonal phase of the system, which is the subject of the present model, the fishery management agency attempts to realize the optimum escapement to the spawning ground determined in the interseasonal analysis. This is a difficult task because objectives are often incompatible with the alternatives available. As adult fish pass through the fishing grounds on their way to the spawning grounds, the only action available to the manager is to open or close various parts of the fishery. The manager operates with imperfect preseason forecasts of the size of run, noisy information about escapement while the run is in progress, and with a group of fishermen whose actions are not entirely predictable. The problem may be further complicated by the existence of two or more species in an area. In this situation closing the fishery may allow the proper number of one species to escape to the spawning grounds, but too many of a second, while opening the fishery may permit the proper number of the second species to escape, but an insufficient number of the first.

The type of fishery being considered is referred to as a gantlet fishery, because as the fish pass through the fishing areas they are intercepted by the fishing gear. Because of the homing nature of salmon, future availability of stock in a particular fishery is partly a function of the number which pass through the fishery and escape to the spawning grounds.

The fishery management agency functions to make a series of decisions relative to opening and closing the fishery during the salmon run, a period which may range from about two weeks to several months. The timing of decisions is important, but the manager is hampered by the quality of information available. This information concerns the size and the composition of the run, weather and water conditions, and location and effectiveness of fishing gear. As the season progresses the management agency gathers information, updates preseason forecasts of run size and composition, and regulates fishing in each subarea to obtain desired escapement for each major species of fish. As the fishing season progresses information improves, but management's ability to affect the total outcome diminishes because an increasing proportion of the total run will have already passed through the fishing area.

Intraseasonal Gantlet Fishery Model

A DYNAMO simulation model has been developed to aid in analyzing the intraseasonal management of a gantlet fishery.[3] The model, which is designed to simulate a single fishing season, is comprised of over 1200 equations.

The basic structure of the model is illustrated in Figure 1.[4] It consists of five interrelated sectors: (1) fish migration sector, (2) fixed fishing gear sector, (3) mobile fishing gear decision-making sector, (4) fishing sector, and (5) fishery management sector.

The fish migration sector represents the movement of two species of fish, called a target species and a diffusion species, through the fishery which consists of three fishing areas. The target species and the diffusion species differ in their migratory behavior as they pass through the fishing areas. (Both species pass through fishing area 1.) That portion of the target species not caught in fishing area 1 moves on into either areas 2 or 3 before escaping to the spawning grounds. The target species is comprised of 3 simultaneously entering stocks (or homogeneous groups). As the diffusion species moves through the three fishing areas a portion of them escapes continuously to the spawning grounds. Each fishing area in the model is divided into 3 subareas, each having provisions for fish to be caught and for fish to escape. The three subareas in series comprise a third-order exponential delay.

Two types of fishing gear are represented in each sector of the model, although only one area is shown in the illustration. Fixed fishing gear consists of nets or traps, and fishes whenever the fishery is open. Thus its operation depends only upon its location and the management decision to open or close that particular area. Mobile fishing gear consists of fishing boats and can move from one area to another or it can enter port in any area.

The mobile gear decision-making sector is the most complex part of the model. It represents the decision of fishermen operating mobile gear to fish or not and at what location. The decision to fish is made in a three-step sequence. The first step is to forecast future catch and its value for each species and each fishing strategy. Three strategies are available to the mobile gear fishermen: to fish in their present area, or to move to one of the other two areas. The catch forecast is made each day by estimating the present daily catch per unit of mobile gear in each area, estimating the population currently in each area, and constructing a forecasting ratio of present population abundance to long-range abundance forecasts. This ratio when exponentially smoothed is used to adjust the long-range forecast to obtain a short-range forecast of abundance in the area. Then the expected catch for the coming week is forecast and the expected dollar value of the catch for each species for each area for the next week is determined. The replication necessary to represent this forecasting procedure for the two species for each fishing area contributes significantly to the large size of the model.

The second step in the decision process is tentatively to choose one of the three fishing strategies, based upon a comparison of expected catch value for each alternative strategy. DYNAMO table functions are used to represent the fraction of mobile fishing gear tentatively choosing a strategy of moving from its present location to another area.

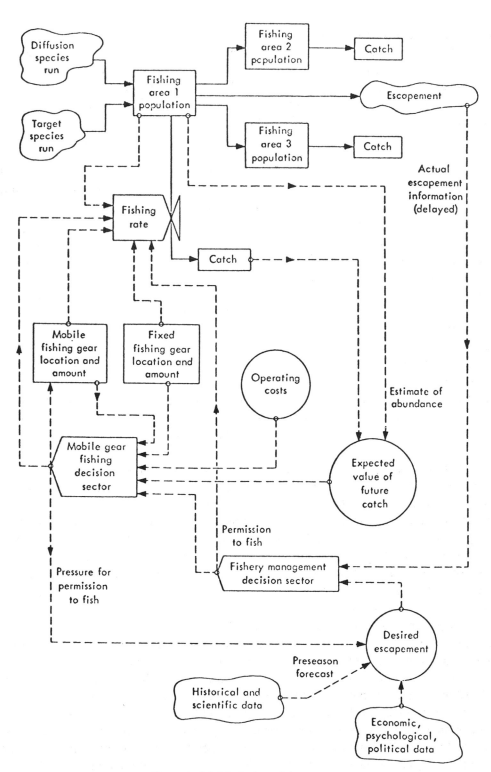

Figure 1   Model of salmon fishery system

In these tables expected catch value is the independent variable and fraction choosing to move is the dependent variable. If an area is presently closed by the management agency then the alternative of moving into that area is excluded.

The third step in the mobile gear decision-making process is to decide whether or not to fish. The decision is based upon a comparison of expected catch value and operating costs for the strategy tentatively chosen in step 2. The fraction actually deciding to fish is used later in the fishing sector of the model. Provision is made in the model for three classes of fishermen referred to as optimistic, normal, and pessimistic. The three degrees of optimism are related to the proportion that will actually choose a fishing strategy for the particular expected catch value. For a given expected catch value a higher proportion of optimistic fishermen will choose to fish than will pessimistic.

In the fishing sector of the model the actual catch is determined for each species in each subarea. The catch in each area depends upon the amount of fishing gear and the amount of fish in the area. The abundance of fish is the function of the number of fish in the fishery, their migration patterns, and the size of catch in the other subareas. Provision is made to reduce the effectiveness of fishing gear as gear concentration increases in a particular area, because of competition among the various units of mobile gear.

In the fishery management sector of the model the management agency acts to open or close each fishery area; it has no direct control over gear movement between areas. Before the season opens a basic regulatory policy is chosen. This policy is modified as the season progresses. Comparisons of estimates of actual escapement are made with the interseasonal analysis which determines the desired escapement of each species. Noise and time lags are introduced into the flow of information about actual escapement. As the season progresses the forecast of run size is improved, but as noted earlier, the proportion of the total run under management control is continuously decreasing. The model also provides for pressure on the management agency for permission to fish. This pressure is used to modify strict adherence to regular decision rules.

In the initial formulation of the model, parameters were chosen which called for the following decision rules:

1) Desired escapement equal to estimated escapement: all areas open.

2) Estimated escapement less than desired escapement but greater than 90 percent of desired escapement: fishing area 1 closed.

3) Estimated escapement less than 90 percent of desired escapement: all fishing areas closed.

Provision is made in the model to alter operations without restructuring. By changing constants and taking advantage of DYNAMO's rerun facility, characteristics of the run, number of species, nature of migration through the three areas, restrictions on gear movement, quality and timing of information, and management decision-making rules can all be changed.

The model has proved useful in providing a means to describe the dynamics of this type of system. It is planned to use this model as a basis for a man-machine simulation model which can be used by students and professionals to explore consequences of different management policies under varying conditions.

Prison Management System Model

As has been pointed out in the literature, the industrial dynamics approach to analysis of feedback system structure and dynamics lends itself to application to the study of organization change processes. These processes involve psychological and sociological variables in organization systems. The problems of gathering and quantifying data for these types of studies are more difficult than for studies involving modeling physical phenomena.

Much quantitative research into sociological and psychological variables has been done using sample surveys to identify conditions at a particular point in time. Less has been done with collecting data on organization change over time or with the study of complex causal relationships and feedback structures of organizations. One of the purposes of the model presented here is to illustrate how these variables may be represented in a simulation model and what the data requirements are. As an example, the table function in DYNAMO provides a very convenient way of specifying non-linear relationship between two variables. Using this table function it is not necessary to develop elaborate mathematical functions to describe variable interrelationships.

Several years ago a study was published which reported on the impact of change in the social system of a prison.[5] The situation observed was of the change from an authoritarian prison administration with a custodial goal to a new administration emphasizing the rehabilitation function. Barton and Anderson have used this case study as a basis to illustrate some aspects of applying systems analysis to such systems.[6] They illustrated how some of the interrelations in the system can be formulated into an arithmetic model of the social control system at work in this situation. However they did not have access to simulation techniques and the flexibility in modeling which they provide. Consequently their model included only linear relationships and did not explicitly include some of the complex time lags in the system.

The prison management system model presented here, the structure of which is shown in Figure 2, is built upon that work. As the model is still under development, it is planned to report more fully on it at a later time.

Five major groups which represent the structure of the system are portrayed in the model: (1) the top level administration of the prison centered around the warden; (2) the custodial staff which consists of the guards and their officers; (3) the treatment staff consisting of the supervisors of the rehabilitation workshops and the prison psychiatrist; (4) an elite group of prisoners who had certain privileges and power in the system; and (5) the rest of the inmates of the prison.

Central to the operation of this system is communication between the various groups and control exercised over this communication. Space does not permit developing all these interactions in detail, but the basic structure of influence is depicted in the flow diagram of the model (Figure 2).

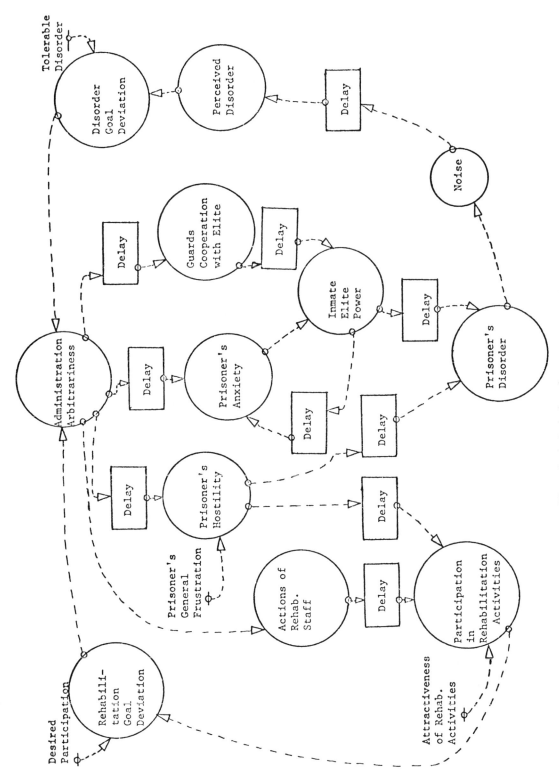

Figure 2   Authoritarian prison management system

Actions of the administration are influenced by the relative weighting it gives to disorder and participation. In the custodial-oriented administration high emphasis is placed upon keeping disorder within tolerable limits. Some consideration is given to the desired participation in rehabilitation activities, but very little weight is given to it. The actions of the administration, which for lack of a better term we have referred as the administration's arbitrariness, combined to perpetuate the system of interaction. This arbitrary administrative behavior was characterized by little communication between the administration and the inmates and between the custodial staff and the inmates. It was seen to be unpredictable and arbitrary in allocation of rewards and punishment. This served to maintain a high level of hostility on the part of the prisoners and a good deal of anxiety.

The anxiety strengthened the power of the inmate elite group, which power they exercised because of the custodial staff's desire to keep disorder at very low level. The guards cooperated to maintain the privileged position of this group through sanctions and willingness to ignore minor rule infractions. A positive feedback loop exists in the system at this point. The inmate elite group was able to use some of its power to hold down the rate of disorder which gave them something to offer the custodial staff who in turn continued to maintain them in their privileged position. Consequently while the level of hostility was high, the power exercised by the inmate elite group was sufficient to keep the level of disorder within tolerable limits.

On the other hand the high level of hostility and the lack of support of the rehabilitation staff by the administration combined to keep down the degree of participation in rehabilitation activities. Information about this participation and the level of disorder is fed back to the administration.

One of the most important aspects of this system is the set of time lags or delays which exist in the various channels. The length of total delays in the chain going from administration to custodial staff cooperation to inmate elite power to prisoners' disorder is much shorter than the delays affecting hostility of the prisoners. Also there appeared to be a long time lag leading to changes in participation in rehabilitation activities.

Consider the impact of these time lags on the change in administration activities. A sudden reduction in arbitrariness would have the effect of reducing the power exercised by the inmate elite group and reducing prisoners' hostility, which should result in an increase in participation in rehabilitation activities at a continued low level of disorder. However the short time lag required to undercut the power of the inmate elite group relative to that required to reduce hostilities works to stimulate a sudden and rather dramatic rise in the level of disorder.

This situation is depicted in Figure 3 which represents a run of the simulation model in which the information feedback to the prison administration has been eliminated. Observe that following the reduction in administration arbitrariness, the power of the inmate elite group drops away much more rapidly than does hostility. This results in a rather dramatic rise in disorders in the prison. In the situation studied by McCleery, a situation similar to this did ensue when a new prison warden took over and set about to try to increase participation in rehabilitation activities. He opened

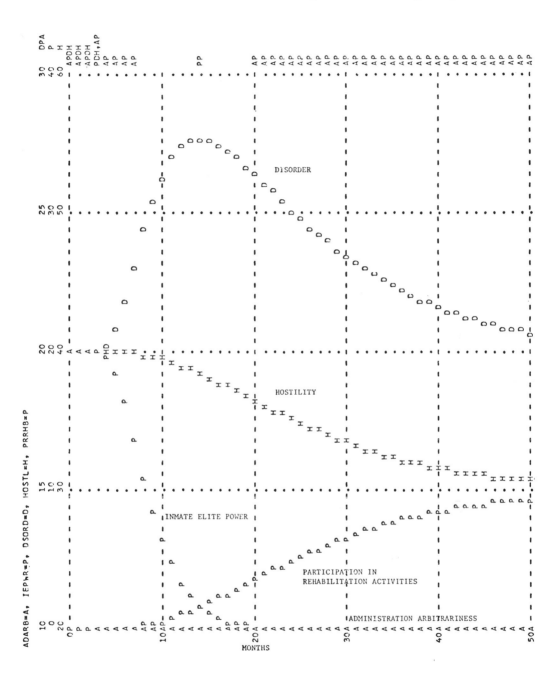

Figure 3   Response of prison system to a reduction in arbitrariness

direct communication channels with the prisoners and took other actions designed to reduce arbitrariness. This had the effect of undercutting the informal control system which had worked to maintain the system in equilibrium and to keep the rate of disorder low. A result of undercutting the informal control mechanism and reducing the power of the inmate elite group more rapidly than hostility was reduced was a rise in disorder which culminated in a riot.

In order to maintain low levels of disorder it is necessary to maintain the existing set of policies, but this is done at the expense of participation in rehabilitation activities. The study done by McCleery and the results of this simulation model point out the necessity of recognizing time lags in the system and recognizing the need for careful structural change if the prison administrator wishes to increase prisoner participation in the rehabilitation program.

In the absence of physical units of measure, arbitrary scales have been used in this model which are intended to represent the nature of relationships and not specific physical units. Future work by sociologists may develop scales for measuring certain of these phenomena which would be very useful in models such as this.

Notes

1. Readers are referred to the following three works for a description of industrial dynamics and the DYNAMO simulation language: Jay W. Forrester, *Industrial Dynamics* (Cambridge, Mass.: The MIT Press, 1961); Alexander L. Pugh III, *DYNAMO User's Manual* 2nd ed., (Cambridge, Mass.: The MIT Press, 1963); and Robert C. Meier, William T. Newell, and Harold L. Pazer, *Simulation in Business and Economics* (Englewood Cliffs, N.J.: Prentice-Hall, Inc., 1969), chap. 3, "Industrial Dynamics and Large System Simulation."

2. G. J. Paulik and J. W. Greenough, "Management Analysis for a Salmon Resource System" in *Systems Analysis in Ecology*, Kenneth E. F. Watt, ed. (New York: Academic Press, Inc., 1966), chap. 9.

3. Joseph W. Greenough, Jr., "Simulation Model of a Hypothetical Intraseasonal Gantlet Fishery", unpublished MS thesis (Seattle: University of Washington, 1967).

4. Robert C. Meier, William T. Newell, and Harold L. Pazer, *Simulation in Business and Economics* (Englewood Cliffs, N.J.: Prentice-Hall, Inc., 1969), p. 106.

5. Richard Mc Cleery, *Policy Change in Prison Management* (East Lansing: Michigan State University, Governmental Research Bureau, 1957).

6. Allen H. Barton and Bo Anderson, "Change in an Organizational System: Formalization of a Quantitative Study", in Amiti Etzioni, ed., *A Sociological Reader on Complex Organizations* (New York: Holt Rinehart and Winston, Inc., 1969).

Appendix A:
Equations for the
Production-Distribution Model
Edited by Edward B. Roberts

The Chapter 2 model of the production-distribution system embodies three main sectors, representing the retailers, distributors, and factory-and-factory warehouse of a mature industry. The system is sufficiently general to represent many industrial situations, but decision functions and parameters have been selected to apply particularly to the manufacture and distribution of consumer durables, such as household electrical appliances. The flows included in the model are materials and orders, and those information flows needed to support the material and order rate decisions.

Equations for the Retail Sector

Customer orders enter the retail sector and add to the pool of unfilled orders awaiting shipment. The equation for unfilled orders is a simple level equation, as explained in Chapter 1, adding orders received and subtracting orders shipped. The initial condition of the unfilled order level is equal to the average order rate times the delay that these orders would await shipment, on average. This average delay has two components, a minimum handling time and an average delay due to out-of-stock conditions.

$$\text{UOR.K} = \text{UOR.J} + (\text{DT})(\text{RRR.JK} - \text{SSR.JK}) \qquad \text{1,L}$$
$$\text{UOR} = (\text{RSR})(\text{DHR} + \text{DUR}) \qquad \text{2,N}$$

UOR—Unfilled Orders at Retail (units)
DT—Delta Time, the time interval between calculations of
    the equations (weeks)
RRR—Requisitions (orders) Received at Retail (units/week)
SSR—Shipments Sent from Retail (units/week)
RSR—Requisitions Smoothed at Retail, i.e., average sales
    (units/week)

The equations presented here are drawn by the Editor from Chapter 15 of J. W. Forrester's *Industrial Dynamics* (Cambridge: M.I.T. Press, 1961). For more complete justification of the formulations, the reader should refer to that text. The equations are nearly similar to those used to develop the results shown in Chapter 2 of this volume.

DHR—Delay due to minimum Handling time required at Retail (weeks)

DUR—average Delay in Unfilled orders at Retail caused by out-of-stock items when inventory is "normal" (weeks)

The customer orders entering the retail sector are averaged, formally or implicitly, to become the basis for determination of target inventory and other retail management concepts. Equation 3 represents the average as a first-order exponential smoothing of RRR over the time-period DRR, which is taken as 8 weeks. The average is set initially equal to customer orders.

$$RSR.K = RSR.J + (DT)(1/DRR)(RRR.JK - RSR.J) \qquad\qquad 3,L^{*}$$
$$RSR = RRR \qquad\qquad 4,N$$
$$DRR = 8$$

RSR—Requisitions Smoothed at Retail (units/week)

DRR—Delay in smoothing Requisitions at Retail, the smoothing
time constant (weeks)

RRR—Requisitions Received at Retail (units/week)

With average sales known, we can now calculate desired inventory for the retail sector as a simple multiple of average sales. About two months' equivalent of sales rate is a reasonable target inventory for a retailer. Average sales also become the basis for computing the desired amount of orders that retailers would like in their supply pipeline, taking into account the several delays that orders will encounter. Finally, the average sales variable permits determination of the normal level of unfilled orders, which concept recognizes the normal delays in processing customer shipments.

$$IDR.K = (AIR)(RSR.K) \qquad\qquad 5,A$$
$$AIR = 8$$
$$LDR.K = (RSR.K)(DCR + DMR + DFD.K + DTR) \qquad\qquad 6,A$$
$$UNR.K = (RSR.K)(DHR + DUR) \qquad\qquad 7,A$$

IDR—Inventory Desired at Retail (units)

AIR—proportionality constAnt between Inventory and average
sales at Retail (weeks)

RSR—Requisitions Smoothed at Retail (units/week)

LDR—pipeLine orders Desired (necessary) in transit to supply
Retail (units)

DCR—Delay in Clerical order processing at Retail (weeks)

DMR—Delay in order Mailing from Retail (weeks)

DFD—Delay (variable) in Filling orders at the Distributor (weeks)

DTR—Delay in Transportation of goods to Retail (weeks)

UNR—Unfilled Normal level of orders at Retail (units)

DHR—Delay in Handling time at Retail (weeks)

DUR—Delay in Unfilled orders at Retail (weeks)

---

*DYNAMO II permits the same equation to be written using the SMOOTH macro: RSR.K = SMOOTH(RRR.JK,DRR). For further details see A. L. Pugh III, *DYNAMO II User's Manual*, 4th edition (Cambridge: M.I.T. Press, 1973).

In contrast with these ''desired'' values, the ''actual'' values indicate the real condition of inventory, orders in the supply pipeline, and unfilled orders (previously defined as Equation 1,L). Inventory requires a simple accounting of goods received and shipped. Initially it is set equal to desired inventory. The pipeline of orders merely sums the several stages through which retailer purchases pass, between the retailer decision and the eventual receipt of goods from the distributors.

$$\text{IAR.K} = \text{IAR.J} + (\text{DT})(\text{SRR.JK} - \text{SSR.JK}) \qquad\qquad\qquad 8,\text{L}$$
$$\text{IAR} = \text{IDR} \qquad\qquad\qquad 9,\text{N}$$
$$\text{LAR.K} = \text{CPR.K} + \text{PMR.K} + \text{UOD.K} + \text{MTR.K} \qquad\qquad 10,\text{A}$$

IAR—Inventory Actual at Retail (units)
SRR—Shipments Received at Retail (units/week)
SSR—Shipment Sent from Retail (units/week)
IDR—Inventory Desired at Retail (units)
LAR—pipeLine orders Actually in transit to Retail (units)
CPR—Clerical in Process orders at Retail (units)
PMR—Purchase orders in Mail from Retail (units)
UOD—Unfilled Orders at Distributor (units)
MTR—Material in Transit to Retail (units)

Based on information now defined the retailer purchase decision can be made. This equation is not an attempt at creating an ''optimal'' decision; rather, it seeks to reflect reasonable and representative behavior by retailers. The amount of goods purchased is set equal to the orders received from customers plus an attempt to adjust gradually (over DIR weeks) for any perceived imbalance between desired and actual inventory, pipeline, and unfilled orders.

$$\text{PDR.KL} = \text{RRR.JK} + (1/\text{DIR})((\text{IDR.K} - \text{IAR.K}) + (\text{LDR.K} - \text{LAR.K}) +$$
$$(\text{UOR.K} - \text{UNR.K})) \qquad\qquad 11,\text{R}$$
$$\text{DIR} = 4$$

PDR—Purchasing rate Decision at Retail (units/week)
RRR—Requisitions Received at Retail (units/week)
DIR—Delay in Inventory (and pipeline) adjustment at Retail (weeks)
IDR—Inventory Desired at Retail (units)
IAR—Inventory Actual at Retail (units)
LDR—pipeLine orders Desired in transit to supply Retail (units)
LAR—pipeLine orders Actually in transit to Retail (units)
UOR—Unfilled Orders at Retail (units)
UNR—Unfilled Normal level of orders at Retail (units)

Once the purchasing decision has been made it must go through an internal clerical processing delay and an external mail delay before the purchases show up as requisitions received by the distributor. Each of these two delays has been represented as a third-order exponential delay of the sort explained in Chapter 1.

$$\text{CPR.K} = \text{CPR.J} + (\text{DT})(\text{PDR.JK} - \text{PSR.JK}) \qquad\qquad 12,\text{L}$$
$$\text{CPR} = (\text{DCR})(\text{RRR}) \qquad\qquad 13,\text{N}$$

$$PSR.KL = DELAY3(PDR.JK,DCR) \qquad\qquad 14,R$$
$$DCR = 3$$
$$PMR.K = PMR.J + (DT)(PSR.JK - RRD.JK) \qquad 15,L$$
$$PMR = (DMR)(RRR) \qquad\qquad 16,N$$
$$RRD.KL = DELAY3(PSR.JK,DMR) \qquad\qquad 17,R$$
$$DMR = 0.5$$

CPR—Clerical in-Process orders at Retail (units)
PDR—Purchasing rate Decision at Retail (units/week)
PSR—Purchase orders Sent from Retail (units/week)
DCR—Delay in Clerical order processing at Retail (weeks)
RRR—Requisitions Received at Retail (units/week)
DELAY3—DYNAMO functional notation for a third-order exponential delay
PMR—Purchase orders in Mail from Retail (units)
RRD—Requisitions Received at Distributor (units/week)
DMR—Delay in Mail from Retail to distributor (weeks)

As the goods are shipped from the distributor to the retailer they pass through a transportation stage that is also represented as a third-order delay.

$$MTR.K = MTR.J + (DT)(SSD.JK - SRR.JK) \qquad 18,L$$
$$MTR = (DTR)(RRR) \qquad\qquad 19,N$$
$$SRR.KL = DELAY3(SSD.JK,DTR) \qquad\qquad 20,R$$
$$DTR = 1.0$$

MTR—Material in Transit to Retail (units)
SSD—Shipments Sent from Distributor (units/week)
SRR—Shipments Received at Retail (units/week)
DTR—Delay in Transportation of goods to Retail (weeks)
RRR—Requisitions Received at Retail (units/week)

The final equations needed for the retailer sector are those that compute the rate of shipping goods from the retail inventory to the customer, in response to customer orders. The shipments are determined by first calculating those that would ordinarily be shipped, given the order-filling delay, and then comparing this amount with the rate that would deplete the retail inventory. Obviously, it is the lesser of these possible rates that will actually be shipped. Discussion of the order-filling delay (DFR) follows this equation cluster.

$$STR.K = UOR.K/DFR.K \qquad\qquad 21,A$$
$$NIR.K = IAR.K/DT \qquad\qquad 22,A$$
$$SSR.KL = MIN(STR.K,NIR.K) \qquad\qquad 23,R$$

STR—Shipping rate to be Tried at Retail (units/week)
UOR—Unfilled Orders at Retail (units)
DFR—Delay in Filling orders at Retail (weeks)
NIR—Negative Inventory limit rate at Retail (units/week)
IAR—Inventory Actual at Retail (units)

DT—Delta Time, solution time interval (weeks)
SSR—Shipments Sent from Retail (units/week)
MIN—DYNAMO functional notation for the lesser of two arguments

The delay in filling orders is some minimum for routine order processing plus a variable time that depends on how long it takes to fill the order due to out-of-stock conditions. That variable delay shrinks toward zero if actual inventory is very large compared to what is needed. Alternately, the variable portion of the delay grows significantly if inventory is low and many out-of-stock situations are encountered.

$$\text{DFR.K} = \text{DHR} + (\text{DUR})(\text{IDR.K/IAR.K}) \qquad\qquad 24,\text{A}^*$$
DHR = 1.0
DUR = 0.4
DFR—Delay in Filling orders at Retail (weeks)
DHR—Delay in Handling time at Retail (weeks)
DUR—Delay in Unfilled orders at Retail (weeks)
IDR—Inventory Desired at Retail (units)
IAR—Inventory Actual at Retail (units)

Equations for the Distributor Sector

The distributor sector of the model parallels exactly the retail sector. Equations 25–48 are comparable to Equations 1–24 just defined, and no further explanations will be provided.

UOD.K = UOD.J + (DT)(RRD.JK−SSD.JK)	25,L
UOD = (RSD)(DHD+DUD)	26,N
RSD.K = RSD.J + (DT)(1/DRD)(RRD.JK−RSD.J)	27,L
RSD = RRD	28,N
DRD = 8	
IDD.K = (AID)(RSD.K)	29,A
AID = 6	
LDD.K = (RSD.K)(DCD+DMD+DFF.K+DTD)	30,A
UND.K = (RSD.K)(DHD+DUD)	31,A
IAD.K = IAD.J + (DT)(SRD.JK −SSD.JK)	32,L
IAD = IDD	33,N
LAD.K = CPD.K + PMD.K + UOF.K + MTD.K	34,A
PDD.KL = RRD.JK + (1/DID)((IDD.K−IAD.K) + (LDD.K−LAD.K) + (UOD.K−UND.K))	35,R
DID = 4	
CPD.K = CPD.J + (DT)(PDD.JK−PSD.JK)	36,L
CPD = (DCD)(RRD)	37,N
PSD.KL = DELAY3(PDD.JK,DCD)	38,R
DCD = 2	
PMD.K = PMD.J + (DT)(PSD.JK − RRF.JK)	39,L

*Present versions of DYNAMO would permit formulating the same equation as a TABLE function with IDR.K/IAR.K as the input.

$$PMD = (DMD)(RRD) \qquad 40,N$$
$$RRF.KL = DELAY3(PSD.JK,DMD) \qquad 41,R$$
$$DMD = 0.5$$
$$MTD.K = MTD.J + (DT)(SSF.JK - SRD.JK) \qquad 42,L$$
$$MTD = (DTD)(RRD) \qquad 43,N$$
$$SRD.KL = DELAY3(SSF.JK,DTD) \qquad 44,R$$
$$DTD = 2.0$$
$$STD.K = UOD.K/DFD.K \qquad 45,A$$
$$NID.K = IAD.K/DT \qquad 46,A$$
$$SSD.KL = MIN(STD.K,NID.K) \qquad 47,R$$
$$DFD.K = DHD + (DUD)(IDD.K/IAD.K) \qquad 48,A$$
$$DHD = 1.0$$
$$DUD = 0.6$$

Equations for the Factory Sector

Many of the order-filling activities at the factory level of the model are represented as similar to those at retail and at the distributor. Equations 49–53 parallel Equations 1–5 and 25–29 and need no further explanation.

$$UOF.K = UOF.J + (DT)(RRF.JK - SSF.JK) \qquad 49,L$$
$$UOF = (RSF)(DHF+DUF) \qquad 50,N$$
$$RSF.K = RSF.J + (DT)(1/DRF)(RRF.JK - RSF.J) \qquad 51,L$$
$$RSF = RRF \qquad 52,N$$
$$DRF = 8$$
$$IDF.K = (AIF)(RSF.K) \qquad 53,A$$
$$AIF = 4$$

The factory warehouse is assumed to be adjacent to the factory. Therefore, the factory sector does not include mail or transportation delays between the factory and the warehouse. Furthermore, the pipeline delay now must reflect the factory's production lead-time.

$$LDF.K = (RSF.K)(DCF+DPF) \qquad 54,A$$

LDF—pipeLine orders Desired in transit through Factory (units)
RSF—Requisitions Smoothed at Factory (units/week)
DCF—Delay in Clerical processing of manufacturing orders at
     the Factory (weeks)
DPF—Delay in Production lead time at Factory (weeks)

Equations 55–57 parallel Equations 7–9 and 31–33, and need no further explanation.

$$UNF.K = (RSF.K)(DHF+DUF) \qquad 55,A$$
$$IAF.K = IAF.J + (DT)(SRF.JK - SSF.JK) \qquad 56,L$$
$$IAF = IDF \qquad 57,N$$

The actual pipeline order variable now reflects the simpler factory delay conditions.

LAF.K = CPF.K + OPF.K   58,A
LAF—pipeLine orders Actual in transit through Factory (units)
CPF—Clerical in-Process manufacturing orders at Factory (units)
OPF—Orders in Production at Factory (units)

The manufacturing rate decision is represented as being equivalent in form to the retail and distributor purchasing decisions. However, account is taken of the possibility that factory capacity may limit the actual production orders. Capacity is initially set so high as to guarantee no constraint.

MWF.K = RRF.JK + (1/DIF)((IDF.K−IAF.K) + (LDF.K− LAF.K) +
        (UOF.K− UNF.K))   59,A
MDF.KL = MIN(MWF.K,ALF)   60,R
DIF = 4
ALF = (1000)(RRI)
MWF—Manufacturing rate Wanted at Factory (units/week)
RRF—Requisitions Received at Factory (units/week)
DIF—Delay in Inventory adjustment at Factory (weeks)
IDF—Inventory Desired at Factory (units)
IAF—Inventory Actual at Factory (units)
LDF—pipeLine orders Desired in transit through Factory (units)
LAF—pipeLine orders Actual in transit through Factory (units)
UOF—Unfilled Orders at Factory (units)
UNF—Unfilled orders, Normal, at Factory (units)
MDF—Manufacturing rate Decision at Factory (units/week)
ALF—constAnt specifying manufacturing capacity Limit at Factory (units/week)

The manufacturing decision goes through a clerical delay before becoming a set of manufacturing orders. These in turn enter the actual production process which is represented as a third-order exponential delay that transforms the orders into shipments delivered into the factory inventory.

CPF.K = CPF.J + (DT)(MDF.JK−MOF.JK)   61,L
CPF = (DCF)(RRF)   62,N
MOF.KL = DELAY3(MDF.JK,DCF)   63,R
DCF = 1
OPF.K = OPF.J + (DT)(MOF.JK−SRF.JK)   64,L
OPF = (DPF)(RRF)   65,N
SRF.KL = DELAY3(MOF.JK,DPF)   66,R
DPF = 6.0
CPF—Clerical in-Process manufacturing orders at Factory (units)
MDF—Manufacturing rate Decision at Factory (units/week)
MOF—Manufacturing Orders into Factory (units/week)

DCF—Delay in Clerical processing at Factory (weeks)
RRF—Requisitions Received at Factory (units/week)
OPF—Orders in Production at Factory (units)
SRF—Shipments Received at Factory inventory (manufacturing output) (units/week)
DPF—Delay in Production lead time at Factory (weeks)

The shipping rate and delivery delay equations at the factory level parallel those at retail and distributor. Equations 67–70 duplicate the earlier Equations 21–24 and 45–48 and need no further explanation.

STF.K = UOF.K/DFF.K	67,A
NIF.K = IAF.K/DT	68,A
SSF.KL = MIN(STF.K,NIF.K)	69,R
DFF.K = DHF + (DUF)(IDF.K/IAF.K)	70,A
DHF = 1.0	
DUF = 1.0	

Input Equations

The basic input to the production-distribution system model is the flow of customer orders into the retail sector. In the actual model this equation, RRR, was set up so as to provide opportunities for testing the system's response to step, sine wave, random, and other changes in retail sales, as illustrated in the discussions of Chapter 2. Here we shall only indicate that intended input variability.

RRR.KL = test inputs	71,R
RRR = RRI	72,N
RRI = 1000	
RRR—Requisitions Received at Retail (units/week)	
RRI—Retail Requisitions, Initial rate, constant (units/week)	

Appendix B:
Equations for the Precision Case
Ole C. Nord

This appendix presents in detail the equations which describe the system of interrelationships underlying the fluctuating workload of the Precision Company, discussed in Chapter 10 of this volume. This system is divided into two sectors, an internal Precision Company sector and a customer sector. The latter part of the appendix presents in detail the equations for the improved policies for Precision.

Precision Company Sector

This section formulates Precision's response to incoming orders. It describes how production and employment levels are determined and how efforts for generating new business are allocated.

The first equation to be written defines the backlog of orders at Precision. An order from the customer stays in the backlog as an unfilled order until it is produced and shipped to the customer. At Precision, finished goods waiting to be shipped are kept to a minimum, and we assume that the shipment rate equals the rate at which production is finished. For the backlog we write:

$$BL.K = BL.J + (DT)(OR.JK - PFR.JK) \qquad 1, L$$
$$BL = (OR)(NDD) \qquad 2, N$$

BL	—BackLog (units)
OR	—Order Rate (units/week)
PFR	—Production Finishing Rate (units/week)
DT	—Delta Time (weeks) - the solution interval for the system of equations
NDD	—Normal Delivery Delay (weeks)

All levels require initial values. In this model initial conditions are based upon the assumption that all variables are initially in a steady-state relationship. For the initial value of the backlog, we have indicated in Equation 2 that the backlog contains the number of orders usually received during the normal delivery delay period.

Permission to reprint has been granted by Ole C. Nord, who authored the original version of this model when he was a Research Assistant at M.I.T. In original form, this appendix appeared as staff memos D-583-2 of the M.I.T. Industrial Dynamics Research Group, October 22, 1963, and D-691, dated January 20, 1964. They have been edited to be consistent with the model and results described in Chapter 10.

The time lapse before orders can be filled is determined by the size of the order backlog relative to the expected production rate. This ratio serves as the basis for the delivery delay estimate supplied to the customer. The expected production rate is taken to be equal to the recent average production rate. The initial delivery delay is set equal to the company's normal delay, which in turn is assumed as ten weeks.

$$DD.K = \frac{BL.K}{APFR.K}$$ 3, A

$$DD = NDD$$ 4, N

$$NDD = 10$$ 5, C

DD   — Delivery Delay (weeks)
BL   — BackLog (units)
APFR — Average Production Finishing Rate (units/week)
NDD — Normal Delivery Delay (weeks)

The average production finishing rate is a short-term average of the production finishing rate. We can write it as a first-order exponential smoothing equation, using DYNAMO's SMOOTH function.

$$APFR.K = SMOOTH (PFR.JK, DAPFR)$$ 6, L

$$APFR = PFR$$ 7, N

$$DAPFR = 4$$ 8, C

APFR   — Average Production Finishing Rate (units/week)
SMOOTH   — DYNAMO notation for a first-order
               exponential averaging function
PFR   — Production Finishing Rate (units/week)
DAPFR   — Delay in Averaging Production
               Finishing Rate (weeks)

Written out fully the equation for APFR would be:

$$APFR.K = APFR.J + (DT)(1/DAPFR)(PFR.JK - APFR.J)$$ L

The delivery delay estimate also indicates to management how well demand is being met. A long delay results from production not keeping up with demand; therefore, more production is required. A short delay indicates that demand is slack, and more effort is needed to increase demand. Equation 3 expresses the current delivery delay as estimated by Precision. It is unreasonable to assume that management is responding to this value where hiring or bidding is concerned. Instead, it is likely that management will be concerned with an average delivery delay, perceived over some longer period of time.

$$ADD.K = SMOOTH (DD.K, DADD)$$ 9, L

$$ADD = DD$$ 10, N

$$DADD = 6$$ 11, C

ADD   — Average Delivery Delay (weeks)
DD   — Delivery Delay (weeks)
DADD   — Delay in Averaging Delivery Delay (weeks)

Formulated next are the hiring and firing policies of Precision. As suggested above, the average delivery delay influences hiring and firing, but the actual action may take some time. The average delivery delay has therefore been delayed again to account for delays involved in decisions on hiring and firing employees.

ADIHF.K = SMOOTH (ADD.K,DHF)   12, L
ADIHF = ADD   13, N
DHF = 4   14, C
ADIHF   — Average Delivery delay Influencing
             Hiring and Firing (weeks)
ADD   — Average Delivery Delay (weeks)
DHF   — Delay for Hiring and Firing decisions (weeks)

A high delivery delay indicates to management that production abilities are inadequate and should be increased by hiring more men. We assume that the maximum number of new people hired per week is equal to 2 percent of the existing labor force, however big the delivery delay becomes. We also assume that the hiring rate is zero for low delivery delay. This suggests a relationship between delivery delay and fractional increase in work force, as shown in Figure 1.

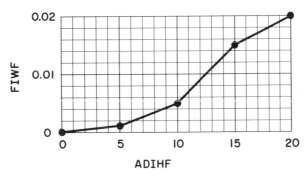

Figure 1   Fractional increase in work force vs. average delivery delay

FIWF.K = TABHL(TBFIW,ADIHF.K,0,20,5)   15, A
TBFIW* = 0/0.001/0.005/0.015/.02   16, C
FIWF   — Fractional Increase in Work Force (1/weeks)
ADIHF   — Average Delivery delay Influencing
             Hiring and Firing (weeks)
TBFIW   — TaBle for Fractional Increase in Work Force
TABHL   — DYNAMO notation for curve representation
             by means of a data table

The actual hiring rate is therefore equal to the fractional increase multiplied by the actual work force at Precision.

WH.KL = (FIWF.K)(WF.K)   17, R
WH   —Workers Hired (men/week)
FIWF   —Fractional Increase in Work Force (1/weeks)
WF   —Work Force (men)

The newly hired workers do not become productive at once. First, they must be trained. This model assumes a constant average training delay. For simplicity it also assumes that no workers leave the company during the training period. The number of workers in training is written as a level equation with newly hired workers flowing in and newly trained workers flowing out.

NTW.KL = DELAY3(WH.JK,DTRN)   18, R
DTRN = 6   19, C
WIT.K = WIT.J + (DT)(WH.JK−NTW.JK)   20, L
WIT = 3   21, N
NTW   —Newly Trained Workers (men/week)
WH   —Workers Hired (men/week)
DTRN   —Delay in TRaiNing (weeks)
WIT   —Workers In Training (men)
DELAY3   —DYNAMO notation for a third-order
            exponential delay

The trained work force is formulated as a regular level equation with an inflow of newly trained workers and an outflow of workers leaving Precision, with an initial pool of 100 trained employees.

TWF.K = TWF.J + (DT)(NTW.JK−WL.JK)   22, L
TWF = 100   23, N
TWF   —Trained Work Force (men)
NTW   —Newly Trained Workers (men/week)
WL   —Workers Leaving (men/week)

The total employed work force equals the sum of trained workers and the workers in training.

WF.K = TWF.K + WIT.K   24, A
WF   —Work Force (men)
TWF   —Trained Work Force (men)
WIT   —Workers In Training (men)

We now represent the rate at which workers leave Precision. This rate comprises both the firing decision at the company and the natural attrition of workers to other jobs or retirement. If the delivery delay is low, more people leave due to both firing and the insecurity of jobs. As the delivery delay increases, less people leave. This relationship is shown in Figure 2.

FDWF.K = TABHL(TBFDW,ADIHF.K,0,20,5)   25, A
TBFDW* = 0.02/0.015/0.005/0.001/0.001   26, C

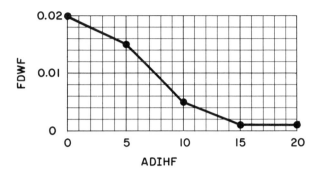

Figure 2 Fractional decrease in work force vs. average delivery delay

FDWF — Fractional Decrease in Work Force (1/weeks)
ADIHF — Average Delivery delay Influencing
Hiring and Firing (weeks)
TBFDW — TaBle for Fractional Decrease in Work force

The actual leaving rate is therefore equal to the fractional decrease multiplied by the work force.

$$WL.KL = (FDWF.K)(WF.K) \qquad \text{27, R}$$

WL — Workers Leaving (men/week)
FDWF — Fractional Decrease in Work Force (1/weeks)
WF — Work Force (men)

The production starting rate depends upon the trained work force and the productivity of each worker, including his overtime effort.

$$PSR.KL = (TWF.K)(PROD.K) \qquad \text{28, R}$$

PSR — Production Starting Rate (units/week)
TWF — Trained Work Force (men)
PROD — PRODuctivity ((units/week)/man)

We assume that an average time of four weeks is required for the production process.

$$PFR.KL = DELAY3 (PSR.JK, DPROD) \qquad \text{29, R}$$
$$DPROD = 4 \qquad \text{30, C}$$

PFR — Production Finishing Rate (units/week)
PSR — Production Starting Rate (units/week)
DPROD — Delay in PRODuction (weeks)

Two factors influence the production starting rate (Eq. 28): the work force and the productivity factor. By productivity we mean the weekly production of each worker, a factor that can vary considerably by applying overtime. For a low delivery delay management will tend to allocate workers to clean up and repair work so that basic productivity will be lower. Basic productivity, without inclusion of the overtime effect, has therefore been represented as a function of average delivery delay estimates, as shown in Figure 3, and indicates the possibility of some increased output due to workload pressure.

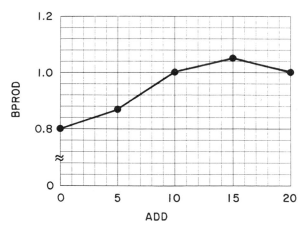

Figure 3 Basic productivity vs. delivery delay

PROD.K = BPROD.K + OPROD.K   31, A
BPROD.K = TABHL (TBPRO, ADD.K, 0, 20,5)   32, A
TBPRO* = 0.8/.87/1.0/1.05/1.0   33, C
PROD   — PRODuctivity ((units/week)/man)
BPROD   — Basic PRODuctivity ((units/week)/man)
OPROD   — Overtime PRODuctivity ((units/week)/man)
ADD   — Average Delivery Delay (weeks)
TBPRO   — Table for Basic PROductivity

Overtime too has been represented as dependent upon average delivery delay, with overtime being used increasingly as the delay rises above normal, as shown in Figure 4.

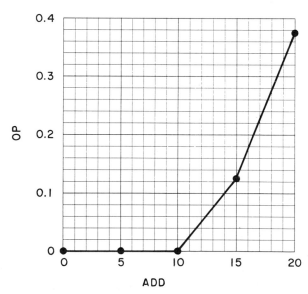

Figure 4 Overtime percentage vs. delivery delay

OP.K = TABHL (TBOP,ADD.K,0,20,5)   34, A
TBOP* = 0/0/0/.125/.375   35, C
OP   — Overtime Percentage (dimensionless)
ADD   — Average Delivery Delay (weeks)
TBOP   — TaBle for Overtime Percentage

    Overtime activities are less productive than regular production. This is caused by fatigue, incomplete work crews, etc. Figure 5 reflects the diminishing productivity contribution of overtime work.

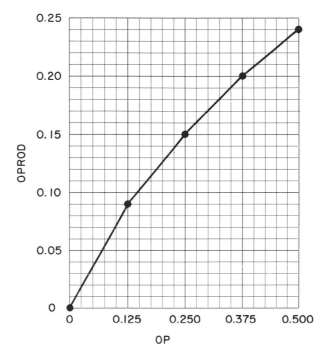

Figure 5   Overtime productivity vs. overtime percentage

OPROD.K = TABHL (TOPRO,OP.K,0,.50,.125)   36, A
TOPRO* = 0/0.09/0.15/0.20/0.24   37, C
OPROD — Overtime PRODuctivity ((units/week)/man)
OP   — Overtime Percentage (dimensionless)
TOPRO — Table for Overtime PROductivity

    For use later in calculating Precision's profitability, we calculate the number of overtime hours worked each week, assuming a 40 hour normal week.

OH.K = (NWHPW)(OP.K)(WF.K)   38, A
NWHPW = 40   39, C

OH   — Overtime Hours (man-hours/week)
NWHPW — Normal Work Hours Per Week (hours/week)
WF   — Work Force (men)
OP   — Overtime Percentage (dimensionless)

To complete the Precision sector of the model, we must describe management efforts toward generating new bids. Such management efforts are assumed to be dependent upon the average delivery delay. As delivery delay increases, management is required to spend most of its time straightening out production problems, and little effort is available for generation of new business. Some efforts are still spent in this direction, however, because a few people are specifically assigned to this function. Figure 6 shows the relationship between fraction of management efforts for bidding and the average delivery delay.

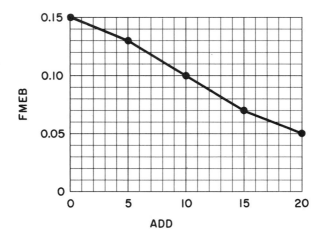

Figure 6   Fraction of management efforts on bids vs. delivery delay

FMEB.K = TABHL(TBFEB,ADD.K,0,20,5)   40, A
TBFEB* = .15/.13/.10/.07/.05   41, C
FMEB   — Fraction of Management Effort on
            Bidding (dimensionless)
ADD   — Average Delivery Delay (weeks)
TBFEB   — TaBle for Fraction of Effort on Bidding

The amount of effort on bidding is therefore equal to the total amount of managerial time multiplied by the fraction on bidding

MEB.K = (FMEB.K)(MT)   42, A
MT = 200   43, C
MEB   — Management Efforts on Bids (managerial hours/week)
MT   — Management Time (managerial hours/week)
FMEB   — Fraction of Management Efforts on
            Bidding (dimensionless)

Customer Sector

This section formulates the aggregate of customer responses to Precision's actions. The important linkages between Precision and its customers are the delivery delay estimates and the managerial efforts on the bids. Price and quality of the product are essentially constant and equal for all competitors, so they do not bear upon the dynamics of the interactions between the company and its customers. On the basis of delivery delay, management efforts, and time to evaluate bids, customers generate an order rate to Precision.

Customers do not respond immediately to changes in quoted delivery delay or bidding effort. Rather some average value of these quantities enters a customer's decision. We therefore formulate two equations providing average values for delivery delay and bidding efforts.

$$\text{ADDC.K} = \text{SMOOTH(DD.K,DADDC)} \qquad \text{44, L}$$
$$\text{ADDC} = \text{DD} \qquad \text{45, N}$$
$$\text{DADDC} = 20 \qquad \text{46, C}$$

ADDC   —Average Delivery Delay recognized by
            Customers (weeks)
DD   —Delivery Delay (weeks)
DADDC —Delay in Averaging Delivery Delay at Customer (weeks)

and

$$\text{AMEB.K} = \text{SMOOTH(MEB.K,DAMEB)} \qquad \text{47, L}$$
$$\text{AMEB} = \text{MEB} \qquad \text{48, N}$$
$$\text{DAMEB} = 4 \qquad \text{49, C}$$

AMEB   —Average Management Efforts on Bids
            (managerial hours/week)
MEB   —Management Efforts on Bids (managerial hours/week)
DAMEB —Delay in Averaging Management Efforts on Bids (weeks)

We now formulate an equation describing the generation of prospective bids, i.e., the bids that are accepted by the customer and eventually will become firm orders. The number of prospective bids for Precision can be viewed as a normal number of bids, identified here as the potential customer business, modified by the influence of delivery delay and bidding effort.

$$\text{PB.KL} = (\text{PCB.K})(\text{DDIB.K})(\text{MEIB.K}) \qquad \text{50, R}$$

PB   —Prospective Bids (units/week)
PCB   —Potential Customer Business (units/week)
DDIB   —Delivery Delay Influence on Bids (dimensionless)
MEIB   —Management Effort Influence on Bids (dimensionless)

The potential customer business is formulated as a constant that reflects potential customer business multiplied by a test function that will allow us to test the model's sensitivity to external disturbances.

PCB.K = (PCBB)(TEST.K)   51, A
PCBB = 100   52, C
PCB   — Potential Customer Business (units/week)
PCBB   — Potential Customer Business, Baseline (units/week)
TEST   — TEST (dimensionless)

The assumed influence of the average delivery delay recognized by the customer on the number of prospective bids is seen in Figure 7. For a low delivery delay, there is little influence. As the delivery delay increases, the customer expends more and more effort finding another supplier that can deliver the product faster than Precision. As far as this is possible, an increased delivery delay leads to fewer prospective bids for Precision. Since there may be certain product types that only Precision can supply, the curve in Figure 7 does not approach zero.

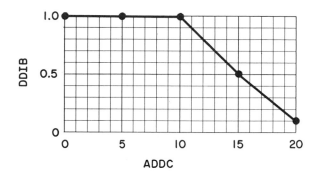

Figure 7   Delivery delay influence on bids vs. average delivery delay
recognized by customer

DDIB.K = TABHL(TBDD,ADDC.K,0,20,5)   53, A
TBDD* = 1/1/1/.50/.10   54, C
DDIB   — Delivery Delay Influence on Bids (dimensionless)
ADDC   — Average Delivery Delay recognized
          by Customer (weeks)
TBDD   — TaBle for Delivery Delay influence

We formulate the influence of management efforts on bids in a similar way. For very low effort few bids are accepted, and for a large amount of effort many bids are accepted. Both an upper and lower limit exist on the influence of management efforts.

MEIB.K = TABHL(TBMEI,AMEB.K,0,40,10)   55, A
TBMEI*= .25/.50/1.0/1.5/1.75   56, C
MEIB   — Management Effort Influence on Bids
          (dimensionless)

AMEB — Average Management Efforts on Bids
(managerial hours/week)
TBMEI — TaBle for Management Effort Influence

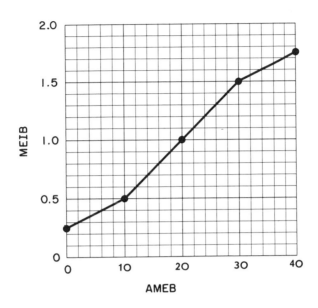

Figure 8 Management efforts influence on bids vs. average management efforts on bids

The prospective bids do not immediately result in an order rate to Precision. First a one- to two-month delay occurs in consideration of the bids prior to customer issuance of the orders. This can be written as a third-order delay.

OR.KL = DELAY3(PB.JK,DCB)   57, R
DCB = 6   58, C
OR   — Order Rate (units/week)
PB   — Prospective Bids (units/week)
DCB   — Delay in Consideration of Bids (weeks)

The order rate flows out of the pool of bids being considered by customers into the backlog at Precision (Equation 1, L).

BUCC.K = BUCC.J + (DT)(PB.JK-OR.JK)   59, L
BUCC = (OR)(DCB)   60, N
BUCC   — Bids Under Consideration by Customers (units)
PB   — Prospective Bids (units/week)
OR   — Order Rate (units/week)
DCB   — Delay in Consideration of Bids (weeks)

Test Inputs.   Remaining to be formulated is the test function TEST appearing in the equation for potential customer business.

TEST.K = 1 + STEPF.K + SINEF.K + NOISF.K   61, A
TEST   — TEST inputs (dimensionless)
STEPF   — STEP Function (dimensionless)
SINEF   — SINE Function (dimensionless)
NOISF   — NOISe Function (dimensionless)

The step change is set to occur at TIME equal to 5 weeks. Its amplitude is set equal to zero for the present.

STEPF.K = STEP(STH,5)   62, A
STH = 0   63, C
STEPF   — STEP Function (dimensionless)
STH   — STep Height (dimensionless)
STEP   — DYNAMO notation for step function

The sine function is formulated with zero amplitude and a period of 52 weeks.

SINEF.K = (AMP)SIN((2PI)(TIME.K)/PER)   64, A
AMP = 0   65, C
PER = 52   66, C
SINEF   — SINE Function (dimensionless)
AMP   — AMPlitude (dimensionless)
TIME   — TIME (weeks)
PER   — PERiod of sine wave (weeks)
SIN   — DYNAMO notation for sine function

The noise function allows us to test the model with random variations of order input. It is formulated with zero amplitude for the present.

NOISF.K = SAMPLE(SNOIS.K,ST,0)   67, A
SNOIS.K = (1)NORMRN(0,STD)   68, A
ST = 5   69, C
STD = 0   70, C
NOISF   — NOISe Function (dimensionless)
SNOIS   — Source of NOISe (dimensionless)
ST   — Sampling Time (weeks)
STD   — STandard Deviation (dimensionless)
SAMPLE   — DYNAMO notation for sampling a variable
NORMRN   — DYNAMO notation for normally-distributed random
                 number generator

As a final equation we calculate Precision's profitability, based on a net price per unit (materials and overhead excluded). Wage costs, accounting for the time-and-one-half bonus for overtime pay, are subtracted to generate the weekly profit rate.

PROF.KL = (NPPU)(PFR.JK) - (WGR)(WF.K)(NWHPW) - (WGR)(1.5)
        (OH.K)

NPPU = 250   72, C

WGR = 5   73, C

PROF   — PROFits ($/week)
NPPU   — Net Price Per Unit ($/unit)
PFR   — Production Finishing Rate (units/week)
WGR   — WaGe Rate ($/man-hour)
WF   — Work Force (men)
NWHPW   — Normal Work Hours Per Week (hours/week)
OH   — Overtime Hours (man-hours/week)

Improved Policies for Precision.   Chapter 10 in part presents a rationale for and the
results of designed improved policies for Precision. The corresponding equations·
are developed here.

The objective is the design of new policies which significantly increase the system
stability. We require of the new policies that they utilize only information available for
management. The information does not necessarily have to be accurate, but the system
must be insensitive to plausible errors in estimates. We also require that the new
policies improve behavior not only for a particular set of selected parameters, but that
they also improve behavior for a wide range of reasonable parameter values. The new
policies involve changes in both manpower and bidding policies.

Manpower Policy.   Instead of responding to delivery delay for hiring and firing, the
new policy responds to the order rate and the backlog. Information about order rate and
backlog is used to determine a desired employment level. Actual employment is then
gradually adjusted to the desired level.

First we formulate an equation for desired production rate. Desired production is
based upon incoming orders and backlog position. To prevent production from fluctuating along with random disturbances, we base the desired production on the average
order rate. Production should also gradually adjust backlog to desired level.

$$PRD.K = AOR.K + \frac{BL.K - BLD.K}{TABL}$$ NP-1, A

TABL = 10   NP-2, C

PRD   — Production Rate Desired (units/week)
AOR   — Average Order Rate (units/week)
BL   — BackLog (units)
BLD   — BackLog Desired (units)
TABL — Time to Adjust BackLog (weeks)

The average order rate is formulated as an exponential average of actual order rate. The smoothing time is taken as 12 weeks.

$$\text{AOR.K} = \text{AOR.J} + (\text{DT})(1/\text{DAOR})(\text{OR.JK} - \text{AOR.J}) \qquad \text{NP-3, L}$$
$$\text{AOR} = 100 \qquad \text{NP-4, N}$$
$$\text{DAOR} = 12 \qquad \text{NP-5, C}$$

AOR   — Average Order Rate (units/week)
OR   — Order Rate (units/week)
DAOR   — Delay in Averaging Order Rate (weeks)

Desired backlog is set equal to the normal delivery delay times average order rate.

$$\text{BLD.K} = (\text{DDN})(\text{AOR.K}) \qquad \text{NP-6, A}$$
$$\text{DDN} = 10 \qquad \text{NP-7, C}$$

BLD   — BackLog Desired (units)
DDN   — Delivery Delay Normal (weeks)
AOR   — Average Order Rate (units/week)

Dividing production rate desired by the normal productivity yields desired work force.

$$\text{WFD.K} = \text{PRD.K}/\text{PRODN} \qquad \text{NP-8, A}$$
$$\text{PRODN} = 1 \qquad \text{NP-9, C}$$

WFD   — Work Force Desired (men)
PRD   — Production Rate Desired (units/week)
PRODN — PRODuctivity Normal ((units/week)/man)

It is neither reasonable nor feasible to adjust the labor force immediately to desired work force. A gradual adjustment is more reasonable to account for time lags in searching for, interviewing, and employing new men. The time lag is taken as 10 weeks. We write the equation for change in work force:

$$\text{WCH.K} = \frac{\text{WFD.K} - \text{WF.K}}{\text{TAWF}} \qquad \text{NP-10, A}$$
$$\text{TAWF} = 10 \qquad \text{NP-11.C}$$

WCH   — Work Force Change (men/week)
WFD   — Work Force Desired (men)
WF   — Work Force (men)
TAWF — Time to Adjust Work Force (weeks)

A positive value on work force change WCH indicates hiring, and a negative value indicates firing. Figure 9 indicates the actual hiring decision. For a large positive value of work force change WCH, workers hired WH is equal to work force change. For large negative values, workers hired is equal to zero. Even if desired work force is equal to actual, some specially skilled people may still be needed. The hiring rate is set equal to .5 for work force change equal to zero. Figure 10 describes the actual leaving rate of workers.

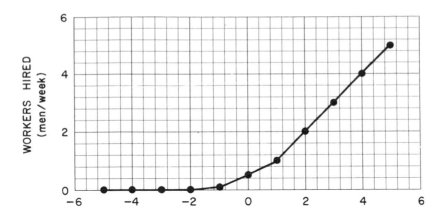

Figure 9   Hiring decision at Precision

Figure 10   Leaving decision at Precision

For a large negative value on work force change WCH, workers leaving WL is equal to work force change. For large positive values, workers leaving is equal to zero. For work force change WCH equal to zero, some people (here .5 men per week) may still be leaving Precision.

    We write the equations for hiring and leaving:

WH.KL = TABHL(TABWH,WCH.K,-5,5,1)   NP-12, R (replaces Eq. 17, R)
TABWH* = 0/0/0/0/.1/.5/1/2/3/4/5   NP-13, C
WL.KL = TABHL(TABWL,WCH.K,-5,5,1)   NP-14, R (replaces Eq. 27, R)
TABWL* = 5/4/3/2/1/.5/.1/0/0/0/0   NP-15, C

WH   —Workers Hired (men/week)
TABWH   —TABle for Workers Hired
WCH   —Work force CHange (men/week)
WL   —Workers Leaving (men/week)
TABWL   —TABle for Workers Leaving

This completes the new manpower policy.

Bidding Policy.   The old bidding policy was based upon pressure from delivery delay. For a high delivery delay, management withdrew bidding efforts. The new policy suggests that management respond directly to market and employment conditions. If the present manpower level can handle more business than is expected from the customers, bidding should be increased, and vice versa.

First, we formulate an equation describing desired work load at the company. Equation NP-16 states that the company desires a work load equal to normal production capability of the trained work force.

DWL.K = (TWF.K)(PRODN)   NP-16, A
DWL   — Desired Work Load (units/week)
TWF   — Trained Work Force (men)
PRODN — PRODuctivity Normal ((units/week)/man)

Next we formulate an equation for the anticipated level of business. It is set equal to average order rate modified by estimates of effects of delivery delay and bidding efforts on the order rate. These estimates cannot be generated accurately, and we therefore require that the model behavior be insensitive to errors in estimates.

ALB.K = (AOR.K)(EDDIB.K)(EMEIB.K)   NP-17, A
ALB   — Anticipated Level of Business (units/week)
AOR   — Average Order Rate (units/week)
EDDIB   — Estimated Delivery Delay Influence
                 on Bids (dimensionless)
EMEIB   — Estimated Management Effort Influence
                 on Bids (dimensionless)

Management knows that for delivery delay higher than normal a fraction of the normal business level is lost. It also knows that more-than-normal amount of management efforts toward bidding generates more accepted bids. Figures 11 and 12 show

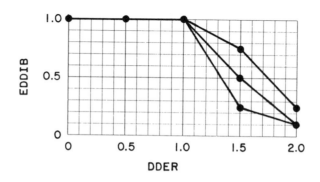

Figure 11   Estimated delivery delay influence on bids vs. delivery delay estimated ratio

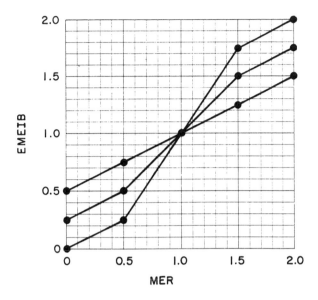

Figure 12   Estimated management effort influence on bids vs. management effort ratio

three sets each of estimates of the influence of delivery delay and management effort. As the initially estimated values, we have used the same values as in the basic model. The model tests that embody errors in these estimates are reported on pp. 182 and 183 of Chapter 10.

EDDIB.K = TABHL(ETBDD,DDER.K,0,2,.5)	NP-18, A
ETBDD* = 1/1/1/.5/.1	NP-19, C
DDER.K = EADDC.K/DDN	NP-20, A

EDDIB   — Estimated Delivery Delay Influence
           on Bids (dimensionless)

ETBDD   — Estimate TaBle for Delivery Delay

DDER   — Delivery Delay Estimate Ratio (dimensionless)

EADDC   — Estimated Average Delivery Delay at
           Customers (weeks)

DDN   — Delivery Delay Normal (weeks)

EMEIB.K = TABHL(ETBME,MER.K,0, 2.0, 0.5)	NP-21, A
ETBME* = .25/.5/1/1.5/1.75	NP-22, C
MER.K = EAMEB.K/NME	NP-23, A
NME = 20	NP-24, C

EMEIB   — Estimated Management Effort Influence
           on Bids (dimensionless)

ETBME   — Estimate TaBle for Management Efforts

MER   — Management Effort Ratio (dimensionless)

EAMEB   — Estimated Average Management Effort
           on Bidding (managerial hours/week)

NME   — Normal Management Efforts (managerial hours/week)

The above equations have not been based on instantaneous values for delivery delay and management effort. Management knows that customers respond slowly to conditions at Precision.

EADDC.K = SMOOTH(DD.K,DEADD)   NP-25, L
EADDC = DD   NP-26, N
DEADD = 20   NP-27, C

EADDC   — Estimated Average Delivery Delay at Customer (weeks)
DEADD   — Delay in Estimating Average Delivery Delay (weeks)
DD   — Delivery Delay (weeks)

EAMEB.K = SMOOTH(MEB.K,DEAME)   NP-28, L
EAMEB = MEB   NP-29, N
DEAME = 4   NP-30, C

EAMEB   — Estimated Average Management Effort
          on Bidding (managerial hours/week)
DEAME   — Delay in Estimating Average Management Effort (weeks)
MEB   — Management Effort on Bidding (managerial hours/week)

The equations above assume accurate estimates of the market's delay in responding to bidding efforts and delivery delay. Model tests for sensitivity to these parameters are reported on pp. 182 and 183 of Chapter 10.

The next equations describe the effort allocation. The desired work load compared to the anticipated level of business determines available capacity for additional production.

$$FCAAP.K = \frac{DWL.K - ALB.K}{DWL.K}$$ NP-31, A

FCAAP — Fraction of Capacity Available for Additional Production
        (dimensionless)

DWL   — Desired Work Load (units/week)
ALB   — Anticipated Level of Business (units/week)

When excess capacity exists—i.e., the desired work load exceeds the anticipated level of business—additional effort is allocated for bidding. When the desired work load is below the anticipated level of business, bidding efforts are reduced. The new policies also indicate that the company always puts in at least a minimum amount of bidding effort and never exceeds a maximum level. Our representation of the relationship between bidding efforts and available capacity for additional production appears in Figure 13.

FMEB.K = TABHL(TBFEB,FCAAP.K,-.2,.2,.1)   NP-32, A (replaces Eq. 40, A)
TBFEB* = .05/.07/.1/.13/.15   NP-33, C (replaced Eq. 41, C)
FMEB   — Fraction of Management Efforts on
          Bidding (dimensionless)
TBFEB   — TaBle for Fraction of Effort on Bidding
FCAAP   — Fraction of Capacity Available for Additional
          Production (dimensionless)

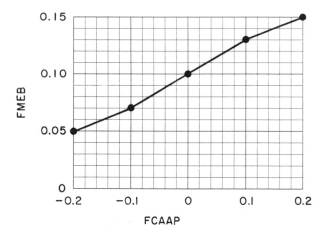

Figure 13 Management effort on bidding vs. fraction of capacity available for additional production

This completes the specification of equations for the changes in policies at Precision. Originally, the company responded to organizational pressures from delivery delay. The new policies are based instead upon planned actions initiated by average order rate and backlog.

Specific Conditions for Producing the Simulation Results

The simulation results described and presented in Chapter 10 of this book were generated using the Precision models detailed in this appendix. In the table below the Basic Model refers to Equations 1 through 73 of this appendix. The Improved Model refers to the introduction of Equations NP-1 through NP-33 in the Basic Model.

Simulation Results (Chapter 10)	Model Conditions
Figure 11	Basic Model, with STH = 0.20
12	Basic Model, with STD = 0.20
13	Basic Model, with STH = 0.20 and TBOP* = 0/0/0/0/0
14	Basic Model, with STH = 0.20 and TBOP* = 0/0/0/0.25/0.50
15	Basic Model, with STH = 0.20 and TBFEB* = 0.1/.1/.1/.1/.1
16	Basic Model, with STH = 0.20 and TBFEB* = 0.05/.07/.10/.13/.15
17	Basic Model, with STH = 0.20 but the following cluster of equations substituted for Equation 44: ADDC.K = FDD.K; FDD.K = DD.K + (FT) (RCDD.K); FT = 10; RCDD.K = DD.K − ADD.K

FDD — Forecast Delivery Delay (weeks)
FT — Forecasting Time period (weeks)
RCDD — Rate of Change of Delivery Delay
                    (weeks/week)

24   Improved Model, with STH = 0.20
25   Improved Model, with STD = 0.20

Pages 182 and 183 of Chapter 10 discussed sensitivity tests of the improved Precision model. Using the Improved Model, the simulation results described were generated by making the following changes:

1. Changing estimated management effort influence
    (a) High estimate   STH = 0.20, ETBME* = 0/.25/1/1.75/2.0
    (b) Low estimate   STH = 0.20, ETBME* 0.5/.75/1/1.25/1.5
2. Changing estimated delivery delay influence on bids
    (a) High estimate   STH = 0.20, ETBDD* = 1/1/1/.75/.20
    (b) Low estimate   STH = 0.20, ETBDD* = 1/1/1/.2/.1
3. Changing delay in averaging management effort on bidding
    (a) STH = 0.20, DAMEB = 2
    (b) STH = 0.20, DAMEB = 8
4. Changing delay in averaging delivery delay influence
    (a) STH = 0.20, DADDC = 10
    (b) STH = 0.20, DADDC = 40
5. Changing customer delay in consideration of bids
    STH = 0.20, DCB = 12
6. Changing productivity to be constant
    STH = 0.20, TBOP* = 0/0/0/0/0, TBPRO* = 1/1/1/1/1

Appendix C:
Equations for the Everdry Case

Edward B. Roberts

This appendix lists the DYNAMO equations for the model of the Everdry Company, used in the analysis described in Chapter 13 of this book.

The model as listed generated Figures 8, 9 and 11 of Chapter 13. Figures 13 and 14 were produced in the DYNAMO rerun mode by setting MPS = 1.5/0.

```
NOTE              PROMOTIONAL MARKET SECTOR
NOTE
R    TDGSL.KL=(ECON.K)(TPPRO.JK)(EADV.K)  TOTAL DEMAND GENERATED SALES
A    EADV.K=EAD   EFFECT OF ADVTG ON SALES
C    EAD=60
N    TDGSL=IDGSL
C    IDGSL=.32    MILLION UNITS
R    TPPRO.KL=DELAY3(TDADV.JK,BGDEL)   TOTAL PROMOTIONAL EXPENDITURE
R    TDADV.KL=(TADPL.K)(TDGSL.JK)   TOTAL PROM EXPEND PLANNED
A    TADPL.K=.025  INDUSTRY PER CENT OF SALES ON ADVTG
C    BGDEL=12 MONTHS  BUDGET DELAY
A    CSMDM.K=(.5)(PRINN.K)+(1)(RELPP.K)   COMPANY'S SHARE OF MARKET DEMAND
R    CDGSL.KL=(TDGSL.JK)(CSMDM.K)   COMPANY'S DEMAND GEN SALES
N    CDGSL=IDGSL/160
A    PRINN.K=TABHL(RINN,RAINP.JK,0,1,1)   PRODUCT INNOVATION EFFECT
T    RINN=0/.1
A    RELPP.K=TABHL(RADE,RLADE.JK,0,1,.1)   REL PERF IN PRODUCT PROMTION
T    RADE=0/.01/.03/.1/.2/.3/.4/.5/.65/.8/1
R    RLADE.KL=CPPRO.JK/TPPRO.JK   REL ADVTG EXPEND
R    CPPRO.KL=DELAY3(CDADV.JK,BGDEL)   COMPANY PROMOTIONAL EXPENDITURE
R    CDADV.KL=(CADPL.K)(CDGSL.JK)   COMPANY PROM EXPEND PLANNED
A    CADPL.K=.025   PER CENT OF SALES ON ADVTG
NOTE
NOTE             BASIC MARKET SECTOR
NOTE
R    TBLSL.KL=(EECBS.K)(BASE.K)   TOTAL BASIC LINE SALES
A    BASE.K=2   MILLION BASIC ANNUAL MARKET FOR GARMENTS
A    EECBS.K=TABHL(ECBS,ECON.K,0,2,2)   EFFECT OF ECONOMIC CONDITIONS
T    ECBS=0/2
R    CBLSL.KL=(TBLSL.JK)(CSRQ.K)(RELPS.K)   COMP BASIC LINE SALES
A    ECON.K=TABHL(CON,TIME.K,0,120,12)   ECONOMIC CONDITIONS
T    CON=1/1/1/1/1/1/1/1/1/1/1
NOTE
NOTE             COMPANY SALES SECTOR
NOTE
A    DESLS.K=CDGSL.JK+CBLSL.JK   DESIRED TOTAL SALES
R    SLS.KL=CLIP(DESLS.K,ECAP.K,ECAP.K,DESLS.K)   SALES RATE
```

655

```
L     CAVSL.K=CAVSL.J+(DT)(1/TACS)(SLS.JK-CAVSL.J)   CURRENT AVERAGED SALES
N     CAVSL=TCVSL
C     TCVSL=.2    MILLION UNITS
C     TACS=3  MONTHS   TIME TO AVG CURRENT SALES
L     LAVSL.K=LAVSL.J+(DT)(1/TALS)(SLS.JK-LAVSL.J)   LONG TERM AVGD SALES
N     LAVSL=ILVSL
C     ILVSL=.2  MILLION UNITS
C     TALS=18 MONTHS   TIME TO AVG LONG TERM SALES
A     SPERF.K=(CAVSL.K/LAVSL.K)-GRSTD.K    SALES PERFORMANCE
A     GRSTD.K=1.1
A     SLMTV.K=TABHL(MLTV,PRSLM.K,-1,0,1)  SALESMAN TURNOVER RATE
L     PRSLM.K=PRSLM.J+(DT)(1/TBP)(SPERF.J-PRSLM.J)  PRESS ON SALESMAN
N     PRSLM=-.1
C     TBP=24  MONTHS TIME TO BUILD PRESSURE TO CHANGE JOBS
T     MLTV=2/1
NOTE
NOTE            PRODUCT LINE SECTOR
NOTE
L     NPPL.K=NPPL.J+(DT)(RAINP.JK-RARP.JK)  NUM PRODUCTS IN LINE
N     NPPL=INPPL
C     INPPL=30 PRODUCTS
R     RARP.KL=RARP.JK+(1/TCP)(EMPS.K-RARP.JK)  RATE OF REMOV PRODUCTS
N     RARP=IRARP
C     IRARP=0    PRODUCTS PER MONTH
C     TCP=24 MONTHS   TIME TO CLOSEOUT A PRODUCT
A     EMPS.K=TABHL(MPS,MPRPS.K,0,2,2)  EFF OF MGT PERC SERV
T     MPS=.2/0
R     RAINP.KL=DELAY3(DEINP.JK,DLINP)  RATE OF INTROD NEW PRODUCTS
C     DLINP=12 MONTHS  DELAY IN INTROD NEW PRODUCTS
R     DEINP.KL=DEINP.JK+(1/TMRSP)(NDVNP.JK-DEINP.JK)   DEC TO INTR NEW PRD
N     DEINP=IDINP
C     IDINP=.1
C     TMRSP=12 MONTHS   TIME TO RESPOND TO SALES PRESSURE
R     NDVNP.KL=TABHL(DVNP,SPERF.K,-1,0,1)   NEED TO DEV NEW PRODUCTS
T     DVNP=2/.2
NOTE
NOTE            PRODUCTION CONTROL SECTOR
NOTE
L     PRDCL.K=PRDCL.J+(DT)(RAIPC.JK)  PRODUCTION CONTROL CAPABILITY
N     PRDCL=IPDCL
C     IPDCL=.2
R     RAIPC.KL=DELAY3(DECIP.JK,DLIPC)  RATE OF IMPROVING PROD CONTROL
C     DLIPC=48 MONTHS  DELAY IN IMPROVING PROD CONTROL
R     DECIP.KL=DECIP.JK+(1/TRPP)(PIPC.K-DECIP.JK)  DEC TO IMP PROD CONT
N     DECIP=IDCIP
C     IDCIP=0
C     TRPP=24 MONTHS   TIME TO RESPOND TO PRESS TO IMP PROD CONT
A     PIPC.K=TABHL(IPC,BAWFW.K,0,1,1)  PRESS TO IMPROVE PROD CONTROL
T     IPC=.1/0
A     ENPBW.K=TABHL(NPBW,NPPL.K,0,60,60)   EFF NUM PROD ON BAL OF WORK F
T     NPBW=1.5/.5
A     ELTBW.K=TABHL(LTBW,LATVR.K,0,2,2)   EFF LAB TRNV ON BAL OF WORK
T     LTBW=1.5/.5
A     BAWFW.K=(EPRCL.K)(ENPBW.K)(ELTBW.K)   BAL OF WORK FLOW
A     EPRCL.K=PRDCL.K/CPCTY.K   EFFECTIVE PROD CONTROL
A     EBAW.K=TABHL(BAW,BAWFW.K,0,2,2)   EFF BAL OF WORK ON SERVICE
T     BAW=0/2
NOTE
NOTE            RETAILERS SECTOR
NOTE
L     NCRO.K=NCRO.J+(DT)(RARO.JK-RLRO.JK)   NUMBER OF COMP RETAIL OUTLETS
N     NCRO=INCRO
C     INCRO=1000   UNITS OF RETAIL OUTLETS
R     RARO.KL=TABHL(ARO,RPCCP.K,0,2,2)   RETAILERS ADDING LINE
T     ARO=0/2
R     RLRO.KL=DELAY3(RRODC.JK,CLDEL)   RETAILERS DROPPING LINE
```

```
C    CLDEL=24 MONTHS  CLOSEOUT DELAY
R    RRODC.KL=ERPCP.K/RELPS.K   RATE RETAILERS DECIDE TO CLOSEOUT
A    ERPCP.K=TABHL(RPCP,RPCCP.K,0,2,2)   EFFECT OF COMPETITIVE POSITION
T    RPCP=2/0
A    RPCCP.K=CSMDM.K/CSRO.K   RETAILERS PERCEPTION OF COMPETITIVE POSITION
A    CSRO.K=NCRO.K/TRO.K   COMPANY'S SHARE OF RETAIL OUTLETS
A    TRO.K=10000   TOTAL RETAIL OUTLETS
A    RELPS.K=EBAW.K/SLMTV.K   REL PERF IN SERVICE TO RETAILER
A    BRPS.K=(MGTB.K)(RELPS.K)   BIASED REL PERF IN SERVICE
A    MGTB.K=1.5   MGT BIAS ON REL PERF IN SERVICE
L    MPRPS.K=MPRPS.J+(DT)(1/TRRPS)(BRPS.J-MPRPS.J)   MGT PERC OF REL PERF
N    MPRPS=1.3
C    TRRPS=12 MONTHS TIME TO RECOGNIZE REL PERF IN SERVICE
NOTE
NOTE           CAPACITY SECTOR
NOTE
A    ECAP.K=(CPCTY.K)(EBAW.K)   EFFECTIVE CAPACITY
A    CPCTY.K=.2   MILLION UNITS
NOTE
NOTE           . LABOR SECTOR
NOTE
A    EESLT.K=TABHL(ESLT,ESTAB.K,0,2,2)   EFF OF EMPLOY STAB ON LABOR TURN
T    ESLT=1.2/.8
A    ESTAB.K=TABHL(STAB,BAWFW.K,0,2,2)   EMPLOYMENT STABILITY
T    STAB=0/2
L    BLATV.K=BLATV.J+(DT)(1/TLRES)(EESLT.J-BLATV.J)   NORMALZD LABOR TRNVR
N    BLATV=ILATV
C    ILATV=1
C    TLRES=6 MONTHS  TIME FOR LABOR TO RESPOND TO EMPLOYMENT STABILITY
A    LATVR.K=(BLATV.K)(ECON.K)/ASKLF.K   LABOR TURNOVER RATE
N    LATVR=1
A    DISL.K=TABHL(TDISL,LATVR.K,0,2,2)   ATTRACT OF IND FOR SKLLD LAB
T    TDISL=.0005/-.001
R    RACSL.KL=RACSL.JK+(1/TLSI)(DISL.K-RACSL.JK)   CHNG OF AVG SKILL LVL
N    RACSL=RACSI
C    RACSI=-.00025   INITIAL RATE OF CHANGE OF SKILL LEVEL
C    TLSI=24 MONTHS TIME FOR LABOR TO CHANGE INDUSTRIES
L    ASKLF.K=ASKLF.J+(DT)(RACSL.JK)   AVG SKILL LEVEL OF LAB FORCE
N    ASKLF=1
NOTE
NOTE           CONTROL CARDS
NOTE
PLOT CDGSL=C,PRINN=I(0,.08)/CSMDM=S(0,.04)/TDGSL=T(0,3)
PLOT CDGSL=C(0,.1)/CBLSL=B,SLS=S,ECAP=E(.1,.2)
PLOT SLS=S(.1,.2)/SPERF=P(-.2,.2)/SLMTV=T(1,1.4)/NDVNP=N(0,.5)
PLOT DEINP=D,RAINP=A,RARP=R(0,.6)/NPPL=N(0,50)/BAWFW=B(.75,1.05)
PLOT BAWFW=B(.75,1.05)/PIPC=P(0,.03)/RAIPC=R(0,.005)/EPRCL=E(.9,1.2)
PLOT BAWFW=B(.65,1.05)/ESTAB=E(.75,1.15)/LATVR=T(.98,1.1)/ASKLF=S(.95,1.
X    05)
PLOT RARO=A(0,.5)/RRODC=D,RLRO=R(2,2.5)/RELPS=S(.5,1)/NCRO=N(850,1050)
SPEC DT=1/LENGTH=60/PRTPER=0/PLTPER=1
NOTE
```

Appendix D:
Equations for the Vertically-Integrated Firm Model

Edward B. Roberts, Dan I. Abrams,
and Henry B. Weil

This appendix lists the DYNAMO equations for the model of the vertically-integrated bakery company, used in the analyses described in Chapter 25 of this book.

The model is listed in the format of DYNAMO I, the simulation language available for system dynamics modelling at the time of the bakery project. Issues of compatibility between DYNAMO I and the currently used DYNAMO II language are discussed in Alexander L. Pugh III, *DYNAMO II User's Manual* (Fourth Edition) (Cambridge: The MIT Press, 1973), pp. 75–76.

```
NOTE      TRANSFER PRICE DECISION
NOTE
20A       BAKR.K=BP.K/CUMIN.K                               MFG BAKERY ROI
6N        BAKR=0.00957
1L        CUMIN.K=CUMIN.J+(DT)(INVR.JK-0)                   CUMULATIVE INVESTMENT
6N        CUMIN=1200000
3L        SMBR.K=SMBR.J+(DT)(1/TSBR)(BAKR.J-SMBR.J)         SMOOTHED ROI
6N        SMBR=BAKR
C         TSBR=4
12A       AROI.K=(SMBR.K)(52)                               ANNUAL EFFECTIVE ROI
7A        BP.K=BIC.K-DO.K                                   BAKERY PROFIT
14A       BIC.K=-BCEDO.K+(BSA.K)(BTP.K)                     INCOME CONTRIBUTION
6N        BIC=15700
7A        BCEDO.K=BCED.K+DEPR.JK                            COSTS EX DEPT OVERHEAD
59A       BCED.K=TABLE(CTAB,BSA.K,0.0,2E6,2E6)              COSTS EX DEPRECIATION
C         CTAB*=20680/370680
21A       ICV.K=(1/BRIC.K)(BRIC.K-BIC.K)                    INCOME CONT VAR
3L        SMICV.K=SMICV.J+(DT)(1/TSIV)(ICV.J-SMICV.J)       SMOOTHED ICV
6N        SMICV=0.0
C         TSIV=4
59A       BWO.K=TABLE(B1TAB,PV1.K,-2.0,2.0,1.0)             BAKERY WIL TO OVERPROD
C         B1TAB*=1.0/1.0/1.0/2.0/2.0
59A       WLP.K=TABLE(B2TAB,PV1.K,-2.0,2.0,0.5)             WILLINGNESS TO LOWER TP
C         B2TAB*=1.0/1.0/1.0/1.0/1.0/0.8/0.75/0.75/0.75
59A       RPLP.K=TABLE(B3TAB,DIRS.K,-1.0,2.0,1.0)           RETL PRESS TO LOWER TP
6N        RPLP=1.0
C         B3TAB*=1.0/1.0/0.5/0.5
12A       PPV.K=(OR.K)(BWO.K)                               PLANNED PROD VOLUME
59A       BPIRS.K=TABLE(B4TAB,SMICV.K,-2.0,2.0,1.0)         BAKERY PRES TO INC R SA
C         B4TAB*=1.0/1.0/1.0/4.0/4.0
20A       CPU.K=BCEDO.K/BSA.K                               COST PER UNIT
```

659

```
31      CUS.K=CUS.J+(DT)(1/TSU)(CPU.J-CUS.J)          COST PER UNIT SMOOTHED
6N      CUS=0.2385
C       TSU=4
12A     ADNS.K=(NORMS.K)(ADFAC)                        ADJUSTED NORMAL SALES
C       ADFAC=1.0
7A      SABN.K=BSA.K-ADNS.K                            SALES ABOVE NORMAL
59A     QDIS.K=TABLE(QDTAB,SABN.K,-4E5,8E5,2E5)        QUANTITY DISCOUNT
C       QDTAB*=1.0/1.0/1.0/0.75/0.5/0.5/0.5
12A     VMU.K=(CMU)(QDIS.K)                            VARIABLE MARKUP
C       CMU=0.039
7A      FP1.K=CUS.K+VMU.K                              TP WITH QUANTITY DISC
7A      FP2.K=CUS.K+CMU
49A     FTP.K=SWITCH(FRTP.K,NEWTP.K,SW1)               FUTURE TP
C       SW1=0
49A     NEWTP.K=SWITCH(FP1.K,FP2.K,SW2)                NEW TP POLICY USED
C       SW2=0
6A      BCT1*1.K=PPV.K
37B     BCT1=BOXLIN(3,1)                               PRODUCTION LEAD TIME
36N     BCT1=BOXLOAD(1.0,PPV)
6A      BSA.K=BCT1*3.K                                 MFG BAKERY UNIT SALES
6N      BSA=400000
39R     MRRP.KL=DELAY3(RPLP.K,MRD)                     MFG RESP TO RPLP
C       MRD=8
12A     LP.K=(WLP.K)(MPRP.K)                           EFF PRESS FOR RED TP
51A     ADWLP.K=CLIP(1.0,LP.K,PV1.K,0.0)               ADJUSTED WIL TO LOWR PR
49A     PV1.K=SWITCH(SMICV.K,SMTPV.K,SW5)              PROFIT VARIANCE NO. 1
C       SW5=0
12A     FNTP.K=(NORTP)(ADWLP.K)                        FUTURE NORMAL TP
C       NORTP=0.2775
12A     FBTP.K=(FNTP.K)(DHGM.K)                        FUTURE ACTUAL TP
6A      BCT6*1.K=FTP.K
37B     BCT6=BOXLIN(5,1)                               TP CHANGE DELAY
36N     BCT6=BOXLOAD(1.0,FBTP)
6A      RTP.K=BCT6*5.K                                 ACTUAL BAKERY TP
6N      RTP=0.2775
1L      BINV.K=BINV.J+(DT)(INVR.JK-DEPR.JK)            BAKERY INVESTMENT
6N      BINV=1200000
12R     DEPR.KL=(DEPF)(BINV.K)                         DEPRECIATION RATE
6N      DEPR=4620
C       DEPF=0.00385
8A      BRIC.K=CBBIC.K+SBBIC.K+RBBIC.K                 BUDGETED INC CONTRIB
6A      CBBIC.K=15700
45A     SBBIC.K=STEP(ISS,53)
6N      SBBIC=0.0
C       ISS=6024
47A     RBBIC.K=RAMP(IRS,53)
6N      RBBIC=0.0
C       IRS=250
59A     DO.K=TABLE(DOTAB,TIME.K,0,260,52)              DEPT OVERHEAD
C       DOTAB*=4217/4217/4217/4217/4217
41R     INVR.KL=PULSE(4E6,53,300)                      INVESTMENT RATE
6N      INVR=0.0
NOTE    SALES PRESSURE ON RETAIL DIVISION
31      SMBSV.K=SMBSV.J+(DT)(1/TSSV)(BSV.J-SMBSV.J)    SMOOTHED SALES VAR
6N      SMBSV=0
C       TSSV=4
14A     PCBS.K=SPLI+(DIBS.K)(SW4)                      PRES ON CQ TO INC SALES
C       SPLI=0
C       SW4=1
13A     DIBS.K=(GPIS.K)(SMBSV.K)(BPIRS.K)
59A     WLRP1.K=TABLE(D1TAB,DIBS.K,-1.0,2.0,1.0)       WILLINGNESS TO LOWER RP
C       D1TAB*=1.0/1.0/0.5/0.5
13A     RPBM.K=(WLRP1.K)(NORMP.K)(WLRP2.K)             MINIMUM PRICE
```

```
51A      FRPB.K=CLIP(RPBM.K,RPRC.K,RPBM.K,RPRC.K)       FUTURE RP
59A      PANS.K=TABLE(PATAB,NBS.K,5,6,1)                PRICE ADJ NO. OF SPECLS
C        PATAB*=1.0/0.95
12A      AFRPB.K=(FRPB.K)(PANS.K)                       ADJ FUTURE RP
6A       BCT2*1.K=AFRPB.K
37B      BCT2=BOXLIN(5,1)                               PRICE CHANGE DELAY
36N      BCT2=BOXLOAD(1.0,AFRPB)
6A       RPB.K=BCT2*5.K                                 RETAIL PRICE
6N       RPB=0.37
59A      SM3.K=TABLE(S3TAB,RPB.K,0.0,0.54,0.18)
C        S3TAB*=3.0/3.0/1.0/0.5
59A      VDPB.K=TABLE(D2TAB,DIBS.K,-1.0,2.0,1.0)        VAR DOLLARS TO PROMOTN
C        D2TAB*=0.0/0.0/4000/4000
8A       DPB.K=VDPB.K+CDPB.K+CDOL                       DLLRS TO PROMOTE BAKERY
C        CDOL=2000
45A      CDPB.K=STEP(PRSS,PRST)
6N       CDPB=0
C        PRSS=0
C        PRST=0
6A       BCT3*1.K=DPB.K
37B      BCT3=BOXLIN(3,1)                               PROMOTION LEAD TIME
36N      BCT3=BOXLOAD(1.0,DPB)
6A       PEF.K=BCT3*3.K                                 PROMOTION EFFECT
6N       PEF=2000
59A      SM1.K=TABLE(S1TAB,PEF.K,2000,14000,4000)
C        S1TAB*=1.0/1.8/2.0/2.0
59A      NBS.K=TABLE(D3TAB,DIBS.K,-1.0,2.0,0.25)        NO. BAKERY SPECIALS
C        D3TAB*=5/5/5/5/5/5/5/6/6/6/6/6/6
6A       BCT4*1.K=NBS.K
37B      BCT4=BOXLIN(5,1)                               DECISION DELAY
36N      BCT4=BOXLOAD(1.0,NBS)
6A       SEF.K=BCT4*5.K
6N       SEF=5
59A      SM2.K=TABLE(S2TAB,SEF.K,5,6,1)
C        S2TAB*=1.0/1.2
13A      MSM1.K=(SM1.K)(SM2.K)(SM3.K)
13A      PSAR.K=(NORMS.K)(MSM1.K)(MSM2.K)               POTENTIAL RETAIL SALES
15A      RBDS.K=(RBSAR.K)(RPB.K)+(EXP.K)(REDPR.K)       RET BAK DOLLAR SALES
6N       RBDS=148000
12A      REDPR.K=(0.67)(RPB.K)                          REDUCED PRICE
54A      RBSAR.K=MIN(PSAR.K,BSA.K)                      RET BAKERY UNIT SALES
21A      BSV.K=(1/BBSM.K)(BBSM.K-RBDS.K)                BAKERY SALES VARIANCE
6N       BSV=0
7A       NORMP.K=STNP.K+CONNP                           NORMAL RETAIL PRICE
C        CONNP=0.37
45A      STNP.K=STEP(PSS,PST)                           STEP CHANGE IN NORMP
6N       STNP=0
C        PSS=0
C        PST=104
8A       BBSM.K=CBS.K+SBS.K+RBS.K                       BUDGETED SALES BAKERY
6A       CBS.K=148000
45A      SBS.K=STEP(74000,53)
6N       SBS=0
47A      RBS.K=RAMP(SALR,53)
6N       RBS=0
C        SALR=711.54
59A      GPIS.K=TABLE(SPTAB,TIME.K,0,260,52)            GEN PRES TO INC SALES
C        SPTAB*=1.0/1.0/1.0/1.0/1.0/1.0
8A       NORMS.K=CNS.K+SNS.K+RNS.K                      NORMAL SALES
6A       CNS.K=400000
45A      SNS.K=STEP(200000,53)
6N       SNS=0
47A      RNS.K=RAMP(575,53)
```

```
6N      RNS=0
NOTE    RETAIL PROFIT PRESSURE
12A     DIBP.K=(GPIP.K)(PV2.K)                          DESIRE TO INC RK PROFIT
49A     PV2.K=SWITCH(SMGMV.K,SMTPV.K,SW5)               PROFIT VARIANCE NO. 2
59A     WLRP2.K=TABLE(WTAB,DIBP.K,-1.0,2.0,1.0)         WILLINGNESS TO LOWER RP
C       WTAB*=1.0/1.0/1.5/1.5
7A      GMB.K=RPB.K-BTP.K                               BAKERY GROSS MARGIN
15A     GMD.K=(RBSAR.K)(GMB.K)+(EXP.K)(RGM.K)           GROSS MARGIN DOLLARS
6N      GMD=37000
7A      EXP.K=BSA.K-RBSAR.K                             EXCESS PRODUCTION
14A     RGM.K=-BTP.K+(0.67)(RPR.K)                      RED GM ON EXCESS
21A     GMDV.K=(1/BGM.K)(BGM.K-GMD.K)                   GMD VARIANCE
6N      GMDV=0.0
20A     GMP.K=GMD.K/RBDS.K                              GROSS MARGIN PCT
21A     GMPV.K=(1/BGMP.K)(BGMP.K-GMP.K)                 GM PCT VARIANCE
49A     GMVR.K=SWITCH(GMDV.K,GMPV.K,SW3)                GROSS MARGIN VARIANCE
C       SW3=1
3I      SMGMV.K=SMGMV.J+(DT)(1/TSGM)(GMVR.J-SMGMV.J)    SMOOTHED GM VARIANCE
6N      SMGMV=0.0
C       TSGM=4
14A     PCIG.K=PLI+(DIBP.K)(SW4)                        PRES ON CQ TO INC GM
C       PLI=0
12A     REDS.K=(RGM.K)(EXP.K)                           REDUCED SALES
12A     NORMR.K=(PERS)(RBDS.K)                          NORM REDUCTIONS
C       PERS=0.02
21A     RV.K=(1/NORMR.K)(REDS.K-NORMR.K)                REDUCTION VARIANCE
51A     RVM.K=CLIP(DIBP.K,0.0,DIBP.K,0.0)               RED VAR MULTIPLIER
18A     EFRV.K=(RV.K)(1+RVM.K)                          EFFEC RED VAR
3I      SMRV.K=SMRV.J+(DT)(1/TSRV)(EFRV.J-SMRV.J)       SMOOTHED EFRV
6N      SMRV=-1.0
C       TSRV=4
59A     DLR.K=TABLE(DLTAB,SMRV.K,-4.0,4.0,1.0)          DESIRE TO LOWER RED
C       DLTAB*=1.0/1.0/1.0/1.0/1.0/0.97/0.94/0.94/0.94
6A      PNO.K=DLR.K                                     PRES ON STORES NOT OVOR
6A      PCNO.K=DLR.K                                    PRES ON CQ NOT OVORDER
59A     GPIP.K=TABLE(PPTAB,TIME.K,0.0,260,52)           GEN PRESSURE INC PROFIT
C       PPTAB*=1.0/1.0/1.0/1.0/1.0/1.0
5A      BGMP.K=CGMP                                     BUDGETED GM PERCENTAGE
C       CGMP=0.257
8A      BGM.K=CGM.K+SGM.K+RGMD.K                        BUDGETED GMD
6A      CGM.K=37000
45A     SGM.K=STEP(GSS,53)
6N      SGM=0.0
C       GSS=18500
47A     RGMD.K=RAMP(GRS,53)
6N      RGMD=0.0
C       GRS=177.89
NOTE    SECONDARY MERCHANDISING
7A      SARS.K=RBSAR.K-SARI.K                           SALE OF SPECIALS
3I      SMSS.K=SMSS.J+(DT)(1/TSS)(SARS.J-SMSS.J)        SMOOTHED SARS
6N      SMSS=SARS
C       TSS=4
18A     ESAR.K=(SMSS.K)(1+RNA1.K)                       EST SALES
33A     RNA1.K=(CQEV)NOISE
C       CQEV=0.0
7A      OR.K=ORS.K+OSS.K                                ORDERS FROM RETAIL
13A     OSS.K=(ESAR.K)(WRO.K)(PCNO.K)                   ORDER OF SPEC ITEMS
59A     WRO.K=TABLE(C1TAB,PCBS.K,-1.0,2.0,1.0)          WIL RISK OVER-PROD
C       C1TAB*=1.0/1.0/1.25/1.5
6A      PSC.K=PCBS.K                                    PRESSURE ON STORES
13A     RPBC.K=(CNP.K)(CWLP1.K)(CWLP2.K)                RP DESIRED BY CQ
7A      CNP.K=CSTNP.K+CONST
C       CONST=0.37
```

```
45A      CSTNP.K=STEP(CPSS,CPST)                    STEP CHANGE IN DES RP
6N       CSTNP=0.0
C        CPSS=0.0
C        CPST=104
59A      CWLP1.K=TABLE(C3TAB,PCBS.K,-1.0,2.0,1.0)   CQ WIL TO LOWER PRICE 1
C        C3TAB*=1.0/1.0/0.5/0.5
59A      CWLP2.K=TABLE(C4TAB,PCIG.K,-1.0,2.0,1.0    CQ WIL TO LOWER PRICE 2
C        C4TAB*=1.0/1.0/1.5/1.5
59A      DHGM.K=TABLE(C5TAB,PCIG.K,-1.0,2.0,1.0)    DES FOR HIGHER GM
C        C5TAB*=1.0/1.0/0.95/0.95
59A      EIS.K=TABLE(C2TAB,P1.K,-1.0,2.0,1.0)       ELASTICITY OF SPECIALS
C        C2TAB*=1.0/1.0/1.25/1.5
49A      P1.K=SWITCH(PCBS.K,TOTPC.K,SW6)            PRESSURE NO. 1
C        SW6=0
7A       TOTPC.K=PCIG.K+PCBS.K                      TOT PRESSURE ON CQ
6A       SM4.K=BCT5*5.K
6N       SM4=1.0
37B      BCT5=BOXLIN(5,1)
6A       BCT5*1.K=EIS.K
36N      BCT5=BOXLOAD(1,EIS)
NOTE     STORE LEVEL DECISIONS
12A      SARI.K=(RBSAR.K)(PNS.K)                    SALES REGULAR ITEMS
31       SMRSA.K=SMRSA.J+(DT)(1/TSRS)(SARI.J-SMRSA.J)  SM SALES REG ITEMS
6N       SMRSA=SARI
C        TSRS=4
18A      ES.K=(SMRSA.K)(1+RNA2.K)                   EST SALES REG ITEMS
12A      ORS.K=(PNO.K)(ES.K)                        ORDER OF REG ITEMS
33A      RNA2.K=(SLEV)NOISE
C        SLEV=0.0
6A       PSIS.K=GPIS.K                              PRES ON STORES INC SAL
14A      DAB.K=PSC.K+(PRE.K)(PSIS.K)                DAIRYMAN ATT TO BAKERY
56A      EB.K=MAX(0.0,DAB.K)                        EFFORT TO BAKERY
59A      SM5.K=TABLE(S5TAB,EB.K,0.0,4.0,1.0)
C        S5TAB*=0.75/1.0/1.25/1.3/1.3
13A      MSM2.K=(SM4.K)(SM5.K)(SM6.K)
7A       SM6.K=RNA3.K+1.0
33A      RNA3.K=(SVAR)NOISE
C        SVAR=0.0
6A       PRE.K=CE                                   PERCEIVED ELASTICITY
C        CE=1.0
6A       PNS.K=CP                                   PERCENT NOT SPECIALS
C        CP=0.5
NOTE     ACCOUNTING DATA
7A       TPROF.K=GMD.K+BIC.K                        TOTAL SYSTEM PROFIT
6N       TPROF=52700
7A       BTPRF.K=BGM.K+BBIC.K                       BUDGETED TOT PROFIT
21A      TPV.K=(1/BTPRF.K)(BTPRF.K-TPROF.K)
31       SMTPV.K=SMTPV.J+(DT)(1/TSTPV)(TPV.J-SMTPV.J)  SM TOTAL PROFIT VAR
6N       SMTPV=0
C        TSTPV=4
1L       CPROF.K=CPROF.J+(DT)(TPROF.J-0)            CUMULATIVE TPROF
6N       CPROF=0
12A      ATSP.K=(TPROF.K)(52)                       EFFECTIVE ANNUAL TPROF
1L       BCT7*1.K=BCT7*1.J+(DT)(BIC.J-0)
37B      BCT7=BOXLIN(1,52)
36N      BCT7=BOXLOAD(52,BIC)
6A       ABIC.K=BCT7*1.K                            ANNUAL BIC
6N       ABIC=816400
1L       BCT8*1.K=BCT8*1.J+(DT)(GMD.J-0)
37B      BCT8=BOXLIN(1,52)
36N      BCT8=BOXLOAD(52,GMD)
6A       AGMD.K=BCT8*1.K                            ANNUAL GMD
6N       AGMD=1924000
```

```
1L      BCT9*1.K=BCT9*1.J+(DT)(RBDS.J-0)
37B     BCT9=BOXLIN(1,52)
36N     BCT9=BOXLOAD(52,RBDS)
6A      ARS.K=BCT9*1.K                              ANNUAL SALES
6N      ARS=7696000
1L      BCT10*1.K=BCT10*1.J+(DT)(BAKR.J-0)
37B     BCT10=BOXLIN(1,52)
36N     BCT10=BOXLOAD(52,BAKR)
6A      ANROI.K=BCT10*1.K                          ANNUAL TOTAL ROI
6N      ANROI=0.49764
NOTE
NOTE    CONTROL CARDS
NOTE
PRINT   1)RBDS,BBSM/2)GMD,BGM/3)BSV,GMDV/4)BIC,BBIC/5)GMP,BGMP/6)TCV
PRINT   7)TPROF/8)CPROF/9)ABIC/10)AGMD/11)ARS/12)ANROI
PLOT    TPROF=T/CPROF=C/ATSP=A/AROI=R/DPB=P
PLOT    RBDS=S,BBSM=B,GMD=G,BGM=D/BIC=I,BBIC=C
PLOT    RBDS=S,GMD=G/BAKR=R/DTBS=X,DIBP=Y,DAB=Z
PLOT    OSS=E,RBSAR=U,BSA=A,SARI=I,ORS=O/BTP=T,RPB=P
SPEC    DT=1.0/LENGTH=260/PRTPER=52/PLTPER=4
```

Index

"The immense value of this book is the void it fills—it is the first major work to appear dealing with managerial applications of system dynamics since Forrester's original publication of *Industrial Dynamics*. It is relatively self-contained, well edited, and provocative. Whether your flair is management, management science, management cybernetics, modeling, planning, or forecasting, you will find a collection of articles in this volume that will certainly whet your appetite. This book merits a place in your library; its appearance should enable graduate schools of business to effectively integrate system dynamics into their curricula."—*Technological Forecasting and Social Change*

"The [36] contributions are grouped under six themes: basic concepts, manufacturing, marketing and distribution, research and development, management control and financial applications, and societal problems. . . . The collection is an excellent instructional and reference book. It was used in draft form for teaching system dynamics at MIT in graduate and middle management executive development programs."—*R&D Management Digest*

Edward B. Roberts is David Sarnoff Professor of Management at MIT's Sloan School.

The MIT Press
Massachusetts Institute of Technology
Cambridge, Massachusetts 02142

ROBMP